Alan Levy was born in New York City in 1932 and educated at Brown University and the Columbia University Graduate School of Journalism. After seven years as a reporter for *The Louisville Courier-Journal* and another seven years freelancing in New York, he took his family to Prague in 1967 on an assignment to adapt a play for director Miloŝ Forman. *Rowboat to Prague*, Levy's eyewitness account of the 1968 invasion of Czechoslovakia (published in England as *So Many Heroes*), was hailed by *Newsweek* as 'the definitive book about a tiny nation's hope and tragedy, written with an intimacy of detail and emotion that transcends mere journalistic reporting.' For it, he and his family were expelled and deported in 1971. After nearly two decades in Vienna, Alan Levy returned to Prague in late 1990 and, the following autumn, became the founding editor-in-chief of a pioneering English-language weekly newspaper, *The Prague Post*. When this book was first published in England in 1993 as *The Wiesenthal File*, it was on Best of the Year lists for the *Good Books Guide* and *The Observer*. Published in America a year later, it earned Levy the 1995 Author of the Year award from the American Society of Journalists & Authors.

Praise for *The Wiesenthal File*:

'Wiesenthal has played his part in a disturbing episode of post-war history. He deserves this readable and intelligent book.'

Norman Stone, *The Times*

'This biography of famed Nazi-hunter Simon Wiesenthal is so well written that it often seems like a thriller.' *Kirkus Reviews*

'Levy is ruthless in his determination to make every act of barbarity clear. It is impossible to turn the pages without feeling not just despair but revulsion . . . A valuable addition to the literature of Nazi atrocities.'

Caroline Moorehead, *New Statesman & Society*

'There is scarcely a page from first to last when one does not flinch, take a deep breath and consider what it is to belong to the species that could bring such nightmares on the world . . . Alan Levy writes affectingly and simply of great tragic matters.'

Simon Ward, *Literary Review*

Photo opposite: Alan Levy & Simon Wiesenthal, © Horst Tappe

'This moving account . . . is filled with Wiesenthal's outspoken comments and impromptu recollections . . . As much suspense and high drama as a thriller.' *Publishers Weekly*

'His approach to Wiesenthal is fair minded and critical.'
International Herald Tribune

'[This book] should be read, lent, and referred to.' *Observer*

'*The Wiesenthal File* is more than the sum of its parts. It throws light on themes such as the nature of evil, and is also a portrait of a man the author knows intimately and obviously admires.'
Emma Klein, *The Tablet*

'[A] thorough, objective book . . . compellingly detailed.'
Good Book Guide

'Alan Levy's biography presents us with the real Wiesenthal, warts and all. It is a candid exploration of a man whose image as an avenger of the Holocaust has, in the popular mind, reached almost biblical proportions.'
Bernard Josephs, *Jewish Chronicle*

'Levy recounts the complex events so skilfully that the book does full credit to Simon Wiesenthal . . . one of the most readable fact-bulging Holocaust reports yet . . . [a] dark, disturbing and brutally honest volume.' *Austria Today*

'Despite the book's sober topic, the author packs in revealing anecdotes and rich detail that capture the ironic humour of Wiesenthal.'
American Booksellers Association, Bookman's Weekly

'Alan Levy can write of truly horrendous acts of inhumanity with clarity and restraint.' Fergus Pyle, *Irish Times*

NAZI HUNTER
THE WIESENTHAL FILE

ALAN LEVY

ROBINSON
London

Constable & Robinson Ltd
3 The Lanchesters
162 Fulham Palace Road
London W6 9ER
www.constablerobinson.com

First published in the UK as *The Wiesenthal File* by
Constable Publishers 1993

This revised edition first published in the UK by Robinson,
an imprint of Constable & Robinson Ltd 2002

A copy of the British Library Cataloguing in
Publication data is available from the British Library

ISBN 1-84119-607-X

Printed and bound in the EU

10 9 8 7 6 5 4 3

To
Cyla and Simon Wiesenthal
and to
Lisa Keloufi
born 3 September 1993
and to
Mélina Keloufi
born 26 September 1996

Contents

PART IV: JOSEF MENGELE

PART V: FRANZ PAUL STANGL, GUSTAV WAGNER, HERMINE BRAUNSTEINER RYAN

PART VI: BRUNO KREISKY, KURT WALDHEIM

PART VII: EPISODES AND EPILOGUES

Illustrations

Prologue: Anti-Semitism without Jews

Bregenz, the capital of Austria's westernmost province, the Vorarlberg, is less than two hours and seventy-seven miles by train from Zürich, Switzerland, but, to the federal capital in Vienna, it is an all-day trip of almost 500 miles on the crack Bodensee Express. Settling into the dining car with Austria's weightiest daily, *Die Presse,* in hand in the early 1970s, a gentleman in his sixties was paired for breakfast with a Vorarlberger in his twenties who boarded in Bludenz almost an hour later, when there were no empty tables left. Discovering that the man opposite him was reading the other side of his paper, the older man was amused and asked, before turning the page, if he was finished. Flustered, the younger man tried to pretend he wasn't reading the other's paper, but he accepted when his neighbour said he'd finished the first section and wouldn't he like to look at it?

The Vorarlberger punctuated his reading of the news with interpretive comment: 'Another traffic detour in Innsbruck! Those Jews in City Hall are always messing things up for the rest of us.' . . . 'The price of gas is going up! It's all because of what the Jews have done to the Arabs.' . . . 'A bomb went off in the South Tyrol! The Italians say German extremists did it, but it's all the work of the Jews.'

'There are still Jews in the South Tyrol?', the older man wondered gently.

'You can't believe what you read in the papers anyway,' the Vorarlberger replied. 'They're all run by Jews!' Passing through some of the most gorgeous mountain scenery in the world, the older man tried not to focus on the ugliness he was hearing.

Finally, though, he could bear it no more, so he asked: 'Do you know any Jews?'

'Of course not!' the man replied proudly. 'I am from Bludenz, where there *are* no Jews.'

'Would you ever sit at a table with one?'

'Certainly not!'

'Well, you're just as wrong about that as you've been about everything else you've said today. You just had breakfast with a Jew.'

The man stood up spluttering 'Waiter! Waiter! I want to pay.'

'But I haven't brought you the second coffee you ordered,' the waiter protested.

'That's all right. I'll pay for it,' the man insisted, thrusting an exorbitant tip at him and exiting in haste.

Simon Wiesenthal reflected on the encounter all the way home. That night, over dinner, he told his wife Cyla and a couple of friends about it. The next morning, he went to the Austrian National Library and did a little research before writing a feuilleton for the *Salzburger Nachrichten*.

'There is only one person who has declared himself a Jew in the whole Vorarlberg,' Wiesenthal reported, 'out of a quarter-million people. Statistically, that means my breakfast guest had a fifty times better chance of being hit by a car while waiting on the sidewalk in Bludenz than of having anything to do with a Jew. And yet he was a confirmed anti-Semite.' To me, Wiesenthal added when we met soon thereafter: 'Even if Hitler had succeeded in exterminating us, we still would have been a menace to the Nazis. They don't need a living Jew. The phantom of a Jew is already enough.'

Part 1
Wiesenthal's Wars

Have you ever heard of Simon Wiesenthal? He lives in Vienna. Jewish chap, came from Polish Galicia originally. Spent four years in a series of concentration camps, twelve in all. Decided to spend the rest of his days tracking down wanted Nazi criminals. No rough stuff, mind you. He just keeps collating all the information about them he can get; then, when he's convinced he has found one, usually living under a false name – not always – he informs the police. If they don't act, he gives a press conference and puts them on the spot. Needless to say, he's not terribly popular with officialdom in either Germany or Austria. He reckons they are not doing enough to bring known Nazi murderers to book, let alone chase the hidden ones. The former SS hate his guts and have tried to kill him a couple of times; the bureaucrats wish he would leave them alone, and a lot of other people think he's a great chap and help him where they can.

– Lord Russell of Liverpool
in Frederick Forsyth's novel, *The Odessa File* (1972)

– 1 –

Deputy for the dead

Coming back to the office from an early lunch on a day when he hoped to win the Nobel Peace Prize, Simon Wiesenthal met a mailman who handed him a hate letter addressed simply to '*Saujude Wiesenthal, Wien*' ('Jewish Pig Wiesenthal, Vienna').

'There are nine Wiesenthals in the Vienna phone book,' Simon protested. 'How do you always know to send this kind of mail to me?'

Confronted by this bustling elder – whose smallish, balding head protruding from a surprisingly tall body made him look like a snail in a grey tweed suit – the Viennese mailman weaselled: 'Well – er – we just send it to *S.* Wiesenthal.'

'But there are two other *S.* Wiesenthals in the phone book and I'm not even *in* the book,' said Simon Wiesenthal, who keeps himself unlisted.

The mailman – a cherubic, ageing Hitler Youth – could have avoided misadventure just by saying from the start: 'It was obviously meant for you.' After all, hardly a day goes by without the Austrian Post & Telegraph Office finding the addressee of missives aimed at 'Simon Wiesenthal, Office of Humanity, Vienna' or 'Nazi-Hunter Wiesenthal, Europe'. Instead, however, the mailman blustered: 'I'm sorry. Just give it back to me and we'll deliver it to one of the other S. Wiesenthals.'

'No,' said Simon Wiesenthal, holding the letter tantalizingly out of reach. 'I want it because I have a standing offer from an American collector. I get two hundred dollars for every one of these.'

That exit line, he could see, hit the mailman where he lived. A few minutes later – telling this tale to a group of friends assembled for the Nobel news on the midday broadcast from Oslo and speaking

German, English, Polish, and Yiddish with the rolled *r*s that spell origins east of Vienna – Wiesenthal's baritone rose to a high cackle and his bristling moustache began to crinkle benignly, as befits any good story-teller easing pain with laughter. But that day's damage was so minor – a familiar insult and no Nobel – that Wiesenthal wanted to leave his well-wishers laughing.

The Nobel Prize he never won, though he was nominated four times by such varied sponsors as Nobel Laureates Henry Kissinger* and Betty Williams† as well as a Dutch parliamentary group. Favoured for it throughout the early eighties, Wiesenthal came closest in 1983, when the Norwegian selection committee would have given it to him if the prize had put their first choice, Lech Walesa, at too much risk with Poland's Communist authorities. When the embattled Polish labour leader (who later became President of his country) won, Wiesenthal rejoiced for him. For a couple of years thereafter, there was talk of Simon sharing the honour with the holocaust novelist and activist Elie Wiesel. Then, in 1986, the Nobel Peace Prize went to Wiesel alone.

Simon Wiesenthal's office when I first met him in 1974 was on the Rudolfsplatz an undistinguished inner-city square surrounding an unappetizing playground which never seemed to have any children in it. Rudolfsplatz Number 7 was a drab postwar apartment house in which Wiesenthal had maintained an office for a decade. When I reached the third floor (American fourth floor), I rang the bell beside a white door that said 'DOKUMENTATIONSZENTRUM'. A recorded voice asked me in German to speak my name and the purpose of my visit. The entrance's peephole, I could see, was a closed-circuit camera lens.

Before I'd finished announcing my name and that I had an appointment, the door swung open and a pretty red-haired secretary named Sonja greeted me and showed me down a narrow hall to a small office where Simon Wiesenthal was waiting with right hand outstretched. At sixty-five, Wiesenthal was already a living legend: fictionalized as 'Jakov Liebermann' in Ira Levin's *The Boys from Brazil* and portrayed as himself in *The Odessa File*. (In their film versions,

*Former US Secretary of State and co-winner for 1973 with his North Vietnamese negotiating partner, Le Duc Tho, who refused the prize because they had not negotiated true peace.

†Co-winner for 1976 with Mairead Corrigan for their peace efforts in Northern Ireland.

he was played in the former by Sir Laurence Olivier, who received an 'Oscar' nomination, and in the latter by Israeli actor Shmuel Rodonsky, who came out looking more like Simon than Simon himself.) Frederick Forsyth had found Wiesenthal 'bigger than . . . expected, a burly man over six feet tall, wearing a thick tweed jacket, stooping as if permanently looking for a mislaid piece of paper.' Levin, who hadn't yet met Wiesenthal, had nonetheless described him fairly astutely as 'a considerate bear with something contagious [who] carries the whole damned concentration-camp scene pinned to his coat-tails.' Sir Ben Kingsley, who would portray Wiesenthal in a made-for-television film of *The Murderers Among Us,* told me in 2001 that 'he is a man whose emotions are very close to the surface. Which makes him a great storyteller, a great balladeer. Simon's song is "Never Forget" and he wanders the world with it.'

This was the self-styled 'researcher' whose discovery of Adolf Eichmann's hideout had led to the Nazi genocidist's abduction from Argentina by Israeli agents in 1960 and his hanging in 1962 for the murders of six million men, women, and children . . . the unrelenting pursuer who had Franz Stangl, commandant of the extermination centres in Sobibor and Treblinka, extradited from Brazil, and Hermine Braunsteiner Ryan, 'the mare of Majdanek' who stomped hundreds of Jews to death, extradited from Queens to spend the rest of their lives in German jails . . . the demonic detective who was always, eternally, one phone call away from apprehending Dr Josef Mengele, the 'Angel of Auschwitz'. Since 1947, Wiesenthal had brought 1100 important Nazis to trial in different parts of the world and made countless others uncomfortable.

'In the moment when the Germans first came into my city in Galicia,' he said in heavily accented but always eloquent English, 'half the population was Jewish: one hundred fifty thousand Jews. When the Germans were gone, five hundred were alive. Five hundred in a hundred fifty thousand! One out of three hundred! Many times I was thinking that everything in life has a price, so to stay alive must also have a price. And my price was always that, if I lived, I must be deputy for many people who are not alive.'

We talked that day about his latest 'clients', as he calls Nazis he's brought to justice; until they're in custody, he labels them, with matching irony, 'the heroes'. One of the clients – in Graz, Austria's second-largest city – was pleading that he did only what everyone in his unit was doing, but Simon said: 'Camaraderie ends when crime begins.'

Then we talked of 'leftist fascism' and how the Russians and their Stalinist puppets in Eastern Europe issued decrees with the same wording used by the Nazi occupiers. As Simon put it: 'The world is round. If you go right, right, right, you come out on the left.'

We talked of his past and we talked of his unpaid helpers around the world. One, in Australia, was a nun: 'I don't ask her background, but I am sure it is maybe Jewish.'

He told of a fifteen-year search for 'a very little killer' he had just unearthed as a Buddhist monk in Katmandu: 'I have heard what that life is like; he is either punished every day or he repents every day. So I will close his file. To bring such a man before a court can only build him sympathy.'

By the end of a couple of hours together, Simon and I were on a first-name basis – a relationship which, in Austria, can take years, or forever, to ripen. It was late afternoon and he offered me a ride home in his small car. On our way out, we met an elderly couple who averted their eyes and said nothing when Simon greeted them.

'They are Jewish,' he whispered when we were one landing down. 'I meet them in the elevator and they are looking on me like I am their murderer.'

What had happened, he explained on the ride home, was a 'blackmail letter' campaign by 'the heroes' addressed to everybody in the building on Rudolfsplatz *except* Wiesenthal. The letter warned his fellow tenants that, 'when the Documentation Centre is bombed, you and your apartments are likely to perish in the blast, too.' All the neighbours – including the Jewish couple, who'd survived the death camps – had signed a petition and started a legal action to evict Wiesenthal as a threat to their security. (They succeeded a few months later, before the case ever came to court, when Simon moved one block away to the Salztorgasse.)

I invited him to my home for our next meeting. Whether or not he carries six million dead Jews on his coat-tails when he enters a room, there was something of a stage play or a grainy old black-and-white film about the way Wiesenthal bustles into any scene – as though something momentous is about to happen or be announced. My daughters, then ten and eleven, took his topcoat and hat. A minute or two later, one of them tiptoed into the living-room and whispered, 'Daddy, that man has a gun in his pocket.'

I asked Simon and he said, yes, the police had told him, in lieu of a bodyguard he'd declined, to carry the snub-nosed revolver he now showed us and then pocketed in his tweed jacket. (My daughters always frisked his topcoat on subsequent visits and never again struck heavy metal.) He certainly had good reason to carry his own protection. The neo-Nazi World Union of National Socialists had recently put a price of $120,000 on his head – dead, not alive. As a fugitive in Bolivia, Klaus Barbie, 'The Butcher of Lyon', once inquired into paying for Wiesenthal's assassination and, in Brazil, one of Dr Josef Mengele's hosts offered to 'put a steel cable to the leg of Simon Wiesenthal and drag his carcass behind my car.' Later, Simon learned of a Palestine Liberation Organization plot to kidnap and kill him, but the world's most notorious terrorist at the time – a mysterious Venezuelan named Ilich Ramirez Sanchez, but called 'Carlos' – was said to have vetoed the contract because the target was, after all, anti-fascist. Still later, in 1982, a bomb planted by neo-Nazis would destroy much of Simon's modest home in a garden district of Vienna and shatter what was left of his wife's health. (The following year, when Wiesenthal testified at their trial, one of the culprits leaped to his feet and tried to throttle him on the witness stand.)

Over vermouth and mineral water, he told how he'd been visited by an Austrian who'd served five years in the French Foreign Legion (fighting in the decisive Vietnamese battle of Dien Bien Phu in 1954) and another four and a half years in an Austrian prison for rape. On the day he was freed, a man named Robert was waiting at the gate to offer him a job: 100,000 Deutschmarks (almost $35,000 at the time) to kill Wiesenthal.

The Legionnaire, having been 'put on ice for four and a half years just for rape', didn't want to risk a murder rap, though he wasn't averse to fraud. So he came to Wiesenthal and said: 'I have been offered one hundred thousand marks to kill you. Maybe we can make a deal and split the money.'

'You mean I die and my widow gets fifty thousand?' Wiesenthal asked incredulously.

'You don't die. You don't play dead,' his caller assured him. He would meet with Robert and the four businessmen backing him –

three Germans and an Austrian – and negotiate an advance. Then Wiesenthal would call a press conference and reveal plot and plotters. He and the Legionnaire would split the advance – and let the 'heroes' try to get their money back!

Wiesenthal agreed, but brought in the Austrian police, too. They infiltrated two meetings and took pictures. The 'heroes', it turned out, were playing the Legionnaire for a fool, too. Not only did they decline to give him an advance, but the eavesdropping ascertained they had no intention of paying him when the job was done, either. Nevertheless, Wiesenthal took them to court to put their plot on the public record. Both Robert and the native businessman fled Austria, as did the three Germans, who had been using false names.

'The "heroes" are tired,' Wiesenthal concluded. 'I know it when they need outside help like a French Foreign Legionnaire to do their dirty work for them. But do you know something else? I am tired, too. I cannot teach my work to other people. There is nobody to succeed me, nobody left who is much younger, who would have my experience or could find out all that I carry in my head. But I will never retire . . . If I ever close my Centre here, I will have nothing to do but wait for my death. Besides, there are others waiting, too. For if I closed my office, it would be a Nazi holiday and a Jewish defeat – a defeat for humanity, a defeat for justice, too. And, believe me, the "heroes" will celebrate it as a victory – and they will begin again that much sooner.'

He denied he was 'some kind of modern Don Quixote or Jewish James Bond. Yes, my work is an adventure, but there are no romantics about it. You could make thriller after thriller out of my files, but I am not like James Bond because the results are not immediate; they can come in years, they may take generations. And Don Quixote I am not. Yes, many times I am fighting against imagination or a world that doesn't understand, but my fight is not without results.'

On his way out, he confided: 'I will tell you a secret. For a man who was in a ghetto and in concentration camps and lost all his blood relatives, my biggest personal satisfaction is not in having a Nazi arrested. It comes when two Nazis have a quarrel and one threatens the other with "I will go to Simon Wiesenthal about you." And he does! They are my best informers.'

At subsequent meetings, I was treated to a display of intellectual fireworks by a collector of circumstantial evidence on why, for example, Christopher Columbus's crew had to be on board the *Pinta*, the *Nina*, and the *Santa Maria* a day ahead of schedule and why Hitler hated the Jews. On the latter, Wiesenthal had this to say:

'I am sure Hitler had syphilis. His paranoia in the last days of the war was typical of a man with syphilis. I have the feeling – though I have no real evidence for it yet – that he contracted this syphilis in the time he was in Vienna before the war. I have been reading all these people like Joachim Fest and others who write books about Hitler that are supposed to tell you all, but in thousands of pages I see not one single word about the sickness of Hitler.'

Actually, the 1960 revised edition of Alan Bullock's *Hitler: A Study in Tyranny* did allude to his catching a venereal disease from a prostitute, but Wiesenthal first heard the theory propounded in the mid-sixties in Munich by a City Councilman named Fackler, who said he'd heard it from Ernst Hanfstaengel, a Harvard-educated local Nazi to whose country home Hitler fled after his abortive Beer Hall *Putsch* in 1923. According to Hanfstaengel, his good friend Hitler told him that, as a lance-corporal fighting in Flanders' fields in the First World War, he'd nearly been court-martialled for 'self-mutilation' when syphilis was diagnosed, but had escaped trial by proving he already had the condition before entering the Bavarian Army and therefore hadn't done anything new in the war to jeopardize his military service.

In Albert Speer's later years, Hitler's master builder and diarist of Nazi times had struck up what could not be called a friendship, but a research relationship with Wiesenthal.* So Simon didn't hesitate to try out his theory on Speer, whose reply came from Heidelberg

*Speer (1905–81), Hitler's wartime Minister for Armaments and War Production, was considered Nazism's second most powerful official and the only top Nazi leader at the Nuremberg trial in 1945–6 to shoulder responsibility for war crimes, for which he served nineteen years' imprisonment in Spandau fortress in West Berlin. An unsuccessful architect until he started winning commissions to co-design Nazi Party headquarters in major cities in the late 1920s, Speer became Hitler's chief architect at the age of twenty-eight soon after the Nazis came to power in 1933.

in an elegant envelope with an 'A.S.' monogram and no return address:

> I can't answer your question completely. Hitler in my presence never spoke of a syphilitic disease, though this does not mean he might not have had one some time earlier. What I can tell you is that his private doctor, Theo Morrell, used to hang his shingle on the Kurfürstendamm in Berlin as 'Specialist in Skin and Venereal Diseases'. From the moment he became the chief official physician of Hitler in 1936, however, that listing of his specialty disappeared.

This intrigued Wiesenthal, who told me: 'I am working on it in my spare time. If I can find a solution in another five or ten years, I would be very happy because this would give the whole story of Hitler and the Jews a different picture.'

'But where do the Jews enter that picture?' I asked him.

'Ah!' said Simon, slapping his knee. 'I haven't told you something else. A few years ago, I have a talk with a man who went to school with Hitler. I ask him what Hitler was like in school and he says, "Normal. But maybe this hatred began after he got this infection from a Jewish whore." . . . So I am looking now for names and details. I am just in the first stages, but I am telling you that if I can find out with evidence that Hitler's anti-Semitism was the aftermath of an infection from a Jewish prostitute, then all the Nazi racial theories sink a layer lower in the sewer. All the Nazis were anti-Semites, but hardly any of them had any personal experience with Jews. If Hitler did, this gives an answer to why he hated Jews the way he did.'

When I met him, Wiesenthal's research had brought him in contact with an expatriate physician, Edmund Ronald, then living in Portugal. In the early 1950s, while working in a Seattle hospital, Dr Ronald had met a young Austrian doctor from Graz who said his late father, also a doctor, had treated Hitler for syphilis long ago. After Austria had been annexed by Germany in 1938, Gestapo agents had confiscated all of his father's files on that particular patient, but the father had informed his son that Hitler told him he'd caught the disease from a Jewish prostitute before World War I. Though Dr Ronald gave Wiesenthal the name of his source, the young doctor from Graz later settled in the US and has not proved traceable.

In 1977, there was a medical debate over whether Hitler was sterile or impotent and Dr Ronald wrote from Bordighera, Italy, to the *International Herald Tribune* that

> Hitler was rather unlucky in his sexual affairs. He caught – according to Dr Anwyl-Davies, the eminent London venereologist – syphilis from a Jewish prostitute in Vienna in 1910 and had to have anti-syphilitic treatment on and off for the next twenty years and it is not certain that he [was] ever completely cured.

Dr Ronald, who subsequently died, went on to note that Hitler's love affair with his Viennese niece, Angela 'Geli' Raubal, ended with her unexplained suicide in 1931 at the age of twenty-three. Wiesenthal suspects she killed herself after her uncle infected her with syphilis.

Wiesenthal's work on Christopher Columbus had been more concentrated and productive. 'In my research on anti-Semitism throughout history,' he explained, 'when I concentrated on the Spanish Inquisition, I discovered an amazing coincidence. The two most important events of 1492 – both of which determined the entire future of Spanish history and much of world history – were the expulsion of the Jews from Spain and the discovery of America. All Jews had to be off Spanish soil by midnight of August second.

'Now Columbus didn't sail for "India", as they called all of Asia in those days, until August third, as scheduled. But his sailors had orders to report on the night of the second. This was not customary: a sailor's last night in port was sacred to him and was usually spent with his family or girlfriend before he came on board next day. I asked myself why.

'The tides weren't right for an earlier departure. And why did Columbus personally supervise the roll-call? So I began to look at the roll he called. One tenth of his crew was Jews; some of them, I learned later, may have been rabbis. But, even though nine-tenths of the crew wasn't Jewish, there was no priest aboard. Very unusual at sea!

'Then I am looking into the financing of his voyage. This business of Queen Isabella hocking her jewels to pay for it is all legend. With the help of *Marrano* ministers of hers, the mission was entirely financed by Jewish money.' A *Marrano* (from the Spanish word for 'pig' or 'damned') was a Jew who, in Wiesenthal's words, 'outwardly pretended to be a Christian, but secretly remained a Jew', while a *Converso* was 'a convert who broke off all relations with Jews and assimilated'. Both were suspect. It had been the discovery of *Marranos* partaking of a Passover seder in 1478 that led to the creation of the Spanish Inquisition, which used the rack, the pyre, the wheel, branding-irons and blinding-rods as well as bizarre pure-blood laws (direct ancestors of Hitler's Nuremberg Laws of racial purity) to get to the very bottom of a victim's religious beliefs.

'I began to ask myself,' Simon went on, 'why the Jews financed Columbus when all others had refused for years. Who was he and what did the Jews want from him?'

Cristoforo Colombo (1451–1506), an Italian mariner known to Spaniards as Christóbal Colón, came from a family of 'Spanish Jews settled in Genoa', according to his contemporary biographer, Salvadore de Madariaga, who believes the Colóns converted to Christianity during Spanish persecutions in the fourteenth century. Around 1479, Columbus married a Portuguese noblewoman of *Marrano* descent. After some preliminary study, Wiesenthal went to Spain to examine materials preserved in the Biblioteca Columbina (Columbus Library) in Seville. In the archives, Simon found a dozen intimate letters from Columbus to his son, Diego. All of them bore not just the obligatory cross at the top, but also a strange boat-like symbol in the upper left-hand corner.

With the help of an American Jewish scholar named Maurice David, Wiesenthal deciphered it as two Hebrew characters, *beth* and *hei*, standing for *baruch hashem*, meaning *Praised be the Lord*. It was, Wiesenthal thinks, Columbus's way of reminding his son: 'Do not forget where you come from. The cross is a tribute to the religion you now follow, but within the circle of your family give the sign *beth hei, so* that they remember their origins.' In one of the letters, Wiesenthal adds, he discussed with Diego the possibility of marriage to a *Marrano*.

'I spent a lot of time in Seville,' Wiesenthal went on. 'I had in my hands all his writings that have survived – not just letters, but books he had read, with his jottings in the margins, and books he valued enough to have copied for himself at his own expense: usually by hand, because this was very soon after Gutenberg.* Now why

* Johann Gutenberg (1397–1468), a German printer, invented movable type in the late 1430s.

would you imagine that a Christian sailor five hundred years ago would make a copy of a work by Rabbi Samuel Jehudi urging Jews to accept conversion, even forced baptism? There were just too many coincidences.

'In all, I find two hundred and fifty references by Columbus to Jews. He knew the Jewish calendar, the Jewish prophets, and his diary showed a deep knowledge of Jewish history. The beliefs of Columbus were a mixture of Christianity and Judaism. In a book of history by Pope Pius the Second, he makes a marginal note that the year 1481's Jewish equivalent was 5241. He writes that Adam lived to be one hundred fifty years old and, when he tells how the Second Temple of Jerusalem was destroyed in the year Seventy by the Romans, he calls it *Casa secunda*, the Second House. Only Jews use that phrase; in no non-Jewish publication have I ever met this idiom, Second House.

'But the most important marginal note I find is the one that tells me Columbus knows the diary of Rabbi Benjamin of Tudela, who travelled in the east three centuries before him and came to the conclusion that the ten lost tribes of Israel were in "India". I have this book in my own library. So now I go back to the register of the crew and look a little closer. Not only are there a number of Jewish names, but later I learn that several in Columbus's crew spoke Hebrew and a couple of them may have been rabbis. And who was the interpreter on board? Luis de Torres, who had been interpreter for the Governor of Murcia, which had a large Jewish population. It took me two weeks to confirm that Luis de Torres had been the governor's interpreter of Hebrew. Now the only possible explanation of this is that Columbus expected to reach countries in which Jews lived and governed.'

From research on Columbus that began around 1965, Wiesenthal was convinced 'that the Jews, concerned about their deteriorating situation in Spain,† were looking for a homeland, a place to flee to, where they would find a protector. And so, in the belief that the ten lost tribes had found refuge in "India", they financed the expedition of Columbus: a man they could trust.' Simon says

†With the expulsion of 1492, some 100,000 *Marranos* settled in Portugal and thousands of others in Italy and North Africa. Spain never recovered from this loss of heart, mind, and money.

...mbus was surely a *Converso* and quite likely a *Marrano*: 'I am ...onvinced he was following the Law of Moses. But I'm not saying to the bitter end that I'm sure he's Jewish. I make the matter open.'

Still, when Simon wrote a book-length manuscript that became *Sails of Hope: the Secret Mission of Christopher Columbus*, he hesitated to offer it to publishers because 'I feel when I give out that Columbus had a Hebrew interpreter, people will think I am absolutely crazy or else some Jewish fanatic. So I cannot publish the book. But then I have an idea. I was invited to lecture in Lisbon, so I am going to the Royal Library there and looking on the documents of Vasco da Gama, who was also looking for a way to India and really found it.* He had also an interpreter for the Hebrew language. When I saw this, now I should publish.'

When Wiesenthal's French literary agent, Charles Ronsac, sold *Sails of Hope* to six European publishers and Macmillan in America (1973), an editor in the New York office objected facetiously: 'The Italian Mafia will kill us!' and Wiesenthal said: 'After this book is published, all Jews will have three holidays: Rosh Hashonah, Yom Kippur, and Columbus Day.'

Actually, the only problem came in Spain, where a Wiesenthal reference to three Franco families who sailed to the New World in 1510 was punctuated with: 'Franco was a common Jewish name in the fifteenth, sixteenth, and seventeenth centuries.' This did not sit well with the fascist dictatorship of Generalissimo Francisco Franco (1892–1975) and *Sails of Hope* was banned in Spain. Wiesenthal says the reference was no accident and was, in fact, his way of thanking Franco for his reluctance to repatriate Jewish refugees who escaped to Spain during the war.

During my dialogues with Wiesenthal, I wondered what the Hebrew interpreter Luis de Torres, who was the first member of the expedition to set foot in the New World, might have said to the 'Indians' when the *Pinta*, *Nina*, and *Santa Maria* landed in the Bahamas on 12 October 1492: 'Did he address them in Hebrew?'

'That I don't know,' Simon said, adding deadpan, 'But I can tell you what the Indians said back to the white man: "Now begins the *tsuris*."'†

*Vasco da Gama (1469–1524) sailed around the Cape of Good Hope on his epochal voyage of 1497–9 for King Manuel I of Portugal.

†*Tsuris*: Yiddish for *troubles*.

– 2 –

The many liberations of Szymon Wiesenthal

When Simon Wiesenthal turned ninety on 31 December 1998, many well-wishers thought he had already been eighty all year because his date of birth was in 1908 – but barely. Bare is how he was born half an hour before midnight on New Year's Eve 1908 in his parents' bedroom in the small town of Buczacz (pronounced *Boo-tchotch*) in Galicia, then the eastern part of the Austro-Hungarian Empire and now the western part of the Ukrainian republic. 'Through half an hour, I am older by a year,' he says with a laugh whenever an interviewer, subtracting 1908 from the present, overestimates his age. When the midwife emerged with the news that a healthy boy was born, Asher Wiesenthal opened a bottle of schnapps and, with a handful of relatives and neighbours, toasted a particularly Happy New Year.

The midwife dutifully registered Szymon's birth in the town office, but his superstitious maternal grandfather, believing that 1909's first-born would win God's special favour, took the liberty of also enrolling him at the top of the new year's book of life. The old man's wife was something of a mystic, as befits a woman whose maiden name was Freud. She liked to take her grandchild on outings to various 'miracle rabbis' of Galicia and have special blessings bestowed upon the boy. 'All my education before school was my grandmother,' Simon recalls, 'with her stories of rabbis and miracles. Through this education, I not only tend to think in a Talmudic way, but I can always reason with rabbis and other religious people because I speak their language.'

The map of Europe in 1909 was vastly different from (and in some ways similar to) the Continent we know now. There were no countries called Yugoslavia or Czechoslovakia, but there were prickly nations known as Serbia, Macedonia, and Montenegro. Albania was a monarchy and Bulgaria and Romania were major powers. Poland was part of Russia, though the city of Cracow was Austro-Hungarian. Austrian might extended from the Alps southward into Italy (a vestige of the Habsburg dynasty's reign until 1806 as Holy Roman Emperors) and nearly a thousand miles eastward from Vienna. With the annexation of Bosnia and Herzogovina a few weeks before Szymon was born, Austria – already a formidable naval force through its port of Trieste – ruled the Adriatic.

In the Austrian crown-land of Galicia – with its 1,700,000 Ukrainians, 1,000,000 Poles, and 800,000 Jews – smouldering tensions enabled the Viennese Habsburgs to divide and rule with deceptive ease. In Buczacz, however, Jews were no minority, for the land's ethnic mix was reversed: of the town's 9000 inhabitants, 6000 were Jews, 2000 Poles, and, at the bottom of the local ladder, 1000 Ukrainians, mostly poor and of peasant origin.

A Jew could hold his head up high in Buczacz, says Simon, though Galicia in general, he hastens to add, was traditionally the land of pogroms: 'Nowhere else have the Jews suffered so much for so long.' His own father used to tell him how a village priest, who loved his schnapps, but couldn't always pay for his drinks, left his church key as security with a Jewish tavern-owner one Saturday night, promising to settle his debt out of Sunday's collection. Next morning, when his Ukrainian parishioners couldn't get in to attend mass, he told them: 'The dirty Jew at the pub has locked you out. Go get the key from him!' They did – by beating the Jewish pub-keeper within an inch of his life, smashing or drinking everything in his tavern, celebrating mass, and then extending the celebration with a little local pogrom, amen!

The Ukrainians of Galicia were descendants of sixteenth- and seventeenth-century Cossacks whose leaders made an unfortunate alliance with the Grand Duchy of Muscovy (now Moscow) in 1641. It imposed the Czar's yoke upon the whole Ukraine, a territory of 232,000 square miles, which exceeds the areas of France and England. Devoutly Catholic and fiercely independence-minded, the Ukrainians were neither the first nor the last people in the world to hold the Jews somehow responsible for their plight. To this day, Simon Wiesenthal is still battling Ukrainians – in Canada, the US, and elsewhere around the world, if not in the Ukraine itself.

Asher Wiesenthal, a 1905 refugee from the pogroms of czarist Russia, had established himself in Buczacz as a solid citizen trading in sugar and other wholesale commodities. Simon's own memories of early childhood are pleasant ones of going to his father's warehouse and erecting his first houses and castles with white sugar cubes. They were the Lego of yesteryear for one who would grow up to be an architect and 'learn to build houses according to certain structural rules so that they could withstand an earthquake' – only to change careers after discovering the hard way that '"The Final Solution of the Jewish Question" was the kind of earthquake for which there was no building code.'

Wiesenthal remembers, too, the Passover table with an extra, ornate cup set for the prophet Elijah. After a special prayer, Szymon – and later his brother, for this was the youngest's honour – would open the door and leave it ajar, for, sometime that evening, the prophet was expected to enter the room and sip from his cup. In the same way that other children elsewhere in the world wait up for Santa Claus on Christmas Eve, the Wiesenthal boys would watch the door with wide eyes that narrowed as the night wore on. 'But, of course,' says Simon, 'nobody came.' Their grandmother, however, insisted that Elijah really drank from the cup and, when they found it full, she would say: 'He doesn't drink more than a tear.'

* * *

With the outbreak of world war in 1914, Asher Wiesenthal, a reservist in the Austro-Hungarian Army, was called up to active duty and sent to the eastern front. There he died in combat in 1915 – fighting for the same cause for which Lance-Corporal Adolf Hitler was soldiering on the western front. In a war that would cost the world eight and a half million deaths and nearly thirty-eight million casualties, Szymon and his brother wept for their father as the only one among many.

Around that time of bereavement, the town of Buczacz became a battleground. When the Czar's Cossacks conquered Galicia, the bereaved Wiesenthals were forced to flee because, as Simon recalls, 'someone told the Russians that my father was not only an enemy soldier who had died fighting Russians, but a refugee from Russia and therefore we were Russians who killed Russians. We didn't know what they would do to us, but we knew they'd find an excuse to do something, so my mother and brother and I escaped to the Austrian part of the empire and I was a refugee in Vienna for the first time around.'

They took rooms on the Bäuerlegasse in the Jewish quarter known as 'Matzoh Island' between the Danube Canal and the river. Both Wiesenthal boys started school in the Austrian capital where, from 1907 to 1913, the Austrian-born, possibly syphilitic Hitler had tried to show the world he was a painter. Twice rejected by the Academy of Fine Arts, Hitler noted that four of the seven professors who denied him admission were Jewish and wrote to the Academy that 'for this the Jews would pay.' And, in his autobiographical *Mein Kampf (My Struggle)*, Hitler wrote that Vienna was 'the hardest, though most thorough, school of my life' – the place where he learned his anti-Semitism from the ideas of the German nationalist Georg von Schönerer (1842–1921) and the utterances of Karl Lueger, mayor of Vienna from 1896 until his death in 1910

Simon has few memories of his stay in Vienna as a six- and seven-year-old – except that it was a relatively happy time before the glory and jubilation of war gave way to hunger and defeat. A Jewish family whose patriarch had perished on the Russian front was welcomed and even honoured in a city that was thriving on wartime prosperity and patriotism even while Franz Joseph slowly breathed his last in Schönbrunn palace and the dead and dying piled up in cattle trucks on railway sidings throughout his doomed empire.

After Franz Joseph died on 21 November 1916, the Wiesenthal boys had a day off from school to watch the Kaiser's black funeral coach crawl through the city, but they were hardly aware that an era had ended. The austere but beloved Kaiser (Emperor) had reigned for nearly sixty-eight of his eighty-six years. His twenty-nine-year-old grandnephew, who became Emperor Karl I, would preside irresolutely over the dissolution of the 640-year-old Habsburg monarchy, which had less than two years to live.

In 1917, the Russians retreated from Galicia and the Wiesenthals returned to Buczacz, where they were caught up in the swirl of history. 'I come from a very windy corner of Europe. Our part of Galicia changed hands so often that I was six times "liberated" before I finished high school,' Simon recalls with irony. 'After the Cossacks liberated us from the Austrians and then the Austrians liberated us back, it was the Ukrainians' turn to liberate us and, for three months after the armistice in 1918, eastern Galicia was the Western Ukrainian Republic. Then the Poles liberated us and we became Polish. After the Polish-Bolshevik War began in 1920, the Soviets liberated us. Then the Poles came back. To survive under such circumstances is a school, I tell you. Nobody could teach *us* anything new until, a couple of liberations later, we got Hitler.'

Of all the early 'liberations', the brief Ukrainian postwar interim was the most painful for young Szymon. Like their Cossack forebears, the Ukrainians robbed, raped, and killed, but their fuel was alcohol and their troops could drink the Czar's army (as well as themselves) under the table. One afternoon, their high command gave the Jews of Buczacz an ultimatum to deliver 300 litres of schnapps by five o'clock or their homes would burn. Szymon and his brother and mother and every Jew in town scoured Buczacz for booze and, when the Ukrainian demand was met, they stayed indoors for the long night of revelry ahead.

The next day, as drunken soldiers still staggered and slept in the streets, women were afraid to venture outdoors, but Szymon's mother thought it safe to send her ten-year-old son across the road to borrow yeast from a neighbour for baking. As Simon returned, a soldier on horseback gave chase and, just for fun, lunged at him with a sabre, slashing his right thigh. Simon collapsed, but neighbours carried him into his house. The doctor who stitched the wound had to reach his patient by a labyrinthine route through cellars and back yards. Wiesenthal still wears that scar across his upper thigh, but insists quite sincerely that 'some of my best friends are Ukrainians. One of them saved my life in 1941.'

As the Red Army, founded by Leon Trotsky, overran the Ukraine, the newly independent Poles pushed the Ukrainians out of Galicia and went to war with Russia themselves. The Ukrainians' various successors were less brutal, but scarcely benevolent. Attending the local academic high school (Humanistic Gymnasium, it was called) in the 1920s, Simon recalls, 'we would get up in the morning not knowing which regime was in power. When we were asked to who we swore our eternal loyalty, we had to look at the picture on the wall above the teacher's table. One week it was Lenin, the next there was a Ukrainian, and then it was the Polish Marshal Pilsudski.

The Bolsheviks rounded up all the *bourgeoisie* and made them pay ransom. My mother and other Jewish women were made to clean up the local sports hall, which the Russians had turned into a stable.' Memory of this humiliation still smarts; eyes and mouth narrow as he relates it.

As for the Poles, 'they did not like us Jews – and that was no new thing. Our fathers had crept out of the confines of the ghetto into the open world. They had worked hard and done all they could to be recognized by their fellow creatures. But it was all in vain. If the Jews shut themselves away from the rest of the world, they were foreign bodies. If they left their own world and conformed, they were undesirable immigrants to be hated and rejected. Even in my youth, I realized I'd been born a second-class citizen.

'A wise man,' Wiesenthal goes on, 'once said that the Jews were the salt of the earth. But the Poles thought their land had been ruined by over-salting. Compared with Jews in other countries, therefore, we were maybe better prepared for what the Nazis had in store for us.' And maybe, he adds, 'made more resistant.'

At the Humanistic Gymnasium of Buczacz – where Jewish parents and ambitious Poles sent their children to learn Latin and Greek in hope of going on to university in Lwów or Warsaw – Szymon met a comely dark-blonde Jewish classmate, Cyla Müller, a distant relative of the Moravian-born Viennese psychoanalyst Sigmund Freud (who was, in turn, no relation to Wiesenthal's maternal Grandma Freud). Szymon and Cyla fell in love and it was taken for granted by all who knew them, including their parents, that the high-school sweethearts would one day marry.

Though that day didn't come until 1936, when Szymon was twenty-seven, the young couple kept close company even after Szymon's mother remarried in 1925 and moved to the town of Dolina in the Carpathian Mountains, where her new husband owned a tile factory. Though his brother went with her, Szymon remained in Buczacz to finish his studies. He visited his family often and took to the Carpathian countryside with zest, riding horses and hiking as well as vacationing whenever he could in the mountain resort of Zakopane, where 'in summer were the woods, sunshine, peace; in winter was good skiing.'

Early in 1926, in the final hour of which he turned eighteen, Szymon registered with the Polish military authorities for future conscription. The following year, however, his grandfather's favour of enrolling him as the first baby of 1909 came home to haunt him. Two policemen arrived to arrest him for failing to register for military service in 1927. Facing jail or immediate induction, Szymon protested that he'd registered in 1926. This was to no avail: boys born in 1909 had to register in 1927. The 1908-model Szymon Wiesenthal was not their concern, the authorities said, unless this Szymon they had in custody could prove conclusively that he was one and the same. A Polish magistrate told Wiesenthal to produce two witnesses to swear affidavits that they knew him during the half-hour of his life that he purported to have spent in 1908.

Having to prove his existence hardly fazed the early Wiesenthal. Scouring Buczacz for 'witnesses who'd remember, to the exact minute, something that had happened almost twenty years ago', he found two neighbours who *did* remember the midwife's announcement *preceding* the proud father's uncorking a bottle of schnapps at midnight. That detail, says Wiesenthal, 'convinced the magistrate and settled the matter, so my birthday was legally recognized and they had to look elsewhere for the younger Szymon Wiesenthal.' Still, this first formal brush with bureaucracy set him thinking about his identity crisis: 'What if it had not been New Year's Eve? What if it had been just an ordinary night with no party, no witnesses? Then where would I be?'

His status clarified, he was now able to obtain a student deferment to study architecture – not at the Technical University in Lwów, the Galician provincial capital where there was a Jewish quota, but at the Czech Technical University in Prague. The golden city on the Moldau* proved not only an architectural revelation, but also – in the post-World War I democracy that Czechoslovak President Tomáš G. Masaryk created with the help of his friend Woodrow Wilson – a truly liberating experience to a young Polish Jew who had been 'liberated' too many times by vicious anti-Semites.

It was in the student cellars of Prague that the gregarious raconteur his friends now know emerged from the shadows of caution and discretion to shine as a master of ceremonies and even a stand-up comedian. Later, back in Lwów, he would edit a satiric student weekly called *Omnibus*, which made fun of communists and Nazis

**Moldau* in German is now *Vltava* in Czech.

and of which he suspects 'the Polish Ministry of Interior must have a complete archive because every week the censor confiscated us for one reason or another' – an offending cartoon or a biting feuilleton. 'We had many a joke together,' he recalls of his student days, 'we who were young with life stretching before us.' But Simon, at least, could sense the most ominous shadow enveloping Europe.

In 1932, Simon's senior year, Adolf Hitler was storming the threshold of power in Germany and, near Prague's ghetto of the golem† and Franz Kafka, Wiesenthal was a regular attraction at a Jewish students' cabaret. 'You know,' he told an appreciative audience of Jewish and Gentile students in the spring of that year, 'we Jews have always managed to get something good to eat out of even our worst tragedies. After Pharaoh, we have matzoh for Passover. After Haman, we have *Hamantashen*‡ for Purim. And, after Hitler, oh what a feast we'll have!'

Sixty years after he told it, I asked Simon Wiesenthal what he thought of his joke now. 'It may have been funny then, but it isn't funny now,' he replied. 'Normally, when you have a problem, if you can make from it a joke, you can, with ten words, say more than in a book. But nobody could imagine what was Hitler. Yes, Pharaoh and Haman had hate, too, but Hitler had the technology of genocide.' And little did Wiesenthal know that his mother and eighty-eight other relatives would vanish into Hitler's boxcars, gas chambers, and ovens.

Implicit in this contemporary analysis of his own joke are two themes that recur in conversations with Wiesenthal. One is 'humour as the weapon of unarmed people: it helps people who are oppressed to smile at the situation that pains them.' In the 1960s and 1970s, Wiesenthal published several volumes of Polish underground humour clandestinely in Poland, but under the pen-name of 'Mishka

†*Golem:* A legendary robot said to have been invented by Judah Löwe, a real rabbi in seventeenth-century Prague, to protect the Jews from anti-Semitic plots. Widely known from the 1916 German novel by Gustav Meyrink and the 1920 Yiddish play by H. Leivick.

‡*Matzoh:* The unleavened bread eaten in the thirteenth century BC by Jews fleeing from Egypt without waiting for the dough to rise. *Hamantashen:* A triangular poppyseed pastry prepared for the joyous religious holiday celebrating the deliverance of the Jews from their Persian oppressor, Haman, as chronicled in The Book of Esther.

Kukin' – not just to protect his serious image in the West, he explained to me in 1976, but also 'because ninety-five per cent of Polish jokes in Poland are making fun of the government. I had to deal with communist authorities and they would be in trouble if they were giving information to someone who pokes fun at the regime. Even though everybody knew "Kukin" was me, they could pretend not to know.'

His other theme stems from his half-century of experience with genocide – too much of it first-hand – in which he has discerned that 'in the whole human history, whenever a crime was committed against an innocent people, there were always the same six components:

'*Hatred* is the juice on which those two monsters of human history, Hitler and Stalin, survived. In all countries of the world, most people want to live in peace. It is only the extremism of their leaders that makes them hate and develops their hatred. None of my "clients" – not Eichmann, not Stangl, not Mengele, and not even Hitler or Stalin – was born a criminal. Somebody had to teach them to hate: maybe the society, maybe the politics, maybe just a Jewish prostitute.

'*Dictatorship* is the second component. What connects two thousand years of genocide? Too much power in too few hands. An emperor, a king; a pope, a bishop or archbishop; a president, a general, a committee or a commission like the Spanish Inquisition that has the power in a dictatorship of hatred needs . . .

'*Bureaucracy*: not just people sitting behind desks, but people who follow orders to kill people. The ones who operated gas chambers or guillotines or ran torture cellars: they were bureaucrats who became murderers. The Germans of the 1940s had many of the same slogans as the Spanish inquisitors of the 1490s, and when the Russians took over from the Germans they used very often the same wording for their decrees. Even the Nuremberg Laws of racial purity* were nothing new; they were a Spanish invention. But the

*Promulgated in 1935, the Nuremberg Laws divided the population into two classes: *Reich citizens* 'of German or related blood' with full civic rights, and *State subjects,* whose rights were curtailed. One of these regulations, the Law for Protection of German Blood and Honour, specified in its first article: 'Marriages between Jews and citizens of German or related blood are forbidden. Marriages contracted in contravention of this law are invalid, even if contracted abroad . . .' The second article prohibited 'extramarital relations between Jews and citizens of German or related

Nazis only went back three generations while the Inquisition's "Certificate of Good Blood" went back seven generations. No, my friend, Hitler invented absolutely nothing, but what he had going for him was the . . .

'*Technology* of our times, which gave him the possibility to fulfil the dream of thousands and thousands of haters for many, many centuries: a world without Jews. If the Inquisition five hundred years ago had had the technology of Hitler, they would not have given Jews choices like "baptize or die!" or "baptize or go out of the country". From the annals of the Inquisition, I find that around 1485, they were looking for an inventor to make a machine that could kill seven people all at the same time. Believe me, if they'd had the technology they wanted, no Jew would have survived in Spain, no Protestant in France, and maybe no Catholic in England.

'*A crisis or a war* is the next component. In what other time is it easiest to kill innocent people? In a crisis, you need scapegoats and a diversion from your own problems. In a war, the country is closed and, even in a democracy, you have secrecy. So there is no way for people to look, see, and ask questions.

'*A minority as victim* is the last component. It can be a racial, social, or political minority that the dictators and their bureaucrats – those with power, hatred, and technology – can hold responsible for a situation.'

Wiesenthal goes on to say that 'when the Turks killed a million and a half Armenians almost a hundred years ago, those six components of genocide were there and they were there, too, when the Spanish Inquisition put twenty people on a stake and burned them. And I can promise you that Hitler has studied very carefully both those holocausts.'

To Simon Wiesenthal today, hatred is the fuse which he fears will ignite the next world holocaust: 'Technology without hatred

blood.' In the SS, sexual relations with Jewish prisoners were punishable by beheading. 'An SS member's sexual organ,' said SS chief Heinrich Himmler, 'being the portion of his anatomy with which he makes possible the perpetuation of the Aryan race, must never be befouled through coitus with Jewesses or women of other subhuman races.' Other Nuremberg Laws established elaborate provisions for 'scientifically' determining percentages of Jewish blood in one's pedigree.

can be a blessing, though not always. Technology *with* hatred is always a disaster. What will happen to this world when the haters of today, the terrorists, come into possession of the technology of our time?'

When Wiesenthal reads of disarmament negotiations in Geneva, Vienna, Washington, and Moscow, he wonders whether 'it is more important to reduce weapons than to reduce hate. I am more optimistic about their reducing weapons than about their reducing hate. Right now, we have the technology to kill each of us eight times. I like to think that, in my lifetime, the super- and not-so-superpowers can get together and reduce it to four times. Then I might die more hopeful for my daughter and grandchildren.'

Wiesenthal, who would experience both Hitler and Stalin, says today that 'the biggest difference between the two as criminals is that Hitler told the truth about what he would do to Europe, what he would do to the Jews, but nobody believed him. Stalin lied about his genocide, about the gulag, and the world believed him, so he lasted longer and got to kill more people than Hitler did.'

In 1934 and 1935, Wiesenthal apprenticed as a building engineer in Soviet Russia. He spent a few weeks in Kharkov and Kiev, but most of those two years in the Black Sea port of Odessa, which he remembers as 'a lovely city' in the Ukraine 'where I spent twenty-one months learning dictatorship from Stalin. When I saw what the Soviets did to their own people – arrests right and left – this was for me not only very good preparation for the Nazis, but also what would happen if we ever came under Russian control.' What disturbed him almost as much at the time, however, was that 'on the streets, all people looked alike: Ukrainians, Russians, Jews, even ethnic Germans. They wore the same clothes, they had the same faces set in the same attitude, they seemed to have the same character: everything under Stalin was drab and uniform. When Hitler came, he would have a hard time figuring out which were the Jews and which were the other "sub-humans". I myself stood out in the crowd just by being me.'

Returning to Galicia at the end of his Russian apprenticeship, Wiesenthal was at last allowed to enter the Technical University of Lwów for the advanced degree that would allow him to practise architecture in Poland. For a while, he roomed on Janowskà Street: future site of the concentration camp in which he would live much of the war. Geographically, it was an easy stroll to the Technical University on Sapiehy Street, which also housed Loncki Prison, a future Gestapo torture centre. Even then, Jewish students took the long way around, bypassing Sapiehy Street, for its residents were Polish officers and officials, professionals and businessmen, whose sons comprised most of the student body of Lwów's Technical and Agricultural Universities. These 'gilded youths' would fasten razor blades to sticks as weapons with which to attack Jewish students and leave them bleeding on the pavement.

'In the evening,' Wiesenthal recalls, 'it was dangerous to walk Sapiehy Street if you so much as looked Jewish, especially at times when the young National Democrats or Radical Nationalists were turning their anti-Jewish slogans from theory into practice. And there was never a policeman in sight.'

What perplexed Wiesenthal was that 'at a time when Hitler was on Poland's frontiers, poised to annex Polish territory, these Polish "patriots" could think of only one thing: the Jews and how much they hated them. In Germany, at that time, they were building new weapons factories, they were building strategic roads straight towards Poland, and they were calling up thousands of Germans for military service. But the Polish parliament paid little notice to this menace: it had "more important" things to do – new regulations for kosher butchering, for instance – which might make life more difficult for the Jews.'

The Technical University's yellow and terracotta neo-classical main building stood behind a low stone wall with a high iron fence. Inside lay no sanctuary. In the upper hall were the offices of Professor Derdacki, for whom Wiesenthal did his diploma work by designing a tuberculosis sanatorium, and Professor Bagierski, who corrected many of his essays. Both were notorious anti-Semites. When Bagierski had to confer with a Jewish student, Wiesenthal remembers, 'he seemed to lose his breath and stutter more than usual.' In 1936, a roving band flung a Jewish student over the ornate balustrade just outside the dean of architecture's office.

In 1937, while Wiesenthal was still formalizing his degree, the Polish Radicals proclaimed their provisional utopia: a 'Day without Jews', usually during examination periods, as a way to reduce the already tiny number of Jewish students. Though beribboned fraternity brothers lay in ambush with spiked clubs, the faculty wouldn't grant make-up exams, so the Jews ran their gauntlet. On the 'Day without Jews', ambulances waited just outside the campus, which was off limits to the Polish police.

Poland wouldn't mobilize against her real enemies until 31 August 1939, the day before Germany invaded. The country's cavalry, booted and spurred, rode into gallant but hopeless action against Hitler's tanks and dive-bombers. So much for 'Polish romanticism', which Szymon Wiesenthal experienced at the cutting edge. 'Where are they now, these super-patriots who dreamed of a "Poland without Jews"?' he would ask. 'Perhaps the day when there would be no more Jews was not far off and their dream would be realized. Only there wouldn't be a Poland either!'

In 1936, soon after his return from Odessa, Szymon and Cyla had married, though the threat of Hitler was enough for the couple, both nearing thirty, to defer bringing a child into their perilous world. Yet, even before he had his Polish diploma in hand, Szymon Wiesenthal was confident enough to open an architectural office in Lwów. He specialized in elegant villas, which wealthy Polish Jews and Gentiles were still building without even trying to read Hitler's handwriting on their walls. 'Right to the end,' says Wiesenthal, 'people surrounded themselves with possessions. They must have thought that somehow property would protect them. Maybe, in those days, I thought that way, too.'

While many architects in Lwów favoured façade over function, Wiesenthal's thinking fell somewhere between the philosophies of two Viennese architectural pioneers: Adolf Loos's 'ornament is crime' and Otto Wagner's more reticent view that function can be ornamental. To Wiesenthal, 'when you start from the outside, eventually you have to cripple function to fit façade. But when the function works, the façade will be absolutely right.' The Wagner-Loos influence is just one reason why Simon takes particular pride in the day in 1990 when, decked out like a Medici cardinal, he received an honorary Doctorate of Architecture from the University of Vienna.

★★★

So far as Simon Wiesenthal knows, none of the housing he built in Galicia still stands. The two houses he remembers most fondly are the first and the last. Toward the start of his career in 1936, he built a rustic villa in Dolina for his mother and stepfather. His final commission came in early 1939 from 'a very rich man, a *nouveau riche* Jewish man, who said to me when I asked what kind of programme he had for his house: "I buy this piece of land. I wish to make a house. You want to know my programme? I have many enemies. So my programme is that when my enemies see this house, they should die of envy."'

Wiesenthal put everything he had into this job, which he finished just before 23 August 1939, when Hitler and Stalin signed a 'non-aggression' pact partitioning Poland between them with secret provisions for incorporating the independent Baltic states of Estonia, Latvia, and Lithuania into the Soviet Union the following year. World War II began a week later when Germany invaded Poland from the west shortly before Russia invaded from the east. When the Red Army occupied Dolina, it paid the thirty-year-old architect a dubious tribute by picking 'the best house in town' for its regional commander's residence and evicting Simon's elders.

In late September, after the Red Army had conquered Galicia, plainclothesmen from the NKVD, the Soviet security police, rounded up Jewish 'bourgeois' merchants and industrialists, including Simon's stepfather, who died in a Soviet prison. Simon's mother came to live with him and Cyla in Lwów, which was now called Lvov in Russian. Though Daylight Saving Time hadn't come to Europe yet, the Galicians got it first, for they had to set their clocks ahead two hours to conform to Moscow time.

In Lvov, Wiesenthal's *nouveau riche* client's enemies were envious, all right, so they denounced the man as a capitalist to the Russians, who could see the truth of it with their own eyes. Deported to Siberia, he never came back – and it could be said that, thanks to the house that Wiesenthal built for him, it was the client who died of envy.

Four weeks after Lwów became Lvov, everybody had to register for a new passport: 'valid five years and renewable thereafter', they were told optimistically. Anyone who declared himself a merchant or property-owner, however, was deported to Siberia. Jewish intellectuals – including doctors, lawyers, and teachers – had the designation '§11' stamped on their passports, marking them as second-class citizens banned from living in large cities or anywhere within a hundred kilometres (sixty-two miles) of the border. A few months later, all holders of Paragraph 11 passports were deported to Siberia as security risks. Not too many survived the war.

Later, Wiesenthal would observe that one difference between Soviet and Nazi genocide was that the Russians liquidated the capitalists first and then the intelligentsia, but the Nazis did it the other way round in order to learn and master the Jewish businesses they took over. With his clientele depleted and materials pillaged by the Red Army, Szymon survived in Soviet Lvov not as an architect, but as a mechanic in a bed-springs factory. By bribing an NKVD commissar, he was able to obtain normal passports for his wife, his mother and himself.

In Lvov, all businesses and houses were nationalized; an occasional homeowner was allowed to stay on as superintendent of his former property – with tenants chosen by the government. No visitor was allowed to stay overnight without permission from the nearest militia post, which made frequent middle-of-the-night spot checks.

Next in the Sovietization process came shortages. Waiting in line for a loaf of bread took two to three hours; for a kilo (2.2 pounds) of sugar, four to five hours. A new industry arose: line-standing. One could hire a professional line-stander for several times the price of the goods. This, in turn, spawned a thriving black market selling sugar for twenty-five times the official price.

With Russian soldiers and officials sometimes buying out everything in a store and promising to pay later, and with their women buying nightgowns and wearing them as evening dresses . . . with jail sentences for coming late to work and constant parades and mandatory free elections to participate in, the people of Lvov accepted their latest 'Liberation' with resignation and almost relief. 'It was not as grim as some of the others,' Wiesenthal concedes, deflecting the pain with a Czech riddle about what would happen if the Soviets had fulfilled their dream of African expansion and taken over the Sahara.

Wiesenthal's answer: 'For two years, nothing would happen – and then they would have to import sand.'

By mid-1940, the arrests and midnight raids had ceased – and enough normalcy had returned that it was safe for Szymon's design for a sanatorium finally to be accepted by Professor Derdacki. 'With generally satisfactory grades' on his tests, Wiesenthal was granted a diploma on 25 June and licensed as an architectural engineer. He gave up his job of twisting bed-springs to take a clerical post in a construction company which had little or nothing to erect. But an agricultural co-operative near Odessa needed outbuildings for feather-plucking, so Szymon returned twice to the city of his apprenticeship and worked his way up to chief engineer of the firm.

'I could still be happy designing huts for chicken feathers,' he remembers, 'because, back in Lvov, my work as an architect still stood – though the people I built for were gone. No matter how primitive they are, Russian people – even occupying soldiers – have great respect for property because they don't have any of their own. But when the Germans came in 1941, I saw my houses demolished in seconds – and, with this, my world was already destroyed.'

– 3 –

Now begins the dying

When Polish *Lwów* became Soviet *Lvov* in 1939, the inhabitants found themselves in a vestibule of hell with a revolving door to the nether world, but at least a little hope of redemption. True, Simon's stepfather passed through the revolving door to perish in Siberia. True, Simon went in an architect and came out a mechanic in a bed-springs factory; by 1940, however, he was working his way back up the ladder from a new bottom with the resilience which people in his part of the world have always needed just to survive. But a few weeks after he'd built all the chicken-feather huts that were wanted in Odessa and returned home to Lvov to seek new opportunities, the steel door to the outside world was bolted shut on 22 June 1941, when Hitler broke his pact with Stalin and invaded the Soviet Union.

Eight days later, when the Red Army left Lvov to regroup in the east, the city reverted overnight to its old Austrian name of *Lemberg*. But the first German invaders had more familiar faces, for they were the hated Ukrainians: auxiliary troops who had fled the Soviet side of a partitioned Poland for the German side and had been trained there. They celebrated their return with a pogrom that lasted three days and three nights. Any Jewish male they laid hands on was offered a choice of deaths: hanging, shooting, or beating. Others were trampled to death or crushed beneath the wheels of cannons. When the pogrom was over, 6000 Jews were dead.

On the heels of the Ukrainians came the *Einsatzgruppen*, SS 'Special Action Groups' which entered behind Hitler's conquering armies and whose only combat mission was to destroy civilian 'enemies', starting with Jewish intellectuals, communists, and gypsies. First unleashed in Austria and Czechoslovakia, they were the brutal fist that hammered home Hitler's furious words to an incredulous world.

'On the first of July,' Simon recalls, 'I was in the apartment of a friend, around eleven in the morning, when we heard a loud screaming in the street. We went to the window and saw German soldiers and Ukrainian civilians insulting Jews in the street, dragging Jews from their homes, undressing and beating them. Two civilians and a soldier were beating six Jews with sticks. Near the curb, a boy of twelve or thirteen had been knocked down by a soldier, who was now kicking him in the head with his army boot. A few yards away, two women were lying on the ground; their hair had been pulled out and it was lying beside them.

'A few minutes later, a group of about sixty unsuspecting Jews wandered into this scene from a side street and were greeted with sticks and stones by the Ukrainians and beaten with rifle butts by the Germans. But suddenly the beatings stopped. An open car – I think it was a Mercedes – arrived with a German general wearing gold braid on his shoulders. He was standing up in the car and a cameraman was filming him. The soldiers all stood at attention and gave him a military salute. The people they were beating had to stand up straight and give a *Heil Hitler* salute. The general waved and, when the car pulled away, the beatings resumed.'

Wiesenthal stayed out of sight during the pogrom and was playing chess in the cellar of his house with a friend on Sunday afternoon, 6 July 1941, when a Yiddish-speaking Ukrainian policeman barged 'right through the front door and went downstairs to tell us to come with him,' Wiesenthal recalls. 'We were on a list he had and he made it sound like we should be honoured.'

The two chess players were taken to Brigidki Prison. In a courtyard, some forty other Jewish professional men were standing around: lawyers, doctors, engineers, and teachers. Wiesenthal and his friend were invited to join them. 'Later,' says Simon dryly, 'they would throw the same sort of garden party for the Polish intelligentsia of Lwów' – mostly university professors plus one of Poland's best-known writers, Tadeusz Boy-Ẑelénski.

The centrepiece of the courtyard was a table covered with bottles of vodka, sausages, plates of hors d'oeuvres, and bullets. For their crimes of being Jewish and educated, the guests would partake only of ammunition.

Some wooden crates were brought in: one for each Jew to stand next to. Lined up facing a wall with arms crossed behind necks, they were shot one by one in the neck by a Ukrainian executioner. After killing three or four men, he would go over to the table and help himself to a drink and some food while another Ukrainian reloaded the weapon. Two other Ukrainians would shove each body into a crate and haul it away.

Seeing men he had known for years crumple, bleed, and die in seconds before his eyes, and knowing that their fate awaited him, too, Simon Wiesenthal realized that he was no longer a hostage to the random, often drunken, violence of the Ukrainian cavalryman who had slashed his thigh as a boy in Buczacz, or the Polish fraternity men who lay in ambush for Jewish students outside the Technical University. 'What I saw for the first time,' he told me, 'was systematic extermination that had no motive except to kill every Jew, starting with the ones who looked the most dangerous to Hitler. And done by people who took real pleasure in killing us.'

As the shots and shouts of the boisterous Ukrainians drew closer to Wiesenthal, he heard a new sound: church bells. The Ukrainians heard it, too. Good Orthodox Catholics all, they laid down their arms for evening mass.

Wiesenthal and his friend had stood five or six bullets away from extinction. Reprieved overnight, they and eighteen other survivors were marched to two large cells where their belts and shoelaces were taken from them. Suicide was forbidden; not for the last time would Wiesenthal learn that, under the Nazis, a Jew could not choose when to die.

During the night, as Simon dozed uneasily on the floor, a flashlight picked him out and a faintly familiar Ukrainian voice said in Polish: 'Engineer Wiesenthal! What are you doing here?'

'Who are you?' Simon asked the beam of light.

The man behind it was his former construction foreman, Bodnar, remembered by Wiesenthal as 'a very good stonemason I tried to use on every building I built.' Though Bodnar now wore the arm-band of the Ukrainian Auxiliary Police, he was still loyal to his former employer.

'I've got to get you out of here,' he whispered. 'You know what they'll do tomorrow morning.'

Wiesenthal asked him to help his chess partner, too. Thinking aloud, Bodnar mused: 'The important thing is to get you out of this building, no matter what the excuse.' He decided to tell his Ukrainian bosses that he'd unmasked a couple of very important Soviet spies among the Jews in custody. 'I'll ask them whether to take you to Sapiehy Street or Academy Street for further questioning,' Bodnar told them. 'Either way, once I get you out of this place, I can lose you.' Sapiehy Street, where the Technical University lay, also housed Loncki Prison, which the Gestapo was converting to a 'research centre': a Nazi euphemism for torture chamber. Academy Street meant the Ukrainian commissar's headquarters.

An hour later, both prisoners were dragged from the cell and mauled by their Ukrainian jailers for a decent interval – long enough for Wiesenthal to lose two front teeth – until Bodnar shouted: 'Enough! We need names and information from them *before* we kill them.'

On their way out, Bodnar tried to tiptoe past the courtyard where the execution squad, having prayed but not having put away their weapons, were still finishing their food and drink by candlelight while celebrating their day's accomplishments. They were oblivious to all, but had been joined by a German sergeant, who spotted Bodnar and his prisoners and asked where he was taking them. Bodnar, who spoke no German, told Wiesenthal to answer.

In his best German, Simon told the sergeant: 'This is a Ukrainian policeman. We are Jews. He should bring us to his commissar.'

The German sergeant, already a little drunk, slapped Bodnar's face and said: 'Then what are you standing around for? If this is what you people are like, then later we'll all have troubles. Report back to me as soon as you deliver them.'

'Safely' outside, Wiesenthal apologized to Bodnar for the abuse he'd caused him. Bodnar was more concerned, however, that now he had to account, verbally at least, for his two prisoners.

They trudged through the silent streets of Lemberg, where there was now a curfew for Poles and an earlier one for Jews. Bodnar took them past the sentry at Ukrainian headquarters and deposited them in the commissar's office, which Wiesenthal and his friend proceeded to clean. When the commissar arrived that morning, he asked them what the hell they were doing there.

'A German sergeant sent us over to clean your office,' said Wiesenthal, 'and it was too late for us to go home when we were finished.'

'So go home,' the Ukrainian said brusquely, though obviously pleased that he mattered so much to his German masters. Wiesenthal and his friends were home in time for breakfast.

Now the revolving door whirled so fast it was coming unhinged. Three days later, Wiesenthal was netted in a round-up of able-bodied men for work details. He and a hundred others were sent 'to a storage ground where they broke us into small groups and had us move armour plates from one place to another. These plates were too heavy for us to lift, particularly when we were being beaten by two German soldiers to encourage us. One of them was from Leipzig and he kept saying he'd known lazy Jews in Leipzig, too, and had settled their accounts. The armour plates had very sharp edges that cut our hands, but the soldiers wouldn't let us wash off the blood or put something on the wounds. We worked without a midday break while the two soldiers took turns having lunch.

'In the afternoon, they had us carry heavy oxygen bottles, some of them weighing ninety to a hundred ten kilograms (198 to 242 pounds) for a distance up to three hundred metres (985 feet). We worked in pairs and, late that afternoon, one couple stood still for a while and were beaten by both the soldiers. One of the men fell and was kicked some more in the face. He lay on the ground unconscious. His partner was sent to work in another group. When we went home in the evening, he was still lying there and we never saw him again. It was nine o'clock – an hour past curfew for Jews – so they gave us passes to go home and report back there next day.'

His life, his career, his hours, days, and sometimes his nights were no longer his own. Then the Germans started building a ghetto with Jewish labour. Wiesenthal remembers this phase well:

'First, they fenced off part of the old town . . . Next, they pulled out the cobblestones, turning the streets into a quagmire. That was part of the systematic method of creating sub-human living conditions. On rainy days you couldn't cross the street without wading in mud up to your ankles. It was impossible to clean oneself. We must have looked like animals, or phantoms from a nether world. And on the worst days, SS leaders and army officers would arrive, with some women, in their big cars, and they would watch us and laugh and take photographs of the strange species of sub-humans.

They sent these pictures home, and everyone said, "Look at those Jews! Hitler is right! They aren't even human."'

The Wiesenthals and his mother managed to stay out of the ghetto until late summer, when an SS man sauntered into their apartment with a Polish prostitute on his arm. Looking right through them, the whore sized up their flat and said, 'Yes, it'll do.' An hour later, the Wiesenthals went to the ghetto, leaving all their heirlooms behind. The new mistress of the house wanted to take it furnished.

A little more than a month later, on 21 October 1941, the SS held a 'registration'. Simon Wiesenthal had learned the new meaning of the word: 'The more often they registered us, the fewer we became. In SS language, registering was not a mere stocktaking. It meant much more . . . From bitter personal experience, we mistrusted words whose natural meaning seemed harmless. The Germans' intentions toward us had never been harmless.'

Simon and Cyla were sent to Janowskà, a concentration camp the Germans were developing in the sands and woods of Lemberg's western city limit. His mother was permitted to remain in their seven square metres (eight and a half square yards) of ghetto squalor. At their hasty parting, Simon gave her 'the last of what we had: a gold watch' in case she needed to buy her safety.

The gateways to hell were segregated by sex. Loaded on to separate trucks and herded by Ukrainians and Askaris (Soviet prisoners of war who'd gone over to the German SS), Simon and Cyla were driven to the men's and women's camps of Janowskà. In each case, the vestibule was a shack where a pair of German officers ordered the prisoners to give up the few belongings they'd brought with them and state their names, ages, and work qualifications. Then, after cursory physical examinations, they were sent through the back door into Hades.

Each prisoner's bread ration was three ounces per day. At the end of a hard day's labour enlarging the camp, quarrying stone, digging burial pits for the day's dead, or (when there was no work to be done) breaking ground and then restoring it or carrying heavy stones from here to there and then back again, the men would stand evening inspection – and those who were visibly sick would be barred from the barracks 'to prevent infection of the healthy'. Instead, they would spend the night out in the cold taking what the Germans called 'a fresh-air cure'. After eight at night, there was a curfew, and the Askaris on the watch-towers had orders to shoot anyone who stood or moved, so the condemned men had to lie on the frozen ground all night. In the Galician winter, none of them arose in the morning, for the 'fresh-air cure' was fatal. Some, however, took a short-cut to oblivion by standing up in the night and inviting the Askaris to shoot them. The Askaris always obliged.

In Janowskà's early days, escape attempts proliferated even when the number of captives executed for each try was doubled from five to ten. The first successful escape meant twenty-five camp killings plus even more drastic consequences: a truck drew up to the man's home in the ghetto and took his entire family – plus some visitors who had dropped by – to the camp as hostages awaiting his return. They were placed in solitary confinement without light or food. Their ordeal lasted three days – until the remorse-stricken escapee returned and was beaten to death before the eyes of his family and their friends, who were then released. The next time a man escaped, the procedure was repeated. After three days, when he hadn't turned himself in, his mother, sister, niece, sister-in-law, and a neighbour's child were shot to death. After that, escape attempts were few.

Toward the end of 1941, by coincidence, Simon and Cyla Wiesenthal were both transferred to a special forced labour camp near the Lemberg railyards. A satellite of Janowskà, it lodged prisoners serving the Eastern Railroad Repair Works. Cyla was sent to the locomotive workshop to polish brass and nickel. For a while, she saw Simon daily, for he was put to work painting swastikas on captured Russian locomotives. When he was promoted to sign-painter for the entire Eastern Works, she saw less of him, but his new job won him a mobility that would later save their lives.

Wiesenthal's work – and the man himself – caught the eye of the Eastern Works' head railwayman, Heinrich Günthert, a civilian, 'because he always walked with his head up and looked me straight in the eye.' Günthert subsequently told Wiesenthal's postwar Boswell, the late Joseph Wechsberg: 'The SS men said that Wiesenthal was impertinent. I didn't argue with them, but I admit that I was impressed by the man's erect bearing. He had a thoughtful expression in his eyes, as though he knew that we Germans might one day have to account for all this.' With God on leave and His anointed deputy, Pope Pius XII, strangely silent, it seemed as if

Simon, little thinking he would ever survive the war, had already stepped into the shoes of Deputy for the Dead.

Upon learning that Wiesenthal was a licensed architect, Günthert – a Nazi who'd already had trouble with the SS guards for treating his Jewish labourers humanely – gave him work as a technician and draughtsman. Günthert's deputy, Adolf Kohlrautz, also a Nazi, not only shared his chief's attitudes, but was immensely grateful for the praise and promotions that came his way thanks to Simon's technical drawings, which were submitted under Kohlrautz's name. Kohlrautz would tell Simon the news he'd risked his neck to hear over the BBC (British Broadcasting Corporation) and smuggle food to Simon's mother in the ghetto.

The ghetto, not the Janowskà camp, felt the first wave of organized deportations to unknown destinations; in Janowskà, you generally finished your life there, sooner or later. Those 'privileged' to remain in the ghetto were mothers and children as well as older people. The more able-bodied among them, however, were forced to labour outside the ghetto by day, during which SS body-snatchers would raid the compound to relieve it of 'non-working, useless mouths'. A woman might return home from a hard day's slavery to find her children gone forever. After desperate mothers managed to conceal their children in stoves and closets or behind false walls, the SS police chief of Lemberg, Friedrich Katzmann, tried another tactic. He announced a relaxation of discipline and, as a token of good faith, he opened a kindergarten for ghetto children. It offered extra rations of milk and cocoa.

The mothers watched warily, but first their hungry children and then their own aspirations for the next generation got the better of them. One afternoon, however, the kindergarten was closed forever. Three SS trucks had taken the class on an outing from which it would never return.

Next to be weeded out as 'useless' were ageing women. Working in the railway yards in the summer of 1942, Simon Wiesenthal watched helplessly as the SS crammed elderly Jewish women into a freight train – one hundred to the car – and then let it stand for three days in the blazing sun while the women begged for water. Hearing their cries, he could only pray that his mother was not among them, but God was on leave and Rosa Wiesenthal was aboard that train.

'My mother was in August 1942 taken by a Ukrainian policeman,' Simon says, lapsing swiftly into the present tense as immediacy takes hold. 'She gives him my gold watch and he says OK and goes away. An hour later, he comes back and this time she has nothing to give him, so she is gone. A neighbour told me this.' Dragged from the ghetto, Rosa Wiesenthal was put aboard a truck that took her and two dozen others to the freight cars waiting in the yards. They all perished in Belzec, a new extermination camp on the road from Lemberg to Lublin. Rosa Wiesenthal was sixty-three.

Around the same time, Cyla Wiesenthal learned that, back in Buczacz, her mother had been shot to death by a Ukrainian policeman as she was being evicted from her home. 'She wasn't moving quick enough,' says Simon, 'so he shot her on the steps of her own house.' In all, the Wiesenthals lost eighty-nine relatives to the Second World War – and it is for them, among millions of others, that Simon stands deputy.

– 4 –

Simon and the sunflower

Imprisoned in the Janowskà concentration camp, where brutality and torture reigned, Simon Wiesenthal was often put on work details outside the camp – which should have been a relief, but wasn't. Marched through the streets of his city, he could read on the faces of passers-by – even, in one encounter, an ex-classmate's – that he was in a parade of the legion of the dead, with each marcher carrying around his own death certificate from which only the date was missing. A year earlier, in the squalor of the ghetto, where each Jew was allotted two square metres (less than two and a half square yards) of living space, a friend of Simon's had overheard an old woman's answer to how God could allow such suffering. She said simply: 'God is on leave.'

At such times, Wiesenthal was convinced the world had conspired to accept, without protest or compassion, the fate Hitler had decreed for the Jews. Having lived among Poles from birth, grown up with them, and attended their schools, Simon knew that 'to them we were always foreigners. Mutual understanding was out of the question. And even now that the Poles, too, had been enslaved and were next on Hitler's list for extermination, nothing had changed: there were still barriers between us.' Sometimes, this estrangement grew so strong that Simon 'no longer even wanted to look at Poles. In spite of the conditions and the risks inside the camp, I would have preferred to stay there. But I didn't always have the choice.'

On an October morning that would mark him for the rest of his life, Simon Wiesenthal's work detail was herded past passive Polish faces on Janowskà Street, left on to Sapiehy Street, and then right into the Technical University, where he had earned his engineering diploma in architecture; his alma mater was now a military hospital for German troops wounded on the Russian front. Before the prisoners could be put to work emptying round-the-clock rubbish from busy operating rooms, a nurse accosted Wiesenthal with 'Are you a Jew?'

The answer was so obvious that Simon didn't respond. Satisfied by his silence, the nurse said 'Come with me' and led him inside the main building and up the stairs into, of all places, what used to be the dean of architecture's office, where Wiesenthal had handed in his assignments in happier times. Now a sick-room, it was the death chamber of a mortally wounded twenty-one-year-old SS soldier from Stuttgart who had asked not for a priest, but for a Jew to hear his confession.

In the Ukrainian city of Dnyepropetrovsk before he was hurt, the young SS man had participated in a round-up of some 400 Jews, who were packed into a house that was then incinerated. Acting on orders, his unit had gunned down victims leaping from the flaming building. Now, blinded by a bombshell in the siege of Taganrog weeks later, he still had before his eyes a vision of a family that had perished in the Dnyepropetrovsk massacre: a father, his clothes afire, shielded his son's eyes before leaping with the child in his arms. The mother jumped a moment later. 'Perhaps they were already dead when they hit the pavement,' the dying SS man said to Wiesenthal. 'It was frightful. Screams mixed with volleys of shots probably intended to drown the shrieks. I can never forget – it haunts me.'

Despite additional brandy rations, many of the young SS men in his unit hadn't slept well that night. Their platoon leader rebuked them next morning: 'You and your sensitive feelings. Men, you cannot go on like this. This is war! One must be hard! They are not our people. The Jew is not a human being! The Jews are the cause of all our misfortunes! And when you shoot one of them, it is not the same thing as shooting one of us: it doesn't matter whether it is man, woman, or child. They are different from us.' But one SS man, at least, could no longer believe these words he'd heard half his life.

In the battle of Taganrog, when he and his comrades left the trenches to storm a Russian position, this one man suddenly stood rooted to the ground. His hands, holding his rifle with fixed bayonet, quivered. For, before him on the battlefield, he saw the burning family – the father with the child and behind them the mother –

coming towards him. The thought, *'No, I can't shoot at them a second time!'* crossed his mind as a shell exploded in his face.

What the dying man wanted now was absolution to be given by the anonymous Jew brought before him. He told Wiesenthal: 'I have longed to talk about it to a Jew and beg forgiveness from him. Only I didn't know whether there were any Jews left. I know what I am asking is almost too much for you, but without your answer I cannot die in peace.'

Left alone with the young German, Wiesenthal had time to reflect that true repentance had brought together a dying 'murderer who didn't want to be a murderer, but had been made into one by a murderous ideology' with a Jew doomed to die at the hands of these same murderers, but resisting death because he 'yearned to see the end of all the horror that blighted the world.' And he knew that he 'was not yet ready to be touched by the hand of death.'

As the SS man's hand groped for his, Simon held it out of reach and sat in the shadow of death contemplating bright sunlight outside and almost envying the dying murderer the traditional sunflower that would soon decorate his grave 'to connect him with the living world. Butterflies will visit . . . For me there will be no sunflower. I'll be buried in a mass grave, with corpses piled on top of me. No sunflower will ever light my darkness and no butterflies will ever dance on my terrible tomb.'

Words gave way to silence as the dying man's confession petered out with a plea that it not go unanswered.

Having heard him out, Wiesenthal left the room without speaking a word. The SS man died a few hours later.

Back in Janowskà that night, Wiesenthal told a handful of his fellow inmates what had happened to him. One of them exclaimed: 'One less!' and another said, 'So you saw a murderer dying? I would like to see that ten times a day.'

A more thoughtful companion named Josek remarked: 'When you started telling us, I feared at first that you had really forgiven him. You would have had no right to do this in the name of people who hadn't authorized you to do so. What people have done to you yourself, you can, if you like, forgive and forget. That is your own affair. But it would have been a terrible sin to burden your conscience with other people's sufferings.'

This terrible burden, however, would prove to be Wiesenthal's vocation for more than four postwar decades. Nor would he let go of the moral issue he faced at the death-bed of a man who wished to die in peace, but couldn't because his terrible crime gave him no rest.

The Talmud had taught Wiesenthal that, even on Yom Kippur, the Day of Atonement, one cannot be cleansed of one's sins against other mortals through sincere repentance alone. One must first obtain the forgiveness of those one has wronged before asking divine mercy. Even God Himself can only forgive sins committed against Himself, not against man – and certainly not against mankind!

In the New Testament, too, the Lord's Prayer (Matthew VI: 9–13) asks forgiveness not just for our trespasses, but for those who trespass against us and, earlier in the Book of Matthew (V:23), Jesus says: 'If thou bring thine offering to the altar and thou remember there that thy brother has aught against thee, leave thy offering there before the altar, and go, first be reconciled to thy brother, and then come and bring thine offering.'

Only God, still on leave, might have known how many priestly confessors as well as postwar courts would grant absolution to Nazi mass murderers who expressed guilt or did minor penance for sins that surpassed all biblical reckoning.

Two and a half years later, in the death barracks of the concentration camp at Mauthausen, Austria, Simon broached his dilemma to a bunkmate named Bolek, a Polish Catholic who had been studying for the priesthood in Warsaw when the Germans shipped him to Auschwitz. Simon's summary concluded with a barrage of questions: 'What do you think I should have done? Should I have forgiven him? Did I have any right to forgive him? What does your religion say? What would you have done in my position?'

After some thought, Bolek replied: 'I don't think the attitude of the great religions to the question of forgiveness differs to any great extent. If there is any difference, then it's more in practice than in principle. One thing is certain: you can only forgive a wrong that has been done to yourself. Yet, on the other hand: where would the SS man turn? None of those he'd wronged were still alive.'

'So he asked something from me that was impossible to give?' Simon asked hopefully.

'Probably he turned to you because he regarded Jews as a single condemned community,' Bolek surmised, going on to conclude that since he 'showed signs of repentance, genuine, sincere repentance for his misdeeds . . . then he deserved the mercy of forgiveness from you.'

They argued this point from then until parting – a few days after liberation on 5 May 1945, when Bolek headed home to Poland and *his* God. The more they talked, says Simon, the more 'Bolek began to falter in his original opinion . . . and for my part I became less and less certain that I had acted properly.'

– 5 –

When a Jew chooses to die

It was Simon Wiesenthal's good fortune that he spent most of the war imprisoned in his own home city of Lemberg without being shipped from the Janowskà concentration camp to Sobibor, Belzec, or any of the nearby extermination camps that took the lives of his mother and eighty-eight other relatives. Whenever he was working as a sign-painter at the Eastern Railroad Repair Works, which was most of the time, he had the chance to see his wife, Cyla, polishing nickel and brass in the locomotive workshop. But, in between rounds at the railway works, he was sometimes yanked back to Janowskà, where he had to look at the broad and beaming face of the deputy camp commandant, Lieutenant Richard Rokita, a chunky Silesian in his late thirties who used to be a café violinist.

'We called Rokita "the friendly murderer",' Wiesenthal recalls. 'He never beat anybody. He never screamed at us. He just shot prisoners politely. One day, Rokita goes strolling through the camp and sees an old Jew, too weak to be of any use to the Third Reich. The old man salutes him. Rokita greets him cheerfully, drops a piece of paper, and tells the old Jew to pick it up. When the old man bends down, Rokita shoots him dead. Like I said, a friendly murderer.'

Rokita's pet project was the camp orchestra, which he formed from a wide selection of first-rate musicians imprisoned in Janowskà. Sometimes he conducted evening concerts of Bach, Grieg, and Wagner for the SS cadre, and even appeared as a violin soloist. Mostly, however, his sixty-man orchestra piped the prisoners out in the morning when they left for work details in the city and serenaded them when they returned in the evening. When a well-known Lemberg songwriter, Zygmunt Schlechter, fell into his hands, Rokita commissioned him to compose a 'Death Tango', which the orchestra played at public executions of escapees and unregistered Jews caught hiding in the city.

These events took place periodically at the far end of 'The Pipe', a six- or seven-foot wide corridor in the no man's land between the barbed-wire fences of the prison compound and the administrative quarter. No prisoner had ever walked through 'The Pipe' and lived, for it led to a sandpit that was the shooting-ground. Sometimes, doomed inmates were left to linger several days in 'The Pipe' without food or drink. The SS found it wasteful to execute fewer than ten Jews at a time – and equally wasteful to feed those whose end was imminent.

Once, the amiable Rokita was leading a work detail past 'The Pipe' when he saw a handful of condemned men starving as they awaited execution. He ordered a guard to bring them food. As soon as the prisoners had the first morsels in their mouths, Rokita and the guard opened fire, killing them all. The condemned men had eaten their last meal.

'Come on, let's go,' Rokita told his appalled work detail. 'You have nothing to fear . . . You're healthy, aren't you? These fellows were sick. It was a happy release for them.'

Janowskà was ruled by two SS rivals: First Lieutenant Fritz Gebauer, the camp's Gestapo chief, and Second Lieutenant Gustav Wilhaus, who ran its everyday operations. Both men despised each other – to such an extent that Wilhaus called his dog Fritz. Though outranked, Wilhaus could get away with such gestures as well as open defiance, for his brother-in-law was SS Major-General Friedrich Katzmann, the police chief of Galicia who'd treated the children and tricked the mothers of Lemberg ghetto in 1942.

Disregarding all the Nazi proscriptions against relations with Jews, Gebauer kept a young Jewish mistress at the camp. His wife consoled herself by sleeping with her Jewish chauffeur. To inmate Leon Weliczker, the impression made by Gebauer, a Berliner in his early thirties, was 'striking. He had more than average good looks. He was tall and broad-shouldered. He usually held himself bowed slightly forward, which suggested an aristocratic stance. Most striking of all were his jet-black deep-set eyes, which sparkled . . . He had a very pleasant, melodic voice with a pronounced masculine tone, and in general seemed to have some kind of inner life.'

Despite this inner life and his marriage's sexual affinity for Jewish lovers, Gebauer had celebrated the Jewish feast of Purim early one spring by forcing six Jews to spend Purim's first night outside the barracks in freezing weather because they 'look sick' and might infect the others. 'In the morning,' Weliczker testified at the Eichmann trial, 'all six people were frozen lying down where they were put out the night before: completely white like long balls of snow.'

On another freezing morning, Gebauer picked eight Jews out of a roll-call line-up because, he said, 'they don't look too clean.' They were ordered to undress and soak in a barrel of cold water – all day and all night. 'Next morning,' said Weliczker, 'we had to cut the ice away' from their corpses.

'Wilhaus,' says Wiesenthal, 'was a perfect sadist. He lived in a house inside the camp with his wife, Hilde, and his daughter, a blonde six-year-old named Heike. One morning, several Jewish labourers were putting up a building near his house. Eye-witnesses saw Wilhaus on the balcony of his villa with his wife and Heike. He pointed at the masons as they bent down, working on the brick wall. They must have reminded Wilhaus of the figures* used as targets on the shooting-range, for suddenly he took his gun, aimed carefully, and fired. A man fell. Heike thought this was a wonderful game. She clapped her hands. Papa aimed carefully again and hit another target, killing the man. Then he handed his gun to his wife and told her to try. She did. Down went the third Jewish mason.'

On Tuesday, 20 April 1943, Wilhaus decided to celebrate Adolf Hitler's fifty-fourth birthday by sacrificing fifty-four Jewish intellectuals. There were, however, only some forty professional men and women left in Janowskà, so Wilhaus ordered a round-up of others who were on work assignments outside the camp. A blank-eyed, slit-mouthed Silesian SS killer named Richard Dyga was dispatched to fetch Wiesenthal and two other men from the Eastern Railroad Repair Works. Though their German civilian boss, Adolf Kohlrautz, pleaded that he needed them, Dyga insisted he

* In Janowskà's Death Brigade of Jewish prisoners who buried and burned the bodies, corpses were called 'figures'. The same abstraction was used by Franz Stangl when he commanded Sobibor and Treblinka.

had his orders and Kohlrautz bade Wiesenthal farewell with a sorry shrug.

Along their way back to Janowskà, Dyga rounded up other educated Jews and delivered them all to 'The Pipe', where the rest of the camp's intelligentsia, including a handful of women, were already assembled, making their peace with life in silence. When attendance was complete, six SS men – one of them carrying a submachine-gun – marched the prisoners through the barbed-wire corridor, two abreast.

'Each of us walked by himself,' Wiesenthal recalls. 'Each of us was alone with himself, with his thoughts. Each was his own island of solitude. That was our privilege, our strength.'

An April shower burst as they reached the rim of the sandpit, where they could gaze down at naked corpses from earlier executions. Nearby, a truck waited, its motor running. The new victims were told to take off all their clothes, fold them neatly, and place them on the truck in individual piles so they could be sorted by size.

'Now one could have no illusions; the end was surely near,' says Wiesenthal. 'The Nazis killed you only when you were naked, because they knew, psychologically, that naked people never resist.'

The truck drove off with their clothes. The fifty-four naked men and women stood in a single row along the rim as the executioner lifted his submachine-gun and began to mow them down with one burst apiece. After the fifth or sixth shot, there was a brief delay when one man fell backwards on to the ground instead of into the pit. An SS man had to go over and kick him in. Then the shooting resumed.

Through the pelting rain, as Wiesenthal waited for the end, he vaguely heard a whistle and some shouts, but the sounds of this earth no longer penetrated his senses. The man next to him, however, heard the word '*Wie-sen-thal!*' and, almost as if relaying a phone call, said, 'It's for you.'

Just outside 'The Pipe', an SS corporal was asking, 'Is Wiesenthal in there? Where's Wiesenthal?' Simon snapped to attention and said 'Here!'

'Follow me!' the corporal commanded and, to Simon's amazement, led him back out through 'The Pipe' for the first and last time any prisoner ever made a round trip.

'I staggered like a drunk,' he recalls. The SS corporal had to slap his face twice 'to bring me back to earth.'

The executioner, too, was flabbergasted. He was supposed to shoot fifty four people, not fifty-three. 'What do we do now?' he asked the corporal.

'Continue!' the corporal commanded. Before Wiesenthal was out of earshot, fifty-three Jews were dead. He never asked if the SS found a fifty-fourth, but suspects they did. All he knows is that 'for a long time, I was the only person I knew in the camps who still believed in miracles.'

The corporal marched him to a warehouse, where the truck had not yet unloaded his clothing or the fifty-three other piles to be fumigated for redistribution. After dressing quickly, he was escorted back to the railway works where he had started his day an eternity ago.

Kohlrautz was grinning from ear to ear as he welcomed Simon back. He had been on the phone with Wilhaus, Gebauer, and others to convince them that Wiesenthal was the best man alive in Lemberg to paint a giant poster – with swastika, white letters, and red background – proclaiming 'WIR DANKEN UNSEREM FÜHRER' (We Thank Our Leader) for the birthday celebration.

'You know, Simon,' said Kohlrautz a few minutes later, 'it's not only Hitler's birthday today, but it's yours, too.'

Kohlrautz, who was killed in the battle of Berlin in 1945, never asked any questions about the two pistols he let Simon store in his desk drawer. Simon had obtained them from the Polish underground cell in the railway works. In his capacity as sign-painter, he had freedom to roam the yards. The Polish resistance figured he might be useful in future sabotage, since their eventual plan was to blow up the Lemberg railroad junction at a crucial moment. Besides, he was an architect, engineer, and draughtsman who could draw maps pinpointing the most vital and vulnerable positions. Would he co-operate?

Yes, said Simon, for a price: his wife's freedom.

Cyla Müller Wiesenthal was blonde and could pass for a Pole. The underground smuggled her out of the yards one night and gave her the identity of 'Irene Kowalska' with which she took a morning train to Warsaw and settled into an apartment that was waiting for her at 5 Topiel Street. Cyla found herself sharing the flat with the wife of the Polish poet Jerzy Lec, but Mrs Lec was also using a pseudonym, so neither woman knew the other's identity – or that the other was Jewish, too.

Still quite sure he wouldn't survive the war, Simon rejoiced that his wife might. Soon, virtually all Jewish women in ghetto and camp were liquidated, so he knew he had made the right move for Cyla. Now he had to look after himself. In late September 1943, when word came down that Jewish prisoners who lived at the railway works would soon be spending their nights at Janowskà, Wiesenthal read between the lines and concluded it would be fatal for him to go back there. Even Kohlrautz kept looking at him and asking: 'Simon, what are you waiting for?'

Kohlrautz often sent Simon, guarded by a Ukrainian policeman, into town to buy art supplies and run other errands for him. On Saturday, 2 October 1943, Wiesenthal and Arthur Scheiman, a former circus director, requested passes to go shopping before the stores closed. Kohlrautz was glad to oblige. While the German boss went looking for a particularly stupid Ukrainian to accompany them, Wiesenthal and Scheiman fished the two pistols out of Kohlrautz's drawer. He came back with a real prize: a Ukrainian who was new to Lemberg and didn't know the city. With a wink, a wave, and a sly *'auf Wiedersehen!'* ('See you again!'), Kohlrautz sent them off to town.

They visited a stationery store that had front and back entrances. They told their guard to wait for them at the cashier's desk near the front. Knowing that nobody could leave without paying, he assented. Then they left by the back door.

A Polish friend from the underground sheltered them in his apartment for a couple of days. Then Scheiman rejoined his wife, a Ukrainian seamstress, who hid him in her clothes closet by day when her customers came for fittings. The partisans moved Simon to a nearby village, Kulparkow, where the parents of a Polish girl who worked at the railway yards hid him in the attic of their house. From this base, he helped the partisans build bunkers and lines of fortification. 'I was not so much a strategic expert as a technical expert,' he recalls, telling how he worked closely with the partisans in the region.

A little nomenclature is necessary here. By late 1943, two main groups of Poles-in-exile were already competing for control of postwar Poland: Stalin had allowed his Polish prisoners of war – taken by the Red Army between 1939 and 1941, when Russia and Germany were allies – to form a military corps under General Wladyslaw Anders which fought with distinction against the Germans. But the Soviet Union and the Polish government-in-exile in London had broken relations earlier in 1943 over a German revelation which, for once, was all too true: in a forest near the Polish village of Katyn, the Germans had found the mass grave of some 4250 Polish officers massacred by the Russians in 1939.* In eastern Poland almost five years later, there were two main underground groups fighting the Germans: The Polish National Resistance Movement, or Home Army (*Armja Krajowa*, known by its initials *A.K.*), supported from and by England, and more nationalistic, anti-Semitic, and anti-Soviet than *A.L.*, the People's Army, which was supported by the Russians. Nevertheless, *A.K.* and *A.L.* didn't fight each other. But, says Wiesenthal, 'there were also partisan groups which were friendly with the Germans. One was *UPA*, the Ukrainian Partisan Army. It had support from the German Army to fight other partisans. It was anti-Soviet and it received its equipment from the Germans.'

Wiesenthal, whose rescuers were from the pro-Soviet *A.L.* partisans, says that 'most of our battles were against *UPA*. But there were cases when our group was bombarded by Soviet planes, since the circumstances in this area were such that we were concentrated there together with four or five other partisan groups. There was such confusion by January of 1944 that no one knew who was with who and who was fighting who. Whoever stuck his head out of the forest got shot at.'

While Simon was in hiding with the *A.L.* partisans in the area between Lemberg and Tarnopol,† a Hungarian division and the Ukrainian SS Division 'Galicia' and a Ukrainian auxiliary police

*Though the Russians claimed the men had been executed by the Germans, the obvious truth of the Katyn massacre was only later acknowledged by the governments of Russia and Poland. In the rift between Stalin and the Polish government-in-exile, General Anders evacuated his army to the West. Its veterans and former *A.K.* partisans were branded as 'traitors' by Poland's postwar communist regimes.

†The Polish city of Tarnopol is now Ternopol in Ukraine. It is about sixty miles from Lvov.

division were combing the woods for partisans. As in Vietnam years later and perhaps in all wars throughout history, the body-counts to headquarters often seemed more important than the actual results. 'Quite often,' Simon recalls, 'a group from the Field Police, the Ukrainian auxiliary police, would come up to the edge of the forest. Then fifty men would go in about a hundred metres [110 yards], shoot off a few rounds – and then we would receive a report that about a hundred partisans had been killed and ten bunkers had been discovered.'

Toward the end of 1943, the Germans liquidated much of the Janowskà concentration camp. Most of the prisoners were shot, but others fled. As the Gestapo scoured the countryside for them, Simon had to leave his attic in Kulparkow and join the A.L. partisans, who didn't mind having Jews in their ranks if they could help. Two Jews, Tanenbaum and Mogely, were already there – until early 1944, when they were 'sent to Biasky, a village nearby,' Simon explains, 'to see a friendly farmer who kept a supply of food [and] to deliver money. We had to pay in dollars.'

The idea of dollars circulating in the backwoods of Nazi-occupied Poland in 1944 astounds his listener, but Simon ploughs on:

'The Russian partisans had dollars, as a rule: one-hundred-dollar bills. We buried at least seventy or eighty thousand dollars. In any case, our Russian liaison man who was with us was always well supplied with dollars. Even if one had to pay only twenty dollars, a hundred would be paid, with no change in return. The Polish zloty was worthless: just like now. But Mogely and Tanenbaum were caught and we found them two days later with their eyes gouged out and their tongues cut off, and one of them appeared to have had his genitals worked over with a wire.'

Together with the farmer with whom they traded, they had been caught by the Secret Field Police or Ukrainian auxiliaries. 'As the farmer's widow told us later on,' Simon remembers, 'the Secret Field Police first brought her husband before a field court and then to Lemberg, where he was shot dead.'

This was a more merciful death than Mogely's and Tanenbaum's or those of three hostages Simon says 'a neighbouring group of us once liberated' from German Army capture: 'The three persons had been forced into a very little room. For seventy-two hours, they did not get anything to eat. This room was in a farm where sausage was being smoked and dried. The three people were in this room while the stove was constantly heated, so that there was a temperature of over fifty degrees Celsius [122° F] in this room. We found these three men in a condition so that they were like boiled. One of them lived for another five days. The other two were unconscious and never came out of it. A doctor gave the living person several injections and treated him with water, but it was no use.'

In February of 1944, Wiesenthal goes on, 'our group was encircled. It was hopeless to stay there, for the Germans were approaching from all sides. During one night, we decided to split up into as many parts as possible by dividing into groups . . . Four of us made our way through and arrived together in Lemberg. We entered the apartment of a Pole, pistols in hand, but he wasn't in. So we helped ourselves to his civilian clothes there, and left in pairs, forty metres [44 yards] apart.'

The only partisan address they had in Lemberg was that of the liaison man for *A.K.* the pro-British, but anti-Semitic, underground group: '*A.K.* did accept Jews in Lemberg all the same because the pressure of the Germans was much stronger there than in any other territory. So the *A.K.* liaison man did offer an apartment to the four of us belonging to friends who were in the field.' His Gentile comrades accepted the invitation, but Simon, feeling uncomfortable about his hosts, went looking for his original escape partner, the circus director Scheiman.

Scheiman was still crouching in the closet of his wife, the Ukrainian seamstress. He invited Simon to join him. 'The next eight days were almost as bad as the concentration camp,' says Wiesenthal. 'Scheiman and I spent our days squatting on low stools in the left-hand half of the closet. The other half, filled with clothes, was kept open. Twice, the police came looking for Scheiman, but when they saw the open closet, they went away again. The air was suffocating in there and we were afraid to cough. A few feet away, Mrs Scheiman's Gentile customers were dressing and undressing for their fittings. It was a totally risky situation.'

Mrs Scheiman wasn't happy with the situation either, so the two men swallowed their pride and took sanctuary in the *A.K.* apartment, where Simon's partisan friends had hollowed out a 'grave' – big enough for a pair of people to recline – in the sand beneath the ground floorboards. The two Jewish fugitives spent most of their time above the earth, but, whenever there was a search, they would climb into their grave and the Poles would cover them with three boards and a heavy table. Eventually, Scheiman (who survived the war) couldn't take this 'life' and returned to his wife's closet. Simon stayed on – savouring the extra elbow room.

In early June 1944, during a drinking bout in a neighbouring house, a chief inspector of the German railways was beaten and robbed by his Polish companions. A house-to-house police search was ordered. Simon reburied himself several times and was in his makeshift coffin on Tuesday, 13 June 1944, when more than eight months of cramped and perilous 'freedom' came to an end. As the Gestapo entered the courtyard of the house, the Polish partisans fled, leaving Wiesenthal trapped beneath the earth 'in a position where I couldn't even make use of my weapon.'

A minute later, he heard heavy boots tramping above. Two Polish detectives – who knew exactly where to look – slid back the table, took away the boards, and pounced upon him. They seized his pistol and a diary Simon had been keeping while hiding. Simon won't say whether he thinks one of the *A.K.* partisans betrayed him. He was bundled into a car and slapped around before being delivered to the Germans.

Possession of a pistol was grounds for immediate execution. Fortunately, the two Polish detectives didn't turn the weapon in to the Gestapo, but took it for themselves to sell on the black market. They did, however, deliver Wiesenthal and his diary to the Germans – which proved to be a stroke of luck, too. In the book, he'd recorded not just the doings of SS men in Janowskà – from Dyga and Blum (in charge of the Askaris) up the ladder to Rokita, Gebauer, and Wilhaus – but also, in recent weeks, maps and diagrams (coded so that only he could explain them) of partisan emplacements to help the advancing Red Army make contact with their allies. 'I owe it specially to these circumstances that I was not killed right away, as so many other Jews,' he says, 'for these records seemed to be very valuable partisan documents.'

Simon was sent to what was left of Janowskà: a penal colony of tailors, shoemakers, plumbers, gravediggers, body-burners, and other craftsmen still needed by the SS for a while. 'The Pipe' was still there, too, and, while the Gestapo studied his diary, Wiesenthal readied himself for the inevitable second and final trip through 'The Pipe'.

Two nights later, a truck with two Gestapo agents came for Wiesenthal. When he saw that one of them was Master Sergeant Oskar Waltke, chief of the Jewish affairs section in Lemberg, Wiesenthal's heart sank, for this was a man whose misdeeds (mentioned by Wiesenthal in his captured diary) had made him the most feared man in Galicia. Waltke has been described by Wiesenthal as 'a cold, mechanical sadist', a heavy-set man with reddish blond hair and steely grey eyes who called his prisoners his 'children' and knew how to savour and prolong their agonies. 'Waltke's speciality', says Wiesenthal, was 'to make Jews with false Polish papers admit they were Jews. He tortured his victims until they confessed and then he sent them to be shot. He also tortured many Gentiles until they admitted to being Jews just to get it over with.'

When Waltke saw Simon, he smiled and beckoned him into the truck, saying 'Get in, my child', in such a gloating manner that Wiesenthal was sure Waltke had read every word of his diary. 'I knew I was finished. The only question was how he would finish me. I didn't want to know the answer.'

As he climbed aboard, Wiesenthal took out a small razor blade he'd concealed in his cuff. With two swift strokes, he cut both wrists. 'With my right hand, I managed well. With my left hand, which I had cut open, not so well,' he says, displaying the scars.

On the truck, he lost consciousness and was driven directly to the Gestapo prison hospital, where he shared a medical cell with two deserters: a German SS man and a Ukrainian. Later, he learned he was the first Jew ever admitted to this hospital. The doctor told him he had lost two thousand grammes of blood. Waltke had left orders to feed Wiesenthal a special diet of hearty soups, liver, and vegetables so he could interrogate him sooner.

This meant Waltke hadn't been able to decipher the tactical parts of the diary. Rather than risk betraying the partisans who'd sheltered him, Wiesenthal opted again for suicide:

'When I went to the doctor for him to change my bandages, I stole a jar of pills. They were very little, so I thought I had better take them all – four or five hundred of them – to finish myself off.

'So I waited until midnight and got them all down me. And do you know what they were?' he asks with a twinkle. 'Five hundred tablets of saccharin!'

While Wiesenthal was recovering from this minor stomach upset, Waltke paid him a visit and told him: 'That wasn't necessary, child. We aren't monsters. Now get well soon so you and I can have a long talk.'

Wiesenthal tried suicide one last time. He threw his belt over a bar of the high cell window. When he climbed up on the toilet seat to put the belt around his neck, however, his bandaged wrists went numb and his weakened system made him dizzy. 'My veins hadn't grown together yet,' he said later, 'so I was bound to fall.' He pitched forward in a dead faint which awoke his cellmates, who called the guards. Tied to his bunk, Wiesenthal decided to let Waltke do the work that he'd botched thrice. 'What will come will come,' he told himself, 'but no more suicide. Let them kill me.'

Soon, Waltke paid him another visit and said: 'You are looking well, my child. In two days, we will have our first talk.'

Waltke would be hard pressed to find time for their talk. The days were numbered, for, late in 1942 and early in 1943, the Red Army had taken the offensive after encircling and capturing or killing the Germans trying to cross the Volga at Stalingrad. By mid-July of 1944, the Red Army was within twelve miles of Lemberg. During the next two nights, Wiesenthal's troubled sleep was jarred by the din of planes, sirens, and heavy artillery, but all these sounds were like music to him, even though he suspected that they might hasten his end.

At dawn on the morning of Wiesenthal's date with Waltke – Tuesday, 18 July 1944 – all the cell doors of the Gestapo prison opened and the inmates filed into the courtyard, where Waltke and an SS officer were selecting prisoners 'for further disposition'. On the left side stood a group of Jewish slave labourers who had serviced the prison and were now ticketed for liquidation at Janowskà. Their last job had been to dig a mass grave – not for themselves, but for those who were standing on the right and would not leave the courtyard alive: Russians, Ukrainians, Poles, and German deserters.

When Wiesenthal's name was called, Waltke said, 'That's the one I told you about', and, with just a perfunctory flicker of interest, the SS officer sent Simon to the right: the Gentile side.

'I looked at the others like some people on an airplane look at their fellow passengers,' Wiesenthal remembers. 'If the plane should crash, I am thinking, these will be my companions in death. Across the courtyard, I see the group of Jews and wish I could be buried with them, not with Gentiles and Nazis. But how to get there? In that moment, there is a roar in the sky above us and an explosion shakes the courtyard. From Sapiehy Street, a cloud of fire and smoke shoots up in the air. The files on the table in front of Waltke and the of officer are scattered all over. Quickly, in the confusion, I run across the courtyard and join my own people. After the air raid, there is an air-raid warning; a car with sirens drives around for this purpose. But there is no air raid and, an hour later, after the all-clear sounds, two SS men put us on a truck and bring us back to the Janowskà concentration camp for the last time in my life.'

The truckload of Jews was greeted by the new camp commandant who had succeeded Wilhaus. Friedrich Warzok was a chunky, ruddy, cold-eyed killer Wiesenthal credits with the deaths of 70,000 Jews in his various posts. Warzok's first question was: 'Who from you was here before?'

Ready – almost eager! – to die, only Wiesenthal stepped forward.

'Very good!' said Warzok. 'We like to welcome back old guests – lost sheep who have come back to their flock. When were you here last?'

'Last summer,' Wiesenthal replied.

'And what should we do with you?'

'Please, shoot me,' Wiesenthal said with resignation.

'No!' said Warzok decisively. 'A Jew should never die when *he* wishes, only when *we* wish.'

– 6 –

A Polish odyssey 1944

The last time Simon Wiesenthal saw Lemberg – on Wednesday, 19 July 1944 – he and thirty-three other survivors of Janowskà were marched through the city, under heavy Red Army artillery fire, to the railway yards where he and Cyla had worked before their escapes and where his mother and thousands of other ageing women had stood suffering for three days without water in crammed freight cars beneath blazing summer sun not quite two years earlier while awaiting deportation to the fires of Belzec.

Put aboard a freight car, Simon and his fellow hostages worried whether they were going to be gassed – until SS man Blum, who'd been in charge of the Askaris, added two more passengers: his dog and, in a cage, his canary. 'That was the best news,' says Wiesenthal, 'because the SS men all loved their pets and would never be so unhuman as to gas *them*. Blum said we'd all be shot if anything happened to his bird or his dog. So we took extra special care of them.'

They reached the city of Przemysl, 125 miles west of Lemberg, the next morning and were transported to the town of Dobromil, where the railroad tracks gave out. Then they were marched along the main road west, already clogged with civilians fleeing the Russians. The 200 SS men guarding the thirty-four Jewish slave labourers were running for their lives, too, and when a horse-drawn convoy of *Volksdeutsche* (ethnic Germans from Poland) overtook the group, Warzok – Janowskà's runaway commandant – halted them and commandeered thirty of their forty wagons.

With each wagon piloted by a Jew and six or seven SS men riding shotgun to 'guard' him, this cowardly caravan caught up near the last bridge across the River San with a German Army column retreating from the Red Army, which was coming closer and closer. If the soldiers with their heavy equipment crossed the bridge first, the Russians might well catch up with 'SS Construction Staff Venus', as Warzok called his bootleg work force.

Though only a captain – but an SS captain! – Warzok pulled rank and a weapon on the Army major commanding the retreating unit. With his pistol held to the major's head and other SS men covering the column with submachine-guns, Warzok ordered his wagons to cross the bridge first and then took two Army engineers across with him while keeping the major and his officers covered with a submachine-gun. The bridge had already been planted with dynamite for eventual destruction, but Warzok had the engineers do it now – leaving their unit and its furious major to be captured by the Red Army while Construction Staff Venus went unscathed and unreported.

Near the Polish city of Grybow, Warzok's crew of captors and captives pitched camp in the middle of a large field. Wiesenthal painted a sign proclaiming it headquarters of SS BAUSTAB VENUS and, for more than a month, the war and the world passed them by without asking any questions.

One September day, however, an SS *Rottenführer* (corporal) named Merz asked Wiesenthal a question of his own. Merz, whom Wiesenthal considered a relatively decent *Rottenführer,* had gone foraging for food and taken Simon along because he spoke Polish. Now, toting two sacks of potatoes, they relaxed beside a babbling brook at the edge of a rustling forest. The weather in Eastern Europe is at its best in September and, stretched out on his back, Merz studied the hazy sky above and let his mind wander.

'Suppose an eagle took you to America, Wiesenthal,' he asked. 'What would you tell them there?'

Fearing a trap, Wiesenthal said nothing. But Merz persisted: 'Don't be afraid. You can talk frankly.'

Wiesenthal evaded the question: '*Herr Rottenführer,* how could I get to America? I might as well try to go to the moon.'

Rottenführer Merz wouldn't let Simon off the hook: 'Just imagine, Wiesenthal, that you're arriving in New York and the people ask you, "How was it in those German concentration camps? What did they do to you?"'

Taking his life into his mouth, Wiesenthal replied haltingly: 'I believe – I believe I would tell the people the truth, *Herr Rottenführer.*'

Merz didn't shoot him. He simply said: 'You would tell the truth to the people in America. That's right. And do you know what would happen, Wiesenthal? They wouldn't believe you.'

With these words, Merz reinforced Wiesenthal's will to live – and prove him wrong.

Merz Schmerz was what Wiesenthal would call the pain caused by daily fulfilment of the cynical but wise *Rottenführer's* prophecy. Still, as the war neared its inevitable end – painfully, usually fatally, slowly for those caught in the camps – the need to bear witness gave thousands of the doomed, many of them more than half dead already, a new grip on survival: a reason for enduring. At Treblinka, would-be suicides who wrapped ropes around their necks were often talked down from their improvised nooses by other Jews who convinced them their testimony would be needed.

As the Germans stepped up their programme of deportation and gassing, hundreds of Jews launched their own programmes of writing and recording. Mordecai Tenenbaum, a Jewish resistance leader in Vilna and later in Bialystok, kept a journal with names and dates and details throughout his adventures and told his fiancée, Tamara Sznajderman, a courier for the Jewish Fighting Organization, to 'live, live at any price so you can tell the story; you are so good at that.' After she was killed in combat in the Warsaw Ghetto in early 1943, a few months before he led an uprising in which he perished in Bialystok, Tenenbaum buried his journal in the ground for posterity to unearth. Its opening words were: 'Greetings, unknown seeker who discovers these pages.'

Way back in 1933 in Warsaw, a far-sighted young Jewish historian named Emanuel Ringelblum had started collecting documents and taking notes on Hitler's earliest decrees in neighbouring Germany with an eye to how they might affect Polish Judaism and inspire 'Jewish countermeasures'. Even before the Jews were arbitrarily moved by the German occupiers into what became the Warsaw Ghetto in 1940, Ringelblum was noting such everyday details as 'Dr Cooperman was shot for being out after eight o'clock. He had a pass', and a ban on the posting of obituary notices. Later, Ringelblum would record the gallows humour of the ghetto: 'If the Germans win the war, twenty-five per cent of the Jews will be dead by then. If the British win, seventy-five per cent will be dead – because the English will take so long.'

Deported in early 1943 to a labour camp, Ringelblum was smuggled out and back to Warsaw by the Jewish resistance because his mission was so vital. In hiding, he continued his chronicles, even though he was on a list of nineteen key resistance figures whom the London-based Polish government-in-exile had agreed to bring out to freedom. By the time action was possible, sixteen were dead. Ringelblum and the other two refused to be rescued 'because we must fulfil our duty to society.' Arrested again that March with thirty-seven other Jews hiding in a bunker, Ringelblum was tortured by the Gestapo and then executed with his wife and son a few weeks before the twenty-eight-day Warsaw Ghetto uprising of April 1943: the war's most heroic armed conflict and a resounding rebuttal to Jewish submission to genocide.

When the ghetto was liquidated, 56,000 of its 60,000 Jews were dead; most of the rest were deported to the death camps. But Ringelblum's notes and other archives (including the first eye-witness account of exterminations at Treblinka)) were found in milk cans and tin boxes dug up in the ruins of the Warsaw Ghetto in 1946 and 1950. In the ashes of Auschwitz-Birkenau between 1945 and 1962, searchers in the bone-riddled earth near where the crematoria once burned day and night unearthed five manuscripts of workers in the *Sonderkommando* whose job was to destroy the remains of the gassed; late in 1980, a sixth – written in Greek and preserved in a buried Thermos – was discovered by Polish schoolchildren planting a tree. All these manuscripts were posthumous – but their authors' words lived to tell the truth.

The posthumous 'diary of Salomon Tauber' – a *Kapo* (Jewish policeman) in the ghetto of Riga, Latvia, who packs his wife into a gassing van – triggers the plot of a living work: Frederick Forsyth's 1972 novel, *The Odessa File*. There is not a word of invention in this fictional 'diary', for it is drawn from depositions in Simon Wiesenthal's office.

Thus, Wiesenthal himself looks upon his conversation with *Rottenführer* Merz and the spiritual pain that followed as a moment of truth that opened unto him his future as an archangel of revelation and retribution. He uses it without any comment or embellishment as a closing postscript to his 1967 memoir, *The Murderers Among Us*. Asked about it now, he recalls that only after he left Lemberg could he consider any horizon wider than his wife's safety somewhere in

Warsaw and his own survival from day to day, or dawn to dusk. But his Polish odyssey – in the custody of 200 SS killers who needed him and some thirty other Jews to keep themselves alive – opened his eyes to the reality that Germany was actually about to lose the war and his captors were looking for ways to melt into the mass of German society which had embraced Hitler without committing the crimes he'd entrusted to the SS. To Wiesenthal, even while hauling potatoes with no end in sight except extinction, the prospect of their postwar assimilation was intolerable.

'I learned later,' he says, 'that ninety-five per cent of the real criminals survived the war through tactics like Warzok's. But I could see even then that the real soldiers on both sides were fighting and dying – and against them the odds were much higher. And for us, the Jews in German or Ukrainian hands, we would be lucky if five per cent survived. A soldier is not a killer. He fights with the risk he can kill or be killed. And this risk was too high for SS killers like Warzok and Dyga and Blum. Helpless people in a camp or a ghetto can be killed without any risk – without *any* risk!' Unable to ride on the wings of Merz's mythical eagle or a magic carpet that would bear him to America to tell the truth about the camps to an unbelieving, uncaring world, Prisoner Number 127371 began at potato level to dig for data and descriptions, recorded at first only in a retentive mind, which would document the destruction of a people at the hands of the Nazis and bring more than a thousand perpetrators to some semblance of justice.

As the Russians neared Grybow, SS Construction Staff Venus pulled up stakes and moved west again, stealing food as it went. Drawing near the German border, Commandant Warzok knew he would have to present his superiors with a more rational military profile than 200 SS men guarding fewer than three dozen Jews. Thus, in Chelmiec, his SS men surrounded a church during mass and kidnapped all the worshippers – men, women, and children – to work for Venus.

Near Neu Sandez (now Nowy Sacz), Warzok summoned Wiesenthal's engineering skills to survey terrain for building anti-tank barricades along a steep, narrow dirt road which ended atop a lonely hill. *'Herr Kommandant,'* Wiesenthal pointed out respectfully, 'this road leads nowhere. No tank would ever come here.'

Slapping his holster, Warzok barked: 'Did I ask for your military opinion?' Wiesenthal recognized that Warzok was merely making work to keep out of a war that was already lost.

'For a while,' Wiesenthal recalls, 'we built defences against tanks that would never come. Then the Russians came closer, so we moved again, this time to the Plaszow concentration camp just outside the city of Cracow, and there Dyga and another SS man took most of the Jews into the nearby woods and shot them' after the camp authorities had performed a perfunctory 'selection' of which ones they would take.

A German general had discovered the Venus hoax, dissolved the 'construction unit', and shipped Warzok and his SS men back to the front. 'Warzok is still around somewhere,' says Wiesenthal, 'and I hope I'll find him before the biological solution catches up with us both.'

Some of Warzok's Polish captives were executed, too, but the rest were sent home to Chelmiec while a handful of able-bodied Jews was turned over to what Wiesenthal still calls 'the terrors of Plaszow', a labour camp where the hardier survivors of Cracow's ancient ghetto had been moved in late 1942; the others were shipped directly to the death camps.

Licensed architect Simon Wiesenthal did well to lose himself among the faceless slave labour at Plaszow. He survived there until late 1944, when the Red Army neared and the camp was liquidated. To cover their tracks, the Nazis had the inmates dig up mass graves and burn the bodies.

At the end of 1944, Plaszow's survivors were 'relocated'. Women and children went to Auschwitz, not quite forty miles away, and were rarely heard from again. Able-bodied men, still including Wiesenthal, were marched to Gross Rosen, a vast quarry near Breslau, Germany (now Wroclaw, Poland) in Lower Silesia. There, the German Earth and State Works, an SS contractor, worked its Jews to death instead of wasting bullets or gas on executing or exterminating them.

In Gross Rosen, they were joined by prisoners taken in the latest Warsaw uprising. Sixteen months after the ghetto and its heroes had been destroyed in four weeks of April 1943, a nine-week non-Jewish Warsaw uprising of 1944 had begun in August when the Red Army had appeared – briefly – on the eastern outskirts of the capital. While the Russians never even attempted to liberate Warsaw until the following year, the Poles had persisted and the SS had defended the city to the death: the death of more than 200,000 civilians and 15,000 Polish underground fighters as well as 10,000 Germans (another 7000 Germans vanished from Warsaw during the battle). Augmented by brigades of Russian deserters and German convicts, the SS brought its own brand of brutality to desperate street fighting which gave Poland's Gentiles a harsh taste of what the Jews had been experiencing and what awaited them in the next round of the Final Solution. As food, medicine, and, finally, water gave out, disease spread and virtually no children survived. Thousands of Poles were shot in cold blood and much of the city was razed, for Hitler had promised his foes naught but scorched earth to conquer.

Worried about his wife, Cyla, who had been planted by the Polish underground at Topiel Street number 5 in Gentile Warsaw as 'Irene Kowalska', Wiesenthal asked the Warsaw survivors whether anybody was from Topiel Street. One of the men said he'd lived at number 7. Without hinting he was married to her, Wiesenthal asked him if he knew Irena Kowalska.

'The blonde woman? Yes, I remember her well,' he replied – adding, however, that she was no more. 'My friend, *no* one in Topiel Street survived. The Germans surrounded one house after another with flame-throwers and afterwards blew up what was left of the houses. There is no hope, believe me. Topiel Street is one big mass grave.'

Remembering that moment of 'truth', Simon Wiesenthal says now: 'That night, I went to sleep a widower.' Cyla Wiesenthal had shared a similar experience during the uprising; a Polish underground courier from Lemberg had 'informed' Irena Kowalska that 'Wiesenthal was arrested by Gestapo man Waltke (*which was true*), cut his wrists (*also true*), and is dead.'

– 7 –

The last liberation 1945

Looking back on early 1945, Simon Wiesenthal says: 'It was a stinking time then and it is a stinking time for me to investigate now. It was a time when Nazi criminals became Allied helpers because they wanted to save their own lives. Everybody has his pet Jew, his own character witness who could testify in good faith that this killer or that one had spared his life. Only the Eichmann forces, which were scattering, were still one hundred fifty per cent Nazi; all the other Nazis were looking for a way out or at least a foot in the gate of the other camp.'

It was worse than a stinking time for Wiesenthal: a sinking time when, as he puts it, 'my way of life was twelve hundred miles of concentration camps' and there were a million ways of death, starting with starvation, disease, decay, fever, frost, incineration, sadism, and summary execution. As the Red Army neared Gross Rosen at the beginning of 1945, the inmates – still heavily guarded – were dispatched on death marches in different directions. Though the war was lost, the Germans would still decide when and where their Jews would die. Those who faltered or fell were shot on the spot.

Wiesenthal's way was across Silesia to Chemnitz (later Karl-Marx-Stadt in East Germany) . . . through frozen fields and icy woods to Weimar, where democracy had bloomed briefly after Germany lost the First World War . . . and then by cattle car to Buchenwald. 'The man in charge was one of the nastiest guys I have ever met,' Wiesenthal recalls. 'Not only did he call us names I'd not yet heard, but he complained about undercrowding when we were loaded one hundred to a freight car, so they had to bring the number up to a hundred forty-five. The soldiers guarding us didn't let us fetch water or make water at the railway stations. At the station in Leipzig, some civilians tried to give us some bread, but the soldiers drove them away with their rifle butts. There were about forty dead in each railroad car when we reached Buchenwald.'

Buchenwald was perhaps the worst of all the concentration camps within Germany. In the last months of the war, 56,549 prisoners perished there, and it is no accident that the definitive book on the mechanism of the concentration camps, *The Theory and Practice of Hell*, was written by a survivor of six years in Buchenwald, Eugen Kogon (1903–87), a German writer and editor. It was at Buchenwald that the commandant, Karl Koch, made himself a millionaire through private exploitation of slave labour while his wife, Ilse, 'The Bitch of Buchenwald', had her lampshades made from the skins of murdered inmates.* When Buchenwald was finally liberated in April 1945, most of its Jews had been killed or evacuated elsewhere, but one of them, eight-year-old Israel Lau, was pulled alive from a pile of corpses by an American Army rabbi, who burst into tears as he asked him in Yiddish: 'How old are you?'

'Older than you,' the boy replied.

The rabbi had to laugh, but the child told him: 'Look, you cry and laugh like a little boy, but I haven't laughed for years and I don't even cry any more. So tell me: who is older?'

Wiesenthal hadn't lingered long in Buchenwald. In early February 1945, he and some 3000 other prisoners had been loaded on to open trucks, 140 to a truck. Their destination was unknown to them – and, it sometimes seemed, to their drivers, who kept them standing on the trucks for a day before departing south and eastward once again. During the six-day trip, there was no food or water.

'The dead stood quietly among the living,' Wiesenthal recalls. 'We would throw them out of the trucks, but when the civilians living along the route protested, the SS men warned us we'd be shot if we threw more bodies out along the highway. So we stuck the stiff bodies on the floor of the truck, like wooden boards, and sat on our dead comrades.'

*Convicted of corruption in 1944 by an SS court, Karl Koch was executed by Nazi justice. For his wife's war crimes, postwar justice handed Ilse Koch a life sentence, which was commuted to four years and she was released. Re-arrested in 1949 after press and public protests, she was tried for murder and again given life imprisonment. She committed suicide in a Bavarian prison in 1967.

When the convoy arrived at the railroad station at Mauthausen in Upper Austria on a cold, clear Friday night, only 1200 of the original 3000 passengers were still alive. Another 180 died on the four-mile uphill hike they were forced to make from the station to the camp.

Wiesenthal was almost one of the casualties. Trudging over frozen snow, with each man's steps crackling thunderously like drums of doom in the silence of the night, he linked arms with a Polish prince named Radziwill, a relative of the one who later married Jacqueline Kennedy Onassis' sister Lee Bouvier. For a while, Wiesenthal and Radziwill kept each other up, but when they couldn't go any farther, they simply sank into the snow.

'Are you alive?' a voice barked in German and, to remedy this condition, its owner fired at them. But the SS guard's hands were cold and his shot landed in the snow between Wiesenthal and Radziwill. Then the two men drifted into sleep as life and death passed them by.

Well before dawn, the camp authorities sent trucks down to collect corpses and spare the sensibilities of villagers going to work in the morning. Frozen stiff, Wiesenthal and Radziwill were taken for dead and flung aboard with a pile of bodies. Simon doesn't know whether it was the motion or the warmth of the other bodies that revived them a little, but when the truck delivered them to the camp crematorium, the prisoners working there noticed that both men weren't quite dead. They carried Wiesenthal and Radziwill to a shower-room, removed their clothes, and immersed them in cold water. When both were conscious, though faint and dizzy, they were smuggled into the 'death barracks', where prisoners too weak to work were left to die.

There Wiesenthal lay for almost three months: a hundred-pound cadaver who drank down his daily ration of 200 calories of soup that stank. So did the barracks – with the smells of sickness, pus, death, and prisoners sleeping two or three to a bunk, some never to awaken. So awful was the stench that the SS men wouldn't even poke their heads inside. A guard would simply stand outside the door and take a one-question morning census: 'How many died last night?' Later in the day, a crematorium detail would collect the corpses.

'Sometimes,' says Wiesenthal, 'we thought we were the last men alive on earth. We had lost touch with reality. We didn't know whether anybody else was still alive.'

As Simon Wiesenthal lay dying in Mauthausen in the last weeks of the war, he used the pencils and paper he had acquired to draw the living (and dying) hell just outside the door of the death barracks. For the concentration camp, which supplied paving stones for Vienna and other Austrian cities, was built around a 186-step-deep rock quarry. Here, Jews and other enemies of fascism – Spanish republicans, gypsies, homosexuals, Jehovah's witnesses – were worked or shot or flung to death. Only ten per cent of the prisoners were German or Austrian. On 31 March 1943, to entertain Heinrich Himmler on an official visit, a thousand Dutch Jews had been tossed off the rim of the pit to smash to death 165 feet below; from then on, the SS referred to this recurrent ritual as 'parachute jumping'.

In the first four months of 1945, more than 30,000 perished at Mauthausen: many from brutality, but more from exhaustion, starvation, and disease. Mauthausen was a slave-labour camp for men* – and they died 'natural' deaths which caused the fewest extermination problems for the SS. By April, there was no water for washing in the camp. 'We were swarming with lice and filth,' a survivor remembers. 'We would sometimes pull out some two hundred lice on each of us. When I would sit down and try to rise, I would get dizzy and see nothing for a couple of minutes. That's how weak we were.' After an Allied air raid, prisoners ate the flesh of fallen inmates who died when a bomb hit part of the camp.

Rarely able to venture from his bunk, but allowed the privacy of the dead, Wiesenthal sat up to sketch the sadistic commandant, Franz Ziereis, who boasted of giving his son 'fifty Jews for target practice' as a birthday present and over whose desk was framed a poem that read:

Shame on the man
Who can't strike blows.
Heed the command:
Beat to death! Beat to death!†

*On the rare occasions when women were imprisoned in Mauthausen, a 1943 decree specified that 'corporal punishment for Russian women is to be performed by Polish women, and for Polish and Ukrainian women by Russian women' – tribal enemies who would, presumably, show each other no mercy.

†Ziereis was shot by two American soldiers in late May 1945. Wiesenthal later published his death-bed confession.

He drew the stone quarry as the gateway to Dante's inferno and later, for a 1946 booklet honouring the first year of liberation of Mauthausen, he captioned what it showed: 'Building the pyramids was a preview in which hundreds of thousands of slaves perished. In the stone quarry, every SS bandit felt like a pharaoh. Just as in ancient Egypt, giant blocks of stone – never lighter than 110 pounds, by Himmler's order – were carried by human bodies. An SS man sat atop such a block, cracking his whip to make work merrier – for him!' Today, Simon Wiesenthal cannot bear to look at the pyramids of Egypt without thinking of Mauthausen and the tiny Jewish slave at the bottom bearing the wonder of the world on his frail shoulders.

He drew a uniformed Hitler peeling off his moustached mask to reveal the SS death's head beneath it. And a portrait of a larger-than-life Himmler etched into the brick wall of a crematorium with a long line of human fuel marching into the door of his fiery gut. With polemic passion, he wrote beneath it: 'Insatiable, the death factory works day and night – insatiable as the devil's helper Himmler himself: "The smoke clouds must roll toward victory! Too little raw material for the chimney! Too few dead! Too few dead! Too few!"' Between 1938 and 1945, more than 130,000 died in Mauthausen.

On Friday night, 4 May 1945, the last SS men disappeared from the camp. The next morning, nobody came to count or collect the dead. An emaciated Wiesenthal, weighing just ninety pounds, struggled out to the courtyard to see for himself that there was no roll-call. It was a bright, sunny spring morning with a scent of pine in the air rather than the usual smell of burning flesh from the crematorium. Toward ten o'clock, instead of Himmler's smoke clouds, a big grey tank with a white star on its side rolled in flying an American flag from its turret.

'Every star was a star of hope,' says Wiesenthal. 'I was about a hundred fifty yards away from the first tank, but I wanted to touch one of those stars.' From the death barracks staggered other living corpses, waving their own long-hidden national flags or newly woven versions of the Stars and Stripes. 'I had survived to see this day, but I couldn't make the last fifty yards.' When his knees crumpled, he fell on his face.

An American GI in green combat fatigues lifted him up. Wiesenthal couldn't speak, couldn't even move his mouth, but he pointed to the tank and was brought to it. Touching the white star of hope on the cold grey armour, he fainted into freedom for the ninth liberation of his life.

– 8 –

Mornings in Mauthausen

Upon seeing the skeletons who staggered out to greet them on 5 May 1945, the Americans of the 65th Division who rode to Mauthausen's rescue had requisitioned every potato in the area. For many that they 'saved', however, it was already too late. Some 3000 inmates died in the weeks *after* the liberation of Mauthausen. Some were too weak or sick to recover from their ordeal. Others left the camp too soon, for one had to be strong to survive in war-ravaged Europe.

Simon Wiesenthal awoke on his bunk to the aroma of real soup. It was so delicious that he took too much of it – and threw up. But he survived his good fortune and the American medics nursed him back to health. 'Others were not so lucky,' he says. 'There were those who died *because* they were being helped. The Americans gave out canned lard and corned beef, which can be fatal in big doses to those who have been living on four hundred calories a day. So they survived hell only to die at the gate of paradise.'

No sooner could he navigate on his own, after about ten days, than he set out for a walk in the surrounding countryside. Past a pastoral scene of children playing and farmers tilling their soil, he strolled towards the village until, after not quite a mile, he felt weak and fatigued. At a farmhouse, he asked for a glass of water and was given grape juice by a strapping Austrian peasant woman who could tell, by one glance at his gaunt face and loose clothes, whence this scarecrow hailed. Nodding in the direction of the camp, she asked him: 'Was it bad over there?'

'Be glad you didn't see the camp from the inside,' Wiesenthal told her.

'Why should *I* have seen it?' she said. 'I'm not a Jew.'

Wiesenthal winced with what he calls *Merz Schmerz*: the pain caused by first fulfilment of *Rottenführer* Merz's prophecy, in Poland less than a year earlier, that nobody after the war would care to believe his testimony. He drank his grape juice and left.

Implicit in the response of this woman – relatively well fed, but generous and surely not guilty of any wrong-doing – was a prevailing attitude of 'this is what happens to Jews' and 'this is what happens to the rest of us'. But the *Merz Schmerz* that the Upper Austrian farm woman unwittingly handed to Simon to digest with his cup of grape juice was part of the potion that transformed a ninety-six-pound victim and survivor of the Holocaust into its avenging arch-angel.

In the weeks, months, and years to come, Wiesenthal would hear many Austrians and 'good Germans' volunteering to him that they 'knew nothing about what was happening' or had even 'saved some Jews'. To this, his private reaction is vehement:

'If all the Jews had been saved that I was told about in those first few months, there would have been more Jews alive at the end of the war than when it began. I also stop believing after a while when people try to convince me they knew absolutely nothing. Maybe they knew not the whole truth about what went on inside the death camps. But all of them must have noticed *something* after Hitler invaded Austria on March eleventh, 1938. They couldn't help seeing Jewish neighbours taken away by men in black SS uniforms. Their children came home from school and reported that their Jewish classmates had been kicked out. They saw the swastikas on the broken windows of looted Jewish stores. They had to walk around the rubble of synagogues destroyed during *Kristallnacht* in 1938. People knew what was going on, although many were ashamed and chose to look the other way so they wouldn't see too much. Soldiers and officers on leave from the eastern front came home and talked about massacres of the Jews there. People knew much more than they admitted, even to themselves, which is why today so many suffer from an acute sense of guilt.' Wiesenthal's words are as good a diagnosis as any of what is now known in Austria as *Waldheimer's Disease*.

Retreating from the traumas of *Merz Schmerz* and pre-*Waldheimer's Disease*, Wiesenthal returned to the Mauthausen camp, where a new blow awaited him. The stronger survivors who had no place to go yet were running the barracks. A Polish trusty named Kazimierz Rusinek pounced on Simon for no good reason and knocked him unconscious. When Wiesenthal woke up, friends had carried him to his bunk. 'What has he got against you?' one of them asked.

'I don't know,' Simon said. 'Maybe he's angry because I'm still alive.'

His friends told him: 'You must report this to the Americans.' . . . 'We're no longer sub-humans; we're free men.' . . . 'We'll go with you tomorrow, when you're feeling a little better.'

Wiesenthal agreed to go because 'if you can beat a skeleton, what else could such a person have done?' When they went to the camp headquarters next morning, the commander, Colonel Richard Seibel, listened and said: 'We have a special branch for that. It's called War Crimes.'

At an office with a handwritten sign, a young lieutenant named Mann heard Wiesenthal's story, his witnesses, and the words of a doctor who'd treated him. 'You'll hear from us,' the officer said brusquely.

That night in the barracks, Rusinek apologized to Wiesenthal before all his friends and extended his hand. Wiesenthal accepted his apology, but did not give him his hand. Though Rusinek later became communist Poland's Vice-Minister of Culture and a leading anti-Semitic propagandist, Simon says that at the time 'he wasn't important. He was already part of the past. What was important was what else I'd seen at the War Crimes office: SS men being interrogated by the Americans, begging cigarettes from their captors, being guarded and translated by former prisoners, and cringing whenever their paths crossed a Jew's. One of them used to whip us in the face if we didn't get out of his way fast enough; now he was trembling, just as we had trembled before him. I had seen nervous German soldiers before, but never a frightened SS man. I used to think of the SS as the strong men, the élite, of a perverted regime. But now I saw that supermen become cowards in the moment they are no longer protected by guns. Only two weeks had gone by and the élite of the Thousand Year Reich were fighting each other for cigarette butts.'

A few days later, he went to the War Crimes Office to thank Lieutenant Mann and offer his services. The young officer listened to him sympathetically, but pointed out that Simon had no investigatory experience. And besides, he added, 'How much do you weigh?'

'Fifty-six kilos [123 lbs],' Wiesenthal lied.

Laughing, the lieutenant told him: 'Wiesenthal, go take it easy for a while and come back and see me when you really *do* weigh fifty-six kilos.'

The Americans tried to persuade him to return to Poland, where architects were sorely needed. 'First you'll be sent to a sanatorium to build you up,' they told him. 'Then you'll go home and build houses for people who need them.' His home city of Lvov, however, was already being absorbed into the Soviet Union, where he knew private housing had no priority at all. But that wasn't why he told them thank you, but no, thank you.

'Every house I built is gone. I have lost my mother, my father, my wife, and ninety relatives in Poland,' he explained. 'Poland is for me a cemetery. Every tree, every stone would remind me of whole tragedies. How can you ask me to live in a cemetery?'

The image he used was hardly amiss, for Poland was worse than a cemetery for many like him. Even though the Poles had lost the second-highest number put to death by the Nazis (three million, including half of those who had higher educations), anti-Semitism was even more rampant among the living than before the war. Jewish survivors were shunned as ghosts returning from the dead to reclaim property that Poles had long since appropriated.

In his definitive 1985 chronicle of *The Holocaust*, the Oxford historian Martin Gilbert – who also co-scripted the 1983 Academy Award-winning documentary *Genocide* for the Simon Wiesenthal Centre in Los Angeles – writes that 'within seven months of the end of the war in Europe, and after a year in which no German soldier was on Polish soil, 350 Jews had been murdered in Poland.' Among them were Chaim Hirszman, one of the only two miraculous survivors of Belzec (where Wiesenthal's mother and half a million others perished in 1942), and five survivors of Auschwitz, Buchenwald, and Mauthausen – one of them a twenty-two-year-old woman – who were flagged down at what looked like a police checkpoint along the main road to Nowy Targ on Easter Sunday of 1946, ordered out of their car, shot to death on the spot, stripped of their clothes, and left naked on the highway. Their uniformed killers were former Polish partisans.

No wonder that, learning of these events and even losing an acquaintance or two in Poland's postwar holocaust, Simon Wiesenthal saw his native land as one vast Jewish cemetery. What he didn't know yet was that the casualty who mattered most to him, his young wife Cyla, was alive in that cemetery.

As 'Irena Kowalska', Cyla hadn't died in the German attack on Topiel Street after the Warsaw uprising; she had slipped away into darkness a few minutes before flame-throwers illuminated and incinerated the whole block. When the battle was over and survivors rounded up, she, as a 'Gentile', had 'only' been deported to forced labour in a German machine-gun factory near Gelsenkirchen, which was liberated by the British on 11 April 1945, while her 'late' husband lay dying in Mauthausen.

Having believed for almost a year that her husband had slashed his wrists in Gestapo custody, Cyla Wiesenthal told the British authorities that she was not Irena Kowalska, but a Jew and the widow of an architect named Simon Wiesenthal. At British headquarters, she was persuaded she had no choice other than to return to Lvov and begin life anew in Soviet Russia. She was given a railroad ticket and, in June, she and a woman friend headed behind the Iron Curtain on a journey which, if completed, surely would have been one-way. At one point, they passed within thirty miles of Simon.

With a little weight under his belt and some improvised rouge on his cheeks to give an illusion of good health, Simon Wiesenthal applied again to the War Crimes office at Mauthausen.

'Hey, Wiesenthal!' Lieutenant Mann greeted him. 'Did that Polish fella beat you up again? Your face is all red.'

Wiesenthal assured him he would heal overnight and came to the point: 'You liberated me, you saved my life, but I don't know what to do with my life. I have nobody and nothing to live for, but I could find a meaning for my life by helping you with your work. I've seen a lot and I have a good memory. Men and women have been murdered before my eyes. I can give you names and dates and sometimes addresses. I can help you find the criminals and, when you interrogate them, the most important thing is to ask the right questions – and those I have.'

Mann had him write a letter to Colonel Seibel, to which he appended accounts of crimes he had witnessed or learned about. To Simon's own amazement, his chronicle contained 'the names of ninety-one men who had to be brought to trial if my need for justice was to be satisfied.'

Three weeks after the liberation of Mauthausen, Simon was accepted. He was sent out with a US Army captain and his jeep-driver to patrol the Mauthausen area for former SS guards from the camp who were hiding in the countryside. 'You didn't have to go far,' he remembers. 'You almost stumbled over them.' After a while, the captain, bored with the sameness of it all and tired of plucking quavering ex-supermen from their wives or girlfriends, would send Simon inside to make the arrests.

Wiesenthal's first 'client' had the everyday name of Schmidt. Taking him into custody was almost situation comedy. Schmidt lived up two steep flights of stairs, and Wiesenthal arrived out of breath to arrest him. On the way down, Wiesenthal – still weak from the ordeals Schmidt and his superiors had inflicted on him at Mauthausen – felt so faint that he had to sit down hard on a step. After a couple of minutes, 'Schmidt helped me as we walked down the stairway together. He could have easily tried to run away. If he had given me a slight shove, I would have fallen down the stairs and he could have escaped out the back door. But Schmidt didn't even think of running away. Instead, he held me by the arm and helped me down. It was absurd – like a rabbit carrying a hunting-dog.'

In the jeep, Schmidt began to cry. 'I was only a little person,' he blubbered. 'I just obeyed orders. Why pick on me and let the big fish swim free? I've done nothing wrong. I swear to you: I risked my own neck just to help prisoners.'

Now the ex-prisoner he had just helped down the stairs turned on Schmidt with a sarcastic snarl: 'Yes, you helped prisoners. I saw you often. You helped them on the way to the crematorium.' Schmidt was silent for the rest of the trip.

When Austria was partitioned for a decade by the Americans, British, French, and Russians, Mauthausen fell into the Soviet military zone of occupation. The US War Crimes Office moved its operations across the Danube to Linz, the capital city of the province of Upper Austria. Mauthausen inmates working for the Americans were lodged in a Displaced Persons camp in the public school of

Leonding, a small town near Linz. That school was where Adolf Hitler had begun his education, and Wiesenthal remembers: 'We slept on cots in a classroom whose windows looked out on a small house that was the former home of Hitler's parents. They were buried in the cemetery at the end of the road. I didn't particularly like the view from the room and moved out of the school after a few days. I rented a modest furnished room on the Landstrasse in Linz. Not much of a room, really, but from the window I could see a small garden.'

By taking that room with a view at Landstrasse 40, Wiesenthal had once again jumped from frying-pan to fire. Not only was his new address conveniently just two doors up from the War Crimes Office at Landstrasse 36, but it was only two more doors away from Landstrasse 32, the house where one Adolf Eichmann – born in the German city of Solingen thirty-nine years earlier – had spent his youth and where his father and stepmother still lived. They were known as the 'Elektro' Eichmanns, for Karl Adolf Eichmann, head of Linz's electric streetcar works for many years, now owned an electrical appliance store there.

Having begun to hear from Hungarian Jews at Mauthausen about Adolf Eichmann as the driving force behind their deportations, Wiesenthal was one of the first on his trail. At Simon's behest, the Americans searched the father's house and found no traces of the eldest child. When they sought a photo of the prodigal son – considered the least successful of the five Eichmann offspring – there wasn't any. Besides, Adolf Eichmann had taken care never to discuss his work or encourage picture-taking.

On 1 August, Wiesenthal received a tip that Eichmann was hiding at house number 8 in Fischerndorf, a section of the village of Alt Aussee, near the war's last SS redoubt. He notified Army Counter-Intelligence (CIC), which asked the Austrian police to bring Eichmann in. The police went by mistake to number 38, where they found an SS captain named Anton Burger with a formidable cache of weapons and ammunition. They arrested him and called it a day's work well done.

Burger, a former deputy commandant of the Theresienstadt concentration camp at Terezín in what had been (and was again) Czechoslovakia, had also served on Eichmann's staff. Wiesenthal often cites this case of mistaken identity as an example of the postwar chaos with hot- and cold-running SS men seemingly lurking behind every door. But he was not too surprised, for so much Nazi loot was hidden in the *Ausseerland* that its population of 18,000 in 1944 had more than quadrupled in 1945. 'Allowing for a few thousand German soldiers,' Wiesenthal wondered, 'who were these sixty thousand civilians who'd arrived during the months before the collapse of the Third Reich?' The answer was that the people who'd known where the bodies were buried now knew where the SS's stolen treasure was buried – and wanted to stay close to it.

When Wiesenthal learned that the Austrians had netted Burger instead of the bigger fish he was seeking, he asked the CIC to do the job itself. An American agent went to Fischerndorf 8 and found a woman named Veronika Liebl, which happened to be Frau Adolf Eichmann's maiden name. Yes, she was the same Veronika Liebl, she said, but she'd divorced her husband in Prague that April and hadn't seen him since. She had their three sons – Klaus, Dieter, and Horst – with her and wouldn't say why she had divorced their father. Wiesenthal told the CIC she bore watching in case her 'ex-husband' paid a visit.

In Linz, Wiesenthal worked mornings for the War Crimes Office and afternoons for a new Jewish Committee, of which he became vice-chairman. Later, its two rooms became the headquarters of the Jewish Central Committee for the US Zone in Austria – and a Mecca for displaced Jews asking the eternal question after a disaster: *'Who else is alive?'* But unlike an earthquake or even a nuclear attack, the Holocaust had scattered its survivors and victims across the map of Europe, with most records of them strewn to the wind, destroyed, or non-existent.

The same chaos and lack of communications enabled the criminals who had torn these families apart, usually forever, to live in American custody under their own names, as Dr Josef Mengele and Franz Stangl did, or under such pseudonyms as 'Memling' for Mengele and 'Lieutenant Eckmann' for Colonel Eichmann. And it meant that the tide of human misery and eternal hope would drive many of these refugees behind what would not formally be identified as an Iron Curtain until 5 March 1946 (by Sir Winston Churchill in a speech in Fulton, Missouri), but was already enmeshing much of Eastern Europe and enveloping hundreds of thousands of innocents in its swirls even before Hitler's machinery had ground to a halt.

As with all of Wiesenthal's postwar organizations, the Jewish Committee's basic function was making lists, not righting wrongs. From information can come justice – which is why the Soviets were suppressing facts. Survivors who came to Wiesenthal to ask after loved ones or friends were asked where *they* were from. Lists of known survivors, arranged by city or town, were compiled at Committee headquarters. Wiesenthal and his colleagues worked nights transcribing names from all sources while, outside their door, anxious people waited in line all night for what Wiesenthal called 'a glance that might mean hope or despair'. Sometimes, there were brawls and scuffles and once, in a fight for the same list, two men tore it up. On another occasion, two men in line argued impatiently over who was next to see a list that a third man was studying. When it became a face-to-face confrontation, they suddenly embraced – for they were brothers who had been seeking each other for weeks.

Wiesenthal recalls 'moments of silent despair when someone discovered that the person he was looking for had been there only a few days before, looking for him. They had missed each other. Where should one look now? Others scanned the lists of survivors, hoping against hope to find the names of people they had seen killed before their very eyes. Everybody had heard of some miracle.'

Wiesenthal, who at that time hardly believed in God, rabbis, or miracles, seldom studied his lists, for 'I had no hope my wife was alive. When I thought of her, I thought of her body lying under a heap of rubble and I wondered whether they had found the bodies and buried her. In a moment of illogical hope, I wrote to the International Committee of the Red Cross in Geneva. They promptly answered that my wife was dead.'

Knowing that his mother had no grave in the ashes of Belzec, he hoped that at least his wife did. A decent burial had become an ambition – even an obsession – to Wiesenthal when, on work details in Lemberg, he was marched past the German soldiers' cemetery where 'on each grave there was planted a sunflower, as straight as a soldier on parade.' (This theme would give thrust and title to his best book, *The Sunflower*, in 1970.)

One night in the summer of 1945, while working on the list of survivors from Cracow, he came across the name and address of a former high-school classmate of his and Cyla's from Buczacz: a Dr Biener. Wiesenthal wrote a letter to Cracow, telling Biener that

Cyla was dead. Just in case her body still lay beneath the ruins of Topiel Street number 5 in Warsaw, some 150 miles away, would Biener please go there and see what he could find? Since there was no postal service to Poland, Wiesenthal gave the letter to an illegal courier who specialized in moving mail across Czechoslovakia to Poland for a price.

Cyla Wiesenthal's welcome to Poland was typical of the times. After crossing the frontier from Czechoslovakia at Bohumin, she and her friend boarded a night train to Lvov. The train went as far as Cracow before a four-hour delay was announced. In the Cracow station, Cyla's suitcase – containing everything she owned – was stolen.

To cheer Cyla up, her companion suggested they take a stroll through the medieval city, miraculously spared a few months earlier. Mined and wired for destruction by the retreating Germans, Cracow had survived when Polish partisans cut the main detonator cable at the very last minute. Glorious Cracow, however, was foggy and dreary that summer morning – until Cyla heard her name being called. Out of the fog stepped a dentist named Landek, whom she and Simon had known in Lvov. Landek 'knew' that Simon was dead and expressed his condolences. Then he told Cyla that perhaps Dr Biener might know more about how her husband met his end.

'Dr Biener from Buczacz?' said Cyla. 'Is he in Cracow?'

'He lives five minutes from here,' Landek told her, giving her the address.

Reaching Dr Biener's home, Cyla asked her friend to wait downstairs so she could receive the grim details of Simon's demise in private. Then she climbed up three flights and rang a bell marked BIENER.

When Dr Biener answered, he *knew* he was seeing a ghost, so he slammed the door in her face.

Cyla had come prepared to be upset, but not rebuffed. Pounding on the door, she shouted: 'Open up! It's Cyla! Cyla Wiesenthal! Cyla Müller from Buczacz! Simon's wife!'

Dr Biener opened the door cautiously and said: 'But you're dead. I just got a letter.'

'I'm very much alive,' Cyla assured him. 'You'd look half-dead, too, if you'd had the train ride I'd had.'

Dr Biener let her in and explained: 'Yesterday, I had a letter from your husband. Simon says you died when the Germans destroyed your house in Warsaw.'

Now it was Cyla's turn to blanch: 'Simon? But he's been dead for more than a year.'

'Then who is writing to me from Linz?' Biener responded. 'Here, read his letter.'

Cyla called to her travelling companion to come upstairs and pinch her in case she was dreaming.

Simon Wiesenthal has believed in miracles ever since: 'If my letter hadn't reached Dr Biener the day before, if Cyla's train hadn't been delayed, if she hadn't gone for that walk, if she hadn't met Landek, if Dr Biener hadn't been at home, then the two women would have gone back to the station and continued their journey to Russia. Cyla might have wound up anywhere in the Soviet Union and it would have taken years to find her again, let alone get her out of there.'

It was much harder to send letters from Cracow to Linz than in the other direction. While Cyla was writing three identical letters to Simon, Dr Biener hunted up illegal couriers who wanted payment in advance, but wouldn't guarantee delivery. Only one of the letters ever arrived: the one that went the longest way around – via Budapest.

It took five weeks, but it will take more than Simon Wiesenthal's lifetime for him to forget the moment he saw his wife's familiar handwriting on an unexpected letter from the 'dead'.

By then, Simon's employer was the office of Strategic Services (forerunner of the Central Intelligence Agency) in Linz. His captain wouldn't give him permission to travel through the Soviet military zone to fetch his wife because he possessed so much confidential knowledge of American security. The OSS did arrange travel documents for Cyla, but since there was no postal communication, someone very reliable would have to take them to her.

A friend from the Jewish Committee, Dr Felix Weisberg, a PhD from Cracow, offered to be Cyla's escort. His romantic mission was as fraught with fear and miscalculation as any in *Romeo and Juliet*. Crossing Czechoslovakia, Weisberg saw an NKVD road-block up ahead and was warned it was 'very strict'. Fearing what the Russians might do to anyone carrying *Amerikansky dokumenty,* Weisberg destroyed them. But the NKVD didn't even search him, and it was only after he was safely past that he realized he had destroyed Cyla's Cracow address and couldn't remember it at all.

Undaunted, Weisberg made his way to Cracow and posted a notice on the bulletin board of the Jewish Committee there: 'Would Cyla Wiesenthal please get in touch with Dr Felix Weisberg, who will take her to her husband in Linz?'

Since a good many people wanted to get out of Poland by then, three women showed up claiming to be Mrs Simon Wiesenthal. 'Poor Felix Weisberg!' says Wiesenthal. 'He had a bigger problem than the judgement of Paris. He didn't know my wife. I hadn't given him any physical description of her. Very easy could he have brought back the wrong Mrs Wiesenthal.'

The woman who told the straightest story was the one Weisberg liked the best, so he bought false travel papers for her on the black market and brought her safely to Linz. There he made her wait outside while he explained all his difficulties at great length and with profuse apologies to Simon, concluding: 'I lost my wife in the war. If this one isn't yours, I'll marry her myself.'

But when Cyla Müller Wiesenthal stepped into the room, Felix Weisberg slipped away, still unmarried and virtually unnoticed.

– 9 –

'Don't forget our murderers!'

Both nearing forty, Cyla and Simon Wiesenthal wasted no time making up for the lost years. Their only child, Pauline Rosa, was born in Linz on 5 September 1946, barely a year after their sudden and suspenseful reunion among the living. 'Nobody has ever wanted a baby as much as we did,' Simon says succinctly.

In the postwar summer of 1946, on a picnic in the rolling hills of Upper Austria, Simon spotted a bush and, behind it, a sunflower. As he drew closer, he saw other sunflowers and now, after more than a year of liberation, he thought back to 1942 in Lemberg: first of the military cemetery, and then of the dying SS man to whom he had denied absolution four years earlier. Surely there was a sunflower growing on his grave and a cross with his name on it. Though Wiesenthal tried to think of the unmarked, unknown last resting places of his eighty-nine relatives who had perished in the Holocaust, he could think only of that young man who had pleaded on his death-bed for a word of forgiveness: an episode he remembered so vividly that he could still see the Stuttgart address on a bag of the SS man's personal effects which the nurse was sending to his mother the next day, while telling Simon the young man had died.

With the sight of sunflowers, all of Simon's questions came back in a rush of doubts. 'Have I anything to reproach myself for?' he wondered. He would be travelling to Munich on business two weeks later, and decided to venture 150 miles farther – to Stuttgart – and visit the SS man's mother. 'It was not curiosity that inspired me,' he explains, 'but a vague feeling of duty . . . And maybe the hope of exorcizing forever one of the worst experiences of my life.'

Badly bombed, Stuttgart still lay in ruins when Wiesenthal found the indelible address in a particularly devastated district. The fragile woman who received him had been twice bereaved, having lost her husband as well as her only child in the war. Of the latter, she had been told only the official truth: that her son had been wounded in battle on the Russian front and died in a military hospital in Lemberg. Showing her visitor the same bundle he'd seen the hospital nurse wrap, she asked how he had come to know her son.

Improvising, as he calls white-lying, Simon told her he'd been working on the railroad in the Eastern Yards of Lemberg when he was handed a note from a hospital train with her address and a message to send a son's greetings to the mother of one of the wounded. 'So you never actually saw him?' she said.

'No. He was probably so badly wounded he couldn't come to the window,' Wiesenthal *improvised*.

Recognizing that he was a Jew, the woman assured him that 'in this district we always lived with Jews in a very peaceful fashion. We are not responsible for their fate.' When Wiesenthal started to argue this with her, she deflected him blandly, but in all sincerity, with 'I can't really believe the stories they tell. I can't believe what they say happened to the Jews', and struck him speechless when she said: 'So many dreadful things happened, but one thing is certain: my son never did any wrong. He was always a decent young man.'

Realizing that this exchange of half-truths had brought him not a single step closer to solving his own dilemma, Wiesenthal left 'without diminishing in any way the woman's last surviving consolation: faith in the goodness of her son.' In her circumstances, he adds, to take that from her might also have been a crime.

Tuviah Friedman – a Polish refugee who started *his* Eichmann hunt in Vienna around the same time as Simon in Linz, and later, in Israel, headed the Haifa Institute for the Documentation of Nazi War Crimes – remembers the 1946-model Wiesenthal with whom he used to compare notes as 'an embittered, ruthless, vengeful pursuer of Nazi criminals. I understood him perfectly.'

A few months later, Wiesenthal took into criminal custody a minor SS torturer who was in an American prisoner of war camp. When the military police searched him while Wiesenthal watched, 'they found this picture on him', Simon told a visitor years later, producing a photo of a naked Jew suspended from a meat hook by his penis, with arms and legs dangling. 'When I saw that this was what he carried around as a memento, I leaped at him with a roar. I lost all control of myself. It's the only time I ever wanted to kill a man and I almost did. Two American GIs had to pull me off him.'

By then, the American soldiers who had liberated the concentration camps and shared some of Simon's outrage had been rotated home and replaced by newcomers from the US or the Far Eastern front. Wiesenthal had trouble communicating the urgency of his or their own mission to his new American superiors: 'They thought those of us who were intent on seeing justice done were eye-for-an-eye avengers and alarmists who would always see the world through a barbed-wire screen.' The Cold War had not yet heated up, but, even before seeing Red, these new Americans abroad saw postwar Europe through the red-white-and-blue standards of their own democratic experience. Wiesenthal was shocked when a captain whose job was to educate Germans explained to him: 'There'll always be people with different viewpoints. At home we have Democrats and Republicans. Here you have Nazis and anti-Nazis. That's what makes the world go round. Try not to worry too much about it.'

Such mentalities, which made no effort to learn German and relied on native interpreters, usually female, often fell prey to what Wiesenthal calls 'the Nazis' best secret weapon: The *Fräulein* Factor. Any young American was naturally more interested in a pretty, obliging girl than in one of "those SS men" everybody wanted to forget like a bad dream.'

When Wiesenthal arrested an SS man in Upper Austria, the prisoner's comely seventeen-year-old daughter, dressed in her lowest-cut dirndl, appeared in the office to ask the captain-in-charge for permission to bring her father food. The captain filled out a form while admiring hers – and made a date. Three days later, Wiesenthal learned that the SS man had been freed on 'captain's orders'.

Simon stormed into the captain's office and asked him why. The captain told him to 'shut up!'

'Ah, so,' said Wiesenthal. 'This is also an answer. You don't have to tell me another thing, Captain.'

His rage seemingly under control, Wiesenthal left the office in Linz and drove directly to US Army of Occupation headquarters in Salzburg, eighty miles away. There, talking to the captain's superiors, he began to sob as he told them: 'Please call the captain and tell him that the next Nazi I find, I will kill – but the responsibility for the killing will be the captain's. He will make me into a murderer.'

Simon created such a commotion that the captain was quickly transferred to Heidelberg. His parting words to Wiesenthal were: 'You're a son of a bitch.' To which Wiesenthal's response was: 'This is nothing. In my opinion, you are a Nazi.'

It got so, says Wiesenthal, that 'if I would arrest a criminal during the afternoon, the next morning he would be free because one of my bosses slept with his wife or daughter.'

Even greater disillusionment came when one of the few superior officers he respected, a Harvard professor, said to him one day: 'Simon, you must emigrate to the United States. People like you can make great careers back home. You work hard, you're intelligent, enthusiastic, idealistic. You will become a big shot in the US because you're Jewish, too. Listen, Simon, in America, the red and green lights regulate traffic and everything else is run by the Jews.'

The man meant it as a joke, but Wiesenthal looked right through him coldly and said: 'From tomorrow, you must find a replacement for me. This is the last day I am working for you.'

His chief apologized, but Wiesenthal resented his remark as 'a slap in the face – that an officer in the US Army which liberated me can talk like a Nazi. So the birth of the Jewish Documentation Centre came from a bad joke. That night, I rounded up thirty survivors – desperados like me, people without a future and with a very bad past and no money, and I said: "I am no longer working for the Americans. Life is too simple to them. They think that in America they have cowboys and Indians and in Europe we have Nazis and Jews. I feel it is our duty to do this job with our own hands." And so we built the Jewish Historical Documentation Centre in Linz without money, without any detective background, and without any official auspices because we all felt we had – we have! – the right of the victim.'

Simon Wiesenthal thinks that the biggest postwar mistake of the Jews was that they settled for material rather than moral restitution.

For a long time, Wiesenthal himself refused to accept restitution money that was legally his from the West German government, which agreed in the 1950s to indemnify Jews for their homes, business, property, and health* – all or some of which Wiesenthal had lost to the Nazis. It took him almost eight years to swallow the idea of taking money from Germans. When he did, he ploughed more than half of it into his Documentation Centre.

Though he didn't open the centre at Goethestrasse 63 in Linz until 1947, his initial costs were minimal. The rent was paid by a $50-a-month voluntary contribution from a former Polish Member of Parliament, Dr Aaron Silberschein, who had become an industrialist in Geneva. Most of Simon's 'desperados' were still living in Displaced Persons (DP) camps, where their food and shelter needs were met and witnesses were always at hand. 'Desperados' became 'correspondents' of the Jewish Historical Documentation Centre and, in each camp, they were provided with typewriter and paper on which to record depositions.

Wiesenthal's greatest resource was the body of lists he'd compiled during his year with the Americans. Every former concentration camp inmate he or his network of correspondents met in the DP camps around Germany and Austria was interviewed about brutality, torture, and killings which he or she had witnessed or experienced; no hearsay evidence was accepted, and exact names and dates were more important than gory details. Wiesenthal kept one card-file by geographic place; before 1946 was out, he had more than a thousand locations listed in alphabetical order. A second card-file listed criminals by name; whenever he obtained photos of them, he circulated them in the DP camps, for many were known only by title or nickname ('Angel of Death', etc.). A third file listed thousands of witnesses, most of whom had already given affidavits.

Virtually all of his correspondents being DPs awaiting emigration to other parts of the world, the turnover was high, but they kept in touch and word soon spread across America, Australia, and Palestine, as well as the continent of Europe, that, back in Linz, a man named Wiesenthal was compiling evidence against Nazi criminals. Hundreds

*West German reparations to Jews exceeded $37 billion and were crucial to the early survival of Israel. Austria, pleading that it was the 'first victim' of the Nazis itself, and the former East Germany, contending that its communist regime had severed all ties with the Nazi past, paid no more than token reparations. In 1988, the Austrian Parliament voted to offer Austrian victims one-time payments ranging from $208 to $416 per person.

of unsolicited depositions poured in and were followed up. Wiesenthal established relations and exchanged information with the Allied Historical Commission in Munich, the *Centre de documentation juive contemporaine* in Paris, and Jewish community associations in Prague, Bratislava, Budapest, Italy, and Greece.

As word of his work spread, mail addressed to just 'Wiesenthal, Austria' began to reach him in Linz – and almost every envelope contained a matter of life and death. In March 1947, he shared an experience which sealed his destiny:

'Three rabbis were coming to me in Linz to report that in a castle near Villach in Carinthia was a whole library of Jewish religious books. Hitler had planned to make many museums and libraries of an extinct race – the relics of a people he had extinguished – and this must have been meant to be part of it. For this purpose, they took away Jewish books instead of burning them; for this purpose, Mengele and many other camp doctors had instructions to send "special Jewish types" to the University of Strasbourg, where they were killed with injections and either embalmed like mummies or cooked until they were skeletons to be presented in hundreds of years as "typical Jews from the twentieth century".

'There was nothing to be done about the people "preserved" this way except to give them decent burials. But the relationship of a religious Jew to a religious book is like a human relation, so there was desperation in these rabbis' eyes when they pleaded with me to "please help us save these books".

'I rode with them through the mountains in heavy snow to Villach, where we spent the night. In the morning, we went to the castle and I spoke to the manager, who opened it up to us. From cellar to attic was nothing but books: bibles, prayer books, Talmuds, bookmarks, silver page-markers, and labels of the owners. This one was from Vilna, that one from Paris, Cracow, Prague . . .

'To these three rabbis, it was like they had liberated a concentration camp. The youngest of them was from Carpathorussia; he had lost his entire family in Treblinka. He would pick up a book from the piles, look at it, kiss it very gently, and then put it back exactly where he'd found it. After he'd done this any number of times, he picked up another book, started to read it – and fainted!

'One of us had some schnapps and when we brought him around, he took a sip and began to cry. "It's my own prayer book," he explained. Then he opened the covers and handed it to me. "Here is a message from my sister." On the first page was a woman's handwriting in the Yiddish language:

> Whoever will find this prayer book, give it to my beloved brother, Rabbi Joshua Zeitman. The murderers are in our village. They are in the next home . . . Please don't forget us! And don't forget our murderers! They . . .

'The writing trailed off there. Her brother was quiet now and spoke almost calmly. "If you don't mind," he said, "I would like to keep the book." I closed the book and gave it to him. But I still see it before me – and hear it: that book with the strong covers that I snapped shut. Because this was not only a message of a sister to a brother or of a Jewish woman to a rabbi. This was a message to me: from the millions who died to us the survivors. It could have been written by a Czech woman in Lidice, from a Frenchwoman in Oradour,* from an Italian woman in Marzabotto.† For me, this letter was the last will and testament of eleven million dead and, in the car on the way back to Linz, I decided to carry out its bequest.

'Long after I stepped out of that car, this is what drives me – and always will.'

*Oradour-sur-Glane: a village in central France where all but ten of its 652 inhabitants were massacred by the SS *Das Reich* Division on 10 June 1944.

†Marzabotto: a town in northern Italy where nearly 2000 civilians were massacred in September 1944 by SS troops under the command of an Austrian major, Walter Reder.

– 10 –

Wiesenthal's law

The end of the war did not mean the end of violence against Simon Wiesenthal. Within days of his ultimate liberation by the Americans, he had been beaten up in Mauthausen by a future Polish Vice-Minister of Culture. A little more than a year later, in a Displaced Persons camp near Linz, he had been attacked by a knife-wielding ex-Gestapo agent named David Zimet – a Jew!

Zimet had been a ghetto policeman in the southern Polish city of Tarnów and, says Wiesenthal, 'the right hand of a very known Gestapo sadist with the name of Grunov. Later, Zimet was sent to Mauthausen to work in the crematory. His family stayed in Tarnów. When the Russians came near Tarnów on their way to fight for Cracow, the Germans started more deportations of the few hundred Jews that were left from twenty thousand before the war, most of whom died in Belzec in 1942. Since there were no more trains, they sent them in trucks. In one truck of Jewish women were the wife and the daughter of Zimet. And the hatred against him was so great that the Jewish women in that truck taking them all to die killed his wife and his daughter then and there.'

By 1946, Zimet was a DP in Austria and was recognized by several survivors from Tarnów. Wiesenthal was still collecting testimony about him in the DP camp when Zimet learned that Simon was, as he puts it, 'occupied with his case, so at seven o'clock in the morning he is coming to my office there with a knife. He was a big, strapping healthy man back in '46 while we were all still so thin. He had lived good in the ghetto and, in the crematorium at Mauthausen, they were all given double food . . . No, I didn't know him in Mauthausen. I see him for the first time when he bursts in and attacks me. I pick up the inkwell from my desk and throw it at his face to protect myself and I shout so loud that people come running to help me and he is arrested. Zimet was four weeks in jail for this. But then, because he had worked in the crematory, they need him for the Mauthausen trial and bring him to Germany as a witness. From Germany, he emigrates to Canada.'

Years later, Wiesenthal was looking over a confidential list of cases being investigated by the Royal Canadian Mounted Police when he read:

> ZIMET, David: A policeman in ghetto in Tarnów. Witnesses have attested to his brutality.

'Zimet!' Wiesenthal exclaimed. 'This is my old case!' He informed the Canadian authorities of his evidence against Zimet, but they proved unwilling to prosecute a Jew for Nazi crimes. The Canadian Jewish Committee intervened and Zimet agreed to submit to a council of arbitration established by the committee.

'Nothing ever came of it,' says Wiesenthal, 'because the Jewish community was reluctant to publicize the case since Zimet was himself Jewish. This is so terrible! Through this false attitude that we must ignore Jewish helpers of the Nazis, we are losing credibility when we say we are acting against all people that commit crimes. If everybody could see that we are not looking only for Germans and Ukrainians, but even for our own Jewish criminals, then we would have much less opposition.'

'I first saw Jewish collaborators in the ghetto of Lwów,' Simon Wiesenthal says in his memoirs, 'and later I saw them in various concentration camps. There were some shocking cases, and when I talked about the problem after the war, many Jews were perturbed. Perhaps they had expected the Jews to be immune from corruption. Like all races, we have had our saints and our sinners, our cowards and our heroes.'

Reinhard Heydrich, who engineered the Final Solution, believed that the secret of manipulation lay in involvement and collaboration. With the appointment of Jewish councils of elders, even rabbis, to enforce Gestapo edicts, Heydrich's hatchet-man Adolf Eichmann could compel each Jewish community to co-operate in its own destruction.

Wiesenthal acknowledges that 'the hardest duty' of the Jewish

Councils the Germans organized in every ghetto and concentration camp was 'deciding which names should be put on "transport lists" for the death camps. The Nazis had established certain criteria for inclusion (health, age, and so on), but . . . they often left the final selection to the Jews themselves.' When Jew listed Jew for extinction, the Germans could claim that the Jews had wiped themselves out.

He also concedes that there were heroes and martyrs among the councilmen, starting with the Zionist physician, Dr Elchanan Elkes, who became mayor of the ghetto of some 60,000 Jews in the Lithuanian city of Kaunas (Kovno in the former Soviet Union). Not only did Elkes resist and impede his German overlords in every way he could, and assist many of his constituents to escape, but, in 1944, when the ghetto was liquidated and its last survivors deported to Dachau, he declined an offer from the Jewish underground to smuggle him to safety. Instead, Elkes elected to accompany his constituents (and patients) to Dachau, where he died on 17 October 1944 and is honoured with a granite memorial. Even Elkes, however, had to issue limited quantities of work permits and, while he tried to give them to heads of large families, thereby sparing a maximum number from deportation, he was dooming many of those he reluctantly rejected.

'A man who had the power to save also had the power to condemn,' Wiesenthal points out. 'The SS and the Gestapo were not welfare organizations. They wanted a list of so many people to put on the train next Tuesday – and not one person less. There was no room for bargaining. The people were to be there at twelve-thirty next Tuesday, not twelve-forty. So I am very sceptical about people who say: "This man, he saved my life." Who could save lives? Only a functionary.'

Once, a character witness asked Wiesenthal to go easy on such a functionary because 'he crossed my name off the transport list.'

'And whose name did he put on it instead of yours?' Wiesenthal asked. The man could not, did not answer.

Of Elkes and a few others, Wiesenthal says: 'Naturally, of those people they saved, many of them survived. They can bear witness. But we lost six million other witnesses who might have something else to say.' He adds that some Jewish Council members 'did the only thing they could, under the circumstances, by following Nazi regulations to the letter. Others were corrupted. They accepted favours, juggled names, hoping against hope that they might save their own skins. Other Jews collaborated with the Nazis or bartered others' lives for their own. Some Jews were concentration camp trusties. Sometimes they helped their fellow inmates; sometimes they didn't.

'After the war, I not only arrested Jews who were Nazi collaborators, but, from the committees running the Displaced Persons camps and the former concentration camps, I expelled people who could not bring evidence about their activities during the Nazi time. I made a rule that was approved by the American military government authorities and became known in the camps as *Lex Wiesenthal*: Latin for Wiesenthal's Law. It was very simple: *Whoever had a function of authority in the Nazi period could not have a function in postwar Jewish life*. I wasn't saying such a man was a criminal. I wasn't even looking into whether he was good or bad. But I needed to protect our Jewish society from more bad surprises.'

'Don't push it, Simon,' a friend he describes as an 'official Jew' pleaded with him. 'What you are doing will only diminish the guilt of the Nazis.'

'No,' said Simon, 'this is an extension of the guilt of the Nazis. When they brought pressure on Jews to work against other Jews, then they were guilty of corrupting hundreds of Jews as well as murdering millions of us.'

Wiesenthal noted that 'in many cases, such people after the war found jobs with Jewish organizations. Maybe they were trying to atone; maybe they thought this was the best place to hide. Once, I was going special to Paris to see the director for Europe of the Joint Distribution Committee, because working for him was a man – a Jew! – who had been in a concentration camp the head of the transports to the death camps.'

According to Wiesenthal, the JDC director, an American, responded, 'So what? This was a time when everyone had to serve.'

'Yes, I know,' Wiesenthal told him. 'Your employee had in his hand power to send people to extermination or take them out. I don't know how he handled it. But suppose somebody will come to you and say, "My father was sick and he put him on transport" or "My father was well enough to work, but he put him on transport", what will you say? The accuser may not have any witnesses. Your man may or may not have witnesses. But you will have a bad conscience. And, if you don't, I will make you such publicity that you will fire him.'

Which the director did.

PART II
Adolf Eichmann

Wherever the murderer may hide away,
There shall we be, night and day,
Our eyes will be fixed on him
As the sunflower follows the sun.

–Nathan Alterman

– 11 –

Eichmann the Zionist

On Monday, 23 May 1960, the day Israel announced that Adolf Eichmann, abducted from Argentina, was 'at present in prison here,' Simon Wiesenthal received an official cable from Jerusalem at his home in Austria: 'CONGRATULATIONS ON YOUR EXCELLENT WORK.' *He studied it with satisfaction and then handed it to his teenaged daughter Pauline, saying: 'You never saw your father when you were a baby. You were asleep when I went to work looking for this man and asleep by the time I came home. I don't know how long I will live. I don't know if I will leave you any fortune at all. But this cable is my gift to you. Because through this cable I am now a part of history.'*

Simon Wiesenthal is in possession of the devil's soul: Eichmann's autobiography, a thousand-page document Eichmann dictated in the 1950s and put finishing touches to in Buenos Aires just before his capture. Suppressed by Israeli authorities on the ground that it is his family's property (but not given to his survivors for fear it might become a bible to neo-Nazis whose old testament is *Mein Kampf*), it begins in silky Satanic style:

> Today, fifteen years and a day after May 8, 1945,* I begin to lead my thoughts back to that nineteenth of March of the year 1906, when at five o'clock in the morning I entered life on earth in the aspect of a human being.

The eldest of six Eichmann children (he had four brothers and a sister), young Adolf established himself early as a failure in life: the

*VE Day, when World War II ended in Europe.

only one who didn't finish high school. The first high school he didn't finish was Linz's Kaiser Franz Federal Scientific Secondary School, which yet another Adolf – Hitler – had attended at the turn of the century. After a couple of unsuccessful years there, Eichmann transferred to the Federal Vocational School for Electrical, Mechanical, and Structural Engineering, from which he also didn't graduate. In both cases, he told an Israeli interrogator, 'my father took me out of school because – I may as well admit it – I hadn't been exactly the most conscientious of students.'

Always polite, and so self-effacing that he looked like a composite portrait of his brothers, he worked at whatever his father's connections could find for him – three months as a miner in the Untersberg between Salzburg and the German border; a couple of years as a radio salesman for Austrian Electrotech – before his father, who felt he wasn't getting anywhere, suggested he become a travelling salesman.

At this point – in 1927, when Eichmann was twenty-one – his stepmother intervened; his mother had died in 1916 of bearing too many children too close together, according to Eichmann, and his father had remarried in the same year. The second Frau Eichmann had a cousin in Vienna who was president of the Austrian Automobile Club and married to a Czech Jewish woman. The cousin, whom Eichmann called 'Uncle', contacted a Herr Generaldirektor Weiss, the Jewish head of the Vacuum Oil Company, and, within a fortnight, Eichmann was trained, employed, and given exclusive rights to sell Sphinx gasoline and Gargoyl-Mobiloil in the *Mühlviertel* (Mill Quarter), a region encompassing half of Upper Austria.

For almost five years during a time of worsening worldwide depression, Adolf Eichmann, the travelling petroleum salesman, made a good living on the road. But he was back in Linz in 1932, when Austria's National Socialist German Workers (Nazi) Party held a rally in the Märzenkeller, a big Bavarian-style beer hall in Linz. Eichmann attended and, during a lull in the diatribes, he was approached by a giant of a man, nearly seven feet tall, with massive broad shoulders, thick arms, rectangular chin, and duelling scars on his face from his student days at the University of Graz. Eichmann knew him by sight as a young lawyer from Linz, three years his senior, named Ernst Kaltenbrunner. 'We'd seen each other around,' Eichmann recalled. 'His father and my father had had business connections for twenty years; Ernst Kaltenbrunner put it to me straight from the shoulder: "You're going to join us." That's how it was done in those days, all very free and easy, no fuss. I said "all right". So I joined the SS.'

Adolf Eichmann enrolled as Nazi party member number 889,895 and SS number 45326 on April Fool's Day, 1932. His recruiter, Kaltenbrunner, a chain-smoker who was already an alcoholic, soon became the spokesman for the Nazi Party in Upper Austria and provided legal services to its members while commanding the underground Austrian SS. In early March of 1938, as Austria's tottering Catholic fascist regime bargained with the Nazi fascists, Kaltenbrunner was named Minister of State Security. A week later, when Hitler annexed Austria and the country he had betrayed ceased to exist, Kaltenbrunner also became a member of the *Reichstag,* the German parliament. After the assassination of Reinhard Heydrich in Prague in 1942, Kaltenbrunner was named to succeed him as chief of the Reich Main Security Office in Berlin, which controlled not only the Gestapo, but also the concentration camp system and the machinery of the Final Solution. The Gestapo was Bureau IV of Kaltenbrunner's empire. Sub-section IV B 4, with Eichmann in charge, would be created to cope with assembling and transporting Jews to the death camps. After the war, Kaltenbrunner was hanged in Nuremberg.

All their way up the ladder from young bourgeoisie playing at patriotism to relentless chief exterminators, Kaltenbrunner kept an eye out for Eichmann as his protégé, but patronized him as his mental, physical, and social inferior. Kaltenbrunner, after all, came from two generations of lawyers, had his own law degree and the right to call himself Doctor (of Law), while Eichmann hailed from a public utilities background and never finished school or excelled in sports. Eichmann was, however, an unquestioning follower of orders: his father's, his employer's, and now his party's.

'I was a relatively young man and used to being led, in business and in everything else,' is how he put it. The political philosopher Hannah Arendt (1906–75), herself a refugee from Nazi Germany, put it another way in her profound but tendentious account of his trial, *Eichmann in Jerusalem,* subtitled *A Report on the Banality of Evil*:

> From a humdrum life without significance and consequence the wind had blown him into History, as he understood it, namely,

into a Movement that always kept moving and in which somebody like him – already a failure in the eyes of his social class, of his family, and hence in his own eyes as well – could start from scratch and still make a career.

His career with Vacuum Oil stopped mattering to him as much as pulling Friday-night SS duty at the party's Brown House in Linz, where he slept on a straw pallet, stood guard, and 'since I was one of the few who was working and making good money', bought the boys beer and cigarettes at the tavern next door. On Sundays, his SS regiment – whose members came from Salzburg and Linz – would be driven across the border from Salzburg in Austria, where their uniforms and parades (and, from 1933, their party) were forbidden, to Freilassing in Germany, where an SS auxiliary police unit played host to their training and marching.

Living for his weekends with 'the boys', it hardly mattered to him when, in the spring of 1933, 'Director Blum said to me: "We've got to cut down on personnel." He said I was the only unmarried salesman and that's why he'd hit on me. So they gave me notice.'

Cushioned by five months' severance pay (one month for each year with the firm), he stayed with his family in Linz, where his father had opened his own appliance store, Elektro-Eichmann. While looking around for work in Austria, where the Austro-fascist dictator Engelbert Dollfuss had just outlawed the Nazi Party, it occurred to him that he might be better off in Nazi Germany, where Hitler had just come to power. Since the Eichmann family had never relinquished German nationality when moving from Solingen to Linz in Adolf's childhood, 'I said to myself: "After all, I'm a German citizen.* Why not go to Germany and try my luck?"'

Armed with letters of introduction from Kaltenbrunner, he crossed the Danube from Upper Austria into Passau, Germany. There he looked up the SS *Gauleiter* (regional commander) who had been the main speaker at the rally where he'd been recruited a year earlier. Eichmann asked for help finding a job with the Bavarian branch of Vacuum Oil, but the Gauleiter suggested he become a storm trooper

*At his trial in Jerusalem nearly thirty years later, when Eichmann's defence attorney sought his extradition to West Germany, where he stood a stronger chance of survival, Bonn refused to co-operate, claiming that Eichmann was not a German national.

instead. Ever one to follow someone else's ideas, Eichmann enlisted: 'I said to myself: "All right, I'll be a soldier." I had no one to provide for.'

He had crossed more than one frontier. Sent first to Lechfeld, an SS and SA camp near a monastery and a brewery, he found himself – despite his German identity – in what the SS called the 'Austrian Legion in exile'. Assigned to shock-troop training, he specialized in street fighting, but distinguished himself in the kind of tedious plodding that wins recognition as true grit in most military or paramilitary organizations:

'Let me tell you a story to show how little I minded the tough training. I used to tell it later on to the officers and non-coms under me. This was still in Lechfeld. A common punishment – later it was forbidden – was to make us crawl through rushes and over gravel. The first time it happened, some of the men went on sick call and got themselves declared unfit for duty. Because I thought we were being treated unfairly, I gritted my teeth and stuck it out. The skin had been scraped off my elbows, but I didn't have them bandaged. After lunch, we had to start in again. The bits of plaster I'd stuck on my wounds were scraped off in a minute. I had no skin left on my elbows at all. But I stuck it out. That way, I attracted attention and got myself promoted.'

He left Lechfeld in late 1933 as a corporal. His next destination was Dachau. The very first Nazi concentration camp, Dachau – on the outskirts of Munich – in those days held more Gentile opponents of Hitler than Jews. More of the former, however, were likely to leave alive, though many came home crushed, intimidated, and unwilling to relate their experiences to others, even to their families. Eichmann's battalion of the Deutschland Regiment, however, was billeted 'just outside the concentration camp, in an enormous iron and concrete hangar formerly used for storing munitions. We slept in triple-decker bunks.'

Dachau had been designed by the SA as a place to *concentrate* – in the physical rather than mental sense – Hitler's enemies for restraint or elimination. First came revenge: the head of the Bavarian state government, which had suppressed Hitler's 'beer-hall putsch' in 1923, was hacked to death with pick-axes in Dachau in 1933. Then came the suppression of dissent: political opponents, outspoken clergymen, liberal editors, balky Nazis who asked aloud whether

Hitler was going too far or too fast, and others who uttered their thoughts were flogged and tortured, sometimes murdered, at Dachau. Next would come 'undesirables' – homosexuals, gypsies, Jews. On 12 April 1933, four Jewish prisoners – three merchants and a Nuremberg lawyer – were ordered to fall out of ranks and were shot to death by storm troopers before the eyes of their fellow prisoners, who were told the four Jews had been 'hostile elements that had no right to live in Germany' and had 'received their due punishment'.

By the time Eichmann reached Dachau, some fifty concentration camps had mushroomed around Germany, with the SS taking over from the SA to streamline them for specialization and ruthless efficiency: Sachsenhausen for Berliners, Ravensbrück for women, etc. Though terror and brutality reigned, it was on a relatively individual basis. Not until well into the 1940s did the needs of the Final Solution create *extermination* camps like Belzec and Sobibor, where victims were gassed *en masse* upon arrival.

At Dachau in 1933–4, the concentration camp was guarded by Bavarian SS men wearing a skull on their collar patch. 'We called them Death's-headers,' Eichmann recalled. His unit, commanded by Prussians, wore the lightning SS symbol with the number 1. They were foot-troops. Given regular German Army training and strict military discipline, Eichmann preferred this diet to 'the shock-troop nonsense we'd had in Lechfeld', but chafed at the 'crushing monotony' of military life – 'day after day always the same, over and over again the same' – and schemed to escape the routine.

When he heard that the SS's own intelligence service, the SD, was recruiting from the ranks, he applied. In the fall of 1934, Eichmann received orders to travel immediately to Berlin.

SD headquarters in the Hohenzollern Palace on the Wilhelmstrasse proved doubly disappointing to Eichmann: 'I expected to see what I'd seen in the illustrated magazines: SS commandos riding in cars behind high party leaders; men standing on running boards.' He had confused the SD (*Sicherheitsdienst*) with the bodyguard branch of the Reich Security service, but, never having learned the right bureaucratic word, *Begleitkommando,* he couldn't complain. It is typical of Adolf Eichmann's career that the aimless, boyish mishmash of misinformation and mistaken identity that brought him to Berlin landed him in the information department of the SD as his first step up the ladder of extermination.

He was put to work on a file of suspected freemasons – classifying their cards in alphabetical order. Masonic lodges, with their mystic rites and secret signs, had long perturbed the Roman Catholic Church and the Habsburgs; almost two and a half centuries earlier, the libretto for Mozart's opera *The Magic Flute* was written in code to conceal its parallels to masonic initiation. The Nazis were quick to lump masons into their early witches' stew of enemies along with Jews, communists, and gypsies.

Though he tried to wriggle out of the work by claiming he knew nothing about freemasonry and had never even heard of it, he didn't persist, for he had tracks to cover. A born joiner who had belonged to the Young Men's Christian Association in elementary school and a couple of German youth movements in high school on his way to the Nazi Party and the SS, he'd been on the verge of joining the Schlaraffia lodge of freemasons in Linz in 1932 when Kaltenbrunner had warned him this was incompatible with Nazism. No wonder the new work in Berlin gave him 'the creeps'.

To make matters worse for Eichmann, his section was inspected every second or third day by either Heinrich Himmler, the failed chicken-farmer who headed the SS, or Kaltenbrunner. Knowing that Kaltenbrunner was aware of his flirtation with freemasonry, the inconsequential Eichmann was quick to endorse (or at least pay lip-service to) his mentor's eugenics: compulsory child-bearing for all Aryan women under thirty-five; if their husbands couldn't or wouldn't father their children, or if women weren't married, then fathers of families with more than four children should be made available for stud duty. On the other hand, Jews should be exterminated and Slavs extinguished via sterilization and the annihilation of their leaders.

After three weeks in this uneasy seat in the information department, however, Eichmann was made an assistant to a curator creating a freemasonry museum made up of materials seized from lodges across Germany: aprons, medallions, seals, photos, whole libraries: 'One room was supposed to represent a St John's Temple and another a St Andrew's Temple. My work was to classify, catalogue, and label thousands of "ritual objects". It must have kept me busy for five months.'

One day in 1935, an Austrian Nazi aristocrat named Leopold von Mildenstein stopped by Eichmann's desk in the St John's Room and asked him to explain his work. Impressed by Eichmann's capability as a custodian of cults that would soon be extinct if Hitler had his way, von Mildenstein said he had just organized a Jewish department at SD headquarters and asked the young clerk to come to work for him. Eichmann didn't hesitate: 'I'd have gone in with the devil himself just to get away from those seals!'

One can wonder now who would have become the senior partner in such a union. At the time, Eichmann impressed his superiors only with his diligence in doing whatever was asked of him. Though one of his colleagues described him as 'a most colourless creature – the typical subordinate: pedantic, punctilious [and] devoid of any thorough knowledge', he did have an ingratiatingly subservient manner, springing to attention and clicking his heels whenever an officer passed in the hall.

As part of Eichmann's on-the-job training, von Mildenstein, who had served as the SD chief of intelligence in Palestine, gave him Theodor Herzl's seminal work, *The Jewish State* (1896), to read and report back on. In doing so, he inadvertently converted Eichmann to Zionism.

Yes, Zionism! 'The book interested me very much,' Eichmann would recall later. 'Up until then, I had no knowledge of such things. Somehow . . . this book touched a chord in me and I took it all in . . .

'When I'd finished reading, I was told to make an abstract of it to serve as an orientation booklet for the SS general staff and also for the specific use of the SD. . .

'In it, I described the structure of the Zionist world organization, the aims of Zionism, its sources and the difficulties standing in its way. I also stressed the need to encourage it, because it fell in with our own desire for a political solution: the Zionists wanted a territory where the Jewish people could finally settle in peace. And that was pretty much what the Nazis wanted.' Perhaps, under the relatively benign (compared to Kaltenbrunner) influence of von Mildenstein, Eichmann sincerely believed for a time that there was a political solution to the Jewish problem.

By 1936, Eichmann had become the SD's leading expert on Jewish problems. Citing Herzl and reading further – starting with the

Encyclopedia Judaica and Adolf Böhm's *History of Zionism* – he gave lectures and wrote pamphlets. Among the documents Simon Wiesenthal came across in his postwar manhunt was a mid-1930s application by Eichmann for 'special funds' to enable him to study Hebrew with a rabbi. Though Eichmann noted that the lessons would cost only three marks – 'a real bargain', Wiesenthal insists – his Nazi chiefs turned him down for fear of further contamination.

Nevertheless, Eichmann started studying the Hebrew alphabet by himself. And, whenever the occasion arose, he would advocate putting 'some firm ground under the feet of the Jews'; Palestine in preference to crematoria; a political solution rather than a 'physical solution'; emigration over expulsion over extermination. In the all-consuming crucible of Nazism, these were relatively humane beginnings for a genocidist who would become the ultimate Grand Inquisitor of European Jewry. Looming above all else, however, was his stolid acceptance and relentless expediting of whatever evil was decreed from above.

Late in 1936, he was joined at the SD's Jewish Desk by another von Mildenstein protégé: Otto Albrecht Alfred von Bolschwing, twenty-nine, a Prussian nobleman who had opened a building supply firm in Palestine in 1933 and spied for von Mildenstein there until the British intercepted his reports. In early 1937, Bolschwing initiated contacts between the SD, which wanted the Jews out of Germany, and the Zionist movement, which wanted German Jews in Palestine. He began by informing Eichmann that 'a gentleman from Haganah' – the Jewish defence force in Palestine – was visiting Berlin. Eichmann took Commander Feivel Polkes, a Polish-born accountant, out to lunch twice and went back to the office with an invitation to visit Palestine to discuss the trade-off further.

Von Mildenstein, a civil engineer by profession, had transferred to the road-building Todt Organization,* the same enterprise to which Simon Wiesenthal and thirty-three other hostages would be sold in 1944 as 'non-German forced labour'. His successor, Herbert Hagen, elected to make the trip to Palestine with Eichmann in late

*This slave-labour organization was named for Hitler's Minister for Armaments and Munitions, SS General Fritz Todt (1891–1942), who created Germany's high-speed *Autobahn* network. Upon Todt's death, he was succeeded by Albert Speer.

1937. Outfitted with press credentials from the *Berliner Tageblatt* – once a liberal Jewish newspaper until the Nazis took it over – Hagen and Eichmann set sail on a Romanian steamship in a bizarre and futile pilgrimage to the Holy Land.

Eichmann and Hagen spent just two days in Palestine. While their ship was in the harbour of Haifa, Eichmann took a taxi to the top of Mount Carmel. Near Tel Aviv, he and Hagen visited a kibbutz and a German colony in Sarona which was a refuge for transplanted freemasons belonging to the forbidden order of Knights Templar. Commander Polkes didn't catch up with them until they'd moved on to Cairo, and he had nothing concrete to offer them. In Cairo, Eichmann and Hagen did meet with the fanatical Grand Mufti of Jerusalem; already banished from Palestine for fomenting riots, he would spend the war in Berlin broadcasting for Hitler. When the two German 'journalists' wanted to return from Egypt to Palestine to pursue their Haganah negotiations, however, the British Consulate, having learned of their contacts and seen through their press credentials, refused them visas.

Returning home from his Holy Land pilgrimage on an Italian ship, Eichmann caught paratyphoid fever, which he termed 'the pathetic end of what had looked to be a promising trip.' Discharged from the ship's hospital only when the boat landed in Bari, Eichmann wrote 'a detailed report absolutely negative in substance' upon reaching Berlin; it purported to quote disgruntled German Jews in Palestine as saying it was better to be in a concentration camp back home. SD chief Heydrich scrawled 'Good' at the bottom of it.

Blundering onward and upward, Eichmann left the enlisted ranks on 30 January 1938, when he was commissioned a lieutenant and commended for his 'comprehensive knowledge of the methods of organization and ideology of the opponent, Jewry.' For all his later power, though, he never rose above lieutenant-colonel; no higher hierarchical slot had been designated for coordinating mass extermination.

When Adolf Hitler annexed his native Austria on 12 March 1938, and German troops received a jubilant welcome, an SD team was dispatched there, too. Adolf Eichmann was certain he'd be chosen to go on that mission to his family's adopted homeland, but when he wasn't, he swallowed his disappointment: 'Orders are orders. You've got to obey, and that's that.'

As it turned out, Hitler and Himmler and Heydrich and Hagen all had higher hopes for him. A week later, he was sent to Vienna as head of the Centre for Emigration of Austrian Jews.

While Eichmann had been chafing in Berlin for an Austrian assignment, Baron Louis von Rothschild, head of the international banking family, was taking Sunday dinner in his Viennese palace on the Prinz Eugen-Strasse on 13 March 1938, when six steel-helmeted Gestapo men arrived to arrest him. His butler made them wait in a vestibule until the Baron finished his meal. Then they marched Baron Rothschild off to a prison cell and, later, internment in a Gestapo hotel until a ransom could be negotiated with the House of Rothschild. The Nazis asked for twenty million dollars, but received considerably less. It was still a time when one could do business with Hitler.

Upon arrival in Vienna, Adolf Eichmann was given 'a small room with nothing in it but a desk' in the glittering, chandeliered Palais Rothschild: his headquarters for what he would later look back on as the best year of his career. It was here that he discovered his two true talents: he could organize ruthlessly, and he could negotiate from a position of strength, real or illusory.

'I've tried to find out exactly when Eichmann turned from a theoretical expert on the Jewish question into an executioner,' says Simon Wiesenthal. 'When he came to Vienna, he was still talking politely about "forced emigration". I've talked to Jews who remember Eichmann from those days. All of them say he was different from the rest of the SS hoodlums. His attitude was unyielding, but always icily polite.'

Eichmann's mission at the time was economic: to extract as much money and treasure as possible from wealthy Jews who wanted to emigrate and raise additional foreign currency to pay for the emigration of poorer Jews. He set the machinery in motion overnight. When a seventeen-year-old Viennese Jew named Arthur Pier went to the police station to apply for a passport and saw the long line of desperate people, he decided this kind of discomfort wasn't for him. Instead, he went to the post office and mailed in his application. Forty-eight hours later, a passport arrived by return mail. 'I took a train to Greece,' he recalls, 'and three weeks later I was in Palestine', where he eventually changed his name to Asher Ben Nathan and came back to Europe after the war as an Eichmann-hunter, a Wiesenthal partner, and, later, Israel's first ambassador to its erstwhile arch-enemy, Germany.

Early in his Viennese tenure, Eichmann sent for the leaders of the Jewish community, all of whom had been locked up in the Nazi takeover. Looking for a Jew he could work with on 'stepped-up emigration', he confronted one Dr Josef Löwenherz, who was still so indignant about his arrest that he insulted Eichmann.

'Anger got the better of me,' Eichmann recalled in 1960. 'I lost control, which very seldom happened. I don't know what got into me. I let myself go and slapped him in the face. It wasn't the kind of slap that hurt, I'm sure of that. I haven't got that much muscle. But I never concealed that incident. Later on, when I was a commandant, I spoke of it in the presence of my subordinate officers *and* Dr Löwenherz – and begged his pardon. I did that deliberately . . . because in the department I ran later, I did not tolerate physical violence. That was why I apologized in uniform and in the presence of my staff.' Nothing is more important to a desk murderer than clean hands. Jolted by his treatment yet tantalized by Eichmann's offer to aid Jewish emigration, Dr Löwenherz elected to work with him throughout the war: drawing up draft proposals for deporting four million Jews to Palestine instead of Poland . . . negotiating with Eichmann over housing for evicted Jews . . . setting extortionate exit fees and foreign currency exchange rates for Jews able to buy their way out of Austria . . . and even contacting an American Jewish organization, the Joint Distribution Committee, in an effort to raise further foreign funds for ransoming the Jews of Austria. He was, Hannah Arendt wrote, an historic figure, for he became 'the first Jewish functionary actually to organize a whole Jewish community into an institution at the service of the Nazi authorities.'* If, as she claims, the Jews co-operated in their own destruction, then the process began when Eichmann slapped Löwenherz.

*Unlike most of Eichmann's official Jewish collaborators, Löwenherz survived the war in Vienna and lived long enough to tell his tale. Emigrating to England and then the US after the war, Löwenherz died shortly after Eichmann's capture. But he left behind some valuable reports, written during and shortly after the war, which were used as vital evidence by Israeli prosecutors in Eichmann's trial.

In Berlin on the morning of Wednesday, 9 November 1938, Eichmann's chief, Reinhard Heydrich, explained to Hermann Göring, the portly, bemedalled Nazi air marshal and military commander, that the expulsion process was going fast in Austria, more slowly in Germany, and not fast enough in either place: 'The problem is not to make the rich Jews leave, but to get rid of the Jewish mob.' The death in Paris that afternoon of a wounded German Embassy attaché, Ernst vom Rath – shot two days earlier by a seventeen-year-old Polish Jew, Hirschel Grynszpan – was the signal which triggered the *Kristallnacht* (Night of Broken Glass) pogrom in which Jewish shops and synagogues were systematically smashed and torched across the Third Reich.

Simon Wiesenthal says the big change in Eichmann came with Kristallnacht: *'Heydrich's orders to Vienna specifically asked that Eichmann be notified. So people saw him going from one synagogue to another, helping with his own hands while personally supervising total destruction. They say he seemed exhilarated. A few days later, the leaders of the Jewish community in Vienna noticed that, when Eichmann summoned them, he no longer offered them chairs. They had to stand up, three steps away, at attention.'*

By early 1939, the personality change in Eichmann was visible to all. Dr Franz Meyer, a German Zionist who had dealt with him in Berlin, was summoned to Vienna for a session on 'forced emigration' with several other Jewish leaders. At Eichmann's trial, Meyer testified: 'So terrible was the change that I didn't know whether I was meeting the same man. Here I met a man who comported himself as a master of life and death. He received us with insolence and rudeness.'

In the spring of 1939 – when Adolf Hitler invaded an already dismembered Czechoslovakia and re-formed the Czech Lands into a Protectorate of Bohemia-Moravia adjoining a puppet Slovak fascist state – Adolf Eichmann, thirty-three, was transferred to Prague. In the greying golden city on the Vltava River (which reverted to its Habsburg name of Moldau), he was sorry to say that the Jews he dealt with 'were calmer and more easy-going and, for that reason, neither side registered the same success as in Vienna . . . Maybe it was their Czech accent that kept us from – how shall I say? – making contact.' This despite the fame enjoyed by the German-language

Jews of Prague – whose numbers once included Kafka* and Rilke – for speaking the purest German heard anywhere in the world! And this from a high-school drop-out whose own atrocious German, overlaid by a thick Upper Austrian dialect acquired during his years in Linz, made him difficult for both Berliners and Viennese, let alone Praguers, to comprehend.

Nor did he show any respect for history or tradition. When he informed the president of Prague's Jewish community that 'the Jews must go – and fast!', the man remonstrated that, after all, the Jews had lived in Prague for 1100 years and couldn't vanish overnight, for they were indigenous. Eichmann shrieked: 'Indigenous?! I'll show you what's indigenous!' The first shipment of Jews was deported the next day.

During his six-month stint in Prague, Eichmann was a driving force in reorganizing the Empress Maria Theresa's old fortress town of Theresienstadt (Terezín) on the banks of the Elbe River as a prison camp purporting to be a 'privileged ghetto'. Half-Jews, Jewish civil servants, and Jews who'd served on the German side in World War I or married Aryans would be eligible, as would wealthy Jews willing to buy their way into 'protective custody' there by voluntarily relinquishing their fortunes. Though Theresienstadt didn't open until 1941, by which time Eichmann had left Prague, he claimed 'paternity' of it and took credit for its 'success' as a 'humane' showcase to reassure International Red Cross inspectors alarmed by reports of atrocities in the camps. Replete with family housing and its own Jewish mayor and orchestra, Theresienstadt had only one 'defect', as Eichmann would conclude later with regret: it was too small for its purpose, so, by 1943, to make room for new arrivals, surplus Jews were either transported to extermination camps or shot on the spot. Some 33,500 would perish in Theresienstadt; for another 84,500, it would be an anteroom to extermination.

The Final Solution, however, had not yet been invented when the 'phoney war' that Hitler had been winning by annexation and

*Elli, Valli, and his beloved Ottla, the three younger sisters of Franz Kafka (1883–1924), all perished in Nazi death camps, as did two other women in his life: Milena Jesenská-Pollak, to whom he wrote his *Letters to Milena,* and Grete Bloch, who in 1915 gave birth to a son who was presumed by some biographers to be Kafka's only child; the boy died at the age of seven and Kafka never knew of his existence.

acquiescence in Austria, partition and subversion in Czechoslovakia, exploded into violent combat and World War II with his blitzkrieg of Poland in September 1939. Eichmann – by then a captain – was transferred back to Berlin as head of the Reich Centre for Jewish Emigration.

Early in his pursuit of Eichmann, Simon Wiesenthal sought to ascertain not only what his quarry had done, but why he did it. He tried to talk to schoolmates from Linz and comrades from his SS days in the early 1930s, but they had little to say to him. One of the Eichmann family's good friends, who had not been a Nazi, simply refused to believe the accusations against 'that oafish, lacklustre Adolf who never spoke up and often seemed to get stupidly stuck on just one idea.' Wiesenthal said later: 'The man didn't realize how well he'd characterized Eichmann – how right he was and, at the same time, how wrong.'

In 1985, Wiesenthal told me: 'I made a mistake in looking for a motive in his early life. There was no motive, no hatred, no anti-Semitism. When I said some of this in my memoir, people think I'm crazy. But I say no. He was such a product of Nazi indoctrination that if they had given him a direct order to take the telephone directory and kill all the people whose names began with K, no matter if Jewish or not, he would have done it – including the Kaiser. Or all people with red hair. During his interrogation in Israel, he acknowledged that, if his bosses had ordered him to kill his father, he would have. And, if Hitler had ordered him to ship the Jews to Palestine, instead of Theresienstadt and Auschwitz, and let them start a Jewish state, he would have done so.

'In this respect, he was a typical product of not only the Nazi years, but of any dictatorship. Eichmann could have been a communist taking orders from Stalin or a mafioso from his godfather. In every dictatorship, the appeal to such people is the same: you let the Führer think for you.'

Wiesenthal says that many of his 'clients' were good neighbours and even pillars of their prewar and postwar communities.

'Look, I've studied the life stories of too many Nazi murderers. Nobody was born a murderer. They'd mostly been farmers, workers, clerks or bureaucrats – the kind of people you meet every day. Some had good early childhoods; some didn't. Almost all had religious instruction of some kind; none had a prior criminal record. Yet they became murderers – expert murderers! – out of conviction. I can't possibly know their reactions to their first crimes and they might not even remember, but I do know that every one

of them later murdered wholesale. It was like they put on their SS uniforms and replaced them in the closet by hanging up their consciences with their civilian clothes. In the moment Eichmann put on the swastika, the first casualty he deported was not a Jew, but his own conscience.'

– 12 –

Wannsee: the final solution

Safe in Berlin during the first two years of the war, Adolf Eichmann saw his somewhat passive efforts to expedite Jewish emigration grind to a standstill as the widening conflict closed off frontiers and communications. With Hitler's rapid conquest of Europe and with expansion of the war to Asia and perhaps even the US imminent, there were no havens left for Eichmann to seek on behalf of his Reich Centre for Jewish Emigration.

Much of his time was spent plotting a nebulous programme to transplant four million Jews to the French island of Madagascar on Africa's south-east coast. Eichmann called this 'a dream once dreamed by the protagonist of the Jewish state idea', his idol Theodor Herzl, but here (as was often the case) he didn't have his facts straight: Herzl had considered Uganda, not Madagascar. In any event, the proposal was never taken seriously by his higher-ups, so the in-house Zionist was available for other chores, such as scouting Polish farmland for extermination sites and even ordering – in October 1941, three months before the Final Solution was formalized – the experimental gassing of eighty Jews in Riga, Latvia, while they were travelling in mobile vans. Eichmann's participation marked another milestone along his road to hell: the transition from conspirator to mass murderer.

In mid-1941, Eichmann was promoted to major and named head of Section IV-B-4: the 'Jewish desk' at Gestapo headquarters in Berlin. Section IV was the Gestapo, headed by Heinrich Müller; sub-section B handled 'Sects', and then there were four 'decks': 1: Catholics; 2: Protestants; 3: freemasons; and 4: Jews.

With genocide as with Germany, Hitler had been expanding eastward, dodging and feinting whenever thwarted, and, when threatened by a warning finger, backing off, but gobbling the arm the next time. Having conquered Poland and absorbed much of Eastern Europe through such tactics, he could now practise genocide on a grander scale unfettered by the prying eyes of his citizens and churchmen whose revulsion at his early experiments at gassing mental and physical 'defectives' as ' useless mouths' to feed had forced Hitler to beat a tactical retreat. When he decided to extend his extermination programme to the Jews in a place where protest would be minimal, Poland, with its long history of anti-Semitism, seemed an ideal setting, for there would be plenty of willing hands to stoke the ovens of hatred.

Though Hitler had publicly advocated 'the annihilation of the Jewish race', it was his heir apparent, the blimpy Reichsmarshal Hermann Göring, who, on 31 July 1941, first entrusted SD head Reinhard Heydrich with 'making all necessary organizational, practical, and financial preparations for bringing about the final solution of the Jewish problem in the territories within the German sphere of influence in Europe.'

Nowhere in Göring's three-paragraph memo to Heydrich was anything specific spelled out. Nowhere was there a concrete blueprint or outline saying, 'Now the Jews will be killed.' All was left to inference from words like 'final solution' or ' total solution' or 'territorial solution'. But, as Holocaust historian Raul Hilberg points out, these euphemisms were nonetheless a clear authorization to invent: to initiate action that could not yet be articulated. In every aspect of this operation, invention became the partner of necessity. For every agency involved, says Hilberg, 'every problem was unprecedented. Not just how to kill the Jews, but what to do with their property thereafter. And not only that, but how to deal with the problem of not letting the world know what had happened.'

In late August or early September of 1941, Adolf Eichmann had been summoned to Heydrich's office in Berlin. Heydrich seemed almost ill at ease, Eichmann recalled in his memoirs and his interrogations in Israel. 'The *Führer*, well, emigration is. . .' Heydrich began stumblingly. Then he veered off into what Eichmann called 'a little speech about emigration', which had virtually ceased, before coming to the point: 'The *Führer* has ordered the physical extermination of the Jews.'

'Those were his words,' Eichmann would recall of Heydrich. 'Then he remained silent, which was not his way, as if he wanted to test the effect of his words on me. I can still remember that. In the first moment, I didn't grasp the implications because he chose his words so carefully. When I did understand, I didn't say anything, because there was nothing to say any more. I had never thought of such a thing – of such a solution through violence. I now lost everything, all joy in my work, all initiative, all interest. I was, so to speak, blown out' – though he did recover his zest all too soon.

Christian Wirth, a genocidist known as 'the savage Christian' had already been sent east to set up an experimental death camp in Chelmno, a Polish village some 125 miles north-west of the city of Lodz, which once had a large Jewish population. Originally intended to revive the euthanasia programme on the eastern front by 'treating' 25,000 tubercular Poles in the castle of Chelmno, Wirth's project was instead transformed into the testing-ground for *Aktion Reinhard*, to which Heydrich would ultimately bequeath his own first name. *Aktion Reinhard* was nothing less than the extermination of the Jews of Poland.

According to Franz Schalling, a German policeman (not SS) who served as a security guard in Chelmno that first winter, the SS made him and his police colleagues sign a pledge 'promising to shut up about whatever we'd see.' After they'd signed, they asked what their top-secret mission was. They were told: 'The final solution of the Jewish problem.'

At Chelmno, where he took to rattling a can of gold fillings taken from the teeth of his victims, Wirth worked with 'moving vans' that met arriving Jews at the freight station and gassed them en route to the camp. Disguised as Red Cross ambulances and known to their operators as 'Black Ravens', these mobile gas chambers pumped exhaust fumes from their engines into the backs of the vans as they pulled away from the station. Passengers were delivered directly to the crematorium dead on arrival. Each van's rear end could be tilted to unload its cargo directly into a pit for burning.

Later, when this system proved impractical because there was too much to clean up before the vans could be used again, Wirth equipped Chelmno's fixed gas chamber with shower fixtures, as he had at Brandenburg in his German euthanasia days, to disguise it as a bath and lull the suspicions of victims who died wondering when water would start flowing from that hissing faucet.

There is a church in Chelmno – and there the Germans would bring naked Jews whenever the mobile and fixed gas chambers were overtaxed or broken and mow them down with machine-guns in the courtyard before the uncaring eyes of the locals. An uncaring world was given an early warning on 19 January 1942, when Jakub Szulman, the rabbi of Grabow, a dozen miles from Chelmno, wrote to Jewish leaders in Lodz:

> My very dear friends:
>
> I waited to write to confirm what I'd heard. Alas, to our great grief, we now know all. I spoke to an eyewitness who escaped. He told me everything. They're exterminated in Chelmno, near Dombie, and they're all buried in Rzuszow forest. The Jews are killed in two ways, by shooting or gas. It's just happened to thousands of Lodz Jews. Do not think that this is being written by a madman. Alas, it is the tragic, horrible truth.

Though it had been in operation for months, 'the final solution of the Jewish problem' wasn't formalized until the day after Rabbi Szulman wrote this warning. On Tuesday, 20 January 1942, at a villa on the Wannsee – a suburban lake to the west of Berlin – Heydrich convened fifteen State Secretaries: the civil servants in charge of the day-to-day running of ministries and key departments. The Ministries of Justice, Interior, and Foreign and Eastern Territories were represented, as were the Nazi party chancellery and the agency for Göring's Four-Year Plan for economic self-sufficiency. Also on hand was Gestapo chief Heinrich Müller.

'At least seven of the fifteen people who met at Wannsee had doctorates, mostly PhDs,' says Simon Wiesenthal with utter scorn. 'And these educated men – these esteemed Doctors of Philosophy and Medicine and Law – who also had the knowledge of what was happening in Poland, sat around a table in the most civilized surroundings and formulated the greatest genocide, the most barbaric slaughter of innocent civilians in human history.'

One of the lowest-ranking persons present was SS Major Adolf Eichmann, who, as head of Gestapo bureau IV-B-4, had sent out the invitations and helped prepare statistics (largely inaccurate) for Heydrich's opening speech. The Final Solution Conference, as it was called, had been previously set for 10 December 1941, but postponed by the Japanese bombing of Pearl Harbor three days earlier and the German and Italian declarations of war upon the United States that week. With the war now global, Nazi Germany had no inhibitions about totally abandoning its initial solutions to the Jewish problem – evacuation and emigration – and moving beyond the interim solution of concentration to the final solution: extermination.

It was Eichmann who kept the minutes of the Wannsee Conference, which began at 11 a.m. on the third Tuesday of 1942. It took the dozen doctors, diplomats, and generals – plus a colonel, a captain, and an awestruck Major Eichmann – a little less than an hour and a half to formulate the fate of eleven million European Jews and seal the doom of six million of them.

Eichmann's minutes show that Heydrich opened the meeting by announcing that Marshal Göring had given him 'the responsibility for working out the final solution of the Jewish problem regardless of geographical boundaries. Emigration has now, with the *Führer's* approval, been replaced by another solution: the evacuation of the Jews to the East. The present actions, however, must be viewed as mere expedients, but they offer a source of practical experience of the utmost importance with a view to the final solution to come.'

'What does all this mean?' Eichmann was asked by his Israeli interrogator almost twenty years later.

Readily, Eichmann translated from the bureaucratese: 'Since emigration was now prohibited, they were to be deported to the East.'

'What is meant by "practical experience"?'

Eichmann conceded that this was the systematic rounding up and shooting of Jews, which had already begun in Russia and Poland – as Wiesenthal was witnessing and experiencing by then.

'Within the framework of the final solution,' Eichmann's minutes went on, 'Jews will be conscripted for labour in the eastern territories under appropriate leadership. Large labour gangs of those fit for work will be formed, with the sexes separated. They will be made to build roads as they are led into these territories. A large percentage of them will undoubtedly be eliminated by natural diminution.'

'What is meant by "natural diminution"?' Eichmann was asked.

'That's perfectly normal dying,' he replied. 'Of a heart attack or pneumonia, for instance. If I were to drop dead just now, that would be natural diminution.'

His Israeli interrogator, Captain Avner Less, persisted: 'If a man is forced to perform heavy physical labour and not given enough to eat, he grows weaker, and if he gets so weak that he has a heart attack . . . ?'

'That,' said Eichmann, 'undoubtedly would have been reported as natural diminution.'

Heydrich's opening remarks went on: 'The remainder who survive – and they will certainly be the ones with the greatest physical endurance – will have to be treated accordingly. For, if released, they would, as a natural selection of the fittest, form a germ cell from which the Jewish race could build itself up again. This is the lesson of history.'

'What does "treated accordingly" mean?' Less asked Eichmann.

'That – that. . .' stammered Eichmann the stenographer, seeking to dissociate himself from the minutes he'd taken. 'That comes from Himmler. Natural selection – that's – that was his hobby.'

'Yes, but what does it mean here?'

'Killed, killed. Undoubtedly.'

Heydrich concluded that, 'in the course of implementation of the final solution, Europe will be combed from West to East . . . For the moment, the evacuated Jews will be brought little by little to so-called transit ghettoes from where they will be transported farther to the east.' These were ghettoes that would be or had been decimated of local Jews to make way for the newcomers who wouldn't linger there long. Heydrich then went over the specifics country by country: in France, 'the seizure of Jews for evacuation should in all likelihood proceed without major difficulty.' Romania would be more of a problem because 'even today a Jew there can buy for cash appropriate documents officially certifying him as a foreign national.' In Hungary, 'it will be necessary before long to impose upon the Hungarian government an adviser on Jewish questions.' (As it turned out, that adviser would eventually be Eichmann and his principal adversary would be a Swedish diplomat named Raoul Wallenberg.)

When Heydrich had finished, the Foreign Office's Undersecretary of State, a former furniture-mover bearing the proud name of Martin Luther, suggested that the 'deeply penetrating treatment of this problem' (to use yet another euphemism) would encounter difficulties in the Scandinavian countries under German occupation.

Luther recommended that Norwegian and Danish Jews be 'treated' last.

The highest official attending from occupied Poland, Dr Joseph Bühler, warned that Poland's remaining two and a half million Jews (their number was diminishing daily) constituted a great danger as black marketeers and bearers of disease, most of them unfit to work. 'I have only one favour to ask,' Bühler concluded, ' – that the Jewish problem in my territory be solved as quickly as possible.'

Reviewing the record of Wannsee years later, Israeli interrogator Less asked Eichmann: 'What is Bühler suggesting?'

'He is suggesting that they should be killed.'*

As euphemism washed over euphemism on the shore of the Wannsee, the word *extermination* was never spoken, but so clear was Heydrich's and Eichmann's bureaucratese that nobody present harboured any doubt as to their meaning. Thirty copies of Eichmann's conference record, distributed to high SS headquarters and the ministries and agencies represented at Wannsee, became the blueprint of the Final Solution.

Butlers poured brandy as the participants stayed for lunch and, without qualms, toasted a morning's work well done. When the others were gone, Eichmann and Müller and Heydrich sat around a cosy fireplace and talked with satisfaction of the day's results. 'This was the first time I ever saw Heydrich smoke and drink,' Eichmann recalled. The more they drank, the happier they grew. Soon the three of them – even the stolid Gestapo chief Müller! – were singing and, according to Eichmann, 'after a while, we climbed on to the chairs and drank a toast; then on to the table and traipsed round and round – on the chairs and on the table again.'

'There are probably only a handful of people in this world who know that the Wannsee Conference . . . was held at the headquarters of Interpol,' Simon Wiesenthal confided in his 1988 memoir. The International Criminal Police Commission, to call Interpol by its full name, was a Viennese invention in 1923. After Hitler annexed Austria in March 1938 and the US, curiously, joined Interpol that May, Heydrich became president of Interpol and had it moved to Berlin, with the villa in Wannsee as its base. After the

*Bühler was tried in Warsaw and executed in Cracow in 1948.

war, Interpol moved to Paris, but Wiesenthal has accused a couple of its postwar presidents, Florent Louvage of Belgium and Paul Dickopf of West Germany, of having less than honourable wartime records: Louvage for 'co-operating' with Heydrich and Kaltenbrunner; Dickopf as an SS officer and member of the security service. Simon says that during Dickopf's 1968–72 tenure as president of Interpol and of the Federal Criminal Office in Wiesbaden, co-operation from both sources was 'as little as one could expect'.

If Wannsee meant the beginning of the end for nearly six million Jews, it also marked the end of Eichmann the Zionist: a commitment no less shallow than his earlier dabblings in education, freemasonry, and soldiering. Singled out by Heydrich for inclusion in 1938's *Kristallnacht* orgy in Vienna, he had gone and pillaged synagogues. Dispatched by Müller to Minsk and by Heydrich to Chelmno, he knew first-hand – and at least as well as anyone at the Wannsee Conference – what all the euphemisms he was transcribing were about. Now, having sat in with 'the most prominent people, the Popes of the Third Reich', as he termed them, and cavorted with the charismatic Heydrich and 'that Sphinx, Müller', he could see for himself that even the élite of the German Civil Service were competing to hammer nails into the crucifixion of the Jewish people.

With its elegantly civilized trappings and convivial camaraderie, Wannsee dispelled all doubt in Eichmann about what he knew to be 'such a bloody solution through violence'. Testifying in Jerusalem, he waxed biblical: 'At that moment, I sensed a kind of Pontius Pilate feeling, for I was free of all guilt . . . Who was I to judge? Who was I to have my own thoughts in this matter?'

Barely four months after his *danse macabre* with Eichmann and Müller at Wannsee, Heydrich was dead. Since the previous September, he had been doubling as *Acting Protector* of 'Bohemia-Moravia', the remains of the Czech Lands dismembered from Slovakia in the betrayals of 1938–9. On 27 May 1942, as Heydrich's open-topped Mercedes rounded a bend in the district of Prague where I now live, two refugee Czechoslovak commandos, parachuted into their homeland by the Royal Air Force, ambushed him with a British Army Sten gun and a high-impact bomb. The gun jammed, but the bomb blew him up. His spine shattered and spleen infected, Heydrich died of blood poisoning on 4 June.

His assassins took sanctuary in the crypt of the Orthodox Church of Sts Cyril and Methodius in Prague, where they shot themselves to death when the Gestapo closed in. In retaliation, the church's bishop, two ministers, the chaplain, and the chairman of its parish council, as well as more than a hundred Czechs accused of aiding the assassins and another 1357 accused of 'approving of the assassination' were massacred by the SS. Less than a week after Heydrich died, the Czech village of Lidice was destroyed in his memory.

Though Lidice still lives in the world's memory of Nazi atrocities, it was just the visible tip of Operation Reinhard, which Hitler and Himmler dedicated to the memory of their martyred murderer whose 'final solution' outlived his life and outdid his death. Another 3000 Czech Jews were uprooted from Eichmann's 'privileged ghetto' of Theresienstadt and 'deported to the east', never to be seen again. In Berlin, 152 imprisoned Jews were killed in homage to Heydrich, who was replaced as head of the SD by Kaltenbrunner. Throughout the Third Reich, the tempo of the Final Solution accelerated.

– 13 –

Eichmann the genocidist

With the extinction of the Warsaw Ghetto in 1943, the only large Jewish community left in the Third Reich was in Axis-allied Hungary, where territorial acquisition and an influx of refugees had doubled the Jewish population to more than three-quarters of a million. Half-heartedly but effectively, Admiral Miklos von Horthy, an ageing anti-Semitic, but not genocidal, regent had protected his Jews from deportation. On 19 March 1944, however, Hitler forced Horthy to appoint a more militantly anti-Semitic government which immediately stripped all Jews of their jobs, property, civil rights, and citizenship, ordered them to wear the Star of David, and herded them into ghettoes where they were systematically starved. German troops occupied friendly Hungary for the first time and Adolf Eichmann was dispatched to Budapest to expedite the Final Solution. As the Axis war machine wore down, the German machinery of genocide sped up to fulfil at least one of Hitler's missions on earth.

'I wanted to send the Master personally,' Heinrich Himmler said when he ordered Eichmann to Budapest. The final step of the Final Solution, the martyrdom of the Hungarian Jews, was to be the culmination of Eichmann's career: the blaze of glory in which the Third Reich would crumble into ashes.

Whether Germany won or lost the war, Eichmann was convinced that if he could 'succeed in destroying the biological basis of Jewry in the East by complete extermination, then Jewry as a whole would never recover from the blow. The assimilated Jews of the West, including America, would . . . be in no position (and would have no desire) to make up this enormous loss of blood and there would therefore be no future generation worth mentioning.' So fanatical was Eichmann by the end of 1944, says Simon Wiesenthal, that 'when even Himmler ordered Eichmann to stop the killing in Hungary, he no longer understood the word "Stop!" any more.'

In April, the Germans started a systematic sweep of the provinces, uprooting Jews from the land for deportation to Poland in sealed boxcars holding as many as seventy people and two buckets: one for water, one for human waste. Heat and suffocation took their toll – and, in Hungary at least, there could be no 'good Germans' contending they had no idea what was going on, for the Hungarian press reported the deportations and one newspaper boldly described the deaths of three Jewish women in a cattle car. Their ages were given as 104, 102, and ninety-two.

Up to four freight trains a day, ferrying up to 12,000 Jews to the death camps, crawled through the Hungarian countryside and paused at city stations. The cries and moans of men, women, and children were audible to all. At Auschwitz-Birkenau, Dr Josef Mengele and his colleagues had their hands full at selections as gas chambers and ovens went on round-the-clock duty to roast the new shipments of what they called 'Hungarian kosher salami'. An extra railway siding was built at Birkenau to deliver the deportees directly to death's door and, when crematorium capacity was overtaxed, Commandant Rudolf Höss ordered new burning-pits dug. The cadre of Jewish death commandos manning the gas chambers was quadrupled. Between May and July of 1944, some 600,000 Jews were deported from Hungary as Eichmann tightened the vise around the 200,000 remaining in the capital.

'You know who I am, don't you?' he introduced himself to the Jewish Council of Budapest. 'I'm the one they call "The Bloodhound".'

In 1944, Rudolf Höss paid three visits to Eichmann in Budapest to coordinate the stepped-up transports to Auschwitz. 'This,' Höss recalled at Nuremberg after the war, 'gave me the opportunity of observing Eichmann's methods of negotiating with the Hungarian government departments and the army. His manner of approach was extremely firm and matter-of-fact, but nevertheless amiable and courteous, and he was liked and made welcome wherever he went. This was confirmed by the innumerable private invitations he received from the chiefs of these departments. Only the Hungarian army showed no pleasure in Eichmann's visits. The army sabotaged the surrender of the Jews whenever they could, but they did it in such a manner that the Hungarian government was unable to intervene.'

On the other hand, Eichmann played the Jewish Council of Budapest like a violin virtuoso, telling Dr Rezsö Kastner, one of its leaders, 'Kastner, your nerves are shot. Shall I send you to Theresienstadt to recover? Or would you prefer Auschwitz?' while bargaining for Jewish freedom by offering to sell one million Jews on a cash basis. 'Blood for money, money for blood,' said Eichmann with a grandiose wave in May of 1944. Later that month, trucks and goods were substituted for money and a wandering Jew named Joel Brand, an official of the Zionist Relief and Rescue Committee of Budapest, was sent to Turkey with Eichmann's offer: *For up to 10,000 trucks, he would free one hundred Jews per truck*. The trucks were to be winterized for use on the Russian front.

The Jewish Agency for Palestine's representative, Moshe Shertok (later Prime Minister of Israel), was supposed to meet Brand in Ankara, but British authorities in Jerusalem refused to give Shertok travel papers – partly because England wouldn't welcome the tiniest fraction of a million new Jews in Palestine and mostly because they looked upon Eichmann's proposal as a transparent plot to divide the Allies, which it was. Meanwhile, tired of waiting for Shertok in Turkey, Brand took the Taurus Express for Aleppo, Syria, in the hope of a meeting with Shertok there or in Palestine. Instead, as he stepped off the train in Aleppo, British security agents arrested him. They interned him in Cairo and he spent the rest of the war in British custody.

It is not likely that either side ever seriously considered meeting the terms of the 'Jews for trucks' deal. Eichmann couldn't have cared less about supplies for the eastern front and was known to have sidetracked troops and supplies bound for combat to make way for trainloads of deportees, but hope and involvement kept the Hungarian Jews working with him instead of against him. Although a strategy of stalling for time while bargaining might have slowed the deportations and saved thousands of lives, when the Russians learned in June 1944 that there was an offer involving equipment to be used against them, Deputy Foreign Minister Andrei Vishinsky vetoed all negotiations whatever.

'The worst story I can ever tell you about Adolf Eichmann,' says Simon Wiesenthal, 'took place during the time he was in Budapest. In the fall of

1944, a group of high-level SS officers were sitting in the SS casino there. And one of them asked Eichmann how many people had been exterminated already.

'Eichmann said: "Over five million."

'Well, because he was among comrades and they all knew it was only a matter of months before they would lose the war, one of them asked whether he was worried about what would happen to him.

'Eichmann gave a very astute answer that shows he knew how the world worked: "A hundred dead people is a catastrophe," he said. "Six million dead is a statistic."'

– 14 –

Eichmann the fugitive

Eichmann left Budapest on Christmas Eve 1944, fleeing the flames as the Red Army encircled the city. From Sopron, the new Hungarian capital, he was recalled to security headquarters in Berlin in January 1945. There, to his disappointment, 'serious work was out of the question. Uninterrupted air raids were wreaking worse and worse devastation. Every day the communications network was repaired and every night it was disrupted again. Without communications, evacuations were inconceivable. I paid no more attention to State Police work because nobody paid any attention to me. I spent more time looking around in the ruins than at my desk. . .'

Every day, his boss and former mentor, Kaltenbrunner, would lunch with all his department heads except Eichmann, who was never invited. Covering their tracks to avoid postwar retribution, most of them avoided this pariah who had executed their wishes; ironically, Kaltenbrunner and several of the others were hanged long before Eichmann. Their daily snub seldom bothered him.

What did annoy him was the discovery that one of the bureau heads was working full-time at making out false documents, certificates, and IDs: 'He was working for the security police in Section IV, who wanted to change their names and prove they'd been insurance agents or something during the war.' Invited to partake, Eichmann said he could do without. 'That absurd business with the false papers sickened me,' he told his Israeli interrogators years later. 'I'd rather have put a bullet through my brain than issue myself an official document.'

Aside from giving visiting Red Cross inspectors a couple of guided tours of Theresienstadt, his showcase concentration camp in Bohemia, Eichmann hung around Berlin until early April. From his field headquarters in a nearby castle, Heinrich Himmler ordered Eichmann to go back to Theresienstadt, which was due for liquidation as the Allied armies approached. He was to select 100 to 200 prominent Jews and bring them to a safe place in the Austrian Tyrol as pawns in possible negotiations with the Allies' supreme commander, US General Dwight D. Eisenhower. From all realms of his empire of death, Himmler was collecting hostages who might keep him and Germany from going down in flames with Hitler. Among these pawns were former French Prime Minister Léon Blum, imprisoned in Austria, and 'the Jewess Gemma LaGuardia Glück, born in New York on 24 April 1887 and imprisoned in Ravensbrück.' She was the sister of New York City's most popular mayor, Fiorello H. LaGuardia (1882–1947); their father was Italian, their mother and Gemma's husband Jewish.

Though Eichmann looked upon Himmler as the most prominent rat deserting the sinking ship, and had even harangued his Red Cross guests against 'Himmler's humane line', he was not one to disobey an order unless he could exceed it. Hurrying to Theresienstadt by car, he put the Jewish Council there to work drawing up a 'Who's Who' without telling them its benign purpose. When he saw Rabbi Leo Baeck, one of the leaders of modern Jewry, passing by, he expressed surprise that Baeck was still alive. The Council members held their breath, but Eichmann wasn't dealing out death that day; he simply told them to put Baeck's name at the top of their list of bargaining chips. Just before leaving, however, he told his terrified puppets: 'Jewish death lists are my favourite reading matter before I go to sleep.' Then he took a few from another pile and sauntered off.

After a brief stop in Prague, Eichmann headed into Austria to search for a mountain sanctuary for his hostages. In the Tyrolean town of Brixlegg, where there was a heavy-water plant, he was caught in a fierce bombardment, but survived. In Innsbruck, the Tyrolean capital, the *Gauleiter* was too busy to see his visitor from Berlin and sent word out, according to Eichmann, 'that he had other things on his mind than to bother about Jews.' One of his department heads, however, found a couple of villages in the Brenner Pass between Austria and Italy which had empty hotels, and these were put at Himmler's disposal.

By then, however, Bohemia was encircled and the roads to Theresienstadt were blocked by the Red Army. After frantic visits to Linz and Prague, with no communications open to Berlin, Eichmann retreated to the SS's last resort: the Austrian spa of Bad Aussee in the remote reaches of the Styrian Salzkammergut, the salt-mine district. This *Ausseerland* had been christened the 'Alpine fortress' by propaganda minister Goebbels, who saw it as a Wagnerian setting for Nazism's heroic last stand. Instead, it proved to be a secret treasure chest, where SS intelligence and counter-intelligence agencies stashed their loot to finance a Fourth Reich or, more likely, to save their own skins. Art masterpieces from Italy, France, Belgium, Denmark, and Holland were stored in an abandoned salt mine; their value, when recovered by the Austrian resistance in May of 1945, was estimated at two and a half billion dollars.

Far more negotiable were the assets of the Reich Main Security Office which were shipped by its chief, Kaltenbrunner, from Berlin to the town of Altaussee early in the spring of 1945: 110 pounds of gold bars; fifty cases of gold coins and other gold articles, each case weighing one hundred pounds; two million US dollars; two million Swiss francs; five cases of diamonds and precious stones, and a stamp collection worth at least five million gold marks.

'Later,' says Simon Wiesenthal, 'we found evidence that during the first days of May 1945, the Reichsbank's special department that handled loot from concentration camps had sent several boxes containing "tooth gold" to Aussee.' Wiesenthal explains that gold teeth and fillings pried loose from prisoners in the camps were all sent to a central depot in the Oranienburg concentration camp and then to the DEGUSSA* company, which smelted the gold into bars. 'Some DEGUSSA gold was later found in the Tyrol in the form of camouflaged gold bricks in the roofs of houses after one overloaded roof collapsed.'

Kaltenbrunner and the other higher-ups who'd holed up with their hoard in Aussee were neither happy to see Eichmann nor the least bit interested in his and Himmler's Theresienstadt-to-Tyrol fantasy. They put Eichmann to work giving weapons training to Romanian fascists who had fled the victorious Allies and were to go back to their homeland as partisans helping to bring about a

*DEGUSSA is an acronym for *De*utsche *G*old *u*nd *S*ilber *S*cheiden*a*nstalt for the extraction of precious metals.

Fourth Reich. When an order came down from Himmler that 'no one is to fire on English and Americans', the training was abandoned.

After Adolf Hitler committed suicide in his Berlin bunker on 30 April 1945, and was burned along with his bride, Eva Braun (who had married him a day earlier and swallowed poison two minutes before Hitler shot himself through the mouth), his will repudiated Himmler for making overtures to the Allies. Named instead as his successor was Admiral Karl Doenitz, who swiftly surrendered. Himmler was apprehended by British troops on 21 May in Flensburg, a German city near the Danish border; the ex-chicken farmer was disguised as an army private with a black patch over his left eye. Two days later, during a medical examination by British doctors, Himmler bit on a vial of potassium cyanide he'd concealed in his gums and died in twelve minutes.

Early that May, Eichmann reported back to Bad Aussee for reassignment. The hulking Kaltenbrunner, playing solitaire and waiting for the end, didn't even greet his most notorious Nazi Party recruit, but simply told him to 'get the hell out'. Taking him at his word, Eichmann headed for Germany armed with the kind of false papers he had so despised in Berlin. These identified him as *Luftwaffe* (Air Force) Corporal Adolf Barth.

'Corporal Barth' was taken into custody in the Danube city of Ulm by the Americans, but escaped when Army Intelligence probed too deeply for his taste. He didn't go far, landing in another US prisoner-of-war camp in Weiden, where he managed to obtain a new identity for later use. Thrice transferred in the next month – to Camp Berndorf near Rosenheim in late May; to a special camp for SS men in Kemanten in early June; and to a work camp at Cham, a half-timbered medieval town in the Bavarian Forest near the Bohemian border, in mid-June – he recommissioned himself along the way as an officer: a 'Lieutenant Eckmann', no less!

To Rudolf Scheide, the German civilian in charge of work details at Cham, 'Lieutenant Eckmann' confessed that he really was a 'Major Eichmann'. The name meant nothing to Scheide, who told him: 'It's your own business what you want to call yourself.'

Eichmann worked on a thirty-man construction detail that was marched by a pair of American military policemen into the town to rebuild Cham, which later became a prime Marshall Plan beneficiary. On 30 June 1945, someone told Scheide who Eichmann was and a little of what he had accomplished in the war. This was too much for Scheide, who notified the camp's resident CIC (US counter-intelligence) man. He and Scheide were waiting for 'Eckmann' when the work detail returned that night. Only twenty-nine men came back. Eichmann, alerted, had disappeared.

Under yet another alias, Otto Heninger, he found work with a farmer in Prien, on the Chiemsee, Bavaria's largest lake. Then he made his way north into the British Zone of Germany. In the spring of 1946, in the town of Eversen in Lower Saxony, 'Heninger' registered with the police as a forestry worker and quickly found employment in that labour-starved timberland. A few months later, a currency reform bankrupted his employer, but 'Heninger' headed north again – stopping just short of Hamburg at the Lüneburg Heath, where the brother of a friend found him work as a lumberjack. Later, 'Heninger' leased a little land, on which he raised chickens, in Altensalzkoth, near the north German city of Celle.

Back in Eichmann's home town of Linz, Wiesenthal was keeping tabs on his quarry's relatives and had made his first contact with the future Israelis – then represented fairly furtively, but aggressively, in Austria by *Bricha* (which means *escape*), the Jewish organization that smuggled displaced persons into what was still Palestine, and *Haganah*, the secret Jewish defence army. Both were headed in Austria by a tall, slim, dapper man known only as 'Arthur', who managed to look aristocratic to Wiesenthal even while smoking cigars and wearing what Simon saw as 'an inter-Allied fantasy uniform that looked like – and was meant to look like – a confusing combination of American, British, and French fashions.' The debonair 'Arthur' was the former Arthur Pier, who, as a teenager early in Eichmann's 1938 tenure in Vienna, had applied by mail for his emigration papers rather than condescend to stand in line. In Palestine, he had joined *Haganah* while working as a journalist, changed his name to Asher Ben Nathan, and, in 1944, in a small office near the port in Haifa, started collecting the stories of arriving survivors and drawing up a list of Nazi criminals in order of importance. Returning to his native Vienna in November 1945, he'd reassumed his identity of Arthur Pier and arrived with a suitcase whose false bottom secreted not just gold to finance clandestine Jewish emigration to Palestine, but even more vital cargo: microfilmed dossiers on many of the major missing Nazi genocidists, with Adolf Eichmann at the top of the list. Under the auspices of the Association of Jewish Students, 'Arthur' had set up the first Documentation Centre in Vienna. Most of his agents – including his eventual successor, Tuviah Friedman – were enrolled at the University of Vienna, which gave his operation a cloak of legitimacy.

'Arthur' preached to all his associates that they must never take the law into their own hands. 'Only the legal authorities and properly appointed judges have the right to punish criminals,' he told them. 'Our job is to find wanted Nazis and have them arrested by the Allies. Acts of personal revenge can only harm our cause, which is not only justice, but sending as many Jews as possible to Palestine.' And, belligerent though he still was, Wiesenthal had already subscribed to some of this reasoning.

After exchanging data on Eichmann's crimes, past, and reported whereabouts, 'Arthur' and Simon decided to send a seducer to visit Eichmann's grass widow in Altaussee to try to penetrate the 'divorcée's' veil of silence. 'Arthur' picked Henyek Diamant, a handsome Polish Jew from Katowice who, while his family was being herded into a cattle truck bound for Auschwitz, had simply put on his best suit and, carrying a bunch of red roses, pretended to be a Gentile passing by on his way to a wedding. Blessed with blue eyes to begin with, he bought a Tyrolean hat, grew a Hitler moustache, bleached his hair and eyebrows, and fitted a plastic sheath over his penis to conceal circumcision when stopped by German street patrols. In 1943, he arrived in Hungary, where he walked into a hospital and introduced himself as a surgeon named 'Dr Ulensky'. Nobody asked for his medical credentials and he was put to work dissecting corpses. He fought in the Hungarian underground and, when the Germans grew suspicious of him in 1944, he became 'Dr Yanovsky' in eastern Hungary, where he helped Jews escape into Romania after it declared war on Hitler that August. From his helping hands as well as his career as a bogus surgeon, he was nicknamed 'Manos' (Spanish for *hands*).

Manos didn't relish his newest assignment. 'That's a terrific idea, Arthur,' he responded sarcastically. 'You want me to become that bitch's lover. Are you crazy? I have feelings, too. You want me to kiss the same mouth that Eichmann kissed? You want me to move right in and live with her? Hah!' When he calmed down, he agreed to try.

In Aussee, posing as a Dutch collaborationist named Henryk van Diamant, Manos charmed some SS 'widows', but had no success with Vera Eichmann, though he delighted her sons. One day, he reported to Wiesenthal by phone that he was taking the three boys rowing the next day. Something in his voice made Simon drop everything and hurry to Aussee to take a walk along the lake with Manos.

'You lost your family in the camps, Manos,' Wiesenthal said. 'Were there children?'

'Two brothers and a sister,' Manos replied, looking away.

'And you think you could get back at Eichmann by having an "accident" out there?' Simon said, beckoning towards the water. He spent the next half hour talking Manos out of killing Eichmann's sons, eventually convincing him that 'a man who unemotionally ordered the death of one million children would show no emotion for his own.'

Returning to Linz, Wiesenthal phoned Arthur and they agreed to find another mission for Manos. Everywhere Eichmann went, he'd had mistresses. Maybe one of them still cherished a photo of her infamous lover which could be circulated on 'Wanted' posters: a far more urgent need than revenge on his family.

A Margit Kutschera in Munich had been his mistress in Hungary. She told Manos there had been photos of herself with Eichmann, but she had last seen them in her hotel suite in Budapest, which she'd fled during the Allied bombings in 1944, leaving everything behind. Manos went to Budapest, but found the suite and hotel had long ago been looted by the Red Army.

In 1947, Wiesenthal learned that another ex-mistress of Eichmann's, Maria Masenbacher, was living in Urfahr, a suburb across the Danube from Linz. Arthur sent for Manos again. As in Aussee, Manos pretended to be a Dutch SS man who didn't dare return home. He frequented a café where Frau Masenbacher, a striking woman nearing forty, was a steady customer, and it wasn't long before she allowed him to buy her a drink. Soon she was sharing her home and her confidences with him – and, one day, her photo album. As they flipped the pages, Manos spotted a picture of a well-dressed man in civilian clothes taken just before World War II. 'Who's this?' he asked.

'Oh, a friend,' she said, flipping the page quickly. 'He died in the war.'

A few hours later, when she was gone, Manos was joined by a detective friend of Wiesenthal's from Linz. The man had been a neighbour of Eichmann's. When he said 'That's the rascal!' Manos lifted the photo from the album – and, within hours, Wiesenthal was circulating copies of it. Though taken in 1939, it was clear and sharp, lending itself to reproduction. For a long while, however, it led only to a 'Lieutenant Otto Eckmann' who had walked out of American custody on 30 June 1945.

Though Wiesenthal no longer worked for the Americans, he and they continued to co-operate. Late in 1947, the CIC in Bad Ischl informed him that Veronika Liebl had applied to the district court for a death certificate for her 'ex-husband' Adolf Eichmann 'for the sake of the children.' She had submitted an affidavit from one Karl Lukas of Prague, who swore that he had seen Eichmann shot to death during street fighting in the Czech capital on 30 April 1945.

Wiesenthal asked the CIC to seek a postponement of the hearing: these cases were normally expedited in two weeks to enable widows either to draw their husbands' pensions or remarry or both. Granted an extra fortnight, he produced testimony sworn at the Nuremberg trials by SS Major Wilhelm Höttl that he had seen Eichmann alive in Bad Aussee on 2 May 1945, and by Rudolf Scheide, the German overseer in Cham to whom Eichmann confessed his identity in mid-June 1945. To clinch the case, Wiesenthal sent a man to Prague, where he learned that the 'eye-witness' to Eichmann's 'death', Karl Lukas, an employee of the Czechoslovak Ministry of Agriculture, was married to Frau Eichmann's sister, Maria Liebl.

Upon examining Wiesenthal's evidence, the Austrian judge threw out Frau Eichmann's application as well as Frau Eichmann herself, warning her that he would have her prosecuted if she ever tried such a trick again. Fifteen years later, after Eichmann's capture, Wiesenthal, in a rare act of vindictiveness, informed Czechoslovak authorities about Lukas's affidavit. Lukas was fired immediately by the Ministry of Agriculture.

'I am convinced,' says Wiesenthal, 'that my most important contribution to the search for Eichmann was destroying the legend that he had died. If he had been legally declared dead, then his name would have disappeared from all the "Wanted" lists and officially he would no longer exist. His case would be closed. Around the world the search for him would end. A man presumed dead is no longer hunted. Many SS criminals were never caught because they had themselves declared dead and then lived happily ever after under new names. Some of them even remarried their own "widows".'

ODESSA, in capital letters, is not the Soviet seaport where Simon Wiesenthal spent two years apprenticing as an architect and another year designing huts for chicken feathers, but an acronym for ***O**rganisation **d**er **E**hemaligen **SS-A**ngehörigen*: Organization of SS Members. As amorphous as the Mafia, which exists even when one cannot prove it exists, ODESSA, like the Cosa Nostra 'families', forms and re-forms to fit the occasion or need. Under such aliases as 'Spider', 'Sluice', 'Silent Help', 'The Brotherhood', 'Association of German Soldiers', 'Comradeship', or even 'Six-Pointed Star' (not the Star of David, but an escape network in Austria's six principal cities), it denies its existence and shrugs off Frederick Forsyth's best-selling 1972 thriller, *The Odessa File*, for the fiction it is, even though Forsyth's novel features such real-life heroes as Simon Wiesenthal and Lord Russell of Liverpool as well as, for a villain, Eduard Roschmann, 'The Butcher of Riga' who, as second-in-command of the Latvian capital's ghetto, was responsible for 35,000 deaths and deportations. In his foreword, Forsyth dissociates fiction from fact by pointing out that 'many Germans are inclined to say that the ODESSA does not exist. The short answer is: it exists.'

Wiesenthal won't waste his time or anyone else's arguing this question. He insists ODESSA was founded in Augsburg or Stuttgart in 1947, when higher-ranking Nazis in the SS and wartime German industry saw that, despite Allied disinterest, the revelation of war crimes and the question of accountability were not going to die a quiet death. With the impending new state of Israel and dedicated survivors like Wiesenthal determined to keep the fires alive, the Fourth Reich wasn't about to happen very soon. Using just a portion of their plunder, which Wiesenthal values at between $750 million and 1 billion, they were able to set up three escape routes: from the north German seaport of Bremen to the Italian seaport of Genoa, where Christopher Columbus was born and, centuries later, Adolf Eichmann and Josef Mengele set sail for the New World: from Bremen to Rome, where the Vatican and the International Red

Cross, wittingly or unwittingly, stood ready to expedite their escapes; and from Austria to Italy, which is the way Franz Stangl went.

'ODESSA provides its members with material aid, organizes social activities, and, when necessary, helps ex-Nazis escape to foreign countries,' said prosecutor Gideon Hausner at the Eichmann trial. 'It has its headquarters in Munich with branches all over Germany and Austria as well as in South American countries. The German community at Hohenau in Paraguay is dominated by ODESSA.'

'ODESSA was organized as a thorough, efficient network,' says Simon Wiesenthal. 'Every forty miles was a shelter manned by a minimum of three and maximum of five people. They knew only the two surrounding shelters: the one from which the fugitives came to them and the one to which they were to be delivered safely.' Ironically, some of the inns and farmhouses along ODESSA's 'rat line', as the escape routes became known, were also used by Jewish refugees making their way illegally to what was still Palestine under an expiring British mandate which sought to maintain the population balance between Arabs and Jews. For some Displaced Persons, it was harder to leave Germany and Austria than it was for their former captors. Wiesenthal says: 'I know of a small inn near Merano, in the Italian Tyrol, and another place near the Resch Pass between Austria and Italy, where illegal Nazi transports and illegal Jewish transports sometimes spent the night without knowing of each other's presence. The Jews were hidden on the upper floor and told not to move. The Nazis, on the ground floor, were warned to stay inside.'

There was also substantial two-way commuter traffic of wanted Nazis across the border between Austria and Germany. Wiesenthal says that ODESSA used German drivers, hired in Munich under their own names or aliases, to deliver *Stars and Stripes*, the US Army's daily newspaper printed in Germany, to the troops in Austria. Military Police would wave these US army vans through the border crossing on the Munich-Salzburg *Autobahn* and sometimes the drivers would repay the favour by handing them a few free copies while a Nazi fugitive crouched behind bundles of *Stars and Stripes*.

The recruitment section of the French Foreign Legion, which asked no questions and into which scores of low-ranking SS men fled in the last days of the war, also served ODESSA well. In early 1948, Roschmann, the Graz-born 'Butcher of Riga', escaped from Austria into Italy with five other Nazi fugitives in a car with French licence plates and a Foreign Legion chauffeur outfitted with papers enabling the car to cross borders without being searched.

Though he found himself bored to death in northern Germany, 'Otto Heninger' stayed until he'd saved enough money to finance an ocean voyage. According to Hannah Arendt: 'Early in 1950, he succeeded in establishing contact with ODESSA, a clandestine organization of SS veterans, and in May of that year, he was passed through Austria to Italy, where a Franciscan priest, fully informed of his identity, equipped him with a refugee passport in the name of Richard Klement and sent him on to Buenos Aires.' The priest in Rome was actually Father Anton Weber at the St Raphael Society, who, years later, boasted of the hundreds of 'baptized Jews' (converts to Catholicism) he'd saved from Hitler and then admitted that 'yes, someone called Richard Klement came to me. He said he came from East Germany and didn't want to go back there to live under the Bolsheviks, so I helped him.' How Father Weber, himself a Bavarian, failed to hear Eichmann's thick Austrian accent must remain an ecclesiastical mystery.

With Weber's help, Eichmann arrived in Argentina in mid-July 1950 as 'Ricardo Klement, thirty-seven, stateless, Catholic'. By 1951, Simon Wiesenthal was back on his trail. Early that year, 'a former member of German counter-intelligence who had good ODESSA contacts told me Eichmann had been seen passing through Rome last summer, probably bound for South America.'

Further confirmation came a few months later in a personal visit from ODESSA itself. After publishing magazine articles on treasure-hunters seeking Eichmann's hidden store of gold melted down from his victims' teeth and jewellery, Simon was called upon in his office in Linz by a slim, dapper Austrian aristocrat whom he identifies in his memoirs as 'Heinrich von Klimrod'. His guest came right to the point: 'I represent a Viennese group of former SS men. Our mutual interests converge at one point. We know that you are a fanatical idealist. You want to find Eichmann to bring him to justice. We, too, want him – for a different reason. We want his gold. I believe we could establish a useful collaboration.'

Not willing to go into partnership with former SS men or make a deal for gold 'that doesn't belong to me and doesn't belong to Eichmann either' (and, he added to himself, 'may have come from my eighty-nine relatives who had been killed by Eichmann's men'), the 'fanatical idealist' declined the offer – but not before eliciting from 'Klimrod' that Eichmann was probably in South America after being sheltered in a Capuchin monastery in Rome and helped by a Father Weber and a Father Benedetti. The one name he didn't have was 'Ricardo Klement.'

– 15 –

The Eichmann abduction

'The 1950s were bad years for Eichmann-hunters,' says Wiesenthal. 'The Cold War had reached its climax and the former Allies were dug in on both sides of the Iron Curtain. The Americans had their hands full with the war in Korea. No one was interested in Eichmann or the Nazis. When two Nazis met, they would say "A new wind is blowing!" and slap each other on the back.'

It seemed to Arthur Pier's (Asher Ben Nathan's) successor, Tuviah Friedman, that 'only the two of us – Wiesenthal and I – cared about Eichmann. Everyone else had forgotten. The Jews who had remained in Germany were involved in her postwar business recovery. Many were living as Gentiles and had married Gentile girls.' By the end of 1951, most Displaced Persons who were Jewish had resettled in Western Europe, Israel, Australia, and the Americas. The stream of witnesses flowing into Wiesenthal's Documentation Centre in Linz and Friedman's in Vienna had slowed to a trickle.

Upon learning that Eichmann had escaped from Europe, Simon could maintain just two frail links with his quarry. In terms he never uses now, he told Friedman how he haunted Eichmann's family:

'I'm in their filthy store every few weeks. I ask them if they've heard from Adolf lately, where is he writing from these days, and always they have the same answer for me: "Please, leave us alone, we don't know anything, leave us alone." Do you know how many times I've been to Frau Vera Eichmann's place? Ask me and I'll tell you. Her three bastard sons know me on sight already.'

In the spring of 1952, his next-to-last link was severed when Eichmann's wife and three boys vanished from Altaussee. Wiesenthal fell into a deep depression. 'Obviously, no one cared,' he said. 'Even the Israelis had more cause to be concerned about Nasser* than Eichmann.'

While ODESSA viewed Wiesenthal as an unco-operatively 'fanatical idealist', Tuviah Friedman has described the Cold War Wiesenthal as 'a right-wing Zionist, a militant who admired the policies of extremists like Menachem Begin.'† Although Friedman is not to be trusted as an historical source and Asher Ben Nathan calls him 'abnormal', 'indiscreet', 'unreliable', and a 'braggart' and a blabbermouth from whom truly important secrets had to be concealed, Simon Wiesenthal says that, between 1946 and 1952, Friedman and he 'worked together well – possibly because we were almost two hundred kilometres [125 miles] apart, him in Vienna, I in Linz. We exchanged information and supplied each other with evidence.'

In 1952, Friedman gave up the ghost – in Austria, at least. 'My files were bulging with documents, with sworn affidavits,' he recalls. 'But nobody clamoured to get at them and use them to prosecute Nazis. The Germans didn't want them, the Austrians didn't want them, and neither did the Western Allies or the Russians.' Upon learning that the Yad Vashem Historical Archives – sponsored by the Israeli government and the world's Jewish communities – had been set up in Jerusalem as an on-going centre for information on and documentation of and memorial to 'the Six Million', Friedman packed his files into two large trunks, arranged for the Israeli Consulate to ship them to Yad Vashem, and shut down his Vienna office.

'One file I did not send to Jerusalem,' he notes. 'That was the file on Adolf Eichmann.' He took that with him when he emigrated to Israel later that year – 'vomiting all the way,' he remembers.

Later that year, Friedman emigrated to Haifa, married a Hungarian doctor he'd known in Vienna on her way to Israel, and returned to Austria to wind up his university studies there. Toward the end of

*Egyptian General Gamal Abdel Nasser (1918–70) led the army coup that deposed King Farouk in 1952 and seized power as Premier in 1954. In 1956, he was elected the first President of the Republic of Egypt and fought wars against Israel in 1956, 1967, and 1969.

†Menachem Begin, founder of the Irgun Zvai Leumi (National Military Organization), a militant Zionist underground group that fought the British in Palestine, became the Likud party's Prime Minister of Israel from 1977 to 1983.

1952, Friedman paid a farewell visit to Wiesenthal in Linz and copied *his* Eichmann files – just in case. Simon's despair had deepened; he hardly ate, drank, or slept and, if his wife Cyla had to ask why, he'd reply: 'The Nazis lost the war, but we are losing the postwar.' Yet he was still fighting his private war when he escorted Friedman to the Linz railroad station and told him:

'Tadek, you go back to Israel and don't let them push you around. Keep reminding the Israelis about Eichmann. Don't let them tell you to forget about him. Let the Israel Government do everything it wants to do: build houses for immigrants, teach everybody Hebrew, make a strong army. Fine! Very good! But they must also start looking for Eichmann. And only you can nag at them and make them do something.'

As they embraced on the platform, Simon added:

'Just think of it, Tadek! When Eichmann is caught, he will be tried by a Jewish court in a Jewish state. History and our people's honour – both are at stake.'

The depression into which Simon Wiesenthal fell in 1952, upon learning that first Eichmann and then his family had disappeared from Europe, mostly took the form of insomnia. In the sleepless midnight hours, while others lay awake counting sheep or naming stars, he watched the dead – first his family, then his friends, then the thousands he met in the camps, and then the cases that crossed his desk every day – parade before his eyes, always with Eichmann, sometimes cracking a whip, bringing up the rear. Simon never had nightmares, for his nights were waking hours spent with ghosts. A doctor he consulted told him he needed relaxation, diversion, a hobby.

'I have a hobby,' Wiesenthal told him. 'I collect witnesses.'

'And from this hobby you are sick,' the doctor said. 'You are prolonging the concentration camp for yourself. When your witnesses cry, you cry, too. And when they suffer, you suffer. How many victims were there? Six million? Well, you will be number six million and one unless you get yourself a real hobby, like stamp-collecting.'

Wiesenthal plunged into philately with the intensity he brings to everything else. Instead of taking his mind off Nazis, however, his hobby focused it on crucial details which, in the end, revitalized his work. Some of mankind's greatest revelations have come only when scientists, researchers, even artists, have taken necessary breaks or detours after intensive concentration: the mind at play can sometimes energize the mind that's at its wits' end. Once, Wiesenthal's contribution to a war crimes trial was calling the judges' attention to the stamp on an envelope addressed home from Poland. Its date of issue contradicted an SS man's alibi that he was back in Germany by the time of an atrocity in Poland.

The matching up of Ricardo Klement with Adolf Eichmann was as painstaking a process as the mounting of a Penny Black or Twopenny Blue in a stamp album. And the breakthrough, though it wasn't recognized at the time, came from Wiesenthal's hobby. At a philately exhibition in Innsbruck in late 1953, he met an old baron who invited him home to his villa in the Tyrol to look at his collection. Over a bottle of wine, the baron – a lifelong Catholic and ardent monarchist who had suffered for his views under Hitler – told his Jewish guest how dismayed he was to see prominent Nazis regaining high positions in the Tyrol 'as if nothing had changed. And it's not only here.' Rummaging in a drawer for a recent letter from a friend in Argentina, he handed it, still in its envelope, to Wiesenthal. 'Beautiful stamps, aren't they?' the baron remarked. 'But read what's inside.'

His friend, a former lieutenant-colonel in the German army who had never concealed his dislike for Hitler, had gone to Argentina as an instructor to Juan Perón's troops. He wrote to the baron:

> There are some people here we both used to know . . . A few more are here whom you've never met. Imagine who else I saw – and even had to talk to twice: that awful swine Eichmann who commanded the Jews. He lives near Buenos Aires and works for a water company.

'How do you like that?' the baron remarked. 'Some of the worst of the lot got away.'

Wiesenthal played it cool, for the baron could convey some of his excitement to his friend, who might mention it in conversation that could alert 'that swine Eichmann'. But he memorized that passage and all the other names in the letter as well as the sender's address. Declining to finish his wine for fear it might blur his memory, he made his excuses early, returned to his hotel, and wrote everything down.

Upon his return to Linz, Simon phoned the Israeli consul in Vienna, Aryeh Eschel, and then prepared two complete dossiers on Eichmann. 'By late 1953,' says Wiesenthal, 'I had definite knowledge of where Eichmann was in Argentina and where he worked. I had everything but his name, which a trained, trustworthy Jewish investigator could have ferreted out easily from what else I had. So I wrote up a full report on Eichmann, complete with the photograph of him and copies of his letters in his own handwriting.' Concluding with the passage from (but not the source of) the baron's letter, Wiesenthal gave one copy to Eschel for forwarding to his government in Jerusalem and sent the other to Nahum Goldmann at the New York headquarters of the World Jewish Congress, an umbrella organization that claims to speak on behalf of Jewish communities in seventy countries.

A dynamic Polish-born scholar who had founded the WJC in 1936 to warn the world against Nazism and prevent persecution of Jews, Nahum Goldmann (1894 – 1982) was its president as well as head of the World Zionist Organization – a man so powerful that, on one of his frequent visits to the young state of Israel, he cut short a meeting with Prime Minister David Ben-Gurion because he was 'too busy'. A feisty autocrat given to categorical statements that ninety per cent of Israel's people live outside its borders and (according to Simon Wiesenthal) that 'only I can decide what is good for the Jews', Nahum Goldmann had headed the postwar International Claims Conference which negotiated with governments for compensation to be awarded to persecuted Jews. When Austrian Chancellor Julius Raab had greeted him with 'Jews and Austrians are both the victims of Nazism!', Goldmann had put Raab in his place with biting sarcasm: 'Yes, Herr Chancellor, that is why I have come to ask you how much money the Jews owe the Austrians.'

There was no reply from Israel, but Wiesenthal to this day is angrier at the answer he did receive after two months from New York, where Goldmann had turned his material over to Rabbi Abraham Kalmanowitz, president and dean of the Mirrer Yeshiva Central Institute. Writing in German, the rabbi acknowledged receipt and asked for 'Eichmann's full address in Buenos Aires'. Politely reiterating that he didn't yet have that, Wiesenthal replied that he could send a Spanish-speaking investigator there to do the job if the

WJC would pay travel expenses plus 500 dollars. Rabbi Kalmanowitz wrote back insisting that Wiesenthal forward Eichmann's address and enclosing a letter from Nahum Goldmann saying, as Simon puts it, 'that anyway Eichmann wasn't in Argentina, but in Damascus.'

Part of the problem, Wiesenthal won't quite admit (but won't deny), was the barrage of false clues given out by Tuviah Friedman (Eichmann was in Syria, Eichmann was in Kuwait) in an effort to smoke out real leads. But he blames Nahum Goldmann more: 'This man blocked everything. When organizations asked for money, he always said no. Once I asked him why and he said: "I don't like independent organizations." But I argued that my kind of work can only be done by independent individuals and small groups. No matter. He wanted to have a monopoly.'

The antipathy between Wiesenthal and the World Jewish Congress, which exploded in 1986 during the campaign of Kurt Waldheim for the Austrian presidency, had its roots in the Eichmann hunt – which Wiesenthal almost, but not quite, gave up in March 1954 when, in despair at the lack of results, funds, and outside interest, he shut down his Documentation Centre in Linz and sent 532 kilos (1170 pounds) of files to the Yad Vashem Historical Archives in Israel. But, like Friedman when he emigrated, he held on to one dossier: Adolf Eichmann's.

The hunt for Eichmann would languish for at least five years. 'The next time I saw Nahum Goldmann, in 1956,' Simon recalls ruefully, 'I told him I'd had to close my Centre. He had no reaction, none at all, not even a word of sympathy.'

Was there no way to track down Eichmann when Wiesenthal came so close? Surely, even then, 500 dollars was not an impossible hurdle for a determined fund-raiser like Simon to clear. But he needed auspices as well as money. 'I was alone in Linz,' he explained. 'Suppose we did find Eichmann living near Buenos Aires and working for a water company, how could we get him? What would I, a private citizen half a world away, do? The Germans were a strong political force in Argentina. German soldiers were training Perón's army. German experts were running Argentine industries. Millions in German capital was invested in Argentine banks.'

Simon Wiesenthal estimates the value of the wealth that the Nazis smuggled out of Europe at close to a billion dollars. 'After the war,' says Wiesenthal, 'the Nazis sent experts and money to Argentina.

Perón himself, according to an investigation made in Buenos Aires after his downfall, was given around $100 million. Buenos Aires became the south terminal port for ODESSA. The Germans took over hotels and boarding houses, gave new SS immigrants jobs and identity papers, and had excellent connections with the highest government officials. At one time, a group of Argentinian Germans plotted to fly to Germany and set free all the Nazi criminals in Landsberg Prison.'

Back in 1954, Wiesenthal guessed that 'Eichmann must feel quite safe in Argentina or he wouldn't have sent for his family. Maybe he has powerful friends there. Otherwise he wouldn't dare live in or near a city with more than 200,000 Jews. Even though his victims seldom saw him, who knows? Somebody from the Jewish Councils in Vienna or Prague or Budapest just might recognize him.'

Actually, Eichmann had hardly been in Buenos Aires during the first three years of his stay in Argentina. 'Ricardo Klement' had arrived wearing dark glasses, a Hitler moustache, and a hat pulled low over his eyes, but had been met by SS friends who quickly put him in touch with the head of CAPRI, a firm founded by Germans to provide work for postwar refugees. Some 20,000 of their countrymen had arrived within a few months after the war ended. CAPRI offered 'Klement' work in Tucumán, some 600 miles from the capital.

CAPRI was a contractor to the Argentine government, prospecting for water power and planning hydroelectric plants and dams. 'Klement' was put in charge of a crew of native workers and, determined organizer of labour that he was, soon excelled and was given promotions, responsibility, and raises that enabled him to send for his family within two years. Vera Liebl, the 'ex-Frau Eichmann', had received a letter – from a 'stranger' whose handwriting she recognized – saying that 'your children's uncle, whom everybody believed to be dead, is alive and well.' When she and her sons had joined 'Uncle Ricardo' in Tucumán on 15 August 1952, the boys had been told that he was 'your dead father's cousin', and they liked him so much that they rejoiced when their uncle married their mother and she had a fourth son: Ricardo Francisco, the middle name in honour of a Franciscan friar who had helped the proud father escape through Italy.

With their mother masquerading as a remarried divorcée to some and a widow to others, their father pretending to be their uncle and stepfather, and their half-brother really their brother, family life for the Eichmann boys sounds more complicated than it was. Even when the baby was baptized 'Ricardo Francisco Klement *Eichmann*', his brothers asked no questions. They were dull boys – like their father had been. He once complained that they showed 'absolutely no interest in being educated' and didn't ' even try to develop their so-called talents.'

In retrospect, says Simon Wiesenthal, 'Adolf Eichmann's undoing was his family feeling. He wanted to resume relations with his wife, he cherished family celebrations, and he wanted his sons by his side. He fitted into the middle-class mould, just the way Mafiosi do – and it was this loyalty that eventually helped us pick up his traces.'

Having lost its government contracts when its protector – Perón's wife, 'Evita' – died of cancer at the age of thirty-three in 1952, CAPRI went bankrupt the following year. Thus, by the time Wiesenthal read the letter from the baron's informant in Buenos Aires, it was obsolete, for Eichmann's water company had gone down the drain. Still, he was back in Buenos Aires looking for work and might have been easy to trace.

The 'Klement' ménage rented a small house on the Calle Chacabuco in Vicente Lopez, a suburb of the capital. With two other Nazis as partners, Eichmann started a laundry business that failed. Then he left his family behind while he worked on a rabbit farm for a few months and, after that, he found an office job in a fruit-canning factory, but it, too, was short-lived. In and out of town, in and out of work, even down and out in Buenos Aires, he barely managed to provide – but he always did. His landlord, Francisco Schmidt, a Jew, had only good words to say about his tenant.

In his first five years in Argentina, only a handful of trusted SS friends knew that 'Klement' was Eichmann. Anybody could guess that he was a Nazi fugitive, but there were thousands of those. Such Germans as the baron's friend who recognized him as 'that swine Eichmann' usually didn't learn – or want to learn – too much about his Argentine identity. Now, however, in financial distress, he turned to a couple of the Nazi help organizations in Argentina, even though they might be infiltrated by informers.

Call them arms of ODESSA, if you will, but these groups were too far above ground to resemble, in any way, an underground railway for escaping Nazis. More of an 'old boys' network', they quickly recognized Eichmann's growing notoriety and rewarded his past work with a job at the Mercedes Benz factory in Suarez, near Buenos Aires. Starting as a mechanic, he was quickly promoted to foreman and then department head.

Scarcely bothering to conceal his identity any more, Eichmann started cutting a celebrity's swath through Argentina's ample Nazi colony. In 1955, he even gave an interview to a Dutch SS man named Willem S. Sassen, who had been dabbling in journalism ever since his arrival in South America in 1948, around the time that Belgium condemned him *in absentia* to death as a war criminal. In his session with Sassen, Eichmann explained his dedication to 'the Final Solution' by saying that Hitler 'may have been wrong all down the line, but one thing is beyond dispute: the man was able to work his way up from lance-corporal in the German Army to Führer of a people of almost eighty million . . . His success alone proved to me that I should subordinate myself to this man.'

Having given up his Documentation Centre in Linz, Simon Wiesenthal had gone into refugee work, first with persons still displaced by the war and then, starting in 1956, from anti-communist upheavals in Poland, Hungary, and East Germany. 'For a while, after the Hungarian revolution,' he recalls, 'I was director of eight schools for vocational re-training of refugees: teaching them jobs that would be necessary in the West, like TV repairmen and automobile mechanics; I trained 8000 workers for Opel. And we tried to find work that would tide over professional people who had to learn languages and pass examinations before they could practise in their new countries. So a lawyer became a notary public, a doctor a laboratory technician . . .'

Simon also represented various Jewish agencies in Austria, though being in Linz, a provincial capital, instead of Vienna, two hours away, was a handicap. Still, he was unwilling to leave Linz because he wanted to keep an eye on Adolf Eichmann's family. The Eichmanns lived only two blocks away from the Wiesenthals. And every day, at least twice, Simon had to pass their electric store with its sign proudly proclaiming ADOLF EICHMANN, the name he could not let go of.

In the evening hours, he freelanced as a journalist, writing for such survivor publications as *Die Mahnung* (The Warning) in West Berlin and *La Voix Internationale de la Résistance* in Brussels as well as any Austrian newspaper (more often in Linz than in Vienna and

Salzburg) that would print his unsolicited contributions. After a while, 'the editors would come to me if they had to have something on such subjects as Nazi crimes because I had a monopoly: I was the only person writing about it in Austria. But it wasn't a career and certainly not a living.'

Like 1938 and 1939, 1968 and 1989, the year 1956 was one of those watershed years in history whose effects are still being felt in various parts of the world – not just in Eastern Europe. A 1956 Middle Eastern event that looked like a disaster to Simon Wiesenthal and everybody else proved to be quite the reverse: the great Suez Canal fiasco turned the tide for Nazi-hunters. That July, Gamal Abdel Nasser nationalized the Suez Canal, inciting Israel to invade the Gaza Strip and Sinai Peninsula in late October and prompting France and England to attack Egypt a week later. Though US and UN pressure forced all three to withdraw, its initial military success made Israel feel secure that its Arab neighbours were not going to 'sweep it into the sea', as they repeatedly said they would. Now the security services could spare some time, however belatedly, for the other enemy: Nazi criminals still at large.

On Wednesday morning, 22 April 1959, Simon Wiesenthal picked up the Linz newspaper *Oberösterreichische Nachrichten* (Upper Austrian News). On the back page was word that Frau Maria Eichmann, stepmother of his quarry, had died. The obituary listed survivors: Adolf Eichmann was not among them, but his wife Vera was. 'People usually don't lie when they write obituary notices' says Wiesenthal. 'It said "Vera Eichmann". Apparently Frau Eichmann had neither divorced nor remarried.' He cut out the article, put it atop his Eichmann file, and sent word to the Israeli consul in Vienna as well as to Tuviah Friedman, Asher Ben Nathan, Yad Vashem, and a few others in Israel who might care.

Somebody high up in Israel *did* care. That summer, Wiesenthal's information went to Isser Harel, the head of Israel's secret services. Wiesenthal's information corroborated reports Harel was receiving from West Germany. He went to Prime Minister Ben-Gurion and told him: 'We have proof that Eichmann is in Argentina. Can I give orders for my men to get on his track?'

'Yes,' said Ben-Gurion, 'bring back Eichmann dead or alive. But I'd rather you brought him back alive. It would have great meaning for young people.'

Two young Israeli agents visited Wiesenthal in Linz and asked him to pick up where he'd left off in 1954. Knowing he would have no luck with the bereaved Eichmanns in Linz, Simon sent a man around to visit Maria Liebl in Germany in quest of the whereabouts of her daughter, Vera Eichmann. Frau Liebl shut the door in the man's face, but not before telling him Vera had married some man named 'Klemt' or 'Klems' in South America.

Wiesenthal reported this to Israel. Again, it corroborated a German source which said Vera Eichmann was living 'in fictitious marriage' with a German named Ricardo Klement.

'I was sure it was a real marriage – that Frau Eichmann was living with her husband Adolf Eichmann,' says Wiesenthal. 'Otherwise the Eichmann family in Linz wouldn't have listed her as Vera Eichmann in the obituary notices. The Eichmann boys lived in Buenos Aires with their parents. It occurred to me that they would probably be registered there at the German embassy, since they would soon reach military age. I asked a friend to make a cautious inquiry. He notified me yes, the Eichmann boys were registered there, under their real name.'

This was enough for the Israelis to move a team of three secret agents into a house on the Calle Chacabuco, opposite 'Ricardo Klement's' residence. With telescopic lenses from their windows and attaché cases that were really hand cameras, they photographed 'Klement' on the street, on buses to and from work, on his lunch hour, and every time he went into or out of his house or appeared at a window. In early 1960, when 'Klement' and his family moved into a primitive brick house – with no electricity or running water – which he and his older sons had been building themselves, the Israelis moved with them and continued the surveillance. The house was on Garibaldi Street in San Fernando, one of the more run-down suburbs of Buenos Aires.

Because its agents were operating illegally on foreign soil, Israel needed to take every precaution before abducting Eichmann. They had to net the right man. A misfire or an embarrassing case of mistaken identity could rupture diplomatic relations with Argentina, an important trading partner and home of many thousands of Jewish refugees as well as Nazi fugitives. Despite the fact that they had photographed 'Klement' up, down, and sideways, the Israelis were handicapped by the scarcity of early photos of Eichmann and by the fact that he had aged badly and lost weight. 'Klement' had the same thin-lipped, cruel mouth, but none of the dapper arrogance of the high-living officer who had romanced Maria Masenbacher and Margit Kutschera. Even those who had known him personally in the past were reluctant to swear that this meek, shabby family man with the pallid, lined face was what had become of Adolf Eichmann. Until they were sure that Eichmann and 'Klement' were one and the same, the Israelis would not move to seize him.

On Saturday, 6 February 1960, Wiesenthal read in the paper that Eichmann's father had died the day before – following his wife to the grave (as is more often the case than we read about) by less than a year. Learning that the funeral would not take place for another five days because the family was 'expecting relatives from abroad', Wiesenthal notified the Israelis, though he warned them that this might refer to one of Adolf Eichmann's four brothers, Emil, who lived in West Germany. His two young contacts came to see him. Though someone would monitor the funeral for them, they told Wiesenthal their bosses were almost as hungry for a current photo of Eichmann as they were for the man himself.

Two days before the funeral, Wiesenthal went out to the cemetery, found the Eichmann family burial plot, and scouted not just the location of the grave, but the terrain for several hundred yards around it. 'I thought what I had in mind could be done, especially on a dark winter day,' he recalls in his memoir. He took a train to Vienna and went to the Concordia Press Club, where he sought out two photographers who were also trusted friends. 'I asked them to come to Linz and photograph the whole Eichmann family while they stood around the grave during the funeral. I told them it was essential that they remain unseen. They did a fine job. Hiding behind large tombstones at a distance of about 200 yards, they made sharp pictures of the members of the funeral procession, although the light was far from perfect.'

Eichmann did not come to his father's funeral. Five hours after the ceremony, however, Wiesenthal held photos of his quarry's four brothers – Emil, Friedrich, Otto, and Robert – in his hand. Reaching into his drawer, he exhumed the 1936 photo of Adolf Eichmann that 'Manos' Diamant had pried loose from Frau Masenbacher near Linz more than a dozen years earlier. He put it in the pack with the other four. 'Next to today's pictures of the four brothers, Adolf, the eldest, looked like a younger brother. I took out a magnifying glass and studied the features of the five brothers. Many people had told me that Adolf Eichmann most closely resembled his brother Otto. Looking at the photographs through the magnifying glass, I suddenly understood why so many people had sworn they'd seen Adolf Eichmann in Altaussee since the war when they were really seeing one of his brothers. The family resemblance was astonishing. . .

'If "Ricardo Klement" in Buenos Aires was identical with Adolf Eichmann, his face must have gone through the same evolution as the faces of the four brothers. I cut from the photographs the faces of the four brothers who had been at the funeral, and the face from the old picture of Adolf Eichmann. I shuffled the faces like playing cards and threw them on the table. Somehow a composite face emerged: perhaps Adolf Eichmann.'

When the two young Israelis came to call, Wiesenthal performed his Eichmann card trick. 'This is how he must look now – probably closest to his brother Otto,' he told them. 'All five brothers have the same facial expression. Look at the mouth, its corners, the chin, the shape of the skull.'

'Fantastic!' one of them exclaimed. 'May we take the pictures with us?' the other asked.

They were out the door with them before he could say yes: 'Suddenly, they were in a hurry. I didn't want to detain them, not for a second. I didn't hear from them, so I assumed that they didn't need my help. There was nothing else I could do.'

With Wiesenthal's portraits in their possession, the Israelis needed to play one more card before they could make positive identification of Eichmann with 'Klement' – and he played right into their hands. On his way home from work on Monday, 21 March 1960, 'Ricardo Klement' did something he had never done before in the months the Israelis had him under surveillance: he bought his wife a bouquet of flowers.

Checking his Eichmann file, the leader of the mission read that Adolf Eichmann had married Vera Liebl on 21 March 1935. This was their silver wedding anniversary – and his sentimental gesture did him in. That very night, a three-word cable reached Harel in Tel Aviv: 'HA'ISH HOU HA'ISH.' ('The man is the man.')

In early April, while the surveillance team kept watch on Eichmann, a six-man 'kidnap commando' was installed by Israel in Buenos

Aires. Four were Israelis who had arrived via different routes and were equipped with false identification papers and cover stories that would hold water. Two were Argentinian Jews, recruited locally and warned they might have to leave Argentina for good – particularly if 'Operation Eichmann' proved successful.

When an intelligence report reached him that 'Klement' had been seen 'with another high-ranking Nazi in the neighbourhood of La Gallareta, in the province of Santa Fé. The description of that other man corresponds to that of [Dr] Josef Mengele', Harel decided to double the stakes by going to Argentina himself and taking charge of Operation Eichmann while keeping an eye out for the Auschwitz medical experimenter as well. When a couple of Israeli Cabinet members who were entrusted with the details of what was afoot complained about committing a large passenger jet *and* the head of Mossad (Israel's centralized intelligence organization) just to bringing back Eichmann, Harel told them blithely: 'To make the investment worthwhile, we'll try to bring Mengele with us, too.'

A long-scheduled visit to Argentina by Abba Eban, Foreign Minister of Israel, provided Operation Eichmann with a respectable cover. Argentina was observing its 150th anniversary of independence in May 1960, and Eban would be leading Israel's delegation to the sesquicentennial celebration. El Al, the Israeli government airline, would also be inaugurating air services between Tel Aviv and Buenos Aires at that time. The large prop-jet that brought Eban and his entourage on Wednesday, 11 May would, if all went well, fly home in a matter of hours or days with Eichmann and his captors. As Harel and his team began renting 'safe houses' (seven in all) in which to hide Eichmann or themselves, they swore their landlords to silence with the story that Eban wanted to hold secret meetings with Arab diplomats to discuss peace in the Middle East.

The kidnapping of Adolf Eichmann was set for 6.30 p.m. on 11 May. Early in May, however, the Argentine government postponed the Israelis' arrival by eight days because its leaders could not receive them before 2 p.m. on 19 May. Rather than alter a well-laid plan, Harel decided to stick to his schedule, but to use the extra week of holding Eichmann captive in Argentina to try to snare Mengele, too.

On 11 May, the bus from the Mercedes Benz plant dropped Eichmann at his corner, as usual, at one minute before the half-hour. It was autumn in Argentina (in the southern hemisphere) and night was falling. A car was parked on Garibaldi Street with its hood raised and three men bent over the engine. A fourth man, apparently the owner, was pacing impatiently. Another car was parked nearby.

As Eichmann passed the 'disabled' car, he reached into his pocket. The car's back door had just begun to open, but now – fearing he would produce a gun – the three 'mechanics' who were supposed to abandon their engine to shove him inside couldn't risk waiting the extra fraction of a second. One of them made a flying tackle, diving to deflect Eichmann's hand, and knocked him to the ground. As they thrashed around, he and Eichmann rolled into a ditch, into which the other two 'mechanics' jumped to subdue their quarry. The fourth man slammed the 'disabled' car's hood shut and then stood lookout while the driver started the engine and the two men in the back seat made room for a third.

Eichmann tried to shout for help, but his false teeth had been dislodged by the tackle and were rattling around his mouth, almost choking him. When his three assailants flung him on to the floor of the car, the two back-seat passengers pinned him down and searched him. The 'weapon' he had been reaching for was a flashlight, which he would have used to find his way in the gathering dusk to his unlit door, which he never saw again.

'One move and you're a dead man!' the driver said over his shoulder. He was Zvi Aharoni, chief interrogator for Israel's domestic equivalent of the Federal Bureau of Investigation and a key figure for the days of dialogue with Eichmann ahead. The three 'mechanics' raced for the other car. The look-out ambled back to the Israeli spy-house to keep watch on what the 'Klements' did when they realized that the head of the house had disappeared. With Eichmann still in Argentina for the next eight or nine days, who knew what might be done to retrieve him or block their exit?

Only twenty-seven seconds had elapsed between the moment Eichmann had reached for his flashlight and the car's take-off with him being bound and gagged in the back. Opaque goggles served as a blindfold. Taking side streets rather than main arteries, Aharoni drove for an hour – with the second car checking that there were no pursuers – before arriving at a villa code-named 'Tire' in the Florencio Varela district of Buenos Aires.

Inside the house, they searched their captive's mouth for a vial of poison and found none. Then they looked at his left armpit and found the telltale scars where his SS tattoo had been removed. Only then did Aharoni ask him in German: 'Who are you?'

Eichmann didn't evade the question by pretending to be Ricardo Klement. '*Ich bin Adolf Eichmann*,' he answered. After a pause, he added wearily but almost with relief: 'I know I'm in the hands of Jews. I am resigned to my fate.'

In the next week, Eichmann talked freely with Aharoni and even wrote a three paragraph statement which began:

> I, the undersigned Adolf Eichmann, hereby declare of my own free will that, as my true identity has been discovered, I realize there is no possibility of trying to escape the course of justice. I agree to be taken to Israel and there stand trial before a qualified tribunal.

Vera Eichmann waited three days before approaching anyone about her missing husband. She made the rounds of hospitals and morgues while her sons contacted Nazi welfare and Argentine fascist organizations, none of which paid much heed to an obscure émigré named Klement who seemed to have left his family. When the police finally were notified, their inquiries, too, were strictly routine. Eichmann's oldest son, Klaus (who preferred to call himself Nikolaus), said in 1965 that he did activate 'one of father's friends, also an SS member', in an effort to intercept Eichmann when his abductors tried to transport him out of the country. 'He organized a network of checks . . . There was no harbour, railway station, airport, or important intersection that didn't have one of our men stationed there.'

Around 14 or 15 May, one of the Israeli commandos thought he saw suspicious activity outside the hideaway, so Eichmann, his interrogator and guards were transferred to another villa. Otherwise, his brief incarceration in Argentina went smoothly and undetected. Harel's only disappointment was that Eichmann maintained he hardly knew Mengele and had certainly not seen him lately. When Eichmann said that Mengele might have gone where most Nazis went when they were between addresses – Gilda Jurmann's boarding house in Vicente Lopez – Harel ordered a stake-out there, much to the dismay of Aharoni and other members of Operation Eichmann, who felt this was jeopardizing their mission.

'Mengele burned like a fire in my bones,' Harel admitted later in explaining why he dispatched agents to every one of Mengele's former addresses. Only on Friday, 20 May, the new date set for the arrival of Abba Eban's delegation on El Al, did Harel concede that Mengele had vanished without a trace.

The 'Whispering Giant' Britannia prop-jet landed in Buenos Aires at 5.52 p.m. with an unusually large staff of nineteen – including a well-rested cockpit crew for the return flight. After the passengers had disembarked and been welcomed, the plane was towed into a hangar for servicing. Three hours later' crew members who weren't working the return flight, but were riding it home, came drifting back from downtown Buenos Aires in varying condition. One uniformed 'steward' was in such bad shape that he had to be driven to the plane's side and helped up the stairs by two of his colleagues. 'I'm glad there are no passengers,' an Argentine airport guard remarked. 'I'd hate to be served by him.'

The 'drunken steward', listed as 'George Doron', was, in fact, the principal passenger. Adolf Eichmann had been uniformed, fed a soporific, and doused with whisky just before leaving the villa. The plane took off without incident. With a refuelling stop in Dakar, Senegal, it touched down in Tel Aviv just before dawn the next day.

The following afternoon, Prime Minister Ben-Gurion addressed the Knesset, Israel's parliament:

'I must inform the Knesset that the security services of Israel have just laid their hands on one of the greatest of the Nazi criminals, Adolf Eichmann, who was responsible with other Nazi leaders for what they called the "Final Solution of the Jewish Problem" – that is to say, the extermination of six million European Jews. Eichmann is already under arrest here in Israel, in accordance with the law on the crimes of the Nazis and their collaborators', which specified that crimes against the Jewish people could be punished in Israel even if they took place outside the country and before it existed.

The reaction in Argentina was swift and vehement, but too late. On 5 June 1960, at Argentina's request, the United Nations Security Council voted unanimously to condemn Israel for violating Argentine sovereignty with its 'illicit and clandestine transfer' of Eichmann. Even before then, the 'transfer' had unleashed a pogrom across South America. Home-made bombs were thrown at Israeli embassies and consulates, Hebrew schools and synagogues, Jewish cultural and community centres, and homes of prominent Jews. Cemeteries were desecrated, kosher restaurants machine-gunned, and 'Death to the Jews' scrawled on walls in Buenos Aires, Asunción, Montevideo, Bogota, Rio, and São Paulo. Argentina's fascist organization, *Tacuara,* to whom the Eichmann boys had turned for help in finding their father, plotted to kidnap the Israeli ambassador and blow up his embassy. (West German Nazis put a price on the head of Isser Harel.) A noted Argentine Jewish scholar, Maximo Handel, was beaten unconscious by Nazi thugs who cut swastikas in his body. A young Jewish woman, Merta Penjerek, said to have brought food to the villa where Eichmann was held, was abducted and murdered. The pogrom would continue until 1 June 1962, the day after Eichmann was executed, when a *Tacuara* gang kidnapped Graciella Narcissa Sirota, daughter of the owner of the same hideaway, and tortured her, abused her sexually, and burned a swastika into her breast with their cigarettes.

And in Vienna around the time Ben-Gurion was addressing the Knesset, Simon Wiesenthal received a cable from Yad Vashem that congratulated him on his work well done.

– 16 –

Should Eichmann die?

'I saw Adolf Eichmann for the first time on the opening day of his trial in the courtroom in Jerusalem,' Simon Wiesenthal says in his 1967 memoir. *'For nearly sixteen years I had thought of him practically every day and every night. In my mind I had built up the image of a demonic superman. Instead I saw a frail, nondescript, shabby fellow in a glass cell between two Israeli policemen; they looked more colourful and interesting than he did. Everything about Eichmann seemed drawn with charcoal: his greyish face, his balding head, his clothes. There was nothing demonic about him; he looked like a bookkeeper who is afraid to ask for a raise. Something seemed completely wrong, and I kept thinking about it while the incomprehensible bill of indictment ("the murder of six million men, women, and children") was being read. Suddenly I knew what it was. In my mind I'd always seen SS* Obersturmbannführer *[Major] Eichmann, supreme arbiter of life and death. But the Eichmann I now saw did not wear the SS uniform of terror and murder. Dressed in a cheap, dark suit, he seemed a cardboard figure, empty and two-dimensional.'*

Noticing that witnesses, too, had trouble identifying the shabby little civilian in the bullet-proof glass booth as the awesome Eichmann they once knew, Wiesenthal suggested to Gideon Hausner, the chief prosecutor, that Eichmann should wear a uniform. Hausner rejected the idea because, while emotionally right, it would give the whole event the theatrical aura of a show trial. And, with Israel already in the international limelight for having abducted the defendant, the whole world was watching critically to see that Eichmann was treated humanely even while it heard hour after hour of his inhumanity.

Simon had another suggestion, to which he also knew Hausner would say no. There were fifteen counts in the indictment: 'causing the killing of millions of Jews', placing 'millions of Jews under conditions which were likely to lead to their physical destruction', 'causing serious bodily and mental harm' to them, 'directing that births be banned and pregnancies interrupted among Jewish women', 'racial, religious, and political persecution', 'plunder of property' by means of murder, the expulsion of 'hundreds of thousands of Poles from their homes' and 'fourteen thousand Slovenes' from Yugoslavia, and the deportation of 'scores of thousands of gypsies' to Auschwitz. Fifteen times, Eichmann was asked how he pleaded, and fifteen times, he answered, 'Not guilty.'

To Wiesenthal, this procedure seemed inadequate: 'I thought that Eichmann should have been asked six million times, and he should have been made to answer six million times.'

Since the trial would last eight months, Hausner's negative reply could be anticipated. But, a dozen years after Adolf Eichmann was hanged in 1962, when Wiesenthal confessed to me that he wondered whether his quarry should have been executed, it was on this same ground: 'When you take the life of one man for the murder of six million, you cheapen the value of the dead. It means, if you look at it a certain way, that one German life is worth six million Jewish lives. In general, I am against the death sentence, though I can understand that Eichmann is a special case. But, in the moment they killed him, the case was closed. Yet, even today, there are people appearing with new testimony, new evidence against him. Maybe it would have been better to give him six or eleven million life sentences and kept him in prison as a warning to the murderers of tomorrow and, each time new charges surface, to bring him back into the glass booth and let him answer them and let a judge decide. The trial is a lesson. But I don't know.'

What was the lesson of the Eichmann trial? At a time when the world was distancing itself from the Holocaust as a historical aberration and neo-Nazi revisionists were beginning to claim that Auschwitz and Anne Frank never really happened, Eichmann's testimony belied these lies. And, as Wiesenthal put it in the original German version of the 1988 memoir, *Justice, Not Vengeance*: 'The Eichmann trial conveyed an essential deep understanding of the Nazi death machinery and its most important protagonists. Since that time, the world now understands the concept of "desk murderer". We know that one doesn't need to be fanatical, sadistic, or mentally ill to murder millions; that it is enough to be a loyal follower eager to do one's duty for a *Führer*, and that mass murderers absolutely need not be – indeed, cannot be! – asocial. On the contrary, mass murder on a large scale presupposes a social conformist for a murderer.' To which he added in an interview: 'These people were often good family men, good fathers. They gave to the poor. They loved flowers. But they killed people. Why? Because they had the idea that they did not need to think. Hitler would think for them. Not one was born a murderer.'

Criticism from Israel hurts Simon. In practically the same breath, Tuviah Friedman claimed that Eichmann's first words to his captors were 'Which one of you is Friedman?' and complained that 'They always talk about Wiesenthal, never about me.' And Isser Harel, leader of the Eichmann abduction, not only made Wiesenthal a non-person in his 1975 memoir, *The House on Garibaldi Street* (even though Simon had supplied Harel's publisher with an important postwar, pre-capture photo of Eichmann, available nowhere else, to illustrate it), but, when questioned about the omission by a Dutch interviewer, said of Simon that 'his information didn't lead to Eichmann's tracks.'

Wiesenthal's response back in 1975 was to term Harel's words 'an assault on the credibility of my Documentation Centre. Harel is trying to get even more honour than he has coming, although I'm not trying to belittle his accomplishments of arresting and kidnapping Eichmann. Look, the capture of Eichmann was a mosaic, a picture puzzle, and in it I had my place. Harel is trying to deny me this and I protest this.'

Over the years, Harel kept bad-mouthing Wiesenthal. He was cited in a footnote to a 1986 book, *Mengele: the Complete Story*, as telling co-authors Gerald L. Posner and John Ware that neither Friedman nor Wiesenthal played any role in finding Eichmann. On a 1989 trip to the US, Harel found that 'everywhere I visited, people would say, "Where is Wiesenthal in the [Eichmann] operation?" because he was telling everybody he was behind all this. I was obliged to tell them it's not true.' Finally, in May 1991, when Harel went to New York to be honoured by the World Jewish Congress, he gave an interview to the *Jerusalem Post's* correspondent there, Jonathan Schachter, which the newspaper headlined: WIESENTHAL HAD "NO ROLE" IN EICHMANN KIDNAPPING'.

Producing a 278-page unpublished manuscript dissecting Wiesenthal's two memoirs and dismissing many of his claims – including ever having written to Nahum Goldmann about Eichmann – as 'a legend woven after the capture of Eichmann, so that Wiesenthal could take credit for a significant role in the tracing of Eichmann, and hence for his capture', Harel told Schachter: 'All of the information supplied by Wiesenthal before and in anticipation of the operation was utterly worthless, and sometimes even misleading and of negative value.' Harel said that one of Wiesenthal's many pronouncements that Dr Mengele was in Argentina may have interfered with Mengele's capture and jeopardized the Eichmann operation.

The World Jewish Congress – still embroiled in its feud with Wiesenthal from his Nahum Goldmann days to the Kurt Waldheim presidency – first denied the existence of any Wiesenthal-Goldmann correspondence; then retracted when Wiesenthal sent the WJC a copy of his four-page letter of 30 March 1954 to Goldmann, but then retracted its retraction by saying it had no proof the letter was ever sent or had even existed at that time, for it had not been found in the late Dr Goldmann's archives. Wiesenthal countered with Rabbi Kalmanowitz's reply of 21 May 1954, thereby proving that his letter had indeed reached the WJC in New York.

It would be pointless to cite and refute each argument of Harel's; besides, this job is done in an admirably documented, if rabidly pro-Wiesenthal, 1992 book called *Documents against Words: Simon Wiesenthal's Conflict with the World Jewish Congress,* issued in Holland but written in English and compiled by Richard A. Stein, president of the Foundation for the Fight against Anti-Semitism (STIBA) in Rotterdam. The spectacle of old men – Friedman, Harel, Wiesenthal – squabbling over scraps of glory well earned years ago is more tarnishing than edifying; if it does none of them any credit, though, it takes the least away from Wiesenthal.

Simon suspects that Harel's vendetta stems from his business, financial, and personal difficulties in the dozen years between his being ousted in 1963 as head of Israel's secret services in a dispute with Prime Minister Ben-Gurion and publication of his memoir in 1975. Most of all, Harel must have chafed at the veil of secrecy he was pledged to wear even after leaving Mossad.

Simon remembers how tight it was in the sixties: 'In those days, the Israeli government was pretending they had nothing to do with the kidnap – that Eichmann just showed up on Israel's soil and was brought before justice. Since what they had done was counter to international law, they just denied everything – including my role.

'Around then, Yad Vashem asked me to give a talk there about my role in tracking down Eichmann. But first, the director of Yad Vashem warned me not to mention, under any circumstances, that my dealings had been with the Israeli Embassy and Israeli intelligence. So I just told about these "Jewish friends of mine" who helped get Eichmann's picture and compared the photos of his brothers. So what happens? Harel feels slighted because he hears I don't mention him and, when he publishes his memoirs in the 1970s, he makes no mention of me or my work. For him, I don't exist, and later I hear Harel is saying I have nothing to do with his great accomplishment. And this is what they call Intelligence?!'

Part III
Raoul Wallenberg

When they came for the Jews, I was not a Jew, so I did not protest. When they came for the trade unionists, I did not belong to the trade union. When they came for the Catholics, I was not a Catholic. When they came for me, there was no one left to protest.

– Martin Niemöller,
Protestant pastor imprisoned by Hitler from 1937 to 1945

– 17 –

Wallenberg the searcher

Genocidists, killers, and 'desk murderers' are the human beasts that Simon Wiesenthal hunts, but another species of war criminal is not yet fair game: the 'desk undertaker' who shuts a door or closes a drawer on human lives, thereby committing crimes of omission which can cause calamity. Assassins of the spirit and muggers of the soul, the 'desk undertakers' were in command at Evian-les-Bains in 1938, when thirty-one nations of the world turned their backs on Jewish immigration and only one tiny Caribbean nation, the Dominican Republic, committed itself to accepting more than a mere handful of refugees . . . in Havana harbour in 1939, when a change in Cuban visa requirements left 930 Jewish refugees from Germany stranded aboard the luxury liner St Louis, *which subsequently was not allowed to land in Panama, Argentina, Paraguay, Uruguay, the United States, or Canada and had to return to Europe, where most of its passengers perished . . . in Ottawa, where immigration director Frederick Blair required written proof from children whose parents had perished in Hitler's ovens that they were orphans before they could be rescued by Canada . . . and in the US State Department, where bureaucrats concealed the truth about the exterminations of the Final Solution for fear that public compassion would burst open the floodgates of immigration. As it was, only 21,000 refugees were allowed to enter the US during the war with Germany: barely a tenth of the quota in normal times. With the end of the war, the 'desk undertakers' did not relinquish their grip on power; on the contrary, nowhere was it asserted more lastingly than in the case of Raoul Wallenberg.*

'The Second World War had no heroes,' Simon Wiesenthal says bluntly. It is the kind of overstatement with which Wiesenthal so often snares the world's attention' even at the risk of alienating widows and patriots, but he persists: 'The heroes from yesterday' –

and here he means previous wars, for World War II is still *today* to him – 'were people with courage in combat. The Second World War was a technical fight with no space for personal bravery, but Raoul Wallenberg is one of its rare exceptions.'

Raoul Gustav Wallenberg Jnr – who would save 100,000 Hungarian Jews from the jaws of extermination, only to vanish into the Soviet gulag himself – was born on 4 August 1912, at his maternal grandparents' summer home. He never met his father, Raoul Snr, a naval officer who died of cancer at twenty-three in May 1912, three months before his son was born. But he bore the illustrious name of a long line of Lutheran bankers and industrialists as well as diplomats; advisers to Crown and Cabinets; grey eminences whose family motto, '*Esse, non Videri*', meant '*To be, not to be seen*'. Through their Enskilda Bank (founded in 1856), the Wallenberg dynasty had a finger in or a grip on every major Swedish industry: steel, iron ore, ball bearings, blast furnaces, timber and then whole forests for pulp and paper, tobacco, electronics, communications, railroads, ferries, the East Asiatic Steamship line, Saab and Volvo autos, and the airline that is now SAS (Scandinavian Airlines System).

Though his mother, Maj, was the daughter of a prominent neurologist, she was hardly a Wallenberg for having been married to one for less than a year – and she shed the name when Raoul was still little by marrying Fredrik von Dardel, a Health Department official. Thus, Raoul was never in the mainstream of power which swept his cousins, Jacob and Marcus, to the pinnacle of the Wallenberg empire. Not quite the black sheep of the family, but a bit of a stray lamb, the little boy with curly locks, full lips, and intense, questioning eyes grew up fearless. Once, in a thunderstorm which had his friends hiding beneath their beds, he ran outside shouting, 'Let's see God's fireworks!' Hating hunting, he liberated the hounds from their kennel the night before a big foxhunt. A solitary hiker, he shunned competitive sports to such an extent that his classmates christened him 'The Only Child'.

He had a passion for planes and trains and boats. He knew all the types of World War I battleships by heart, but a naval career was ruled out when he drew green horses grazing on red grass and it was discovered that he was colour-blind. Curious how everything was put together, he would visit construction sites and converse with bricklayers. And he liked to draw on any surface he could find. Architecture loomed as a likely outlet for his interests and, after an obligatory year in the Swedish Army upon graduation from high school, he set off for the United States in 1931 to attend the University of Michigan's College of Architecture and Design in Ann Arbor.

His professors and classmates remembered him as a charming, conscientious student who lived in the architecture fraternity for a while and then boarded off-campus. The late Dr Jean Paul Slusser described Raoul as 'one of the best and brightest in thirty years' experience as a professor of drawing and painting' – despite his colour-blindness. To his freshman humanities courses, he brought some of the worldly wisdom he had acquired in his travels, writing:

> The open-mindedness of humanity, even in our generation, is a myth. Maybe the individual is open-minded on one question, but on this question he generally belongs to the minority. In most other things, he generally is extremely reactionary.

Another part of his American education was his discovery of hitchhiking. He thumbed his way to the 1932 summer Olympics in Los Angeles and, the following summer, to the Chicago World's Fair, as well as periodically to his mother's sister in Greenwich, Connecticut. 'Bus and train trips are predictable,' he wrote to his grandfather, 'but hitchhiking offers the thrill of the unknown.' Besides, it was cheap: 'I went three hundred miles on fifty cents.' The real prize of hitchhiking, however, was 'the great practice it offers in the art of diplomacy and negotiating. You have to be on your guard. And it brings you into intimate contact with so many different kinds of people.'

At the 1933 World's Fair in Chicago, he worked in the Swedish Pavilion, where, for three dollars a day, he washed windows, sold souvenirs, arranged displays of glass and porcelain, manned the cash register, and moved heavy equipment. His greatest contribution to his native land that sweltering summer, however, was teaching the pavilion's manager a cheap visual trick any architect knows: by mounting spotlights on a nearby skyscraper, they could illuminate the otherwise drab Swedish Pavilion and bathe it in an aura of distinction it didn't really have.

During his student years in Ann Arbor, Raoul Wallenberg acquired the only girlfriend he is known to have had: Bernice

Ringman, an instructor at nearby Michigan State Normal College (now Eastern Michigan University) in Ypsilanti. A physical therapist in a pioneering programme of special education for handicapped children, she laughed with him at Laurel and Hardy and Marx Brothers films, went into Detroit with him to watch Fred Astaire tapping on tour, and danced with Raoul at college proms. He often called for her in the late afternoon and helped her with her patients. When she had to bring them from hospital to homes, he would carry those who couldn't walk. Bernice, in turn, taught him to drive. In 1934, he bought a jalopy and, instead of hitchhiking, drove to Mexico. To pay his way, he sketched farmhouses and landscapes and then sold his drawings to the locals for cash or lodging.

Bernice Ringman never married. In her eighties, she was living in Los Angeles and sometimes came over to the Simon Wiesenthal Centre to talk to school groups about Raoul Wallenberg and his bravery. Once, though, she recounted his aspirations and insecurities: 'He always wanted to do something outstanding in some way in some field. He was always planning something. As far as he was concerned, it was never Sunday; there was always something to do next.'

With his curly brown hair already receding and a prominent nose that was often described as aristocratic, Raoul Wallenberg was still a much-sought-after bachelor when he returned to Stockholm in 1935 with a Bachelor of Arts degree in architecture from the University of Michigan, after completing the four-and-a-half-year course in three and a half. Out of a class of 1100 Students, he won its only medal from the American Institute of Architects. On the boat home, he prepared his entry for a major Swedish architectural competition to rehabilitate the waterfront near the Royal Palace. Raoul's design – which included a museum, an outdoor swimming-pool, and a public park along the embankment – won second prize: an astonishing feat for a newcomer up against all of Sweden's best-known architects. But, in a cautious country still reeling from the Depression and girding to stay out of the Second World War, not even first-prize winners were being built; as fulfilled after the war, the project bears closer resemblance to Raoul's runner-up than to the winning design.

Another obstacle to instant success in his homeland was that his American diploma didn't entitle Raoul to practise architecture in

Sweden and nothing he saw on the horizon encouraged him to study for his licence there. Instead, he was persuaded by his grandfather to acquire some commercial experience as a trainee with a trading company in South Africa for six months, and then to apprentice with a bank in Palestine. To a friend, Gustaf Wallenberg wrote of his grandson:

> Most of all, I want to make a man of him by giving him a chance to see the world and, through mixing with foreigners, to acquire what most Swedes lack: an international outlook.

Based in Cape Town, Raoul travelled the length and breadth of an uneasy, but seemingly placid, British dominion to sell chemicals, timber, and building materials for the Swedish-South Africa Export-Import Company. His employer wrote to his grandfather: 'I have found him a splendid organizer and negotiator. He has seemingly boundless energy and vitality as well as great imaginative powers: an original mind.' Another partner wrote that Raoul had the 'remarkable gift of quickly and thoroughly acquainting himself with whatever he sets his mind to.' Sharpening these skills with international experience was preparing Raoul Wallenberg for a mission which not even his great imagination and original mind could have envisioned in 1936.

From South Africa in 1936, Raoul moved on to Palestine, which England had conquered in World War I and, under League of Nations mandate, ruled imperiously as if it were an unruly British colony. His clerking for the Holland Bank branch in Haifa went unpaid, for no Swede could obtain a visa to work in a Dutch bank under the tight British population control.

In the bustling port of Haifa, he encountered the first flood of Jewish refugees from Germany to Palestine. Stripped of their proud past, their wealth and position in society, brutalized and terrorized by storm troopers who sang of '*When Jewish blood spurts from the knife*' at every parade, degraded and deprived of German citizenship by the Nuremberg Laws of 1935, they were the lucky ones who escaped early. Struggling for survival and a fresh start, these bedraggled burghers of Berlin, Munich, Stuttgart, and Hamburg touched a chord in a displaced architect in search of himself.

Palestine – which then included what are now Israel and Jordan – had been pledged as a Jewish homeland by Britain's Balfour

Declaration of 1917. It should have been the one place in the world where Jews fleeing Hitler could find a haven in the early days of the Third Reich, but now the territory's Arab natives worried that the Jewish influx would drive them out. Fuelled by the Grand Mufti of Jerusalem, Haj Amin el Husseini, a rabid Jew-hater and Nazi sympathizer, and a young nationalist named Fawzi al-Qawukji, who openly imitated Hitler, the combustion point came on 19 April 1936, when Palestinian Arabs set fire to Jewish villages and ambushed hundreds of Jewish settlers.

From the outset of their Palestinian mandate, British policy had been to divide and rule. It was the same tactic they took in India, playing Hindus against Moslems, and the one the Habsburgs had used with the peoples of Galicia and the Balkans. In an effort to keep the balance of power and control the Suez Canal, their lifeline to India and their Asian colonies, the British insisted after the 1936 riots that Palestine could not absorb large numbers of immigrants. Now the desk undertakers took control. Entry requirements were tightened: a prelude to 1939's shameful 'White Paper' limiting Jewish immigration to 1500 a month for the next five years – while the Holocaust raged hottest! – and shutting it off entirely from 1944 on 'unless the Arabs of Palestine are prepared to acquiesce in it.'

In relatively peaceful Haifa in 1936, Raoul Wallenberg roomed for a while in a kosher boarding house with one of the early Displaced Persons, Ariel Kahane, a Berliner with architectural training. They talked late into the night about villas and public buildings. Kahane, who went on to become a notable Israeli town planner, would later recall: 'He was a princeling and I was at the nadir of my career. I was possibly the poorest architect of the time and he probably the richest, but we talked on completely equal terms.'

If anything, Raoul Wallenberg might have envied Kahane, for the penniless German had every opportunity while the wealthy Swede felt hemmed in by his background and profession. After three months 'engaged in routine work' at the foreign exchange desk of the Holland Bank in Haifa, he wrote to his grandfather:

> I am not made to be a banker. There is something about the profession that is too calm, cynical, and cold for me. I think that my talents lie elsewhere. I want to do something more positive than sit behind a desk all day saying no to people.

In closing, he reiterated his passion for architecture – if only there were buildings to build in pre-war Sweden!

Upon his return to Stockholm in 1937, he applied for jobs with architectural firms and submitted plans and designs – all to no avail. By early autumn of 1938, when architect Simon Wiesenthal, twenty-nine, was building his last houses in Lwów, Raoul Wallenberg, twenty-six, had yet to receive his first commission.

It was around that time that he met the actress Viveca Lindfors, then sixteen or seventeen, at a family party. Though they danced so far apart that another couple could easily have danced between them, Lindfors recalled in a 1980 interview that afterwards 'he invited me up to his grandfather's office – I thought to make love to me. But he spoke to me in an intense voice, very low, almost a whisper, of the terrible things that were being done to the Jews of Germany. I just didn't understand what he was talking about. I thought he was trying to win my sympathy or something. I was just a dumb girl at the time and I had a cold Swedish soul. I wasn't ready to appreciate a man like that.'

Other cold Swedish souls were warning against a 'Jewish invasion' of German refugees who would take jobs away from Swedes. When Stockholm University invited nine notable Jewish professors banned from teaching in Germany, the medical students demonstrated against them. In this behaviour, Sweden was hardly unique so much as symptomatic of the world's indifference to the plight of the Jews. The American Medical Association recommended that only US citizens be permitted to practise – which meant a five-year wait. The British Medical Association threatened a strike to keep 'the country [from being] inundated with émigrés' after Hitler annexed Austria. Even socialist doctors, at the 1938 conference of their Medical Practitioners union, warned of 'the dilution of our industry' with non-members, but they were outdone by Tories typified by this editorial in Lord Beaverbrook's *Sunday Express*:

> Just now, there is a big influx of foreign Jews into Britain. They are over-running the country. They are trying to enter the medical profession in great numbers. They wish to practise as dentists. Worst of all, many of them are holding themselves out to the public as psychoanalysts. A psychoanalyst needs no medical training, but arrogates to himself the functions of a doctor. And

> he often obtains an ascendancy over a patient of which he makes base use if he is a bad man.

Among these sinister figures was the father of psychoanalysis, Dr Sigmund Freud himself, who arrived in London that June and died fifteen months later.

As the war widened and Hitler kept winning, Raoul's range expanded from Berlin and Budapest to all the other places his Hungarian Jewish partner in an import/export firm, Kalman, Lauer, could no longer visit: occupied Paris and Vichy France, Norway and Denmark, Belgium and Holland. Wherever he went, Wallenberg saw shame, fear, and an indifference that seared his sensitive soul. But he also learned, in negotiating sales and licences, that one could do business with Hitler's henchmen, for not far behind the sinister spout of ideology lay the saving vices of greed and corruption. Plus an awe of authority that could be exploited to intimidate even killers running amok.

– 18 –

'I came to save a nation'

The Moscow Declaration issued by Roosevelt, Churchill, and Stalin in the autumn of 1943 was the first joint statement by the Allies to address the issue of postwar retribution for Nazi atrocities:

> Germans who take part in the wholesale shooting of Italian officers or in the execution of French, Dutch, Belgian, or Norwegian hostages or of Cretan peasants, or who have shared in slaughters inflicted on the people of Poland or in the territories of the Soviet Union which are now being swept clear of the enemy, will know that they will be brought back to the scene of their crimes and judged on the spot by the peoples whom they have outraged.

But there was no mention of the Jews. The desk undertakers were burying them even faster than the Nazis were obliterating them.

This omission outraged US Treasury Secretary Henry J. Morgenthau, who happened to be Jewish and suspected it was no accident. He asked three of his Protestant aides – Randolph Paul, John Pehle, and Josiah E. DuBois Jnr – to prepare a secret eighteen-page report which bore the shocking title 'On the Acquiescence of This Government in the Murder of the Jews'. It was a devastating wartime weapon of bureaucratic in-fighting: an inter-departmental attack on State Department officials who 'have not only failed to use the Governmental machinery at their disposal to rescue Jews from Hitler, but have even gone so far as to use this Governmental machinery to prevent the rescue of these Jews.'

On 22 January 1944, six days after reading the Treasury Department report, President Franklin D. Roosevelt created the War Refugee Board (WRB), a special agency 'to forestall the plot of the

Nazis to exterminate the Jews and other persecuted minorities of Europe.' Pehle was named director; DuBois, general counsel.

The WRB hit the ground running – by warning the Axis leaders and all Axis satellites that, after the war was won, the Allies would hold them accountable for their treatment of the Jews. While the Nazi chiefs were already far beyond redemption, uneasy puppets twitched on their strings, for the Second World War's outcome was no longer in doubt by the beginning of 1944.

The WRB's first field representative – sent to non-aligned Turkey – was Ira A. Hirschmann, a New York department-store executive who had gone straight from the Evian conference in 1938 to Vienna and stood as personal financial guarantor for importing two hundred Austrian refugees to the US. Based in Ankara for the WRB, Hirschmann quickly persuaded the Romanian government, through its Turkish legation, to empty its concentration camps in Transnistria and return the 18,000 surviving Jews to their homes to fend for themselves. Since this wasn't enough to protect them from Eichmann or home-grown fascists, Hirschmann used funds from Jewish welfare organizations to pay Black Sea captains to activate their antiquated ships and ferry Jews from Constanza in Romania to Istanbul. Between April and August of 1944, some 4000 Jews were evacuated in this way from the Balkans and transported from Turkey to Syria by train and then delivered to Palestine.

The War Refugee Board appealed to Pope Pius XII to exert his influence upon the devout Admiral Horthy, but the passive Pope waited a month before sending his personal plea. The WRB also urged neutral nations to increase their legation staffs in Budapest. Its hope was that the presence of foreign observers might moderate Nazi brutality. This hope proved futile when only one neutral showed sustained interest. That nation was Sweden. Thus was the door pried open to admit Raoul Wallenberg.

In the spring of 1944, as the noose narrowed around the necks of the Jews of Hungary, Raoul Wallenberg had offered to visit Budapest again to see what he could do for his partner Kalman Lauer's in-laws, still trapped there. Raoul had, however, been refused a visa. In early June, another opportunity presented itself when the War Refugee Board convinced Sweden it should add a special representative for humanitarian affairs to its Budapest legation. In an elevator, the WRB's Stockholm representative, Iver C. Olsen, met Lauer, who recommended Raoul for the job.

That was how Raoul Wallenberg became an American agent. Lauer approached Raoul when the Swede returned from weekend duty as an officer in the Home Guard. Raoul's response was immediate: 'I will do it gladly if I can be of help to people in need.' On 9 June 1944, Olsen met with Raoul, who had just turned thirty-two, and was impressed by his vitality and resourcefulness. With the help of US Ambassador Herschel V. Johnson, the Swedish Foreign Ministry was persuaded to name him Second Secretary of its embassy in Budapest and to give him access to funds – raised by Hungarian Jews for a rescue operation – that had already been turned over to the Swedish government. Since the WRB's total operating budget worldwide was a modest one million dollars, its spending power had been augmented by an American Jewish philanthropy, the Joint Distribution Committee, which had raised $100,000 for deposit to Raoul's account at his family's Enskilda Bank for the Budapest rescue operation. A two-week delay came from Stockholm's chief rabbi, Marcus Ehrenpreis, who hesitated over Raoul's youth and naïveté as well as the blunt cynicism with which he spoke of needing plenty of cash for bribing German and Hungarian officials.

Raoul Wallenberg had no scruples about bargaining with the devil. It was what he was being sent to Budapest to do. Besides, it was his belief that, in unlawful times such as Hitler's, any lie, any trick that defends decency or delays indecency, is not only acceptable, but urgent. As one of his assistants in Budapest would put it a short time later: 'Whatever is illegal becomes legal. The main thing is to help.'

Eventually, Rabbi Ehrenpreis was won over by Raoul's salesmanly charm and the commanding German he spoke so fluently. The rabbi bade him farewell with a Talmudic saying: 'Those who set off on a mission of humanity can be assured of God's special protection.'

On 6 July 1944, Raoul Wallenberg flew to Berlin and spent the night sitting up talking with his half-sister, Nina, and her husband, Gunnar Lagergren, a diplomat in the Swedish Embassy there. An air-raid alarm interrupted their marathon conversation, but they continued it in the bomb shelter.

Though the Swedish ambassador had reserved a night sleeper to Budapest for his guest on 9 July, Raoul knew how fast Eichmann was working and insisted on taking the first train out. Without a reservation, he perched in a corridor and leaned on his only luggage, two knapsacks, as he listened to German soldiers discussing their conquests (by that stage of the war, only romantic ones) and to air-raid sirens that made the train pull over to sidings several times during the delayed overnight journey. As Wallenberg's passenger train rolled south towards Budapest, cattle cars were carrying the Jews of Hungary north to death.

In one of his knapsacks was a cheap second-hand revolver. 'I don't want to waste money I could use to bribe Nazis,' he told a friend who wondered why he didn't buy a better weapon. 'Besides, the gun is only to give me courage. I don't plan to use it.'

Simon Wiesenthal has reflected on how a Jewish Nazi-hunter and a righteous Gentile saviour of the Jews could both have started out in the same profession as Hitler's chief engineer of destruction: 'The first time Albert Speer visited me, his first words were, "We are both architects." And I say, "Excuse me, we built in different directions." From then on, we are not more talking about architecture.' Suppose, I asked Wiesenthal, Wallenberg had come to him and said, 'We are both architects'? Without hesitation, Wiesenthal replied: 'Today I would say to him: "We were both engaged not only in building houses, but in building justice."'

As befits an architect, Raoul Wallenberg was a student of dents and precedents: dents in the armour of Eichmann's death machine and precedents for going around it.

Before his arrival, the Swedish Embassy had been giving out a limited number (some 700 in all) of provisional passports to Hungarians with established Swedish connections or reasonably official travel plans. Whether the Hungarian authorities accepted these documents was another matter – particularly where Jews were concerned – and then there was the question of crossing Nazi Germany with such a flimsy credential. Nevertheless, one Jewish merchant, Hugo Wohl, had hired a lawyer who argued that Wohl's provisional passport made him a Swedish citizen not subject to wearing the yellow star on his clothes and door. Wohl had won his case. Another Budapest businessman, Wilhelm Forgacs, working in a Jewish forced labour unit, had been rounded up for deportation. In desperation, he had brandished his hitherto futile Swedish provisional passport one last time. A Hungarian officer had hesitated and put him instead into an internment camp, from which the Swedes were able to rescue him.

'Wallenberg considered these two stories carefully. They offered amazing insight into the psychology of bureaucracy. People ready to send their fellow human beings off to untold suffering and death without a qualm could be stopped dead by the sight of an official-looking document. This was something to build on!' writes Elenore Lester in *Wallenberg: the Man in the Iron Web* (1982).

'I think I have an idea for a new and perhaps more effective document,' Wallenberg informed the Swedish ambassador at their first meeting in Budapest. What Wallenberg invented was the *Schutzpass*, a protective passport which said the bearer was emigrating to Sweden and was therefore not only under Swedish protection, but, in effect, a Swedish citizen. Wallenberg relied upon his draughtsman's training to design a document that was particularly impressive visually. Bearing a photograph of the recipient, engraved with Sweden's three-crown emblem in full blue and yellow, it looked so official that even an Eichmann might flinch at violating it.

Authorized to issue 4500 *Schutzpässe*, Wallenberg printed many times that number and extended their protection to the families of bearers. He was absolutely reckless, which shook some of his staid diplomatic associates. When he proclaimed to them, 'I came to save a nation', the unspoken question arose: '*Which nation? Hungary? Or Sweden's soul?*'

He carried his disarming arrogance to new heights in his first meeting with the Hungarian regent, Admiral Horthy, to present his credentials. At seventy-six, the towering Horthy was astonished to be lectured on humanitarianism by a very junior Swedish diplomat who warned him that he would be held accountable after the war for the fate of Hungary's Jews. Though Horthy stood a good half-foot taller than the medium-sized Wallenberg, the latter wrote home to his mother that 'I felt taller than he was.'

Raoul also wrote to his mother about his business partner's relatives:

> Please be so good as to inform Dr Lauer and his wife that I have unfortunately found out that his parents-in-law and also a small child belonging to his family are already dead. That is to say that they have been transported abroad where they will not live for very long.

In six weeks, Wallenberg had mastered the arithmetic of the Final Solution which had eluded the Allies for six years.

Had the Schutzpass *been Wallenberg's only contribution to history, he might have merited the Nobel Peace Price for which Wiesenthal keeps nominating him on the assumption that he is still alive until proven dead. 'He developed as a hero from the moment he was sent to save lives,' says Simon. 'Soon, helping others became for him more meaningful than his own life. Many times he risked his life. Eichmann tried a few times to kill him, but he could also have been killed whenever a transport of people was going out and he, with his great courage, would follow the transport in his car. When the transport stopped at a station, he would go to the prisoners and pass out as many Swedish protection passports as he had. Then he would race ahead to the next station and, when the transport arrived, make a scandal for the SS about their deporting Swedish citizens. In that way, he saved thousands from odds that were ninety-nine to one . . .'*

'Against them?' he is asked.

'Against him,' Wiesenthal clarifies, for hope was less than even one in a thousand for Hungarian deportees in the Holocaust's final fury: no more 'selections' awaited them at Auschwitz, where they were sent directly to death. And Wiesenthal wonders rhetorically: 'What did a second secretary of a little land like Sweden matter to an SS man or a Hungarian Nazi with gallons of blood on his hands already? Wallenberg's only weapons were that official-looking Schutzpass *and his personal courage.'*

There are many accounts of Raoul rushing to assembly points for deportations and asking, 'Who here has Swedish papers?' Sometimes people without passes would hold up driver's licences, prescriptions, or other Hungarian documents the Germans couldn't read. Wallenberg would issue *Schutzpässe* and then proclaim their rights before the ink was dry.

In the summer of 1944, Dr Alice Breuer was in Kistarca, a collection camp for Jews ticketed for Auschwitz. 'Suddenly,' she recalls, 'a guard came and ordered me to come along. He said I was to be released. I didn't believe him, but when I arrived at the camp exit, a car with Hungarian police was waiting. I was taken, together with three others, to the Swedish Embassy in Budapest. There I met Raoul Wallenberg for the first time. He offered me chocolate, handed me a large document, and explained that I was now a Swedish citizen with nothing to fear from the Germans and the Hungarian Nazis. "Remember that your connection with Sweden is AB Kanthal Hallstahammar," he said. "This is important. Don't forget it. Now hurry home to your husband and his parents. They are waiting for you."'

Rarely was his intervention so indirect. More than once, he stood on the roof of an outbound freight train passing out *Schutzpässe* to all within reach while the engineer sounded his whistle impatiently. At least once, German soldiers fired warning shots in the air. One jolt of the engine, one flinch by Raoul, one stray bullet, and he would have perished then and there. Sometimes he stepped in front of German guns, placing his own body between Jews and deportation. More than once, he was manhandled by guards and threatened with worse, but he would not stop. Nobody had ever seen such a man!

Hearing of Raoul's efforts, Eichmann sped up deportations. When there weren't enough trains, thousands were penned in makeshift camps near the railway yards. In the middle of the night, a young man tiptoed into the shed where Agnes Adachi and a hundred others waited for the end and, lowering his voice, apologized for stepping over them, 'but I am here to help you, so don't worry.' While they wondered to each other who this angel was who still talked to them as though they were human, Wallenberg stepped outside and started screaming at an SS officer in German: 'What are you doing with our protected people? I am taking them all with me right now!' And he did.

When Wallenberg paid his first visit to the Jewish Council of Budapest, these beleaguered bargainers mistook him for a senior Gestapo officer because he strode in and spoke German so aggressively, so intimidatingly, that any bureaucrat – Aryan or not – would quake in his boots. When he talked to their oppressors – German or Hungarian – he threatened trials and hinted that he had the power to grant immunity. 'He acted,' says one observer, 'as if the war was over and he was the victors' first emissary to Hungary.'

As soon as he'd organized a new Section C for humanitarian affairs at the Swedish Embassy on the Buda side of the Danube, he moved its operations across the river to Pest, where most of Budapest's Jews lived; he was anticipating that the Red Army, already advancing upon the capital, would enter from the Pest side sometime that autumn. Though his largely unpaid Section C staff grew to 400 Jews – for all of whom he won an exemption from wearing yellow stars and the freedom to move around the city – the first two he hired were Forgacs and Wohl, the two businessmen who had fought to win the protection of their Swedish provisional passports before he'd invented the *Schutzpass*. They had the kind of initiative Wallenberg wanted.

Edith Wohl, who went to work in Section C with the rest of her family, has recalled Raoul's impact upon his staff:

'He gave us courage. He was so courageous that he made the rest of us ashamed to be afraid. Because of him we all became more optimistic.

'He also shocked us by his behaviour. Here he was, an Aryan who didn't believe that Jews were something vile and despicable. He even socialized with us as if we were normal people. This was amazing.

'After a while, it became impossible for us to consider him a normal human being. We didn't ask ourselves the normal objective questions about his background. In fact, we didn't even know that he was a member of the Wallenberg family. Instead we came to see him as superhuman; someone who had come to Budapest to save us, a Messiah.'

With the Red Army within artillery range and the Germans poised to burn their bridges behind them, real estate was cheap in Budapest, so Wallenberg was able to buy thirty buildings in Pest which he made into 'safe houses' flying the Swedish flag and offering shelter and refuge to thousands of Jews. Some of the younger inhabitants vowed to protect Raoul's property and he even, on occasion, dressed some of his more Aryan-looking Jews in SS uniforms to stand guard outside his safe houses.

Eichmann and Wallenberg – two losers in civilian life who, in wartime, built their names in different directions – first met in late July or early August of 1944 in the Arizona night club in Budapest: at Wallenberg's instigation but Eichmann's invitation. There they discussed the possibility of Sweden buying real estate from the Nazis. Wallenberg offered 200,000 dollars for forty houses. Eichmann, who knew the Swede wanted them for sanctuaries, brushed him off lightly with: 'Surely, Mister Secretary, you can't be serious. Why, the that autumn. Though his largely unpaid Section C staff grew to 400 Jews – for all of whom he won an exemption from wearing yellow stars and the freedom to move around the city – the first two he hired were Forgacs and Wohl, the two businessmen who had fought to win the protection of their Swedish provisional passports before he'd invented the *Schutzpass*. They had the kind of initiative Wallenberg wanted.

Edith Wohl, who went to work in Section C with the rest of her family, has recalled Raoul's impact upon his staff:

'He gave us courage. He was so courageous that he made the rest of us ashamed to be afraid. Because of him we all became more optimistic.

'He also shocked us by his behaviour. Here he was, an Aryan who didn't believe that Jews were something vile and despicable. He even socialized with us as if we were normal people. This was amazing.

'After a while, it became impossible for us to consider him a normal human being. We didn't ask ourselves the normal objective questions about his background. In fact, we didn't even know that he was a member of the Wallenberg family. Instead we came to see him as superhuman; someone who had come to Budapest to save us, a Messiah.'

With the Red Army within artillery range and the Germans poised to burn their bridges behind them, real estate was cheap in Budapest, so Wallenberg was able to buy thirty buildings in Pest which he made into 'safe houses' flying the Swedish flag and offering shelter and refuge to thousands of Jews. Some of the younger inhabitants vowed to protect Raoul's property and he even, on occasion, dressed some of his more Aryan-looking Jews in SS uniforms to stand guard outside his safe houses.

Eichmann and Wallenberg – two losers in civilian life who, in wartime, built their names in different directions – first met in late July or early August of 1944 in the Arizona night club in Budapest: at Wallenberg's instigation but Eichmann's invitation. There they discussed the possibility of Sweden buying real estate from the Nazis. Wallenberg offered 200,000 dollars for forty houses. Eichmann, who knew the Swede wanted them for sanctuaries, brushed him off lightly with: 'Surely, Mister Secretary, you can't be serious. Why, the citizen with nothing to fear from the Germans and the Hungarian Nazis. "Remember that your connection with Sweden is AB Kanthal Hallstahammar," he said. "This is important. Don't forget it. Now hurry home to your husband and his parents. They are waiting for you."'

Rarely was his intervention so indirect. More than once, he stood on the roof of an outbound freight train passing out *Schutzpässe* to all within reach while the engineer sounded his whistle impatiently. At least once, German soldiers fired warning shots in the air. One jolt of the engine, one flinch by Raoul, one stray bullet, and he would have perished then and there. Sometimes he stepped in front of German guns, placing his own body between Jews and deportation. More than once, he was manhandled by guards and threatened with worse, but he would not stop. Nobody had ever seen such a man!

Hearing of Raoul's efforts, Eichmann sped up deportations. When there weren't enough trains, thousands were penned in makeshift camps near the railway yards. In the middle of the night, a young man tiptoed into the shed where Agnes Adachi and a hundred others waited for the end and, lowering his voice, apologized for stepping over them, 'but I am here to help you, so don't worry.' While they wondered to each other who this angel was who still talked to them as though they were human, Wallenberg stepped outside and started screaming at an SS officer in German: 'What are you doing with our protected people? I am taking them all with me right now!' And he did.

When Wallenberg paid his first visit to the Jewish Council of Budapest, these beleaguered bargainers mistook him for a senior Gestapo officer because he strode in and spoke German so aggressively, so intimidatingly, that any bureaucrat – Aryan or not – would quake in his boots. When he talked to their oppressors – German or Hungarian – he threatened trials and hinted that he had the power to grant immunity. 'He acted,' says one observer, 'as if the war was over and he was the victors' first emissary to Hungary.'

As soon as he'd organized a new Section C for humanitarian affairs at the Swedish Embassy on the Buda side of the Danube, he moved its operations across the river to Pest, where most of Budapest's Jews lived; he was anticipating that the Red Army, already advancing upon the capital, would enter from the Pest side sometime

Americans once offered us two million dollars for the Jews of Slovakia!* Why should the Hungarian Jews be worth less?'

Eichmann dismissed his visitor as 'soft . . . another decadent diplomat' and, says Wiesenthal, 'in his memoirs, Eichmann has just four lines about Wallenberg.' But, by the time the first deportation of Budapest's Jews was announced for 25 August 1944, Wallenberg had rallied the handful of other neutral nations represented there. A Jewish glass and ceramics manufacturer turned a building over to the Swiss legation and this 'Glass House' became another centre of sanctuary and occasional salvation for Budapest's desperate Jews. Despite friendly relations with Hitler, the Spanish and Portuguese dictatorships set up small programmes to shelter Sephardic Jews in Budapest. And the Manfred Weiss family, owners of Hungary's largest steel and munitions work, went around Eichmann to bargain with SS Major Kurt Becher, who was, literally, Heinrich Himmler's horse-trader. A long-time Himmler confidant who was sent to Hungary by the SS personnel department to buy 20,000 horses for its troops, Becher wound up acquiring the Weiss combine and becoming the head of it in exchange for the emigration to Portugal of forty-eight Weiss family members, who were flown there in two German planes. Eichmann was furious and called Becher's coup a '*Schweinerei*' (dirty trick), even though it had Himmler's tacit approval.

Monsignor Angelo Rotta, the papal nuncio in Budapest, went far beyond the realm of Hungary's Catholic Church, which concerned itself only with winning for Jews who'd been baptized as Catholics the right to wear a cross next to the yellow star. Not only did Rotta warn Admiral Horthy face to face that 'the whole world now knows what *deportation* means in practice', but he also conspired with the apostolic delegate to Turkey, Monsignor Angelo Roncalli, to provide baptismal certificates to thousands of Hungarian Jews, with or without ceremony or obligation. The instigator of this scheme had been Ira Hirschmann of the WRB, who had approached Roncalli at his summer residence on an island near Istanbul on 1 August. Without being asked, Roncalli (later the

*There is no record of such an offer, though Eichmann's deputy in Bratislava, Dieter Wisliceny, is known to have taken 50,000 dollars in 1942 from the Jewish Relief Committee there for delaying deportations.

beloved Pope John XXIII) also managed to wangle some immigration papers to Palestine from the balky British and sent those along, too.

On 21 August, as the deadline for deportation loomed, Wallenberg organized a meeting of the neutrals in Budapest which resulted in an appeal to the Hungarian government signed by the papal nuncio, the Swedish ambassador, and the Portuguese, Spanish, and Swiss chargés d'affaires, deploring and denouncing 'the deportation of the Jews', a euphemism of which they said they 'all know what this means, even though it be described as "labour service".'

Their declaration coincided with other bad news for Horthy. On 24 August, Hungary's southern neighbour, Romania, not only capitulated to the Russians, but left the Axis and declared war on Germany and Hungary. Reading the handwriting on the wall and in his hands, Horthy cancelled all deportations from Hungary.

When Himmler in Berlin upheld Horthy because Hungary was now vital for supply lines and troop movements to and from the Balkans, Eichmann asked that his SS special unit be recalled to Germany because 'they have become superfluous.' His request was granted and he was decorated with the Iron Cross Second Class for his work to date in Hungary. But Eichmann did not retreat far. Some of his key officers sprinkled themselves around the Hungarian countryside and Eichmann himself stayed on in a castle in Velem near the Austrian border as guest of the Hungarian Minister of Jewish Affairs. His host also lost his post at the end of August when Horthy, emboldened by his own move against deportations, installed a more moderate government. While proclaiming publicly that Hungary would fight to the death for the Axis, Horthy privately urged his new cabinet and Prime Minister to work toward regaining Hungarian sovereignty, liquidating the war in an honourable fashion, and 'putting an end to the inhuman, foolish, cruel persecution of the Jews.'

Throughout September, the Hungarian government made clandestine efforts to negotiate an armistice with the Allies. Toward the end of the month, Horthy sent special emissaries to Moscow to arrange Hungary's surrender. With the Red Army just fifty miles south of Budapest, and with virtually every Jew in the city outfitted with some credential or other – Swedish or Swiss, official or counterfeit – Wallenberg gave thought to winding down his Section C. He wrote to his mother:

Treblinka extermination camp

Auschwitz inmates. Children liberated from the camp in 1945

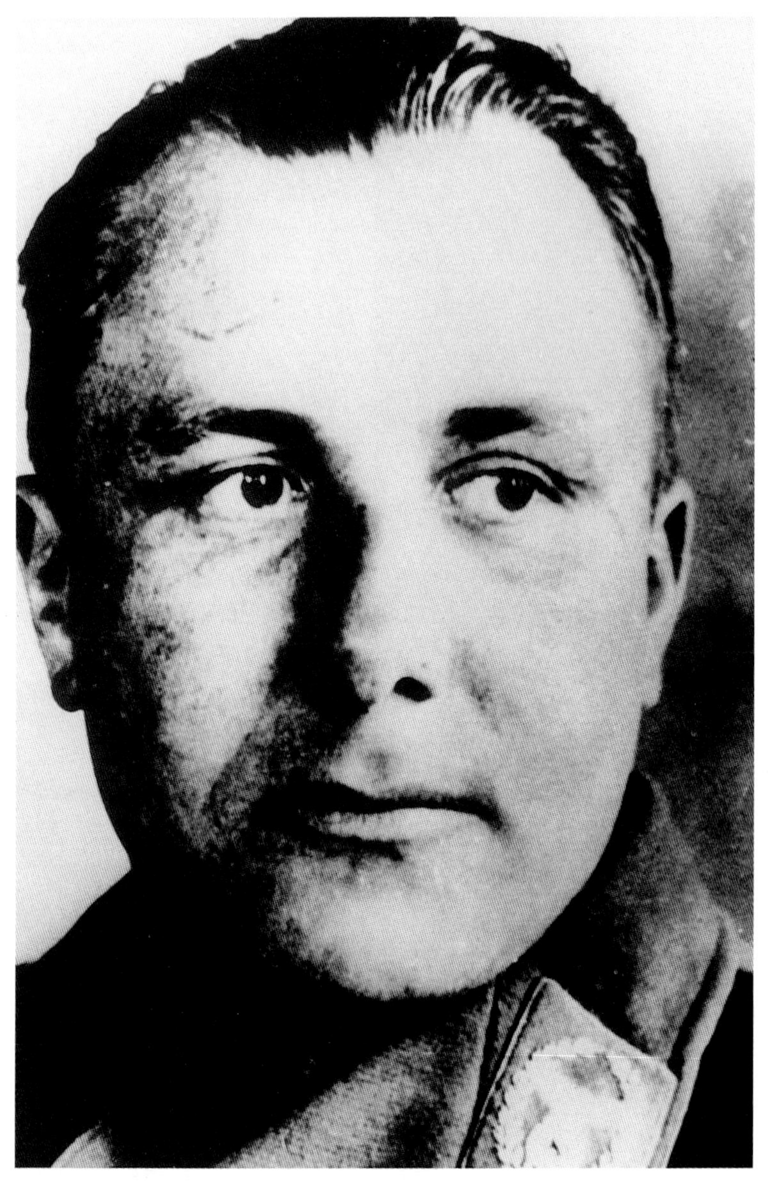

Martin Bormann

Adolf Eichmann

Eichmann on trial in Jerusalem

Raoul Wallenberg

Josef Mengele

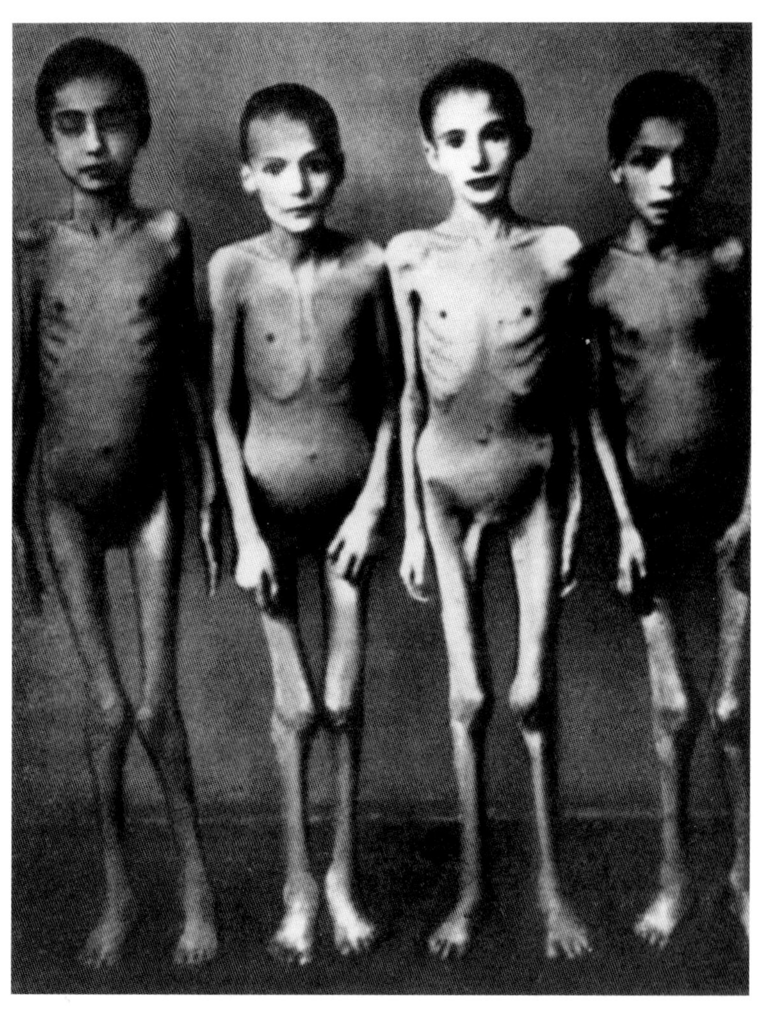

Mengele's experiment victims from Auschwitz

The Federal Police in São Paulo, Brazil released these photographs of the man they believed was Josef Mengele. They were found in the house in which he was said to have lived.

> I am doing everything in my power to return home quickly, but you understand that one cannot disband a large operation such as this on a moment's notice. When the invasion comes, the disbanding will take place more swiftly and I will try to return home in eight days.

On 29 September, he notified his home office:

> The agreement reached [in August] between the Hungarians and Germans that all Jews were to be evacuated from Budapest to the countryside outside the capital has been completely sabotaged by the Hungarian authorities and has not yet resulted in a single Jew leaving Budapest.

Nevertheless, he urged caution, for the Germans surely knew about Horthy's overtures to Moscow and seemed to be concentrating SS units in and around Budapest. Indeed, Berlin had just advised Eichmann and the officers of his seemingly dissolved SS unit to remain in Hungary in October 'in anticipation of a political change.'

As late as 12 October 1944, Raoul's dispatch to Stockholm was cautiously optimistic:

> The Russian advance has increased the hope of the Jews that their unfortunate plight will soon end. Many have voluntarily stopped wearing the Star of David. Fears that the Germans might, at the last moment, carry out a pogrom remain, despite no positive signs of such an occurrence.

Indian summer, however, was coming to an end for the Jews of Budapest. On Sunday afternoon, 15 October 1944, Horthy took to the air with a prerecorded broadcast proclaiming Hungary's withdrawal from the war: 'Hungary was forced into war against the Allies by German pressure . . . Today it is obvious to any sober-minded person that the German Reich has lost the war. We shall not become . . . the Reich's rear-guard combat zone. We have agreed to abandon further participation in the fight against the Soviet Union.' Horthy went on to say that 'under the cover of the German occupation, the Gestapo confronted the Jewish question in a manner incompatible with the dictates of humanity.' He concluded by ordering the armed forces to stay loyal and follow his instructions.

Hungary was out of the war for just a few minutes. As the people danced in the streets, as the Jews of Budapest ripped off their remaining yellow stars, as Hungarian soldiers distributed weapons to the Jewish forced labourers they'd been guarding, saying, 'We're on the same side now', the first rebroadcast of Horthy's proclamation was followed by an ominous silence and then martial music – the Hitlerite *Horst Wessel Song* – and then an announcer's voice saying flatly that the war would continue and then more martial music. Budapest was bewildered.

The explanation was simple and sinister: that morning, the Germans had kidnapped and wounded Horthy's only surviving son, Miklos Jnr. (An older son, Istvan, a pilot, had been shot down by the Russians in 1942.) Confronted by German tanks planted on the lawn of Buda Castle with their guns pointed at his windows, and told that his son would be shot if the father uttered another word of 'treason', Admiral Horthy capitulated to save his son; his nation, he now knew, was beyond rescue. He stepped down and was escorted into exile in a Bavarian castle; his son was held hostage in two concentration camps: first, Mauthausen (Simon Wiesenthal's final wartime destination), and, later, Dachau.

Surrounding Budapest with four armoured divisions, the Germans handed the country over to the Arrow Cross, Hungary's fanatical Catholic fascist movement with its own army of teenage toughs armed by the Nazis. Adolf Eichmann returned to Budapest. The real bloodbath had begun. The 'blue' Danube, normally muddy-brown around Budapest, would flow red for months.

In the first twenty-four hours of the Arrow Cross regime, some 600 Jews were dragged off the streets and out of their homes and other refuges to be murdered and dumped into the Danube. Swedish and Swiss 'safe houses' became torture chambers with a ready supply of victims. The executions provided new sport for the Arrow Cross punks. Rather than 'waste' bullets on individual Jews, they killed them three at a time by stripping them naked, tying them together, standing them in the waters of the Danube, shooting the middle one, and watching his weight drag the other two into the river. Dozens of other despairing Jews committed suicide.

On Monday afternoon, Jewish homes were padlocked for ten days 'to prevent further rioting.' Some 6000 Jews, including the chief rabbi of Budapest, were rounded up and herded into two synagogues and held for days without food or water. Borrowing a bicycle from a woman, Wallenberg – whose car had been confiscated, and whose chauffeur, a Jewish engineer named Vilmos Langfelder, had been arrested – stormed into Arrow Cross headquarters and retrieved both car and chauffeur as well as custody of the Swedish safe houses. Then he went to the Dohany Street synagogue, the largest in Europe, brushed past the Arrow Cross thugs at the door, strode down the aisle to the Ark, and asked for Jews with Swedish *Schutzpässe* to identify themselves. To others who claimed that theirs had been lost, confiscated, or torn up by the Arrow Cross, he issued blank replacements, and then formed his Jews into columns, with bearers of the most impressive documents on the flanks, and marched 300 of them past the astonished Arrow Cross men to very temporary sanctuary in the Swedish safe houses.

Two days later, prodded by Eichmann, the new Hungarian Minister of the Interior decreed that 'I recognize no letter of safe conduct of any kind nor any foreign passport which a Jew of Hungarian nationality may have received from whatever source or person.'

This surely meant the end of the *Schutzpass,* but Wallenberg had another card to play. He had befriended Baroness Elisabeth Kemény, the brand-new bride of Hungary's new Foreign Minister. She was a young and sheltered Austrian aristocrat who'd had no idea of what the man she'd just married stood for – until her honeymoon ended in Budapest, by which time she was pregnant. Wallenberg preyed on her fears that her child would grow up fatherless if her husband went to trial as a war criminal* and used her to bait another trap: like most outlaws in power, the Arrow Cross thirsted for the respectability of diplomatic recognition by such certified neutrals as Sweden and Switzerland. While Sweden had no intention of recognizing the new Hungarian regime, Wallenberg hinted that he might intervene to change his Foreign Ministry's mind.

Baron Gabor Kemény pleaded that he was the youngest and least powerful member of the new cabinet, but his bride said that if he didn't act, she was 'going home to Mother'. So persuasive was the Baroness that she accompanied her husband to the radio station on 20 October to make sure he broadcast a proper rendition of the decree Wallenberg had drafted in his name. It restored recognition of foreign passes, exempted Jewish bearers from wearing yellow

*Her husband was indeed hanged after the war.

stars, and granted extra-territorial protection to safe houses owned by neutral legations. When they returned home, the Baroness found a floor-to-ceiling plant waiting with a tiny gift card that read, 'Thanks, Wallenberg.' Her husband was furious and jealous. Meanwhile, the Arrow Cross men continued their rampage: sometimes respecting the rules, sometimes not. Every delay, however, helped.

With Jews unable to leave their homes, let alone buy food or medicine, Wallenberg bought supplies with funds channelled through Sweden by the Joint Distribution Committee. His young Zionist storm troopers and 'monsignors' delivered them to the embattled Jews of Pest. He distributed another 5000 *Schutzpässe*. When all ration cards for Jews were voided and it was decreed that all without ration cards must be deported, Wallenberg and his staff worked through the night printing and issuing 'Swedish ration cards'. Forty doctors recruited by Wallenberg moved through the ghetto inoculating its inmates against typhoid, paratyphoid, and cholera.

By early November, when Adolf Eichmann summoned Raoul Wallenberg to Gestapo headquarters in the Hotel Majestic, each was well aware of the other's work. Eichmann greeted Raoul with an intimidating question that showed he'd been looking into his adversary's past: 'Why did you go to Palestine in 1937?'

'Because it interested me,' Wallenberg answered coolly, and then, casually letting on that he'd done his homework, too, he alluded to Eichmann's 'Zionist' past by adding: 'I believe the Jews should have a state of their own, don't you?'

'I know all about you!' Eichmann screamed. 'You're a Jew-lover who receives all his dirty dollars from Roosevelt. We know that the Americans have put you in Budapest and we know that your cousin Jacob is another Jew-lover and an enemy of the Reich.' In Berlin, where Jacob Wallenberg headed the Swedish trade mission to Germany, a close German friend of his had been executed after the botched 20 July attempt to blow up Adolf Hitler. The Wallenbergs were warned to stay out of Germany. 'We have proof enough to arrest you because of your association with Jacob Wallenberg,' Eichmann bullied Raoul.

Not many men faced down Adolf Eichmann in wartime and lived very long, but Raoul was one of them. 'All right,' he said blandly. 'I'll admit that Jacob Wallenberg is an enemy of Nazism. So what? That's none of my concern.'

Infuriated by Raoul's nonchalance, Eichmann ranted: 'We know about your so-called passports. They're all frauds! The Jews who've escaped to Sweden with them are all enemies of the Reich. We know they're helping Jews escape from Denmark, too.' With no home-grown fascist movement, the Danes had been a thorn in Eichmann's side, for, even under German occupation in 1940, they had refused to persecute their 6400 Jews or even hand over 1300 German Jews who had taken refuge in Denmark before the war. When the Nazis tried to introduce the yellow star, they were told the King would be the first to wear it. Workers in Danish shipyards refused to repair German vessels. The Germans hadn't cracked down until October 1943, but the Danes hid the Jews so well that barely 500 Jews were apprehended – and even they were sent to the 'privileged' ghetto of Theresienstadt, where ninety per cent survived. Another 6000 Jews or endangered relatives (half-Jews; non-Jewish spouses, etc.) were smuggled to Sweden in late 1943, which explains Eichmann's outburst.

Wallenberg didn't even dignify Eichmann's attack with a cool answer. Instead, he presented Eichmann with a bottle of Scotch and a carton of cigarettes, for, while Raoul's research had shown that Eichmann was incorruptible and treacherous, he had also recognized that the vocational school dropout and middle-class hardware heir from Linz would be awed by an aristocrat treating him as an equal.

After they'd shared a couple of shots of Scotch, Eichmann calmed down and admitted: 'You know, Wallenberg, I have nothing against you personally; actually, I rather like you.' He even offered to allow a trainload of 'your protected Jews' to travel to Sweden if Raoul would raise a ransom for them. Wallenberg hesitated because he smelled the kind of rat that might allow Eichmann to deport the rest of Budapest's Jews while the neutral nations were applauding his token generosity.

Eichmann's good humour was short-lived. A few days later, an International Red Cross official who had been encouraged by Raoul's example to speak up to Eichmann drew this withering response: 'I am going to kill that Jew dog Wallenberg.'

Soon after this was reported back to Raoul, a sympathetic Hungarian policeman warned him that he had orders to kill him. A little later in November, a German armoured truck rammed the

Swedish second secretary's car at high speed, but Wallenberg was using another vehicle. He also took to sleeping at different addresses from night to night.

'You see, I am back again,' Eichmann had greeted the Jewish Council of Budapest in mid-October after Horthy fell. 'You forgot that Hungary is still in the shadow of the Reich. My arms are long and I can reach the Jews of Budapest as well.' He vowed that they would 'be driven out on foot this time.'

On 8 November 1944, after the Allied armies finally cut off the rail routes to Auschwitz, Eichmann ordered a death march to the Austrian border for as many Jews as could be rounded up in Budapest. Nazi Germany's official excuse for this newest atrocity was that its vast underground aircraft and armament works in Austria were running short of forced labourers, but no trains were available to transport replacements. Since any surviving able-bodied Hungarian Jewish males and females were already in labour service companies, most of the death marchers proved to be children, mothers and middle-aged women, and older folk of no use to the Third Reich's manpower needs. The pretence that these people were being sent to work in Austria was merely the paperwork of extermination, which continued to take lives long after the machinery of Auschwitz and other death camps had been dismantled.

Though it was a bitterly cold November on the Hungarian plain, some 30,000 men, women, and children were rounded up in Budapest and sent off in groups of a thousand to walk to the border, 150 miles away, without any food, shelter, or medical care. Women in high heels and men who had been working without jackets when they were grabbed were paraded down the boulevards and across the Danube bridges as 'the Jews lent to Hitler to help Hungary win the war.' Whipped forward by Hungarian guards, those who faltered were shot on the spot. Bertha Schwartz, seventy-four, reached towards a guard for support and was killed before her hand ever touched him.

In several hundred hours of audio-visual history – 'Testimony to the Truth', unrehearsed videotaped interviews with survivors – the Simon Wiesenthal Centre in Los Angeles has gathered many accounts of that death march. Susan Tabor, later a librarian at Hebrew Union College in New York City, has recalled what happened soon after it began for her and her mother:

'When we reached the outskirts of the city, we were herded into a brick factory. There were holes in the floor, which could not be seen in the darkness. Some people fell and were trampled over because the guards hurried us mercilessly into the building. Once we were all in, there was hardly room on the floor for everyone to sit. There was no light, no water, no food, no doctors, no first aid, no sanitary facilities, no one was allowed outside. Armed Nazis walked around stepping on people, abusing them, cursing and shooting. We were beaten because our spirit was broken.'

Elaborating in 1985 upon her experience, Susan Tabor explained: 'We didn't talk to each other. We were treated like animals and we felt like animals. One Nazi couldn't stand the screams of a woman who had a broken foot and couldn't move, so he stamped on her head. Her brains came out. We still didn't talk to each other.'

Before dawn the next day, when those who survived the night were supposed to set out for the border, there was the blare and glare of loudspeakers and lights and then, amidst all the black uniforms and jackboots, a man in civilian clothes materialized in the doorway. It was Wallenberg, whom she remembers as 'a frail-looking man with a sensitive face. We just stared at him, not even realizing that he was talking to us, not even comprehending what he was saying. He was telling us he had negotiated with the Nazis for the release of those of us with *Schutzpässe*. When the Germans weren't looking, he slipped extra passes to some women. He also gave us food and medical supplies.'

Even more than that, says Susan Tabor, 'he gave us hope. He gave us back our dignity, our humanity. Can you fathom the impact of what his being there meant to us? Someone cared, someone thought we were human beings worth saving. Someone who had no obligation to us fought for us! He saved our lives just by caring about us. We began to care about ourselves.'

Unblessed with *Schutzpässe,* Susan and her mother were nonetheless so emboldened by Wallenberg's visit that, a few hours later, they quietly gave their Yellow Star coats to a couple of shivering friends and slipped away from the death march: 'We didn't know if we were going to be shot in the back or not. Nazi soldiers were all around. No one stopped us and we just kept walking' – back to Budapest, where Christian friends hid them until the war was over.

Though Wallenberg freed a few hundred, many thousands of others had to make the death march to the border crossing at Hegyeshalom – and almost a quarter of them died en route. At Issaszeg, seven men too sick to walk were shot and their wives were ordered to dig their graves. Then the widows, too, were shot. A Red Cross officer – bearing food and medicine for the marchers, but not always allowed to deliver his vital cargo – has described the view from the open road to Hegyeshalom:

'Endless columns of deported persons were marched along: ragged and starving people, mortally tired, among them old and wizened creatures who could hardly crawl. Gendarmes were driving them with the butt-end of their rifles, with sticks and with whips. They had to cover thirty kilometres [nearly nineteen miles] a day until they came to a "resting place". This generally was the market-place of a town. They were driven into the square and spent the nights in the open, huddled together and shivering with cold in the chill of a November or December night. On the morning following the "rest", we saw the number of corpses that would never again rise from the frosty ground of the market square.'

On 16 November 1944, the head of the *Waffen SS*, General Hans Jüttner, drove from Vienna to Budapest with Rudolf Höss, commandant of Auschwitz, to consider alternative deportation routes. Halfway to the Hungarian capital, Eichmann's alternative came to them with what Jüttner described in 1948 testimony as a 'truly terrifying impression': columns of women, spaced twenty-five or thirty kilometres apart. 'Between the individual columns, we met stragglers who had been unable to march on and lay in the road ditch. It was immediately apparent that they would never be able to march as far as the frontier.'

Upon arrival in Budapest, General Jüttner* pulled rank on Eichmann and ordered the death march to stop immediately. The next day, 7500 Jews on the road were brought back to Budapest. Four days later, with his VIP visitors gone, Eichmann gave orders to resume the death march.

Around that time, the US State Department cabled Iver Olsen, the WRB representative in Stockholm, to 'PLEASE TRANSMIT TO THE

*General Jüttner, who was also the long-time Chief of the SS Operational Main Office, became director of a sanatorium in the German spa of Bad Tölz after the war.

SWEDISH GOVERNMENT THIS GOVERNMENT'S SINCERE APPRECIATION OF THE HUMANITARIAN ACTIVITIES OF THE SWEDISH GOVERNMENT AND OF THE COURAGE AND INGENUITY DISPLAYED BY MR WALLENBERG IN RENDERING ASSISTANCE TO THE PERSECUTED JEWS IN HUNGARY.' While Raoul hadn't directly influenced the four-day suspension of the death march, Eichmann somehow held him and Charles Lutz, the Swiss Consul, 'responsible for this outrage' through their 'abuse' of safe-conduct passes, he told Dr Kastner of the Jewish community on 21 November. Lutz had gone so far as to list 957 'protected' Jews on a single Swiss passport he'd issued.

With the resumption of the death march, Wallenberg set up checkpoints along the route where his men and others from neutral nations could hinder deportations of people holding protective papers. Then he drove with two Hungarian Jewish aides – his chauffeur, Langfelder, and Jonny Moser, his very Aryan-looking errand boy – and a Swedish Embassy colleague, Per Anger, to the village of Gönyü, a 'resting place' where a thousand Jews were lodged in two barns and hundreds more on moored barges. There they rescued more Jews with Swedish papers and unloaded sacks of food for them. As they worked, they heard the screams of those who could stand no more agony and were leaping to death in the icy river. What they didn't know was that, in the morning, those unfit to walk were pushed into the Danube by SS and Arrow Cross men.

Back on the road, Per Anger recalls passing 'masses of unfortunates, more dead than alive. Ashen-faced, they staggered forward under proddings and blows from the soldiers' rifle butts. The road was edged with bodies. We had the car full of food, which we succeeded in passing out despite such help being prohibited' but it did not go very far. At Hegyeshalom, we saw how those who arrived were turned over to an SS unit under Eichmann, who counted them like cattle. "Four hundred eighty-nine – check!" The Hungarian officer received a receipt that said everything was in order.'

Several cattle cars had been loaded with a hundred Jews each. Other boxcars waited with open doors as new hundreds were counted and assembled on the platform. Most were ticketed for Strasshof, the nearest Austrian concentration camp.

Wallenberg's pleas were ignored by Eichmann, who withdrew frostily, and were heard perfunctorily by his deputy, Wisliceny, who had already shown 'mercy' by rejecting a few handfuls of dying marchers as too weak to travel. When the Hungarians refused to accept them, they were turned loose and told to walk back to Budapest. Not one of them survived the return death march.

With time running out, Wallenberg left Wisliceny and ran towards the deportees on the platform. Shouting that those with Swedish passes should join him, he was stopped by Arrow Cross bayonets prodding his chest. Retreating, Raoul ran around to the other side of the train and climbed atop the sealed boxcars to shout through the slats: 'Are there any Swedish-protected Jews in there who've lost their papers?' To answering cries, Wallenberg shoved blank *Schutzpässe* through the openings and at any hands or fingers that appeared at his feet.

As he ran from freight car to freight car, leaping from roof to roof like a lithe movie hero, the Arrow Cross fired a volley over his head. He climbed down, but returned a few minutes later with a squad of Hungarian soldiers and a gendarme officer he'd bribed with rum and cigarettes.

By then, Wisliceny had withdrawn from the never-ending confrontation and the Arrow Cross allowed Wallenberg to set up his tables and open up his large leather-bound Register of Protected Swedish Jews. Reciting the most common Jewish names, he gave out 'replacement' *Schutzpässe* to those who stepped forward; he vouched personally for those he pretended to recognize. All the while, Jonny Moser circulated among the Jews murmuring 'Raise your hands!'

He saved 300 of the 3000 Jews assembled at Hegyeshalom on 23 November 1944. To a listless grandmother, he apologized softly: 'I am sorry. I want to save you all, but they will let me take only a few. So please forgive me, but I must take the young ones first because I want to save a nation.'

Six days later, when Eichmann found freight cars to ferry the remaining Jews directly from Budapest instead of littering the road with their corpses, Raoul saved another 300 Jews at the Josefvaros Station even after a young SS officer pointed a revolver at his stomach. Hearing about this confrontation, Eichmann dispatched a trusted aide, Captain Theodor Dannecker – who had been in charge of deporting the Jews of France, Italy, and Bulgaria to the death camps as well as the attempt to kill Raoul in a convenient auto 'accident' – to the station to chase Wallenberg away. Dannecker did so at pistol point – and another 17,000 Jewish 'workers' were sent to die in 'labour camps' in Western Hungary.*

Wallenberg and Eichmann – life and death sparring with each other while wrestling with the clock, or, as Wiesenthal puts it, 'two enemies with the same enemy: time' – had one last face-to-face encounter in December 1944, with the sound and sight of Soviet artillery fire, already on the outskirts of Budapest, as backdrop.

Hearing that Eichmann had said 'I know the war is lost, but I'm still going to win my war', Wallenberg had invited him to his apartment for dinner in one last effort to dissuade him. Then, in his flurry of activity and changes of address for safety from Eichmann, Dannecker, and others, Raoul forgot about the event.

He happened to be at home, but was taken aback when Eichmann and an aide, both in full uniform, appeared at his door. After serving his guest a drink, he ducked into another room and phoned Lars Berg, a Swedish Embassy attaché who had a cook and some food on hand. Dinner, Raoul then informed his guest with debonair aplomb, would be at Berg's on Gellért Hill.

During an elegant meal on fine china with rare wines, they talked about everything but war. Over coffee and brandies in the sitting-room, however, Wallenberg extinguished the lights and treated his guest to a picture-window view of the Red rockets' glare and the rolling thunder of an artillery barrage. 'Look how close the Bolsheviks are,' he told Eichmann. 'Your war is almost over. Nazism is doomed, finished, and so are those who cling to this hatred until the very last. It's the end of the Nazis, the end of Hitler, the end of Eichmann.'

Several of the people in that room quavered, but Eichmann didn't flinch at Raoul's attack. 'All right, I agree with you,' Eichmann admitted calmly. 'I've never believed in all of Hitler's ideology, but it has, after all, given me a good career, a good life. You're right, Wallenberg. Soon, very soon, this comfortable life will end. No more airplanes bringing women and wine from France. The Russians will take my horses, my dogs, and my palace on Rose Hill. They'd probably shoot me on the spot. For me there's no escape, no

*Dannecker committed suicide in American custody in Bad Tölz on 10 December 1945.

liberation. There are, however, some consolations. If I continue to eliminate our enemies until the end, it may delay our defeat – even for just a few days. And then, when I finally do walk to the gallows, at least I'll know I've completed my mission.'

This was a rare burst of eloquence for the socially ill-at-ease Eichmann, particularly among hostile neutrals, but Simon Wiesenthal feels it was quite honest, for 'there was no question Eichmann knew the war was lost, but he wanted it to be won on one front: the liquidation of the Jews.'

After Wallenberg persisted with 'Why don't you call off your people? Why not leave now while you still can?', Eichmann pulled himself together and declared stiffly, 'Budapest will be held as though it were Berlin.' Saying his farewells, he thanked his hosts for 'an exceptionally charming and interesting evening', and then added to Wallenberg: 'Now don't think we're friends. We're not. I plan to do everything I can to keep you from saving your Jews. Your diplomatic passport won't protect you from everything. Even a neutral diplomat can meet with an accident.'

When Wallenberg nodded and mentioned his car's ramming, Eichmann practically promised him another. Neither man could have imagined the accident of history that awaited Wallenberg less than a month later.

Eichmann fled Budapest a few nights later when the Hungarian government fled to Sopron on the border of what used to be Austria. For a few terrible weeks, Budapest belonged to the rampaging Arrow Cross hoodlums plus such freelance fanatics as Mrs Wilmos Salzer, a society lady who liked to burn naked Jewesses with candles . . . Kurt Rettman, a former telephone company official who believed in shooting Jews on sight . . . and Father Andras Kun, a Minorite monk clad in black cape and carrying giant crucifix in one hand, snub-nosed revolver in the other, and hate-literature in his robes. All three practised what they preached – and so did their followers. As his executioners aimed their rifles at Jews they had tortured within an inch of their lives, Father Kun would give the command: 'In the holy name of Jesus, fire!'

The Swedish mission declined to follow the fascist government to Sopron, but, amidst the anarchy that reigned in besieged Budapest, diplomacy was obsolete in early 1945. Raoul Wallenberg roamed

Rettman's torture chamber to pluck out those for whom he could find rescuing words or lies. He would descend at dawn upon Danube embankments where Father Kun's teenage Sunday-schoolers waited for their mentor to come and bless them before pushing the 'Christ-killers' – already packaged in bundles of three – into the river. Ironically, to bully them into untying their prey, Raoul's best bribes no longer were rum and cigarettes, but Swedish *Schutzpässe* which might help these killers elude justice when the Allies won. Though some say these documents, found on wanted men when they were apprehended, eventually compromised Wallenberg in Red Army eyes, he nevertheless dispensed them freely, for a life saved now meant more to him than a criminal caught later.

The German troops doomed to defend Budapest to the last had no time to spare for the Final Solution. When their commandant ordered the central ghetto liquidated, Wallenberg informed him: 'If you go ahead with this, I will personally see that you are hanged as a war criminal.' The general rescinded his order. Seventy thousand lives were saved.

Playing for high stakes sometimes made Wallenberg exultant. 'I *like* this dangerous game!' he told an aide. 'I *love* this dangerous game!' Only once was it too much for him to bear. Arriving too late at a 'safe' house that had been emptied of its Jews, he found it guarded by a frightened fourteen-year-old who told him in gestures that all the inhabitants had been marched into the Danube and were dead. Then the boy made one more gesture. Having given information to the enemy, he held out his hand for a tip. Instead, Raoul burst into tears.

The last time Wallenberg's diplomatic colleague Per Anger saw him was on Wednesday, 10 January 1945, when Anger pleaded with Raoul to stay with all the other Swedes in the more secure diplomatic quarter of Buda while the battle of Budapest raged through Pest. Wallenberg, however, insisted on staying in Pest, where the last of his surviving Jews were fighting for their lives against time and the Arrow Cross.

As they drove through Pest, Anger remembers that 'again and again we had to hit the brakes of the car, for the streets were blocked by dead bodies, horses, toppled trees, and shattered buildings. But Wallenberg never hesitated at the danger.'

Anger asked him if he ever grew frightened.

'Sure, it gets a little scary sometimes,' Wallenberg conceded, 'but for me there's no choice. I've taken on this assignment and I'd never be able to go back to Stockholm without knowing inside myself I'd done all a man could do to save as many Jews as possible.'

When Wallenberg confessed to fear, Anger thought to himself: 'Only a man who can admit that is genuinely courageous.'

In its reign of terror's final days, the Arrow Cross – seeking to settle the score with Wallenberg by taking his life for all those he'd saved – raided his safest 'safe house', on Jókai Street, in the middle of the night and tore it apart looking for him. Failing to find him, they carted away all 280 Jews living there and, in the custody of the perverted Mrs Salzer and the fanatical Father Kun, 180 of them perished within a week. One who barely survived the raid was Alice Breuer, the Jewish doctor who had been rescued from a transport to Auschwitz by Wallenberg the previous summer. That had been many lives ago – for her entire family had been deported to Auschwitz and murdered there. Now she and a handful of other surviving 'Swedes' stood on a bank of the Danube – facing the river with a firing squad behind them so they could fall right into their watery grave. Instead of shots, however, a voice rang out: 'These are Swedish citizens! Release them immediately and return their belongings to them!'

For Alice Breuer, it was the Second Coming of the messiah who had already saved her once: 'For an instant, I thought: "*God has come to save us*." Then I recognized Raoul Wallenberg. To our astonishment, the executioners obeyed him. He seemed very tall indeed – and strong. He radiated power and dignity. There was truly a kind of divine aura about him on that night.'

Today, Dr Breuer lives in Stockholm, where Raoul Wallenberg doesn't.

With the fascists still hunting him, Wallenberg and his driver, Langfelder, caught what sleep they could at an International Red Cross house on Benczur street in Pest. There, on Saturday morning, 13 January 1945, Wallenberg met his first Soviet 'liberators'. He and Langfelder and the other transients had taken refuge in the basement kitchen while the heaviest fighting raged outside. The Russians were advancing not only in the streets, but through ancient cisterns and corridors that connected the cellars of Pest. In the early hours, fifteen Russian soldiers pounded a hole through the kitchen wall and entered in a cloud of plaster and dust.

Wallenberg immediately produced papers in Russian certifying that he was a Swedish diplomat and asked to see their commanding officer. Within hours, and sporadically throughout the next three days, he was interrogated by both the NKVD (the Soviet secret police) and the Red Army.

Between sessions with the Russians, Wallenberg moved freely through the liberated areas of Pest, resisting pleas from his friends to take sanctuary while the fighting still raged around him. He was scheming to meet Marshal Rodion Malinovski, the Red Army commander who, while reconnoitring Pest, had spotted so many foreign flags that he'd wondered aloud whether he was liberating a Swiss or Swedish city instead of a Hungarian one.

What Wallenberg wanted, first and foremost, was to warn Malinovski that the last of the SS still planned to liquidate the central ghetto of Budapest. But he also wanted to discuss a postwar Wallenberg Institute for Support and Reconstruction of all of Hungary, not just its Jewry. Repatriation, restitution, and return of property as well as reunion of families, creation of employment, medical care, and rebuilding of homes and cities were among his most ambitious goals. Having already drafted the blueprint and a first fund-raising appeal, he was impatient to begin. And naïve.

Anybody who has been 'liberated', willingly or unwillingly, by the Red Army will recognize that Wallenberg presented a profile sure to excite Soviet paranoia: wealthy; capitalist; philanthropic; an arrogant neutral ready to take bold risks; not just a friend of the Jews, but more and more willing to admit that he was an agent of both the American government and a Jewish agency. What's more, Iver Olsen, the American who hired Wallenberg for the War Refugee Board, happened to be affiliated with the Office of Strategic Services (OSS), wartime forerunner of the Central Intelligence Agency (CIA). That this was known to the Russians, if not to Raoul, made it all the more incriminating.

Simon Wiesenthal, however, says that 'what happened to Wallenberg had nothing to do with the Jews or the OSS. The Soviets were suspicious of him right away because he spoke Russian to them. In those days, a foreigner who spoke Russian was immediately a spy because the Russians themselves didn't know other languages. In Russia at that time, the only use for a foreign language was in espionage. The second thing was that Wallenberg had with him various hard currencies – dollars, Swedish crowns, British pounds – just like all spies were supposed to.'

★ ★ ★

Late on Tuesday, 16 January 1945, which proved to be his last night in Budapest, Wallenberg loaded his car with food packets and, in the fuel tank, he and his chauffeur, Langfelder, and another Jewish aide, György Szöllös, hid what Szöllös said was 'a great quantity of gold and jewels that Wallenberg was taking with him' on what he hoped would be an imminent visit to Marshal Malinovski. While it is presumed that this wealth had been entrusted or donated to Wallenberg by Hungarian Jews fleeing for their lives, this aspect has been neglected by most chroniclers of the Wallenberg case – as if it could tarnish Wallenberg's heroism!

Taking it into consideration, however, is important in trying to comprehend his incomprehensible fate, for we can only guess what the Russians thought he was up to. It is quite possible that, upon discovering the gold and jewels in his fuel tank, the Russians mistook Wallenberg for a black-marketeer. And it has only recently become significant that the Soviet unit which took Raoul into custody, the 18th Army, had as its chief political officer a newly promoted Major General, Leonid I. Brezhnev.

In interviews with Szöllös and others in Budapest right after the war, Hungarian historian Jenö Lévai made no effort to explain why Wallenberg took along this treasure, but in their 1982 book, *Lost Hero*, Swedish-born Rabbi Frederick E. Werbell and writer Thurston Clarke theorize that he planned to use it to bribe the Russians to liberate the ghetto as swiftly as possible and spare the ravaged Jews the looting and raping by Soviet troops going on elsewhere in the city: 'He had had great success bribing the Germans and their Hungarian allies; why, he must have reasoned, should the Soviets and *their* Hungarian allies be any different?' Other theories range from buying Soviet support for the Wallenberg Institute's postwar recovery plan to a well-founded fear that anything he left behind in Budapest would be pillaged by Russian soldiers.

Wiesenthal has a simpler explanation of why Wallenberg went so well heeled: 'At that time, when the world was coming to an end for the Axis, nobody would accept their paper money – Hungarian pengös, German marks – because everybody knew that, in a few weeks, you might as well eat the money for all the food it would buy.'

On the morning after he loaded up his car, Raoul Wallenberg visited the Hungarian Jew in charge of the Swiss safe house (formerly the US Embassy) and told him he was leaving for Russian headquarters in Debrecen, 125 miles to the east. Raoul remarked: 'I seem to have formed a good relationship with the Russian military.' Then he and his driver, Langfelder, visited the Benczur Street refuge and told the Jewish leader there: 'I need to pick up all my possessions because I'm leaving today for Debrecen. Please thank everybody for their hospitality and I'll call on you as soon as I return.' He estimated that he might be gone as long as eight days.

When his host pleaded with him to defer his departure, for there were still snipers and house-to-house fighting, Raoul pointed through the window. Outside, near where his own car and driver stood, were two Red Army soldiers astride motorcycles. They wore full battle dress and were armed to the teeth. In the sidecar of one motorcycle sat a squat Soviet officer, Major Dimitri Demchinkov, wearing an olive-drab greatcoat.

'They have been ordered especially for me, but I don't know whether I'm going as their guest or their prisoner,' Raoul said, almost proudly.

Flanked by his Soviet military escort, Wallenberg paid his last call in Budapest at the Swedish Hospital. En route, his Studebaker collided with a Soviet troop transport. Furious, the Russian truck-driver was ready to kill Langfelder until Major Demchinkov pulled rank, warned him he had hit a diplomatic vehicle, and ordered him off. Outside the hospital, there was a second accident: Wallenberg slipped and fell on the icy pavement. He seemed hurt, but, as he picked himself up, he deflected his friends' concern by pointing to three men emerging from the hospital and taking their first timid steps towards freedom. Each still wore a yellow star on his overcoat, but Wallenberg smiled and spoke his last recorded utterance as a free man: 'I am happy to see that my work has not been completely in vain.'

By the time the central ghetto of Budapest was liberated that night, Raoul Gustav Wallenberg had vanished from view: the first victim of the Cold War to come. It took less than a week for the hero who had fought, bluffed, and outsmarted Eichmann, the Third Reich, the Final Solution, and the Arrow Cross, saving tens of thousands of Jewish lives at great risk to his own, to be enmeshed for life (and, perhaps, death) in another criminal bureaucracy: the Iron Curtain with which Stalin had already begun to blanket Eastern Europe.

Accounts of what happened after he left Budapest for Debrecen come from prisoners and a few other civilians who saw or talked with Wallenberg or his driver, Langfelder, in the Soviet penal system. The two men told their story whenever they could in the hope that these casual contacts, if they ever went free in the West, could send word to a mostly uncaring world.

At a checkpoint on the outskirts of Budapest, NKVD officers in green uniforms with red shoulder-boards slashed Wallenberg's tyres, transferred him and Langfelder to an official Soviet car, and dismissed the military escort. Not for another thirty-six years did it become public knowledge that their abduction had been ordered by a Red Army political commissar (*politrak*), Major General Leonid Brezhnev, who later ruled the Soviet Union from 1964 until his death in 1982: a period of stagnation from which he is remembered as a coveter of fast cars and expensive trinkets.

In 1981, former Red Army officer Yaakov Menaker, who had emigrated to Israel, told a Stockholm newspaper, *Aftonbladet*, that he had met several of the officers involved at a veterans' reunion and they had referred to Wallenberg's arrest as a 'successful secret operation' directed by Brezhnev. A few days later, former Swedish Supreme Court Justice Ingrid Gärde-Widemar, head of the Swedish Wallenberg Committee, acknowledged that 'we have known since last fall that Brezhnev personally ordered the arrest of Raoul Wallenberg in Hungary in 1945 when he was a Soviet Red Army *politruk*. We are one hundred per cent sure the information is correct, but our big problem was whether we should make this public or not. We decided to keep silent in order not to jeopardize our efforts to seek Wallenberg's release.'

Brezhnev died the following year. Two years later, a Ukrainian Catholic activist, Yosyp Terelia, published in an underground journal, *Chronicle of the Catholic Church in the Ukraine*, a letter claiming that Brezhnev's main objective had been Raoul's dented Studebaker.

Terelia said he had two witnesses who had participated in the arrest, one of whom later became a Catholic and confessed his role to his priest:

> Over the years, this man had become a devout believer and told his confessor what had happened. Thus we managed to establish that Raoul Wallenberg had been arrested without the knowledge of the supreme command. He had, in fact, been arrested on the direct orders of Brezhnev. The captain of Brezhnev's guards robbed Wallenberg and confiscated his diplomatic car. Wallenberg demanded his car back, but Brezhnev had made a present of the car to one of his superiors. Knowing that Wallenberg would protest to Marshal Malinovski, Brezhnev ordered the arrest of the Swedish diplomat.

For this and other efforts, Terelia was sentenced in 1985 to twelve years of hard labour and exile.

Little knowing that they were under arrest and charged with being 'German spies' and 'not in possession of valid papers', the diplomat and his chauffeur were driven to their destination, Debrecen, but not to see Marshal Malinovski. Instead, Raoul was told he would have to confer with civilian higher-ups in Moscow Then, with four armed escorts, he and Langfelder were put aboard a train headed towards the Russian border.

Both men must have recognized that, particularly under communism, it is hardly customary to ship a chauffeur as a passenger along with an invited guest. Indeed, the decisions about Wallenberg's fate were already being taken in the Kremlin, for, in a message dated 16 January 1945 – the eve of Raoul's departure for Debrecen – Soviet Deputy Foreign Minister Vladimir Dekanosov had sent a note to Swedish Ambassador Staffan Söderblom in Moscow that 'First Secretary Raoul Wallenberg of the Swedish Legation in Budapest has gone over to the Russian side. Measures have been taken by the Soviet military authorities to protect Mr Wallenberg and his property.' Meanwhile, back in 'liberated' Budapest, the NKVD began interrogating and sometimes imprisoning those who had ever worked with Wallenberg.

Simon Wiesenthal says that 'for years after the war, there would be so many diplomats and other foreigners shuffling back and forth through Russia and its prisons that one Swedish first or second secretary wouldn't normally have worried Stalin.' But the war was not yet over in January of 1945, and Wiesenthal thinks that what *did* worry the Russians was Raoul's link with the War Refugee Board, which Stalin perceived as a front for US intelligence and for 'separate peace' negotiations by the Americans and British with Nazi Germany instead of the 'unconditional surrender' demanded by all the Allies. Indeed, the WRB's field representative in Turkey, Ira Hirschmann, had been bargaining in Ankara and the Middle East with Nazi go-betweens while other intermediaries were in contact with Heinrich Himmler, who was hoping to come to power and negotiate a 'conditional surrender' if Hitler faltered. And the 'condition' Stalin feared the most was a fantasy occasionally voiced among both Axis and Allies: what if America and Britain (and perhaps the Free French) signed a separate peace with Germany (and perhaps Japan) and victors and vanquished united to wipe out godless Bolshevism once and for all?

Learning of Hirschmann's negotiations, the Soviet Foreign Ministry vehemently vetoed all such dealings. W. Averell Harriman, the US Ambassador to Moscow, was obliged to cable Washington that the Soviet Union was not interested in the Jewish problem.

None of this was known to Raoul Wallenberg and Wilmos Langfelder who, still treated courteously as though in protective custody, bore the discomforts of a 1500-mile rail journey, largely through war-torn Romania, which took two weeks. After a brief stop at Focsani at an internment camp for foreigners, they ate dinner with their escorts at a restaurant called Luther in Iasi, the Romanian town on the Russian frontier. Then they boarded a Soviet train that took them through the Ukraine to Moscow.

No official car awaited their arrival on Wednesday, 31 January. Instead, their escorts took the Swedish diplomat and his Hungarian chauffeur on a tour of the newly completed Moscow subway: each station a museum of Russian art, some of it revolutionary, some of it Stalin Gothic. To Wallenberg as an architect, these were to be his last images of freedom. Alighting at the Dzerzhinskaya station that evening, he and Langfelder were led into a floodlit former hotel flying a red flag. This was Lubyanka Prison, headquarters of the NKVD and last known address for hundreds of thousands of political prisoners.

There Wallenberg and Langfelder were separated. There they faded from sight. By March of 1945, the Soviet-controlled Kossuth

Radio in Budapest was claiming Wallenberg had been murdered en route to Debrecen by Hungarian fascists or 'agents of the Gestapo'. This became the official Soviet line for more than a decade.

It would be more than two decades before another 'liberated' architect, Simon Wiesenthal, would first hear the name of Raoul Wallenberg and drop everything to enter his case. 'For us Jews,' says Wiesenthal today, 'human life is very holy and there is a passage in the Talmud that is maybe 1500 or 2000 years old, but it applies to Wallenberg right now. It says that when you save one human life, you save the whole world.'

– 19 –

The Wallenberg disappearance

Throughout the 1950s, as foreign captives trickled back to the West from Soviet prison camps, one could chart Raoul Wallenberg's movements (and some of his driver, Wilmos Langfelder's) from 1945 onward, if never upward, through the Gulag Archipelago: ex-citizen Alexander Solzhenitsyn's designation of his native land's vast clandestine penal system which 'begins right next to us, two yards away from us' and in which, said Solzhenitsyn in 1975, 'Raoul Wallenberg, the Swedish diplomat . . . has been imprisoned for thirty years and they will not yield him up.'

Gustav Richter, former German police attaché in Bucharest, shared cell 123 in Moscow's Lubyanka Prison, Wallenberg's first port of call in the gulag, with him for more than a month in 1945. He said Raoul asked several times: 'What will my relatives say when they learn I'm in prison?' Richter replied: 'Under the circumstances, I think you have no cause for shame.'

Twice a month, prisoners were allowed to petition any Soviet official, even Stalin. Raoul wrote to the prison director, protesting his arrest and treatment and demanding the right to contact the Swedish Embassy in Moscow. His petition went unanswered. During their time together, Richter said Raoul was taken out for interrogation only once – 'for an hour or an hour and a half,' after which he reported that he was accused of espionage and told: 'Well, we know who you are. You belong to a great capitalist family in Sweden.'

In mid-March 1945, Raoul was transferred to another Lubyanka cell which had just been vacated by Langfelder. When Wallenberg learned of his chauffeur from his cellmates, he was overjoyed and asked the prison duty officer to deliver his own cigarette ration to Langfelder. But Langfelder had been transferred to Lefortovo Prison in Moscow, after which he vanished into the more remote reaches of the gulag.

Claudio de Mohr, former Italian cultural attaché in Bulgaria, was in Lefortovo when Wallenberg was transferred across town from Lubyanka in April 1945. De Mohr was in cell 152 when new prisoners were brought into cell 151. As usual, they communicated by tapping in code on their walls, which is how de Mohr learned that one of his new neighbours in the gulag's diplomatic ghetto was 'Mr Raoul Wallenberg from the Swedish legation in Budapest.'

Bernard Rensinghoff and Ernst Wallenstein, former German attachés in Bucharest, learned from Wallenberg's tappings that he was interrogated frequently and told only that 'for political reasons, you will never be sentenced'. According to Rensinghoff, an inspector interrogating Raoul had told him 'that he was a political case. If he considered himself innocent, it was his responsibility to prove this. The best proof of his guilt was that the Swedish legation in Moscow and the Swedish government had done nothing on his case. Raoul Wallenberg had asked the inspector . . . to be allowed direct contact with the Swedish legation in Moscow or the Red Cross or at least to write to them. This request was refused with "Nobody cares about you. If the Swedish government or its legation had taken any interest in you, they would long ago have contacted you."'

The NKVD had a point. When he'd disappeared, there was heavy cable traffic about his case between Washington and his recruiter, Iver Olsen, the Treasury Department's and War Refugee Board's representative in Stockholm who also worked for the OSS. On a memo about Wallenberg, Treasury Secretary Morgenthau pencilled a note: 'I am personally interested in this man.'

Washington instructed the US Ambassador to Moscow, W. Averell Harriman, to offer the Swedes any American assistance that could hasten Raoul's return. Interviewed by a team from the Simon Wiesenthal Centre shortly before his death at ninety-four in 1986, Harriman recalled:

'I did a quite natural thing. I went to see the Swedish Ambassador and asked if there was anything we could do to help. I offered American aid and he said no, there was not a thing we could do and, under those circumstances, there wasn't.'

On 12 April 1945, around the time Wallenberg was transferred from Lubyanka to Lefortovo, Harriman cabled Washington about his meeting with the Swedish Ambassador: 'THE SWEDES SAY THEY HAVE NO REASON TO THINK THE RUSSIANS ARE NOT DOING WHAT THEY CAN AND THEY DO NOT FEEL AN APPROACH TO THE SOVIET FOREIGN OFFICE ON OUR PART WOULD BE DESIREABLE.' His cable was sent at 10 a.m. That afternoon, Franklin Delano Roosevelt died in Warm Springs, Georgia, and there was a new President, Harry S. Truman, a new attitude toward winning the war without looking back, and, before long, a new cabinet. If anyone glanced at Harriman's cable on that memorable day, it and Wallenberg were quickly forgotten in Washington. The cable was buried even before FDR was. For not the first of many times, Raoul Wallenberg was betrayed by an accident of history. It would be thirty years before America would take any further action on his behalf.

That left Wallenberg's destiny in Swedish hands. But the Swedish Ambassador in Moscow who had declined Harriman's aid Staffan Söderblom, who, as head of Foreign Ministry's political department in 1942, had buried the first eyewitness account of gassings at Belzec – handed by an appalled German technocrat named Kurt Gerstein to a Swedish diplomat, Baron Guran von Otter, on a train from Warsaw to Berlin because he 'judged it too risky to pass information from one belligerent country to another'. Face to face and behind the scenes in Budapest, Wallenberg had thwarted Eichmann, the ultimate 'desk murderer' who seldom saw his victims, but, in jail in Moscow, he was in no position to cope with a prototypical 'desk undertaker' who could bury all hope through inaction or wishful thinking.

Like Wallenberg, the staff of the Swedish Embassy in Budapest had been taken into custody by the Red Army. Shipped to Bucharest by bus and then to Odessa and Moscow by train, they wondered all the way whether they were prisoners or honoured guests. Worried that their train might be shunted to Siberia, Söderblom met them in Moscow with one repeated admonition: 'Remember, when you get home to Sweden – not one harsh word about the Russians!' Wallenberg's closest colleagues, Per Anger and Lars Berg, agreed to comply. Later, Anger would recall ruefully: 'We never suspected then that when we'd passed through Moscow, Raoul was right there, confined in Lubyanka.'

During their stay in Moscow, Berg – who had hosted Raoul's memorable dinner with Eichmann – was questioned by the NKVD about Wallenberg. On the first day, Berg was asked whether Wallenberg was a German spy. Scared though he was, Berg burst into laughter – and then told the Russians they were out of their minds.

The next day, his interrogators were back with another approach: had Wallenberg been spying for the Americans? If he wasn't working for one, he must have been working for the other. Their mentality could never understand a man who came to save a people – and, to a considerable extent, did.

Eventually, the Swedish contingent went on by train to Leningrad and then Helsinki and the Finnish port of Turku. They swallowed hard when, arriving in Stockholm on a Finnish ship on 18 April 1945, they were met by their own relieved relatives plus Raoul's mother, Maj von Dardel, who had come down to the pier just in case her son was aboard. 'Where is Raoul?' she pleaded. 'I had hoped he was with you.'

Maj von Dardel had been hoping against hope ever since early February, when she'd called upon the Soviet Ambassador to Sweden, Alexandra Mikhailovna Kollontai, and been told: 'He's safe. Don't make a fuss and he'll return.'

Madame Kollontai cuts an ambiguous figure in the Wallenberg saga. Daughter of a Czarist general, she was nonetheless a close associate of Lenin and heroine of the Soviet occupation of the Alexander Nevsky Monastery in the Revolution. A fashionable clothes-horse and friend of Raoul's banker cousin, Marcus Wallenberg, she led a movement back home to expel all non-proletarians from the Communist Party and fire all technicians trained before the Revolution. The Simon Wiesenthal Centre says she fell into disfavour with Stalin and was recalled to Moscow in 1946 because of the indiscreet assurance she gave Raoul's mother.

On the other hand, Wallenberg's Budapest ally and confidante, Baroness Elisabeth Kemeny, the Austrian bride of the Hungarian Foreign Minister who was hanged after the war, says Raoul was in contact with Madame Kollontai and not only told her his ambitious plans to rebuild the Hungarian nation and reconstruct its Jewish community, but also asked her to help the Kemenys – all of which, says Baroness Kemeny, Madame Kollontai reported to the Kremlin, thereby convincing Stalin that Raoul was a threat to the spread of communism.

Meanwhile, in Moscow, Swedish Ambassador Söderblom – prodded by Wallenberg family influence and Raoul's friends in the Foreign Ministry – made five or six perfunctory inquiries about his missing fellow diplomat. Whether the latest rumour was that Raoul had died in an auto accident or that he was alive and well and living under a pseudonym in Budapest or missing in an air raid, Söderblom invariably would caution Stockholm that this was not the time to bait the Russians, and what if Wallenberg turned up to 'tell sensational stories to the press' against Sweden's powerful and menacing eastern neighbour? Per Anger, who was reassigned to Cairo in 1946, says that 'the Foreign Office had to urge Söderblom not to fall into passivity.'

Söderblom had not even consulted with Stockholm before refusing Averell Harriman's offer. Later, Söderblom gave his Home Office to understand that the US itself had decided not to intervene. In October 1945, he reported that 'the Americans have not made any approach to the Soviets' – without mentioning who had discouraged them.

Of all the muffed opportunities to retrieve Wallenberg, the most maddening came on 15 June 1946, when Söderblom's stint in the Soviet Union was nearing an end. The only ambassadors Stalin normally saw were the US and British envoys, *when* they had special messages from their President or Prime Minister for him. The austere 'man of steel' *never* met with diplomats from small neutral nations. Well, almost never, for he granted a farewell interview to Söderblom in the Kremlin.

This rare face-to-face confrontation was the high point of a curious figure's diplomatic career, and he knew it even then. In an absolutely fawning report to the Foreign Ministry, made public only in 1980, Söderblom wrote that he found Stalin in his marshal's uniform looking 'fit and in vigorous health. His short but well-proportioned body and his regular features made an especially agreeable impression. His tone of voice and demeanour gave an impression of friendliness.' In an interview in the 1980s for an Australian film documentary, *Between the Lines*, produced by the Simon Wiesenthal Centre, Söderblom went a few steps farther, on camera. An ageing, twisted man – still full of himself in retirement – Söderblom told how his host 'shook hands with me and', as if he needed any introduction, 'said "Stalin." I nearly got tears in my eyes.'

Proud that he spoke Russian and all the more humble because he wasn't speaking through an interpreter, Söderblom told Stalin: 'I am grateful to Your Excellency that you have agreed to receive me before my departure from Moscow. I do not want to take up much more of your valuable time as I have no reason to plead with you on any matters, nor do I wish to approach you regarding any difficult problems.' He proceeded to present greetings from his King and Prime Minister before expressing Sweden's desire to live at peace as a good neighbour to the Soviet Union.

Then Stalin, every inch the gracious monarch of Marxism-Leninism and the gulag and nearly a quarter of a billion people, asked Söderblom: 'Do you have any special requests?'

To this breathtaking, but anticipated, question, Söderblom replied: 'I have nothing special to take up with you, but since you ask, I would like to mention one matter.' After sketching Swedish intervention on behalf of humanity in Budapest, he said that 'among those who saved twenty-five to thirty thousand Jews was a Swedish diplomat, Wallenberg', who was last seen with Russian soldiers when 'he disappeared without a trace.'

Stalin smiled benignly and said: 'Of course we shall look into this matter for you, Mr Ambassador. I shall write down the name to make sure I remember. The name was Wallenberg? If, as you suggest, there is any chance he is in the Soviet Union, our investigation will provide an answer.'

We all have moments when we regret saying too much. What happened next made Tage Erlander, Sweden's Prime Minister from 1951 to 1969, declare when he found out about it that the conversation between Söderblom and Stalin was 'dangerous and perhaps disastrous . . . It would have been better if it had never taken place.' Perhaps in his soul of souls, which only an Ingmar Bergman might penetrate, Söderblom lived to regret the words he volunteered when he saw the almighty Stalin actually jot down the name on a pad and stick the scrap of paper into his uniform jacket:

'*I, personally, think Wallenberg was a victim of robbers, or perhaps an accident in Budapest,*' said Söderblom.

Stalin smiled knowingly and puffed on his pipe. The audience was over. The same undertaker in diplomatic pinstripes who had once buried the Final Solution's first revelation in the files had now embalmed his countryman and colleague by shredding his last hope of intervention from above. No wonder Wallenberg's NKVD interrogator was so sure nobody cared.

While Söderblom and Stalin were consigning Raoul to oblivion or worse, Rensinghoff and Wallenstein, the German diplomats whose cell was above his, helped him with his French for an appeal he addressed to Stalin in what was then the language of diplomacy; it went unanswered. In the spring of 1947, Wallenberg tapped hastily on his ceiling, 'We are being taken away.'

Unlike the German and Italian 'enemy' diplomats, most of whom were eventually repatriated, Wallenberg the 'neutral' was absorbed into the mainstream of Soviet political prisoners shipped to Siberia, which lends credence to the theory that the Russians believed Sweden had disowned him. According to one who was in the transit room at Lefertovo when Wallenberg was shipped out, he said bitterly: 'They just want to make me disappear into darkness and fog.'

As if to make this perception of his official, on 18 August 1947, Soviet Deputy Foreign Minister Andrei Vyshinsky issued a note declaring that Wallenberg is not in the Soviet Union and he is not known to us.'

What about the 16 January 1945 letter from Soviet Deputy Foreign Minister Dekanosov to Ambassador Söderblom that Wallenberg was in Red Army hands? That, said Vyshinsky, was based on 'indirect information from a commander of infantry troops fighting for Budapest. At the time, it was impossible to verify the report. Since then, a thorough investigation has failed to produce a positive result. The Soviet officer who provided the information about Wallenberg has not been found. Nor has Wallenberg been found in the camps for prisoners of war and internees.'

Vyshinsky went on to 'draw your attention to the fact that Wallenberg in January 1945 was in a war zone where Soviet troops were involved in violent fighting at a time when anything could have happened. He could, on his own initiative, have left the region that was occupied by Soviet troops. There might have been an enemy air attack. He could have perished under enemy fire or fallen victim to an assassination attempt . . . Our own hypothesis is that Wallenberg either died during the fighting in Budapest or was abducted' by the Arrow Cross.

Though Vyshinsky's message was so self-serving that it might have been scripted by Söderblom for Stalin, there were those who still wanted very badly to believe the Big Lie. Erlander's new Swedish government was Social Democratic and its Foreign Minister, Östen Undén, was a Marxist law professor with infinite faith in the Soviet experiment. When a Wallenberg Action Committee visited Undén with evidence that Raoul was still alive in the gulag, the Foreign Minister turned to one of the members, Birgitta de Wylder-Bellander, and asked: 'Mrs Bellander, do you think Vyshinsky is lying?'

Considering that Vyshinsky had prosecuted Stalin's great purges of the 1930s, winding up many a courtroom harangue with 'Shoot the mad dogs!' Mrs Bellander's affirmative answer should not have surprised Undén the way it did. 'But this is terrible, terrible!' he burst out. 'It is quite unthinkable!' Indeed, he and most of the Foreign Ministry – to whom Wallenberg was an outsider, a wartime addition who was never 'one of us' and who might have endangered his colleagues by his boldness in Budapest – steadfastly declined to think the unthinkable

In 1947, the year Vyshinsky denied Wallenberg's presence inside the Soviet Union and presumed he had died in Hungary, Albert Einstein (1879–1955) wrote a personal letter of inquiry to Stalin, who answered the scientist with written assurance that he knew nothing about the missing Swedish diplomat. Less trusting than Raoul's own employers, Einstein joined three deputies from Sweden's Parliament the following year in nominating Wallenberg for the Nobel Peace Prize, which goes only to living persons.

There were rumblings, too, within the Swedish Foreign Ministry. According to Rabbi Abraham D. Cooper, associate dean of the Simon Wiesenthal Centre in Los Angeles, 'Lars Berg got so fed up that, after the war, he quit Sweden and quit the Foreign Service. Later, he turned up in Rio [de Janeiro] and became the Swedish Consul there . . . But he wrote a book about Wallenberg that was published in 1947 in Sweden. It was on the stands for one day. All the copies were bought up by persons unknown – presumably from the Foreign Ministry.'

To placate the Wallenberg agitators, whose efforts had made Raoul a national hero, Per Anger was assigned to pursue the case upon his return from Egypt in 1948. During Anger's two years on the job, he says, 'Undén persisted in his negative attitude, and many times I was ready to give up. I had not gained the slightest attention at the highest level for my conviction that Wallenberg was in Russian imprisonment, or for what I thought should be done to set him free.'

Late in 1950, on their way to a conference in Oslo, Undén invited Anger into his train compartment to talk over Wallenberg. Anger reiterated his certainty that Wallenberg was still alive in Soviet custody and stated his opinion that 'the only language the Russians understand in a situation such as this is: meet force with force, or offer something in exchange.' The Swiss and the Italians had retrieved their diplomats by exchanging them for Soviet agents. A Dane named Hakon Dahl, who had been in the gulag for six years, had been exchanged for a Russian jailed in Copenhagen. 'I added,' Anger remembers, 'that we in Sweden had given the Russians a billion crowns in credits during our 1946 trade negotiations without asking anything in return. We'd had several spy cases in Sweden in which Soviet citizens were involved. Was it not conceivable that instead of expelling a spy, we could hold such a person, expecting to exchange him for Wallenberg?'

'The Swedish government does not do such things,' Undén answered frostily, turning his attention to other matters. Soon after, Anger was granted a transfer.

Simon Wiesenthal concurs with Anger's viewpoint: 'There was another time when Sweden could have got Wallenberg back. The Swedish government could have exchanged him for Colonel Stig Wennerstrom, the Swedish military attaché in Moscow who was spying for the Russians for fifteen years and had the rank of a general in the KGB. When the Swedes caught him in 1963, he was sentenced to twenty years. That was before I was involved, but I have the feeling the Soviets would have given back Wallenberg for Wennerstrom. Naturally, it would have been up to Wennerstrom whether he would go – because, when he was convicted, he didn't lose his Swedish citizenship, just his freedom.'

For more than a decade, Raoul was lost from view while his mother and stepfather, his half-sister and half-brother, and a handful of his diplomatic colleagues, led by Per Anger, kept his cause alive, despite Soviet denials that Wallenberg was ever on their soil. Undén and other desk undertakers in his Swedish Foreign Ministry rebuffed and even denounced them as people who wanted 'to declare war on Russia' for one man's sake and endanger Sweden's neutrality.

To his dying day, Söderblom would argue, as he did in 1980, that he was defending Sweden's precarious neutrality in the Cold War by soft-pedalling Wallenberg in his approaches to the Kremlin: 'The political climate was such that I thought it unwise to provoke the Russians. The Soviet government had been very positive and friendly toward Sweden. I therefore considered it inappropriate for me as ambassador to make unsuitable hints or innuendoes.'

While Söderblom's defence might have looked good in the 1950s, it hardly held water in the 1980s, when Per Anger, not long after his retirement from diplomatic service as Swedish Ambassador to Canada, contended that 'a tremendous responsibility weighs upon the postwar Social Democratic governments . . . They have deliberately lain low and been unwilling to take any action they feared might have serious consequences for our relations with the Soviet Union. Were they, at first, so anxious to preserve our neutrality in the Cold War then starting, that Wallenberg was sacrificed on the altar of neutrality?'

In 1956, Prime Minister Erlander paid Sweden's first official visit to Moscow since the Revolution of 1917. At a meeting in the Kremlin, Erlander presented the new Soviet leader, Nikita Khrushchev, with the testimony of more than a dozen witnesses to Wallenberg's presence in Lubyanka and Lefortovo between 1945 and 1947 along with a strongly worded request that his fate be investigated. The hope was that a reformed regime might not only blame a miscarriage of justice upon the excesses of its Stalinist predecessors, but seek to make amends.

Only half this hope was fulfilled ten months later. On 6 February 1957, Deputy Foreign Minister Andrei Gromyko (later Foreign Minister and President) reported to the Swedish Ambassador in Moscow that Soviet authorities had made a 'thorough investigation' of the Wallenberg case and, while 'none of these efforts provided the smallest indication that Raoul Wallenberg had spent time in the Soviet Union . . . in the course of their research, the Soviet authorities had the occasion to examine the files of prison infirmaries. They discovered in Lubyanka a handwritten report which may refer to Wallenberg. The report is addressed to [V. S.] Abakumov, Minister for State Security, from A L. Smoltsov, the head of the prison hospital service. It is dated July 17, 1947: "I am writing to inform you that the prisoner Walenberg [*sic*], known to you, died suddenly in his cell last night. He was apparently the victim of a myocardiac infarctus. In view of your instructions to me to supervise Walenberg personally, I ask you to let me know who should conduct the autopsy to ascertain the cause of death."

'The same report contains a second manuscript note from Smoltsov: "Informed the minister personally. Order given to cremate the body without autopsy. 17 July 1947."'

Gromyko's memorandum went on to add that no further information, documentation, or testimony had been found: 'Smoltsov died on May 7, 1953. The above-mentioned facts lead one to conclude that Wallenberg died in July 1947. Evidently he was arrested, like many others, by the Russian Army in the area of fighting. That he was later detained in prison and that false information was given about him to the Foreign Ministry by the Chief of State Security over a number of years is one aspect of the criminal activity of Abakumov. As is well known, the latter was sentenced by the Supreme Court of Justice and executed for serious crimes.

'The Soviet Union expresses its sincere regret in relation to these circumstances and assures the government of the Kingdom of Sweden and the family of Raoul Wallenberg of its profound sympathy.'

Neither his family nor his government could accept Raoul's suffering a convenient heart arrest at thirty-four, just a few months after the last witnesses had him leaving Lefortovo for the gulag. Sweden later condemned the 'autocratic manner' in which the Soviet security police made 'a diplomat of a neutral country a prisoner' and kept him in jail. The official Swedish reply added, 'Expressing its regrets, the Soviet government has admitted its responsibility', and went on to reserve judgement, indicating that, to his fellow Swedes, Wallenberg was still alive until proven dead.

In the next three years, their faith was rewarded by testimony from four veterans of the gulag – a Swiss, an Austrian, and two Germans – placing Wallenberg in Vladimir Prison, 150 miles east of Moscow, between 1953 and 1959.

The Swiss prisoner had never seen Wallenberg, but had conversed with him in 1954 by tapping on walls. One day, Raoul had tapped: 'When you are freed, report to a Swedish consulate or legation. I am not allowed to write or receive letters.'

In early 1955, the Austrian prisoner had been put in Wallenberg's cell by mistake. Wallenberg told him he'd been kept in solitary confinement for years and implored him, upon his release, to tell any Swedish legation he'd met Raoul Wallenberg. If he couldn't remember the name, 'a Swede from Budapest' would suffice. The next day, a Soviet political officer had the Austrian removed and warned him never to tell anybody about his encounter with Wallenberg.

The two Germans told of meeting a Georgian prisoner named Simon Gogoberidse in Vladimir in 1956. Gogoberidse, an occasional cellmate of Wallenberg's, said he was told by a prison official around the time of Prime Minister Erlander's 1956 visit: 'They'll have to look for a long time to find Wallenberg.' Gogoberidse, an exiled Social Democrat who had been kidnapped from Paris by the KGB, said Wallenberg was always made to share cells with Soviet citizens serving long sentences, not with foreigners, to minimize risk of his whereabouts reaching the West.

Although Wallenberg was reported in remarkably good health (one witness later described him taking full advantage of his exercise periods, scooping up handfuls of snow and rubbing them into his face, chest, and arms to warm up before systematically exercising his whole body in the narrow pen), he went on a hunger strike in 1959. When he became ill a few months later, he was taken to the hospital wing of Moscow's Butyrka prison, whose grim high wall stretches for two blocks and, says Solzhenitsyn, makes 'the hearts of the Muscovites shiver when they see the steel maw of its gates slide open.' The earliest victim of the Cold War had slipped through a crack in history.

On March 29, 1971, Maj von Dardel wrote to Simon Wiesenthal in Austria. She told him she had read his 1967 memoir and had followed with fascination his unearthing of Eichmann and Stangl. 'If you were able to find Eichmann,' she wrote, 'surely you could find my son.' Her letter ended with 'If before I die, I could embrace my own beloved son, this is all I ask.'

Wiesenthal recalls: 'She told me that nobody cared now, that the various Wallenberg Committees exist only on paper, that there is just a mother, a father, a sister and a brother working for Wallenberg, and her son is a victim. I was going to Sweden soon, so first I sent her a letter saying I hadn't known that nothing was working. I never get involved in things other people are already occupied with. When I visited Stockholm, I met her and her husband: a lovely, charming old couple with this one sadness in their life. She lost her composure only once – when she told me she had been reading about Soviet mental hospitals – and then *she* apologized to *me* for *her* reaction: "Mr. Wiesenthal, you may imagine my feelings as a mother to think that my son Raoul is in one of these hospitals and I cannot help him." She gave me all their information and documents and I said to her: "I see I must reopen the case and bring it to life."'

'I was very busy at the time, but I told myself: "The Nazi criminals can wait, but this case cannot."'

'Because he might still be alive?' I ask him.

'Yes,' says Simon, 'and because the murderers are living free, but he is not. And one other reason: We Jews have a long historic memory. Throughout our history, we record and we remember not only the sins and crimes and atrocities against us, but all the people who have helped us in the worst of times. When I am looking for Wallenberg, not only am I doing for the Jews, I am also doing for someone who did for the Jews.'

– 20 –

Enter Wiesenthal

When Simon Wiesenthal entered the Raoul Wallenberg case a quarter of a century after his disappearance, he says there was 'no organization – just the family force – and no clamour.' To generate clamour, Wiesenthal employed the same hit-and-miss publicity-seeking technique that would work with Gustav Wagner, who succeeded Franz Stangl as commandant at Sobibor when Stangl moved up the extermination ladder to Treblinka, but would cost truth dearly in his quest for Dr Josef Mengele. This time, it worked extremely effectively in bringing Wallenberg's fate out of the gulag's darkness into the angry glare of the public eye.

A few minutes before his next scheduled press conference, Wiesenthal approached a friendly journalist and asked him 'to ask me what I am working on now. When he did, I answered that "except for the Nazis, I am preoccupied with the Wallenberg case." Well, ninety-five per cent of the journalists in that room had never heard of Raoul Wallenberg, so now I was telling the whole story to the press. It got the case more publicity outside Sweden than it had in the past twenty-five years. Then I wrote articles about him for the Dutch press, in *Der Spiegel*, in our annual report, which is distributed worldwide.'

In 1972, Moshe Leder, who had been Wiesenthal's secretary for eighteen years, emigrated to Israel to head the Russian section of Israeli Radio. Wiesenthal asked Leder 'at least once a month in your Russian and Yiddish broadcasts to the Soviet Union, please to mention the name of Raoul Wallenberg. From time to time, somebody coming out of Russia may bring news or have a reaction.' Wiesenthal recognized that he would first have to prove that Wallenberg was alive *after* 17 July 1947, the date on which Andrei

Gromyko (a decade later) had pronounced Raoul dead, before he could hope to find him – dead or alive.

When the Swedish Foreign Minister, Christer Wickman, came to Austria later in 1972, Wiesenthal – who would hold a credential from the Foreign Press Association of Vienna for twenty-eight years – attended his news conference as a journalist and asked him: 'What is the latest about the fate of Wallenberg?'

'As far as the Swedish government is concerned, the Wallenberg case is closed,' Wickman replied bluntly.

Simon says he took this personally as 'a slap in the face to me, so I said to him: "For me, it is not closed. And I am sure that, for what you are saying now so quickly and directly, the Swedish people will never forgive you."' Simon realized then and there that the solution to the Wallenberg riddle would never come from Sweden.

Such confrontations, however, made headlines and news – and brought Wiesenthal a phone call in 1974 from his first important witness, a Viennese doctor named Menachem Meltzer, who began: 'You have been talking and writing about a man with whom I met and spoke.'

'Who is the man?' Simon asked.

'Wallenberg.'

'When did you talk to him?'

'Summer of 1948.'

'One year after he died,' said Wiesenthal, probing guardedly.

'According to the Russians,' said Meltzer.

Hearing that, Wiesenthal jumped into his car and drove out to see Meltzer, who lived on the Engerthstrasse at the far end of Vienna's 'Matzoh Island', where the Wiesenthals had lived briefly during the First World War. 'I was so excited,' Wiesenthal recalls, 'that I drove too fast and got a ticket.' He brought along an assortment of photos: Wallenberg alone, other individuals, Wallenberg in groups, other groups without Wallenberg. Every time Raoul appeared, Meltzer identified him correctly. Then Wiesenthal sat back and listened to his story, which he likes to recount with a certain degree of glee:

'Meltzer was a Jewish Austrian communist who in the 1930s went to the Soviet Union to help build a socialist paradise. He got there just in time for Stalin's trials against foreigners, making them out to be spies, while back in Austria, things were going from bad to worse – meaning Hitler. As a wise Jew trapped in a situation he couldn't escape from, he decided not to wait for Stalin to make a trial for him, too: "Before they will send me to Siberia, I will go voluntarily. Once I am in Siberia, they can no longer send me to Siberia."

'So he went to the NKVD and said: "I am a doctor. I am also an idealist. I know that in Siberia there are some places without doctors. I wish to go there."'

Lying low in Siberia with all the aplomb of the Good Soldier Schweik, Meltzer survived the Second World War with a minimum of discomfort, considering his situation. When the war ended, he was chief medical officer for all of Stalin's concentration camps in northern Siberia. In the summer of 1948, he visited a labour camp in the Urals at Khal'mer Yu, which apparently was Wallenberg's second stop in Siberia after a year in Vorkuta, seventy miles north of the Arctic Circle. There Wallenberg had apparently been stripped of all diplomatic privileges in the prisoner hierarchy. His rations reduced, he was sent to work as a slave labourer in the coal mines. The fate that Eichmann would have wished Wallenberg was enforced by Eichmann's enemies, who were fast becoming his successors.

Wallenberg's defiant response was to thrive on hard labour, which led to his reassignment to Khal'mer Yu, farther north than Vorkuta. Dr Meltzer met him when workers were needed to build a dam, and he took twenty doctors north with him to examine the manpower pool at Khal'mer Yu. Meltzer told Wiesenthal:

'All the men were waiting there on long lines and we had everybody's dossier. When I looked at this one dossier and saw the name Wallenberg, that isn't such an unusual name in Russia, where many people, particularly Jews, have Germanic-sounding names. Nor did I look up when I read the first name Raoul, but, knowing that the Russian letter *R* comes out *P* in Cyrillic, I thought it was a mistake and said to the prisoner: "Your first name is Paul, isn't it?"'

'No, it's Raoul,' the man assured Meltzer. 'I am Scandinavian.'

Meltzer glanced up to see a swarthy man of medium height with sharp features and an intense stare, none of which looked very Viking to him. So he said: 'But that's not a Scandinavian name.'

'Yes, it can be,' Raoul replied. 'Do you know the explorer Amundsen?'

'The one who discovered the South Pole?'

'Yes, he was Norwegian and his first name was Roald. I am Swedish and my first name is Raoul.'

That was the extent of their conversation. Meltzer examined Wallenberg and found that, while 'he had a strong heart' (a year after his 'death by heart attack' in Lubyanka), his lungs had not yet recovered from his months in the mines. Meltzer deferred him from heavy labour for three months. Wallenberg seems to have stayed in Khal'mer Yu until early 1951, when he was transferred to a camp for political prisoners at Verkhneural'sk in the southern Urals. After two years there, he left Siberia for Vladimir.

Meltzer, the wandering Jew who had volunteered for Siberia, was repatriated to Austria in 1951. He moved to Israel and died there not long after his disclosures to Wiesenthal. But he had provided Wiesenthal, the world, the Swedish Foreign Ministry (which questioned him in Vienna), and the von Dardel family with the first written official Soviet evidence that Wallenberg was alive and reasonably well in Khal'mer Yu a year after his official demise in Moscow. 'We had proved our point,' says Simon. 'Gromyko had lied and Wallenberg could still be alive.'

In early 1979, responding to Simon's public appeal for information about Wallenberg, the Soviet dissident Yuri Belov, freed from hard labour and deported from his native land, passed through Vienna and paid a call on Wiesenthal. Belov told Simon that, back in 1963 in a Soviet prison camp, he'd been working on a sanitary detail with a Hungarian prisoner. 'The Hungarian took Belov to see an American communist who was dying of cancer in the prison hospital,' Wiesenthal recounts. 'The American had fled the [Senator Joseph] McCarthy era [of 1950s Red-hunts] in the US to escape possible jail and, soon after he settled in the workers' paradise, he tried to organize a strike, so they threw him into the Lubyanka Prison and from there they sent him to the gulag. Like every foreign prisoner, Belov's partner inquired after his own countrymen in case he could tell their families something if he ever went home, but the American said "No, I didn't meet any Hungarians, but there was a diplomat in Lubyanka who'd been working in Hungary. I don't remember his name, but he was Scandinavian – Swedish, I think. He made a hunger strike in one of the camps, so they brought him back to Butyrka Prison in Moscow and put him in the mental hospital."'

Wiesenthal asked Belov when the American had said he'd seen the Swede in Moscow. The answer was 1961. As he had with Meltzer, Wiesenthal took Belov to the Swedish Embassy to swear a deposition. Belov spent the next decade working for the International Society for Human Rights in Frankfurt cataloguing and protesting the misuses of psychiatry and other political persecution in the Soviet Union.

Meltzer and Belov are two key witnesses Wiesenthal has produced to unlock the chain of lies surrounding Wallenberg's undying existence, but he has also screened out many pretenders who come out of Russia hoping to use the name Wallenberg as a ticket to a toehold in the West. Though one or two may have been Soviet 'disinformation' artists – providing false clues which, when debunked, could discredit the whole Wallenberg quest – most were just, in Wiesenthal's words, 'crooks and confidence men without any confidence that they can survive on their own. Seventy years of revolution in Russia didn't improve the people any. They are materialists who worship capitalism so much that they think if they say names like Rockefeller or Wallenberg some of their money will rub off on them. Sometimes I am flying especially to Israel to meet such people with their stories. But as soon as I ask them "Where were you with Wallenberg?", they say to me "No, this is my secret. My life with Wallenberg will be in a book I am already writing, so I cannot tell you this. Later I let you write the preface." So I cut the interview short and go spend a couple of days with my daughter and her family, who live in Israel.'

In a slave-labour camp in the Urals near Sverdlovsk in 1972, two prisoners met and one of them said: 'My name is Asher Hanukajev.'

'I am Raoul Wallenberg,' he says the other said.

'Is Wallenberg a Jewish name?' Hanukajev says he asked.

'No, I'm a Swedish diplomat. I was kidnapped by the Russians from Hungary in 1945.'

Hanukajev says he spent four days with Wallenberg, who 'told me why he'd been kidnapped: for freeing 35,000 Jews from German occupation.' Hanukajev, who still had six years to serve on a twenty-six-year sentence, remembers Wallenberg's farewell to him: 'God help you to get out sooner. Probably they will never let me go.'

Another former Soviet prisoner, Victor Hermann, says that, in 1977, he heard Wallenberg was in 'an intermediate prison' in the central Russian city of Gorki* before being 'sent north' and that other prisoners had seen him as late as 1979. With the Soviet invasion of Afghanistan in the last hours of the seventies, détente crashed to a halt. Emigration slowed to a trickle and so did 'sightings' of Wallenberg. 'Now they mention places so far east in the Soviet Union,' Simon says, 'that they are impossible to check. In the late 1970s and well into the eighties, there were reports he was in a camp near Irkutsk for special people who should not come into contact with ordinary political prisoners. But these are not prisoners they release, so nobody can come out and say "I saw this man there." All they can say is that it is very VIP there, so it is the kind of place where they might hide Wallenberg.' Other reports have placed 'an old Swede' as far apart as the Chinese border (in the Blagoveshensk Special Psychiatric Hospital, used for brainwashing home-grown dissidents) and wandering the streets of downtown Leningrad.

A 1985 Simon Wiesenthal Centre *Trbute to the Lost Hero of the Holocaust* offered one hopeful hearing of Raoul – perhaps! In 1963, Greville Wynne, a British agent imprisoned in Lubyanka for eighteen months, was delivered to his daily airing and exercise in a solitary pen atop the prison. As Wynne reached the roof in a tiny, filthy, cage-like elevator, he heard another cage arriving at the next pen. When its gate opened, a voice called out 'Taxi!'

Wynne chuckled at this defiant humour. Five days later, it happened again.

'Are you American?' he called out.

'No, I'm Swedish!' the voice answered in English before guards subdued both men.

*Formerly Nizhni Novgorod and renamed after the writer Maxim Gorki (1868–1936) who was born there, Gorki was where the dissident physicist Andrei D. Sakharov was banished under house arrest in the 1980s. From his internal exile in Gorki in early 1981, Sakharov wrote to the Wallenberg Committee in Stockholm that 'for about ten years now, I have known about the tragic fate of Raoul Wallenberg. I consider him to be one of those people of the twentieth century to whom all mankind is greatly indebted and ought to be proud of . . . The refusal of the Soviet authorities to release Wallenberg's files would testify to the fact that they have something to hide.'

More ominously and precisely, one later report placed Wallenberg in the early 1960s on Wrangel Island, a remote, icy outpost inside the Arctic Circle some 270 miles north-west of the Alaskan coast. This account – based on the testimony of a former KGB and NKVD agent named Efim Moshinsky, who spent two years on Wrangel Island and later emigrated to Israel – had Wallenberg banished to the island prison-camp's hospital, where Soviet Navy and space scientists were said to perform medical experiments on foreign prisoners the Kremlin had already declared dead. Injected with experimental drugs, exposed to prolonged radiation, fed possibly contaminated foods, immersed under water for long periods, and breathing varying amounts of oxygen, the victims' premature official obituaries quickly became self-fulfilling prophecies.

Given half a chance, Dr Mengele could have picked up his practice there with scarcely any loss of momentum. Such a fate for a liberator like Raoul, however, might have given Kafka pause when writing *In the Penal Colony.* And it is almost unbearable to think that, in the gulag, too, there could have been a whole category of living, dying non-persons like Wallenberg.

Moshinsky said Wallenberg shared a two-room wood hut with another thorn in the Soviet side, a Russian anti-communist leader named Aleksandr Trushnovich. If Moshinsky is to be believed (and, over the years, circumstances have tended to confirm rather than refute his report), then he lends credence to *Lost Hero* authors Werbell's and Clarke's thesis – shared, incidentally, by ex-Prime Minister Erlander – that, for one reason or another, Wallenberg's health worsened on Wrangel Island and he was eventually transferred back to either Vladimir or a special Moscow prison hospital, where he died in 1964 or 1965.

Across Western Europe, Wiesenthal went on organizing Wallenberg Congresses in Austria, Holland, and West Germany. He held hearings every January, the anniversary of Raoul's disappearance, and August, the month of Raoul's birth: there is very good propaganda value, he admits, in reminding the world that Wallenberg is now 'a man nearing ninety, a man almost my age, who is still in the concentration camps of the Second World War.' He prodded Sweden to join the US, England, and Switzerland in bringing the Wallenberg case before European Security Conferences in Madrid and Vienna as a Basket

Three (Reunification of Families) issue of the 1975 Helsinki Treaty, which was reviewed periodically for compliance. He exhorted Sweden to boycott 1980's summer Olympic Games in Moscow unless the Kremlin told the truth about Wallenberg.

As it turned out, sixty-two nations stayed away from Moscow, but Sweden wasn't one of them – and the Soviet invasion of Afghanistan, not Raoul, was their reason.

Prodded by Wiesenthal and Wallenberg's siblings, the Swedish government *did*, in recent years, offer to exchange a captured communist spy or two for Raoul, but the Russians simply smiled and said the Swedes would be fools to exchange anyone for someone who was cremated in 1947. Most Swedish diplomats, too, saw a worrisome precedent: if the Russians wanted to retrieve one of their agents, they could frame a Swede in Moscow and then exchange him (as happened as recently as 1986, when an American journalist in Moscow, Nicholas Daniloff, was ensnared by the KGB after a Soviet spy was caught receiving secret data on a New York subway platform). But Wallenberg's colleague Per Anger said of the new Swedish willingness to barter: 'If only this had happened years ago, then perhaps Raoul would be a free man now.'

In the late 1970s, very late in Leonid Brezhnev's life, Wiesenthal, at Henry Kissinger's suggestion, had persuaded Armand Hammer – the American petroleum magnate who once knew Lenin and therefore was trusted by all his successors – to intervene with the Soviet President and party chief. 'One day, Hammer was talking to Brezhnev,' Wiesenthal reports, 'and Brezhnev answered that he had never heard the name Wallenberg, but added that "I will inform you." Later, he told Hammer: "Gromyko already gave the answer."' At that time, neither Wiesenthal nor Hammer knew that it was Major-General Brezhnev of the 18th Soviet Army in Hungary who had ordered Raoul's arrest in 1945.

Around the same time, a report surfaced in Israel from the dentist daughter of a former Moscow music conservatory administrator who had been jailed for eighteen months as a black-marketeer after he'd applied for an exit visa to Israel. Upon his release from Lubyanka in 1977, Jan Kaplan placed an international call to Dr Anna Kaplan Bilder in Jaffa to tell her he was out. 'How did you manage to live through all that time?' she asked her father solicitously.

'Oh, you can survive for a long time in there,' he responded.

'Why, when I was in the Butyrka prison hospital in 1975, I met a Swede who told me he'd been in prison for thirty years and he seemed reasonably healthy to me.'

Almost immediately, Anna Bilder was invited to the Swedish Embassy in Tel Aviv for an interview. Her father's remarks had coincided with intelligence received from a young Russian Jew who had gone to a May Day party at the Moscow home of a senior KGB officer. 'Much vodka was drunk,' the young man recalled, 'and the younger men at the party began to speak of dissidents and the rough time they must have in prison. The KGB officer burst out and said: "Don't you believe it! Things aren't as tough nowadays as they used to be. You can live a long time in jail now. Why, I have a Swede under my charge in Lubyanka who's been inside for thirty years!"' Only when he emigrated to Israel did the young Russian Jew hear the name of Wallenberg and the story of his disappearance. When he did, he went to the Swedish Embassy and filed a report.

On the basis of its new information, Sweden announced in early 1979 that it was formally re-opening the Wallenberg case and sent a note to the Russians requesting an investigation. The reply from Moscow to this belated inquiry was:

> There is not, and cannot be, anything new regarding the fate of Raoul Wallenberg. As already stated on innumerable occasions, he died July 1947, and the assertions that he was in the Soviet Union as late as 1975 are not in accordance with facts.

There was a more ominous response – in Moscow. On 3 February 1979, the Kaplan home was searched by Soviet criminal investigators and Jan Kaplan was re-arrested. In Israel, his daughter learned this from three anonymous phone calls (one in Hebrew and two in Russian) which warned her, for her father's sake, not to speak of Wallenberg again. As of 1986 Kaplan was still in prison.

* * *

Wiesenthal's greatest service to Wallenberg has been to focus public attention on him. Around 1972, he tried to persuade the novelist Leon Uris to write one of his fact-filled fiction epics about Raoul. But Uris said he was busy with a book about Masada, the one-time fortress of King Herod where 960 Jewish men, women, and children committed mass suicide in AD 73 rather than face total slaughter by 15,000 Roman soldiers.

'Masada has waited 2000 years. Wallenberg cannot wait that long,' Wiesenthal told Uris in vain.

In 1977, a Californian mother named Annette Lantos read a small item in the back pages of the *New York Times* saying that Simon Wiesenthal was sure Raoul Wallenberg had been alive into the 1960s and may have been sighted as recently as 1975.

To Annette Lantos, this was a voice from the dead – the deaths Wallenberg had spared her and her husband, Tom, and the death they thought Raoul had died in 1945 at Nazi hands in the battle of Budapest, as they and all other Hungarians had been told by their Soviet 'liberators' and *their* Hungarian puppets. Since 1972, under the auspices of the Jewish Community Relations Council – which sent Holocaust survivors into schools, clubs, and churches – Annette had been lecturing on the impact of one man, 'the *late* Raoul Wallenberg'.

When Annette Tillemann was twelve, her father had been dragged from a shelter by Arrow Cross men and killed in the street. But she and her mother had been saved by Wallenberg and, after surviving the war, they emigrated to Canada still thanking the 'memory' of Raoul. In 1950, Annette married Tom Lantos, who had escaped from a forced labour camp and hidden in Budapest's ghetto under Swedish protection – only to flee Hungary in 1947 after protesting communism's takeover. Tom became an economics professor at the University of California and a widely known television commentator on world affairs.

That such personally involved and well-informed people as the Lantoses should not have known Raoul might still be among the living not only tells much about official Western unconcern and Eastern disinformation, but also shows Wiesenthal's educational impact worldwide. 'Not only the Wallenberg case, but just his name, had been all but forgotten,' Annette recalls. 'At that time, it seemed that no one but his mother cared whether he lived or died. After reading the story from Wiesenthal, I was determined that from then on the rescue of Raoul Wallenberg would have to be my number-one priority.'

She formed Concerned Citizens for Wallenberg in 1977; later, it became the Free Wallenberg Association. In October 1979, US

President Jimmy Carter promised her the support of the US government in obtaining Wallenberg's release. Though Carter lost his bid for re-election the following year, Annette's husband Tom ran for Congress in the same race and withstood the Ronald Reagan Republican landslide to win election as the Democratic representative from San Mateo County. In Washington, one of his first acts was to introduce a bill making Raoul Wallenberg an honorary citizen of the United States. It passed the House of Representatives by 396 to 2 and the Senate unanimously in the autumn of 1981.

Signing the bill into law at a White House ceremony a few days later, with Wiesenthal and the Lantoses on the platform, President Reagan said that in bestowing honorary US citizenship, 'I think we're the ones that are being honoured. Raoul Wallenberg is the Swedish saviour of almost 100,000 Jewish men, women, and children. What he did, what he accomplished was of biblical proportions . . . Wherever he is, his humanity burns like a torch.' The President noted that 'Sir Winston Churchill, another man of force and fortitude, is the only other person who has received honorary US citizenship.'

In his concluding remarks, Reagan said eloquently:

'I heard someone say that a man has made at least a start in understanding the meaning of human life when he plants shade trees under which he knows he will never sit. Raoul Wallenberg is just such a man. He nurtured the lives of those he never knew at the risk of his own. And then just recently, I was told that in a special area behind the [Yad Vashem] Holocaust Memorial in Israel, Hungarian Jews now living in Sweden planted 10,000 trees in Raoul's honour.'

Turning to Raoul's half-sister and half-brother, who had come from Sweden, the President of the United States said:

'Mrs Lagergren, Mr von Dardel, we're going to do everything in our power so that your brother can sit beneath the shade of those trees and enjoy the respect and love that so many held for him.'

In January of 1981, on the thirty-sixth anniversary of Raoul's disappearance, Simon Wiesenthal convened a formal hearing in Stockholm to review testimony on the Wallenberg case. He was joined on the panel by Gideon Hausner, chief prosecutor of Adolf Eichmann in Jerusalem; Elie Wiesel, conscience and chronicler of the Holocaust (the name of which he coined); and retired Swedish Supreme Court Justice Ingrid Gärde-Widemar.

Held in co-operation with the International Sakharov Committee of Copenhagen, the Wallenberg hearing attracted such witnesses as British Member of Parliament Greville Janner and French Nobel Laureate André Lwoff, chairmen of Raoul Wallenberg Committees in their own countries, as well as Annette Lantos and Elizabeth (Mrs Daniel P.) Moynihan, secretary of the US Senators' Free Wallenberg Committee. Virtually all witnesses spoke of Raoul in the present tense.

Red herrings abound. During the Wallenberg hearing, Wiesenthal introduced excerpts from the diaries of General Gennadi Kuprianov, a Soviet war hero imprisoned by Stalin from 1948 to 1956. General Kuprianov had encountered Wallenberg thrice during his eight years in the gulag: in 1953, 1955, and early 1956. Years later, he mentioned his meetings with Wallenberg to another ex-prisoner, who later emigrated to Israel and told a Russian émigré newspaper about Kuprianov and Wallenberg. Summoned to KGB headquarters in Leningrad early in 1979, the rehabilitated retired general was warned by a colonel not to spread rumours that an officially dead person was still alive.

Four months later, Kuprianov received another ominous green summons from the KGB. This time, the colonel told him that to 'help refute American-Israeli provocations . . . you must go home now and compose your denial of these false reports.'

'But I cannot deny the truth,' Kuprianov insisted. 'I cannot say "No, I haven't met the Swede" when I met him on three different occasions.'

He was told to come back the next day with his denial. That night, the old general told his wife and his former secretary, who had stayed a family friend, that 'I don't know if I'll be able to stand that questioning.'

He went back to the KGB next morning, empty-handed. He never returned. Five days later, his wife received a call from the KGB: 'Your husband is ill. You may visit him in the police hospital.' When she went there, she was directed to the morgue. Like Raoul Wallenberg her husband had been pronounced dead of 'heart failure'.

Kuprianov's ex-secretary – whom Wiesenthal would identify only as 'I.L.' – had an exit visa at that time and came to Vienna with key pages from Kuprianov's diaries, which she had copied before the KGB seized them. Wiesenthal said he had authenticated the documents, but sceptics seized upon Wiesenthal's refusal to identify 'I.L.' and other discrepancies to condemn his hearings. Wiesenthal explained that, while 'I.L.' was now living in the US, she still had relatives in Leningrad she wished to protect. And indeed, in 1986, when I pressed Simon for more details about the Kuprianov affair, he told me to 'forget about Kuprianov; it didn't go anywhere.'

Despite dissent, the Stockholm session overwhelmingly adopted a Wiesenthal resolution pronouncing Wallenberg alive until proven otherwise. 'The family and the world have a right – in fact, a duty – to call for further investigation and clarification,' he insists. 'Until the Russians can give a better accounting than they have in the past, there is no sense debating whether he is dead or alive.'

In 1983, Wiesenthal was instrumental in reviving Albert Einstein's 1948 ploy of nominating Raoul Wallenberg for the Nobel Peace Prize. Since Nobels aren't awarded posthumously, the prize would reaffirm not only the value of Raoul's work, but a predominantly Swedish panel's faith that he is still alive somewhere. Thus far – and, it is likely, forever – the Nobel Prize has eluded both Wallenberg and Wiesenthal.

On 17 January 1985, Simon Wiesenthal sent Swedish Prime Minister Olof Palme a cable:

> FORTY YEARS AGO TODAY, A MAN TO WHOM THE FREEDOM OF OTHERS WAS MORE IMPORTANT THAN HIS OWN LIFE, WAS ARRESTED BY THE SOVIETS. THOUSANDS THANK HIM FOR THEIR LIBERTY. WHAT HE HAS ACHIEVED FOR SO MANY HUMAN BEINGS LIVING IN FREEDOM TODAY CANNOT BE BORNE UNTIL THIS BENEFACTOR AND TRUE HERO OF THE TWENTIETH CENTURY IS HIMSELF RESCUED FROM SOVIET HANDS. I AM TOGETHER WITH YOU THIS EVENING IN A SHARED WISH THAT RAOUL WALLENBERG SHOULD ONCE AGAIN PARTAKE OF THE FREEDOM HE FURTHERED.

Wiesenthal says he received a warm reply from Palme, though his secretary at the Jewish Documentation Centre has been unable to lay hands on it. Not long after Palme's assassination on a Stockholm street in early 1986, his successor Prime Minister Ingvar Carlsson, on an official visit to Moscow, raised the Wallenberg question with the new Soviet leader, Mikhail S. Gorbachev, explaining 'why the fate of Raoul Wallenberg is still important to the Swedish Government as well as to Swedish and international public opinion, and why earlier Soviet statements in his regard could not be considered satisfactory.'

Gorbachev promised to look into the matter and Carlsson wrote to the Simon Wiesenthal Centre: 'You may rest assured that Raoul Wallenberg's fate is very alive in my mind and that the Swedish Government will never relent in its effort on his behalf.'

Once Gorbachev had kicked Andrei Gromyko upstairs to the Soviet presidency in 1985, after twenty-eight years as foreign minister, an editorial crusade by the influential *New York Times* columnist A. M. Rosenthal targeted Gromyko as the 'Kremlin's living link' to Raoul Wallenberg:

> Gromyko [then] a deputy foreign minister, signed that note in 1957 saying that Mr Wallenberg was dead, but he carefully chose words that implied that the finding could be changed. Mr Gromyko now is President of the Soviet Union. He knows.
>
> And Mr Gorbachev knows and can tell the world whether Mr Wallenberg still lives. And if Mr Wallenberg does not, Mr Gorbachev can say in what manner, year, and cell the Swede of the Jews died. It is important for all people to know, particularly Russians.

In 1988, when Gromyko relinquished the presidency to party chief Gorbachev, Abe Rosenthal renewed the campaign by hinting that Gorbachev could gather strength by baring the sins of his predecessors.

In late 1989, a few months after Andrei Gromyko took his secrets to the grave, Wallenberg's half-sister and half-brother were invited to Moscow by the Soviet Foreign Ministry, whose spokesman, Gennadi I. Gerasimov, apologized to them for 'a tragic mistake. Your brother was swept up in the maelstrom of repression.' The KGB gave them a small box of Raoul's belongings: his Swedish diplomatic passport, some old bills, and a few notebooks. The KGB's deputy chairman, Vladimir Perezhkov, expressed his personal admiration for Raoul's bold deeds in Hungary and added that he had even 'become a hero in this country.' But the Russians stuck to the story that the hero died in Lubyanka in 1947. Four days later, the KGB produced the card registering Raoul as a prisoner in Moscow on 6 February 1945; it had just been discovered 'by chance'.

'We simply don't believe them,' said Nina Lagergren. 'We are convinced our brother is still alive in a prison here.'

She and Guy van Dardel visited the prison hospital at Vladimir, where Per Anger, now chairman of the Raoul Wallenberg Association, told them several witnesses had placed their half-brother in 1980. And they appeared on a popular television talk show in Moscow, where viewers were asked to call in 'if you have seen anyone you believe is Raoul Wallenberg.' Fifty callers responded.

And that's where it stood for more than a decade. Early in the twenty-first century, however, there was a brief flurry of addition and subtraction by official Russian and Swedish panels looking into Wallenberg's disappearance. In November 2000, Alexander Yakovlev, head of a Russian presidential commission investigating Wallenberg's fate, announced that he had been executed for espionage in Lubyanka prison in 1947. But on 12 January, 2001, a Swedish–Russian working group issued two different reports. The Russian side went back to his dying of a heart attack in Lubyanka in 1947. The Swedes said that there is no evidence he died.

'The most interesting possibility is death by execution or by violence,' admitted Hans Magnusson, a member of the Swedish panel, 'but we have not been able to find sustainable evidence. Therefore, we cannot exclude that he lived much longer.'

Despite the Kremlin's official wall around the Wallenberg case, Simon Wiesenthal insists: 'What is important is to destroy the legend that Wallenberg died in 1947. What we need from the Soviets is the full truth. If he is alive, where is he? If he is not alive, when and where and under what circumstances did he die? In either event, why, after so many interventions, was the man not released?' He hoped that 'today or perhaps tomorrow, Gorbachev could come out from the shadow of all his predecessors and shed the light of truth on the matter. He was the first to have absolutely nothing to lose from the truth. For finding out the truth there is no statute of limitations.'

I asked Wiesenthal: 'Given so many opportunities to return Wallenberg to freedom, why do you think the Russians chose to destroy him?'

Wiesenthal answered slowly: 'The Soviet Union, like every dictatorship, never recognized a mistake. In all history, no dictatorship ever did. And nothing has really changed from Stalin to a later regime. So long as they stay a dictatorship, even with Gorbachev, there can be no lasting change. Once they make a statement that is false, even when they know it is false, they stick with it. This is the real philosophy of any dictatorship.'

Then, almost as an aside, he added a pearl of wisdom which has eluded not just dictators through the ages, but such presidents of democracies as Richard Nixon and Kurt Waldheim – and sometimes even Wiesenthal himself:

'Brighter people know better. When I admit a mistake, I can only win.'

After the Soviet Union disintegrated in 1991 and Gorbachev became a prematurely elder statesman, I asked Simon Wiesenthal how anyone could believe that Raoul Wallenberg is still alive today. If mortality tables were kept for survival in the gulag, wouldn't the figure for more than forty-five years be as sub-zero as the Siberian temperature? And, to tell the truth, wouldn't Wiesenthal himself be surprised if Wallenberg were to turn up alive?

'A Jew should believe in miracles if he wishes to be a realist,' Simon replied. 'Whoever doesn't believe in miracles is not a realist. Look at me! In a situation where you had to fight every minute of every day for the slimmest chance to stay alive, I tried to commit suicide twice – and I survived. Who gave me the chance to survive? The Gestapo! So I believe in miracles. And I make this formula: *Raoul Wallenberg is alive so long as the Russians don't give us believable information about his death.*'

PART IV
Josef Mengele

Boy, they sure were big on crematoriums, weren't they?

–US Vice President George Bush touring Auschwitz, 1987

– 21 –

Mengele the dilettante

A British writer once asked Simon Wiesenthal in the early 1980s what mistakes he had made in his life.

*Wiesenthal replied that he was not aware of having made any, but, even if he had, he could not discuss them because neo-Nazis would make propaganda out of his admission. On another occasion, when I asked him the same question in 1983, he gave a more mellow answer: 'I know there are thousands of people waiting for me to make a mistake. Look, we had 3000 cases in thirty-eight years, but we managed only 1100 to bring to justice. Of the 3000, only four people ever sue me. Three lose the case and one is pending.' A few weeks later, that last action was dropped by the plaintiff.**

The gap between the wise man who says 'when I admit a mistake, I can only win' and the Wiesenthal who cannot afford to concede error is an age-old chasm straddled by psychiatrists with maladjusted home lives, lawyers who break the law, accountants who neglect to pay their taxes. Situated somewhere between Practice and Preach, it is filled with hundreds of human foibles which are the stuff that drama and newspapers are made of. It was through this Paradox Canyon of what Britain's Observer *rightly called 'empty bombast' by Nazi-hunters 'hot on his trail' that Josef Mengele eluded justice for the last thirty-four years of his life and six years beyond it. At the head of this pack of bloodhounds was Simon Wiesenthal, proclaiming quite sincerely that 'I have a compact with the dead. But if I could get this man, my soul would finally be at peace.'*

*The plaintiff was Friedrich Peter, leader of Austria's third-ranking Freedom Party. Back in 1975, Wiesenthal had unmasked Peter as a corporal who had received a 'battlefield commission' as a lieutenant for his 'valour' in the '1941–2 winter campaign' of the First SS Infantry Brigade: an extermination unit which massacred 13,497 civilians in the Ukraine during that winter.

He didn't and it isn't. But Paradox Canyon has many a twist and turn. Though the dead were denied their day in court with the dapper 'selector' who doomed thousands of them at Auschwitz and mutilated so many survivors in the name of medicine, and though Wiesenthal, with alarming consistency, followed every wrong trail (and just a handful of right ones) while barking up virtually every wrong tree, his 'empty bombast' made Mengele's last years a living hell on earth and the 'Angel of Death' a haunted recluse.

'When I was in the camps,' says Simon Wiesenthal, 'I hardly heard of Eichmann and never of Stangl, but the name of Dr Josef Mengele was known throughout our world, even by inmates who had never been near Auschwitz: he was a Doctor of Philosophy from the University of Munich who had studied Kant's Critique of Pure Reason, *but embraced the racist rubbish of Alfred Rosenberg, Hitler's philosopher. He was a Doctor of Medicine from the University of Frankfurt* who sacrificed thousands of children – twins from all over Europe – to painful injections that tried to change the colour of their eyes from brown to blue . . . Mengele was the perfect SS man; he would smile at pretty girls while he sent them to death. In front of the Auschwitz crematorium, he was once heard to say: "Here the Jews enter through the door and leave through the chimney."'*

Slender and impeccably garbed in his black SS officer's uniform, his boots polished to an unearthly glow, a gold rosette sewn to his lapel, Captain Mengele liked to ride to work on his bicycle. As the most decorated medical officer on the Auschwitz staff, he always wore across his chest the four decorations he'd won on the Russian front. On an occasion when one of his two Iron Crosses fell off, a platoon of prisoners crawled for their lives – scouring the dirt roads connecting the SS officers' quarters, where he lived, with the Auschwitz camp, where he had gone on administrative business, and Birkenau, where, as chief medical officer of the extermination camp, he worked out of a barracks behind the hospital. Fortunately, the medal was found on the ground.

Pedalling blithely along, this doctor in his early thirties seemed immune to the dirt, dust, and grease of the misery around him – none of which was permitted to smudge his attire – or smoke from

*In 1964, both universities revoked Mengele's degrees 'because of the crimes he committed as a doctor in the concentration camp at Auschwitz.'

the crematoria and gas chambers that were his Polish backdrop. He might be humming or whistling a melody – maybe Mozart, sometimes Wagner, but invariably with perfect pitch, for there was much that was musical about this man who lives on in the annals of infamy as Auschwitz's 'Angel of Death' or 'Exterminating Angel' long after his body failed him in the Atlantic waters off Bertioga Beach in Brazil in 1979 and his skull was exhumed and identified in 1985. Even those who saw through his heavenly and earthly disguises when he was lord of their hell were utterly beguiled:

'He stood before us, the handsome devil who decided life and death . . . He stood there like a charming, dapper dancing master directing a polonaise. Left and right and right and left his hands pointed with casual movements. He radiated an air of lightness and gracefulness, a welcome contrast to the brutal ugliness of the environs; it soothed our frayed nerves and made whatever was happening devoid of all meaning . . . A good actor? A man possessed? A cold automaton? No, a master of his profession, a devil who took pleasure in his work . . . With utter docility, the people went to the right or to the left . . . wherever the master waved them. Sometimes a daughter did not want to be parted from her mother, but the words, "You'll see each other tomorrow, after all", would reassure them completely.'

So wrote Grete Salus, a doctor's widow who was the sole survivor of Auschwitz in her family. She could never forget this younger practitioner's death-bedside manner, his 'most persuasive kindness' to those he was beckoning to extinction.

Trainside manner would be more correct. Prisoners who had been deported to Auschwitz usually met Mengele minutes after their freight trains left the main line and backed into Birkenau's drab barbed-wire corridor between the men's and women's sectors. This was the death camp's railway depot, where all the promises and lies they had been told were undone as soon as the doors slid open to the club-wielding SS greeting and rough-and-tumble unloading from unventilated freight cars that were, for many, their last homes on earth; sometimes, forty per cent of a transport was dead on arrival. Wrenched from their baggage and soon to be wrenched from each other, the living were lined up in columns of five and slowly marched past a 'selector' – in too many cases, the dashing Dr Mengele.

The 'selection ramp', where the fates of millions were decided in seconds, was just a low-slung railway platform with a track on one side and two tracks on the other. There he stood, usually with his hands clasped behind his back. His lips were tightly shut, unless he was whistling. (*The Blue Danube Waltz* and an aria from *Tosca* were favourites in his repertoire.) Sometimes he spoke. 'To the right,' he would say casually to a young woman or a strong man. 'To the left,' he would say, with a wink, to a couple of adorable children and their nervous grandmother, for all three of whom his was the last smiling face they would see on earth. Each command would be accompanied by a debonair wave of the appropriate hand. Often he wore elegant white kid gloves, which were never dirty.

Sometimes he would dispatch a child to the left and a mother to the right. 'Please, sir,' the mother would plead timidly, 'I'm the boy's mother and I'd like to go with him.' In such cases, where other SS officers would fly into murderous rages, Mengele would simply reply: 'As you wish. You may both go to the left.'

That day, 'to the left' meant immediate death in one of Birkenau's four chimneys, where, within an hour, mother and son would be smoke and ashes and tiny particles of bone. 'To the right' meant life – for a while, at least. For this group, Mengele chose men, women, and teenagers who looked as though they could work hard in Auschwitz's slave-labour factories and hospitals and on its roads.

For him, 'selections' were a game. Sometimes, he changed the rules of the game and, for a few days, 'left' was life and 'right' meant death. Many healthy mothers, upon arrival, thought they were sparing their sons hard labour when they convinced Mengele to send the lads in the other direction with their sisters and grandmothers; Mengele usually obliged. A woman with whom he worked and who knew the rules once pleaded with him when he dispatched her father to his death. 'Your father,' Mengele said cheerfully, 'is in his seventies. Don't you think he's lived long enough?'

He liked cryptic dialogues in which he understood the subtle nuances, but the other person didn't. 'Have you ever been on the other side?' he asked an ailing woman who didn't yet realize she was ticketed to the gas chamber. 'What's it like over there?'

'I don't understand your question, sir,' said the woman.

'Don't worry,' he assured her. 'You'll know the answer before long.'

Once, he stood before a dozen Yugoslav peasants who had just arrived at Birkenau. 'Sing something from Wagner for me,' he demanded. The Slavs had never heard of Wagner. For that, they died.

At one 'selection', a beautiful young girl caught his eye. 'You look like an educated person,' he told her. Then he whistled a tune. 'Do you know what that's from?' he asked in a puzzled tone.

'It's Wagner,' she said helpfully. 'I'm not sure, but I think it's from *Tannhäuser*.'

'Sorry!' said the genial master of ceremonies. 'The answer is *Lohengrin*.' And for that mistake, she went to the left.

When the first deportations from Hungary delivered a freight car-load of one hundred rabbis – all dressed in black hats and long black satin robes – Mengele formed them in a circle and made them dance. Cracking a whip, he choreographed them faster and faster and made them lift their heads up to the sky and their Lord who was on leave. Then, for entertainment's sake, he commanded them to sing – and, without skipping a beat, humiliation turned to pride as the rabbis chanted the most sublime melody in the Jewish liturgy: *Kol Nidre*, an anguished, plaintive prayer which ushers in the Day of Atonement, *Yom Kippur*, and seems to echo the Jews' long history of torture, flogging, flaying, hanging, rending, burning, and boiling. With that, the party was over for Mengele, as the hundred rabbis straightened their backs, broke their circle, and marched off defiantly to the gas chamber, chanting the Jewish death-bed (and daily) prayer: '*Shema Yisrael, Adonai eloheinu, Adonai echad.*' ('Hear O Israel, the Lord our God, the Lord is one.')

Of the millions he met in the eternal chill before the chimneys of Birkenau, Dr Mengele reserved a special welcome for those who had not been created 'in God's image', for they were laboratory animals for his diabolical pseudo-scientific 'experiments'. The author of *Auschwitz: True Tales from a Grotesque Land,* Sara Nomberg-Przytyk, remembers how 'he once brought a woman to our area who had two noses. Another time he brought a girl of about ten years of age who had the wool of a sheep on her head instead of hair. On another occasion, he brought a woman who had donkey ears.' And, of course, he adored midgets and dwarfs. He rubbed his hands with glee when one transport delivered a whole family of midgets from a circus in Budapest. He was doubly delighted to discover that they had brought their own miniature furniture with them. Personally assigned by him to private quarters, the midgets primped and powdered themselves for his house call. 'How beautiful he is! How kind!' they exclaimed. 'How lucky we are that he became our protector! How good of him to ask if we have everything we need!' When he arrived, the tiny matriarch fell at his feet, hugged his shiny boot, and started to kiss it. 'You are so kind, so gorgeous. God should reward you,' she murmured. With a flick of his foot, Mengele shook her off his boot and sent her sprawling. 'Now tell me how you lived with your midget,' he commanded. 'Speak!' Recovering herself, the woman began to tell how her husband was a loving father, a hard worker, a good provider. 'Don't tell me about that!' Mengele interrupted, frothing at the mouth. 'Only how you slept with him.'

Most of the midgets died slow, but relatively luxurious, deaths as Mengele bled them every few days to ascertain the secrets of their heredity in his 'scientific laboratories'. On blood-letting days, he gave them double rations of bread to reward them for their contribution to German research – and some of the more conscientious midgets even volunteered to be bled at more frequent intervals just to earn extra bread to feed their families.

In late 1944, when the machinery of extermination was taxed beyond capacity, Mengele took 'pity' on seventy aged women from a Jewish old people's home in Slovakia and, to 'spare' them the long death lines, had them delivered to his infirmary instead. One of them called out, 'God bless you for your goodness, that you take such pains to protect us old people!' To which Mengele responded, 'Why are you blessing me before you know me?' A few minutes later, he ordered all the old women killed by lethal injections of phenol to the heart.

Mengele's fame had preceded him when a fourteen-year-old Transylvanian Jewish scholar arrived at Auschwitz in 1944. He remembers 'the notorious Dr Mengele' as 'a typical SS officer' with 'a cruel face, but not devoid of intelligence', wearing a monocle and waving a conductor's baton which sent his subjects either right or left. By lying to Mengele that he was eighteen and a farmer, Elie Wiesel lived to bear witness to the calamity that he was the first to call 'the Holocaust' and tell the truths of the Final Solution to an uncaring world in a way that won him the 1986 Nobel Peace Prize.

In the Auschwitz memoir appropriately titled *Anus Mundi,* Polish survivor Wieslaw Kielar characterizes 'the anthropologist Dr Mengele, who was also camp doctor' as 'an exceedingly elegant and good-looking SS officer who, thanks to his attractive appearance and his good manners, conveyed the impression of a gentle and cultured man who had nothing to do with selections, phenol, and Zyklon B. What he was like in reality was something we were to learn soon enough.'

⋆⋆⋆

As a matter of fact, however, Dr Josef Mengele was no evil mastermind, no ancient dybbuk, no devil incarnate, but a dumb intellectual, a dilettante, a dabbler who used human beings as his guinea pigs. Though better educated and endowed, he was as much a loser in life as Eichmann or Stangl: a bungler whose failures bred failures, aborted starts and abrupt ends that, almost without design, carved a trail of blunders and false clues leading only to Simon Wiesenthal's greatest postwar disappointment. Even Mengele's 1979 drowning in three or four feet of water – which cost the world and Wiesenthal a chance to confront him in court – was banal and stumbling, as befits the man's mediocrity.

Oldest son of Karl and Walburga,* Josef Mengele was born heir to a farm machinery fortune in the Swabian town of Günzburg, which lies between Stuttgart and Munich, on 16 March 1911. In Günzburg – a quaintly half-timbered medieval town of 12,000 on the banks of the Danube near its source in the Black Forest – Wiesenthal says 'the Mengeles have been its first citizens for almost a century and everybody depended on them one way or another', which is why a veil of silence shrouded Josef Mengele's return visits to his home town even when he was the world's most wanted war criminal with hundreds of thousands of dollars of rewards on his head.

*Though among the most German of names, Walburga is derived from the name of an Englishwoman, St Walpurgis, an eighth-century missionary and abbess in Germany. The German *Walpurgisnacht,* witches', sabbath, is supposed to take place on 30 April, the eve of her feast day.

When he went off to university in Munich in 1930, Josef Mengele was noted only for his family name, his ballroom dancing, and the white car his parents gave him as a high school graduation present. Munich, at that time, was still the centre of the swirl of violence which Adolf Hitler had unleashed with his abortive beer-hall putsch seven years earlier, but young Mengele plodded through his PhD studies in the philosophical and medical faculties while staying aloof from current events. Although his parents had embraced Nazism early and his father had donated the Mengele factory hall for a Hitler appearance in Günzburg, young Josef did not join the Nazi Party until 1937 and the SS a year later.

By then, he was a certified physician whose mentor at medical school in Frankfurt was a name to be reckoned with in Nazi Germany: Professor Otmar von Verschuer, a 'race scientist' specializing in twins. Having hailed Hitler in 1937 as 'the first statesman to recognize hereditary biology and race hygiene as leading principles of statesmanship', von Verschuer would proclaim prophetically two years later: 'We specialists in race hygiene are proud that the work normally associated with scientific laboratories or classrooms has extended into the life of our people.'

For von Verschuer, Mengele did his dissertation on cleft palates in children and, after interning at the University Hospital in Leipzig, spent his residency at his mentor's newly endowed Institute for Eugenics at the University of Frankfurt, and stayed on as a physician there.

Early in the war, young Dr Mengele was mobilized as a physician in the *Waffen* (military) *SS* Viking Division. *'A lot of people still think* Waffen SS *means a fighting group,' Simon Wiesenthal told me in 1985. 'Yes, it started that way, but in April 1942, they transferred 34,000 guards from concentration camps and prisons and the* Einsatzgruppen *– those SS "Special Action Groups" that were sent in right behind every conquest to kill off "civilian enemies" – from the regular SS to the* Waffen SS *because they were now needed in combat. Then, in 1943, three brigades – the First and Second Infantry and the First Cavalry:* Sonderkommandos *who operated behind the front in Russia to kill thousands of Jews, gypsies, Russians, and intellectuals – were put into* Waffen SS *regiments like* Der Führer *and* Das Reich, *which already had big reputations for burning villages and slaughtering civilians. This is why, at Nuremberg after the war, the* *whole SS, including the* Waffen SS, *was condemned as a criminal organization.'**

In 1942, on the Russian front, the Viking Division penetrated the Caucasus, some 2000 miles from pre-war Germany, just before the great westward retreat began when the Germans took 300,000 casualties in the battle of Stalingrad: a turning-point in the war. That year in Russia, Mengele won his first Iron Cross for 'rescuing two wounded soldiers from a burning tank under enemy fire on the battlefield and giving them medical first aid', and his second when he was wounded himself.

While recuperating in a military hospital in Germany, Mengele contacted von Verschuer, by then director of the Kaiser Wilhelm Institute of Human Genetics and Eugenics in the Dahlem district of Berlin. In early 1943, around the time that Auschwitz was authorized to establish 'an experimental physiological, pathological station', Mengele volunteered to go there as camp doctor and von Verschuer lined up financing for him to experiment on twins, though Mengele later took advantage of Auschwitz to extend his research to hunchbacks, dwarfs, midgets, and, eventually, foetuses, babies, children, women, men, Jews, Gentiles, gypsies: a doomed cross-section of the whole human race in the Third Reich.

'More than any other SS doctor, Mengele realized himself in Auschwitz,' writes the American psychiatrist Robert J. Lifton in *The Nazi Doctors: Medical Killing and the Psychology of Genocide* (1986). 'There he came into his own – found expression for his talents, so that what had been potential became actual. Intelligent but hardly an intellectual giant, Mengele found expression and recognition in Auschwitz *beyond his talent*. The all-important Auschwitz dimension was added to . . . create a uniquely intense version of the Auschwitz self as physician-killer-researcher.

'Mengele took hold of and maximized the omnipotent authority held by any SS doctor in Auschwitz. He could give a forceful and

*Wiesenthal was talking in the context of a worldwide furore that attended a controversial 1985 visit by US President Ronald Reagan to lay wreaths of reconciliation upon *Waffen SS* graves in a military cemetery in Bitburg, West Germany. 'Those people buried in Bitburg were from *Der Führer* [regiment],' Wiesenthal pointed out, 'and some of them even have Ukrainian names.'

flowing performance in displaying that omnipotence because it blended so readily with the traits and ideology he brought to the camp. In Auschwitz, Mengele was the "right man in the right place at the right time". His energies no less than his ambition were galvanized by this Auschwitz synchronization of all his faculties.'

Hoping it would lead to a postwar professorship, he claimed his research on twins would unlock the biological secrets of multiple birth in such a way that the Master Race could eventually mass-produce its own breed of blond-haired, blue-eyed Aryan supermen: a tribe to which neither Hitler nor Himmler belonged. Neither, for that matter, did the dashing Dr Mengele.

Despite the many 'Angel of Death' accounts that picture Mengele as tall, blond, and blue-eyed, Wiesenthal has always insisted (and the recent autopsies bear him out) that Mengele was 'a small, swarthy, dark-haired man with a slight squint in his left eye and a triangular cleft between his upper front teeth. While still in Auschwitz, he was beginning to go bald. He looked like a gypsy, but wanted to look like an Aryan – which he never did.' His eyes were greenish brown, his hair dark brown, and his height around five feet eight inches.

A woman prisoner who worked as a medical and anthropological artist – diagramming and documenting Mengele's experiments – remembers him graphically as looking 'like Peter Sellers, but better . . . His head was like a cat's head. It was wide at the temples. He had a widow's peak, dark brown hair, brown eyes. His eyebrows made a kind of accent circumflex, like a cat. Using Mengele's own terminology, I would say he had an M-shaped mouth; a straight, short regular-medium nose; a wide, broad head; a mark on his left ear – a flat round disc on his ear cartilage . . . His eyes were like Peter Sellers' eyes – as though only half of the iris would show. They were dead eyes.'

In *Mother Was Not Home for Burial*, the disturbing memoir of a survivor who revisited Auschwitz in 1980 and died of grief in 1985, M. S. Arnoni recalled his one crucial glimpse, as a teenager arriving at Birkenau, of Mengele: 'He was a strikingly handsome young man. He was not huge, like most of the other SS officers. Medium height and build, his facial features were delicate and refined. No Aryan type, he was dark, around his SS officer's cap protruding silky dark hair.'

In his laboratory, an entire wall was lined with human eyes, classified by colour (from pale yellow to bright violet) and pinned like butterflies. He also tried to turn children's eyes blue by injecting them, most painfully, with methylene dye; when the experiment didn't work – and it never did! – the children were gassed. Three pairs of twins, all under ten years of age, particularly interested Mengele because within each pair were two different eye colours. After he had injected chloroform into their hearts so they died virtually simultaneous deaths, he removed their eyes and other organs and sent them to von Verschuer's institute in Berlin in a packet marked 'WAR MATERIALS – URGENT'. With one set of 'heterochromic-eyed' twins – gypsies who had been shipped to Auschwitz as a family – he had the whole family of eight killed and dissected. When Berlin phoned back to say Mengele had sent eight records, but only seven pairs of eyes, he plundered a pair of heterochromic eyes from an unrelated gypsy and rushed them to Berlin. So much for scientific integrity!

He stood children on their heads for hours to compute the speed at which blood drained from their stomachs. He immersed them in cold water to correlate temperature levels with loss of consciousness. Dr Martina Puzyna, a University of Lemberg anthropologist jailed for Polish underground activities and employed by Mengele to measure his victims, despised him as a scientist. She told Mengele biographers Gerald L. Posner and John Ware in 1985 that their subject could 'only be described as a maniac. He turned the truth on its head. He believed you could create a new super-race as though you were breeding horses. He thought it was possible to gain absolute control over a whole race. Man is so infinitely complex that that kind of strict control over such a vast population could never exist. He was a racist and a Nazi. He was ambitious up to the point of being completely inhuman. He was mad about genetic engineering. I believe he thought that when he'd finished with the Jewish race he'd start on the Poles, and when he finished with them, he'd start on someone else. Above all, I believe that he was doing this for himself, for his career. In the end, I believed that he would have killed his own mother if it would have helped him.'

Perhaps his own appearance afforded Mengele an affinity for gypsies. As trainloads rumbled towards him in 1943 and 1944, Mengele never missed a selection. The gypsies arrived wearing gaily coloured shawls. Some were singing; others played bizarre instruments. 'I have seldom enjoyed a selection as much as this one,' Mengele remarked after a few thousand gypsies had passed in review. Some he selected for his pigmentation experiments; a rare condition called 'dry gangrene of the face' was relatively common among gypsies. And one, a four-year-old boy dressed in white, became Mengele's mascot – going everywhere with him, giving command performances of song and dance, even standing beside him at selections in the summer of 1944.

For a while, gypsies fared better at Auschwitz than Jews or other minorities. Some even arrived wearing Hitler Youth uniforms; others greeted their captors with shouts of 'Heil Hitler!' Still others had been plucked from the ranks of the German Army. For them, a special 'Gypsy Camp' was created where they could live with their families (and Mengele could explore their heredity) – until the night in late 1944 when all 4500 of them were annihilated. Twelve pairs of twins were gassed apart from the others so Mengele could dissect their corpses. And, at the very last minute, Mengele pushed his little gypsy pet into the gas chamber, too.

If gypsies were his fetish, twins were his forte. 'Scientists,' Mengele once gloated, 'have always been able to study twins after they have been *born* together. But only in the Third Reich can Science examine twins who have *died* together.' Sometimes, he would even dissect them while still alive. When the first twins were born in Birkenau – boys to a Frenchwoman – he not only presented them with a basket, a blanket, and a pair of baby shirts, but gave their mother an unheard-of white sheet for her stretcher. Yet he took her twins away from her every morning and returned them only at night, weaker and darker from each day of life. Within three weeks, both babies were dead – and their mother, having outlived her usefulness to Mengele, was thrown into an oven.

Miriam and Tovah Fuchs were Polish Jewish twins who had grown up in the ghetto of Lodz knowing nothing but Nazi oppression there from 1939 to 1944. Their parents were taken away in 1942: their mother to an unknown destination, never to be heard from again; their father was burned in Chelmno. At the age of ten, their older sister, Hana, became mother and father to the orphaned twins. When the three sisters were deported to

Auschwitz in 1944, Miriam and Hana were sent to the right with the healthier people, while Tovah was sent to the left with the elderly and infirm. Seeing several twins standing in a small cluster on the right, Hana Fuchs protested to Dr Mengele: 'My sisters are twins and they've never been parted.' Mengele looked from one to the other and, with a flick of a white glove, ordered Tovah to rejoin the living. All the twins were taken to what Miriam has remembered all her life as 'a hospital that wasn't a hospital, but a place where they didn't heal people, where they made well people sick, where you sat up from the injections and transfusions and anaesthetics with new pains in parts that had never hurt before. From then on, I have suffered from ulcers, back pains, headaches, difficulty in concentrating, lapses in memory, and inferiority complexes. To make matters worse, the punishment Mengele inflicted on me has been passed on to the next generation. I gave birth to three children. The first was born with a defective heart and lived only a few hours. The second had to be operated on as a baby for a defective stomach. The third is physically underdeveloped and suffers from damage to both ears and partial deafness as well as jaw defects. He has been in medical treatment ever since birth and will still require several difficult operations. The doctors have certified that all these deformities trace back to the experiments that were made upon me, but I don't need more doctors to tell me what one doctor did to me. My complaints and the experiences that brought them on are the central truths of my existence,' she told me over coffee in my living-room in Vienna in 1988.

Stirring her empty coffee cup aimlessly, she added that her twin, Tovah, now in Israel, has a similar medical history. Also in Israel was their sister, Hana, who was shipped as slave labour to Germany. Hana never forgave herself for the misery she inflicted on her sisters by saving Tovah's life, though they are thankful. As with Simon Wiesenthal after more than half a century, the Holocaust is still with the Fuchs sisters every day of their lives.

Simon Wiesenthal says: 'Always I am thinking about the cruel experiments he made on twins. I ask myself why. Now I will tell you why. The perverted Nazi racism was based on blood: good blood, bad blood, mixed blood, Jewish blood, the Nuremberg Laws. When Himmler decided to kill the *children of Stauffenberg,* it was because they had bad blood. So what kind of experiments did Mengele make? He took blood from twins and transfused it to expectant mothers. Why? Because he thought maybe this blood of twins would give them twins. Later he would try giving twins' blood to young fathers so maybe they will make twins. Have you ever heard of such a thing?' Wiesenthal snorts, his own blood boiling. 'Twin-makers!'*

On the assumption that, whether or not Germany won the war, the Fatherland would want to recoup its casualties by repopulating in Hitler's Aryan image, Wiesenthal says Mengele sought to double the reproduction rate and win glory for himself. He kept his 'Twins' files in bright blue covers. When one prisoner, a physician from Budapest assigned as a research assistant, spilled a spot of grease on to one of Mengele's neatest folders, the young German glared at the Hungarian Jew and asked reproachfully: 'How can you be so careless with these files, which I've compiled with so much love?'

The outraged Hungarian, Dr Miklos Nyiszli, later wrote a book called *Auschwitz: A Doctor's Eyewitness Account* in which he accused Mengele of sending 'millions of people to death merely because, according to a racial theory, they were inferior beings and therefore detrimental to mankind. This same criminal doctor spent long hours at his microscope, his disinfecting ovens and his test tubes, or standing near his dissecting table, his smock befouled with blood, his bloody hands examining and experimenting like one possessed.'

*Claus Philipp Maria Schenk, Count von Stauffenberg (1907–44), a young colonel who had lost his left eye and right hand fighting for Germany, tried to blow up Hitler on 20 July 1944 by planting a time-bomb in Hitler's conference room. It killed several people present, but not Hitler. Stauffenberg and four other conspirators were apprehended and shot to death hours after the bomb went off, but the blood-bath that followed led to 7000 arrests and 5000 deaths – including that of World War II's greatest German hero, Field Marshal Erwin Rommel, 'The Desert Fox' of the North African campaign. Rommel had known some of the conspirators, but refused to participate in their plot. For not giving them away, Rommel was offered the choice of standing trial and jeopardizing his family or taking poison; he chose poison. Though Himmler vowed in August 1944 that 'the Stauffenberg family will be exterminated, root and branch', the Count's pregnant wife and four children survived the war in a concentration camp, where the fifth child was born and their name was changed to Meister.

Nyiszli says that Mengele 'took himself to be one of the most important representatives of German medical science.' Indeed, tattooing a twin with a battery-operated device, Mengele told the child: 'You're a little boy. You'll grow and some day you can say you were personally given your number by Doctor Josef Mengele. You'll be famous. Don't scratch it.'

History, however, has attested to Mengele's mediocrity as a scientist. In the words of his captive assistant, Dr Olga Lengyel:

> His experiments and observations were carried out in an abnormal fashion. When he made transfusions, he purposely used incorrect blood types. Of course, complications followed. He would inject substances and then ignore the results. But Mengele had no one to account to but himself. He did whatever pleased him and conducted his experiments like a mad amateur. He was not a savant. He had the mania of a collector.

In her horrifying 1947 book, published under the titles *Hitler's Ovens* and *Five Chimneys*, Dr Lengyel asked herself: 'What conception could Dr Mengele have had of the medical work he did in the camp?' Her answer: 'His experiments, lacking scientific value, were no more than foolish playing and all his activities were full of contradiction.'

In *Prisoners of Fear* (1948), another of the first postwar memoirs to mention Mengele, Dr Ella Lingens-Reiner – a Viennese Gentile physician who served in the Austrian underground until she was sent to Auschwitz for sheltering Jews and forced to assist him – described his 'scientific method' of weeding out patients by ordering inmate physicians to write out diagnoses and prognoses: 'If we put down that a patient had to remain in hospital for over three to four weeks, he or she was condemned.' If a shorter term was predicted, Mengele would summon patient and physician and scream, 'What! You say you're a doctor and you mean to send this wretched creature out of the hospital in less than four weeks?' Sometimes he would send both to 'The Bakery', as he called the crematoria. Or he might insist upon releasing the inmate on the date specified, which, with enfeebled patients, 'was sometimes nothing short of murder', said Dr Lingens. 'It was often impossible to find a way out.'

Dr Olga Lengyel concurred with Dr Ella Lingens: 'No medical considerations governed his decisions. They seemed entirely arbitrary. He was the tyrant from whose decisions there was no appeal. Why should he trouble to select on the basis of any method? Nor did the state of health have anything to do with his selections . . . How we hated this charlatan! He profaned the very word "science". How we despised his detached, haughty air, his continual whistling, his absurd orders, his frigid cruelty!'

The most perceptive diagnosis of Mengele by anyone who met him and lived to tell the tale was that of a layman. The twin he tattooed personally, Marcus Adler, later described the anomaly of Mengele to biographer Gerald Astor in terms similar to Simon Wiesenthal's characterization of his most elusive quarry. Adler told Astor about 'a doctor of philosophy, a medical doctor, a man who enjoyed music and poetry, and his greatest weapon was his manner. He could get people to do everything by appearing to be decent. He would totally disarm someone. You could not believe he was lying, yet he lied all the time. He acted on the basis that if you tell a Jew good morning, that proves you are a nice person.'

Around 1975, when a medical congress was in Vienna, Wiesenthal was contacted by an eminent German doctor who claimed he had recently lunched with Mengele in a private room of the German Club of Asunción, Paraguay while two bodyguards stood watch. After alluding to articles he'd written for German medical journals in the 1930s, Mengele asked his guest what he knew about his subsequent 'anthropological studies at Auschwitz'. The German – who was no admirer of his host – replied discreetly: 'I know you only from your reputation in the German press.'

'God damn the press and the Jews!' Mengele exploded, pounding the table so hard that crockery and bodyguards jumped. 'What do they want from me? My selections were only to increase the number of living. Without them, everybody would have died.'

Upon hearing this, it was Wiesenthal's turn to explode. 'Why not propose him for the Nobel Prize?' he berated his informant with sarcasm. 'Look, more than two million people were "selected" at Auschwitz. There were twenty-three doctors who had selection duty, but how come Mengele wound up selecting more than 400,000? Why was he responsible for so many? We have the duty rosters. We know that Mengele on his own volunteered to replace the others. He was looking for special people for his terrible experiments and, of course, the other doctors said OK.'

After blowing off steam and then apologizing to the German doctor, who had, after all, sought him out with his seemingly useful information, Simon pondered Mengele's rationalization and realized, as he put it to me in his own English: 'He was preparing his own line of defence. A man who is talking this way is thinking: "What will be my defence when I am catched?"'

If so, Mengele was preparing his defence much earlier. Back in Auschwitz, he once explained to his infirmary's head nurse, an imprisoned German communist named Orli Reichert, why he invariably sent Jewish women with young children directly to their deaths: 'When a Jewish child is born, or when a woman comes to the camp with a child already, I don't know what to do with the child. I can't set the child free because there are no longer any Jews who live in freedom. I can't let the child stay in camp because there are no facilities here that would enable it to develop normally. It would not be humanitarian to send a child to the ovens without permitting the mother to be there to witness the child's death. That's why I send mother and child to the gas ovens together.'

Since Mengele hoped to open an office as a fashionable obstetrician-gynaecologist in postwar Berlin, he practised his profession by delivering as many babies at Auschwitz as he could find time for – sterilizing all his instruments and cutting each umbilical cord meticulously. Thirty minutes later, unless the infant held some 'scientific' interest for him, he would dispatch mother and babe to the gas chamber.

Mostly, though, he didn't have time to waste on pregnant women and sent them directly to their doom. Still, he took a certain prurient interest when an inmate conceived in camp. He would interview the expectant mother and savour every detail of romance behind barbed wire. Then he would throw her away. Once, after asking a pregnant fifteen-year-old the most intimate questions, he patted her belly and sent her off to the gas chamber. 'This camp is not a maternity ward,' he told her.

Of all the hundreds of thousands of 'cases' that Mengele moved through Auschwitz-Birkenau, the one that moves Wiesenthal the most is the saga of Ruth Eliaz, who did not look pregnant when she arrived there in December 1943. By May 1944, however, she had read the writing on the barbed wire and heard from the camp grapevine that, in the wake of Allied bombings, some healthier inmates would soon be sent to Germany to clear the rubble. More than four decades later, Ruth Eliaz recalled her struggle for survival with the immediacy of the present tense:

'I am in the seventh month. I am told that pregnant women are sent to the gas chamber. I am only twenty years old. I want to live. Friends succeed in placing my number on the Transport to Germany list. We young stronger workers are brought to the women's camp. Now there is further selection. This time, Doctor Mengele will personally make the selection. We are naked and must march like geese past Doctor Mengele. A few young women have decided to place me in their midst and thus try to direct the attention of Mengele to themselves. We never get near to him. Is it possible? Doctor Mengele doesn't notice me. I may live? And the new life stirs within me.'

She is sent to Hamburg, where more perceptive authorities take one look at her shape and ship her back to Auschwitz. Perplexed by his oversight, Mengele singles her out for special care in his hospital. When the baby, a girl, is born, Mengele binds her mother's breasts with bandages to keep her from nursing. Ruth Eliaz remembers:

'My child is crying from hunger. She wants to be fed. I chew a tiny piece of bread and place it in my child's mouth. My breasts are full of milk. I am swollen from it up to my neck. Every day, Doctor Mengele comes to enjoy himself by looking at this spectacle.'

Sympathetic nurses smuggle the baby tea, but it is not enough for the starving infant. On the eighth day, Mengele tells the mother: 'Be ready tomorrow morning with your child. I am coming to get you.'

On what she believes to be her last night on earth, Ruth Eliaz clings to her dying daughter until a woman inmate doctor comes to her and says, 'I will help you. Here is a syringe with a strong dose of morphine that will kill your child. It cannot survive. It is starved. Already it has hunger edema.'*

Ruth Eliaz tells the woman to go ahead, but she refuses: 'I am a doctor. I cannot be the one to kill the baby. Look, it has not much more life, but you are twenty years old. You will survive. You will

*edema: swelling due to an excess of fluid in the tissues.

have children. Can you look so on this baby and choose to die with her? Please do it!'

After two hours of soul-searching, she kills her daughter.

The next morning, Mengele asks: 'Where is your child?'

'Died during the night,' she responds listlessly.

'I want to see the corpse,' he says. Satisfied, he tells her: 'You are lucky. You leave for the work camp this morning.'

In early 1985, to observe the fortieth anniversary of the liberation of Auschwitz, a Mengele 'trial in absentia' was held in Jerusalem only a few weeks before his remains surfaced in Brazil. The panel of 'judges' included historian Yehuda Bauer, Nuremberg prosecutor Telford Taylor, Eichmann prosecutor Gideon Hausner, and Simon Wiesenthal.

As Ruth Eliaz testified – telling how her daughter had died slowly, 'very close to me. I can still hear her last breath, her last groan' – Wiesenthal was struck speechless. When he found words, he turned to the other 'judges' and said, 'Please, no questions.'

Later, Ruth Eliaz came up and kissed him for his eloquent plea for silence, which, she felt, honoured her martyred child as no words could. 'I have three children,' she told him, 'three beautiful children, and they thank you.'

Reflecting upon that encounter soon after his return to Vienna, Wiesenthal remarks: 'You can imagine that I am taking with me not only what happened to me in the camps, but what happened to all those witnesses. Some emotions are so mixed that, for me, this was my baby that she killed. You know, after so many years of listening to such stories, people think I should be made from stone. I am not! When people are coming and telling me what happened to them, they start to cry and I cry with them. I feel it. I see it. For only a little while, I can forget. I tell myself that this is 1985 and that was 1944. But then I remember.'

Quivering, then shuddering, Simon Wiesenthal begins to sob.

– 22 –

The world's biggest battlefield

In the beginning, there was a swamp. Early in 1940, a former Düsseldorf businessman named Richard Glücks discovered it in the fork of the Vistula and Sola rivers in the portion of Poland that Germany devoured after Hitler and Stalin invaded and dismembered their neighbour the previous September. For Glücks' purposes, this was an ideal industrial site. Not far from the city of Cracow, it had its own community, Oswiecim, with a small hotel and a population of 12,000 potential workers. It was accessible to Vienna, Warsaw, Berlin, and several other key German cities. Most important of all, it bordered on an important railway junction. In his report back to his chief, Glücks described the swamp and its surroundings as a 'suitable site'.

Richard Glücks was Nazi Germany's new Chief Inspector of Concentration Camps. The superior to whom he reported was Heinrich Himmler, the second most powerful man in Germany. And the 'suitable site' for their largest Polish enterprise, Oswiecim, later became known by its German name, Auschwitz.

In the summer of 1941, Himmler summoned Captain Rudolf Höss,* the first commandant of Auschwitz – by then a year-old slave-labour camp with factories belonging to Krupp, I. G. Farben,

*Rudolf Höss (1900–47), hanged by Poland at Auschwitz after the war, is not to be confused with Rudolf Hess (1894–1987), Hitler's deputy leader of the Nazi Party until May 1941, when, in the delusion that he could make peace with enemy Britain to unite against the Slavs, he flew an unauthorized solo flight and parachuted into Scotland. Jailed by the British for the rest of the war, Hess was convicted at Nuremberg of crimes against peace and sentenced to life imprisonment. The last surviving Nuremberg defendant, he was the only inmate of Spandau Prison in West Berlin when he committed suicide at the age of ninety-three.

Siemens, and other German manufacturers – and told him that the Führer had ordered a final solution to the Jewish problem and the SS must enforce it. Höss returned to Poland from Berlin and, a few days later, Adolf Eichmann joined him.

Höss, a former guard at Dachau and chief warder at the Sachsenhausen concentration camp, had a more criminal past than most SS designated exterminators. In his early days as a Nazi, he had served five years of a ten-year prison sentence for the 1923 vengeance killing of a suspected informer named Walther Kadow in a forest where, after beating him within an inch of his life with clubs and branches, his abductors cut his throat and finished him off with two revolver shots. Kadow had been an elementary schoolteacher, and one of his former pupils, Martin Bormann, was convicted as an accomplice of Höss and sentenced to a year in jail. Bormann later became Hitler's secretary and Höss's protector.

Höss was hanged in the Auschwitz camp on 7 April 1947, from a gallows erected beside the comfortable house where he and his wife and five children resided from 1940 to 1943. At his trial before a Polish military tribunal, he testified that Eichmann discussed with him various methods of extermination and the probable sequence of lands that would lose their Jews: first Russia, Silesia, and Poland; then Germany (including Austria), Czechoslovakia, France, Belgium, and Holland. (Hungarian Jews, still protected by a pro-Axis regime, were not yet on the timetable of the Final Solution.) Höss and Eichmann agreed that shooting and hangings, executions and massacres, which prevailed in the East, were unsuitable for Auschwitz, which was expected to process hundreds of thousands of Jews. Nor could they rely on carbon monoxide, used in the euthanasia programme and the extermination empire 'the savage Christian', Captain Wirth, was setting up in the east of Poland. (Chelmno was already in operation, soon to be followed by Belzec, Sobibor, and Treblinka.) Cost-effective analysis showed carbon monoxide expensive to produce in quantity while killing too few at a time.

'We did not come to any decision at that time,' Höss testified. 'Eichmann was going to find out about some gas which would be easy to come by and not require a big apparatus.

'I drove with Eichmann through the neighbourhood of Auschwitz to look for the most suitable place . . . We found a farm which suited the purpose . . . It was situated a little out of the way, hidden by a little forest, and was close to the railroad. The corpses were to be buried in a nearby field in wide deep trenches. We calculated that, with the right gas, we could kill 800 Jews at one sitting. This calculation later proved to be correct.'

There were actually two farmhouses on the land Höss showed Eichmann. The Germans called them the White House and the Red House, but they belonged to the Harmatas and Wichajs, two peasant families that had intermarried and shared the land. They were evicted and their homes transformed into bunkers for experiments with the new wonder gas, Zyklon B. Under SS supervision, prisoners from Auschwitz, less than two miles away, dug trenches for the disposal of bodies. The first Jews were gassed in the White House in January 1942, shortly before the twentieth of the month, when the Final Solution was formalized at Wannsee.

On 17 and 18 July 1942, Heinrich Himmler, who had visited Auschwitz the year before, came back to look at the new nearby transit-and-extermination camp which was sprouting on the two farms. He liked what he saw and told Höss to expand and speed up the operation by combining gas chamber with crematorium in one all-purpose building. Four such death centres were built in the mushrooming new camp, which had 175 hectares (432.5 acres) of land at Nazi disposal; a fifth was built back in Auschwitz, where the whole camp was only eight hectares (not quite twenty acres) in area. There, the first Zyklon B gassings had been tried in the basement of barracks 11, 'the Death Block', on 3 September 1941. The gas chamber at Auschwitz would be used for prisoners who rebelled or were punished, who were too sick to work, or were weeded out for other reasons. The other four, on the former farmland of the Red and White Houses, were mostly for new arrivals deemed unfit or who were not needed to work themselves to death for the Third Reich.

At first, the new camp was called Auschwitz II, but then, thanks to a cluster of birch trees that had been its only distinguishing feature in the beginning, it was christened Birkenau. Together, Auschwitz and Birkenau formed what the Polish Council for the Preservation of Monuments to Resistance and Martyrdom (in conjunction with UNESCO) calls 'the world's biggest battlefield, where four million people died in World War II.'

On Tuesday, 17 January 1945, with Red Army artillery booming in his ears, Dr Josef Mengele had packed two boxes of files on *his* big projects – the experiments with twins, cripples, gypsies, and dwarfs – and loaded them into a waiting car which took him and several other Auschwitz doctors to the Gross Rosen concentration camp, some 200 miles to the north-west in Silesia. There, they were expected to continue their 'scientific' work.

Thus, the first feasible encounter between political prisoner no. 127371, Diploma Engineer (in architecture) Simon Wiesenthal, and Nazi Party member no. 5574974, Josef Mengele, MD and PhD (in anthropology), would have been in early 1945 at Gross Rosen. Along his 1200-mile death march from the Janowskà and Plaszow camps to Buchenwald and Mauthausen, Wiesenthal's short stay in Gross Rosen overlapped Mengele's for a few days. Fortunately for history, however, Dr Mengele's and Engineer Wiesenthal's paths didn't quite cross at that time.

At Gross Rosen, where bacteriological experiments on Soviet prisoners of war had been going on for three years, Mengele stayed until 18 February. As the Red Army neared Gross Rosen, he flew westward through a landscape littered with corpses and clogged with refugees. Hooking up with a retreating German army unit, he exchanged his SS uniform for a *Wehrmacht* (regular army) officer's. The soldiers stayed in central Czechoslovakia for a couple of months until the Red Army drove them to the west.

At Saaz in the Sudetenland on 2 May, they encountered a motorized German field hospital – one of whose doctors, Hans Otto Kahler, had been a close friend of Mengele's in the Third Reich Institute for Heredity, Biology, and Racial Purity at the University of Frankfurt before the war. Even though Kahler had one Jewish great-grandparent, his twins research was so important to Professor von Verschuer, the director, that Kahler survived Nazi Party efforts to remove him from the staff and eventually was commissioned a *Wehrmacht* officer.

That night, Mengele asked Kahler if he could stay with the field hospital, which specialized in internal medicine. Kahler put in a word with the commanding officer and Mengele was invited to join the staff. Soon after, he had an affair with a German nurse, to whom he entrusted his research files, for nurses were seldom imprisoned or searched by the Allied armies.

He knew his notes were incriminating, even though he didn't

yet know how incriminated he was. Ever since Auschwitz had been liberated on 27 January, his name had recurred in survivors' testimony to American, British, French, Russian, Polish, Yugoslav, and Czechoslovak authorities. Starting in April, his name had appeared high on the lists of major war criminals compiled by the US Office of Special Investigations, the fledgling United Nations' War Crimes Commission, and the Allied High Command in Paris as wanted for 'mass murder and other crimes'. But neither Mengele nor his colleagues had access to such publications, though, on 3 May, the day after he joined the field hospital, his wife Irene heard an Allied broadcast listing the charges against him.

While Kahler knew Mengele was an SS doctor wearing a *Wehrmacht* uniform, he never told anyone. A senior physician in the unit, Colonel Fritz Ulmann, suspected the truth because every day at roll-call, Mengele gave a different name. Though the war in Europe ended on 8 May with Germany's unconditional surrender, Ulmann's and Kahler's and Mengele's field hospital was trapped for six weeks in a twenty-mile no man's land in a forest of Saxony (now in eastern Germany) between the American and Russian lines, while the Allied commands worked out who had jurisdiction. Finally, in mid-June, their unit simply formed up as a medical convoy and passed through the American lines, making their way through several road-blocks into northern Bavaria.

Safe from the Russians, they were apprehended by the US Army in the town of Weiden when their gas supply ran out. They were interned there, but, as anticipated, Mengele's nurse girlfriend was released in a few hours and she headed home to Gera, in the Russian zone, with his research files intact. The officers would have to linger longer while their records were checked.* When Mengele started to give his name as Memling, this was too much for Kahler, an art-lover, who told his colleague this was dishonourable. So Mengele gave his real name.

Even though he was in American custody for eight weeks, nobody ever checked his name against the lists of wanted criminals. The

*Adolf Eichmann, too, was interned in Weiden, but Captain Mengele was in officers' quarters while Colonel Eichmann was masquerading as an enlisted man.

early days of occupation were so chaotic that it is quite possible none of the lists filtered down to the camps he was in. One other detail literally saved his skin: back in 1938, when he'd joined the SS, his vanity had made him evade the tattooing of his blood group on arm or chest. Flaunting his expertise as a physician, he'd persuaded the SS that any competent surgeon would cross-match blood types before giving transfusions rather than rely on tattoos. In 1945, the SS tattoo was the first clue American investigators looked for and a soldier without one was considered relatively clean.

Nonetheless, throughout his stay in American hands, Mengele worried that he might be unmasked. He fell into what Dr Kahler diagnosed as clinical depression and asked Dr Ulmann, who was a neurologist, to treat him. Ulmann voiced his suspicions to Mengele, who broke down and confided just a little of what he had done at Auschwitz. Closing ranks the way the medical profession so often does, Ulmann not only treated Mengele's anxiety, but assuaged it by offering to obtain a second identification for him to use once he was released or if he escaped. Ulmann, whose own release was imminent, was working at camp headquarters, where he was able to obtain an extra set of his own separation papers. Once outside, Mengele was welcome to become Fritz Ulmann.

Believing he was 'clean', the Americans released Mengele at the end of July, and a truck deposited him in the Bavarian city of Ingolstadt on the Danube. He decided to head for nearby Donauwörth, where an old school chum, Albert Miller, was a veterinarian. Borrowing a bike from a friendly farmer, he pedalled to Dr Miller's door and rang the bell.

'Good day, Dr Mengele,' was how Mrs Miller greeted her uniformed caller, who was taken aback to be recognized so readily. She invited him in and, when her husband came home, prepared dinner, during which Mengele told his hosts: 'All the things you will be hearing about me are lies. Don't believe a word of them. I have done nothing wrong.'

Mengele asked the Millers to let his family know he was alive, safe, and free. They invited him to stay the night, but he decided against it when American troops arrived after dinner to arrest Dr Miller for questioning about his wartime Nazi activities. Mengele hid in a back room and, later that night, set out for East Germany to retrieve his precious files.

During Mengele's perilous three-week journey through Russian lines, Dr Miller (who was quickly released) and his wife passed the news of his visit on to the Mengele family in Günzburg. The doctor's wife, Irene, who had moved to a cottage in nearby Autenried after their son Rolf was born in 1944, was relieved to hear she wasn't a widow. On 11 June 1945, three American military policemen had driven up, looking for her husband. Mrs Mengele, who hadn't heard from him all year, had told them with some certitude that he was 'probably dead'.

Bearing Fritz Ulmann's good-conduct certificate from the Americans, Mengele made his way back to Bavaria and knocked on the door of a pharmacist in Munich who had served with him in combat on the eastern front in 1942. The druggist and his wife were friends of the chief pharmacist at Auschwitz, who had told them what went on there and the role Mengele played. They welcomed him to their apartment, where he stayed four weeks and insisted: 'I don't have anything to hide. Terrible things happened at Auschwitz and I did my best to help. One could not do everything. There were terrible disasters there. I could only save so many. I never killed anyone or hurt anyone. I can prove I am innocent. . .'

'You're crazy!' the pharmacist told him. 'It's impossible for you to get a fair trial. If you turn yourself in, you'll either be shot on the spot or else you'll be tried and then hanged. Forget this nonsense about proving your innocence. We must find a place to hide you.'

German medicine closed ranks around its blackest sheep once again. The pharmacist happened to know the real Dr Fritz Ulmann's brother-in-law and his wife, both doctors too. They offered to look for work for the fake Fritz Ulmann on isolated farms in eastern Bavaria, whose young men had been so decimated in the war that few, if any, questions were asked of hired hands. Out of gratitude, Mengele volunteered to alter a few letters which changed the name on his document from *U*lmann to *Hol*lmann.

With Mengele, the Ulmann kin drove around Mangolding, an Alpine farm area near the Austrian border. After being turned down twice by farmers, they were welcomed by the Georg Fischer family, who farmed twenty acres of potatoes and wheat, milked a dozen cows, and needed an extra hand. Mengele was introduced as 'Fritz Hollmann', a refugee from Görlitz in East Germany on the Polish border. The Fischers were sitting down to eat and invited their visitors to join them. Georg's younger brother Alois remembers that Hollmann 'ate as though he didn't get much to eat in the war. He didn't say a word – he just ate an enormous amount of food. My brother told him: "If you work as much as you eat, then you're my man. We will try you."'

Fritz Hollmann, alias Dr Josef Mengele, signed on as a farmhand on Tuesday, 30 October 1945, for ten marks a week.

In a 1987 visit to the scene of Mengele's crimes at Auschwitz-Birkenau, I found only a handful of traces of his deathly work: a detailed packing list (signed by him) which had accompanied the head of a twelve-year-old gypsy boy that was shipped on 29 June 1944 to a research institute in Germany for further analysis; a photo of four gypsies he'd castrated; several pages of his handwritten 'anthropological measurements', and a letter of recommendation from the SS garrison commander at Auschwitz to the Chief Doctor's Office. Dated 19 August 1944, it notes that:

> Dr Mengele has been here since 30 May 1943.
>
> Dr Mengele has an open, honourable, firm character. He is absolutely trustworthy, upright, and direct. His mental and bodily hygiene is outstanding. His appearance indicates no weakness of character, no inclinations or addictions. His intellectual and physical predispositions can be designated as excellent.
>
> In his function as camp physician at Concentration Camp Auschwitz, he applied his knowledge practically and theoretically while fighting grave epidemics. He seized every opportunity, even under difficult circumstances, to improve both his theoretical and practical knowledge. He uses his spare time to search for further opportunities and unusual anthropological materials.

The report concluded by recommending Mengele for promotion, but it was too late in the war for it to be acted upon.

In the Auschwitz archive, I listened to a tape-recording of the disembodied electronic voice of a twin named Emil Reichenberger telling of two years of injections and experiments by Mengele that cost him his larynx, among other parts. 'But I am the lucky one,' the voice concluded. 'My brother died in the same experiments.'

There are only two pictures of Mengele in the archive: SS identification portraits, neither of them from Auschwitz. For all his vanity, he rarely let anyone photograph him because he knew he would one day be held responsible for his crimes against the human race.

– 23 –

Mengele the fugitive

Upon learning in late July 1945 that her husband was alive, Dr Josef Mengele's 'widow', Irene, kept the good news to herself. In 1946, she started taking the train to Rosenheim on weekends whenever farmhand 'Fritz Hollmann' could take time off from the Fischer family to visit his 'girlfriend' in Rosenheim. After making sure she wasn't followed, Irene would walk up the road to Mangolding, encounter 'Fritz', and spend the night with him at an inn on a Bavarian lake called the Sinnsee. Back home in Autenreid and in her husband's family stronghold, Günzburg, she continued the deception by telling friends she was sure she would never see her husband alive and even wearing black widow's weeds to church and asking the priest to pray for the repose of her late husband's soul.

Her father-in-law, Karl Mengele Snr, did his bit by twice telling denazification investigators his son was missing in action and, the third time, that he was dead. Apparently, both he and Irene convinced the authorities, for, when Dr Giselle Perl, his Hungarian Jewish prisoner gynaecologist at Auschwitz, denounced Mengele to the Americans in 1947, she elicited this reply from Brigadier General Telford Taylor, chief US counsel to the Nuremberg war crimes trials, who informed Washington a year later: 'We wish to advise that our records show Dr Mengerle [sic] is dead as of October 1946.'

Back on the Fischer farm in Bavaria, 'Fritz Hollmann' was still remembered in 1985 as 'a very obliging farmhand who never started a fight and was always in a good mood', as Maria Fischer put it to Dr Günther Deschner, a Munich historian on the trail of the late

Dr Josef Mengele. Her brother-in-law Alois told Deschner that Mengele 'was neither friendly nor unfriendly, but always very controlled and disciplined . . . Only once was there a small dispute. He was supposed to work as a labourer, but he gave me an order that I should take the hay down from the threshing fork. I told him he should do it himself. Then he got very angry, only for a short moment, but very, very angry. He looked at me with such fury I actually thought he would attack me. But then he completely controlled himself and such a thing never happened again' during 'Hollmann's' thirty-four months in the Fischers' employ from October 1945 to August 1948.

Toward the end of his days as a farmhand in Bavaria, the 'great selector' of Auschwitz tried to teach the Fischer family to perform 'scientific selection' of their crop in order to breed medium-sized potatoes. Even though the Fischers didn't take Mengele's theories seriously, he found that 'in this way, my mind was kept active.'

In spite of their bi-monthly trysts on the Sinnsee, however, Irene and Josef Mengele's marriage was deteriorating beyond redemption. Insanely jealous of the men she saw in Autenreid and Günzburg between visits to him, he spent most of their time together berating her for her infidelity.

In mid-1948, after a dozen SS doctors, including a couple of his Auschwitz colleagues, had been hanged for offences less heinous (qualitatively and quantitatively) than his, Mengele disappeared from the Fischer farm and returned to Günzburg, where friends and relatives hid him in homes, warehouses, and even at a convent school called the English Institute which, coincidentally, was later attended by Petra Kelly, the half-American Army brat who grew up to be the first Green Party member of Germany's Parliament.

With Karls Snr and Jnr denazified, and Josef's other brother Alois home after four years in a prisoner of war camp in Yugoslavia, the Karl Mengele & Sons machinery company was thriving by making wheelbarrows for the rebuilding of Germany.

In Günzburg, the only person who didn't make Mengele feel welcome was his own wife. When he asked Irene to follow him to South America with their son Rolf soon after he'd send word he'd arrived, she declined. She had already met Alfons Hackenjos, who would become her second husband when she divorced Mengele in 1954.

Günzburg, however, was not a retreat, but a rest stop on Mengele's route to South America. As 'Fritz Hollmann', he crossed from Germany into Austria by train on Easter Sunday, 17 April 1949, and made his way to an inn at Steinach, at the foot of the Brenner Pass. In the early hours of the next morning, with a full moon illuminating the edelweiss, a shepherd – financed by his family through SS contacts in Günzburg – guided him across the Brenner into Italy in barely an hour. From there, he took two trains to Vipiteno, where he registered at the Inn of the Golden Cross. He was there a month.

Whether his well-organized network of helpers were part of ODESSA is still being argued by Mengele biographers Gerald Astor in *The 'Last' Nazi* (1985) and New York attorney Gerald L. Posner and British television producer John Ware in their *Mengele: the Complete Story* (1986). But even Posner and Ware, who dismiss ODESSA as 'mythology', have to concede that there was 'plenty of cloak-and-dagger'.

At the Golden Cross, Mengele met an Italian code-named 'Nino', who asked for a passport photo and then provided him with a German identity card as 'Helmut Gregor'. His next visitor, code-named 'Erwin', was an old schoolfriend, Hans Sedlmeier, who had become sales manager of the Mengele company in Günzburg. Sedlmeier, who would be the family's go-between with its blackest sheep for thirty years, brought the doctor greetings from his father, dollars for the days ahead, and a small suitcase with scientific specimens, including two glass slides with a blood sample between them, plus his precious notes from Auschwitz.

As 'Helmut Gregor', whose listed occupation of 'technician' covered a multitude of sins, Mengele moved on to Bolzano, the capital of the German speaking part of the South Tyrol, which was ceded by Austria to Italy after the First World War. At home among hosts who had hoped Hitler would annex Bozen (as they still called Bolzano) into the Third Reich, 'Gregor' was briefed by a man named 'Kurt' on the last phase of his escape from Europe. 'You will sail in July from Genoa to Argentina', he told 'Gregor'.

Going to Genoa for his emigration documents proved the most perilous part of 'Gregor's' mission. He had no trouble obtaining an International Red Cross passport from the Swiss consulate in Genoa, or passing the physical examination required by the Argentine consulate; 'Kurt' supplied him with a fake vaccination certificate saying he had been inoculated within the past fortnight. When he went for an Italian visa, however, the official whom 'Kurt' kept on a retainer had gone on vacation. His substitutes not only spotted 'Gregor's' documents, particularly the vaccination certificate, as phony, but refused a 20,000-lire (thirty-dollar) bribe and threw him in jail to await investigation of how he'd entered the country.

For three weeks, 'Gregor' languished in an Italian jail with cell-mates he characterized as 'disgusting rural rejects', 'communist rabble', and 'the sewage of the big towns'. These included a dwarf street musician and a morphine-addicted doctor whose withdrawal symptoms Mengele diagnosed as due to 'constitutional inferiority'. Then, just as swiftly as he'd landed in jail, 'Gregor' was released. 'Kurt's' contact had come back from vacation. Suddenly, the police who had been ignoring and insulting 'Gregor' became very obsequious, and one of them even wondered aloud whether he was a Jew because so much influence had been brought to bear on his behalf. By way of amends, 'Kurt's' corrupted Italian official used his own connections to upgrade 'Gregor' from tourist accommodation to second class on the *North King* for no extra charge. He sailed in mid-July 1949.*

In Argentina, Mengele enjoyed easier going than Eichmann from the beginning. Upon arrival as 'Helmut Gregor', he continued to disguise his medical past by taking menial work as a carpenter in Vicente Lopez, the same suburb where Eichmann later lived, because the job came with a room. It also came with a roommate: an engineer whose family boarded next door. When the engineer's daughter took sick, he asked 'Gregor' to treat her – having deduced his room-mate's real profession from the black bag in which he stored his Auschwitz specimens and research notes. Mengele obliged by quarantining the child in the storehouse and prescribing cold compresses, camomile tea, and a sulfa drug.

Having been found out that easily, Mengele gave up manual labour after a few weeks and moved to the Spanish-colonial home of a Nazi sympathizer in a more elegant suburb called Florida. He

*As was to be the case throughout his hunt for Mengele, Wiesenthal was far off target. In his 1967 as well as 1989 memoirs, Simon claimed that Mengele didn't leave Europe until 1951, and via Spain.

bought a dog and made the acquaintance of not just such fellow fugitives as Eichmann and his interviewer Willem Sassen,* the Dutch SS man turned journalist, but legitimate figures like Jewish bridge partners (who accepted him as just another refugee from the war they'd fled) and Colonel Hans Ulrich Rudel (1916–82), Hitler's most decorated air ace, the *Luftwaffe's* 'Red Baron' of World War II.

Credited with 2530 missions and 532 tank kills as well as sinking a battleship and a cruiser, Rudel escaped from Soviet imprisonment the first time he was shot down and lost a leg the second time. After the amputation in 1944, he was entrusted by Martin Bormann, Hitler's deputy, with Operation Land of Fire: the transport (mostly by night flying) of tons of gold, huge bundles of securities and shares, and crates of art to Argentina.

A devout Nazi, though never a war criminal, Rudel was surely in the avant-garde of neo-Nazism. Immediately after the war ended, he emigrated to South America to pursue a lucrative and well-publicized career as a manufacturer's representative and invincible Master Race superman extolling a Fourth Reich and perpetuating SS shrines while serving on Juan Perón's payroll as a consultant to the National Institute of Aeronautics in Córdoba. An ardent sportsman who didn't let an artificial right leg slow down his tennis, skiing, and waterskiing, he also formed Rudel Clubs in Europe and Latin America – ostensibly for flying lessons and competitions, but also as a *Kameradwerk,* an alumni association to assist 'so-called war criminals' in relocating to safer climes. This he admitted in 1960, eight years after a German neo-Nazi newspaper reported that 'Rudel has been proclaimed Führer' of the Fourth Reich.

In his memoir, *Trotzdem* (Nonetheless), published in German in Buenos Aires, Rudel glorified war and Hitler in equal measure. In 1976, two West German air force generals were dismissed for defending his appearance at an official reunion of former *Luftwaffe* aviators.

*It was Sassen who introduced Mengele to Eichmann, but Mengele found Eichmann rather shabby as well as dangerous to be with, and therefore avoided his company, although the two fugitives met from time to time at the ABC Café in downtown Buenos Aires.

Though his biggest clients were aircraft manufacturers, one of the firms that Rudel represented was Karl Mengele & Sons of Günzburg, and so he was privy to the secret of 'Helmut Gregor's' identity. On one of Rudel's frequent trips to Germany, he recommended that 'Dr Gregor' be hired as the family firm's own representative in Latin America, a burgeoning postwar sales area. After Rudel conjured up a vision of a fertile continent laid bare and thirsting to be worked with manure-spreaders, chain saws, and other Mengele exports, the family in Günzburg was convinced.

Around 1951, Mengele had made a business trip to Paraguay with Rudel, who introduced him to his contacts and showed him the territory. 'It was Rudel,' write Mengele biographers Posner and Ware, 'who persuaded Mengele that a lucrative market in farm machinery was waiting to be cornered in Paraguay, a country about the same size as California, especially in the well-watered luxuriant pastures of the south-east.' When General Alfredo Stroessner, a fascist dictator of German extraction, seized power in 1952 and took firm control as President for Life, Paraguay was enhanced for Mengele as a potential escape hatch should the political climate in Argentina ever sour.

In 1953, 'Dr Gregor' moved into the city of Buenos Aires, taking an apartment on the Calle Tacuari. But he had also put down roots in the suburb called Florida by investing in a small carpentry workshop there which made wooden toys for children and odd pieces of furniture. With Mengele's family funds, it expanded into making nuts and bolts for textile factories, and soon was paying dividends which, along with his sales commissions from Karl Mengele & Sons, enabled 'Gregor' to live comfortably and frequent the best restaurants of Buenos Aires.

Though the Mengele family in Günzburg to this day steadfastly denies it paid its prodigal son's way, all evidence is to the contrary. Family ties were so strong that father Karl Snr, who first visited his eldest son in Argentina in 1954 to expedite Josef's divorce from Irene before any court controversy could alert the Allies to his whereabouts, also arranged the fugitive's second marriage: to Martha Weil Mengele, widow of Josef's youngest brother, Karl Jnr, who had died of a heart attack at thirty-seven toward the end of 1949, not long after Josef had landed in Argentina.

While such a union has its roots, ironically, in Jewish tradition whereby a bachelor is expected to marry his brother's widow, it was a corporate manoeuvre by Karl Mengele Snr to keep the business in the family. True, Josef had signed a secret document renouncing his share in Mengele & Sons – just for 'show' in case any prosecutor or victim claiming reparations ever sought to attach or impound the firm's earnings. Now, toward the end of his life, the patriarch worried that Martha, who had inherited her husband's share, might remarry and a non-Mengele might sit in the boardroom; he had already broken up a relationship she was having with a Günzburg businessman. If Josef married Martha, Karl Snr knew his son would share profits and voting power through her.

Martha Mengele required some persuading. This would be her third marriage, and it would uproot her and her ten-year-old son, Karl-Heinz. A voluptuous and sensuous woman, Martha had led a tangled love life which was the talk of Günzburg. Married to a businessman named Wilhelm Ensmann in 1944, when her son was born, she had testified, when divorcing Ensmann in 1948, that Karl Mengele Jnr was really the boy's father – and a regional court in Memmingen had upheld Mengele's paternity. Still 'ravishingly beautiful', according to Josef's son Rolf, she was a hot potato that the other Mengeles were glad to export.

A combined courtship and family reunion was arranged for a ski holiday in Switzerland in March 1956. Bearing an Argentine passport issued to foreign residents, 'Helmut Gregor' flew from Buenos Aires to Geneva, with a two hour stopover at Idlewild (now Kennedy) Airport in New York. He was met at Geneva Airport by Hans Sedlmeier, the family firm's faithful envoy to its most notorious member. Sedlmeier drove Mengele to Engelberg, a Swiss ski resort an hour south of Lucerne. Waiting in the Hotel Engel were Martha, her son Karl-Heinz, and Mengele's own son Rolf, who had been invited along as a playmate for Karl-Heinz and 'to meet your Uncle Fritz from Argentina, who used to take you walking in the woods when you were little.' The Mengeles were playing the same 'uncle' game that had worked with the Eichmann boys.

For ten days, *Onkel Fritz* delighted both twelve-year-old Mengele boys – first cousins who would soon become unknowing step-brothers – with his sagas of derring-do by gauchos and mestizos on the pampas of Argentina, as well as his own exploits against 'partisans' in Europe during the war. According to Posner and Ware, who interviewed the reclusive Rolf Mengele in August 1985: 'Rolf was impressed by his dashing uncle, who dressed formally for dinner, had such exciting tales to tell, and gave him pocket money, his first allowance ever. Rolf recalls: "*Onkel Fritz* was a very interesting man. He told us stories about the war and at that time no adults spoke about the war. I liked him – as an uncle." Rolf also noticed how physically attentive *Onkel Fritz* was to his Auntie Martha, although he thought at the time that it was merely ordinary family affection.'

Emboldened by the ease with which he had transited America and entered Switzerland, *Onkel Fritz* decided to go home to Günzburg with his relatives for nearly a week. There, he continued his courtship of Martha and, when he left, they were informally engaged. Renting a car in Günzburg, he drove to Munich to visit the pharmacist and his wife who had sheltered him right after the war. In Munich, 'Gregor' was involved in a minor auto accident, after which the police warned him, as a foreign resident, not to leave Germany until the case was settled. Alarmed, Mengele phoned his family in Günzburg. Karl Snr drove to Munich and, according to Rolf, 'paid the police some money to forget about the accident.' The next day, 'Gregor' flew to Argentina.

Looking for a home that would be suitable for Martha and Karl-Heinz, Mengele set his sights on a white stucco house at 970 Virrey Vertiz in the Olivos suburb of Buenos Aires. It bordered on the back of what had been Juan Perón's residence until 1955, when the President was deposed by the Argentine Navy and shipped into Paraguayan exile. To take out a mortgage, however, meant furnishing stronger proof of identity than the provisional documents that sustained the myth of 'Helmut Gregor'. With no alarms out, rewards for, or publicity about him, Mengele decided to brazen it out under his real name.

He went to the West German embassy in Buenos Aires and gave a secretary his correct name, date and place of birth, marriage and divorce dates, addresses in Buenos Aires and Günzburg, and swore that he was Josef Mengele and had been living under the false name of Helmut Gregor for seven years. No further questions were asked. The embassy did check with Bonn, the federal capital of West Germany, but nobody consulted the Allied or West German 'wanted' lists; Mengele appeared on several, though his name was just one among many. If any details were verified, they were only the ones he gave.

On 11 September 1956, the German Embassy issued him a certificate of identity as Josef Mengele. He took it to the Argentine National Court, which issued a judicial certificate which he delivered to the federal police, who gave a new identity card, number 3.940.484, to 'Josef Mengele, manufacturer'. Armed with this, Mengele returned to his embassy, which issued him West German passport number 3.415.574.

The following month, Martha Mengele and her son emigrated to Argentina. They moved into the house their host had mortgaged on Virrey Vertiz in the very German suburb of Olivos and, while he and Martha weren't married until 1958, in a civil ceremony in Uruguay, they led a bourgeois married life from the beginning. In 1957, Dr Mengele moved closer to the medical profession he had long ago left by selling his carpentry workshop and investing some $100,000 in founding, with two Argentine partners, a pharmaceutical firm called Fadro Farm. He was now known as Dr José Mengele.

Soon after returning from his honeymoon with his brother's widow in the summer of 1958, Mengele was taken into custody by Buenos Aires police as part of a round-up following the abortion death of a teenage girl. He and a number of other foreign doctors were held on suspicion of practising medicine without licences. While Mengele had no apparent connection with the case, he didn't relish lingering in jail and worrying whether any of his past medical practices might surface. Besides, if any other country should move for his extradition, Juan Perón's successors looked less kindly upon their Nazi constituents. A five-hundred-dollar bribe to two detectives turned Mengele loose after a few hours, but the scare was enough that, in September, he gave his bride power of attorney and set out on a sales trip to Paraguay.

While he had little success peddling Karl Mengele & Sons' new manure-spreader to Paraguayan farmers, he stayed on at the Astra, a German boarding house in the capital city, Asunción, to explore possibilities of settling permanently in General Stroessner's fascistic dictatorship. Martha and her son, Karl-Heinz Mengele, visited him often, though she tried in vain to persuade him he was still safe in Buenos Aires.

He prolonged his ninety-day visa several times and then, in 1959, after renting rooms on the Alban Krug farm in New Bavaria, a German colony of 60,000 near the Argentine border, José Mengele applied for Paraguayan citizenship. Both his residence and his application were arranged by Colonel Rudel. The Nazi air ace introduced him not just to the Krugs, but to Werner Jung, who had been chief of the Paraguayan Nazi Party during the war, and Alejandro von Eckstein, a close adviser to Stroessner. Jung and von Eckstein were Mengele's two sponsors, swearing (falsely) in court that he had been a continuous resident of Paraguay for five years. Rudel also asked the Minister of Interior to expedite Mengele's citizenship, which was granted shortly before the end of 1959.

The Jung family lived in a palatial mansion on Calle General MacArthur in Asunción, and Mengele, who liked to swim in their pool, was always a welcome guest there when he was in the capital. 'We thought very highly of him,' Mrs Jung told Mengele biographers Posner and Ware in 1985. 'He loved classical music, enjoyed reading good German poets, and praised our good and natural way of life. He was very good with the children and helped my second-oldest son pass biology.'

Her husband bore an astonishing facial resemblance to Martin Bormann, Hitler's missing deputy – and this coincidence, combined with one of Mengele's rare attempts to practise medicine, could conceivably have led to Mengele's capture in 1959. One early spring night at dinner, the host took violently ill. When Mengele tried to, but couldn't, treat Jung's stomach seizures, a woman guest went out in search of a doctor and brought back Dr Otto Biss, an Austrian physician practising in Asunción. Jung tried to talk to the doctor in halting Spanish, but Mengele, spotting his "colleague' as a fellow Mitteleuropean, told Jung: 'You may speak German.'

Dr Biss prescribed a treatment for gastritis and left. A few days later, he saw pictures of Martin Bormann and insisted: 'There was no possible doubt. The man I had seen was older than the man in the photographs, but it was the same man. He was certainly Martin Bormann.' A few months later, when Mengele went to the top of the wanted list, just behind Eichmann, Dr Biss would swear that the other doctor in attendance was Mengele.

Since most other experts, including Simon Wiesenthal, eventually were convinced by forensic evidence that a skeleton found near the bunker in which Hitler committed suicide was

Martin Bormann's,* and inasmuch as it was easy to show that the sick man at Jung's address was the host himself, the whole report was discredited. But it was a case of throwing out the baby with the bath water, for little credence was given Biss's correct identification of Mengele.

Mengele's face had become familiar to the world thanks to a joint effort by two Austrian citizens: Wiesenthal, then in Linz, and Hermann Langbein, an earnest, solemn Viennese non-Jew who fought against Franco in the Spanish Civil War and was imprisoned as a communist† first in Dachau and then in Auschwitz, where he used his job as a clerk in the chief physician's office to compile evidence against Mengele and other 'experimenters'. After the war, as general secretary of the International Auschwitz Committee and the Association of Concentration Camp Ex-Prisoners, Langbein, considered the most thorough of all Nazi-hunters, supplied crucial evidence in the trial of Dr Karl Clauberg, chief of sterilization 'experiments', and the extradition of Clauberg's colleague, Dr Horst Schumann, who specialized in X-ray sterilizations, from Ghana, where he was serving dictator Kwame Nkrumah as chief medical officer of the Ministry of Health.

Langbein and Wiesenthal, three years his senior, had united to pressure German prosecutors to indict Mengele in the German university city of Freiburg, where his ex-wife Irene now lived. There, Langbein had found Mengele's 1954 divorce papers and an address on the Calle Tacuari in Buenos Aires buried within the public record. On 5 June 1959, a Freiburg court ordered Mengele 'to be taken into custody . . . on emphatic suspicion of murder and attempted murder.' It listed *only* seventeen counts of premeditated murder,

*In the sixteen-page 'Where is Bormann?' chapter of his 1967 memoir, Wiesenthal concluded that Bormann was 'most probably now living near the frontier of Argentina and Chile as I write this, early in 1966.' In his 1988 memoir's sixteen-page chapter on missing Nazis, 'Declared Dead', Simon devotes only a pair of pages to Bormann and concludes that 'today I harbour no more doubts that the Federal Prosecutor in Frankfurt is correct in his view that, during the night of 2–3 May 1945 in Berlin, Bormann committed suicide when he saw that it was impossible to flee.'

†Langbein broke with communism when the Red Army crushed the Hungarian uprising of 1956.

but the language was strong enough to force action against him for 'killing numerous prisoners with phenol, benzene, and/or air injections [and] in the gas chambers; killing a fourteen-year-old girl by splitting her head with his dagger; injecting dyes into the eyes of women and children, which killed them; killing several twins of gypsy parents either with his own hands or by mixing lethal poison into their food, for the purpose of conducting specious medical studies on their bodies during autopsies; and ordering a number of prisoners to be shot because they would not write to their families saying they were being well treated.'

When Bonn formally asked Argentina for Mengele's extradition later that year, Argentina rejected it because Mengele no longer lived on the Calle Tacuari. The German Ambassador, an active Nazi and former adviser to Hitler's foreign minister, Joachim von Ribbentrop,* wasn't inclined to pursue Mengele's change of address, so Wiesenthal contacted a friend, who, on 30 December 1959, came up with Mengele's last known address on Virrey Vertiz. The warrant was filed again in early 1960 and, this time, Argentine authorities insisted they had to decide whether the charges against Mengele were politically motivated; besides, he was no longer at Virrey Vertiz. All this foot-dragging somehow quickened Israeli hopes that snatching Eichmann might also lead to Mengele.

By then, however, Mengele had returned to Buenos Aires several times to wind up his affairs there – selling his share of Fadro Farms pharmaceuticals to an Argentine. By 30 June 1960, when Argentina finally ordered Mengele's extradition, he was entrenched in Paraguay, well out of the law's reach. Nevertheless, he had much to worry about. Barely a month earlier, the Israelis had snatched Eichmann, lain in ambush for Mengele, and proclaimed he was next on their list. According to Wiesenthal in the uncharacteristic English translation of his 1988 memoir: 'On the day Eichmann was seized, he skedaddled across the Paraguayan border.' In fact, Israeli agents were shadowing Martha Mengele's occasional visits to Paraguay and had even pinpointed her husband's base as Alban Krug's farm in New Bavaria, though they had yet to find him there when they were. One of their agents, an Englishman, tried to penetrate the

*A wealthy former champagne merchant, von Ribbentrop was hanged at Nuremberg in 1946 for war crimes.

farm by wooing Krug's daughter – to no avail. 'It was not our intention at any stage to try to kill Mengele,' Israeli intelligence chief Isser Harel explained later. 'That would have defeated the whole purpose of the exercise. We wanted him back in Israel for a public trial.'

In the fall of 1960, their prime bait, Martha Mengele, slipped away. She and her husband had agreed that living with a fugitive was no life for her and her son, so they separated and, when she and Karl-Heinz, sixteen, flew to Europe for Christmas in Günzburg, they used one-way tickets.

With West Germany offering a 20,000-Deutschmark ($5000) reward for Mengele, there were enough opportunists around New Bavaria to necessitate another move and a new identity. Besides, even his best friends in Asunción were reading the horror stories from Auschwitz with the kind of disbelief that could turn to aversion or worse if just one per cent of it struck them as true. Even dictator Stroessner began to worry about Mengele. When he asked Rudel about him, the colonel said Mengele was a mere laboratory technician who had done none of the deeds Stroessner was reading in the papers. Stroessner was reassured, but, when Mengele again turned to Rudel for help in relocating, Rudel was more than glad to oblige.

Riding to Mengele's rescue, Rudel sent a former Austrian Hitler Youth chief named Wolfgang Gerhard, editor of an anti-Semitic hate newsletter called *Reichsbrief*, published in German in Brazil. Forever compensating for the misfortune of being born too late to fight at the front for the Third Reich, Gerhard was a man who hung a silver swastika instead of a star of Bethlehem atop his Christmas tree. His Brazilian wife, Ruth, even before she met Mengele, once gave her landlady – in the original 1943 wrappers – two bars of soap made from corpses of Auschwitz inmates. The Gerhards had christened their son Adolf. And Wolfgang Gerhard once said that his dream in life was to 'put a steel cable to the leg of Simon Wiesenthal and drag his carcass behind my car' for miles and miles.

* * *

Miles and miles and, as it turned out, light-years away from his quarry, Simon Wiesenthal boasted in his 1967 memoirs that 'I have now been able to retrace Mengele's movements quite exactly.'

Stepping off on the wrong foot, Wiesenthal cited the early 1960 death of a forty-eight-year-old Israeli spinster named Nora Eldoc, who 'had been sterilized by Dr Mengele' in Auschwitz and found herself face to face with him in the Argentine resort of Bariloche. According to Wiesenthal, 'the local police report does not say whether he recognized her. Mengele had "treated" thousands of women in Auschwitz. But he did notice the tattooed number on her lower left arm.' For a few seconds, says Wiesenthal, victim and torturer stared at each other in silence. Then she turned and left the hotel ballroom without a word, but, a few days later, she disappeared. Her battered body was discovered in a mountain crevasse weeks later and police listed her death as a 'climbing accident'. In telling these details, Wiesenthal wrote: 'I cannot give the source of my information, but I can vouch for its reliability.'

We now leave the realm of euphemism that pervaded so many Nazi reports to enter the world of the 'factoid', a postwar phrase popularized and exploited by Norman Mailer in his non-fiction novels. A factoid is a legend – possibly untrue, possibly exaggerated – that is repeated and embellished so much that it takes on a life, even a sub-culture, of its own. Wiesenthal's 'Nora Eldoc' is one of those factoids: she recurs as Nora Aldot, alias Nourit Eldad, a possible Israeli secret agent, in Michael Bar-Zohar's *Avengers* (1968): as Judith Aldot in Werner Brockdorff's *Flight from Nuremberg* (1969); as Mengele's mistress in the late Ladislas Farago's *Aftermath* (1973); and as Nourit Eddad and Norita Eldodt in other works of 'non-fiction'. Most significantly, she does not re-appear in any form, however, in Wiesenthal's 1988 memoir.

In actuality, she was Norit Eldad, born in 1910 in Frankfurt, though, in Wiesenthal's defence, it was the Argentine hotel register that transformed her into 'Nora Eldoc'. But she had left Germany in 1933 for Palestine and had never been in a concentration camp, never been tattooed or sterilized, and had never heard of Mengele, who almost certainly was not in Bariloche at the time of her death She was visiting her sister, who had emigrated to Argentina in 1933. On a climbing trip with a group of Jewish Argentines, she made a wrong turn on a poorly marked trail and fell off a precipice.

A Buenos Aires newspaper had first muddled the matter by headlining her obituary 'SECRET AGENT, HUNTING NAZI MENGELE, ASSASSINATED IN ARGENTINA' and quoting a local police inspector:

> The apparent motive now is that she was searching for Josef Mengele, the Nazi doctor. Now it is possible that Dr Mengele might have been staying in Bariloche.

Such was the post-Eichmann climate in Argentina that this led to speculation that her Jewish Argentine companions were an Israeli hit team. On 21 March 1961, the Israeli Embassy felt compelled to issue an official denial that this prissy middle-aged secretary was any kind of Mata Hari sent to seduce the elusive Mengele; on the contrary, the embassy described Norit Eldad as 'a timid and nervous person. Certainly it is not possible that she was an agent involved in a mission as difficult as finding Mengele.' Argentine newspapers had refuted the rest of their competitor's 'exclusive' – and all this had been public record for six years before Wiesenthal cited his 'reliable source' in print. *Voilà,* instant factoid!

In 1962, just as Wiesenthal was preparing to go to Israel for the Eichmann trial, a trusted ex-Nazi tipped him off that Mengele was meeting his ex-wife Martha on the island of Kythnos. Hermann Langbein lined up a Greek scientist who had worked as a prisoner under Mengele in Auschwitz while Wiesenthal, short of time and resources, persuaded a large illustrated German weekly magazine to send a reporter to Kythnos, where, if he found Mengele, he would telephone the scientist to come there from Athens, identify Mengele from a short distance, and call the police. When the reporter arrived forty-eight hours later on one of the infrequent passenger ferries to Kythnos, where Wiesenthal said there were only two large buildings – an inn and a monastery – he went to the inn and was told, according to Wiesenthal, that the only guests, 'a German and his wife', had left by yacht twelve hours earlier. From a batch of photos, said Wiesenthal, the innkeeper and a couple of monks who dropped by all identified Mengele. Wiesenthal concluded: 'We had lost another round.'

You can't lose what you've never found. In a 1985 interview, the German magazine reporter, Ottmar Katz, remembered that 'not a single detail was correct' in Wiesenthal's information: 'I spent four or five days on Kythnos. Mengele was certainly not there.

There was no monastery. I spent two days with the local judge, who was strongly anti-Nazi. We inspected the register of the only hotel. The only name we thought worth checking we discovered belonged to a Munich schoolteacher. I explained to Wiesenthal that it was all wrong and then, seven years later, I read his book and he said we'd missed Mengele by a few hours.'

A few months later, when Wiesenthal learned that Martha Mengele had rented a house at Schwimmbadstrasse (Swimming Pool Avenue) 9 near Zürich's Kloten Airport, while her son, Karl-Heinz, was studying in Montreux, he sent a Swiss friend, posing as the landlord's household insurance agent, to check the house for repairs. Martha Mengele showed him around and he ascertained that she seemed to be living alone. Still, her location near a noisy airport hinted at convenient visits from afar, so Wiesenthal asked the Swiss authorities to keep an eye on her. Instead, they asked her to leave Switzerland, for, having stayed out of the war, they wanted to stay out of war crimes extraditions too. She moved to Merano, in Italy's Germanic South Tyrol; in his 1988 memoir, Wiesenthal supplies Martha Mengele's Merano address.

Wiesenthal's third round of shadow-boxing came in March 1964, when, he says, a 'Committee of Twelve' wealthy American survivors of Auschwitz tried to kidnap Mengele from the Hotel Tyrol, a bastion of Paraguay's German colony in Hohenau, near the Argentine border. 'I know about these men,' Wiesenthal later told Michael Bar-Zohar when the Israeli author visited Vienna. 'They came to see me, here in my office. They were after Mengele, and asked me for information where he was hiding.' Their plan, Wiesenthal told Bar-Zohar, was 'to take him to a yacht and judge him when out at sea. Six of them landed in Paraguay, while the others waited aboard the yacht.'

In his first memoir, Wiesenthal said that 'the Auschwitz trial was to begin in Frankfurt in 1964' and contended this time that, instead of justice at sea, the would-be abductors' aim was 'to seize Mengele alive and bring him to Frankfurt.' Simon picks up the yarn with:

> It was a hot, dark night. Half a dozen men had trailed 'Dr Fritz Fischer' to Suite 26 of the hotel . . . A few minutes before 1 a.m., the men entered the lobby of the Hotel Tyrol, ran up the stairway, and broke open the door of bedroom number 26. It was empty.

> The hotel-owner informed them that 'Herr Dr Fischer' had left in a hurry ten minutes earlier, after getting a telephone call. He was in such a hurry that he hadn't even bothered to take off his pyjamas. He had put his suit on over them, raced down the stairway, and disappeared into the night.
>
> Mengele was still odd man out.

Truth will out, too. Odder still, under the circumstances, are the following facts: Paraguay is landlocked – and it would have been easier to fly Mengele to Tel Aviv on an El Al 'charter flight' than bring him to justice at sea, even by yacht. The Auschwitz trial of twenty-one officers, doctors, and guards – in which chief prosecutor Hans Kuegler charged that 'the highest spheres of the Paraguayan government' were 'protecting Mengele' – had already begun in 1963 and was coming to a close in 1964. And the Hotel Tyrol was a rustic one-storey chalet with no upstairs, no room 26, and no telephone to warn Mengele.

In July 1964, Wiesenthal notified Dr Fritz Bauer, the German Jewish Eichmann-hunter who was by then Attorney General of West Germany, that Hans Sedlmeier of the Mengele firm in Günzburg was 'maintaining contact with Josef Mengele.' Acting on the tip, Bauer ordered a midnight raid on Sedlmeier's home and found nothing. Interrogated by the Attorney General himself, Sedlmeier denied all. More than two decades later, it was learned that a friend on the local police force had phoned Sedlmeier to say: 'We are coming to search your house. Make sure we don't find anything.'

Wiesenthal claims it was at this point that the Jewish Documentation Centre (not Simon himself!) made its 'first mistake', which he says was 'our firm conviction that the West German Attorney General had used the information we gave him to have Sedlmeier shadowed by the German police as the most likely link to Mengele.'

According to Wiesenthal, 'Sedlmeier was on the lookout for a woman to manage Mengele's household in South America. From a card index of persons who, over the years, had volunteered their services, I picked a woman and saw to it that Sedlmeier made her acquaintance. He was impressed by her qualifications and, after he'd had her meet Mengele's brother Alois and wife Martha, Sedlmeier offered to pay her travel expenses to Latin America – he didn't say where – and a generous salary for looking after his friend: he didn't say who . . . But all of a sudden the deal was called off by the Mengele family. Alois Mengele was the one who told her. To this day, we don't know why.'

Wiesenthal had kept prosecutor Bauer informed of his effort, for 'we had reason to fear for the woman's safety. Israeli authorities were also notified in order to reduce her risk.' When Wiesenthal visited Bauer in Frankfurt, the two men could only guess what had gone wrong: either someone had talked or Sedlmeier and the Mengeles had smelled a mole on their own, or else the position had been filled by someone already in South America.

Both Wiesenthal and Bauer believed Mengele was still in Paraguay – partly because the last good detective work on the case had been done not by skilled investigators or Nazi-hunters, but by the staff of the West German Embassy in Asunción. In the summer of 1960, a typist from the embassy had dislocated her ankle while vacationing in the south Paraguayan resort of Colonia Independencia. When she limped back to work, she told her boss, Peter Bensch, the chargé d'affaires, that a German doctor named Mengele had treated her, and she wondered why he wasn't on the embassy's list of physicians. Bensch recognized the name and made a journey of nearly 300 miles to seek out Mengele. He never found him, even though he did meet Mengele's host, Alban Krug, who denied knowing him. Anyway, Mengele appeared to have left. Back in Asunción, Bensch reported his clue to Bonn and, receiving no particular encouragement or discouragement from the German Foreign Ministry, went digging into the dictatorship's public records and unearthed José Mengele's acquisition of Paraguayan citizenship in 1959.

Unfortunately, Paraguayan law forbade extradition of its citizens. In 1963, Konrad Adenauer, the eighty-seven-year-old West German Chancellor, had offered Paraguayan President Alfredo Stroessner, fifty-one, ten million Deutschmarks (then some $2.5 million) in aid if he would let Germany lay its hand on Mengele. Stroessner, knowing by then that the game was no longer on his soil and wanting to seem a man of principle, declined without denying Mengele's presence, which tended to reaffirm it.

On 8 February 1964, West German Ambassador Eckhard Briest visited General Stroessner to suggest that, since Mengele had lied in his application that he'd lived in Paraguay for five years, his citizenship could be revoked. Stroessner bristled at this. Pounding his desk with his fist, he told Briest, 'Once a Paraguayan, always a Paraguayan!', and warned the ambassador that he could be declared *persona non grata* if he persisted. As it was, the incident ended Briest's effectiveness in the embassy, and Bonn recalled and replaced him not long thereafter. Although the German Embassy was well guarded by Paraguayan police, semi-official graffiti soon appeared on its walls: 'JEWISH EMBASSY! HANDS OFF MENGELE! THIS IS A COMMAND!' On 23 September 1964, the Paraguayan government issued a statement that Mengele had 'departed Paraguay four years ago.'

This was quite accurate, but who would take Stroessner's word against Wiesenthal's? Three years later, Wiesenthal concluded the Mengele portion of his memoirs with the 'certainty' that his quarry was in Paraguay:

> Mengele now lives as a virtual prisoner in the restricted military zone between Puerto San Vincente on the Asunción-São Paulo highway and the border fortress of Carlos Antonio Lopez on the Paraná River. There he occupies a small white shed in a jungle area cleared by German settlers. Only two roads lead to the secluded house. Both are patrolled by Paraguayan soldiers and police, who have strict orders to stop all cars and shoot all trespassers. And just in case the police should slip up, there are four heavily armed private bodyguards, with radios and walkie-talkies. Mengele pays for them himself.

In truth, Mengele had been living a totally different life in Brazil for nearly seven years as a man called 'Peter'.

Wolfgang Gerhard, the ageing Hitler Youth, had taken Mengele out of Paraguay and into Brazil with him in early 1961, lodged him on his farm at Itapeceria, some forty miles outside São Paulo, and – to see whether the coast was clear – put him to work for a while helping out with routine chores at a textile firm he ran in São Paulo. Mengele, however, did not take to the city where Wiesenthal would soon be hunting concentration camp commandant Franz Stangl.

In the fall of 1961, Gerhard approached Geza and Gitta Stammer, a Hungarian couple who had fled the Iron Curtain in 1948 and were working an eleven-acre farm on the dry plain of Nova Europa, some 200 miles from São Paulo. Gerhard told the Stammers he knew a 'Swiss' named 'Peter Hochbichler', a bachelor who liked the country life, had worked as a 'cattle breeder', and had also inherited some money he wanted to invest in Brazilian property.

To the Stammers, this sounded like manna from heaven. They had their eyes out for a larger property with richer soil. And Geza, a civil engineer who made ends meet by going off on surveying jobs, needed a full-time manager to run the farm. A meeting was arranged and the Stammers found the thin and pale, clean and tidy man Gerhard brought with him 'nothing exceptional', but Mrs Stammer was impressed by his hands, which 'showed he was used to working, for they were full of calluses' (presumably from his days as a farmhand in postwar Bavaria). 'He proved to be very gifted in the garden and with his hands,' she said, 'and all he wanted in return was bachelor quarters, meals, and laundry.' A few weeks later – bearing two suitcases, clothes, and books – 'Peter' moved in with the Stammers to manage their farm.

Though he organized the coffee harvest efficiently, pruned the fruit trees, and built new sheds, 'Peter' was not well liked by the Stammers' farmhands, who called him 'Pedro'. Having lived most of his postwar life alone, and not having formed a lasting relationship with Martha and her son during their two years together, Mengele had grown autocratic, opinionated, intolerant – and pretty intolerable to those who had to work under him. The hired men found it peculiar that their new boss went to work wearing a raincoat with his shirt buttoned at the collar and would pull his hat low to cover his face whenever they approached him. He had very little command of Portuguese or his violent temper. 'He loved giving orders and kept saying we should work more and harder,' one of the hired hands recalled. 'The worst of it was that he didn't seem to understand much about farming or heavy work.'

What did impress them was when Mengele repaired a calf's hernia. 'He reached for some instruments and cut its belly open quite expertly,' said Francisco de Souza, who held the calf. 'He corrected the hernia and sewed up the cut. He said he could guarantee the calf would get better – and it did. I noticed he did everything with a high degree of dexterity.'

Not so when he tried to set up his own mini-Auschwitz to exterminate white ants. 'He made me mount a hook on a cart,' one farmhand recalled. 'On the end of the hook he suspended a 175-pounds weight and with this crazy machine he escorted me around the farm to destroy these huge ant-hills, some of them a yard high. He just stared while I had to pull the weight up and release the rope. Sure, the weight smashed the mounds, but, within a few hours, the ants were making new homes for themselves. We thought it was a crazy idea that took hours and hours to prepare while the ants just worked faster.'

His relations with the Stammers were no better. 'He said we were too soft with our children,' said Mrs Stammer. 'He was always telling us to sack this worker or that one and that we were too slack with them. And he would argue with my husband.' Since, however, 'Peter' asked for no pay and would help finance their move to a new farm, they put up with him as long as they could – which proved to be thirteen years.

Though Mrs Stammer denies it, two recent Mengele biographies strongly suggest she had sexual relations with him. Posner and Ware say point blank that 'Gitta's unswerving loyalty to Mengele appears to be the result of a love affair between them.' The co-authors of *Mengele: the Complete Story* (1986) quote one farmhand as saying she and he were 'always together. They walked everywhere together and were always sitting and talking to each other.' Another hand reported that when the head of the house was free to spend more time away from the farm, the Stammer children 'once told me Pedro and Gitta locked themselves in the bedroom to be by themselves, making it clear they had a romance.' In *The Last Nazi* (1985), Gerald Astor calls it 'not unreasonable' that she had an affair with 'Peter', only ten years her senior. Mengele's diaries contain love poems written to the 'beautiful Gitta'. Interviewed in 1985 by *Der Stern*, Mr and Mrs Wolfram Bossert, an Austrian couple who befriended Mengele as his relations with the Stammers ruptured, insisted that Gitta and 'Peter' were lovers until she 'reached menopause, could no longer achieve orgasm, and was no longer interested in him as a sexual partner' – an interpretation of female sexuality that casts its own dubious shadow.

In July 1962, the Stammers and their manager moved to a 111-acre coffee and cattle farm in Sierra Negra, more than a hundred miles closer to São Paulo. Half the capital for the purchase had been put up by 'Peter', who busied himself with woodworking, carpentry, and, with the help of a local mason, an eighteen-foot-high stone observation tower from which he could scan the countryside with binoculars, watching the approach of visitors from the nearest town, Lindonia, five miles away. Eichmann had been hanged in Israel that June and, although the Mengele manhunt was still focused on Paraguay and Argentina, there were six false-alarm 'sightings' of him in Brazil in less than a year, plus a recurrent rumour that Israeli agents had already abducted Mengele and put him aboard a banana boat heading for Haifa. Reward money had quadrupled.

In 1963, Gitta Stammer read an illustrated magazine article about the missing Mengele and saw a photo of 'a young man, about thirty or thirty-three years old. Then I thought this face was very familiar to me, and his smile with gaps between his teeth.' When she saw 'Peter' that day, she told him: 'This man looks a lot like you. You have many mysteries, but please be honest and say whether it's you.'

He blanched and left the room without saying a word. That night, he was very quiet at dinner – but, after the meal, he told Mr and Mrs Stammer: 'Well, you're right. I live here with you and so you have the right to know that, unfortunately, I am that person.'

Around that time, Mengele noted in his diary: 'Cold wind whistles around the house and in my heart there is no sunshine either.' The Stammers drove to São Paulo and pleaded with Wolfgang Gerhard to take Mengele back and put him somewhere else or they would consider informing the authorities.

Gerhard, whose first reaction had been to tell them they should be proud to have a place in history, now responded: 'Do you really think it might be better that way? You should be very careful, for if you do anything against him, you'll have to take the consequences because he lives here with you. You should think about the future of your children.'

Threatened themselves, the Stammers backed down, but begged him to do something. Gerhard told them to be patient. They would wait another eleven years.

Instead of losing their unwanted guest, who grew more aggressive and abusive each day, the Stammers soon received another guest: a dapper, rotund German named Hans, who arrived bearing money. Hans was Sedlmeier, sent by the Mengele family to make peace. At least 7000 dollars were changed into Brazilian cruzeiros, though much of the money went to Mengele. Sedlmeier promised he would look for another place for Mengele, but, having placated the Stammers, he, too, took his time.

Over the years, Gerhard assured them he was negotiating havens for Mengele in Egypt, Libya, Morocco, or another Latin American country. Meanwhile, tension mounted as Mengele, who rarely ventured far, went nowhere, on the farm or off, without the shrill accompaniment of fifteen stray dogs, most of them vicious. He'd given this pack 'obedience training' to kill on command. One day, Gitta Stammer taunted him with: 'You're such a great man, so why do you live in hiding? At least your colleagues had the guts to live openly and stand trial. Sure, some were hung. Our countrymen in Hungary, too, the non-communists, were killed by the Russians. But they were real men. They didn't hide.'

Mengele raised his hand, but stopped himself from striking her and left the room.

To make matters worse, his hosts' two sons were growing up and refusing to take orders from the star boarder. In 1969, when both boys had finished school, the Stammers gave up farming for a living and bought a four-bedroom house on a two-acre hilltop plot in Caieiras, twenty miles from São Paulo, to enable Geza to work full time as an engineer in the city while their sons went off to the Brazilian naval academy. Mengele paid for half the new house with funds from the sale of the Sierra Negra property.

When he moved in, the domestic war resumed. Once, his Austrian friend Bossert – a one-time German Army corporal whom Wiesenthal identifies as 'a former member of the SS' – took him aside and reminded him quietly that he was merely a guest in the Stammer home.

'Half of this is mine!' Mengele retorted. 'I can do as I please.'

Back in Germany, the Mengele prosecution had been transferred to Frankfurt from his ex-wife Irene's home city of Freiburg. From 1969 to 1975, a diligent Frankfurt investigating judge named Horst von Glasenapp questioned hundreds of witnesses, starting with depositions from those who had given evidence in Freiburg, in order to ensure that, should any of them die before Mengele was brought to justice, their testimony would be in proper legal form to be used against him. According to Wiesenthal, von Glasenapp 'travelled half the world (Austria, Italy, France, Poland, the Soviet Union, Israel, the US, and Canada) to prepare as complete and solid an accusation sheet against Mengele as possible. In September

1970, Sedlmeier was again interrogated, this time by von Glasenapp. And this time Sedlmeier had to admit having met Josef Mengele several times. The last meeting, he claimed, had been in 1961 – a blatant lie.'

Actually, von Glasenapp's formal questioning of Sedlmeier took place on 9 December 1971. While admitting that he had met Mengele during the doctor's 1956 visit to Günzburg and later in South America, Sedlmeier insisted that 'I visited the accused solely for business reasons. If my memory serves me correctly, the last time I saw the accused was about ten years ago. I seem to remember it was at the airport in Buenos Aires. I also heard that, around the time Eichmann was apprehended, the accused went to live in Paraguay. Since then, all connections with the accused have been severed and there has been no further correspondence. I personally am in no position to state where the accused is residing nowadays . . .'

Sedlmeier, of course, knew exactly where Mengele was, stayed in constant touch with him, had recently visited him at his Brazilian hideaway, and helped disinform his hunters by hinting at a Paraguayan address. At the time, though, while von Glasenapp knew Sedlmeier was lying, he couldn't prove it.

Here, says Wiesenthal, von Glasenapp 'made a serious mistake: he forgot to put Sedlmeier's* testimony under oath.' Since Germany had a five-year statute of limitations on the offence of aiding a felon, Sedlmeier could scarcely be prosecuted for the 'ten-year-old' contact with Mengele that he admitted to. Had he been sworn, however, he would have faced a trial for perjury – or the threat of a trial, which could have elicited new information – as soon as any detail of his 1971 testimony proved false.

With Sedlmeier admitting that he'd lied to Fritz Bauer seven years earlier, and with von Glasenapp openly sceptical about his latest testimony, Wiesenthal says 'we took for granted that the Attorney General would at least have Sedlmeier placed under sporadic investigation. We thought his mail would be checked and his telephone tapped intermittently. After all, Sedlmeier had been a key figure since 1964.' And in this assumption, he concedes, 'the

* In his 1988 memoir, Wiesenthal misspells Sedlmeier's name as Sedlm*a*ier.

Documentation Centre committed its second mistake' – which sounds exactly like its first: belief in Bauer.

When Judge von Glasenapp went to Vienna to take testimony from Wiesenthal, he was sorely disappointed. For legality's sake, he arranged for an Austrian judge to repeat his questions at a hearing convened just for Wiesenthal. The German judge began the charade – which sounded like a variation on the *Tell-your-mother-this, tell-your-father-that* overtures of a domestic quarrel – by asking the Austrian judge to ask Wiesenthal, who was present, for the names and addresses of persons who might have accurate information about where Mengele was. According to von Glasenapp:

> Wiesenthal was quite angry that I'd asked him these questions and he refused to answer them. He said he was bound by confidentiality to his informants, which I understood. I left feeling he was eager to convey that he was leading the field on [Mengele], that he was the man out front. Perhaps behind his refusal to answer was a feeling that [his sources] weren't so reliable after all. I myself remained a little sceptical and never raised the subject with him again.

Von Glasenapp later told American lawyer Posner and his British co-biographer, Ware, that 'I met Wiesenthal several times, but never got much out of him. I naturally wanted to know if he really did have something of value. It was difficult to make that judgement from the various newspaper articles I'd read.'

In the early 1970s, a delegation from Asunción's Jewish community council – representing Paraguay's 1000 Jews – visited Wiesenthal in Vienna to plead with him not to do anything against Mengele on Paraguayan soil or they would suffer at the hands of some of their country's 30,000 ethnic Germans *and* its government. When they showed him letters they had received warning them not to molest Mengele, this reinforced his certainty that his quarry was in Paraguay.

Having 'no alternative' to heeding their appeal and having 'received no co-operation from Latin American governments', Wiesenthal says he sought a snatch somewhere outside South America. Back in 1974, he told me: 'I missed Mengele by eighteen hours in Torremolinos in 1971, by two days in Milan at Christmas time 1963, and I could have had him in Bermuda in December

1970, but I was in London when word reached Vienna and then the man I tried to send from New York was in Tokyo, so it took five days before we could get anybody there and Mengele was gone.' Later, records would show that Mengele never was in any of those places at any of those times – or, with the exception of Milan, ever.

Benno Weiser Varon was Israel's first ambassador to Paraguay, serving in Asunción from 1968 to 1972. Like Mengele, Varon had studied medicine. But Varon was forced to flee Vienna when Hitler annexed Austria three months before he was due to become a doctor. During his four years in Paraguay, Varon saw no symptoms of Mengele's presence there, though the man was always on his mind and he followed up every tip that reached him.

'Sometime in the seventies,' says Varon, who later settled in the US, 'Wiesenthal confided to me in Boston that it was not at all easy to keep his outfit in Vienna going. He said that his lecture fees and the contributions of some 17,000 Dutch Gentiles went only so far.' Varon came to the conclusion that, while 'Mengele would be a prize catch for any Nazi-hunter . . . no one has specialized in him. Simon Wiesenthal makes periodic statements that he is about to catch him, perhaps since Wiesenthal must raise funds for his activities and the name Mengele is always good for a plug.' In any event, Varon contended, 'Simon Wiesenthal was always a Nazi-hunter, but never a Nazi-catcher.'

Wiesenthal admits that 'we had to content ourselves with publicizing the Mengele case again and again', a tactic which *The Times* of London – in a scathing 1985 article entitled 'What Next for the Mengele Industry?' – said 'only sustained [Wiesenthal's] self-confirmatory myths and gave scant satisfaction to those who were seriously seeking Mengele.' But Simon's severest critics have to acknowledge his sincerity and dedication as well as his astuteness in latching on to Sedlmeier as the key as early as 1964. Even such Wiesenthal critics as Mengele biographers Posner and Ware, who contend 'financial constraints and a knack of playing to the gallery . . . ultimately compromised his credibility', nevertheless go on to add:

> What no one can take from Wiesenthal is his missionary zeal, his success in ensuring that many people and some reluctant governments pursued Nazis when they would have preferred to forget. One must ask: if not Wiesenthal, who else would

have performed that role? He really was the public conscience of the Holocaust when few others seemed to care. It was largely on Wiesenthal's self-image of a tireless, dogged sleuth, pitted against the omnipotent and sinister might of Mengele and a vast Nazi network, that two full-length Hollywood films were made. Both *Marathon Man* and *The Boys from Brazil* were box-office hits. They played an important part in keeping Mengele at the forefront of the public's mind, an easily identifiable symbol of the Allies' betrayed pledge to pursue Nazis wherever they fled. But these movies also created a mood of despair: Mengele was simply too powerful, he was too clever, he was 'bionic', he would never be caught. And yet . . . he was here, he was there, he was everywhere, said Wiesenthal. He had been seen: he really could be found.

In 1977, Wiesenthal informed *Time* Magazine that Josef Mengele was living in a spacious villa in San Antonio, a Paraguayan village in a remote area south-east of Asunción, and also had a home in Puerto Stroessner, a town at the confluence of the Paraná and Iguaçú rivers. Both lay within a military enclave off limits to outsiders. But Mengele also travelled within the Paraguayan hinterlands, visiting German-owned farms where die-hard Nazis lived in constant anxiety. 'That is a part of their punishment,' Wiesenthal told *Time*.

According to Wiesenthal, Mengele – escorted by four armed guards – would arrive in a black Mercedes 280SL. Prior to his entering even a trusted German home, two bodyguards would go first and make sure it was safe before using their walkie-talkies to sound an all-clear to Mengele and two other guards in the car.

Of late, Wiesenthal went on, Mengele had been seen regularly at the German club in Asunción. Any time a stranger entered the bar, Mengele would don his sunglasses and remove them only when he felt secure. Performing this exercise so annoyed Mengele that, once, he slammed his sunglasses on a table, breaking a lens. On another occasion, after too much to drink, he took out a pistol and waved it wildly. Complete with photos of Wiesenthal, Mengele, and one of the fugitive's 'homes' in Paraguay, *Time* called its story 'Wiesenthal's Last Hunt: Tracking Down the Angel of Death', and gave it a page and a half in the World section.

The only problem was that Mengele hadn't set foot in Paraguay for sixteen years. But even as he perpetuated the myth of the bionic Mengele, his own words fuelled Simon's determination that, as he once put it to me, 'in my lifetime and his, Mengele must be before a court as a man and not roaming free as a legend.'

– 24 –

Death of a bionic 'angel'

In reality, the 'bionic' Mengele had been floundering like a fish out of water since 1971, the year he lost a protector but gained a valuable identity card. Tragedy had struck the family of Wolfgang Gerhard, the forty-six-year-old Hitler Youth who had lodged Mengele with the Stammers. Gerhard's Brazilian wife Ruth was diagnosed as having stomach cancer; his son, Adolf, bone cancer. His textile business and neo-Nazi journalism earnings couldn't meet his doctor bills. Gerhard decided to go back to his native Austria to seek medical help and financial fortune. Before departing, he gave Mengele his Brazilian foreign resident's identity card; one report says Mengele paid 7000 dollars for it. Substituting his own photo, he left all other details, including a fingerprint, the way they were.

In 1972, Mengele's health began to decline – thanks, oddly enough, to the handlebar moustache he'd grown to hide his facial features and gapped teeth. Where others grind their teeth or bite their lips to cope with nervous tension, Mengele's mannerism had been to chew off the ends of his moustachioes. Over the years, these strands had formed a hairball – similar to what befalls cats from licking their coats – blocking his intestines and requiring surgery.

When he checked into a hospital in São Paulo, a doctor noted that 'Wolfgang Gerhard' seemed much older than the forty-seven years shown on his identity card. Wolfram Bossert, who had taken over Gerhard's role as protector and accompanied Mengele to the hospital, hastily explained that the authorities had made an error in recording the birth date and promised to correct it by issuing a new card soon. After his recovery, Mengele used the card as little as possible, but it remained his most plausible permit for being in Brazil and less dangerous than the Paraguayan passport of José Mengele.

Before 1972 was out, Mengele had also been diagnosed as having an enlarged prostate gland and degenerating discs in the lower spine. Another complaint was financial: aside from sending Sedlmeier, bearing cash, at irregular intervals, the Mengele family in Günzburg was letting its notorious black sheep live on an allowance of $100 to $150 a month; although he lived frugally, crafted his own furniture, and never went anywhere, he still felt he deserved more. But the biggest pain in his life was living with the Stammers, which was proving intolerable for everybody. When his relatives in Germany bought a car for the Stammers, Josef Mengele complained that they didn't deserve it, the Stammers complained that it was too small, and everybody complained when the Stammers produced some extra money they hadn't told anybody they had and traded their gift in for a larger auto.

In 1974, Geza Stammer moved out of the house in Caieiras and took quarters in a hotel in São Paulo's red-light district, insisting that he wouldn't come back until Mengele left. Knowing that the police could easily become involved, Bossert sent a warning to Günzburg (via a post office box Sedlmeier kept in Switzerland) that 'the situation is explosive.' Sedlmeier made a flying visit and waved 5000 dollars before the three squabblers, but nobody rose to the bait. That November, the Stammers sold the house in Caieiras and, using Mengele money which they'd hoarded over the years as well as their own savings, they bought a 900-square-metre (10,000-square-foot) villa just outside São Paulo. It was big enough for them and their two sons (both of them officers in the Brazilian merchant marine) and their families. When they moved there the following month, Mengele was not invited to join them. The new owner of the Caieiras house let him stay until February 1975.

The Stammers, never ones to pass up extra income, used Mengele's $25,000 share of the price they received for the house he was living in to buy a bungalow in a seedy suburb of São Paulo, register it in the name of their younger son, Miklos, and then rent it to Mengele. The new tenant's electric bills were in the name of 'Peter Stammer'; the neighbours knew him as 'Don Pedro', and the authorities listed him as 'Wolfgang Gerhard'.

His survival as 'Gerhard' was threatened in 1976, when Brazil changed the format of its foreign residents' identity card. New photos, fingerprinting, and a personal visit to the Department of

Public and Social Order were required to obtain one. When Mengele sent an SOS to Günzburg, Sedlmeier visited Gerhard in Austria, where his wife had died the year before and his son Adolf was undergoing repeated surgery and expensive treatments for bone cancer. The fugitive's stepson, Karl-Heinz, by then a director of Mengele & Sons, was helping with the medical payments. Sedlmeier paid Gerhard to fly back to Brazil and renew his residence permit. While there, Gerhard not only visited Josef Mengele, but looked after his idol's eternal rest by visiting his own mother's grave in Embu and telling the cemetery manager that, now that his wife was interred in Austria, he'd like to be buried in Europe, too, but would the cemetery please reserve the adjacent plot for an ageing relative in Brazil?

On his brief visit to Brazil, Gerhard also asked Ernesto Glawe, a textile engineer of German ancestry, to look in on his ageing relative, 'Peter Gerhard', from time to time. That was why Glawe's young son, Norberto, and his fiancée, were saying goodbye to Mengele on Sunday, 16 May 1976, when he suddenly lost control of speech and movement as a sharp pain stabbed the right side of his head. Within seconds, he could no longer move his left arm or leg. Norberto Glawe drove him to a hospital, where he was admitted and diagnosed as having suffered a stroke. Asked to pay a deposit, he produced a crisp new US hundred-dollar bill.

Norberto Glawe took note of this as well as the identity card on which 'Don Pedro' purported to be the Wolfgang Gerhard the Glawes knew – and mentioned these details to his father. When Mengele, who regained the use of his limbs next day, was discharged from the hospital two weeks later, young Norberto moved in with him for a fortnight as a sort of male nurse. His father dropped around from time to time. When he found a farm-machinery catalogue from Mengele & Sons lying around, Ernesto Glawe says he 'put two and two together', but didn't take his arithmetic to the police. In a letter to Sedlmeier, Mengele complained about having 'to pay friends for their silence'.

'In 1977,' says Wiesenthal, 'we learned from a reliable source that Mengele's son, Rolf, employed by an investment company in West Berlin, was about to travel to Brazil. We intended to let two persons shadow him, as we had no doubt that Rolf would somehow establish contact with his father in Latin America. Unfortunately, the Documentation Centre lacked the necessary funds for their operation. . .

'We therefore approached a popular Dutch newspaper, suggesting they pay the expenses in exchange for exclusive rights to the story of our manhunt. But the Dutch newspaper considered the sum involved – 8000 dollars! – too risky. So we had to call the operation off.'

It is hard to imagine Simon Wiesenthal at that stage of his career – with Eichmann, Stangl, and more than a thousand other Nazi scalps on his belt and a Nobel Peace Prize nomination on the table – being unable to raise 8000 dollars, but this was shortly before the Simon Wiesenthal Holocaust Centre came into being in Los Angeles and went into high fund-raising gear. And perhaps Wiesenthal had cried wolf too often where the wolf was named Mengele. Besides, Rolf Mengele was a lawyer in Freiburg, not a banker in Berlin, 400 miles away; routine fact-checking would have given any editor pause before investing further in such an adventure in pinpointing. As with his 1964 Sedlmeier tip, however, Simon's information about Rolf's first visit to his father in twenty-one years was right on target.

Briefed by Sedlmeier and bearing greetings and 5000 dollars in cash from his cousin and stepbrother Karl-Heinz, and a passport he had stolen from a friend named Wilfried Busse, Mengele's thirty-three-year-old son Rolf stepped off a Varig charter flight from Frankfurt to Rio de Janeiro on Monday, 10 October 1977. After an overnight stay in Rio's most luxurious hotel, the Othon Palace, Rolf took a domestic flight to São Paulo and then three taxis (to make sure he wasn't followed) to Wolfram Bossert's house at Rua Missuri 7. Bossert drove him in an ancient Volkswagen bus to his father's bungalow at Estrada de Alvaranga 555 on an unpaved street in the suburb called El Dorado.

'The man who stood before me,' Rolf recalled years later, 'was a broken man, a haunted creature.' After a distant embrace and a few preliminaries, Rolf asked his father to tell him about Auschwitz and answer the accusations against him. The interrogation went on for days and nights. With lawyerly detachment, Rolf first listened to his father's case, asking as few questions as possible pending cross-examination. Leftist in politics, embittered by the deception that 'Onkel Fritz' was his father, which had kept him in the dark until he was sixteen in 1960, and resentful that his father had always favoured Karl-Heinz over him, Rolf Mengele held no brief for the man he was meeting for the first time in his adult life.

For a fortnight, Dr Mengele assured his son that he had neither invented Auschwitz nor condoned it, but, forced to work there or lose his life, had made the same choices that confront a surgeon in a field hospital: if a dozen dying casualties are brought in, he operates first on the handful that have a chance of survival, dooming the rest to certain death. 'When people arrived at the railhead half dead and infected with disease, what was I supposed to do?' he asked rhetorically, answering that his job was only to classify those 'able to work' and 'unable to work' – and that he was as generous in his assessments as he could afford to be. He took personal credit for rescuing twins for research.

After his father had concluded his case by saying he felt no guilt, no repentance, Rolf asked him why he hadn't turned himself in.

'There are no judges. There are only avengers,' Mengele replied, paying grudging tribute to Wiesenthal, Langbein, and others who, denied their day in court, had nonetheless trumpeted his crimes and reduced him to a recluse in the custody of his own comeuppance.

Later, Rolf Mengele told biographers Posner and Ware: 'I realized that this man, my father, was just too rigid. Despite all his knowledge and intellect, he just did not want to see the basis and rules for the simplest humanity in Auschwitz. He didn't understand that his presence alone had made him an accessory within the deepest meaning of inhumanity. There was no point in going on.'

So the son became a tourist in his father's world. They visited his previous addresses in Sierra Negra and Caieiras and went to Bertioga Beach, where he liked to swim. To his neighbours and cleaning woman, Elsa Gulpian, he introduced Rolf as his 'nephew'. To the Bosserts and Stammers, there was no pretence, though the Stammers begged them not to mention the name Mengele in the presence of their future daughter-in-law.

When father and son parted at São Paulo airport, Mengele's last words to Rolf were: 'We shall try to meet again, very soon, all of us.' But they never did.

In 1978, Wolfgang Gerhard died in Austria under what believers in the 'bionic' Mengele describe as 'distinctly mysterious circumstances':

standing beside his auto, he fell on his head and, while unconscious, died of a heart attack. True, he had outlived his usefulness to the Mengeles, but there is no evidence to suggest anything more sinister than the thought that people who lead peculiar lives often die peculiar deaths.

Biologically, Mengele was deteriorating rapidly. His 1976 stroke had left his left hand twisted. In 1978, he suffered an attack of shingles. To his prostate and spinal conditions were added diagnoses of high blood pressure and an inner ear infection, all of which combined to cause stumbling and near-collapses on the streets of El Dorado. Perhaps out of loneliness and a need to be taken care of, he fell in love with his small, sharp-featured, bleached-blonde, thirtyish housemaid, Elsa Gulpian; bought her a gold bracelet, a ring, and a white woollen shawl, and started taking her out for dinner, movies, concerts, and long walks. He even danced at her sister's wedding. When he asked her to move in with him, she said he would have to marry her first. This he refused, without telling her why. He was still married to Martha and, besides, it was too risky for him to present his falsified identity card at the marriage registry. Elsa left his employ and his life in October 1978 when she became engaged to a dark-skinned Brazilian. 'He is not the man for you,' Mengele warned her in parting. 'You deserve a better, more cultured person.'

South of the equator, the seasons are the reverse of ours. In the midsummer heat of early February 1979, Mengele accepted an invitation to visit the Bosserts at their beach house in Bertioga, some forty miles north of São Paulo. Just before making the two-hour bus trip, he told Ines Mehlich, the maid who replaced Elsa: 'I'm going to the beach because my life is coming to an end.' By then, said Ines, her employer always 'seemed distracted and spoke with difficulty. Once, he nearly fell into the well in the back yard.'

Mengele arrived at Bertioga Beach on Sunday, 5 February 1979, but kept to himself until Tuesday the 7th, when he went for an afternoon walk along the shore with his host and the Bossert children. Perched on a large rock, he looked out to sea and told Wolfram Bossert: 'Over there is my country. I'd like to spend the last days of my life in Günzburg writing the history of my town.' Then, around 4.30 p.m., he went in for a dip.

At Bertioga Beach, the waves are gentle and the Atlantic sand-shelf slopes slowly into the sea. A man Mengele's size could walk out more than half a mile and not be in over his head. Mengele was an accomplished swimmer and there was nothing to worry about. But he had barely reached waist level when Bossert's son, Andreas, on the beach with his father, cried out: '*Onkel!* Come out! The current's too strong for you.' Mengele was thrashing in the sea.

Wolfram Bossert ran and swam to his guest's side as fast as he could. But Mengele had suffered another stroke and was paralyzed. He must have tumbled underwater and now was bobbing lifelessly on the surface. 'I had to swim with one arm and pull him with the other, and the sea was dragging us both out,' Bossert recalled in 1985. Upon fighting his way to shore with his dead weight, Bossert was hospitalized for exhaustion.

No hospital, however, could help Josef Mengele any longer. A doctor on the shore massaged his heart and tried mouth-to-mouth resuscitation. For a second or two, there was a flicker of life – and then eternity. The 'Angel of Auschwitz' had gone to hell.

– 25 –

Post-mortems

In 1978, eighteen years after Dr Josef Mengele left Paraguay, Wiesenthal had written in his annual report: 'Mengele is living in Paraguay, where he is protected by the local junta, which is dominated by ethnic Germans. Mengele is Number One on our wanted list. Although his observation in Paraguay and the monitoring of his occasional trips abroad has cost us a lot of money, we have continued our activities against this arch-criminal through 1977 and intend to do so in the future.' In 1979, Wiesenthal wrote to Kurt Waldheim, then Secretary General of the United Nations, imploring his fellow Austrian to bring pressure on Paraguay:

> I appeal to you, in this International Year of the Child, to use all your influence so that the murder of hundreds of thousands of children by a doctor of medicine, who is enjoying his liberty within a UN member country, will not go unpunished.

Waldheim responded by contacting the Paraguayan authorities, who revoked Mengele's citizenship – for what it was worth to a dead man.

In 1980, barely a year after Mengele drowned, Wiesenthal proclaimed: 'I cannot say where he is, but he has been seen five times recently. I am much closer to catching him than I was a year ago. His capture could come in the next few weeks.'

The following January, he described Mengele in his annual report as:

> . . . a criminal permanently on the run. For a short time, we thought we had located Mengele in the Colonia Dignidad, an isolated German settlement in Chile. But then it seemed we had been misled by people who wanted to give the Colonia Dignidad a bad name . . .

> Later, we managed to localize Mengele in Santa Cruz, Bolivia, where he was together with a doctor friend of his. Unfortunately, he was gone again before we could act. The last serious information places Mengele in Rio Negro, Uruguay, in October 1980. As we are told, his state of health is not good.

Applied to a man who had been dead for twenty-three months, this was the understatement of the year. But Wiesenthal concluded on an optimistic note:

> Now that we know somewhat more about Mengele's friends and his circle of acquaintances, we hope for success at last in 1981.

Mengele's capture, Wiesenthal insisted, 'is only a matter of time.'

In early 1982, the man who couldn't raise 8000 dollars five years earlier posted a $100,000 reward for information leading to Mengele's arrest and said that for such a sum 'even his bodyguards would sell him out.' He added that he was 'checking information that Mengele recently obtained a new passport from a Central American country. There is also a very trustworthy report that Mengele, suffering from stomach cancer, has sent his X-ray pictures to a well-known specialist who is studying them now.' That April, Wiesenthal proclaimed he was 'much closer than ever to capturing him'; that May and again in August he was still 'very close'.

A year later, Wiesenthal, who writes the way he talks, reported:

> According to latest informations – which we publish so that Mengele's friends will know that we know – Mengele was repeatedly seen in Philadelphia in Paraguay. He was there for several short visits to the Mennonite villages located in that region.
>
> His acquaintance with the Mennonites dates back to his long stay in Paraguay. He sometimes gave them medical help and felt safe among them. His last visit took place between December 27 to 30, 1982. We also gave the public prosecutor in Frankfurt the names of several West German doctors of whom we have reason to think that they are still in contact with Mengele.

The Mennonites – a Protestant sect which, along with the Amish, comprises most of the people we call 'Pennsylvania Dutch' – held Wiesenthal's attention into 1985, when he reported

> ever-increasing indications that Josef Mengele is on very good

> terms with the inhabitants of the Mennonite settlements in Paraguay . . . particularly in respect to a group of German Mennonites from Russia who emigrated to Paraguay after the 1918 Revolution, as well as with regard to a group of Mennonites who left Germany and the Netherlands for Paraguay in 1947.

In 1984, Wiesenthal warned Neal Sher, head of the US Justice Department's Office of Special Investigations, on a visit to Vienna, that 'the key to Mengele lies with Sedlmeier', but he says he added naïvely: 'He is surely being watched by the authorities in Frankfurt.' As Rabbi Marvin Hier, head of the Simon Wiesenthal Centre in Los Angeles, pointed out later: 'For twenty years, Simon had been telling this to the German prosecutors and urging them to maybe do at least a telephone tap on Sedlmeier, but nothing was ever done. In those twenty years, he kept getting tips, some of which he thought were serious, so he put out word that he was sure Mengele was hiding in Paraguay. Look, Wiesenthal is an individual. He gets his information from what other people supply: SS men, Displaced Persons, victims, survivors, refugees, informers, people on the run. And, in this case, almost all of them were wrong. But he's not an agency. He's not an intelligence organization with unlimited resources and hundreds of agents to look for one man. He's not the CIA or Mossad [Israeli Intelligence]. Anyway, even the Mossad thought Mengele was in Paraguay. So did the Klarsfelds.'

It was early in 1985 when Serge Klarsfeld – a Romanian-born French lawyer, Nazi-hunter and victim whose father died in Auschwitz – broke the logjam by having a friend search Rolf Mengele's apartment. This turned up the passport he'd stolen from his friend Wilfried Busse. Stamped into it was a 1977 Brazilian visa, confirming Wiesenthal's lead, but Klarsfeld and Wiesenthal never compared notes; Klarsfeld contends that Wiesenthal saw him as a rival instead of an ally. 'He's an egomaniac,' says Klarsfeld. Wiesenthal, in turn, has naught but frosty contempt for Klarsfeld's tactics, of which he considers stooping to burglary just the tip of an iceberg.

Klarsfeld's German-born wife, Beate (who, unlike her husband, is not Jewish), stepped up the pressure by visiting Asunción to prod Paraguay into revealing Mengele's whereabouts. When the government insisted he hadn't been there for twenty or twenty-five, years, she unfurled a banner reading 'PRESIDENT STROESSNER, YOU lie when you say you don't know where ss mengele is' on the steps of the Supreme Court which granted 'the devil's doctor' Paraguayan citizenship a quarter of a century earlier. Police chased her and a small band of supporters back to her hotel, where she was told to pack her bags and leave because she had 'offended the Paraguayan people in the person of the president.' Asked on television to 'tell us where he is', she replied: 'If you think logically, there is nowhere else he could be.' And she added: 'It's up to the government to prove he isn't here.'

Dictator Stroessner had scheduled a state visit to West Germany that July. When Chancellor Helmut Kohl, an admirer of Wiesenthal, wrote to Simon in March for help in assembling information to 'raise emphatically' the issue of Mengele's extradition, Wiesenthal gave Kohl the late doctor's 'latest' Paraguayan whereabouts and said the Stroessner visit offered the best chance of delivering Mengele to justice. After the Klarsfelds made it clear that the general would be hounded by the media about Mengele, Stroessner cancelled his trip.

Earlier, around the time when Serge Klarsfeld was having Rolf Mengele burgled, the Simon Wiesenthal Centre had invoked the US Freedom of Information Act to obtain a 26 April 1947 Counter-Intelligence Corps (CIC) letter from Benjamin J. M. Gorby, stationed in Regensburg, Bavaria, to the commanding officer of the 430th CIC detachment in Vienna, asking him to verify a newspaper report that Dr Mengele 'has been arrested in Vienna' and, if so, to please question him 'with regard to the fate of a group of approximately twenty Jewish children who were alleged to have been removed by him from the Auschwitz camp in November 1944 and taken to an unknown place. The fact of the removal of the Jewish children from Auschwitz by Dr Mengele was confirmed to this office by the father of one of the children . . . Other parents of the children among the group are still alive and most eager to have news from or about their children.'

'The Gorby Document', as it became known, proved to be a false clue that had actually been declassified a year and a half earlier by the Department of the Army after an administrative appeal by biographers Posner and Ware. Nevertheless, by suggesting that Mengele might have been in US custody as late as 1947, 'the Gorby Document' triggered an uproar in Washington. Attorney General

William French Smith ordered an investigatory commission to look into the Mengele case and any US involvement in it. A special unit of US marshals began a country-by-country search for Mengele's whereabouts. The Wiesenthal Centre posted a million-dollar reward, starting a sweepstake which escalated around the world. Israel offered a matching reward of a million dollars and so did the Unification Church guru Sun Myung Moon's *Washington Times* newspaper.

'In order not to be outdistanced,' says Rabbi Hier with some satisfaction, 'the West German government increased its reward to a million marks – about 313,000 dollars at the time – from around 25,000 dollars. But without our publicizing the Gorby Document, the US government never would have entered the Mengele case and none of these other events would have happened so soon.'

The contagion of Wiesenthal assertions and Beate Klarsfeld's stormy visit unleashed a media circus in Asunción. The District Attorney of Brooklyn, ex-Congresswoman Elizabeth Holtzman – herself a twin and Jewish – arrived with a delegation which included the Roman Catholic Bishop of Brooklyn and a member of Children of Auschwitz Survivors. The *New York Times* put investigative reporter Ralph Blumenthal on the case and the Columbia Broadcasting System dispatched a team to Paraguay for its weekly magazine programme, 'Sixty Minutes'. The CBS producer actually found a man who told him Mengele had drowned in Brazil, but nobody believed him. West German authorities received a similar tip that Mengele had perished 'on the beaches of Brazil', but a Brazilian official had responded with: 'Which beach? We have 10,000 miles of beach.'

Back in Europe, the fortieth anniversary of the liberation of Auschwitz rekindled memories of Mengele. In Israel, when Simon Wiesenthal participated in a mock trial of Mengele, he heard dozens of witnesses: twins, midgets, dwarfs, gypsies, many still showing the scars and ravages of the viruses and hormones, chemicals and poisons, amputations and anomalies Mengele inflicted on them and future generations; fathers who lost their whole families to him and mothers like Anna Sussman, who saw Mengele pitch her newborn son into a burning oven, and Ruth Eliaz, who made Wiesenthal weep as she told how Mengele bound her breasts to starve her infant daughter

At the White House, when Elie Wiesel was pleading with Ronald Reagan not to visit the SS cemetery in Bitburg, Germany, the future

Nobel Peace Prize-winner spoke from his own Auschwitz experience of sons seeing their fathers die, mothers watching 'their children die of hunger And then there was Mengele and his selections.'

In early April 1985 in Vienna, Wiesenthal was saying: 'If you ask me in what place I believe he is, he is in Paraguay. That is the safest place for him.' Was he certain? 'Well, we can bring some evidence that six or seven months ago he was there.' A month later, Simon said he had informed German Chancellor Kohl of three independent sightings of Mengele the previous July in the German settlement of Capitán Miranda outside Hohenau in a zone of Paraguay closed to non-residents because General Stroessner had several presidential summer homes there. As late as 20 May 1985, Wiesenthal would declare: 'There is without any doubt that he is alive.'

In Günzburg, the Mengele family, which had stayed silent to protect those who had sheltered its black sheep, was feeling commercial pressure from customers who didn't want *that* name on their tractors and manure-spreaders. Colonel Rudel and Alban Krug, who had shepherded Mengele from Argentina to Paraguay, had both died in 1982; Wolfgang Gerhard, his Brazilian benefactor, was buried in two places: Graz, Austria, and Embu, Brazil. The cemetery-keeper at Embu had prepared the plot Gerhard had reserved for his ageing relative, but when he saw Gerhard's own name on the coffin that arrived in February 1979, he exclaimed: 'It can't be possible! He mentioned an uncle and now here he is himself!'

Making the sign of the cross, the caretaker had suggested that they open the coffin. But he didn't take much dissuading when Liselotte Bossert, whose husband had been hospitalized from trying to rescue Mengele, had hysterics. Remarking that 'a body pulled out of water is not a pretty sight', the man relented – and, as Posner and Ware put it, 'Mengele's secret was taken to the grave.'

Six years later, Karl-Heinz and Dieter Mengele, who were running the firm in Günzburg, decided on damage control: a slow leak that might dredge up their uncle's bones without directly implicating the Bosserts, the Stammers, Sedlmeier, or themselves. Dieter Mengele gave an interview to John Martin of the American Broadcasting Company in which he said blandly: 'I think he's dead. First of all, he'd be seventy-four. If it's true what I'm reading that everybody's looking for him, they'd have found him by now if he's still alive.'

Hearing the ABC interview, Mengele's son Rolf, who hadn't been consulted, remonstrated with his cousins. Reluctantly, they agreed that no further statements would be made until the Bosserts and Sedlmeier were dead.

Sedlmeier had been questioned in December 1984 for only the third time in the two decades since Wiesenthal had warned West German prosecutors that this was the man to watch. A university professor from Giessen had met Sedlmeier and his wife, Renate, at a resort hotel in the Black Forest and, over dinner and drinks, Sedlmeier had waxed expansive, mentioning that he'd sent Mengele money for many years. In the hope of collecting the rewards he'd been reading about, the professor had reported this conversation to the police. Confronted by an investigator, Sedlmeier had said he had no recollection of these words and insisted he hadn't seen Mengele since the early 1960s at Buenos Aires airport. He hadn't even hinted that Mengele was dead.*

On Friday, 31 May 1985, more than five months after his interrogation, the German federal police raided Sedlmeier's house. It was their first raid since 1964, when they'd acted on Wiesenthal's tip and Sedlmeier had been warned by a friend in the Günzburg police department. This time, apparently, he was not forewarned. Whether 1985's raid was prompted by the worldwide clamour for Mengele to stand trial or his nephews' need to purge the ghost is not absolutely certain; Simon thinks it was rather stagey.

Sedlmeier ran for a jacket hanging in his closet. His investigators intercepted him and seized a pocket directory containing addresses and phone numbers, some of them in code. The search bore fruit when, to Sedlmeier's apparent astonishment, the investigators found, in a room used by his wife, a complete photocopy file of letters from and to Mengele, the Bosserts, and the Stammers in Brazil. Renate Sedlmeier, who had been close to Mengele during the war and still had a crush on him, claimed to have copied them before Sedlmeier had them destroyed. 'How could you do that?' her husband wailed, calling her an 'idiot'.

*The professor never collected any cash for his good deed. The reward offerers were so certain Mengele was alive that, in most cases, they called for his capture or information leading to his capture – and seldom specified 'dead or alive'. Information leading to exhumation six years after burial was not deemed worthy of a cash prize.

Sedlmeier, who refused to answer questions, was placed under house arrest while the police sifted their finds. A 1979 letter from Wolfram Bossert reporting 'with deep sorrow the death of our common friend' cracked the case. After phone calls to Brazil and a few hours of interrogation by São Paulo police, the Bosserts broke – and the eyes of the world focused on Bertioga Beach and the hillside cemetery in Embu.

Simon Wiesenthal was en route to New York for his semi-annual lecture tour when the story broke. Met by reporters at Kennedy Airport, he branded it a hoax:

'This is Mengele's seventh death. Only in Paraguay has he been dead three times, always with witnesses who say it's him. On one of those occasions, we found the body of a woman.

'If Mengele really died, then the whole world would have been informed five minutes after, not five years. His wife, children, relatives, besides friends and sympathizers, would have done everything to announce the death of Mengele so they could spend the rest of their lives in peace.'

At best, Wiesenthal said, there was a one per cent chance the man was Mengele. In the ensuing weeks, however – as both 'Wolfgang Gerhards' were exhumed in Graz and Embu; as forensic specialists, including three Americans engaged by the Simon Wiesenthal Centre in Los Angeles and three more by the US government in Washington, converged upon São Paulo to study the skull, a partial fingerprint, hairs and dental evidence – Wiesenthal raised his estimate to 'I think it's fifty-fifty it's him.'

In Günzburg, Hans Sedlmeier refused to co-operate with the police, but no charges could be placed against him, for the West German statute of limitations on the crime of aiding a fugitive – even a wanted war criminal – was only five years. This may have played a part in the surfacing of the letters in his wife's boudoir, which Wiesenthal found 'a little too perfect'.

Rolf Mengele issued a statement confirming that his father had drowned in Brazil in 1979 and explaining that he had remained silent 'out of consideration for the people who had been in contact with my father over the previous thirty years.' His statement, handed out in Munich by his stepbrother Jens Hackenjos at a press conference Rolf didn't attend, also extended 'to all the victims and their relatives my own and our most profound sympathy.' Those minimal remarks earned Rolf the enmity of the Günzburg Mengeles, who no longer speak to him.

By Friday, 21 June 1985, when the bits and pieces of Josef Mengele were exhibited to the press on the twentieth floor of São Paulo police headquarters, Wiesenthal seemed convinced. The 'Wolfgang Gerhard' buried in Brazil was exactly Josef Mengele's height, had his broken left finger, the same gap between two top front teeth, and the degenerating spine Mengele had complained about. A video image of his skull matched up perfectly with an authenticated photo of Mengele on to which it was superimposed. A similar montage matched the skeleton's hip bones with Mengele's medical measurements. John Martin of ABC asked Dr Lowell Levine if there was any doubt at all.

'Absolutely not,' the New York odontologist replied.

Later, after deciphering obscure references in Mengele's diary to a series of dental visits, two US consular officials in Brazil tracked down eight X-rays taken in 1976. Not only did they clearly show the unusual gap between Mengele's two front incisors, but every detail exactly matched X-rays taken of the skull in mid-1985. Dr Levine announced that 'reasonable scientific certainty' had become 'absolute certainty'.

In Israel, when victim Ruth Eliaz heard the news from Brazil, she said: 'Drowning is a horrible death. But, for Mengele, this death was too good, too fast, and too simple.'

* * *

Back in Vienna from his US trip, Simon Wiesenthal told me on 12 July 1985: 'I am not satisfied that he is dead. I had hopes that the victims of his experiments would at least have the occasion to see his trial and tell what he has done to them. So I am dictating a letter to Germany. I am asking only that the million-Deutschmark reward for catching Mengele be divided up among his victims.'

Listening between the lines and recognizing that he was thinking wishfully, I said: 'So you're convinced he's dead?'

'Yes,' Simon admitted. 'In September, he will be declared officially dead.'

'And you won't contest it?'

'No,' he said wearily. 'I am sure he is dead.'

In his annual report for 1985 – dated 31 January 1986 – Simon Wiesenthal wrote:

> A post-mortem examination was carried out following the opening of the grave by an international team of forensic experts, and revealed with near certainty that the body buried in Brazil was that of Josef Mengele. For us, the case is thus concluded.
>
> Naturally, there are people who cannot accept this, and others who attempt from time to time to misinform Jewish organizations with news about Mengele, as has been the case throughout the last years.

Late in 1988, however, it became apparent that one of these doubting troublemakers was Simon Wiesenthal himself.

'I begin to have doubts that the body is the body of Mengele,' he told me, 'when the prosecution in Germany will not declare him dead. So I ask the chief prosecutor in Frankfurt, Dr [Hans-Eberhard] Klein, why not. He tells me that, like me, he keeps getting reports from people who have seen Mengele alive and well in Paraguay. Then there is a woman dentist in Brazil who says she treated Mengele in April 1979, two months after he was supposed to have drowned. The Brazilian police say she is just seeking publicity, but Klein and I would like to hear more from her side of the story. So Klein says that, as long as these reports are not laid to rest, he cannot declare Mengele dead. And I agree . . . Israel, too, still has not declared him dead.'

Tantalized by tidbits, Wiesenthal makes much in his memoirs of a December 1982 visit by Sedlmeier and Mengele's nephew and stepson Karl Heinz to Dr Hans Munch near Munich. Munch – one of Mengele's closest friends at Auschwitz – was an SS lieutenant in a biological research station there who refused to do selection duty at the ramp. At a 1947 war-crimes trial in Cracow, Munch was the only Auschwitz doctor acquitted by the Supreme National Tribunal of Poland; forty other doctors and SS men were convicted. In June 1985, Munch told Mengele biographers Posner and Ware that the visit's apparent purpose was for Karl-Heinz Mengele, with Sedlmeier as his shepherd, to familiarize himself with (and, perhaps, rationalize himself out of) Josef Mengele's actual activities at Auschwitz. Had he been involved in gas-chamber selections? Did he conduct experiments on human beings? Did he ever kill anybody with his bare hands? This was the nature of the questions Munch says he tried to answer as candidly and kindly as an old friend could. But Wiesenthal says the session was a moot-court kind of dry run to determine whether Dr Mengele stood a better chance before a judge if charged with conducting experiments or conducting selections. And he finds it significant that, if both of Munch's visitors knew that Mengele had been dead for nearly four years, they nonetheless referred to him in the present tense. This, however, was Sedlmeier's tactic right up to 1985.

Still, says Simon, 'people who are usually quite busy and tied down to their jobs – like Karl-Heinz Mengele, who is the head of a big factory – don't waste their time asking theoretical questions about someone who is not alive.' He also points out that neither Frankfurt prosecutor Klein nor the Israeli police nor the US Office of Special Investigations will pronounce Mengele dead. Neal Sher, head of the OSI, said Mengele's death, like John F. Kennedy's assassination, will never be laid to rest. But Rabbi Abraham Cooper of the Simon Wiesenthal Centre, who thinks Mengele is dead, finds it significant that, since 1985, nobody has come forward to claim the rewards leading to his arrest.

Wiesenthal pounces on such trivia as an unexplained hole in the spine of the corpse exhumed at Embu (perhaps it was made by a nail hammered in to obliterate a tell-tale detail) and the lack of any discrepancy between the corpse's height of 1.74 metres (5' 8.5") and the identical height listed on Mengele's wartime SS records (even though loss of hair and the shrivelling of age should have subtracted a centimetre or two). He suggests that clever needlework by a dentist or a doctor like Mengele himself could have duplicated the perforation between his front teeth. And he has endless questions about the suspicious behaviour of the Bosserts on the day Mengele died – and the day after, at the cemetery.

'Just today,' Wiesenthal told me happily on 27 December 1988, four days before his eightieth birthday, 'I receive a letter from a Swiss man who says he met Mengele in Paraguay lately. When I come back from Israel, I will look into it.'

A cruel but telling two-part editorial cartoon by Dana Summers in Florida's *Orlando Sentinel* was syndicated worldwide in the summer of 1985. In the left-hand panel, headlined '1945–1984', a moustached man who looked like Wiesenthal sat behind a desk labelled 'Nazi Hunters, Inc.' and, pondering documents, told an aide: 'Nobody has any information on Mengele. He seems to have disappeared into thin air!' In the right-hand panel, titled '1985!!', a news stand featured headlines that shouted: 'I KNEW JOSEF!' . . . 'HOUSEWIFE SAYS – "WE HUNG OUT TOGETHER"' . . . 'JOSEF FATHERED MY BABY!' . . . 'I GAVE SWIMMING LESSONS TO ANGEL OF DEATH!' . . . 'ALIEN BEINGS LIKED MENGELE' . . . and, inevitably, '"WE WERE DRINKING BUDDIES" – SAYS ELVIS' GHOST'.

On the same page as Summers' cartoon, the *International Herald Tribune* excerpted an editorial from *The Observer*, 'Why Wasn't Mengele Found?', which began by asking:

> How was it possible that Josef Mengele eluded capture for thirty-five years? In the light of the evidence, catching him would not have been difficult. His protection and cover in South America was not at all elaborate.

More often than not, the finger of blame for following false trails was pointed at Simon Wiesenthal – most devastatingly by Benno Varon, the ex-Viennese Israeli ambassador to Paraguay, who called Wiesenthal's periodic Mengele 'sightings' and posting of a reward that 'is in no danger of ever having to be paid out' and proclamation of his imminent capture 'subtle inducement for contributing to the Simon Wiesenthal Centre. Who wouldn't gladly part with some money for the prospect of catching a genocidal monster?', and by Mengele's biographers Posner and Ware, who said 'Wiesenthal's pronouncements raised the public's expectations, only to dash their hopes each time.' In *Mengele: the Complete Story*, they remark:

> The extraordinary thing is that the myth of Wiesenthal's hunt remained intact even after Mengele's body was discovered. He told reporters it was he who had tipped off the West Germans and persuaded them to raid the Günzburg home of Hans Sedlmeier. . .

The Wiesenthal Centre rose to Simon's defence. Its director, Gerald Margolis, and Washington counsel Martin Mendelsohn took on Varon in the pages of the influential Jewish magazine, *Midstream*:

> To denigrate Wiesenthal's efforts, as Varon does, is to defame a man who has successfully brought to justice 1,100 Nazi war

> criminals; a man who embarked on his sacred mission in 1945 unlike some recent arrivals who have embarked with much passion and fury and scant results in the 1980s.

And, in a 1986 interview with me, Rabbi Hier drew a bead on New York lawyer-biographer Posner as one of those Simons-come-lately: 'What Posner skips is that he himself had just completed a book and was about two weeks away from publication when the body was found in Brazil. In the book, he was going to give Mengele's "actual" address in Paraguay. Then the events occurred in Brazil which led him to write a new book. So why does he tell the world how wrong Wiesenthal was and forgets to say that he'd seven-eighths published a book of interviews with high Paraguayan officers and generals and was about to pinpoint the exact location of Mengele in Paraguay? And yet he wants to fault someone else for making the same mistake.

'Over the years, you have to remember that, if Simon had not been in there looking for Mengele – and, later, the entry of Klarsfeld as well – the world would have forgotten about him. A guy like Mengele wouldn't have had to spend his last few years watching soap operas on TV in Brazil. He could have been back home in Bavaria or spending more time on the slopes in Switzerland.'

In 1992, a team of British scientists flew to Germany to make DNA genetic tests comparing a blood sample from the corpse in Embu cemetery with a blood sample from Rolf Mengele, who has changed his name. The match-up left the scientists '99.97 per cent certain' that the body was indeed Josef Mengele's. German authorities were quick to embrace these results. 'As prosecutors,' they said, 'we can assure all survivors of the Holocaust and their families that Mengele is dead.'

Simon Wiesenthal is not so sure, but when I called to find out how he was taking the news, he was taking it personally: 'All day my phone has been ringing with people who say they can prove Mengele is alive. And this is Mengele's revenge on me.'

To make matters worse for Simon, who had undergone prostate surgery a few years earlier: 'The urologists are having a convention here. Many of them are Jewish and they all want to talk with me about Mengele. But not one of them is asking how I am pissing.'

Part V

Franz Paul Stangl, Gustav Wagner, Hermine Braunsteiner Ryan

Oh, what a tangled web we weave,
When first we practise to deceive!

–Sir Walter Scott

– 26 –

Stangl the weaver

With a few exceptions (such as the apprehension of Gustav Wagner, which will be treated in this section), Simon Wiesenthal's role as a serious sleuth and Nazi-hunter ended somewhere between the extraditions of Franz Stangl in 1967 and Hermine Braunsteiner Ryan in 1973. In that interim, Wiesenthal became more of a publicist and conscience than avenger and researcher. Nowhere could his good use of his new-found power as a celebrity be better glimpsed than in his crusade for Raoul Wallenberg. Nowhere could his abandonment of his old talents be viewed with more alarm (yet, even here, with some grudging admiration for the pain he caused villains) than in his campaign to unearth Dr Josef Mengele. But now, before exploring the New Wiesenthal of the seventies and eighties, it is time to pause and appreciate the deftness, determination, and persistence of the Old Wiesenthal – and to detail three of his last hurrahs.

Nine months and five days before Simon Wiesenthal's birth in Galicia, Franz Paul Stangl was born on 26 March 1908, in the Upper Austrian town of Altmünster on Austria's deepest lake, the Traunsee, to an attractive young mother and an ageing night watchman. His father, who hadn't wanted him and wasn't certain the boy was his, lived only for his military past in the imperial dragoons. 'His dragoon uniform, always carefully brushed and pressed, hung in the wardrobe,' Stangl recalled in 1971 in an interview with British journalist Gitta Sereny. 'He was a dragoon. Our lives were run on regimental lines. I was scared to death of him.' His brutal father beat him so hard that, more than half a century later, Stangl still recalled not just the pain, but his mother's screams of 'Stop it! You're splashing blood all over my clean walls!'

Too old to fight in the First World War, Stangl's father was nonetheless a casualty of the slaughter, for he died of malnutrition in 1916. 'He was thin as a rake,' the son remembered with no overt pity. 'He looked like a ghost, a skeleton.' A year later, Stangl's mother married a widower with two children of his own. As soon as Franz was fourteen, his hard-pressed stepfather tried to put him to work in the steel mill where he was employed. 'But I had my eye on working for the local textile mill,' said Stangl. 'That's what I always wanted to do, and for that I had to be fifteen. So I got my mother and the school principal to say I had to stay in school another year.'

Leaving school at fifteen to become a weaver, Stangl finished his apprenticeship in three years: 'When I was eighteen and a half, I did my exams and became the youngest master weaver in Austria. I worked in the mill and only two years later I had fifteen workers under me.' Playing the zither in a local club and giving music lessons at night, building his own sailboat on weekends, he remembered those years proudly and fondly as 'my happiest time'.

After five years, however, the happiness was wearing off. When he turned twenty-three in 1931, he realized that 'without higher education, I couldn't get further promotion. But to go on doing all my life what I was doing then? Around me I saw men of thirty-five who had started at the same age as I and were now old men. The work was too unhealthy. The dust got into your lungs – the noise. . .'

And the dragoon uniform hanging in his father's closet was under his skin. He often looked at young policemen patrolling the streets and envied how spruce and secure they looked in their uniforms. He applied to the Austrian federal police and, after an examination and interview, was ordered to report to their barracks in Linz, the Upper Austrian capital, for basic training.

When Stangl gave his notice at the mill, the owner said: 'Why didn't you come and talk to me about it instead of doing it secretly? I was planning to send you to school – in Vienna.'

Telling about this almost four decades later, Stangl wept. When interviewer Sereny, who spent more than seventy hours with him, asked why he didn't change his plans when his boss told him that, Stangl answered through the tears: 'He didn't ask me to.'

Austria was already an armed camp when Stangl donned his police uniform and began courting Theresa Eidenböck, an Upper Austrian perfumer's daughter a year older than he; they met in Linz, where she was studying midwifery at the School of Social Work. Austria's two major contending parties – the progressive (but not communist) Socialists (known as the Reds) and their conservative, heavily Catholic rival, the Christian Social Party (called the Blacks: the colour of priests' robes) – each had its own flag, its own anthem, its own paramilitary force: the leftists' *Schutzbund* (Workers' Militia) vs the rightists' *Heimwehr* (Home Guard). Untrained in democracy after a millennium of monarchy, the Austrian people gave to their political parties the loyalty most people give to their countries.

In 1931, the post-World War I question of Anschluss (which then meant union with Germany, but would later mean armed annexation) was revived. In a 1932 Cabinet crisis, the ruling Blacks' Minister of Agriculture Engelbert Dollfuss became Chancellor, governing with a one-vote majority in Parliament and dependent upon his party's armed *Heimwehr* to keep him in power. Dollfuss, just turning forty, was an unimposing figure, not just because he stood not quite five feet tall, but also as the illegitimate son of peasants. Both his admirers and detractors were quick to nickname him '*millimetternich*' after a more astute statesman and master manipulator who had tyrannized Austria while remaking the map of Europe more than a century earlier. Other enemies termed Dollfuss 'the poisonous dwarf'.

By 1933, with more than half a million Austrians out of work and Hitler taking power in Berlin, talk of Anschluss with their German-speaking neighbours tripped off many Austrian tongues. The domestic Nazi party – hitherto a fringe group that hadn't elected a single deputy to Parliament – made ominous noises amplified by infusions of propaganda and manpower from Nazi Germany. *Der Führer* proclaimed that the unification of Austria and Germany was 'a task to be furthered by every means'. The Austrian province of Styria's *Heimwehr* went over to the Nazis.

Hitler's atheistic fascism was distasteful to Dollfuss, who recognized early that the Nazis, while talking of the historic unity of Christian and German culture, were subverting the former with Teutonic paganism and the latter with racism and terror. Thus, he favoured a more Italian-flavoured, but homegrown, militantly Catholic Austro-fascism – and seized the chance in parliamentary turbulence on 4 March 1933, by declaring that Parliament had 'suspended itself'.

To avoid an election that would surely have won the Nazis some seats, he invoked an obsolete law from 1917 granting the government emergency powers. First, he outlawed the Nazi Party, whose growing numbers, driven underground, turned to grenades, subversion, and infiltration of government organs. The Communist Party, a negligible factor, was banned too.

Until 1933, the Socialists – who could better be classified as 'Social Democrats' – had been *pro*-Anschluss, but the transformation of Germany into a Nazi dictatorship altered their position. Still, such was the mutual detestation between Socialists and Dollfuss that neither side considered uniting against Hitler, who would destroy them both. Otto Bauer, the brilliant Jewish leader of the Socialists, despised Dollfuss personally as a bastard who had usurped power. After all, in the 1930 elections, the Socialists had won forty-one per cent of the vote, making them the largest party in Parliament until Dollfuss abolished parliamentary democracy. Besides, they wanted no part of Austro-fascism or any other kind. When Dollfuss banned the *Schutzbund*, the Socialist militia, as a prelude to forming a one-party regime called the Fatherland Front, Austria was soon as seething a police state as any in the Balkans.

On the morning of 12 February 1934, the inevitable conflict between Reds and Blacks erupted in Linz, where Patrolman Franz Stangl was stationed. Police broke down the doors of a workers' club on the Landstrasse to confiscate arms from the outlawed Socialist militia. The *Schutzbund* greeted them with a hail of bullets which generated a general strike in the Socialist-ruled cities of Austria and a three-day civil war across the nation. When it was over, the victorious government forces – including police, *Heimwehr*, and Austrian army – had lost 128 lives, with 409 more wounded; official figures gave *Schutzbund* and Socialist casualties as 137 dead and 399 wounded, though, by counting families trapped in the bombardment of Socialist housing projects, the roll would come to more than a thousand. The Socialist Party was outlawed. Some of its leaders fled the country. Many of its members were arrested. Nine were executed.

The fighting in Linz lasted just one day, but a rookie cop had his work cut out for him and Stangl could boast: 'The Socialists entrenched themselves in the Central Cinema and we had to fight for hours to get them out. I was the one who flushed the last ones out that night at 11 p.m. – after well over twelve hours. I got the silver Service medal for that.'

He held no grudge against Socialists and, in the beginning, no bent for the Nazis: 'The Austrian police were very professional. Our job was to uphold the law of the land' – by quelling disturbers of the peace, right or left, and by doing a job that had 'nothing heinous or very dramatic about it then. It was just a job one tried to do as correctly – as kindly, if you like – as possible.'

On 1 May 1934 – the Republic of Austria's first May Day without a Socialist Party – Dollfuss's puppet Parliament passed a new Constitution transforming Austria into a 'Christian Corporate State'. By then, Dollfuss had opened detention camps for his opponents: one of them in Wöllersdorf, some thirty miles south of Vienna.

Here, however, any resemblance to Mussolini or Hitler ends. Dollfuss enjoyed neither the power nor the popularity of *il Duce* or *der Führer.* The treatment of political prisoners at Wöllersdorf never rivalled that in Dachau, the first Nazi concentration camp established by Hitler in 1933 on the outskirts of Munich. Dollfuss's fascism was relatively free of the imperialism, racism, anti-Semitism, and anti-clericalism that marked one or both of his neighbours'. And, instead of Anschluss, Dollfuss preached that the Austrians were the better Germans – defenders of a civilized tradition dating back a thousand years to Babenberg dukes who ruled Austria while Teutonic tribes to the west were subsisting on acorns – and affirmed a patriotic doctrine of 'Austrianness', combining German culture with Austrian tolerance: 'Living with other nations for centuries has made the Austrian softer, more patient, and more understanding of foreign cultures, even though he has been and is conscious of maintaining the purity of his own culture and kind.'

These qualities, too, would make Austrians like Stangl excellent exterminators a few years later.

That much-misunderstood historical figure, Dollfuss, was as doomed as his doctrines. On 25 July 1934, in a meticulously bungled putsch called 'Operation Summer Festival', no fewer than 154 Austrian Nazis, wearing military and police uniforms, rode into the courtyard of Dollfuss's Chancellery on the Ballhausplatz in eight trucks which penetrated security just by tagging along behind the regular 12.50 p.m. changing of the guard. They seized the building and shot Dollfuss to death, as intended, but failed to arrest his ministers and install a new government because the cabinet meeting they thought they were raiding had ended forty minutes earlier. Only Dollfuss and his chief of security and the head of the *Heimwehr* were on hand. While the Austrian Army surrounded the Chancellery and the German ambassador negotiated the surrender of the Nazi invaders, the next Chancellor, Kurt von Schuschnigg, thirty-seven, hitherto Minister of Justice and Education, was convening the cabinet elsewhere in town and promising continuity.

As a concerned citizen and professional policeman, Franz Stangl was appalled by the assassination of Dollfuss. A few days later, he discovered a Nazi arms cache in a forest. This won him, along with four colleagues, another medal – the Austrian Eagle with green and white ribbon –and enrolment in detective school. In 1935, he was transferred to Wels, an Upper Austrian hot-bed of Nazism, to investigate illegal political activities.

Since the Nazis, like the Socialists, had enhanced his career, Stangl harboured an occasional kind feeling toward them. He contributed to a Nazi welfare fund to look after relatives of political prisoners. And, for a Nazi lawyer named Dr Bruno Wille, Stangl and his detective partner, Ludwig Werner, did 'the sort of thing one was able to do at times before 1938: just warn someone under suspicion to watch his step.'

In Vienna, the cultured but colourless Schuschnigg governed for nearly four years while Hitler watched Austria's economy erode under German and Italian pressure, such as economic barriers to tourism, until he was ready to pounce. German troops crossed into Austria before dawn on Saturday, 12 March 1938; Hitler rode in triumph that day through his native town of Braunau to his home city of Linz, wildly cheered and welcomed all the way. In Vienna, Schuschnigg was escorted into what became ten weeks of house arrest followed by seven years in Hitler's prisons and concentration camps.* Far more brutally, another 76,000 foes of Nazism were arrested that weekend in Vienna alone.

*Schuschnigg emigrated to the US after the war and spent twenty years as a professor of political science in the Midwest, mostly at St Louis University in Missouri. Naturalized as an American citizen in 1956, he returned to Austria in 1967 to 'live in peace and perhaps do a little writing' and died in 1977 at the age of seventy-nine in rented rooms in a village in the Tyrol.

The first transport of 151 Austrians left Vienna for Dachau on 1 April: Jews, intellectuals, and politicians, including two Schuschnigg supporters who would survive to become postwar conservative chancellors of Austria: Leopold Figl and Alfons Gorbach. Nine days later, Hitler called a 'plebiscite' in Austria and Germany to ratify his Anschluss. With eighteen per cent of the electorate excluded for political or racial reasons, and the rest either feeling coerced or acceding to the inevitable with varying degrees of enthusiasm, 99.75 per cent of Austrians and 99.08 per cent of Germans voted yes.

With Anschluss, Austria literally disappeared from the map. Renamed *Ostmark,* it was later christened 'the Danube and Alpine Reich's Provinces'. The very word 'Austria' was banned. Working in Wels, Franz Stangl was no longer in the province of Upper Austria. Upper and Lower Austria were now called Upper Danube and Lower Danube.

In the bloody purge that followed the bloodless entry of German troops into Austria, the Nazis arrested three of the five detectives who had won Eagles in 1934 for confiscating their weapons near Linz. As Stangl later recalled: 'That left only my friend Ludwig Werner and myself. Meanwhile, in Linz, they'd shot two of the chiefs of our department. People we'd seen just a few days before. No trial, nothing – just shot them. Another one, also a friend of mine, was arrested too.' When one of their colleagues remarked that 'you'd better let your Eagle fly out the window', fear gripped Stangl and Werner. They shredded their whole index-card file of suspected Nazis, communists, and socialists, and flushed it all down the toilet.

Stangl and Werner were given forms to fill out. One of the questions asked whether they had been Nazi Party members back when it was illegal.

Remembering the little favour they'd once done a Nazi lawyer, they went to Dr Wille and asked him to 'remember' that Werner and Stangl had been underground Nazis. Wille obliged by entering their names on his Nazi Party rolls for the previous two years. Then the two worried detectives completed their questionnaires by saying they'd been Party members since 1936.

When Stangl went home that night, he thought his wife would be relieved, too, but instead she accused him of betraying her with 'these swine, these gangsters!' Through his pain, Stangl comprehended that, as an Austrian whose country had just been violated and as a devout Catholic, Theresa hated Nazis with a passion shared by many of her people.

Stangl's interviewer-biographer, Gitta Sereny, in her profound 1974 book, *Into That Darkness: An Examination of Conscience*, draws a fascinating parallel between Franz Stangl's individual and the Vatican's institutional 'step-by-step acquiescence to increasingly terrible acts' before and during World War II. In both cases, she says, 'the very first failure to say "No" was fatal, each succeeding step merely confirming the original and basic moral flaw.' In this morality play, Theresa Stangl emerges as a tragic figure caught between loyalties to the man she loved and the church she revered.

Franz Stangl, on the other hand, looms large as a master weaver who wove a web of death and deception – eventually, self-deception. Having lost the respect of his wife, Stangl lost his self-respect a year later when his new boss, a Nazi from Munich, ordered him to sign a paper renouncing his religion. He never told Theresa he'd signed it.

In 1940, Stangl, after receiving several promotions as a Gestapo agent in Wels, was transferred to Berlin. To his own surprise, the Austrian plainclothes detective was given a green uniform with lieutenant's rank and named police superintendent of a special institute of the General Foundation for Institutional Care at Tiergartenstrasse (Zoo St.) 4. The foundation's fancy title was just a façade for a host of euphemisms which endure today and have even achieved a modicum of respectability: *mercy killing, assisted suicide, euthanasia*. In those days, they meant the slaughter of those deemed mentally, morally, or physically unfit to participate in the lunacies of the Third Reich. *T4,* as the foundation was nicknamed because of its address, was the forerunner of the Final Solution.

The programme had begun when Hitler came to power in 1933 with enactment of the Law for Compulsory Sterilization of those suffering from hereditary diseases. Two years later, a Law to Safeguard the Hereditary Health of the German People legalized abortion where either of the parents had a hereditary disease. At the end of October 1939, a secret decree by Hitler quietly gave his chancellery

> the responsibility for expanding the authority of physicians who are to be designated by name, to the end that patients who are

> considered incurable in the best available human judgement after critical evaluation of their condition can be granted mercy killing.

The first gassings of Germans certified as incurably insane were carried out in December 1939 or January 1940 at a ' psychiatric clinic' in Grafeneck castle and at a former prison in Brandenburg-an-der-Havel, after which two other facilities in Germany and another in Austria were opened to cope with the mentally and physically retarded, the incurably sick, and the very old as well as the insane.

The newly commissioned officer Stangl was sent home to Wels to await further orders. After a day spent relaxing with his wife and two small daughters, he was called for by an unmarked delivery van with a driver in civilian clothes who took him to Schloss Hartheim, a sixteenth-century Renaissance castle in Alkoven, a dozen miles from Linz.

Simon Wiesenthal first heard of Hartheim when he was in the Mauthausen concentration camp toward the end of the war: 'The crematoriums were working overtime. Whenever an oven broke down, the people in charge would send for "an expert from Hartheim" to fix the machinery. Sometimes batches of prisoners were sent over to Hartheim; they never came back. All we were told was that they'd been "permanently transferred." So the word *Hartheim* seemed to spell *death*, but I didn't give it a second thought. Lying on my bunk in the death block, I was too weak to think.'

When Wiesenthal visited Hartheim as a postwar investigator, his architect's eye found it forbidding with its four triangular towers, onion dome, and row after row of windows, though he was impressed by its large courtyard surrounded by an ornate colonnade. At the time, it was known only that 7200 inmates from Mauthausen and 3600 from Dachau had been gassed there in the closing months of the war. Less was known about its activities in the early months of the war.

When the more prosaic Franz Stangl arrived there in late 1940, he found it 'big, y'know, with a courtyard and archways and all that. It hadn't been a private residence for some time; they'd had an orphanage in it, I think, and later a hospital.'* But now Hartheim

*Actually, Hartheim had been a home for retarded children since 1898.

had become Austria's 'euthanasia sanatorium' – or, as Wiesenthal calls it in his memoirs, a 'school for mass murder'. He goes on to say:

> No one will ever know exactly how many people were murdered in the Renaissance castle with the beautiful colonnade. No memorial for the victims of Hartheim, most of them Austrian and German Christians, has been built. The records of the registry office have not been found . . . In 1947, people testified that from thirty to forty human guinea pigs were 'treated' in the cellars every day. That would account for about thirty thousand people in three years. Toward the end, Hartheim became just another place of extermination.

Hartheim still retained the pretence of a hospital, though all but its most retarded 'patients' might have wondered why it had no wards or overnight accommodation. When even the normally unquestioning Stangl asked why the temperatures of the mentally ill were taken upon arrival, his chief, Captain Christian Wirth, explained that 'they must not be allowed to realize they're going to die. They have to feel at ease. Nothing must be done to frighten them.'

At first meeting, Christian Wirth struck Stangl as 'a gross and florid man. My heart sank when I met him. He stayed at Hartheim for several days that time and came back often. Whenever he was there, he addressed us daily at lunch.' By the time Stangl came to work for him, 'the Savage Christian' was supervisor of the Reich's entire euthanasia empire, which performed some 50,000 'mercy killings' between 1939 and 1941.

What Stangl couldn't stand about his superior was the way Wirth spoke bluntly about 'doing away with useless mouths' and 'sentimental slobber that makes me puke' instead of, in Stangl's words, the 'humane or scientific terms' used by the euthanasia doctors and officials, who spoke piously of 'totally painless release from an intolerable life'. Though his career would be entwined with Wirth's for the rest of the war, Stangl could never stomach his chief's directness of phrase.

Franz Stangl's job as security officer at Hartheim was euphemistic as well as euthanasic: to produce death certificates that didn't disclose the truth of how the 'patients' had died: 'It was part of my function to see that, afterwards, families of patients received their effects: clothes and all that and identity papers as well as certificates. I was responsible for everything being correctly done.' The families were told 'the patient had died of a heart attack or something like that. And they received a little urn with the ashes.'

Once, a grieving mother wrote that she had not received, among her late child's personal effects, a candle she'd sent as a present shortly before the sudden death. To retrieve the candle, Stangl journeyed to the church-run institution from which the child had been 'selected' for Hartheim. When he arrived, the Mother Superior, who had found the candle for him, was visiting a ward with a priest. Showing Stangl a small child shrivelled up in a basket, she asked him: 'Do you know how old he is?'

'No,' said Stangl, unwilling to hazard a guess.

'Sixteen,' said the nun. 'But he looks like five, doesn't he? He'll never change, ever. But they rejected him.' She was referring to the Medical Selection Commission, which examined her patients at regular intervals, marking plus signs on the cards of those who would live (until the next selection) and minus signs on those ticketed for Hartheim. 'How could they not accept him?' she complained bitterly while the priest accompanying her on her rounds nodded. 'Just look at him,' the Mother Superior went on, pointing to the basket case. 'No good to himself or anyone else. How could they refuse to deliver him from this miserable life?'

Stangl said this episode 'really shook me. Here were a Catholic nun – a Mother Superior! – and a priest. And they thought it was right. Who was I, then, to doubt what was being done?'

Fearing his wife's certain disapproval, Stangl never told her this self-serving story or anything else about his work at Hartheim until after the war. When he did, years later, she asked: 'Why didn't you tell me? Didn't you know I'd stand by you?'

And Stangl said: 'I didn't want to burden you with it.' He never did tell her the truth about Treblinka or his intermediate station, Sobibor, either.

How close Stangl came to the killings at Hartheim is uncertain, though he must have witnessed some. A defendant in Austria's 1947 Hartheim trial, driver Franz Höldl, testified that Stangl had nothing to do with the killings and was responsible only for police matters. But Hartheim was more than a death clinic for 'defectives'; it was a proving-ground for genocidists.

Simon Wiesenthal says that, at the scientific end, Hartheim was organized like a medical school in which 'students' were taught not to save human life, but to destroy it as efficiently as possible. The victims' deaths were analysed clinically, photographed precisely, and perfected scientifically. Various gas mixtures were tried out for effectiveness. Doctors with stop-watches would observe the dying through a peep-hole in the cellar door, clocking the length of the death struggle to a tenth of a second. Slow-motion pictures were filmed and studied by experts. Victims' brains were monitored to show exactly when death had occurred. 'Nothing was left to chance,' says Wiesenthal.

In 1961, a woman scorned twenty years earlier by one Bruno Bruckner came to Wiesenthal to even the score. 'He can tell you about the nice experiments he photographed in Hartheim,' she assured Simon – and indeed Bruckner did.

Back in 1940, Bruckner, an amateur photographer working nights as a guard at the Linz stockyards, was asked by the Nazis if he could run a first-class darkroom. After a job interview, he signed a pledge that he would talk to nobody about his work and was delivered to Captain Wirth at Hartheim.

Bruckner described 'the savage Christian' as 'a nice guy after working hours, but very strict while you were on duty. He wouldn't hesitate for a moment to shoot you if something went wrong.' Wirth told him to film three portraits of each patient, which Bruckner found hard work: 'Some patients were raving mad and had to be restrained by male nurses. Once or twice, a patient got away before being given the lethal injection and jumped at me. It was tough. And the worst part was that I couldn't eat anything. There was a terrible stench in the air from the cremation ovens. [Hartheim had three.] After a few days, I went to Captain Wirth and said I couldn't stand it. I asked to be released from the assignment.'

Wirth offered Bruckner three alternatives: 'Either you stay here and keep your mouth shut or you'll be sent to Mauthausen. Or, if you prefer, you'll be shot here right away.'

When Bruckner went to his room to think it over, Wirth sent up a bottle of schnapps. Bruckner drank it all and went back to work next day. Later, his duties were expanded to filming close-ups of each victim's death throes. 'I didn't ask any questions,' he admitted in 1961. 'It was a good job. I was paid 300 marks a month and made a little money on the side taking pictures of the staff, with Captain Wirth's permission. The food was good. There was always plenty of liquor. And, at night, lots of parties. Everybody was sleeping with everybody else.'

A chemical worker twenty years later, Bruckner was still sleeping well. Only one little detail troubled his mind: why did Wirth need at least eighty employees to kill no more than thirty-five patients a day?

Wiesenthal had the answer a few weeks later. Although the Austrian authorities did nothing to pursue Bruckner's revelations,* Wiesenthal found in them his answer to a triple-barrelled pedagogical riddle which still perplexes historians and criminologists, psychologists and philosophers. 'How were people selected and trained to carry out the murder of eleven million people and how did they keep their secrets so well that they were not known for years after the war?' he phrased it rhetorically.

'Obviously,' he went on, 'men assigned to gas chambers, who had to watch the deaths of tens of thousands of people day after day and week after week, would have to be trained technically *and* psychologically; otherwise, they might collapse under the continuous stress . . . Machines broke down, but the people handling them never did. How could it be that people operating gas chambers and ovens were more reliable than the machines?'

These questions had bothered Wiesenthal for years, for 'all facts pointed toward the conclusion that special cadres of technically skilled and emotionally hardened executioners were trained somewhere.' With Wirth's breaking of Bruno Bruckner, Wiesenthal first realized that the overstaffing at Hartheim and the other euthanasia centres held the key.

*Dr Rudolf Lohnauer of Linz, chief physician at Hartheim, committed suicide with his entire family after the war; his deputy, Dr Georg Renno, arrested in Frankfurt in 1963, was excused from euthanasia trials due to ill health and lived a good life recuperating in the Black Forest spa area of Germany. Franz Höldl, the chauffeur who wouldn't implicate Stangl in the killings, was given a four-year sentence. Wiesenthal says that a file he handed personally to the Minister of Justice and the Attorney General of Austria in 1964, implicating other Austrians in Hartheim, has never been acted upon.

Their carefully selected staffs didn't know they were really students under surveillance; those who qualified would go on to run the gas chambers and crematoria of the death camps. First, they watched the 'experiments'; later, when they no longer flinched, they carried them out themselves. Security was tight because, Wiesenthal says, 'the Nazis realized that there must be no slip-up. Germans and Austrians were being killed, and there could be trouble.'

There was. On 19 March 1940, Theophil Wurm, the Protestant bishop of Württemberg, wrote an irate letter of protest to the Minister of Interior. On 27 November 1940, the Vatican of Pope Pius XII issued a timid proclamation that 'extinction of unworthy life by public mandate' was 'incompatible with natural and divine law', but, with Benito Mussolini next door in Rome, the Pope's weak words were disseminated only in Latin and not heard in German or Germany until 9 March 1941, when the courageous Bishop of Berlin, Konrad von Preysing, read them from the pulpit of St Hedwig's Cathedral. Bishop von Preysing prefaced the Pope's proclamation with his own ringing words: 'No justification and no excuse can be found for taking away the life of the weak or the ill for any sort of economic or eugenic reason. With the same devotion to principles with which the Church protects the institution of matrimony – the moral focus of the people – she also protects the individual's right to life.'

Then, on Sunday, 3 August 1941, Count Clemens August von Galen, the powerful archbishop of Münster, stood up in St Lambert's Church in that north-German city and attacked the murder of innocents and disregard for the sanctity of human life. He denounced Hitler's whole euthanasia programme as 'plain murder', giving details of transports of patients, dubious death certificates, and the flouting of Catholicism through cremation. He told his congregation he would sue those responsible for these criminal acts under Paragraph 211 of the Penal Code. Copies of von Galen's sermon were mimeographed and distributed throughout the Third Reich and smuggled to soldiers in the front lines, where the Bishop's concern was shared by badly wounded soldiers and their comrades in arms who recognized that they could be killed by their own side if they lost their 'productive capacity'.

That summer, too, Adolf Hitler was actually jeered by a crowd in Hof, near Nuremberg, when his special train and some local traffic were stalled by the transfer of a transport of mental patients who were being loaded from a freight train on to trucks.

In the German towns of Sonnenstein and Grafeneck, there was so much gossip that two of the 'sanatoria' had to be closed. The children of Hadamar were known to shout after the blacked-out buses heading into the 'institute' there: 'Here come some more for gassing!' Only in Hartheim was secrecy sustained – and the credit for that went to security chief Stangl.

'Hartheim graduates later became teachers of future cadres of scientifically trained killers,' says Wiesenthal. 'After some practice, the "students" became insensible to the cries of the victims. The "teachers" would watch the reactions of their "students". It was a brilliant psychological touch to use Germans and Austrians as victims in the basic training for mass murder.' If a 'student' didn't crack under the strain of killing his own people, he was unlikely to feel any guilt while eradicating 'sub-humans' such as Jews. If he did object, he would quickly be reassigned to a front-line suicide squad – or offered Bruno Bruckner's alternatives.

Adolf Hitler, too, was pondering his alternatives. After the outrage in Hof and Bishop von Galen's sermon – the most effective single religious protest in the whole Hitler era – the Führer resisted advice from his deputy, Martin Bormann, to hang von Galen, and from Himmler to jail 'the Lion of Münster', as the courageous Archbishop became known. Instead, Hitler heeded his propaganda minister, Josef Goebbels, who warned that punishing von Galen might cost the Nazis vital support not just in Münster, but throughout German Catholicism.* On 24 August 1941, in a surprise move, Hitler decided to discontinue the whole euthanasia programme. But it was just a tactical retreat.

'At Hartheim,' Franz Stangl told his biographer, Gitta Sereny, 'the winding-up process ran very smoothly, but not everywhere.' In October 1941, he was sent to another 'institute' in Bernburg, near

*Bishop von Galen (1878–1946) was finally arrested after 20 July 1944's assassination attempt on Hitler, but survived the war in the Sachsenhausen concentration camp. He was named Cardinal in 1945, as was the outspoken Bishop von Preysing (1880–1950) of Berlin a year later.

Hanover, to wind up its affairs; the doctor in charge there, named Eberl, would be Stangl's predecessor in Treblinka. 'Bernburg was a mess,' said Stangl. 'There were all kinds of things which had to be settled properly in the institutes. I had to look after property rights, insurance, that sort of thing. After all, some of those who died left children who still had to be properly provided for.'

What Stangl called 'the winding-up process', however, was just the curtain falling after a dress rehearsal. With the conquest of Poland, Hitler had found a vast arena in which to perform the Final Solution on a scale that none of his Hartheim puppets – except, perhaps, 'the savage Christian' – could have envisioned.

– 27 –

The man in the white jacket

Only staff and a few selected slaves stayed overnight at the extermination camps of Chelmno, Belzec, Sobibor, and Treblinka. While Auschwitz did have a gas chamber, the vast complex was primarily a concentration camp for slave labour that had survived 'selections' upon arrival (and during subsequent weed-outs) at its extermination annex, Birkenau, a couple of miles away, where multiple ovens, pits, chimneys, and gas chambers worked around the clock. So as not to turn queasy German stomachs into organized opposition, virtually all extermination facilities were installed in the conquered east, where protest was punishable by summary execution. Only toward the end of the war – as the drive to finish the Final Solution outstripped the machinery of death – did such German concentration camps as Buchenwald (which Wiesenthal survived) and Bergen-Belsen (where Anne Frank died) diversify from starvation, disease, hangings, and firing squads into mass extermination too.

Belzec (where Wiesenthal's mother perished), Sobibor, and Treblinka – the three camps opened by Christian Wirth in Poland in 1942 – were entrusted to alumni of the aborted euthanasia programme. Thanks to his success at Chelmno in 1941, 'the savage Christian' was named supervising inspector of the four extermination camps, all of which used diesel exhausts: Wirth's preferred method of extermination.

Though none of them lasted more than a year at a time, together they destroyed some two and a half million Jews. They shut down only when the extermination of East European Jewry was nearly complete and because carbon monoxide was being out-performed by the new technology of Zyklon B, which Auschwitz commandant

Rudolf Höss had embraced while building his Birkenau extermination branch. Zyklon B was also used in the new gas chambers opened at the Majdanek concentration camp near Lublin in late 1942, around the time one Hermine Braunsteiner arrived there as a guard.

Although Höss had been one of Christian Wirth's tutors in mass extermination, he began referring to Wirth as a 'sloppy amateur' and 'untalented disciple' for resisting Zyklon B. Still, there was something positively gruesome to be said for the savage Christian's recalcitrance; only 114 prisoners – none of them children – survived his four-camp empire,* while more than 100,000 outlived the gassings, shootings, hangings, beatings, lethal injections, 'medical experiments', starvation, exhaustion, and disease that took four million lives at Auschwitz-Birkenau.

On Wirth's recommendation in early 1942, Franz Stangl was commissioned to construct and then command Sobibor, in eastern Poland. While Stangl said he was told Sobibor would be a supply camp for the German Army, his suspicions might have been aroused by the assignment of several other euthanasia alumni to work under him, including Hermann Michel, who had been the chief male nurse at Hartheim. After the Polish labour on hand proved 'lackadaisical', Stangl requisitioned a more driven 'Work Commando' of twenty-five Jewish prisoners plus some Ukrainian guards to drive them. In the beginning, Jews and Ukrainians and Germans all slept in the same hut – the Germans on the kitchen floor; the others in the loft – until more huts were built.

One day, Michel went for a walk in the woods and came back on the run. 'I think something fishy is going on here,' Stangl said Michel told him. 'Come and see what it reminds you of.'

Ten or fifteen minutes into the forest, Michel showed Stangl a new brick building, three yards by four, with three rooms. The

*Only two Jews out of 600,000 survived Belzec: soap manufacturer Rudolf Reder, and metal-worker Chaim Hirszman, who was killed by Polish anti-Semites after the war. Only two out of 400,000 survived Chelmno: Simon Srebnik and Mordecai Podchlebnik, who both went to Israel after the war. Sobibor, which operated from the spring of 1942 until the fall of 1943, killed 300,000; there were fifty survivors. The 400 days of Treblinka (July 1942–August 1943) left 1,200,000 dead; only sixty lived.

moment Stangl saw it, he understood what Michel meant: 'It looked exactly like the gas chamber at Schloss Hartheim.'

How could he, as commandant, not have known it was there until Michel stumbled upon it? Stangl claimed the 'lackadaisical' Poles must have built it before he fired them, though 'they wouldn't have known what it was to be.' While the structure showed on his blueprints, they didn't specify what any of the buildings were for.

Stangl drove to Belzec to find out from Wirth what this was about. If he is to be believed, this visit to Belzec was his first physical encounter with extermination, even though it had been his line of work ever since he had joined the euthanasia programme two years earlier. This is how Stangl described it to Gitta Sereny:

'As one arrived, one first reached Belzec railway station, on the left side of the road. The camp was on the same side, but up a hill. The commandant's headquarters were 200 metres (225 yards) away, on the other side of the road. It was a one-storey building. The smell – oh God, the smell! – it was everywhere.

'Wirth wasn't in his office. They said he was up in the camp. I asked whether I should go up there and they said, "I wouldn't if I were you. He's mad with fury. It's not healthy to go near him." I asked what was the matter. The man I was talking to said one of the pits had overflowed. They had put too many corpses in it and putrefaction had progressed too fast, so that the liquid underneath had pushed the bodies on top up and over and the corpses had rolled down the hill. I saw some of them – oh God, it was awful!*

'A bit later, Wirth came down. And that's when he told me that this was what Sobibor was for, too. And that he was putting me officially in charge.'

Stangl protested that he was a police officer, not an exterminator, and simply wasn't up to such an assignment. Wirth did not argue back, but said his response would be conveyed to higher headquarters in Lublin. In the meantime, Stangl was to return to Sobibor and continue work.

*Such was the stench of Belzec that it penetrated passenger cars of trains passing through the town, even when their windows were sealed. The townspeople of Belzec said that the odour of rotting bodies grew worse each day and even the SS complained when the human cesspool seeped out in front of their barracks and mess hall.

That night, according to Stangl, 'Michel and I talked and talked about it. We agreed that what they were doing was a crime. We considered deserting; we discussed it for a long time. But how? Where could we go? What about our families?'

Once again, where euphemism failed the finicky Stangl, he sought the comfort of verbal abstraction: it was 'what *they* were doing', not what *he* was building. And Michel reminded him of one of Wirth's recurring witticisms: 'If any of you don't like it here, you're welcome to leave – but under the earth.'

The next day, Wirth arrived in Sobibor to supervise the installation of what were now five gas chambers. He ignored Stangl, who busied himself with other construction. Leaving Stangl in nominal charge of the camp, Wirth took Michel into the woods to share his expertise in gassing.

On the third or fourth afternoon, when the machinery seemed in working order and the full force of Jewish prisoners were applying finishing touches, Wirth turned to Michel and said: 'All right, we'll try it out right now with your work-Jews.' With that, the twenty-five slaves were pushed inside and gassed.

That was the baptism of Sobibor. When it turned out that the doors had been put on backward, Wirth cursed the dead Jewish labour inside and lashed out with his whip at the Ukrainian guards and everybody in sight, including Michel. Stangl was summoned to the scene of carnage and told to reverse the doors before burying the bodies. Wirth left in a rage which struck Stangl speechless, though he would later explain that he simply concentrated on completing the camp; Wirth had, after all, put Michel in charge of gassings. Soon after, the first freights of Jews arrived for 'processing'.

Michel, a staff sergeant with the mellifluous voice of a priest in a pulpit, took to his work so well that his 'work-Jews' christened him 'The Preacher'. He would meet each shipment of Jews and tell them:

'Welcome to Sobibor! You will be sent to a work camp. Families will stay together. Those of you who work hard will be rewarded. There is nothing to be afraid of here. We are concerned, however, about diseases and epidemics. So we ask you to take a shower. Men to the right. Women and children under six to the left.'

Sometimes he would add that Sobibor was 'just a transit camp for classification and disinfection. From here, you'll all be going to the Ukraine as soon as the Third Reich can establish an independent

Jewish state there for you.' Since they wanted to believe him, his victims would sometimes cheer or applaud his words. Then 'he would personally escort the people on the special road . . . to the barbers' huts and from there to the gas chambers', one of his ex-'work-Jews', Moshe Shklarek, remembers. 'With his tricks and his slippery-tongued speeches, Michel was more dangerous than his comrades in crime.'*

With Michel doing the meeting and greeting and gassing, Stangl stayed in the background: an executive supervisor presiding over construction and decreeing policy while distancing himself – intellectually as well as physically – from the consequences of his command. It was during Stangl's tenure of slightly less than six months in 1942 that workers on the death detail were forbidden to use such words as *bodies*, *corpses*, or *victims*, and were compelled instead to call them *Figuren* (figures or images, such as puppets or dolls) or *Schmattes* (rags): yet another giant step into the realm of abstraction in which Stangl secluded himself from the reality of his work.

Though Sobibor wasn't 'fully operational' until May 1942, that month it outdid Auschwitz or Belzec or Chelmno by gassing more than 36,000 Jews from nineteen Polish communities. A sixth gas chamber was added – using the 200-horsepower, eight-cylinder engine of a captured Russian tank to pump a mixture of carbon monoxide and carbon dioxide – and the Germans built a power generator that furnished enough light to allow night gassings. A narrow-gauge railway was built from the unloading platform to haul clothing, suitcases, valuables, and the corpses of the Dead on Arrival into the bowels of the camp and to transport gold extracted from the teeth of the gassed in the 'dental workshop', a shed near the 'showers'. By July, Stangl and Michel had streamlined Sobibor into such a showcase for efficient extermination that Heinrich Himmler came from Berlin to see for himself. Prisoner labour – tailors, shoemakers, goldsmiths, and bricklayers – were detached from their regular duties to make the camp shine like a Swiss ski resort. While Himmler was going on to Lublin for lunch, a team of cooks and bakers was assigned to prepare canapés to go with his drinks.

*Hermann Michel escaped to Egypt after the war, Stangl told biographer Gitta Sereny.

Himmler, however, was all business and interested only in extermination. When the luxury cars from Berlin pulled on to the switching-track outside the main gate, Stangl gave Himmler's nine-man delegation (three in civilian clothes and six, including Himmler, in SS uniforms) a welcoming salute and greeting. Then 'Preacher' Michel and Stangl's deputy, Gustav Wagner, gave a brisk tour of the gas chambers, where they and their guests watched a few hundred Jews die.

When they returned to the main gate, Stangl was waiting to answer their questions, welcome their observations, and invite them to stay for a cognac. Himmler asked about many details, but his whole group's impression was highly favourable and Stangl was promised expanded help and facilities. After Himmler declined the cognac and canapés, Stangl and his staff consumed them, but Wagner – in a fit of pique that their culinary efforts had gone unnoticed and untried – dispatched the hors d'oeuvre team to the gas chambers.

A six-foot-four blond Austrian whose bland, handsome face looked as if it had been carved out of soap, Gustav Wagner walked with a distinctive looping lurch and claimed to have participated in the 1936 Olympic Games in Berlin as a javelin-thrower, though Wiesenthal says 'we haven't been able to find his name in any sporting reports or in the Olympics register.' His criminal record began when he joined the illegal Nazi Party in 1931. Three years later, when he was caught painting swastikas and putting up Hitler posters, he fled to Nazi Germany and joined the SA, which posted him on guard duty outside one of its camps.

As a genocidist, Wagner's career paralleled Stangl's, though always on a slightly lower level. At Hartheim, he had served as cremator of corpses from the euthanasia programme. As top sergeant at Sobibor, he started out in charge of 'accommodations' (for the 'work-Jews', since virtually all 'guests' didn't stay overnight) and later succeeded Michel as chief of the gas chambers. On his visit to Sobibor, Himmler personally awarded Wagner an Iron Cross for his proficiency in mass murder.

Known to his victims as 'The Human Beast', Wagner has been described as an insatiable sadist, a brutal thug who incited others to hang, beat, and kill prisoners (in Robert Wistrich's *Who's Who in Nazi Germany*), and 'by all accounts a particularly nasty piece of work' (in Gitta Sereny's *Into That Darkness*). 'He didn't eat his lunch if he didn't kill daily. With an axe, shovel, or even his hands. He had to have blood,' said one survivor. 'He was an Angel of Death. For him, torturing and killing was a pleasure. When he killed, he smiled,' said another.

'Wagner was no desk murderer,' says Simon Wiesenthal. 'He was a murderer the way you imagine murderers to be: huge shoulders, enormous hands, a real picture-book SS man. Any Jews who stepped out of line, even on their way to the gas chambers, were killed by Wagner with his own hands. He had the strength to kill any undernourished, emaciated prisoner just by punching him hard in the stomach or slamming him to the ground. It was the strength of a bully, not of an athlete.'

Franz Stangl may not have known it when he played host to Heinrich Himmler in July 1942, but he was in his last month at Sobibor. Since Wirth claimed never to have elicited an answer from his superiors to Stangl's request for reassignment, Stangl had stayed on the job – pending a decision, he pretended to himself. Now that Himmler's visit had been a scientific 'success', his promotion to a higher command was assured.

More than a third of the 300,000 Jews who died in Sobibor perished during Stangl's brief tenure there – and the camp was 'fully operational' for less than three months of his rule. Several of the few witnesses who survived Sobibor to testify against Stangl have linked him more intimately to the violent deaths that awaited their arrival than his executive detachment might suggest. They remember him standing out in the tumult of the unloading platform – where they were stripped of their clothes, baggage, and belongings – because he wore white linen riding clothes and cracked his whip like a horseman. Washington journalist Richard Rashke, who interviewed eighteen survivors for his book *Escape from Sobibor* (1982), has cited one man's impression of Stangl at the scene:

> Shooting into the air from a platform, while supervising the organized chaos, was a Nazi in . . . a white jacket. He seemed oddly out of place, almost as if he had interrupted his dinner to greet the Jews and was eager to get back to it before it turned cold.

According to Stanislaw 'Shlomo' Szmajzner, who was fourteen when he reached Sobibor on 24 May 1942, Stangl shot into the throng of prisoners around him, as did the rest of the SS men on hand to usher them to their doom. Szmajzner, who was spared the fate of his family because he was an accomplished goldsmith, was one of several hundred Jews who escaped from Sobibor in an uprising in October 1943 (long after Stangl had left for Treblinka) and one of only thirty-two to survive the revolt. After the war, still in his teens, he began a new life in Brazil – only to discover in the 1960s and 1970s that Stangl and Wagner were there too.

Stangl seemed to Szmajzner like a youngish university professor uprooted from his classroom by the war and planted in the sandy soil of Sobibor. Wiry and elegant in bearing, he dressed nattily, with his white coat buttoned from collar to waist, his slacks pressed to a razor-sharp crease, and, above an inevitable film of dust, his boots polished to a dazzling gleam. He always wore white gloves. Beneath the silver skull on his SS cap, light brown hair protruded and there was the hint of a dimple on his chin. Though he appeared vain and slightly foppish, his eyes seemed kindly and he smiled easily. He spoke softly, had good manners, and was always polite – to Jews as well as Germans.

Having kept Shlomo Szmajzner around to melt down gold (from fillings, some with flesh and blood, gums and bone, still on them) and make rings for his SS men, as well as jewellery and monograms for his and their families back home, Stangl took particular interest in the lad. He even used to bring him a special treat on Friday nights, saying, 'Here's some sausage for you to celebrate the Sabbath.'

The idea of tempting an orthodox Jew with pork somehow perturbed many when Szmajzner testified at Stangl's trial in 1970 for more than a million murders, but the defendant maintained that pork sausage was such a luxury in wartime that his well-intentioned gift was 'most probably a mixture of beef and bread crumbs.'

Stangl was so kind to Szmajzner from the start that Shlomo risked a special request: 'My parents and sister came here with me. I miss them. When may I see them?'

Stangl avoided his eye, but spoke in fatherly fashion: 'Don't worry. They're fine. They just went to take a shower. They got new clothes and are working in the fields, happy and well. But they do have to work harder than you do . . . I promise on my word as an officer that soon you'll join your family.'

Later, Shlomo asked again and Stangl continued the deception: 'They are in a much better place. They have everything they need. You'll join them soon, I promise.'

Not from Stangl, but from a friend who worked in the burial pits and smuggled out first a message and then a letter before perishing there, did Shlomo eventually find out what had happened to his family and the thousands of others sent through the gate marked SHOWERS. His friend's message read: 'No one lives . . . Say *Kaddish*' – the Jewish prayer for the dead.

– 28 –

Stangl's inferno

In Jean-François Steiner's *Treblinka* (1966) – the best-known book in the literature of this extermination camp – Franz Stangl doesn't appear by name. Steiner's descriptions of the camp commandant as 'a poor minister gone astray, more sadistic than clever' and 'a sadistic intellectual incapable of directing an undertaking like Treblinka' would seem to refer to Dr Irmfried Eberl, an SS first lieutenant and physician who supervised construction of the camp in the spring of 1942 and was its first commandant. When early exterminations failed to keep pace with the rate of arrivals, Eberl was relieved of his command and replaced by the more efficient Stangl, who had proved himself at Sobibor.

'Stangl?' said SS man Otto Horn, who was in charge of burning the bodies ('The Roasts', his workplace was called), in an interview years after the war. 'I only saw him twice in all the time I was at Treblinka.' Of a dozen former personnel at Treblinka who were tried for crimes against humanity in Düsseldorf in 1964–5, only Horn, a professional male nurse, was acquitted.

'Stangl?' said Joseph Siedlecki, a prisoner who worked in the undressing rooms at Treblinka and later as a *maître d'hôtel* at Grossinger's resort in the Catskills. 'I never saw him kill or hurt anyone. But why should he have? He didn't have to. He was no sadist like some of the others and he was the commandant. Why should he dirty his own hands? It's like me now in my own job; if I have to fire somebody, I don't do it – why should I? I tell somebody else to tell the person he's fired. Why should I do the dirty job myself?'

Treblinka on the day Franz Stangl arrived in August 1942 was, he confessed to Gitta Sereny, 'the most awful thing I saw during all of the Third Reich. It was Dante's inferno. It was Dante come to life.'

When his naturalized British Boswell asked what could shock him after several months at Sobibor, he told her: 'In Sobibor, unless one was actually working in the forest, one could live without actually seeing; most of us never saw anybody dying or dead. But Treblinka. . .'

Chauffeured by an SS driver, Stangl started to smell where he was going when they were still miles away, following the River Bug. Fifteen or twenty minutes before reaching his destination, he began seeing corpses along the railroad tracks: first one or two, then two or three, and finally, upon reaching the Treblinka depot, hundreds that had been there for days, rotting in the heat. In the station stood a train full of Jews: some dead, some still alive, all sealed together for days on end and an eternity to come.

Entering the camp and alighting in the Sorting Square, Stangl 'stepped knee-deep into money. I didn't know which way to turn, where to go. I waded in notes, currency, precious stones, jewellery, clothes. They were everywhere, strewn all over the square. The smell was indescribable; hundreds, no, thousands of bodies everywhere, decomposing, putrefying. Across the square, in the woods, just a few hundred yards away on the other side of the camp, there were tents and open fires with groups of Ukrainian guards and girls – whores, I found out later, from all over the countryside – weaving drunk, dancing, singing, playing music . . . There was shooting everywhere.'

As the pagan bacchanal raged around the inferno, Dr Eberl, the outgoing commandant, greeted his successor, who asked crisply why the treasure they were standing in wasn't going to headquarters. With a straight face, Eberl replied that the transports had been ransacked somewhere along the way.

After a few hours, Stangl drove on to Warsaw and reported to the police chief of Poland, General Odilo Globocnik, a fellow Austrian born in 1904 to Croatian parents. A protégé of Reinhard Heydrich, Globocnik had been removed as the Nazi *Gauleiter* of Vienna in 1939 for embezzling funds and recruiting local débutantes for sex orgies. Himmler, however, had pardoned him and sent him to Poland to 'liquidate Jews, aristocracy, intelligentsia, and clerical elements' there. When Heydrich was assassinated in Prague in the spring of 1942, Himmler had put Globocnik in charge of 'Operation Reinhard' in Poland, where he publicly pledged a million deaths to honour his mentor. Reporting only to Himmler and no intermediate authority, Globocnik – whose domain included Belzec, Majdanek, Sobibor, and Treblinka – tripled his quota and confiscated some $45 million in cash, jewels, and negotiable securities, pocketing $5 million worth for himself before turning the rest over to the Gestapo. An alcoholic who consumed two quarts of vodka a day, Globocnik often boasted that he needed the money to keep himself afloat.

Stangl said that when he tried to tell Globocnik that his mission at Treblinka was impossible, Globocnik showed more interest in the valuables he'd seen strewn around. Captain Christian Wirth – whose jurisdiction as supervisor of death camps in the region included Sobibor and Treblinka – was summoned from Belzec to clean up the mess so Stangl could make a fresh start. Wirth arrived next morning and, after a long meeting with Globocnik, accompanied Stangl back to Treblinka.

While Wirth conferred with Eberl, Stangl went to the mess for coffee and chatted with some of the camp's officers, who told him that Treblinka was 'great fun; shooting was "sport"; there was more money and stuff around than one could dream of, all there for the taking; all one had to do was help oneself. In the evening, they said, Eberl had naked Jewesses dance for them, on the tables.'

What was Stangl's reaction? 'Disgusting – it was all disgusting.'

Franz Suchomel, the SS sergeant in charge of collecting and processing Jewish gold and valuables, remembers that the first suggestion he heard Stangl make was to put buckets in 'The Tube' – the path, thirteen feet wide and 350 feet long, flanked by ten-foot-high barbed-wire fences – leading directly from the undressing rooms to the gas chamber. The women in particular, Stangl told Wirth, defecated on their way in, but, in Sobibor, buckets had helped maintain decorum.

'I don't give a damn what you did with the shit in Sobibor!' Wirth said bluntly. 'Let them shit all over themselves! You can clean it up afterwards.' Later, two Jews were assigned to hose 'The Tube' between transports.

After dinner on his first night there, Wirth announced he would be staying a while. Eberl and four of his officers left the next day for a *Waffen SS* unit on the Russian front.* Wirth rang Warsaw and stopped all transports until Treblinka could be tidied up, which took him and Stangl two weeks before a technocrat called Sergeant Heckenholt could be summoned from Belzec to expand the existing gas chamber with a dozen more cottage-like 'bath-house' annexes which all led to the same end.

Early in the clean-up, the two partners in crime, Wirth and Stangl, stood at the rim of the burial pits filled with black-and-blue bodies. 'It had nothing to do with humanity – it couldn't have,' Stangl said later. 'It was just a mass of rotting flesh.' At the time, though, Wirth asked him, 'What shall we do with this garbage?', and it was his wording, Stangl insisted later, that 'unconsciously started me thinking of them as cargo.'

Almost beside herself, interviewer Sereny said to Stangl: 'There were so many children! Did they ever make you think of *your* children, of how you would feel in the position of those parents?'

'No,' Stangl replied, 'I can't say I ever thought that way. You see, I rarely saw them as individuals. It was always a huge mass.' Inmates of Treblinka have described Stangl standing atop the earthen wall dividing what were actually called 'Death Camp' and 'Living Camp' (Roll-Call Square; housing for 'work-Jews'; stables, textile store, bakery, and coal pile) in his white jacket and riding-pants and boots, 'like Napoleon surveying his domain.' Under questioning from Sereny, Stangl conceded that, as soon as the living were naked in the undressing barracks, they ceased to be human beings to him: 'I avoided [them] from my innermost being. I couldn't confront them. I couldn't lie to them. I avoided at any price talking to those who were about to die. I couldn't stand it.' But he was not too squeamish to stand on the wall and 'watch them in "The Tube" . . . naked, packed together, running, being driven with whips. . .'

'Could you have changed that?' Sereny asked. 'In your position, couldn't you have stopped the nakedness, the whips, the horror of the cattle pens?'

'No, no, no,' Stangl answered. 'This was the system. Wirth had invented it. It worked. And because it worked, it was irreversible.'

*Eberl committed suicide in 1948.

Stangl's propensity for euphemism travelled with him from Hartheim to Sobibor to Treblinka, where 'resettlement' meant death within hours and 'The Tube' was termed 'The Road to Heaven'. Woven into 'The Tube's' barbed wire soon after Stangl took command were pine branches changed daily by a camouflage squad of twenty 'work-Jews'. For it was truly at Treblinka that Stangl emerged as a Master of Illusion in an underworld whose every gateway was inscribed with the myth of '*Arbeit macht frei*' ('Work gives freedom').

For the Christmas season of 1942 – the only Christmas in the camp's year and a quarter of existence – Stangl presented Treblinka with a 'railway station' to enrich the solitary platform at the end of the line where the tracks disappeared into a mound of sand. Adjoining the platform was the windowless rear wall of the Sorting Barracks, where the victims' valuables, clothes, and women's hair (used for stuffing mattresses and insulating submarines) were readied for shipping. On to this wooden wall, Stangl had fake doors and windows painted in pleasing pastels. The 'windows' were lined with cheerful curtains and framed by green blinds: all painted. The 'doors' were stencilled with signs saying 'STATION MASTER', 'TOILET', 'INFIRMARY' (with a red cross), and even 'FIRST CLASS' and 'SECOND CLASS' waiting-rooms. The 'station's' ticket window has been appraised by an artist as a triumph of *trompe l'oeil* which tricked the eye with the false perspective of its painted ledge and vertical grillework barred by a horizontal 'CLOSED' sign. Next to the window, a large timetable announced departures to Warsaw, Bialystok, and Wolkowysk, but the one true destination, Death, wasn't posted. Only the flowers on the front façade were real.

To enhance the mirage of a transit camp, two arrows pointing in opposite directions led to real doors, but both were death's doors. The arrow pointing left 'To BIALYSTOK' took thousands to the undressing rooms to be shorn of all earthly belongings, including female hair, before being put through 'The Tube'. The arrow pointing right 'To WOLKOWYSK' led to one final fatal illusion: a fake 'hospital' with a red cross on its front, but no roof. The old and sick as well as the very young – all those deemed unfit to make their way through the undressing barracks and 'The Tube' – were dispatched to this 'hospital', where nurses undressed them and seated them on the rim of a continuously burning pit. There, an executioner named August Miete shot them in the neck and let them topple in;

the SS called this 'curing with a single pill'. Rather than waste precious bullets on children, Miete might throw them in alive, but more 'humane' SS men would sometimes smash tiny heads against the wall first. That was how the milk of human kindness trickled through Stangl's Treblinka.

Although it took longer to shear the women who went through 'The Tube', a hundred or more females from every transport were sent up 'The Road to Heaven' ahead of the first men who stood naked and shivering in the Undressing Square. 'Men won't burn without women' was one of the 'scientific' truths of Treblinka. Because the female layer of subcutaneous fat is more highly developed than that of males, women's bodies were used to kindle the fires from the bottom. Blood, too, was found to be first-rate combustion material. And young corpses burned faster than old ones, for their flesh was softer, as veal is to beef. At Stangl's request, an instructor in incineration – Herbert Floss, an SS technical sergeant in his forties with a solicitous smile of perpetual care on his face – was sent over from Auschwitz. He was nicknamed *Tadellos* (Perfect) for his favourite expression – 'Thank God, now the fire's perfect' – when, ignited by gasoline, the pyre of corpses would burst into flames.

'Today we burned 2000 bodies,' *Tadellos* told the 'work-Jews' at roll-call one night. 'This is good, but we must not stop here. We will set ourselves an objective and devote all our efforts to reaching it. Tomorrow we will do 3000, the day after tomorrow 4000, then 5000, then 6000, and so on until 10,000. Every day we will force ourselves to increase output by one thousand units. I count on you to help me.'

And, driven by the law of supply and demand – enforced by whipping and killing – they did.

Cosmetically, the finishing touch to the all-important first impression of Treblinka came when Stangl's deputy, Kurt Franz – a former boxer known as 'The Doll' for his puffy, pouty good looks – had a realization that 'a station without a clock is not a station.' The camp carpenters painted the face of a clock on to a wooden cylinder eight inches thick and twenty-eight inches in diameter. The 'hands' of the 'clock' were painted to read three o'clock. Time stood still in Stangl's Treblinka on the edge of eternity.

Some arrived in airless boxcars, defecating on their dead and licking the sweat from each others' skins to slake their thirst. Polish and

Russian Jews travelled in cattle cars; Czechs and Western Jews in passenger coaches or sometimes – as with a trainload of rich Bulgarian Jews – in sleepers with a special baggage car for their valuables. No sooner had they dismounted and disrobed, however, than they were just cattle to be butchered into meat and bones and then burned to ashes and reduced to dust in 120 minutes of orchestrated violence and delusion that gave them no time to think – or resist.

'Faster! Faster!' they were commanded in a rain of clubs and whips punctuated by thunderclaps of pistol shots. Men who lingered for a last look at loved ones were commended to the voracious mercies of a dog called Barry, a mongrel St Bernard which, when presented by Stangl to his deputy, ex-boxer Kurt Franz, was already trained to bite off male genitals on command. All 'The Doll' had to say to his dog was a mocking 'Look, man, that dog isn't working!' and Barry would emasculate the victim, whom Kurt Franz would usually finish off with a bullet. At least three such canine attacks inside and outside 'The Tube' were documented at 'The Doll's' 1964–5 trial in Düsseldorf, where he received a life sentence. Also introduced as evidence was his scrapbook of photos from Treblinka. The album was titled 'The Best Years of My Life'.

'Faster!' and 'Faster!' the victims of Treblinka climbed over each other just to escape from frying-pan to fire, from the terrors of 'The Tube' to annihilation in the thirteen 'bath-houses' (one of them disguised as a synagogue) which disposed of 12,000 Jews in a typical day, but could – and, on occasion, *did* – kill 30,000 *per diem* by working around the clock. To Herbert Floss's perfection of the technology was added Kurt Franz's pugilistic insight into primitive physical medicine: if you make a man run all the way to the gas chamber, he will not only get there sooner, but, already gasping for breath, he will die faster.

On busy days, children, naked and barefoot, stood shivering in 'The Tube' waiting to be gassed. When their feet froze, they had to be ripped from the ground – or torn in half by 'Sepp', a ferocious SS guard who specialized in killing children. Sometimes 'Sepp' couldn't wait until his small 'clients' were in 'The Tube'. He would seize them by the feet upon arrival at Treblinka and smash their heads against boxcars. 'Sepp', later identified as Josef Hirtreiter, was the first Treblinka 'Hangman' to be brought to trial. In Frankfurt in 1951, he was given life in prison.

Most of Treblinka's executioners, however, were not German, but Ukrainian, for Stangl's staff, aside from slave labour, varied from thirty to forty SS and 200 to 300 Ukrainian guards, with the ideal ratio being five Ukrainians to each German. The Ukrainians, who had been at war with the Jews for most of the nearly 2000 years they had been living together, took to the task with unsurpassed zeal. One of them, Fyodor Fedorenko – later of Waterbury, Connecticut* – not only whipped prisoners as he herded them into gas chambers, but shot those who knelt at his feet begging for mercy.

Above the entranceway to the main gas chamber was carved, in gold Hebrew letters, 'THIS IS THE GATE OF THE LORD. THE RIGHTEOUS SHALL ENTER THROUGH IT'. Behind the doors was no Gentile St Peter, but Ivan and Nikolai, two Ukrainians who had joined the SS and operated the machinery of death. Ivan was the taller of the two. He had close-cropped blond hair and grey eyes that seemed kind and gentle until you looked into them – but, if you did, he would shatter your skull with a six-foot-long gas pipe he carried as a club. Nikolai, a pallid miniature of Ivan, brandished a sabre, but he was merely a brute while Ivan was a sadist who recurs in the annals of Treblinka as 'Ivan the Terrible'.

Whenever they needed more bodies for a full load before turning on the gas (throughout its brief history, Treblinka stuck with Wirth's outmoded, but effective, carbon monoxide technology, using motors from captured Soviet tanks and other dismantled equipment), Ivan and Nikolai would step out into 'The Tube' to hurry their victims along. Once, in a fit of frenzy, Ivan the Terrible borrowed Nikolai's sabre and slit open the bellies of a group of women from the Warsaw ghetto. Then, after piling the disembowelled women at the end of the 'Road to Heaven', he forced some male prisoners to mount and have sex with them.

Even before the war had ended, in a 1944 memoir called *One Year in Treblinka,* a 1943 escapee named Yankel Wiernik wrote how Ivan 'enjoyed torturing his victims. He would often pounce upon us while we were working; he would nail our ears to the walls or make us lie down on the floor and whip us brutally. While he did

*Extradited to the Soviet Union in 1984, Fedorenko was executed by a firing squad in 1987.

this, his face showed sadistic satisfaction and he laughed and joked. He finished off the victims according to his mood at the moment.'

At the age of fifty-two, Wiernik had worked in the body-disposal detail. Written in hiding and published underground, his account of life and death at Treblinka was the first to reach England and America and shock the world. He wrote:

> The screams of the women, the weeping of the children, cries of despair and misery, the pleas for mercy, for God's vengeance, ring in my ears to this day, making it impossible for me to forget the misery I saw.
>
> Between 450 and 500 persons were crowded into a chamber measuring twenty-five square metres [thirty square feet]. Parents carried their children in their arms in the vain hope that this would save their children from death. On the way to their doom, they were pushed and beaten with rifle butts and with Ivan's gas pipe. . .
>
> The bedlam lasted only a short while, for soon the doors were slammed shut. The chamber was filled, the motor turned on and connected with the inflow pipes and, within twenty-five minutes at the most, all lay stretched out dead or, to be more accurate, were standing up dead. Since there was not an inch of free space, they just leaned against each other.

'Even in death,' Wiernik noted, 'mothers held their children tightly in their arms. There were no more friends or foes. There was no more jealousy. All were equal. There was no longer any beauty or ugliness, for they were all yellow from the gas.'

At Treblinka, Chiel Rajchman, a textile merchant from Lodz, had worked as a 'dentist' – tearing open the corpses' mouths with pliers and extracting any gold or silver dental work. Escaping in August 1943, he hid in a bunker in Warsaw and jotted his recollections of Treblinka until the Red Army entered in early 1945 and freed him of everything but his recollections:

> On a hot day the Ukrainian helpers feel good. They work with their whips from right to left, in all directions. Nikolai and Ivan . . . they feel very good and happy on such a hot day.
>
> Ivan is about twenty-five years old, looks like a strong, big boss. He is pleased when he has an opportunity to expend on the workers his energies. From time to time he gets an urge to take a sharp knife, stop a worker who is running by, and cut off his ear.

> The blood spurts out, the worker screams, but he has to keep running with the carrier [a stretcher for corpses]. Ivan waits patiently until the worker runs back. He tells him to put the carrier down, tells him to get undressed, to go over to the pit where he shoots him.

Once, Rajchman and another 'dentist' named Finkelstein were working at a well – washing blood and tissue from the gold crowns they had extracted from corpses – when Ivan wandered over with an auger for drilling holes in wood. 'He told Finkelstein to lie down on the ground,' Rajchman recalled, 'and he drilled the metal into his rear end. This was just a joke. The poor man didn't even scream out loud. He only groaned.'

Ivan just laughed and told Finkelstein: 'Lie still or I'll shoot you.'

In 1981, Chiel Rajchman of Montevideo, Uruguay was a key witness in a Cleveland, Ohio trial that led to the revocation of the US citizenship of John Demjanjuk, sixty, a Ford Motor Company mechanic, and Demjanjuk's extradition and deportation to Israel five years later to stand trial for the crimes of Treblinka's 'Ivan the Terrible'. The second man to occupy the glass booth in Jerusalem where Adolf Eichmann had defended himself a quarter of a century earlier, Demjanjuk, too, was sentenced to death (in 1988). Unlike Eichmann, however, he denied everything, including that he, Ivan Nicolaievich Demjanjuk, born 3 April 1920, in Duboimachariwzi in the Ukraine, was the same person as 'the other Ivan', whose name he (and, later, others) said was Marchenko. But Demjanjuk performed the ultimate abstraction when he told the US marshals escorting him to Israel: 'If I was in Treblinka, then I was just a small cog. There was a war on, and there was no choice but to follow orders. But I was never in Treblinka.'*

Aloof and distant, Franz Stangl stood above it all, above the 'dentists' and the 'work-Jews', the victims and their corpses, the driven and their destroyers, the SS and the Ukrainians. He was the master magician tinkering with new illusions to beguile killers and innocents

*Simon Wiesenthal's work in the Demjanjuk case was peripheral until his trial in 1987, when documents supplied by Wiesenthal, plus his expertise, proved helpful to prosecutors seeking to identify Demjanjuk as 'Ivan the Terrible'.

alike: admonitions to 'take soap and towel into the bath-house with you' . . . receipts for clothing to be claimed after 'showering' . . . and, on occasions when traffic needed to be slowed down, a booth along 'The Road to Heaven' would be opened by a Ukrainian to collect a piddling 'one zloty to pay for the bath' . . . or, when traffic needed to be speeded up, a German sat there encouraging them to 'hurry up before the water gets cold'.

Two of Sigmund Freud's sisters, both in their eighties, were transported to Treblinka from Vienna and, on the platform at arrival, one of them went up to the newly commissioned Lieutenant Kurt Franz (whose zeal had won him a rare 'battlefield' promotion from the top enlisted rank of sergeant) and asked to be given lighter work because of her age and health. Franz humoured her with the assurance that she must have been sent there by mistake and would be put on the first train back to Vienna 'as soon as you take a bath.'*

As in Auschwitz and Janowskà, there was a camp band. This one was conducted by a noted Jewish chamber musician, Arthur Gold, to hasten the pace up 'The Road to Heaven' and muffle the cries and moans of hundreds of humans being driven to their deaths like cattle to a pen. To enable inmates to whistle while they worked with the remains of their co-religionists, Kurt Franz wrote a 'Treblinka Song' which Gold set to music and 'work-Jews' had to sing at roll-calls:

Looking straight ahead – brave and joyous – at the world,
We march off to our work.
All that matters is Treblinka;
It is our destiny.

We heed our commandant's voice,
Obeying his every nod and sign.
We march along together
To do what duty demands.

*The Freud sister was either Marie, eighty-two, or Pauline, eighty, both of whom perished in Treblinka. Two other Freud sisters also died in the camps: Rosa, eighty-four, in Auschwitz, and Adolfine, eighty-one, in Theresienstadt.

Work, obedience, and duty
Must be our whole existence.
We want to serve, to go on serving
Until destiny winks its eye. Hooray!

Even with this musical homage to Stangl to inspire them, fifteen to twenty 'work-Jews' committed suicide daily – and, occasionally, so did a Ukrainian or a German SS man.

Like Simon Wiesenthal, a Czech 'work-Jew', Richard Glazar, marvelled at how well the death machinery worked, even when technically imperfect, because the people who ran it rarely failed. Glazar, who survived Treblinka and then twenty years of Stalinism in his native Czechoslovakia before escaping to Switzerland during Alexander Dubček's brief Prague Spring of freedom in 1968, contends that 'only lack of transport, because the Germans needed it for war, prevented them from dealing with far vaster numbers; Treblinka alone could have dealt with the six million Jews and more besides.' Given adequate rail transport, he says, just the German extermination camps in Poland could have liquidated all the Poles, Russians, and other East European 'sub-humans' they planned to kill once the war was won.

The weak link, transport, had become the burden and mission of Adolf Eichmann, who visited Treblinka twice in 1942 – once in the camp's preparatory stages and again, with an SS group from Berlin, when Stangl had it running smoothly.

The first time, he tried not to use his imagination when a police captain in shirt-sleeves whose 'vulgar, uncultivated voice' (Eichmann recalled almost two decades later to his Israeli interrogators) told him in 'some dialect from the south-western corner of Germany . . . how he had made everything nicely air-tight, for they were going to hook up a Russian submarine engine and pipe the exhaust into the house and the Jews inside would be poisoned.' For Eichmann, this was 'monstrous. I can't listen to such things . . . without their affecting me. Even today, if I see someone with a deep cut, I have to look away. I could never have been a doctor. I still remember how I pictured the thing to myself and began to tremble, as if I'd been through something, some terrible experience.' Quite likely, the vulgar captain he described – adding, 'maybe he drank' – was the savage Christian Wirth.

The second time around, 'I expected to see a wooden house on the right side of the road and a few more wooden houses on the left; that's what I remembered.' Instead, Eichmann was pleasantly surprised to see 'a railroad station with a sign saying TREBLINKA, looking exactly like a German railroad station – a replica, with sign-boards, etc.' As a desk murderer who professed to be squeamish about violent death, Eichmann said he 'hung back as far as I could. I didn't push closer to see it all. I saw a footbridge enclosed in barbed wire and over that footbridge a file of naked Jews was being driven into a house, a big . . . no, not a house, a big, one-room structure, to be gassed.'

Anticipation of Eichmann's second visit threw Commandant Stangl into a tizzy of tidying Treblinka. He ordered Staff Sergeant Suchomel (who, in 1965, was sentenced to seven years for his service under Stangl) to 'put everything in order, first in the tailor shop and then . . . make sure about the "gold Jews" shop, too. Mark all trunks and cases very precisely with regard to content and description. He is going to want to see it looking exactly right. And when they are here, you come up to us and make a report in a proper military style.'

Witnesses were scarce. Once upon a time, an 'Aryan' woman – the wife of a high-ranking German Army officer – and her two sons boarded the wrong train in Germany. They wound up in a perfectly respectable passenger coach bound for Treblinka with Jewish veterans who had fought for the Kaiser in the First World War – and their families. It was only on the platform at arrival that the young mother managed to make herself heard while being ordered to undress. She presented identity papers showing she was of pure German stock and, besides, the SS could see that neither of her sons had been circumcised. Yankel Wiernik was there and wrote in *One Year in Treblinka* (1944):

> She was a good-looking woman, but there was terror in her eyes. She clung to her children and tried to soothe them, saying their troubles would soon be cleared up and they would return home . . . She petted and kissed them, but she was crying because she was haunted by a dreadful foreboding.
>
> The Germans ordered her to step forward. Thinking that this meant freedom for herself and her children, she relaxed. But

> alas, it had been decided that she was to perish together with the Jews, because she had seen too much and would be liable to tell all about what she had seen, which was supposed to be shrouded in secrecy. Whoever crossed the threshold of Treblinka was doomed to die. Therefore, this German woman, together with her children, went to her death with all the others. Her children cried just as the Jewish children did, and their eyes mirrored the same despair, for in death there is no racial distinction; all are equal.

Stretched far beyond the parameters of Kant and Nietzsche, the twisted German logic that let lesser thinkers like Stangl and Eichmann live with themselves in World War II has never been articulated more revealingly than in Stangl's dialogues with Gitta Sereny in Düsseldorf in 1971 during the last months of his life.

'It was a matter of survival, always of survival,' Stangl told Sereny. 'What I had to do . . . was to limit my own actions to what I – in my own conscience – could answer for. At police training school, they taught us . . . that the definition of a crime must meet four requirements: there has to be a subject, an object, an action, and free will. If any of these four elements are missing, then we are not dealing with a punishable offence.'

'I can't see how you could possibly apply this concept to this situation,' Sereny protested.

'That's what I'm trying to explain to you,' said Stangl. 'The only way I could live was by compartmentalizing my thinking. By doing this, I could apply it to my own situation. If the *subject* was the government, the *object* the Jews, and the *action* the gassings, then I could tell myself that for me the fourth element, *free will*, was missing.'

On another occasion, Sereny asked Stangl: 'What did you think at the time was the reason for the exterminations?'

'They wanted the Jews' money,' he replied.

'You can't be serious!' she exclaimed.

'But of course. Have you any idea of the fantastic sums that were involved? That's how the steel from Sweden was bought.'

'But,' Sereny argued, 'they weren't all rich . . . There were hundreds of thousands of them from ghettoes in the East who had nothing . . .'

'Nobody had nothing,' said Stangl. 'Everybody had something.'

As if to confirm Stangl's reasoning, Simon Wiesenthal cites a document signed by Stangl: a roster of items delivered by his

Treblinka administration to SS headquarters in Berlin between 1 October 1942 and 2 August 1943:

25 freight cars of women's hair
248 freight cars of clothing
100 freight cars of shoes
22 freight cars of dry goods
46 freight cars of drugs
254 freight cars of rugs and bedding
400 freight cars of various used articles
2,800,000 American dollars
400,000 British pounds
12 million Soviet rubles
140 million Polish zlotys
400,000 gold watches
145,000 kilograms golden wedding rings
4,000 karats of diamonds over 2 karats
120 million zlotys in various gold coins
Several thousand strings of pearls

When Stangl insisted that 'the racial business was just secondary' to the looting, Sereny asked him why, if the Nazis were going to kill the Jews anyway, they humiliated them so cruelly and used so much hate propaganda.

'To condition those who actually had to carry out the policies,' he answered. 'To make it possible for them to do what they did.'

'Well, *you* were part of that,' Sereny pointed out. 'Did *you* hate?'

'Never! I would never let anybody dictate to me who to hate.'

'What is the difference to you between hate and a contempt which results in considering people as "cargo"?'

'It has nothing to do with hate. They were so weak. They allowed everything to happen – to be done to them. They were people with whom there was no common ground, no possibility of communication – that is how contempt is born. I could never understand how they could just give in as they did. Quite recently I read a book about lemmings, who every five or six years just wander into the sea and die; that made me think of Treblinka.'

Simon Wiesenthal says that the first time he came upon the name of Franz Stangl was in 1948, when 'I was shown a secret list of decorations awarded to high SS officers. Most of the recipients were given the Cross of Merit for "bravery beyond the call of duty", "giving aid to comrades under fire", or "escape under especially hazardous circumstances". But after certain names on the list there is just the pencilled notation "Secret Reich's Matters" followed by "for psychological discomfort". The coded Nazi terminology meant "for special merit in the technique of mass extermination". Franz Stangl's name was followed by both the notation and the special remark.'

On 4 October 1943, Heinrich Himmler told a meeting of SS generals in Posen (now Poznan, Poland):

'I also want to speak very frankly about an extremely important subject. Among ourselves we will discuss it openly; in public, however, we must never mention it. . .

'I mean the evacuation of the Jews, the extermination of the Jewish people. This is something that is easy to talk about. "The Jewish people will be exterminated," says every member of the party. "This is clear, this is in our programme: the elimination, the extermination of the Jews. We will do this." And then they come to you – eighty million good Germans – and each one has his "decent" Jew. Naturally, all the rest are vermin, but this particular Jew is first-rate. Not one of those who talk this way has seen the bodies; not one has been on the spot. Most of you know what it is to see a pile of one hundred or five hundred or one thousand bodies. To have stuck it out and at the same time, barring exceptions caused by human weakness, to have remained decent: this is what has made us tough.

'This is a page of glory in our history which never has and never will be written.'

Even the shadowy Stangl, who avoided most contact with Jews at Treblinka, had his own 'decent' Jew: a Viennese named Blau, whom he made a cook because 'I always tried to give as many jobs as possible to Viennese Jews . . . After all, I was Austrian . . . Blau was the one I talked to the most; him and his wife . . . He knew I'd help whenever I could.'

One day, Blau asked Stangl's help. Blau's eighty-year-old father had arrived on that morning's transport. Was there anything Stangl could do?

'Really, Blau, you must understand,' Stangl responded in a kindly voice. 'It's impossible. A man of eighty!'

Blau said of course he understood his father couldn't be put to work and would therefore be a useless mouth. But could he take him to the fake 'hospital' for execution rather than let him be run through The Tube to the gas chamber? And could he maybe take his father first to the kitchen and give him a meal?

Stangl said magnanimously: 'You go and do what you think best, Blau. Officially, I don't know anything; but unofficially you can tell the *Kapo* [prisoner squad leader] I said it was all right.' That afternoon, according to what Stangl told Sereny in 1971, 'when I came back to my office, Blau was waiting for me. He had tears in his eyes. He stood to attention and said: "*Herr Kommandant*, I want to thank you. I gave my father a meal. And I've just taken him to the *hospital*; it's all over. Thank you very much." I said, "Well, Blau, there's no need to thank me, but of course if you want to thank me, you may."'

While the son's wish to show his doomed father how well he was doing under the worst of circumstances may be comprehensible to some, to Gitta Sereny 'this story and the way it was told represented to me the starkest example of a corrupted personality I had ever encountered and came very near to making me stop these conversations. I broke off early that lunchtime and went to sit for nearly two hours in a pub across the street, wrestling with the most intense *malaise* I'd ever felt at the thought of listening further.' Fortunately, she did return and historians probing the depths of the Final Solution are indebted to her intestinal fortitude.

To Sereny, Stangl also described how 'a beautiful reddish-blonde Jewess' was sent up to substitute for an ailing maid who cleaned his living quarters. Just to make chit-chat, Stangl asked her if she had chosen a room for herself in the servant barracks.

The girl stopped dusting and stood very still, looking Stangl in the eye before responding quietly: 'Why do you ask?'

Taken aback by her breach of master-slave etiquette, Stangl blustered: 'Why shouldn't I ask? I can ask, can't I?'

The girl looked right through him for a few seconds before saying: 'Can I go?'

'Yes, of course,' Stangl said. Years later, he recalled how 'I so admired her for facing up to me', but could not remember what became of her. Apparently, the girl, Tchechia Mandel, an industrialist's daughter from Wiesenthal's home city of Lemberg, was still alive and working in the camp kitchen at the time of a 2 August 1943 uprising when 200 militant young Jews (including Richard Glazar and Grossinger's maître d' Siedlecki, 'dentist' Rajchman and lumberman Rajzman) – armed with rifles, revolvers, and hand grenades stolen from the SS arsenal – cut all wires, set fire to the camp, and escaped into the woods with another 400 'work-Jews'. (Four hundred more who couldn't or wouldn't flee were killed in the camp.) Most of the escapees were hunted down and murdered by the Germans, Ukrainians, Polish peasants, and even Polish partisans. Only fifty survived the war.

No women were in a position to escape on that heroic Monday and hardly a handful of them survived the German reprisals. The spirited Tchechia Mandel did, but she was not to be spared.

In the very last days of Treblinka, a sergeant stood up after a good lunch and said to Tchechia and the two other women who had served it to him: 'Well, girls, it's your turn now.'

The other two cringed, but Tchechia laughed in his face and said: 'I never did believe your fairy-tale promises, you pigs. Go ahead and kill us. Just do me one favour. Don't ask us to undress.' When one of the other girls began to weep, Tchechia told her: 'Don't cry. Don't do them the favour. Remember, you are a Jew.' Such people died prouder than Stangl ever lived.

After the revolt, transports continued coming to Treblinka for another fortnight and were liquidated in whatever facilities remained in operation. Stangl produced plans to rebuild the camp more efficiently than ever, but orders came down from Berlin through Globocnik to obliterate Treblinka. The machinery of the Final Solution was running low on Jews to process, and Zyklon B at Auschwitz and Majdanek had more potential than Treblinka's low-grade carbon-monoxide technology. Transports ticketed for Treblinka would be diverted to Sobibor, though not for long: On 14 October 1943, a revolt closed Sobibor. A dozen SS men and more than a dozen Ukrainians perished, as did 200 Jews shot or blown up by mines while trying to escape. Of the 400 who did escape Sobibor, a hundred were later captured and killed. Others joined Soviet partisan units, with which most of them died in combat.

Others died of typhus or were killed by Poles. Only thirty survived the war, among them the leader of the revolt, Alexander Pechersky, a Jewish soldier in the Red Army who would testify to Simon Wiesenthal against his tormentor Gustav Wagner, nearly four decades later.

The last transport – *Pj* (for Polish Jews) 204 – to reach Treblinka arrived on Thursday, 19 August 1943, and its passengers were destroyed the same day. Then Treblinka's remaining buildings were demolished. The grounds were planted with pine trees, which grew astonishingly fast. Bricks of the dismantled 'bath-houses' went to build a farmhouse for a Ukrainian named Strebel who was put in there with his family and told to pretend they had been farming there since 1939. But no lie could long conceal the bones of more than a million men, women, and children. The liquefaction of their imperfectly burned bodies caused the earth to shift. Gases released by putrefaction blew the cosmetic top-soil off the burial pits. The Strebels fled before the Red Army came in late 1944.

Toward the end of August 1943, however, Franz Stangl had at last been able to tell his wife that her wish had come true: he was done with the death camps of Poland and about to be transferred to Trieste, considerably closer to home, for anti-partisan combat duty.

– 29 –

The secret bearers

If power corrupts and absolute power corrupts absolutely, it made monsters of mediocrities like Mengele, Eichmann, and Stangl. If Hitler embodied evil as few, if any, in history ever did, his mastery lay in his grasp and manipulation of power, but did he pose any greater physical danger to individuals and whole societies (Jews, gypsies, freemasons) than did these devoted servants of his who soldiered so zealously to translate his every fevered, far-fetched rant into unspeakable reality for millions? To paraphrase Shakespeare, some are born to power, some achieve power, and others have power thrust upon them. To the man in the street and the Jew in the ghetto of the Third Reich, those *others* were the ones to watch – and watch out for.

Mengele was 'a man who believed in nothing but power, the ultimate cynic', says his unwilling 'Aryan' underling, Dr Ella Lingens-Reiner, holder of law as well as medical degrees from the University of Vienna. 'The trouble with Eichmann,' writes Hannah Arendt, 'was precisely that so many were like him, and that the many were neither perverted nor sadistic, that they were, and still are, terribly and terrifyingly normal.' And Stangl, says Gitta Sereny, had an infinite capacity to manipulate and repress his own moral scruples, which, she insists, unquestionably existed.

If, unlike Mengele's, the names of Eichmann and Stangl were unknown to Wiesenthal during his concentration-camp odyssey, this was because Eichmann worked mainly behind the scenes with fellow Nazis and Gentile collaborators as well as through the Jewish Councils he created and later liquidated. For facelessness, however, none of the others in Wiesenthal's gallery could match Franz Stangl, whose name was unknown to the million and a quarter who passed through Treblinka or even to most of the sixty who survived his inferno.

By late 1943, he was a non-person to Hitler's high command, too. SS Captain Stangl had left Poland for Trieste that September in a convoy with his chiefs, General Odilo Globocnik and Major Christian Wirth, and 120 other men. 'I realized quite well, and so did most of us, that we were an embarrassment to the brass,' he later told Gitta Sereny. 'They wanted to find ways and means to "incinerate" us. So we were assigned the most dangerous jobs. Anything to do with anti-partisan combat in that part of the world was very perilous.'

Yugoslav partisans took no prisoners. Simon Wiesenthal confirms that, in Berlin headquarters' jargon, 'incineration' meant eliminating their own men by sending them to a front from which they were not expected to return. This was the cynical Nazi solution to the problem these technicians of mass extermination posed to their superiors, who called them 'secret-bearers, first class', meaning that they knew too much for their own or the Party's good. After blowing up the camps and planting farms and other cosmetic disguises atop them, as many expert witnesses as possible had to be removed.

With Wirth, it worked. 'The savage Christian' was killed in street fighting on the Istrian Peninsula on 26 May 1944. 'I saw him dead,' Stangl said with some satisfaction. 'They said partisans killed him, but we thought his own men had taken care of him.' A third theory, propounded by British historian Robert Wistrich in his invaluable *Who's Who in Nazi Germany* (1982), suggests that 'he may also have been the victim of a Jewish vengeance squad organized to hunt down Nazis mass murderers.'

Globocnik survived his Adriatic exposure; he had, after all, been born in Trieste and knew the treacherous territory. But the chief exterminator of Polish Jewry had three strikes against him: he was an alcoholic, a plunderer, and, worst of all, a bachelor turning forty. Since it was not considered 'natural' for one to rise so high in the SS without mating and breeding for the future of the 'Master Race', Globocnik was given leave to find a bride. His military travel orders from the highest headquarters deserve partial quotation:

> It is important that SS Major General Globocnik marry soon to fortify him with the strength that only a good wife and home life

can afford him against the rigorous existence of a pioneer. This would undoubtedly enable General Globocnik to conserve his energies for the larger tasks ahead of him, for which he is certainly qualified. Otherwise, there is the danger that, while the rugged and strongly masculine frontier atmosphere of the East would not necessarily destroy him, it might still sap those energies.

Put out to stud, Globocnik went a-courting in his home province of Carinthia (in what had been southern Austria) and found himself a hefty *Hausfrau* named Hannelore. According to Stangl, 'she was a big blonde who was working in a hospital in the city of Klagenfurt', where Globocnik married her in a civil ceremony in October 1944. When the war was over, he made his way back across the Dolomites to reach his Hannelore, but was stopped by a British patrol on 31 May 1945 along the banks of the Weissensee, a pristine mountain lake in Carinthia. There, according to most accounts, Globocnik committed suicide by swallowing a cyanide capsule a few minutes after he was apprehended, though Wistrich again adds that 'according to other versions, Globocnik was hunted down and killed either by partisans or by a Jewish vengeance squad in June 1945.'

For his first three months in the port of Trieste, Franz Stangl was assigned to Transport Security – in charge of guarding the closely watched trains headed north in late 1943 with passengers, plunder, and occasional prisoners. He had one narrow escape at the very end of this stint. Granted Christmas leave, he turned over his reins to Franz Reichleitner, the 'secret-bearer' who had succeeded him at Sobibor. That night, on a regular rural security patrol that Stangl would have made, Reichleitner was ambushed and assassinated by partisans. Intercepted in Udine in northern Italy, Stangl was recalled to hunt Reichleitner's killers and his furlough was cancelled.

Back in Trieste, Stangl assembled twenty-five men 'and we scoured the whole valley all night. There wasn't any sense to it. It poured. It was pitch dark. There could have been a partisan behind every tree and we wouldn't have known or found them. Only the next morning did we learn that while we were out the night before, partisans had marched through a village, singing. Everybody hid them. They were safe at home.'

After a brief assignment either hunting partisans in Fiume (now the Croatian port of Rijeka) or, in Wiesenthal's version, rounding up Jews in Fiume and Abazia (now Opatija) for deportation to the extermination camp in Riseria di San Sabba, Stangl was granted a two-week leave at the end of February 1944 to go home and see his new-born third daughter. His wife was still in bed, recovering from a difficult pregnancy and a cold winter. When Stangl showed up with blankets, down comforters, and bed linens – gifts from the family conscious General Globocnik, he told her – Theresa Stangl said it was 'like Christmas in March'. Stangl stayed a week. He didn't quite say what his work was in Italy, but he did complain that he'd been ordered to stay on the look-out for Jews. 'What do they think I am?' he asked rhetorically. 'A headhunter? They can leave me out of this now.'

Upon his return to Trieste, he was given his longest and biggest assignment there: as special supply officer for a strategic construction project in the Po Valley which involved some half a million Italian workers building last-ditch fortifications under German supervision. Not only was the post in the less perilous Italian portion of Globocnik's command, but it was a position from which he would feather his nest for a postwar escape. 'I was responsible for getting everything: shoes, clothes, food,' Stangl would boast to Gitta Sereny. 'I was the only one who went about in civilian clothes. Everybody, army and SS, had to help me. I carried a paper signed by the general stating that "Captain Stangl is authorized to act in uniform or civvies and all services are requested to give him every assistance in the execution of his command" . . . I had a man with me who had no other job except to carry trunks with millions in cash.'

'Buy whatever you need,' Globocnik had told Stangl. 'Money is no object.' He was free to patronize the black market, which was virtually the only source of gas, tyres, and spare parts. He made many contacts in northern Italy – wheeler-dealers, smugglers, gangsters, and nobility with something to sell – and some of them may have greased his postwar path across their turf.

When the war ended, Stangl made his way to the Attersee, a lake in Salzburg province, to stay with a village policeman he knew. One of his host's colleagues, however, notified the US Army of Occupation that there was an SS officer in town. The Americans sent a car around and hauled Stangl off to the royal spa of Bad Ischl for questioning by US counter-intelligence. He gave his own name.

His interrogators focused on his anti-partisan activities in Yugoslavia and Italy, but he never mentioned his Polish past. Then they sent him to Camp Marcus W. Orr in Glasenbach, near Salzburg, for further investigation. He was there for more than two years.

In Glasenbach – less than a hundred miles from Wiesenthal in Linz – Franz Stangl, whose name didn't enter Simon's card files until 1948, spent twenty-six months in relatively tranquil detention by American counter-intelligence. 'He underwent a routine investigation,' says Wiesenthal. 'Nobody knew he was the former commandant of Treblinka. He was questioned and gave routine answers about his wartime service. Then he went back to his bunk, lay down, smoked an American cigarette, and talked with fellow SS officers about escaping.'

To an alumnus of Mauthausen like Wiesenthal – who visited Glasenbach several times on behalf of the War Crimes Commission, OSS, and CIC – it was virtually a spa: 'The internees were well-fed and sunburned, and they led a pleasant life. They had amusing company from another part of the camp, where wives of high-ranking Nazis and some women who used to be concentration-camp guards were interned . . . The internees of the Americans, at least, lived like guests. They got medical care and cigarettes. In many cases, these "prisoners" were living better than the civilian population outside the gate.'

After more than two years in Glasenbach under very random and casual American investigation, Stangl had not yet been traced beyond Italy and Yugoslavia to Poland; there were so few survivors of Sobibor and Treblinka and he had stayed so aloof from the dirty details that no witnesses had yet surfaced to identify him by name. He might even have gone free in 1947 if his record hadn't shown that, early in the war, he'd worked at Hartheim, the euthanasia castle which was just beginning to interest Austrian authorities. They asked that he be turned over to them for trial and, late that summer, he was transferred to a civilian prison in Linz.

Not only was his new address closer to home in Wels, but Stangl soon had a single room where his wife could pay him conjugal visits. Still not fully aware of his roles at Sobibor and Treblinka, Theresa Stangl confronted her husband with press clippings about the first smaller fry from Hartheim who were already on trial. She said that when he told her 'how ill the patients were; how nobody could be killed without four certificates from the doctors . . . I cannot in all honesty say I felt bad about Hartheim.' Still, she took a day off from her office job in a Wels distillery to attend one day's hearings in the Hartheim trial. It happened to be the day when Franz Höldl, the Hartheim chauffeur, was asked by a prosecutor about Stangl and (in her word) 'exonerated' him of any connection with the killings there. 'I was so happy,' she recalled. 'I can't tell you how relieved I was.'

Upon reading, however, that Höldl had been given a four-year sentence, Theresa Stangl prodded her husband to break out of his comfortable cocoon. 'If this driver gets four years,' she told him, 'what will you get for having been police superintendent of that place?' When she gave him her savings (less than twenty dollars) and her jewellery (a ring and a necklace) to finance his trip, he recognized that these were his marching orders.

'The prisoners were often sent out to clear away rubble and help rebuild bomb damage,' says Simon Wiesenthal, who was living in Linz at the time. 'Later I heard Stangl was with a group of petty criminals who worked at rebuilding the VOEST steelworks in Linz. The prisoners were not heavily guarded. Why would they want to run away? They got more food in the prison than outside. A few kilometres away, at the Enns bridge, Russian soldiers guarded the frontier of the Soviet Zone of Austria. What prisoner would be fool enough to run away *to* there?' Nevertheless, on the night of Sunday, 30 May 1948, Franz Stangl and another prisoner named Hans Steiner were not among those who'd marched out in the morning.

Stangl and Steiner had walked away from their work with a rucksack of canned foods and headed south on foot. The next day, an Austrian police officer called on Theresa Stangl and asked if her husband was at home. That was how she found out that he'd acted upon her advice. She invited her visitor to search her home, but he declined politely, 'No, no, that won't be at all necessary', and left.

'No one had seen Stangl escape,' says Wiesenthal, 'but no one got very excited about it. A notation was added to his file and the file thrown on top of many other files. Neither the American authorities nor the Austrian press was informed.'

Stangl said that he and Steiner walked the 150 miles from Linz, the Upper Austrian capital, to Graz, capital of the Austrian province of Styria. In Graz's Renaissance old town, he sold his wife's jewellery for a tiny sum and then, he later told her, was walking past a construction site where a house was being pulled down when he was recognized – by a labourer who rushed out shouting '*Herr Hauptsturmführer!*' ('*Captain!*') and embraced him. It was ex-Master Sergeant Gustav Wagner, who had served with him in Hartheim and Trieste as well as Sobibor, and, having been more visible as chief of the gas chamber and second-in-command at the death camp, had already been tried *in absentia* and sentenced to death by the Nuremberg Tribunal.

Wagner begged Stangl and Steiner to let him come with them. When they said yes, he walked off his job and joined them on their journey into Italy.

Simon Wiesenthal doubts much of Stangl's and his wife's Wizard-of-Oz version of this journey. It is unlikely that Stangl and Steiner would have walked all the way from Linz to Graz, particularly without a stop-off in Wels, just fifteen miles away. And, despite truth being stranger than fiction, it seems more than 'purely coincidental' that two such closely linked euthanasia and extermination alumni as Stangl and Wagner should get together so accidentally in Graz. 'I am afraid she led you by the nose,' Wiesenthal told a visitor who had just interviewed the Stangl woman.

When the Stangls claimed that he and Steiner and Wagner 'just walked out of Austria' over a mountain pass by night, Wiesenthal exclaimed: 'What nonsense! How could they? Without papers or passports? What about the frontier? It's all lies! They obviously had papers provided by ODESSA.' While Frau Stangl insisted that her husband was 'a very good mountaineer and knew the Tyrolean mountains well from his youth. It was very difficult for the two others, but he managed to get them across', Wiesenthal believes they took the 'monastery route between Austria and Italy. Roman Catholic priests, particularly Franciscan friars, helped pass the fugitives down a long line of "safe" religious houses.'

Many of these monks and other good Christians had sheltered Jews fleeing for their lives during the war. Of Rome's 8000 Jews, at least half survived because they were hidden in convents, monasteries, houses of Catholic orders, and even in the Vatican. (Still others were sheltered by Italian neighbours and friends, but 2000, most of them women and children, died in Auschwitz or in transit.) For better or for worse, by 1945 some of these good Samaritans had been in 'refugee work' for so long that they no longer discriminated among their guests, but simply helped any 'pilgrim' on his way.

By 1947, the Vatican had become 'the largest single organization involved in the illegal movement of emigrants', including Nazis, according to a US State Department report made that year by Vincent La Vista, an American Foreign Service officer in Rome. The document was classified as 'top secret' until 1984, when, after pressure from both Simon Wiesenthal in Vienna and his Centre in Los Angeles, it was made available to historian Charles R. Allen, Jnr.

'In countries where the church is a controlling or dominating factor,' said the La Vista report, 'the Vatican has brought pressure to bear which has resulted in the foreign missions of those Latin American countries taking an attitude almost favouring the entry into their country of former Nazi and former fascist or other political groups, so long as they are anti-communist.' La Vista added that 'the justification of the Vatican for its participation in this illegal traffic is simply the propagation of the faith.'

Whether or not Stangl and his companions reached Rome with church assistance (some of the lay contacts Stangl and Wagner had made during their Italian tours of duty may have helped), he sought it early on. 'I heard of a Bishop Hu*lda* at the Vatican who was helping Catholic SS officers, so that's where we went,' Stangl told Gitta Sereny. Actually, it was not that easy, for he had the name wrong and 'no idea about how one went about finding a bishop at the Vatican' – or, for that matter, about finding the Vatican. The three 'pilgrims' split up, agreeing to rendezvous later. Then, Stangl recalled: 'I walked across a bridge over the Tiber and suddenly found myself face to face with a former comrade: there, in the middle of Rome where there were millions of people. He'd been in the security police in France and they wanted to put him on trial there. He'd been extradited from Glasenbach by the French and escaped in the Tyrol when on the way to France.'

'Are you on your way to see Hu*dal*?' his friend asked.

'Ah, so! Hu*dal*!' Stangl exclaimed. 'Yes, but I don't know where to find him.'

His friend directed him to Bishop Alois Hudal, rector of Santa Maria dell'Anima and father confessor to the German community in the Eternal City. When Stangl reached Hudal's office and gave his name, the Austrian bishop came into the waiting-room, held out both hands, and welcomed him with: 'You must be Franz Stangl. I've been expecting you.'

The name Stangl had in his head, however garbled, the 'meet cute' on the Tiber and Hudal's welcome all spell ODESSA to Wiesenthal. But it is perhaps more edifying to ponder the philanthropy of Bishop Hudal, who had ingratiated himself with Adolf Hitler, another native Austrian, while helping Eugenio Cardinal Pacelli negotiate a 1933 Vatican concordat with the Nazis. Throughout the 1930s, Hudal lobbied for a pan-Germanic federation of Austria with Germany and, after Hitler accomplished that overnight in 1938, for closer collaboration between the Vatican and the Nazis. In all of this, he had the ear of Cardinal Pacelli, a Germanophile who had served as papal nuncio to Bavaria and Berlin from 1917 to 1929 and ascended to the papacy as Pius XII in 1939.

Hudal's postwar 'refugee work' with thousands of SS men – some eighty per cent of whom would have qualified for death sentences had they appeared before the Nuremberg tribunal – earned him the unofficial title of 'chief Scarlet Pimpernel of Rome.'

Simon Wiesenthal sees red when he discusses how Hudal helped not just Stangl, Eichmann, and possibly Mengele, but also Walter Rauff, who invented the mobile gas chambers used in Riga and Chelmno and died in Chile in 1984, and, above all, a Viennese named Otto Wächter, who was not only one of the assassins of Austrian Chancellor Dollfuss in 1934, but one of the murderers of Wiesenthal's mother in 1942.

Rewarded for his earlier crime by being made Vienna's chief of police after Hitler annexed Austria in 1938, Wächter was sent to Poland with the outbreak of war in September 1939: first as governor of the Cracow district and then as governor of Galicia. 'I saw him in early 1942 in the ghetto of Lwów,' Wiesenthal recalls, adding painfully that, seven months later, Wächter was 'personally in charge' of the transport that sent Simon's mother to her death.

'There were 800,000 other people Wächter killed, too,' Wiesenthal adds matter-of-factly. After the war, Wächter escaped from Bavaria to Italy, carrying his complete archives with him, but calling himself 'Otto Reinhardt'. In 1949, when Wächter was dying under an assumed name in a religious college in Rome where he had been given sanctuary, he confessed his identity and sent for his wife and Bishop Hudal.

Hudal gave the dying man last rites of the Church and took charge of his files. After Wächter's death, Wiesenthal asked Bishop Hudal to give him his mother's murderer's files. Hudal refused – arguing that Wächter's records were part of his confessional and had to be respected as secret and sacred. What made Wiesenthal forever equate the name Hudal with the word *chutzpa* (Yiddish for *gall*) was the bishop's last word on the matter: 'I am a priest, not a policeman.'

Simon is certain that the churchman, who died in Rome in 1963, will sizzle for eternity in the hottest reaches of hell. As evidence against Hudal, he cites an excerpt from the bishop's postwar diary, made public in 1985:

> Ultimately, the war of the Allies against Germany had nothing to do with ideals. This war was not a crusade, but a rivalry between economic complexes . . . using catchwords like democracy, race, religious liberty, and Christianity as bait for the masses. This is why I felt duty bound after 1945 to devote my charitable work mainly to former National Socialists and fascists, especially the so-called 'war criminals' who had been persecuted by communists and Christian Democrats.*
>
> For this, I was soon known in the Roman Curia† as a 'Nazi fascist bishop' who was '*troppo tedesco*' (too German) and faulted as incompatible with Vatican policy. But I thank God that He opened my eyes and blessed me with the undeserved ability to visit and comfort many victims of the postwar period in their prisons and concentration camps and that I could also rescue some of them from their tormentors by helping them escape with false identity papers into more favourable countries.

Of Hudal's help, Franz Stangl said:

'First he got me quarters in Rome where I was to stay until my papers came through. And he gave me a bit of money; I had almost nothing left.' Stangl joined 'many, many German civilians' sleeping on mats in a huge Franciscan convent on the Via Sicilia, just off Rome's most fashionable boulevard, the Via Veneto. In the morning,

*Members of Italy's dominant postwar political party, usually closely aligned with the Vatican.

†*Curia Romana*: the papal court.

the men were roused at dawn and, after breakfast, had to leave the convent until evening, though they were given meal tickets for lunch at a mess run by nuns. Since Germans and Austrians without Italian documents were subject to arrest by the *carabiniere*, Stangl wandered the streets as inconspicuously as he could, loitering on benches in the Pincio and Borghese Gardens, where the big danger came from dozing off if the police patrolled. Eventually, to keep out of trouble, he volunteered to do maintenance work for the nuns. Visitors to the Vatican in mid-1948 would have paid little attention to the former commandant of Sobibor and Treblinka carrying a bucket for a nun as she and he crossed St Peter's Square together. For his good work, he wrote home, he was given extra rations and the chance to attend morning mass in St Peter's Cathedral.

Gustav Wagner faded from sight in Stangl's story of his stay in Rome, though his path would parallel his ex-chief's. The third musketeer of their Italian odyssey, Hans Steiner, grew homesick and escaped back to Austria, where he surrendered to the Americans.

After a few weeks, Bishop Hudal handed Stangl a whitish booklet with a red cross on it. It was an International Red Cross passport, issued in Stangl's name to the bishop, who had said the Vatican vouched for Stangl's identity. Dispensing as many as 500 such documents per day, and pressured by the Italians to expedite the exits of unwanted foreigners, the Red Cross's attitude almost forty years later was: 'How could we refuse to accept the word of priests?'

Stangl had one objection to his new credential. 'They made a mistake,' he told Bishop Hudal. 'The name is incorrect. It says Paul Franz Stangl. My name is Franz Paul Stangl.'

Hudal, he says, patted him on the shoulder and suggested: 'Let's let sleeping dogs lie. Never mind.'

The Bishop also gave Stangl a boat ticket from Genoa (in many cases, transportation was paid by the Catholic welfare organization Caritas) and an entrance visa to Syria, where a job in a textile mill awaited 'Paul F. Stangl, weaver'. Egypt, Jordan, Syria, Lebanon, and Iraq had declared war and invaded the new State of Israel in May 1948, hours after it was proclaimed and the British had withdrawn, so Stangl was sailing beyond the reach of Israeli and Western intelligence – and Nazi-hunters like Wiesenthal.

Failing to abort the birth of the State of Israel in 1948, her Arab neighbours tried to pick up where Hitler had left off. Genocide was an idea whose time had come (not for the first time) to Egypt and Syria, which imported their technicians and technocrats from the ruins of the Third Reich.

Most notorious of these was Alois Brunner, an Austrian born in 1912. Brunner was Eichmann's right-hand man in Vienna and Prague in 1938–9 and his successor in Vienna, where Wiesenthal credits him with inventing the Jewish police in the ghettoes to do the work of identification, registration, and deportation of Jews for the SS. Simon also says Brunner conceived the postcards that deportees were ordered to write home while en route to or upon arriving in extermination camps ('*I am in good health and feeling well*'); by the time the postcards reached their destinations, virtually all the senders were dead. 'Among Third Reich criminals still alive,' says Simon, 'Alois Brunner is undoubtedly the worst. In my eyes, he was the worst ever' – even worse than Eichmann, who 'merely' made the plans that Brunner implemented so zealously in Vienna, Prague, Bratislava, Paris, and Greece. Brunner accompanied one of the last transports from Vienna to the east; en route, he personally shot a Jewish banker, Siegmund Bosel, to death. In Greece, Brunner supervised the deportations that Lieutenant Kurt Waldheim 'never saw'. Close to 50,000 Jews were shipped from Salonika to Auschwitz in sixteen freight trains. When several hundred Jews from outlying Greek islands missed the trains, Brunner had them herded into antiquated boats which were then put out to sea and sunk in the Aegean. Surfacing in Damascus after the war as 'Dr Georg Fischer', Brunner became an adviser to the Syrian security services and, well into his eighties, was occasionally consulted on Lebanese affairs and still gave rabid interviews to German and Austrian journalists.

The first major war criminal tried by a West German court under West German law was Franz Rademacher, ex-head of the Jewish Section of the German Foreign Ministry and Eichmann's contact man there. While appealing against a mild sentence of three years and five months for complicity in the murder of 1500 Yugoslav Jews (on his expense account form for a trip to Belgrade, he had filled in 'Purpose of Journey' with 'liquidation of Jews'), Rademacher jumped bail and escaped to Syria.

So hungry were Israel's enemies for German expertise, major and minor, that Simon Wiesenthal says 'the Syrian Embassy in Rome opened a recruiting office which worked like the French Foreign Legion: no questions asked, but, in this case, only if you were German. So when it became embarrassing to the French Foreign Legion that they had Nazi criminals in their midst, certain French officials sold their embarrassments to the Arabs for 350 dollars per man. They were handed over at an Italian port and shipped out on the next boat.'

Walter Rauff's credentials required no recommendations or negotiations when he contacted the Syrians in Rome. As reported in a forty-three-page investigatory report on 'SS Colonel Walter Rauff: The Church Connection 1943–1947' issued in 1984 by the Simon Wiesenthal Centre in Los Angeles, the inventor of the mobile gas chamber would later testify (in Chile) that 'I signed a contract with the Syrian government and went to Damascus as technical adviser to the secret police and the bodyguard of the head of state.'

In the summer of 1948, when Franz Stangl arrived in Syria, his credentials as a genocidist were not yet so well known as Rauff's, so he lived frugally and saved every pound he earned to pre-pay his family's passage to the Middle East. By the time Wiesenthal ascertained Stangl's significance a couple of years later and located his home address in Wels, Theresa Stangl and her three daughters had disappeared too. Neighbours said that the Stangls had left on 6 May 1949, not long after three men from the Viennese movers, Schenker & Co., had come to the house to pack the belongings Frau Stangl had put out on the front lawn – beds and bedding, sewing-machine, china, chairs, table, even the piano – into two large crates which they hauled away. There was nothing furtive about Frau Stangl's departure. After the men had nailed the crates shut, she painted their destination on them in big bold letters: FRANZ PAUL STANGL, HELUANIE 14, DAMASCUS. When she applied for a passport to emigrate and the police asked why, she told them just as boldly: 'To join my husband, who escaped.'

Theresa, Brigitte, Renate, and Isolde Stangl sailed for Syria from Genoa in mid-May 1949. Reunited with the man of the house in Damascus, they first stayed in a pension at 22 rue George Haddat: an address notorious in *Flight from Nuremberg** and other escape

**Flucht von Nürnberg,* published in the Stangls' home town of Wels in 1969, was written between 1964 and 1966 by 'Werner Brockdorff', a pseudonym for Alfred Jarschel, former head of the Hitler Youth. He died in 1967.

literature as ODESSA'S reception centre. Though their first few months together became a struggle when Franz Stangl's employer died and his textile firm collapsed, they found a flat in the rue de Baghdad, where they lived for six months until their furniture arrived from Austria. In early December 1949, Paul Franz Stangl, as he was now called, found well-paid work as a mechanical engineer with the Imperial Knitting Company, and the Stangls moved to larger quarters on the rue de Youssuff in Old Damascus. 'It was a wonderful house, and with our things we made the flat into a real home,' Theresa Stangl later recalled. 'We were the first German family to have our own home, and *all* the Germans visited us.'

The only fly in their ointment was an open one. The chief of police of Damascus lived in the front of their house – with his harem. The Stangls' middle daughter, Renate, was twelve when they arrived in Syria – and, within a year or two, she had caught their neighbour's lascivious eye. 'She was very blonde and very pretty and he really had his eyes on her,' Frau Stangl told Gitta Sereny. 'Renate could do anything she liked. She could do no wrong as far as he was concerned. We got into a panic about it. What could we do – foreigners in Syria – if he took it into his head he wanted her?' Complain to the police?

The concerned parents decided to move from Syria. There were no South American consulates in Damascus, but they made the rounds in Beirut, where the Brazilian consul said his country welcomed mechanical engineers and gave them a visa. In 1951, the Stangls sailed from Beirut to Brazil, via Genoa. On their first day in São Paulo, the usually astute Frau Stangl gave all their cash (worth about forty dollars) to a German woman to exchange on the black market. 'And then she came back and said she'd given it to a man who'd said he'd get cruzeiros at a good rate and he'd made off with it. I couldn't *prove* she was lying' – and, again, there was no possibility of calling the police.

When she told her husband their money was gone, 'he wasn't angry. He was never angry with me, or any of us . . . He never raised his voice, or lost his temper – until much, much later – and never never did he strike or spank the children.' No, the benign, mild-mannered Paul Franz Stangl simply said he had to find a job fast – and, within a week, he was engaged as a weaver by the Sutema textile firm.

– 30 –

The Stangl extradition

For Simon Wiesenthal, the case of Franz Stangl was a classic example of why retribution is always to be favoured over revenge.

'Once I located where Stangl was,' says Simon, 'I could have had him killed for 500 dollars before he was ever extradited. In South America, it is only a matter of money. So many people disappear. Even one of the officials I was bothering hinted to me that I could just write the cheque and soon I would receive Stangl's ears. But this wasn't what I was after. So we ended up with Stangl on trial for six months and, each day, it was in the papers and millions of people were reading about it. If I'd had him killed, Stangl would have amounted to just a corpse, a few lines in the press, and, later, nothing.

'With Stangl, though, it was always a matter of money.'

The first breakthrough came on Friday, 21 February 1964, when Simon, who had been trumpeting Stangl's sins to the press, was visited in his office by a woman in tears. 'Mr Wiesenthal,' she said, 'I had no idea my cousin Theresa was married to such a terrible man.'

'What terrible man?' he asked.

'Franz Stangl.'

Without showing the excitement he felt, Wiesenthal asked almost casually: 'And where is Theresa now?'

'Why, in Brazil, of course,' the woman replied. Then her mouth clamped shut and she took a step back, realizing she had said too much.

Having told the press that Stangl had left Damascus for an unknown destination, Wiesenthal attempted 'to draw the woman out, but she wouldn't say another word, no matter how hard I tried.

And I couldn't break my rule and ask her name. It was already well known in Vienna that I never demand the name or address of anyone who comes voluntarily to give me information. So I had to let her go away anonymous.'

To this day, nobody knows who this cousin was. Theresa Stangl's younger sister, Helene, was already living in Vienna: a restaurant cook and second wife of a Viennese Jewish construction engineer who had escaped to Shanghai in 1939 and returned after the war. They had met at a swimming-pool in 1959 and they visited his daughter and grandchildren on a kibbutz in Israel every year until he died in 1969; she was still doing so when Franz Stangl's biographer, Gitta Sereny, dropped in on her unannounced in 1972. Neither Helene Eidenböck nor her husband had any idea of her brother-in-law's past until they read in the papers in 1964 that Wiesenthal was looking for him. Her husband 'hardly spoke for a week', she told Sereny. 'He was totally shattered by it. I suppose it was worse – even worse – for him than me, because here he was, with me, loving me, and this man, accused of these awful, awful things was my brother-in-law . . . He used to read the papers and then just sit, shaking his head. "You can't really understand," he'd say to me. "Imagine, just imagine, it was your child, your baby they took, and slammed against a wall, shattering its head. Your child before your eyes. . ." Perhaps I didn't understand the way he did, but I felt it. I felt the horror of it all through my body.'

Whoever the woman was who'd called upon Wiesenthal, her visit was followed a few days later by one from a sleazy man with shifty eyes who rubbed his chin whenever he spoke. 'I wasn't surprised when he admitted he'd worked for the Gestapo,' says Wiesenthal, 'but I found him harder to believe when he told me he'd done "nothing bad. They made me join. What else could I do? I'm just a little guy." I said nothing. It was the usual preface.'

Wiesenthal's visitor came to the point: 'I read your story in the papers. About Stangl. It's the big bastards like Eichmann and Stangl who've made it hard for us little guys . . . Look, I know where Stangl is. But it's going to cost you money.'

'How much?'

'Twenty-five thousand dollars.'

'You might as well ask for two million dollars,' Wiesenthal responded. 'I don't have that kind of money.'

The informer shrugged: 'All right . . . I'll make you a special price. How many Jews did Stangl kill?'

Wiesenthal guessed that some 700,000 died in Treblinka while Stangl was the commandant.

'I want a penny for each of 'em,' the man said. 'Let's see. That's 7000 dollars. A real bargain!'

Wiesenthal, who had already seen and heard enough to make him shockproof for life, had to clutch his desk to keep from slapping the man in the face: 'His arithmetic was too much for me.' But he contained his rage, decided to throw him out, stood up – and then sat down again. This might be his only chance to find Stangl.

'Well?' said the man.

'Well, I won't give you one cent now,' Wiesenthal said. 'But if Stangl is arrested on the basis of your information, you'll get the money.'

'Who guarantees you'll keep your word?'

'Nobody. And if you don't like it, get out!'

'All right . . . Stangl works as a mechanic in the Volkswagen factory in São Paulo, Brazil.'

* * *

In retrospect, Stangl should not have been hard to find. He and his family had travelled from Syria to Brazil, via Italy, under their own names in 1951. He always gave his name as either Paul Franz Stangl, to conform to the identity the Italian Red Cross had issued him, or Franz Paul Stangl, to be perfectly honest with others. In 1954, his wife registered the entire family with the Austrian consulate in São Paulo. When he or she or their daughters wrote 'home' to Austria, they put their names and return address on the envelopes. In the mid-1960s, Stangl remarked to his wife: 'You know, if that clever man Wiesenthal is looking for me, surely all he has to do is ask the police or the Austrian Consulate. He could find me at once. I am not budging.'

In his first two years in South America with the Sutema textile firm, Stangl's organizational ability was recognized early and he rose from weaver to chief planner: practically an engineering position. Since it involved frequent travel within Brazil, another of his assets was that he had picked up Portuguese swiftly and easily.

On one of his trips (he confessed to Gitta Sereny in 1971), 'my train stopped next to a slaughterhouse. The cattle in the pens, hearing the noise of the train, trotted up to the fence and stared at the train. They were very close to my window, one crowding the other, looking at me through that fence. I thought then, "Look at this; this reminds me of Poland; that's just how the people looked, trustingly, just before they went into the cans . . ."'

'You said "cans",' Sereny interrupted. 'What do you mean?' But Stangl wasn't listening to her as he continued:

'I couldn't eat canned meat after that. Those big eyes . . . looking at me . . . not knowing that in no time at all, they'd all be dead.' His wife, too, remembered that 'he suddenly stopped eating meat at one point.'

Despite such qualms of the flesh, Stangl prospered – nearly tripling his salary when he left Sutema's employ after a couple of years for similar work with another firm. Over a nine-year period, beginning within weeks of their arrival in South America, he and his family built with their own hands a rambling pink-and-white middle-class chalet in a multi-racial working-class neighbourhood of São Bernardo do Campo. Some twenty miles from São Paulo, São Bernardo do Campo was the Detroit of Brazil: home of a Rolls-Royce parts factory, a Mercedes Benz factory, and Volkswagen's largest plant outside Germany. Starting from scratch, Stangl put in the plumbing and his daughters did the painting. 'We built room after room, first just camping outside, then moving into one room after another, as the house grew,' Theresa Stangl recalls.

There was a serious interruption in late 1955, when Franz Stangl took sick. Though his symptoms were rheumatism and weakness that rendered him unable to walk more than a block or two, or even stand on his feet for more than a few minutes, it proved a prelude to a major heart attack in 1966. While he lay idle in the second half of the 1950s, his women constructed a small workshop across the courtyard and, when he had recovered somewhat but was still unfit to hold a steady job, he bought some second-hand machine parts, built some weaving machines, and soon was making elastic bandages for hospitals. His family took over the selling while Frau Stangl found work at Mercedes Benz as a secretary, working her way up to chief of book-keeping by 1962, with 'seventy girls under me.'

Franz Stangl with daughter

Bruno Kreisky towards the end of his life

This photograph, released by the World Jewish Congress, shows Kurt Waldheim, second from left, at a meeting on 22 May 1943 at an airstrip in Yugoslavia. Flanking him are Italian General Ercole Roncaglia and Waldheim's chief, Colonel Joachim Macholz. Facing General Roncaglia, right, is *Waffen* SS General Arthur Phleps, holding a briefcase.

Oberleutenant Kurt Waldheim (1) relaxing in 1943 at the Hotel Grande Bretagne, Athens with other German army officers: General Glydenfeldt (2), Lt. Col. Willers (3), General Helmut Felmy (4)

Kurt Waldheim takes his seat at the United Nations for the first time as Austrian Delegate, 1955

Dr Israel Singer, Director General of the World Jewish Congress, holds up a 25-page booklet which contains documents alleging links between Waldheim and the deportation of thousands of Italian soldiers to German labour camps and civilian massacres in Nazi occupied Yugoslavia

Simon Wiesenthal in his office with a map of the Third Reich

Four 1992 photographs of Wiesenthal

Renate, the middle daughter who had caught the roving eye of the Damascus police chief, married an Austrian in 1957, as did her older sister Brigitte a year later. In 1959, Franz Stangl's health had improved enough that he could rejoin the salaried work force as a mechanic for Volkswagen. As usual, his diligence and competence caught the eye of his superiors and, with rapid promotions, he wound up in charge of preventative maintenance for the entire plant at three times the salary he'd been earning when he fell ill.

With two of the daughters working too, as secretaries in the Volkswagen works, the Stangls were doing so well that, aided by financing from Mercedes Benz, they bought land on Frei Gaspar in Brooklin, one of the best residential districts of São Paulo, and this time had a house built for them by professionals: more Danish-modern than Austrian-rustic, with picture windows and a two car garage. When they moved in there in 1965, Stangl bought a car and became a commuter.

The two years they spent in Brooklin were 'our happiest in Brazil', Frau Stangl said, despite her husband's heart attack in 1966, from which he recovered fairly rapidly. Back in Austria, however, another heart was pounding as Simon Wiesenthal closed in slowly on his quarry.

Having learned in early 1964 where Stangl was, Wiesenthal had no trouble asking a Brazilian contact to run a 'credit check' on him which ascertained his address and lifestyle without alerting anybody. Then, however, he waited nearly three years before making his next move. He explains:

'By 1964, Stangl was wanted by Austria not just from the Hartheim trials and for escaping from custody, but for his work in Sobibor and Treblinka, too. If I'd gone to the Austrian Ministry of Justice, a dozen people there and in the Ministry of Foreign Affairs would have known about it. And then in Brazil, at least double that number in the Austrian Embassy, the Brazilian ministries, and the Brazilian police would have had advance notice of Stangl's arrest. Now you don't have to believe in ODESSA to be absolutely certain that Stangl would have been warned and even people who didn't know him personally would have helped him to disappear. And then there would be – and, as I told you, there were! – others who wanted to make him disappear for me and just bring me his ears. But I wanted him alive!

'To do that, I knew I would have to go to someone highly reliable in the Ministry of Justice to catch Stangl. But first I had to lay the groundwork in Brazil. I alerted my friends in Rio de Janeiro that I was looking for someone influential and sympathetic to our cause, though I didn't specify it was about Stangl. It wasn't until December 1966 that they sent word a Very Important Personality was travelling in Europe and could receive me in Zurich. I flew there to meet him.'

The Brazilian who welcomed him to his Swiss hotel suite was described by Wiesenthal as 'middle-aged, good-looking, with thoughtful eyes' and a good listener who was clearly well informed. Even before Simon told him where Stangl was working, he guessed: 'I'll bet he's got a job with some German firm. They all do.' Simon remembers that the politician 'gave me his assurance that he would be of assistance in this case. The main difficulty was to find a way to shorten the procedure of the extradition request coming from Austria to Brazil and then, in the normal course of events, to the Ministry of Foreign Affairs, the Ministry of Justice, the office of the Governor, the main police headquarters, the local police, and, eventually, the Supreme Court. This would mean that about forty persons would have to know about the extradition request – and very likely Stangl would be Number Forty-one.

'We agreed that a success would only be possible if one could cut down the number of the people let into the secret. So we reduced with the help of that politician the number of those persons down to six.' Knowing how many eyes and ears would be open, the politician's farewell words to Simon were: 'Write me briefly when I'm back in Rio, but don't send any evidence in the mail.'

Wiesenthal did better than that. In early 1967, he went directly to the Austrian Minister of Justice, Dr Hans Klecatsky, a trustworthy Tyrolean, and, working with just a handful of loyal aides, they assembled excerpts from the thousand-page dossier on Stangl as well as a compilation of the warrants out for him. When they were nearly ready, while Wiesenthal was awaiting further documentation from Düsseldorf, where the 'Treblinka trials' of twelve Stangl subordinates had been held in 1964–5,* he sent his own courier – a

*Only one defendant, male nurse Otto Horn, was acquitted. The stiffest sentence under West German law, life imprisonment, went to Stangl's

young woman, born in Brazil and living in Vienna, who worked part-time for him – to Rio with the Jewish Documentation Centre's own dossier on Stangl.

Upon arrival, she couldn't get near Wiesenthal's high-level political connection. It was Carnival time in Rio and nobody was working. Eventually, she made contact with him and handed the dossier to him personally. By the time she left Rio in mid-February, he had a police friend shadowing Stangl unofficially – but he sent her back with a warning to Wiesenthal that he'd be leaving Brazil for Europe again on 1 March, so Stangl had better be in firm custody by then or anything could happen.

Wiesenthal had to move fast. Less than a fortnight remained to February. Phoning Klecatsky, he explained the urgency to the Minister of Justice, who called him to his office on Wednesday, 22 February. The abridged case against Stangl had just been translated into Portuguese. It was delivered the next day to the Austrian Foreign Ministry, which had a trusted official of the Brazilian Embassy verify and notarize the translation. Now it was ready to cross the Atlantic.

But how? Wiesenthal offered to pay the plane fare of a diplomatic courier, but was told the Foreign Ministry had none for South America. Nor were there direct radio or telex links with Austria's embassies there. Any official trip by a Foreign Ministry employee lasting more than three days had to be approved in advance by the Council of Ministers, which met on Tuesdays; this would mean sharing the secret with twelve more officials. No, thank you, said Wiesenthal. The simplest solution, everybody agreed, was to send the warrant, the extradition request, and the translated dossier excerpts via express air mail in a special envelope signifying to embassy employees that it was to be opened only by the ambassador.

On Friday night, 24 February 1967, Wiesenthal phoned the politician in Rio and asked him to pay a call on the Austrian ambassador on Monday morning to tell him privately what to expect in the mail. When he did, on Monday the 27th, the ambassador had just received the packet. It was delivered to the Brazilian Foreign Office the same day. A few hours later, the chief of the federal

deputy, Kurt Franz, whose scrapbook of Treblinka, 'The Best Years of My Life', was used as evidence against him. He was paroled in 1993 at the age of 79.

police visited the Austrian ambassador, studied additional documents (including Wiesenthal's), and flew to São Paulo to meet with its governor, Abreu Sodre.

The next night, Tuesday, 28 February, family man Paul Franz Stangl stopped for a beer in a bar with his youngest daughter, Isolde, twenty-three, nicknamed Isi, on their way from work at the Volkswagen plant. Then they drove home.

From their two-storey house in Brooklin that day, Frau Stangl had noticed there were no parking places on the street where they lived, but had thought nothing more of it. 'I heard a commotion and went to the window,' she recalls. 'Police cars were drawn across the street, blocking it off on each side. Our car was surrounded by crowds of police. Paul was pulled out of the car – handcuffed. Isi fell to the ground shouting for us – that's what I'd heard when I rushed to the window – but the police car with him in it, followed by a string of others, was off before I could even get out the door. Isi was almost incoherent with shock. She said her father's face went yellow when it happened.'

Unlike the Eichmanns, the Stangls chased around from police station to police station right away, but nobody knew anything until they went to the São Paulo Office of Public Security, where they were told yes, he was in custody, and no, they couldn't see him. 'And they said we should be glad they'd taken him,' Frau Stangl remembers. 'If they hadn't, the Israelis would have picked him up.' Wiesenthal, too, says his sources told him Stangl was 'terrified. He was certain he was being kidnapped by Jewish commandos pretending to be Brazilian police. He was visibly relieved when he was brought to a police prison. He remembered what had happened to Eichmann and considered himself lucky.'

The next morning, 1 March, Simon's Brazilian contact left for Europe, as scheduled, but phoned him first to assure him that Stangl was safely under lock and key. He would be transferred to Brasilia, the country's remote inland capital, to forestall any rescue or escape attempt. That night, the governor of São Paulo officially announced Stangl's arrest. West Germany and Poland immediately asked for his extradition, too.

Lawyers all over the world began wrangling over various statutes of limitations – most notably, Brazil's, which set a twenty-year limit on arrests for murder. But Brazil had signed the International

Convention Against Genocide,* which excludes that most heinous of crimes from any statute of limitations. Besides, Germany's arrest warrant had been issued in 1960, so Stangl was culpable until 1980, by this definition. Austria argued that Stangl's escape from prison in Linz interrupted the statute of limitations. Most significantly, Wiesenthal, who had been heading for New York when he received word of Stangl's capture, made an appointment with Senator Robert F. Kennedy. In Simon's presence, the former US Attorney General weighed in with a phone call to the Brazilian ambassador in Washington stating that he – a potential presidential candidate in the next year's election – would view any evasion of extradition with disfavour. 'What's at stake is justice for enormous crimes,' said Kennedy. 'Brazil now has an opportunity to gain millions of friends.'

In the spring of 1967, when Stangl's family read in the papers that he was in a military prison in Brasilia, they drove there, taking turns behind the wheel. Alone with his wife, he cried and, when she asked about Treblinka, because by this time she'd read so much he hadn't told her, he said: 'I don't know what pictures you saw. Perhaps you saw pictures of other camps.' With his daughters, however, his wife recalls that 'he was so wonderful with them, never gave way, never cried while they were in the room, smiled at them, walked them to the gate and waved goodbye to them. But, of course, this was the first time it became real to them. Seeing him like this, in prison, was a traumatic experience for them.'

On 8 June 1967, the Brazilian Supreme Court ruled unanimously that Franz Stangl should be extradited to West Germany. Two weeks later, he was flown to Frankfurt and put in a prison in Duisburg to await trial. His family moved back to São Bernardo do Campo and rented the house in Brooklin to diplomatic families to help finance his defence and his wife's attendance at the three years of trials in Düsseldorf. She flew there, but went to court only thrice: to testify that he had never told her what was happening at Hartheim; on the day Stanislaw Szmajzner, the Sobibor goldsmith, testified against her husband, and on Tuesday, 22 December 1970, when she saw her husband sentenced to life in prison for having 'supervised the murder of at least 900,000 men, women, and children.'

*The United States did not ratify the Convention against Genocide until late 1988.

Simon Wiesenthal was in the courtroom that day, too. On his way out, he took from his wallet a photo of the man he had stalked for twenty years and tore it up. It had been sandwiched between snapshots of Wiesenthal's wife and daughter as a reminder of Franz Stangl's innocent victims. In finding Franz Stangl – accused of 1,200,000 murders and convicted of more than three-quarters of them – and winning his extradition from Brazil to Germany more than two decades after the Second World War ended, Simon Wiesenthal claims to have given Germany 'its most significant criminal case of the century.'

During her stay in Düsseldorf, Theresa Stangl visited her husband several times a week. 'What was strange,' she says, 'was that often he would hardly talk to me. He'd sit opposite me at the table . . . but he'd chat with the guards, not with me. He'd talk to them about their leaves, their outings, places he knew, had been to. It hurt me, and sometimes I'd say, "Don't you want to talk to *me*?"'

Of course he didn't. To talk about his work from 1940 to 1943 would have been to confess his infidelity to her values and upset the delicate equilibrium of his relationship with her and his family. She, more than he, had long looked the other way. His war crimes were like a mistress that everybody knows the head of the house has, but to openly acknowledge her existence would disturb the harmony of Sunday dinner. So it is perhaps fitting that the only time Stangl ever acknowledged his guilt, in private or in public, was to another woman, Gitta Sereny, on Sunday, 27 June 1971, the day before he died.

In his final interview with her, after reiterating his usual 'I have never intentionally hurt anyone myself', he added, 'But I was there. So yes, in reality I share the guilt. Because *my guilt* – *my guilt* – only now in these talks – now that I have talked about it all for the first time – *my guilt* is that I am still here. That is *my guilt*.'

Those words *'my guilt'* were so foreign to his tongue and mind that it took him almost half an hour to speak those few fragmented sentences, which hit his body like a series of blows to the solar plexus, making him sag before Sereny's eyes. 'Still here?' she repeated gently.

'I should have died. That was my guilt.'

'Do you mean you should have died or you should have had the *courage* to die?'

'You can put it like that,' he said.

'Well, you say that now,' said Sereny. 'But then?'

'That *is* true,' he replied slowly. 'I did have another twenty years – twenty good years. But believe me, now I would have preferred to die rather than this . . .' Looking around at the little prison visiting-room, he added: 'I have no more hope.' His parting words to her were: 'Let there be an end.' He died of heart failure in his cell nineteen hours later – shortly after noon on 28 June 1971.

★ ★ ★

Hard-working, resilient, pulling together rather than apart in times of adversity, and asking little or nothing of their neighbours or their nationalities, the Stangls even more than the Eichmanns embodied the work ethic to which so many still hew and adhere in a fragmenting world. 'Never, never did he strike or spank the children,' Theresa Stangl said of her husband; nor did he ever soil his white riding uniform by laying a hand on any of the more than a million prisoners who perished under his administrations at Sobibor and Treblinka. He was, Frau Stangl went on, 'an incredibly good and kind father. He played with the children by the hour. He made them dolls, helped them dress them up. He worked with them; he taught them innumerable things. They adored him – all three of them. He was sacred to them.'

In Düsseldorf, Gitta Sereny had asked Stangl: 'Did your children know?' His face went red with anger as he replied: 'My children believe in me.'

Sereny persisted: 'The young all over the world question their parents' attitudes. Are you saying that your children knew what you had been involved in, but never asked questions?'

'They – they – my children believe in me,' he insisted. 'My family stands by me.' Then he began to cry.

After Stangl died in 1971, Sereny visited his widow and daughters in Brazil to research her invaluable book, *Into That Darkness: An Examination of Conscience*. Driving her back to São Paulo one night, daughter Renate, by then divorced, told Sereny how her father once said to her that 'if you ever need help, I'll go to the end of the moon for you.'

If his cell in Düsseldorf was the end of the moon for Franz Stangl, then what was Treblinka? Merely the end of the earth for more than a million mortals, many of them as good parents as or even better than he was. Examining his conscience through Gitta Sereny's ears and eyes, we can't help confronting the monster within each of us and asking ourselves what we might have done in his situation. Sereny comes to this conclusion:

> I do not believe that all men are equal, for what we are above all other things, is individual and different. But individuality and difference are not only due to the talents we happen to be born with. They depend as much on the extent to which we are allowed to expand in freedom . . . A moral monster, I believe, is not born, but is produced by interference with this growth.

Is it enough, then, to say, as Simon Wiesenthal said at Stangl's trial, that '*if I had done nothing else in my life but bring this wicked man to justice, I would not have lived in vain*'? Yes, it is truth for Wiesenthal – and we can only admire his giving Stangl and his victims their day in court. When Stangl died barely half a year after sentencing, Wiesenthal told me:

'That is enough for a life sentence. The important thing is that he was brought to trial. The spirit of the law is that every person who is killed has the right to a trial of his killers. Now, if a man is responsible for 10,000 deaths, you cannot make 10,000 trials. So you make one trial. And imprisonment is not only a sentence, it is a symbol of justice. Even if it is of short duration, every son or daughter of his murder victims can at least take a pencil and calculate that, "for killing my mother, he spent two minutes or two days in prison." It is not much, but it is something that helps the survivors to live.'

For each of the 900,000 murders of which Franz Stangl was convicted, then, he served eighteen seconds in jail.

– 31 –

Wearing down Wagner

While Franz Stangl, deported to West Germany, had been awaiting trial there, his wife Theresa was called upon in Brazil by Gustav Wagner, her husband's former colleague at Hartheim, deputy at Sobibor, and fellow escapee from Austria into Italy. Wagner had settled some thirty miles from the Stangls and was in the habit of dropping in unannounced. Franz Stangl had always welcomed Wagner, though his wife found him 'vulgar' and obtrusive.

After a brief expression of sympathy for the Stangls' plight, Wagner told his involuntary hostess that his own wife had just died and would she lend him money to bury her? At first, she refused, but, when he told her he was down and out and worried about Wiesenthal looking for him next, she relented – even though every cent the Stangls could spare was going for her husband's defence.

As he pocketed the money, Wagner looked her over appreciatively and said: 'Say, why don't you and I set up house together? I haven't got anybody any more and, as for Franz, well, they're going to do him in anyway over there and you'll be alone, too.'

She threw him out of the house.

He never repaid the loan, but, according to Wiesenthal, he paid a condolence call on Theresa Stangl after her husband died in jail in 1971. And, this time, he proposed marriage. Again, she threw him out.

'My husband was a decent, proper man who did his duty,' she told some friends with pious sincerity. 'He never laid hands on inmates; at the most, he had to shout at one or two of them. But that Wagner was a notorious sadist. And now he has the nerve to call on me and ask me to marry him!' She told Gitta Sereny that Wagner, at their last meeting, looked 'like a beggar, with torn clothes and shoes', and told her he was going to try his luck in Uruguay.

Simon Wiesenthal had picked up Wagner's trail while chasing after Franz Stangl in the 1960s. Retracing Wagner's escape route, he discovered that, after the two fugitives had parted in Rome, Wagner had travelled to Beirut and then Brazil. By 1967, when Stangl was extradited, Wiesenthal had copies of Wagner's postwar Red Cross passport and his first Brazilian identification card in his possession ('so we had a fair picture of what he might still look like') as well as an early Brazilian address. Elated by the Stangl capture, friends of Wiesenthal put him in touch with a Jewish millionaire who was also a concentration-camp survivor. After Simon explained that a discreet search, which wouldn't alarm Wagner into fleeing Brazil, would be costly, the man pressed all of fifty dollars into his hand.

Wiesenthal was outraged. 'If I could get Gustav Wagner arrested for fifty dollars, I wouldn't have to come to you,' he said as he stalked out of the room.

The man ran after him and spent a quarter of an hour explaining his recent financial reverses. 'If you're so poor,' Wiesenthal told him angrily, 'I can give you a hundred dollars.' He went away thinking that 'if Gustav Wagner has many enemies like such a survivor, then he doesn't need friends.'

For ten years after that, says Wiesenthal, 'I laid low and, in whatever material I gave the media, never mentioned Wagner's name as being on our wanted list. Several times, we try to locate him with help from friends in various Brazilian cities, but no results.'

Then, in the spring of 1978, on a flight from New York to Amsterdam, Wiesenthal was thumbing through the New York *Daily News* when he came across an item about a reunion of old Nazis that had taken place on 20 April to celebrate Adolf Hitler's eighty-ninth birthday. Under the slogan of 'WE ARE NOT THE LAST OF YESTERDAY, BUT THE FIRST OF TOMORROW', this Fourth Reich celebration had lasted three days at the Hotel Tyll in Italiata in the Brazilian province of São Paulo.

From Amsterdam, where his daughter Pauline and her family were living at the time, Wiesenthal contacted a Brazilian foreign correspondent he'd met in Israel, Mario Chimanovich of *Jornal do Brasil,* the country's biggest daily, and asked for photos from the party. A few days after Simon's return to Vienna, Chimanovich phoned to say he had not just a giant photo of all the assembled guests, but also the invitation list. And, suspecting that Simon was on to a story, he agreed to fly to Vienna to deliver them in person.

Wiesenthal had been playing a hunch that Wagner was at the event. Disappointed not to find Wagner's name or recognizable face in the new material, he decided to bluff his trusting friend, Chimanovich, by pretending that a Nazi with big ears in the photograph was his quarry. 'If it wasn't quite kosher, well, I owe this try to a quarter of a million Jews who died in Sobibor,' Simon told himself even as he told Chimanovich: 'Do you see this one here? He's Gustav Wagner and he's showing himself publicly at a celebration of Hitler's birthday in Brazil without anybody paying any notice. And I should think your police know where to find him.'

Armed with Wiesenthal's dossier and documents on Wagner, Chimanovich wrote a story that appeared on the front page of *Jornal do Brasil* on 27 May 1978. Public reaction was fierce upon learning that the deputy commandant of Sobibor was living as a free man among millions of Brazilians. Pleading his innocence and seeking protection, the long-eared Nazi who wasn't Wagner turned himself in to the police. And so did the real Gustav Wagner, whose Red Cross and Brazilian ID photos made him a marked man too. He even told the police nobody had died in Sobibor.

With Wagner in custody and expensive lawyers engaged to set him free, Wiesenthal had forty-eight hours to supply evidence that would 'show cause' for detaining the suspect and to persuade a government to ask for his extradition. Israel responded first, then a reluctant Austria, then Germany and Poland. A dossier of depositions went air-freight to Brazil, while Wiesenthal held his breath about connecting flights and customs delays.

Simon could have breathed easy. In the town of Gojana, 550 miles from São Paulo, Stanislaw Szmajzner, the teenaged Jewish goldsmith who had melted down fillings to make jewellery at Sobibor and testified against Stangl, heard the news and heaved a huge sigh of relief. A few years earlier, when Gitta Sereny had told him Gustav Wagner was still alive and probably in Brazil, 'Shlomo' Szmajzner had gone pale and sat down hard. 'This is the worst, most terrible shock you give me,' he told her, gasping. 'That man! Here in Brazil? To think that I am now breathing the same air as him makes me feel terribly, terribly ill . . . I wouldn't know how to find words to describe to you what a terrible – what a truly terrible man that is! Stangl, he is good by comparison – very good. But Wagner, he should be dead.' Sereny says Szmajzner kept repeating, 'I must do something.'

Now that he had the chance, Szmajzner, by then only fifty, hastened to São Paulo to confront Wagner in a police station.

'How are you, Gustl?' he greeted Wagner.

Wagner looked at him blankly, then recognized him: 'Yes, yes, I remember you well. I must have picked you out of the transport and saved your life.'

'That's right,' Szmajzner replied, 'but you didn't save the lives of my sister, my brothers, my mother and my father. And if you're saying that you saved my life, then you're also saying you had the power to kill the others.'

Whether the authorities accepted this logic, they now rejected Wagner's blanket denials that he'd had anything to do with deaths at Sobibor, where 'nobody died' anyway. Now the question was where to extradite him.

Germany took the lead because, from the Stangl case, it had the best evidence and a solid claim to put Wagner on trial. Transferred to a cell in the capital, Brasilia, he tried to commit suicide by eating his eyeglasses, which he'd crushed with a shoe. A guard intercepted him seconds after he started chewing the ground glass. Treated at a prison hospital and then examined at a psychiatric hospital, Wagner was sent back to jail, where he then suffered a series of heart attacks which Simon says were 'kosher', and attempted suicide again. He went on telling Brazilian authorities that 'I knew what was happening there [in Sobibor], but I never went to see. I only obeyed orders.' Later, in a television interview, Wagner acknowledged the nature of his work, but insisted: 'I had no feelings . . . It just became another job. In the evening, we never discussed our work, but just drank and played cards.'

In June 1979, the Supreme Court in Brasilia threw out the West German extradition request because of a typing error in its Portuguese translation, which said Wagner had been on the wanted list since '1974' instead of '1947'. Brazil's statute of limitations specifies that charges must be preferred within twenty years after commission of a crime. Wagner was set free.

But he was not a free man. With the heinous revelations in the press, even Nazi doors in Brazil were closed to him. He tried suicide twice more in São Paulo: once by stabbing himself with a knife, once by throwing himself in front of a car. Then, around the time West Germany presented the Brazilian court with a properly typed translation of the accusations against him, Wagner vanished – but he didn't go far. At a remote farm fifty miles from São Paulo on 4 October 1980, he finally succeeded at suicide by hanging himself. He was sixty-nine years old.

'For me,' says Simon Wiesenthal, 'Wagner's suicide must serve as a confession. But I wonder whether he felt guilt – or just fatigue.'

– 32 –

The mare of Majdanek went to Germany

Created in 1979, the US Justice Department's Office of Special Investigations pinpointed several hundred Nazis and their collaborators residing in the US and deported (including Ivan Demjanjuk of Cleveland and Andrija Artukovic of Surfside, California, to death sentences in Israel and Yugoslavia,* and Feodor Fedorenko to a Soviet firing squad) in the eighties. But it owes its existence to the day in 1964 when Simon Wiesenthal pointed an accusing finger at Mrs Russell Ryan, wife of a Queens construction worker. Nine years later, Hermine Braunsteiner Ryan became the first war criminal ever to be deported from the US into custody of a country where she had committed some of her crimes. 'I fought for nine years to extradite her to Germany,' says Wiesenthal. 'It was worth it just for her case alone, but it opened the door to dozens of other deportations from the US since then.'

Wiesenthal's foot in the US's revolving door took its first step in April 1964, when a woman recognized him in a Tel Aviv café and told him: 'I was at the Majdanek concentration camp in Poland. There was a guard there named Hermine Braunsteiner who used a

*Artukovic, eighty-eight, who was Interior Minister of the wartime Croatian fascist puppet state, died in a Zagreb prison hospital in 1988, before his execution could be carried out. Demjanjuk was later freed by Israel when it became apparent that some other guard named Ivan was 'Ivan the Terrible.' Demjanjuk returned to Cleveland, where in 2002 a federal judge stripped him of his US citizenship for lying in his application by concealing his past employment at Treblinka and Sobibor.

vicious dog and a whip weighted with lead on women prisoners. She enjoyed flogging us, she enjoyed it when we screamed and even more when we fainted. She was a complete sadist. When mothers with children were brought to the camp, she'd tear the children away. She hated children. Mr Wiesenthal, in Majdanek I saw cruel men and cruel women. The women were worse – and Hermine Braunsteiner was the most vicious of them all. I don't know what's become of her, but she must answer for her crimes. Please try to find her.'

Simon had never heard of Hermine Braunsteiner, but, his interest piqued, he looked up the name upon his return to Vienna. She was, in fact, born in his adopted city in 1919 and had worked as a Viennese housemaid before moving to Berlin when Austria became part of Germany in 1938. In August 1939, she joined the SS and was assigned to the women's concentration camp at Ravensbrück, north of Berlin. There she rose rapidly to guard supervisor and head of the clothing detail by the time she was twenty. In October 1942, she was transferred to Majdanek, a new extermination camp on the outskirts of Lublin. When she left there in early 1944, she was a supervising warden. Reassigned to Ravensbrück, she served as director of a satellite labour camp in nearby Genthin until the Allied armies approached in 1945, when she fled home to Austria.

On 6 May 1946, she was arrested by Austrian authorities on charges of assassination, manslaughter, infanticide, torture, and 'injuring and offending the human dignity of inmates' – but just at Ravensbrück. Released from jail on 18 April 1947, she came to trial in 1948 in Austria's second-largest city, Graz, where she received a three-year sentence. With credit for time served awaiting trial, she was set free on 22 November 1949 and granted an amnesty from further prosecution in her native Austria. According to Wiesenthal: 'Of her activity at Majdanek only little was known. Except for the letter of a Polish woman, which didn't figure in the Graz proceedings, nothing was known. The matter of Majdanek was not mentioned.'

Having told a Viennese neighbour that 'there isn't enough to eat in the city. I think I'll go to live with my relatives in the country', Hermine Braunsteiner had vanished from view right after her release fifteen years earlier. From the neighbour, Wiesenthal obtained the name and village of her country cousins in Carinthia. Since a cosmopolitan foreign-born Jew like Wiesenthal would stand out in an inbred rural society even if he weren't recognized as a celebrity, Simon dispatched one of his many volunteers: the guilt-ridden twenty-four-year-old son of an unrepentant Nazi family. The young man took his vacation in the mountain village and, on the third day, knocked on the relatives' door and told them they had the same last name as *his* relatives in Salzburg province. They never did link their kin, but he ingratiated himself with them and was invited back for several meals. Over lunch one day, he mentioned a 'poor uncle' who had 'done no harm' worthy of his fifteen-year sentence.

'The same thing happened to a relative of mine,' his hostess remarked. 'She was a prison guard and she got three years for boxing a couple of gypsies on the ear . . . But the times are changing and she got lucky. She went to Canada and married an American.' Before departing, Wiesenthal's undercover agent said he hoped to visit Canada and would like to look up their relative. His hosts were sure her name was Ryan and thought she was in Halifax, Nova Scotia. With this to go on, it took a Wiesenthal contact in Toronto only three weeks to trace Hermine Braunsteiner Ryan from Canada to her mail forwarding address in the US.

In the 1950s, Hermine Braunsteiner had met Brooklyn-born Russell Ryan when he took a vacation in Austria while serving as a US Air Force enlisted man in Germany. In 1959, she'd journeyed to Canada to marry him and he brought her to New York to live. There, she found work as a machine-operator in a clothing factory. On 15 January 1963, she had been sworn in as a US citizen at a naturalization ceremony in Brooklyn's federal courthouse.

While the US Immigration and Naturalization Service (INS) then had no provision forbidding admittance of war criminals, all immigrants had to sign a statement swearing that they had never participated in persecution of a minority because of race, creed, or national origin. And they were required to either swear that they had never been convicted of crimes or else explain whether they were political crimes and whether there were any special circumstances. Simon suspected Mrs Ryan had lied in both answers.

After Wiesenthal wrote to inform the US government of her past and received no immediate response, he contacted the *New York Times* with a packet of details. On Monday, 13 July 1964, reporter Joseph Lelyveld* knocked on the door of a one-storey bungalow at 52–11 72nd Street in Maspeth, a predominantly Irish and German district of the Borough of Queens.

Lelyveld was greeted in heavily accented English by a large-boned woman standing five feet six inches tall with a stern mouth, blue eyes, and blonde hair turning grey. Wearing peppermint striped shorts and a matching sleeveless blouse, she had been painting the home that she and her husband had recently acquired.

'Yes, that's me,' she told me. 'All I did was what guards do in camps now. I was punished enough. I was in prison three years. Three years, can you imagine? And now they want something again from me?'

Lelyveld pointed out that, while her punishment had been for crimes at Ravensbrück, now she was accused of crimes at Majdanek. Had she ever been at Majdanek?

Yes, she replied, but for just a year – eight months of which she claimed she spent in the camp infirmary with a serious illness. 'On the radio, all they talk is peace and freedom,' she complained. 'All right. Then fifteen or sixteen years after, why do they bother people?'

When Lelyveld told her the new evidence against her came from Simon Wiesenthal, she turned pale and burst into tears. Crossing her living-room to phone her husband at work, she declared: 'This is the end! This is the end of everything for me.'

Wiesenthal had guessed right. Mrs Ryan hadn't told the US authorities about her past. Nor had she told her husband. Russell Ryan, however, stuck by her. 'My wife, sir, wouldn't hurt a fly,' he told the *Times* by phone. 'There's no more decent person on this earth. She told me this was a duty she had to perform. It was a conscriptive service. She was not in charge of anything. Absolutely not, as God is my judge and your judge.'

'Good!' said Simon in Vienna. 'Then let's let a judge decide.'

Russell Ryan flailed at the Nazi-hunters: 'These people are just swinging axes at random. Didn't they ever hear the expression: "Let the dead rest"?'

*Later a 1986 Pulitzer Prize-winner for his book *Move Your Shadow: South Africa, Black and White.*

And Simon, as deputy for the dead, said: 'A million and a half people who perished at Majdanek will rest better when this woman comes before a court.'

Prodded by the *Times*, the INS said that Mrs Ryan's false swearing 'might' prompt a second look at her immigration and naturalization papers, but indicated that such reviews rarely resulted in withdrawal of citizenship. Pestered by Wiesenthal, the INS applied to the Austrian government for a certified copy of her 1948 conviction in Graz. Obtaining this one document took nearly a year, but, in June 1965, INS sent Mrs Ryan's dossier to the US Department of Justice urging it to file suit for revocation of her citizenship.

Justice examined the file for half a year and then sent it back to INS with a request for more information on her SS activities. INS contacted Wiesenthal – which he considered no small victory, for it was the first time the US government had called upon his expertise in Vienna – and he provided them with two survivors of Majdanek who identified Hermine Braunsteiner as a guard there. In October 1966, INS again submitted the file to Justice.

Back it came two months later. Justice's question: *Were any charges still pending against Hermine Braunsteiner (Ryan) in Austria?*

Seven months later, in July 1967, INS's answer was no.

Justice sat on the case for another year. Then, in July 1968 – four years after Wiesenthal and the *Times* had unmasked Mrs Ryan – Washington sent the file to the US Attorney in Brooklyn, who charged her in federal court with entering the US illegally by concealing her Austrian prison sentence. He asked that her citizenship be revoked.

In Maspeth, her neighbours rallied round her, proclaiming to the press that she was 'a quiet person who never bothers anybody', an industrious housewife fond of dogs and children. They could not and would not believe that she was the 'cruel, brutal, and sadistic woman who unnecessarily beat and tortured defenceless prisoners', as the Justice Department branded her, adding in an affidavit that she was also 'an active participant in one of the most horrible and inhuman projects in history: the systematic imprisonment, torture, and murder of millions of human beings – of many nations, races, and religions – whose lives were deemed to be expendable by the Nazi regime.'

Simon Wiesenthal points out that this is a very common paradox: 'From Eichmann and Stangl on down, ninety per cent of my "clients" were – sometimes before the war and certainly after the war – solid family men and women, devoted to their children, loyal to their relatives, hard-working, tax-paying good citizens and good neighbours who did their duty, tended their gardens, and seldom made trouble for anyone. But when they put on the uniform, they became something else: monsters, sadists, torturers, killers, desk murderers. The minute they took off the uniform, they became model citizens again. But I work only from deeds and eye-witnesses, not from character references or psychoanalysis. Still, so often I think about it. And what I think is that the key is the *did their duty* part.'

Nobody answered the Ryans' front door when newsmen knocked. Reporters who lingered at the kerb were chased away by neighbours.

The case vanished into the back pages for another three years as the wheels of the Federal Court ground slowly towards a confrontation with justice. In 1971, as the case neared court, Hermine Braunsteiner Ryan crossed up her pursuers by signing a consent decree to relinquish her citizenship without a trial. This took the case, for the time being, out of the hands of US attorney Robert Morse, a determined prosecutor. 'We have witnesses who, if this case had gone to trial,' said Morse, 'would be able to testify in support of the allegations in the complaint.' But now the ball was back in the court of the Immigration and Naturalization Service.

Some sources say the plea bargain in this case was that INS would make no effort to deport her as an undesirable or illegal alien. In 1971, soon after she signed the consent decree, Carl Burrows, INS assistant commissioner for investigations, wrote in a memorandum:

> In all probability, there is insufficient evidence of a clear, unequivocal and convincing nature upon which we could initiate deportation proceedings . . .

According to *New York Times* investigator Howard Blum's 1977 book, *WANTED! The Search for Nazis in America,* Commissioner Burrows said to INS chief trial lawyer Vincent Schiano, 'Why punish her twice?', and Schiano replied angrily and dismissively, 'Go pound rocks.'

When he calmed down, Schiano wrote Burrows a memo arguing that 'we must reject the suggestion of "further punishment" by deportations. Aliens become deportable by reason of certain criminal convictions.' Early in 1972, Schiano urged in another memo that 'an investigator be assigned to this case to work under my direction and make proper requests of the various government agencies and take control of overseas leads.' The investigator appointed, Anthony DeVito, was a twenty-year INS veteran who, as a GI in 1945, had entered the Dachau concentration camp hours after it was liberated and witnessed the stoning of a collaborator by fellow inmates.

An admirer of Wiesenthal's, DeVito contacted his hero in Vienna and every other source he could on Majdanek and Ravensbrück. As American Jewish organizations joined Wiesenthal in drumming up a clamour for action, a neo-Nazi fund-raising committee called the Hermine Ryan Defence Foundation was formed to finance further delay.

Just as there are Jewish prostitutes, there are misguided Jewish crazies, too. At 1.30 in the morning on Saturday, 11 March 1972, a young couple at 52–11 79th Street in Queens was awakened by the sound of glass breaking downstairs in their living-room. Seconds later, there was an explosion and their curtains caught fire. Somebody had tossed a fire-bomb through their window.

Gathering up their three small children, the wife ran for help while her husband put out the fire himself. Half an hour later, a New York newspaper received a call from a spokesman for the 'Jewish Resistance Assault Team', who said his 'organization' had just bombed the home of 'Mrs Anna Harmione Ryan'. The 'team' *did* have the right house number, but the wrong street: the Ryans lived at 52-11 *72nd* Street, not *79th* Street.

Until May 1972, Hermine Braunsteiner Ryan had led a charmed life for an accused murderess in America. She had not yet been in custody and wouldn't be for many months. In signing the consent decree, she had made no admission of guilt. Nobody had testified in public against her. But all this was about to change, thanks to Wiesenthal's and DeVito's and Schiano's persistence.

On 1 May, an opening hearing was postponed after a few minutes when Mrs Ryan's attorney, John J. Barry, discovered to his dismay that the court appointed translator of German-language documents was Jewish.

Procedure in a deportation inquiry differs from a courtroom trial. The hearings can be held at widely spaced intervals in the nearest INS office: in this case, on West Broadway in Lower Manhattan. 'They appear and fade away like astronomical phenomena, convening for a day or two to hear testimony of a witness, then recessing for a few weeks, or a month, or longer, until another witness is ready,' writes former US prosecutor Allan A. Ryan Jnr – no relation to Hermine, except that the Justice Department's Office of Special Investigations, which he headed from 1980 to 1983, grew out of her case, as did the title of his incisive 1984 memoir of prosecuting Nazi criminals in America: *Quiet Neighbors*.

The defendant testified first. She said that in May 1950, not long after her release from an Austrian prison, a court in Vienna had told her she never had to report her arrest or conviction to anyone. Therefore, any time the question was raised – in Europe or North America – 'I said no', which she considered 'a truthful answer'.

Starting gently, INS attorney Schiano asked her whether she had ever done anything she was ashamed of while employed at Ravensbrück and Majdanek. Her reply was a firm 'no'.

All that she would acknowledge doing was occasionally hitting prisoners, but 'only with an open hand', never with fist or whip. She claimed not to have been aware of what happened to prisoners in Ravensbrück, a slave-labour camp where doctors made medical experiments upon women, but conceded that she knew Majdanek was an 'extermination camp'. She was 'shocked and appalled', she said, but 'it was not in my power to do anything. I was too little.'

The dimensions of her work loomed larger the next month when Eva Konikowski, also of Queens, swore to tell the truth. A Polish Catholic from Wiesenthal's former home city of Lwów, she had been jailed in 1941 for hiding Jews from the Nazi death squads. As a prisoner at Majdanek in 1943, she saw Hermine Braunsteiner and another guard loading children on to trucks bound for the gas chamber. 'They gave the children some pieces of candy,' Mrs Konikowski recalled, 'but that didn't fool them. They were screaming and crying "Mama!"' Eva Konikowski, too, had screamed – so hard that, later, she had to have an operation on the glands of her neck. She also testified that she had been under psychiatric care for 'what I went through' at Majdanek.

Matter-of-factly, defence attorney Barry asked Mrs Konikowski if she personally had ever seen Mrs Ryan kill anybody. Her answer was no.

That defence tactic, however, was laid to rest on 8 September 1972, when Aaron Kaufman, seventy-one, an Orthodox Jewish survivor of eight Nazi concentration camps who was living in Westchester County, testified that he had seen Braunsteiner whip five women and a child to death on three occasions in Majdanek. This frail elderly gentleman had once been a human 'horse' there, hauling a heavy wooden cart loaded with food and coal. An expression of sympathy from Schiano was waved away politely as Kaufman, speaking English softly with Yiddish inflection, explained he had bribed his way into such a good job; otherwise he wouldn't be alive in New York thirty years later.

Hauling coal one day in May 1942, he had seen five women pulling up weeds within a barbed-wire corridor. Kaufman, who had been about six yards away, told the hearing: 'Suddenly, Braunsteiner appeared, spoke to the women for a minute, then started beating two of them with her whip. Both died.'

Under questioning, he said he had known both victims. One was Sara Fermeinska, about twenty-six, and the other was named Secholovic, about thirty. He added that when it became known he had witnessed their deaths, he was called out from his barracks and given twenty-five lashes across the back.

On another occasion, Kaufman was on a detail carrying lumber. Coming upon a group of women collecting stones and lumber for the men to haul, they stopped to chat. This was unheard of in Majdanek and the guards sounded an alarm. 'Mrs Braunsteiner came along,' said Kaufman, 'and when she saw, she started using her whip again and killed two other ladies.'

In June 1942, Kaufman and other 'horses' were hauling food from the kitchen to the women's camp, about a kilometre away. At the gate, however, they were blocked. 'Three or four hundred ladies were there,' he related. 'Mrs Braunsteiner was telling the ladies they would have to give their children away because the children were going to a summer camp where they would get milk two times a day. The mothers didn't want to give up their children because they knew what would happen. Mrs Braunsteiner started hitting one woman with a child so long the woman fell down. The lady was dead and the child was dead. We had to move them aside and then get our wagons in.'

Kaufman withstood several hours of cross-examination by defence attorney Barry, who asked him if he was seeking revenge.

'No,' said Kaufman. 'I'm just interested in the truth.'

'The truth,' said lawyer Barry, 'is just what I'm after.'

'*Erev Rosh Hashanah*,'* said Kaufman, 'it must be the truth.'

Barry hadn't finished cross-examining the witness on his painful testimony when the hearing adjourned for a fortnight (instead of the scheduled one-week interval) to avoid confrontation with a rally against Mrs Ryan outside INS headquarters. The protest had been announced by a group called the Warsaw Ghetto Resistance Organization. When the hearing did reconvene, Kaufman did not reappear. He had suffered a heart attack and was too sick to testify. This, of course, worked to the defence's advantage: Mrs Ryan had not been given a full chance to confront her accuser. . .

Other witnesses, too, reported strange and sinister happenings after testifying. Eva Konikowski received neatly typed postcards warning that 'dirty Jewish witnesses will be killed.' The day after another survivor, Nuna Wiezbicka, testified, there was a knock on her door. When she looked through the peephole, she saw a man wearing a ski mask and hissing, 'Witness . . . witness . . . witness.' Mary Finkelstein identified Mrs Ryan as Braunsteiner from an old photo and testified that she'd seen her 'clobber' a woman inmate of Majdanek to the ground and scream, 'You pig! You God damn Jew! Stand up straight!' According to Mrs Finkelstein, 'she dropped and didn't get up – ever.' When Mrs Finkelstein returned to her home in Brooklyn, the phone was ringing. A man's voice informed her that 'all Jews will some day be killed.'

That 17 September, thanks to the Ryan hearings, Majdanek Day, the annual return of Polish and other European survivors, was covered by the international press for the first time. Hanna Mierzejewska – a survivor of Auschwitz and Ravensbrück as well as Majdanek who was working at the American school in Warsaw – led reporters past the brooding Stalin Gothic war memorial, drab barracks, rusted barbed wire, and barren fields to 'the real Majdanek memorial': a mound of earth containing the ashes and bones of

*'*On the eve of the Jewish New Year?* . . .'

more than 18,000 Jews who were murdered there in one day: Sunday, 3 November 1943, when Hermine Braunsteiner was still stationed at Majdanek.*

The victims, she said, were 'our Jews and those from two other camps near Lublin. . .' Pointing to a grassy field that stops at the edge of industrial Lublin, she said: 'They were ordered to run down that slope. As they reached the ditches, they were shot with machine-guns. They didn't want the rest of us to hear, so the loudspeakers were turned up and played music all day.'

When she arrived at Majdanek in January 1943, Mrs Mierzejewska – known as 'Pant Hanka' – was chosen as a block leader because she spoke German. In that capacity, she matched wits with Hermine Braunsteiner almost every day: hiding children and sick and elderly women, for which she was often whipped over barbed wire. For the lives she saved and example she set, she was awarded her country's highest civilian decoration, the Poland Reborn medal.

James Feron, who was there for the *New York Times,* reported that when the name of Braunsteiner was raised, the recollections came reluctantly, for the survivors went to this annual reunion 'to greet each other rather than to recall the horrors of this place.' But one woman told him: 'Yes, I remember Braunsteiner. We feared her most of all. She was a big woman [who] used her whip a lot.' Another said that the camp's woman commandant had been captured, tried, and executed by the Poles. Other subordinates had also been extradited to Poland.

A Warsaw woman dentist, Dr Danuta Czaykowska-Medryk, fifty-one, said she was saving her memories for the following week in New York. She was flying there to testify against Mrs Ryan. The case against her was entering a new phase. With Wiesenthal's intervention, an Iron Curtain country was not only supplying evidence, but also allowing residents to travel to the West.

Dr Czaykowska-Medryk and Dr Suzanne Weinstein Lambolez, a Parisian physician, both arrived in New York on 19 September 1972. INS had provided plane tickets and promised them $37 a day in expenses, barely the price of a ratty New York City hotel room. Upon landing, however, they were told the federal funds for their

*In all, some 360,000 prisoners from twenty-nine European countries were murdered at Majdanek during World War II.

stay had not yet cleared. With the stop-and-start schedule of hearings and possible recalls, INS wasn't finished with them until early November. To keep them afloat financially, investigator DeVito passed a hat around the fourteenth floor of the INS building, where he worked, and raised $604. The government's expense money didn't clear until 9 November, the day before the witnesses left the country.

DeVito was convinced that Nazis infiltrated the federal bureaucracy and even INS to put obstacles in his witnesses' way. He cited a call his wife, Frieda, received during the hearings. Speaking German in a calm, unctuous voice, the caller asked her why she was letting her husband hunt Nazis. Didn't she know this could be dangerous? After all, hadn't she been born in Germany and lived through the war there? The DeVitos' phone was unlisted and he felt that 'only someone in the Service' would also have known that his wife was German.

In any event, the two women's trips proved valuable. Slender, pretty, and blonde, Dr Czaykowska-Medryk wasn't Jewish, but Catholic, and had written a book about her resistance to Nazism and the life it had brought her in the camps. In February 1943, a month after she arrived in Majdanek, she was on a detail of women who'd been ordered to carry sand and bricks. 'Overseer Braunsteiner came over with a dog,' she testified, 'and made us run by using a whip. She beat us with the whip . . . She had a cape over her uniform and a dog. I remember distinctly because she was the first woman with a dog. It was a police dog, not muzzled, but held on a leash . . . On her command, the dog would jump towards the prisoners.'

Later that month, on a similar detail, she encountered Braunsteiner again: 'She used the whip and a bat against our legs to make us move faster.' Braunsteiner, she added, didn't need whip, dog, or bat to be a brute. She kicked the witness and other inmates so hard and so often with her steel-studded heavy leather boots that they nicknamed her 'The Mare of Majdanek'.

'Did you ever see a woman bitten by the dog?' lawyer Barry asked blandly. No, she hadn't.

Did she ever see Mrs Ryan kill anyone? To Barry's usual question, the answer was no. But Dr Czaykowska-Medryk had, in August 1943, seen her help select Jewish women for the gas chambers: 'On that day, some Polish women were pulling Jewish women away, trying to hide them. Braunsteiner ran to one of those women who wanted to hide a Jewish woman and kicked and beat her.'

Later that August, she saw Braunsteiner grab children and throw them on to two trucks for delivery to the gas chambers. 'One policewoman refused to help,' she said, 'and Braunsteiner hit her across the face.'

The witness testified in Polish, but the INS special inquiry officer, Francis J. Lyons, had difficulty understanding the interpreter's English, so he sent for another translator and recessed the hearing until after lunch. The delay, the change of translators, and the ominous presence of her one-time tormentor all served to unnerve the Polish woman dentist.

In the afternoon, she was asked whether she could identify Braunsteiner. Pointing to Mrs Ryan, she said: 'The moment I walked in, I recognized her.'

'Easy to say,' Mrs Ryan remarked to her husband.

Hearing that voice after nearly thirty years, the witness turned pale and, after examination by a nurse, was sent home for the day. When the hearing resumed three days later, she was cross-examined by lawyer Barry, who asked her whether she had expressed any concern for the Jewish women in another part of Majdanek.

'I never asked,' she answered. 'Just to ask might bring them closer to death. I was concerned about the few Jews I knew. We were all facing death together.'

'Did you hate Jewish women in the field?' Barry persisted.

'You are trying to make an anti-Semite out of me!' she responded indignantly. The most that Barry was able to show 'against' her was that she'd been approached to testify by the US Embassy in Warsaw and that she'd said yes without consulting her husband. Great emphasis was placed by the defence on Russell Ryan's sitting beside his wife at every hearing. The most that Barry was able to show 'for' his client was the witness's labelling Braunsteiner the 'second cruellest guard' in the camp. Top 'honours', she said, went to a woman named Lotte.

That night, lawyer Barry suffered an attack of bleeding ulcers and the hearings were suspended indefinitely.

When they resumed in early October, the French Dr Lambolez gave a glimpse of Braunsteiner at the peak of her career: as head of her own slave labour camp at Genthin, near Ravensbrück, toward the end of the war. Testifying that she saw her mistreat inmates on many occasions, she said: 'I watched her administer twenty-five lashes with a riding-crop to a young Russian girl suspected of having tried sabotage. Her back was full of lashes, but I was not allowed to treat her immediately.'

'From October 1972 until March 1973,' recalls ex-prosecutor Allan Ryan, 'not a witness was heard, not a day of trial held. The case against the Mare of Majdanek sat on a table in an empty courtroom.' He described its status as 'mired'.

At the European end, however, Simon Wiesenthal was slogging through the mire by prodding Polish and German authorities with his evidence, the hearings' evidence, and hundreds of names of witnesses. On 19 March 1973, Poland asked for Mrs Ryan's extradition to stand trial for participation in gas-chamber selections of women and children at Majdanek. While Barry's law firm was arguing that this was political persecution by a communist regime that could not and would not give their client a fair trial, West Germany upstaged everybody two days later by formally issuing a warrant for her extradition as a fugitive accused of murder.

This took the case out of the INS hearing-room in Manhattan and back into federal court in Brooklyn. Mrs Ryan was arrested and spent her first night in jail on Rikers Island in the East River. When she appeared in court at a hearing for bail, she complained that she had 'slept with prostitutes'. Bail was denied, but she was transferred to the less demeaning Nassau County Jail on Long Island.

Events now moved swiftly and dramatically. The West German warrant, citing nine instances in which 'Hermine Ryan, née Braunsteiner' had played a role in murder or torture at Majdanek, and accusing her of taking part in the consignment of as many as a thousand Jews at a time to death in gas chambers, was followed by a three-hundred-page document of depositions detailing her offences. The first ninety-two pages were made public in English translation by US Attorney Robert Morse on 9 April.

'In the fall of 1942, or the following winter,' the indictment began slightly fuzzily, 'the accused hit an unknown female prisoner on her head and body in such a way that she collapsed and died a day or two later because of her injuries.'

During that period, it went on, 'not only did she push prisoners selected by other SS members into the group destined for the gas chambers, but those who argued for exemption because they were still capable to work were rendered useless by means of lashes or cuts with the whip.'

In September 1943, swore Maria Kaufmann-Krasowski in a deposition, a Jewish girl tried to escape the gas chamber by pretending she was a Gentile. Braunsteiner knew better – and, to set an example for her other prisoners, ordered a special roll-call. Beneath an improvised gallows, she placed a three legged stool. Then an SS man named Enders led the girl in.

'On the way to the gallows,' the witness had testified, 'I had to translate Enders' questions . . . as to whether she was aware that she was to be hanged. She answered that she was aware of it. As the noose was slipped around her neck, she turned to the crowd that was forced to watch and said in Polish: "Remember me."

'There was a great silence. Then Enders pushed away the stool and hanged the girl. Braunsteiner stood right next to the gallows during this hanging. Then the Germans went away. Somebody threw some flowers on the body, and it was taken away . . . All of us went quietly to our barracks, and in my barracks people were praying.'

Russell Ryan was in court. He embraced his wife whenever she was brought in or taken away. 'They talk about crimes against humanity and human dignity,' he declared. 'I think this entire case is a tremendous outrage.' He vowed to 'stick with her to the very end' and follow her to Germany, if necessary.

He must have read the handwriting on the wall. On 1 May 1973, Federal Judge Jacob Mishler ordered Mrs Hermine Braunsteiner Ryan deported to Germany. In a ten-page decision, the judge ruled that 'there is competent and sufficient evidence to establish probable cause to believe that Mrs Ryan committed each of the acts charged in the [German] bench warrant.'

Amidst the uproar in the courtroom, investigator Tony DeVito leaped to his feet and called out to INS attorney Schiano: 'God damn it, Vince, we did it! We made history.' Lunging to embrace his partner, he suddenly remembered the dignity and seriousness of their roles – and the two men exchanged a solemn, deeply felt handshake.

After the US Court of Appeals and Supreme Court Justice Lewis F. Powell Jnr refused to block it, Secretary of State William P. Rogers signed the extradition order at the end of July. On Monday morning,

6 August 1973, Mrs Ryan was taken in handcuffs from her cell at the Nassau County Jail in East Meadow and driven to the federal courthouse in Brooklyn – not for another appeal, but for a final phone call to lawyer Barry. That afternoon, she was driven to Kennedy Airport, where Barry, Russell Ryan, six US marshals (one of them a woman), the counsel of the West German consulate, and a Düsseldorf policeman and policewoman, both in civilian clothes, were waiting. While her husband wasn't allowed to join her in the departure area, the others spent the next ninety minutes with her in a small, secluded room. Completely composed, Mrs Ryan accepted a Coca-Cola, smoothed her make-up, and chatted briefly in German with her Düsseldorf escorts before remarking to some of the others how funny her native tongue sounded to her now that she hadn't spoken it for years. Everybody had the tact to refrain from telling her what she already knew – that she would be speaking German for the rest of her life

When a US customs official popped in to ask her to open her luggage for inspection – not the usual procedure for departing passengers – Mrs Ryan, whose hair had been cropped short for the transfer, said: 'OK, let's get this over with.'

Her only carry-on baggage was a cardboard carton containing her knitting. As she boarded the Lufthansa flight to Cologne, the US marshals removed her handcuffs so as not to alarm the other passengers and, flanked by the German plain-clothes couple, 'the Mare of Majdanek' was kicked out of the United States with far more finesse than any of the exits she had administered.

Upon landing in Cologne the next morning, Hermine Braunsteiner Ryan – the first accused war criminal to be expelled from the US to face trial in Germany – was served with a warrant containing twenty-one pages of murder charges from Ravensbrück and Majdanek and then driven directly to Düsseldorf jail.

A year and a half later, in February 1975, she was indicted with nine other Nazis accused of taking a quarter of a million lives in Majdanek. When the Majdanek Trial, as it became known, opened in 1976, she was freed on bail – for she was the only one of the ten defendants in custody. Her bond, the Deutschmark equivalent of 17,000 US dollars, was posted by Russell Ryan, who had moved to Germany to be at his wife's side.

Ryan raised funds for a futile effort to retain his wife's Austrian nationality long after she'd relinquished her US citizenship. The defence contested the German court's jurisdiction because the offences were committed in Poland and she was an Austrian, though both lands were part of Nazi Germany at the time of the crimes and Austrians had become German citizens overnight in 1938. Besides, the court ruled, she had enlisted in the SS in Berlin.

When a professor of international law at the University of Cologne testified on Mrs Ryan's behalf, Simon Wiesenthal notified the court that the expert's consultancy fee of 2000 dollars had been paid by the 'White Power' movement in the US. When a scholar who had written on SS brutality testified for the prosecution, the defence pointed out that he had done his doctoral work in Berlin under a Jewish professor.

The Majdanek Trial took five years, during which one defendant died of natural causes. Every Tuesday, Wednesday, and Thursday, Mrs Ryan would commute from the nearby Ruhr Valley industrial city of Bochum, where she and her husband had rented a small apartment. 'She hasn't missed a single hearing and is always in the dock on time,' a court official said admiringly. The defendants sat there, one reporter wrote, 'like any row of elderly, modestly dressed passengers on a streetcar in a big German city.'

As in America, the defence tactic was two-pronged: to delay a decision (hopefully by boring press, public and judge to death) and to discredit not just the witnesses, but the dead and even the unborn. One of the defence lawyers actually drew a parallel between abortion today and the gassing of children in Majdanek. Another, representing Mrs Ryan, complained that the relentlessness of the testimony against her was a new form of torture.

Simon Wiesenthal attended the trial and called it 'a circus. A lawyer needs to defend his clients, but not to abuse people. The lawyers are talking to witnesses as though they were criminals. After a Polish lawyer told the court how defendants ordered her to bring the gas to the chamber, the defence lawyers asked the judge to charge her as an accomplice.'

Even in a courtroom circus, however, truth will out – and perhaps the most damaging moment for the defence came when one of its own witnesses, an SS officer, was asked what thoughts went through his head on Friday, 3 November 1943, the day some 18,000 Jews were murdered at Majdanek while he was on duty there. 'I was thinking about my vacation,' he replied.

On Tuesday, 30 June 1981, Chief Judge Günter Bogen read his verdicts. One defendant was released because of insufficient evidence. Seven others – including the deputy camp commandant and a woman accused of direct involvement in murdering 1196 prisoners – received sentences ranging from three to twelve years in jail. But Hermine Braunsteiner Ryan was given a life sentence.

She remained impassive. Not her husband, though. 'American Jews demand these trials,' Russell Ryan intoned, 'and this is what happens.'

He didn't mention the Galician Jew from Vienna who made it all happen. But his wife surely had not forgotten her moment of truth and insight almost seventeen years earlier when she had first learned that Simon Wiesenthal was on her case: 'This is the end of everything for me.'

Part VI
Bruno Kreisky, Kurt Waldheim

A bad memory is a consequence of a bad conscience.

–Erich Kästner

Memory, which recalls 'I have done that', eventually yields to pride, which then argues, 'I cannot have done that'.

–Friedrich Wilhelm Nietzsche

– 33 –

The Jewish Chancellor

In the early 1970s, when a pair of Viennese periodicals 'quoted' Bruno Kreisky as saying he was no longer a Jew, Simon Wiesenthal antagonized Austria's first Jewish Chancellor forever by quipping publicly that 'the only Austrian who doesn't believe Kreisky is Jewish is Kreisky himself.' The barb stung – and, while later lawsuits and denunciations, accusations of 'Jewish fascism' and 'Nazi collaboration' and besmirching of each other's past and present involved other issues, the enmity began there. Though Kreisky, at the peak of power, would brand Wiesenthal 'Public Enemy Number One', Simon would insist to Kreisky's dying day that 'I am not his enemy because I am not a hater, but he hates my guts.'

'There is nobody in this country who doesn't know I'm of Jewish birth,' Kreisky told me when I went to see him in early 1974. 'And I am happy. Ours was a very happy family . . . I never said "I am no longer a Jew." The *Kurier* and *profil* both printed it and it spread into the world press, but when the Austrian Press Council asked them to produce proof, all they could come up with was two tapes, which didn't show I said it. So they were reprimanded by the Press Council for "violating the ethical obligations of the press."'

Since the Austrian Press Council's censure isn't binding, neither publication had retracted the misquote or even mentioned the reprimand. I asked Kreisky what he *did* say.

'I said "I am an Austrian of Jewish origin. I am not a Zionist." And I would say this to you today: "I am of Jewish origin and I am not willing to deny this. But I am not a Zionist and never have been a Zionist." I refuse the thesis that a Jew has to be a Zionist. It is not true.'

When Kreisky insisted that he had 'never suffered religiously, only politically' for his religious origins, I pointed out that he had to leave the country in 1938. He replied: 'Yes, but because I was a Social Democrat. We were in the avant-garde of millions of others. I was arrested by the Gestapo for the first time because I was a Socialist. The Jews were arrested eight months later – in October or November, And they were not the last victims. You know, there were American soldiers who suffered and died, too. All the victims of the war suffered because of Hitler. . .'

In the beginning, there was detachment, distancing, and deflection – shifting the martyrdom to GIs in very much the way others may think they dilute the Holocaust by noting that Gentiles and gypsies and good Germans perished, too. All this was quite remarkable for a man who lost his mother's brother's family to the gas chambers, another uncle to suicide after the Anschluss, and many other relatives to the Nazi camps. In the end, there would be denial (never denying that he is Jewish, but never acknowledging that he was endangered by being a Jew) and deception (not just self-deception). When I read my 1974 conversation with Kreisky to Wiesenthal in 1987, Simon snorted: 'Kreisky is an illusionist. Jews were arrested as Jews from the day Hitler was coming to Austria. He got out only because he had friends who were Nazis.'

Here, Wiesenthal was referring to Kreisky's first jailing (in 1935–6) as a Socialist by the home-grown 'Christian Corporate State' of Dollfuss and his successor, Schuschnigg. From 1933 to 1938, under Austro-fascism, socialists, communists, and Nazis were all looked upon as enemies of the state. Thus, Kreisky found himself sharing a cell with a Nazi named Sepp Weninger and a communist named Auerhahn. They didn't argue politics. They addressed each other as 'Friend', not 'Comrade' or anything else. They shared gifts of food from their families. They complained about the same miseries and, when they talked about the long sentences they faced, Weninger said he'd be freed when Hitler came. Auerhahn said Hitler's failures would surely pave the way for Stalin. Kreisky sat silent, comforting himself with the hope that his Social Democrats would be around to pick up the pieces.

'Hitler was the biggest danger,' Kreisky told me in our 1974 interview, 'not just because he boasted that the Jews must be destroyed. This was only a symptom of a general political ideology and we Socialists always said: "Fascism is starting as a civil war and will end as a world war." In captivity in 1934, the most disturbing note was that many Kreisky met – Nazis, communists, guards, and the professional criminals who ran the jail – seemed to blame their problems on the Jews. Even a few of the imprisoned socialists did.

Of the three cellmates, Weninger underwent the strictest surveillance, for the 'illegal Nazi' was not only politically suspect, but under strong suspicion of having been behind a bombing attack. He was allowed no visitors or other contact with the outside world. Once, when Kreisky was being visited, Weninger asked him to smuggle out a message to his lawyer about where some incriminating evidence was that should be destroyed. The information was written on a cigarette wrapper. As Kreisky entered the reception area, he saw that the guards were making thorough body searches, so he swallowed the cigarette paper – and saved Weninger's life.

In 1938, when Kreisky was jailed by the Gestapo for five and a half months, some of his Nazi fellow inmates from two years earlier were now his guards – and Kreisky acknowledges in his memoirs that they eased the pain of prison life for him in 1938 and may even have played a role in his release. When the transports to Dachau began, he was on the shipment list several times, but Sepp Weninger kept crossing him off every posted roster until he was released on condition that he leave the country.

Weninger became a prominent Nazi in the Ostmark, as annexed Austria was renamed by Hitler. Toward the very end of the war, Weninger served on a tribunal that ordered five balky militiamen, who had resisted dying for a cause that was already lost, to be shot by a firing squad instead. Weninger was sentenced to death as a war criminal. Kreisky, by then an Austrian diplomat in postwar Sweden, sent a plea for mercy on Weninger as a friend who'd saved his life. 'My exoneration didn't help him,' Kreisky said succinctly. Weninger was executed in 1948.

Still reacting to Kreisky's disclaimer of ever having been persecuted as a Jew, Simon Wiesenthal went on: 'And what is this business about Hitler persecuting American soldiers, too? The Nazis didn't have orders to kill every prisoner of war – except maybe the Russian POWs – but they did have orders to kill every Jew. I have no words for this kind of thinking.' Simon being Simon and Kreisky being Kreisky, however, Wiesenthal did find the words to diagnose Kreisky as a case of Jewish self-hate: 'In my opinion, Kreisky is a Jewish tragic figure like we have in every generation. He hates himself because he is Jewish. He is a Jew and an anti-Jew in the same person.'

Austria's two most famous living Jews had been on a collision course from the day Bruno Kreisky took office in April 1970, after the newly elected Chancellor had formed a Socialist minority government. In his inaugural address, Kreisky declared bluntly that every citizen must be given the right to reappraise his or her political views – including those held during the Nazi era – in the light of 'subsequent experience and knowledge'.

Still, it came as a surprise to many when, a few days later, Simon Wiesenthal revealed to the German news magazine *Der Spiegel* (*The Mirror*) and the Austrian Catholic weekly *Die Furche* (*The Furrow*) that four of Kreisky's eleven cabinet appointees – his Ministers of Defence, Interior, Agriculture, and Construction – had been Nazi Party members and two of them, Agriculture Minister Hans Öllinger and Interior Minister Otto Rösch, had darker pasts than that. Öllinger had been a lieutenant in the *Waffen SS*, the military arm of Hitler's blackshirts; not only was Rösch – whose new post made him, in effect Austria's chief of police – a former SA brownshirt, but he had a criminal record as a participant in the founding of a postwar neo-Nazi organization whose main aim was to provide fugitive Nazi war criminals with falsified documents to facilitate their escapes. On 8 December 1947, Rösch, then thirty, had been apprehended with a suitcase full of blank documents and unauthorized stamps, but his defence was that he had no idea of the bag's contents. In 1949, he was acquitted for lack of evidence.

Surprised by Öllinger's record (though apparently not by Rösch's), Kreisky stuck to his choices and argued that his own past permitted him to judge former Nazis, since he had not only been their political prisoner, but had lost twenty-one of his family members to them. Of Wiesenthal, who had lost eighty-nine relatives to Hitler, Kreisky remarked sarcastically that 'I'm waiting now for Mr Wiesenthal to prove that I was also in the SS.'

Investigation showed that Öllinger had quit the *Waffen SS* in 1940 to join the German regular army and had been quickly denazified after the war. Granted clearance, he served only twenty-nine days as Minister of Agriculture, however, after suffering a heart attack and resigning because of ill health. His replacement as Minister, Oskar Weihs, had joined the Nazi Party as early as 1932.

Weihs, Öllinger, Rösch, and the other two ex-Nazi cabinet Ministers were all devoted Austrian Socialist Party apparatchiks; Rösch's membership, in fact, dated back to 1927, a decade before he joined the (then illegal) SA. A genial, silver-haired tennis player and skier, Otto Rösch came into the cabinet with Kreisky in 1970 – serving as Minister of Interior until 1977 and then Minister of Defence – and left office with him in 1983. Though even his enemies tend to concede that Rösch served capably and honourably – and, when I asked Wiesenthal in 1974 whether he had good co-operation from Minister Rösch, he replied, 'In the last time, I must say yes' – nevertheless it must be noted that searches for and apprehensions of Nazi war criminals ground to a virtual halt during his seven years as Interior Minister.

Within Austria back in 1970, few voices other than Wiesenthal's had been raised against Kreisky's appointments. True, Dr Erich Thanner, a distinguished editor, lawyer, aristocrat, and veteran of four years in Nazi prisons, had responded with an article headlined: 'WHO SLEEPS WITH DOGS WAKES UP WITH FLEAS: *The Extraordinary Anti-Semitism of Dr Kreisky*.' But the Blacks and the Blues (the traditionally Catholic-oriented People's Party and the postwar splinter called the Freedom party) rejoiced that, by defending 'his' Nazis, Kreisky had lost any advantage to be gained by condemning theirs. It is symptomatic of postwar Austria that the 1970 uproar was not known as 'the Kreisky affair' or 'the Öllinger affair' or 'the Rösch controversy', but as 'the Wiesenthal case'.

Hatchet-man for the Socialist counter-attack on Simon was the Party Secretary and newly named Minister of Education and Culture, Leopold Gratz, born 1929 and an alumnus of NAPOLA: the Nazi Party's élite secondary school for future political leaders (where Otto Rösch served briefly as a teacher). Though never a Nazi or even a Hitler Youth himself, Gratz had been indoctrinated in that era and spoke its language when he addressed the Socialist Party Congress on 11 June 1970, at the Stadthalle, Vienna's version of Madison Square Garden. Terming Wiesenthal's Jewish Documentation Centre a secret state police spying apparatus which intrigued against the innocent, Gratz warned ominously: 'It will soon be seen whether this country still needs Engineer Wiesenthal's private Inquisition . . . How much longer will we tolerate this private tribunal?' The crowd cheered and Chancellor Kreisky declared himself 'fully' in accord with Gratz, adding that 'in Austria, a Nazi Party member or an SS man can assume any political office provided there is no criminal evidence against him.'

Wiesenthal's response to this was: 'I understand full well that one can't exclude half a million people from public life. So I make this formula: *the Nazis can live, the Nazis can die, but the Nazis should not govern us*. Anyhow, Nazis sit in all public offices – also under Kreisky – so when he even makes them ministers, then he acknowledges that he is giving a blanket acquittal from moral guilt. I am against the theory of collective guilt; but I am also against the theory of collective innocence. Not even the Jews have collective innocence.'

Six days later, Dutch journalist Martin van Amerongen interviewed Kreisky and asked him whether the Socialists were trying to hunt down the Nazi-hunter.

'Nonsense!' Kreisky snorted. 'We're not hunting Wiesenthal. You in Holland are badly informed about Wiesenthal's activities. Just from the standpoint of the importance of people's personal freedom, how can one reconcile this with a private organization that lies in ambush for people? Here one cannot be an onlooker. Wiesenthal is a Jewish fascist. Just the way in which he has reproached our Interior Minister, Otto Rösch, with his Hitler Youth membership* after so long a time . . . Wiesenthal is an extremely reactionary man with close ties to the People's Party.' But he shrugged off Simon's significance by adding that 'one finds reactionaries among us Jews just as there are Jewish thieves, murderers, and prostitutes. That's the way it is. All in all, I don't find the Wiesenthal affair so crucial.'

When Amerongen visited Wiesenthal a few days later, he found him in good spirits. 'Nobody has ever given me a better name in the world than Bruno Kreisky has,' Simon proclaimed from behind a desk littered with telegrams and letters of support, mostly from abroad. They were not just from Jewish and survivor organizations, but, among many others, the fan club of operetta composer Robert

*Coming of age in the month Hitler annexed Austria, Rösch was too old to be a Hitler Youth and neither Wiesenthal nor anyone else but Kreisky has ever accused him of being one.

Stolz and an aristocratic Swiss pianist who not only expressed 'the anger of the world', but added that she'd ascertained 'the former German Chancellor Dr [Kurt Georg] Kiesinger is in accord with me.' Later would come, in Wiesenthal's words, 'a series of demonstrative invitations, among them to a luncheon in the US Senate and a dinner in the House of Commons of the British Parliament at which Winston Churchill's grandson was master of ceremonies for eighty invited guests.'

The influential American Jewish newspaper *Aufbau*, published weekly in the German language, called Kreisky's utterances a 'tasteless' attempt 'to intimidate Wiesenthal.' A telegram from an American asked Wiesenthal: 'PLEASE ANSWER MY QUESTION: IS MR GRATZ A SOCIALIST OR A NATIONAL SOCIALIST?' While Kreisky was calling Wiesenthal a 'fanatic', 'avenger', and 'manhunter', and Gratz was saying he ran a centre for 'informing, spying and inquisition activity', Simon's sources at the Ballhausplatz said that the Chancellor's office had received 600 to 800 protests, mostly from abroad. 'Now Kreisky can start a stamp collection, too,' said Simon, himself a philatelist.

'Do you know,' Simon went on to Amerongen, 'that your interview was the first time in years that Kreisky used the expression "*we Jews*"? He knows only full well that the term "*Jew*" goes over better in the Netherlands than it does in Austria. Kreisky uses his Judaism only for export.'

Was he going to sue Kreisky for calling him a Jewish fascist'? Wiesenthal explained that, under Austrian law, the Chancellor, who was also a Member of Parliament, possessed parliamentary immunity even for words spoken outside Parliament, 'so I can't sue him unless he lets me sue him.' When the bad name his intemperate attack on Wiesenthal had created abroad hit home to Kreisky, the Chancellor issued a denial – *ten days after the words appeared in print!* – that he'd ever called Simon a 'Jewish fascist'. The Dutch periodical's editors were worried. 'Are you going to sue *us*?' they asked Simon over the phone.

'I don't sue you,' Simon assured them. 'I will sue him when first I get the chance. I know he said it. You know he said it. He knows he said it.'

At my own very first meeting with Wiesenthal in 1974, he said that he'd known his adversary only on a handshake basis, though he'd been grateful to him in 1966 when he'd been crusading for a catalogue of Jewish art treasures confiscated by the Nazis and still unclaimed by their rightful owners, to be circulated among Austrian consulates around the world. Kreisky, then Foreign Minister, had supported the project. But 'four Nazis out of eleven ministers is too much. It's even higher than the percentage of former Nazis in the Austrian population. His first Cabinet had even more Nazi Party members than [Schuschnigg's successor, Artur von] Seyss-Inquart had in the first cabinet after the Anschluss. So when I point this out, they attack me in Parliament and the papers. . .

'Look, Kreisky used to say "I am no more Jewish, because in the thirties, I left from the Jewish community." He is an atheist; you know, he is not baptized. That was when I give a statement that "the only person who does not know that Kreisky is Jewish is Kreisky himself." It is coming from me, but my phrase is the answer to why he makes such a big problem. Now the Austrian people can say, "When even the Jew Kreisky can forget about SS or Nazi Party membership, then so can we." But, in Holland, a collaborationist can't even be the mayor of a village and it's the same with Quislings in Norway and Vichyites in France. Even in Italy, where fascism got its name and they change cabinets every three months, there hasn't been a single former fascist minister yet!'

Wiesenthal's greatest fear was that Kreisky would inflict collective guilt on the 6000 Jews of Austria: 'I accept that he will have nothing to do with the Jews, but I am sure that if his politics should go wrong, the people will make the Jews guilty for him. It is not the same fear if Henry Kissinger makes a disaster for the United States because there are so many different groups in the population of America that whatever he does bad for one group is good for another – not like here, where on a particular block, all are Catholics and all are anti-Semite.'

From the outset of the Kreisky era, Wiesenthal had not been impressed 'when many of the Socialists tells me, "You see, this is a miracle. We have a Jew for Chancellor." And I tell them this is not a miracle because the Jews were the founders of the Social Democratic Party in Austria. Always the leadership was Jewish – from Viktor Adler to Otto Bauer. Yes, Adler became a Protestant, but Bauer once said: "I am a Jew, but for me is the Judaism not a nation, not a religion, but a shared fate." And you cannot leave it because then you are a deserter. This is why he remained a Jew – not to go to synagogue, but because he feel it.

'I was this way for a while, too, after the war,' Simon admitted, 'but always in my life I feel Jewish. You know, after 2000 years, so much changes, but what stays common for all Jewish generations over these centuries is the attacks against us – the persecution, from Spain to the Urals, from Latin America to Libya . . . So Kreisky says he learned much from Otto Bauer? One thing he didn't learn is what Bauer knew and others learned from Hitler: you *can change your shirt, but not your skin*.'

In 1988, Simon Wiesenthal declared that Bruno Kreisky 'has a disturbed relationship to Nazism and Judaism.'

'In all my disputes with Wiesenthal,' Bruno Kreisky told me in early 1986, 'I had the feeling that what he wanted the most from me was that I should put loyalty to Israel before my loyalty to Austria. And that I would never do.'

Earlier, Kreisky had informed me: 'Wiesenthal is for me less than a zero . . . He is living from telling the world that Austria is anti-Semitic. What else can he do?'

The antipathies between the two men were obvious. The Chancellor was an assimilated ex-exile seeking to be a political figure of reconciliation between modern Austria and its brown past. The irate Nazi-hunter was a concentration-camp survivor slowly evolving from a symbol of retribution to one of righteousness and 'feeling Jewish' enough to serve on the board of the Austrian Association of Jewish Communities, during which time Kreisky broke with a tradition that the Chancellor honoured the High Holy Days with a Jewish New Year's message to the Association. Kreisky, on the other hand, was a Viennese-born Jew who, like Freud and Mahler (both born in the Czech lands) and many before him, felt at least a little ashamed of the more primitive Jews who flooded their city from the east; for all his education and achievements, Wiesenthal was a transplanted Jew from Galicia. 'The eastern Jews,' Kreisky once declared, 'are alienated from normal ways of thinking.'

Call this 'Jewish self-hate', as Wiesenthal does, or make light of it, as Arthur Schnitzler did ('Anti-Semitism became popular in Vienna only when the Jews themselves took it up'), but the same tensions exist between Berlin Jews and other German and Austrian

Jews and, in Israel, between Oriental and European Jews. Or, as Dr Wilfried Daim, a Viennese analyst who wrote *Depth Psychology and Salvation,* put it to me bluntly: 'To a German-speaking Jew like Kreisky, a Polish-and-Yiddish-speaking Jew like Wiesenthal coming out of the East to haunt him is as much a rebuke as if he had a Southern "darky" for a cousin.'

'For me,' said Kreisky in 1986, 'this whole "Wiesenthal Complex" . . . isn't worth another word. I happen not to like the man and that is my right. Just because we share the same religion, it doesn't mean that we have to love each other. Do all Catholics?'

Kreisky could easily infuriate Wiesenthal, whose only child lives with her family in Israel and whose granddaughter and grandsons have all served in the Israeli Army, just by disparaging Israel's right-wing Prime Minister, Menachem Begin, as 'that Polish lawyer' and 'the son of a little Polish tailor'. Or by complaining that 'Israel is run by Russian and Polish Jews.' Or by proclaiming: 'I have no Jewish fellow citizens; I know only Austrian countrymen.'

Said Wiesenthal: 'One of Kreisky's favourite themes is that the Jews are not a people. He says this is scientific truth and one day he's going to write a book about it. He belabours journalists with endless sermons on this subject and most of them are too polite to interrupt or challenge him.'

One Israeli editor did, however. Menachem Oberbaum of *Al Ahram* asked Kreisky in 1975 how, as a statesman and diplomat, he could criticize Israel, the Jewish people, Begin, and Wiesenthal in such strong terms.

Kreisky's reply was nothing if not vehement: 'Tell me once and for all, Mr Editor, do you come to me wanting information from the Chancellor of the Republic or are you here to interrogate me? When you want to make an interrogation of me, then I'll cancel everything [on the schedule]. The Jews publish so much that is terrible about me that I won't allow this [to happen]. Would you have the nerve to question the French Prime Minister in such a way? This is such impudence that I would gladly throw you out. Why must I really stand for your Questions and Answers? . . . Now I've had enough. I'm not here to answer like a defendant to the Jewish – the Israeli media.' He concluded his tirade with one of his most memorable utterances: 'The Jews are not a people, and if they are, they are a lousy people.'

Calming down to the melting-point, Kreisky answered the rest of Oberbaum's question quite candidly: 'When I hear the name Begin or Wiesenthal, I simply lose control of myself.'

To Wiesenthal, it was quite clear that he and Begin were 'for Kreisky the same "Jews from the east" that we are to many Viennese and he will have nothing to do with us.'

In the autumn of 1975, when Bruno Kreisky stood for re-election, he struck a bargain with Friedrich Peter, head of the small right-wing Freedom Party: if Kreisky's Socialists failed to win a majority in Parliament, his Reds would govern in a coalition with Peter's Blues. Peter would be appointed Vice Chancellor and his party would be given the Foreign Ministry, too. Since the Freedom Party was riddled with Nazis, this alarmed many – but not Simon Wiesenthal. 'Just wait,' he reassured friends. 'First, we must have the election and then we will see the results – but I can guarantee there will be no such coalition.'

Simon gave this assurance because, upon returning from his summer vacation early that September, he had found a new acquisition crowning the clutter on his desk. It was a 1942 roster of the First SS Infantry Brigade, which Wiesenthal calls 'one of the most notorious extermination units of the war.' In 'special actions' against civilians in the Ukraine in 1941–2, it had massacred 13,497 men, women, and children, whose corpses were classified as 'Jews, gypsies, partisans, bandits, and suspected enemies.' From near the middle of the list, one name jumped out at him: SS Lieutenant Friedrich Peter, an Austrian born 13 July 1921.

When that date matched Peter's campaign biographies, Simon made further inquiries and quickly confirmed that this was the same Friedrich Peter who had never denied an SS past, but had hinted he was 'only a lieutenant' in the *Waffen SS*. It did not take Wiesenthal long to establish that Peter had been a corporal in the brigade's Fifth Company on Thursday, 4 September 1941, when, according to a regimental logbook which had, ironically, been issued by a Socialist publishing house in Vienna as a warning against resurgent Nazism:

> . . . the village of Leltschitky was, thanks to strong reconnaissance power, reached and taken without casualties. Seized: sixty rifles, eleven machine guns, fifteen hand grenades, 22,115 bullets; in

addition, thirty-eight prisoners were executed and 1,089 Jews shot to death.

'The massacre,' says Wiesenthal, 'took place just outside the town. The Jews had to dig deep trenches and then climb in, so they could be shot in their grave and buried efficiently.' Not all the victims, however, were shot, but those that weren't were buried alive when the next group of victims had to cover the grave over with sand before digging their own.

For his work in the brigade's 'winter campaign 1941–42', Friedrich Peter earned an Iron Cross and a battlefield commission. More than three decades later, Simon Wiesenthal recognized that 'I had a stick of dynamite in my hand. If I made it public during the campaign, Kreisky and Peter and everybody else would accuse me of meddling in politics.' Anticipating that the volatile Austrian vote might react in favour of Peter or Kreisky as a backlash against the interfering Jew, Wiesenthal decided to maintain silence until after the election, but to show his good faith by delivering Peter's dossier beforehand to the apolitical President of Austria: Dr Rudolf Kirchschläger (predecessor to Kurt Waldheim).

A lanky, pious man who spoke with a quaver that often sounded as if he were about to cry, Kirchschläger wept real tears when Wiesenthal presented him with the Peter papers on Monday, 29 September 1975, a week before the election. 'The President read a few pages and began to shudder and then burst into tears,' Wiesenthal recalls. 'Then he thanked me for not going public with it before the election, so the people would vote on the issues and not on one man's past. He made me feel like a patriot.' Simon said he would make Peter's past public after the election out of fear that he might come to high office then or at a later time. The President, with Simon's permission, sent photocopies of the dossier to Peter and Kreisky. He also indicated to Wiesenthal that he might reject any naming of Peter as Vice Chancellor: calling elections and accepting governments are among the few real powers of the largely ceremonial Austrian Presidency.

In that critical week before the election, Simon says that Peter was very uneasy and offered to bow out of the bargain, but Kreisky told him anything Wiesenthal said could be disregarded. The deal was still on.

Sunday, 5 October's election results nullified all arrangements. The Reds won ninety-three of the 183 seats in Parliament; the

Blacks eighty; and Peter's Blues ten. Kreisky could govern with a clear majority and no partners.

On 9 October, Wiesenthal gave a press conference in the Hotel de France on the Ringstrasse and handed journalists his documentation of Peter's war record. From his party headquarters, Peter told reporters that he had not participated in his unit's dirty work, had known nothing of atrocities, had heard nothing from his comrades-in-arms, and must have been on home leave when the Leltschitky massacre occurred. Wiesenthal was quick to retort that no leaves were granted by the First SS Infantry Division while it was in 'combat' against civilians during the 1941–2 'special actions' and that Peter's Fifth Company was in the centre of virtually every daily extermination during that time. That night, on Austrian television, Peter declared: 'I have never taken part in such an operation, but have only fulfilled my duty as a soldier.'

(Peter's plea of *Pflichterfüllung*, 'fulfilment of duty', may have fallen more sympathetically on President Kirchschläger's ear than Wiesenthal surmised. For, as a captain in the German Army in 1945, Kirchschläger had fulfilled his duty without question by leading 1200 teenagers, the last of Hitler's reserves in Austria, to certain doom from Soviet tanks at the gates of Vienna on the eve of the city's surrender. Badly equipped and without enough weapons to go around, some 200 youths died and another 800 were wounded, as was Captain Kirchschläger. Nowhere did this infamous 'Charge of the Lightly-Armed Brigade' appear in his official biography.)

After Wiesenthal's revelation and Peter's denial in 1975, the response from Chancellor Kreisky – at a press conference with foreign journalists – was massive overkill:

'Look, to close out this whole long chapter, I must say that all this is for me a baroque affair that has materialized only through the efforts of Mr Wiesenthal, whom I know just from secret reports – and they are very negative, positively evil.'

Asked what he was talking about, Kreisky rambled on: 'I can assure you that Mr Wiesenthal maintained a different relationship to the Gestapo from mine – provably! More I cannot say now, but the rest I will say in court . . . I hope it will be a big trial, for, let me tell you, a man like him has no right after all that to play the role of a moral authority. Furthermore, I state that he has no right to earn his living from persecuting other human beings . . . He has no right to meddle in Austrian politics. The man must go!'

As Kreisky went on to call Wiesenthal a spy and a *mafioso* bent on bringing everybody to court, a reporter from United Press International broke in to ask incredulously: 'Are you saying that Wiesenthal was a Gestapo agent?'

'I maintain,' said Kreisky, 'that, in that time, Mr Wiesenthal lived in an area under the Nazi sphere of influence without being persecuted.'

This was reverse character assassination worthy of the Hitler era. Perhaps not as ominous because the consequences weren't immediate, but, even in a democracy – particularly in a democracy! – such a public denunciation by the head of government, calling for Simon's disappearance, was an open invitation to any crazy or Nazi to take a pot-shot at Wiesenthal and even for the police to look the other way. Vienna is an orderly city with an abundance of social services, but it has its share of people who walk down the street backwards shouting to themselves. In late 1975 and well into 1976, it seemed to me that most of them were proclaiming that 'the Jew, Simon Wiesenthal, must go!'

What made this even more terrifying, says Wiesenthal, was that 'in the time of Kreisky, Austria was not a democracy because he so dominated it. Even the Jews here, some of them were so angry at me for making trouble and most of them were worried this would lead to big anti-Semitism.'

Though outraged, Simon Wiesenthal was a little less surprised than many by the nature of the attack on him. Five years earlier, when he was criticizing Kreisky for naming four Nazis to his Cabinet and Kreisky was calling him a 'Jewish fascist', he had learned of feverish inquiries in international Socialist circles for any leads connecting him to a pre-war Jewish-fascistic youth group in Poland. This research unearthed a Polish Jewish youth group called *Betar*, whose members wore greyish brown blouses and blue trousers. 'Unfortunately,' said one Swiss report, 'Wiesenthal did not belong to it; besides, it was not at all fascistic.'*

**Betar* (short for *Berit Trumpeldor*) was an activist Zionist youth movement founded in 1923 in Riga, Latvia. Spreading through Eastern Europe in the late twenties and early thirties, it claimed its brown shirts symbolized the earth of the Jewish homeland. It exists in Israel today as a right-wing youth organization whose anthem calls for a Jewish state 'on both banks of the Jordan'.

Not even this, however, had prepared Wiesenthal for the onslaught of public insults from Kreisky, who disparaged him as 'Simon Wiesenthal, so-called Engineer', and still questioned his right to Austrian citizenship: 'One must at last close the door on these things. Some day there must be an end to this – then how is it that Wiesenthal is allowed to live here anyway?' Most reprehensible to Simon were the accusations and allegations, slurs and insinuations against him without a shred of documentation: the antithesis of the way he worked.

On Austrian television, the Chancellor told millions that Wiesenthal's methods were 'deplorable' and the attack on Peter was, in reality, aimed at Kreisky himself. He had known Peter for years. He believed this stalwart democrat's assurances that he had been involved in no criminality at all – and Peter's word was enough for him. Not for Wiesenthal, however. 'The fact that Friedrich Peter had, until now, never acknowledged his service in the First SS Infantry Brigade,' said Simon, 'didn't seem to disturb the Chancellor at all.'

Wiesenthal says that the next six weeks were 'the worst time I had experienced since the war. I was a leper in my new homeland and only the thought that I hadn't survived Hitler just to escape from Austria kept me from emigrating. What I was up against was Kreisky at the peak of his popularity with a hypnotic, downright magical hold on the people. They saw him as father, emperor, and god in one. Self-critical Austrian intellectuals hung on his lips for every single word; they called him the "Sun King". The journalists of the country, with a few exceptions, ate out of his hand. And, whenever others attacked me, he cheered them on. I had the public image of an insatiable avenger who, every morning, got up and ate some poor innocent little Nazi Party member for breakfast.' (When asked point-blank whether he did indeed devour a neo-Nazi a day, Simon once replied: 'No, I don't eat pork.')*

Around that time, a polling institute in Linz reported the results of its national public opinion survey of Austrian reactions to the Kreisky-vs-Wiesenthal controversy: fifty-nine per cent supported Kreisky; twenty-nine per cent were neutral; thirteen per cent had

*Simon said this in German, in which the last word is more emphatic: *Schweinefleisch*.

no opinion; and only three per cent supported Simon. Among younger interviewees (ages sixteen to twenty-nine), six per cent were for Wiesenthal, but among the over-fifties, his support was so negligible that the computer couldn't even register one per cent.

'WIESENTHAL DISCREDITS AUSTRIA ABOARD', the nation's bestselling daily, the tabloid *Kronen-Zeitung*, howled in a front-page headline. A Freedom Party weekly 'exposed' the regimental war diary as 'a forgery' planted by the Czechoslovak secret police. One of the few editors who did speak up – Peter Michael Lingens of *profil*, who used to be Simon's secretary and who wrote that Kreisky's slurs were 'undignified and immoral' as well as 'monstrous' – was sued by Kreisky, who won at every level of the Austrian courts. Fined a sum equivalent to almost 4000 dollars, Lingens – in a move that would not have occurred to many Austrian lawyers – took his case to one of Kreisky's pet institutions: the European Court of Human Rights in Strasbourg, France. In 1986, more than ten years after the case was initiated, Lingens won in Strasbourg. The European Court, after studying the statements of both sides, said that Lingens had the right of free expression of opinion to call Kreisky's utterances 'monstrous, immoral, and undignified'. The government of Austria was told to vacate the fine and pay Lingens' court costs of some $23,000.

'Do you know how Kreisky "justified" calling me a *mafioso*?' Simon asked me rhetorically in early 1989. 'In Lingens' case, he explained that the abduction of Adolf Eichmann had been conducted like a Mafia operation. Then, in the same presentation, he says, "Wiesenthal had nothing to do with the abduction of Eichmann." Look, his calling me a *mafioso* didn't bother me as much as other people. Three waiters make a strike: their customers call it a Mafia. But, for a Jew to call another Jew a collaborator is to call him a murderer.'

Friedrich Peter sued Wiesenthal as well as *profil* and the *Kurier* for slander. At sporadic court sessions over the next seven years, Wiesenthal produced documents indicating that Peter's SS Brigade killed close to 400,000 people during his twenty months in its service, and showing that another 167 members of the unit were living in Austria. In 1976, Kreisky took former SS Lieutenant Peter with him on a State visit to Czechoslovakia which included a stop in the Theresienstadt (Terezin) concentration camp, where many of the

Jewish Chancellor's relatives perished or passed en route to extermination; Peter stood stony-faced through the short ceremony. In 1977, President Kirchschläger decorated Peter with Austria's highest gold medal for service and, a year later, Peter retired as head of the Freedom Party, though retaining his positions as Member of Parliament and party speaker there. In 1983's re-election campaign, Kreisky announced he wouldn't govern in coalition and, when the Socialists failed to achieve an absolute majority, he stepped aside after thirteen years as Chancellor to let his Socialist deputy, Fred Sinowatz, form a government with the Freedom Party's more respectable new chief, Norbert Steger (born 1944), as Vice Chancellor. Around the time his party achieved a share of power (which lasted until 1986), Peter had his lawyer write to Wiesenthal's lawyer saying that the suit was being dropped because Peter had lost interest in pursuing it.

Simon Wiesenthal tried to sue Bruno Kreisky, but the Chancellor's parliamentary immunity protected him, no matter where and what he spoke. Parliamentary immunity is stronger in Austria than even diplomatic immunity; a drunk-driving deputy who shows his status to a policeman will be waved forward to weave onward – the assumption being that he is going about his government business. Though Kreisky said he would gladly waive his immunity for the 'big trial' against Wiesenthal, he never did and it never materialized. Meanwhile, Kreisky said he would order a special parliamentary commission to investigate not Peter, but Wiesenthal. Information later surfaced that, three days after Wiesenthal's disclosures, the Austrian federal police shadowed and eavesdropped on him in the transit buffet of Vienna's Schwechat Airport as he greeted two friends he encountered while waiting for a flight to Frankfurt:

> WIESENTHAL told the two passengers rather loudly that he would not tolerate PETER's continuing to function as a politician, since he belonged to a murder unit during the war. Furthermore, said WIESENTHAL, he would not permit KREISKY's behaviour against him. He would therefore investigate associates of KREISKY more closely. The investigations would take several months, but, if the occasion arose, KREISKY would have to bear the consequences.*

*From *Staatspolizei* report SCH – P-50.207/75 dated 13 October 1975.

The unlikely truce-maker in this uncivil war between Austria's two best-known Jews was Simon's ailing wife Cyla. After nearly two months of not picking up a newspaper, never turning on TV, seldom leaving the house since being heckled while shopping, and declining to see her friends because she knew what they had on their minds, she told Simon she wanted to lead the normal life of a woman nearing seventy: to sit in a coffee-house, stroll in the park, go to the theatre. She asked him to settle the case. Simon argued that they hadn't survived Janowskà and Mauthausen only to capitulate to Kreisky.

'But we were young then,' Cyla pointed out. 'And it doesn't matter what people think, so long as we can finally enjoy a little peace in our old age.'

The president of B'nai B'rith* in Vienna, a mutual friend of both men, negotiated an uneasy peace between them. Wiesenthal abandoned his efforts to force Kreisky into court while the Chancellor dropped the idea of an investigatory commission and told Parliament grumblingly: 'Incidentally, I want to make it clear that I have never identified Wiesenthal as a Nazi collaborator.'

In 1982, when Israel invaded southern Lebanon, Kreisky declared in an interview: 'Israel's standing is bare of any ethics. Its leadership has shown its true face. The warfare in Lebanon has actually cost Israel the support it secured and received during the past few decades. The insanity of its rulers, who are only relying on their arms, is causing fear in the world at large. With this Israel I don't want to have anything to do any more. Never again!'

In a 1986 interview with me, ex-Chancellor Kreisky elaborated succinctly on why 'this Israel is not my Israel: it has, in my view, a semi-fascist ideology, a policy of force, a regime of apartheid, and it uses the support of the masses for its own ends. I have no sympathy for any of this.'

This viewpoint, of course, did nothing to endear Kreisky to Simon Wiesenthal, but it did endear him to Austrians who said, as one heard all too often: 'We'd have nothing against the Jews if they

***B'nai B'rith* (Hebrew for 'sons of the covenant') is an international Jewish organization founded in New York City in 1843. It institutes and administers programmes to promote the social, educational, and cultural betterment of Jews and of the public at large.

were all like Kreisky.' Or, as Simon Wiesenthal put it succinctly: 'Every anti-Semite had to have a Jew he likes.'

Dr Daim, the Viennese depth psychologist, has examined why Kreisky was particularly well liked by many Austrian Nazis: 'For them, it was a sort of redemption to elect a Jew. And for that very reason, the Nazis were already lucky to have Kreisky, for he alone was in a position to make them socially acceptable again. A Jewish Chancellor could put an end to a past with which they didn't want to have anything more to do' – if Wiesenthal hadn't risen to protest Kreisky's gift of absolution. To make matters worse, Daim adds, 'Kreisky, in the way he attacked Israel's invasion of Lebanon, enabled these people to start thinking of Jews as war criminals.'

Notorious in Austria for his controversial 'psychograms' of Kreisky, Daim actually 'interviewed' his subject at the height of the furore over Wiesenthal's 1975 exposure of Peter. 'It was hardly an interview,' Daim recalls. 'My topic was his attitude toward the Nazis and he spoke for more than an hour without my even having a chance to interrupt and ask a question. But when our time together was nearly up, I managed to thank him for talking about the Nazis and then I asked him: "Mr Chancellor, now what is your relationship to the Jews?' And he replied very sharply: "That has nothing to do with it." But I said, almost as sharply: "Mr Chancellor, it has a direct bearing. One cannot speak about the Nazis without speaking about the Jews." So then he talked in generalities about "these highly intelligent people" and so on.'

'Kreisky is a modern King Midas,' said a People's Party politician. 'When he takes a Nazi in his hand, suddenly he's no longer a Nazi.'

Every now and then, Kreisky repeated one or another of his allegations and insinuations against Wiesenthal – and, each time Simon found out about it, he went through the motions of trying to sue. By November 1986, he could tell me: 'I've sued him five times, but each time Parliament won't lift his immunity.' To avoid making it six, I didn't bother to mention my visit to Kreisky's home on Friday, 24 January of that year: two days after the ex-Chancellor's seventy-fifth birthday.

His 250-year-old rented villa with a discreet modern swimming-pool in the back was already under wraps for winter hibernation. Its tenant would soon be flying off to Mallorca, where he maintained an island home.

The Viennese villa hadn't changed much, but Kreisky had. Upon leaving the Ballhausplatz, he'd let what was left of his reddish greying hair grow long to form a fringe which met a foxy-looking beard he'd grown while hospitalized for a kidney transplant. His *eternal-Lumpenproletariat* look had yielded to a rakish demeanour which, to me, conjured up a bizarre image of Ezra Pound as an elder Jewish wise man.

When we talked about Wiesenthal, he confided that 'my information on him is very, very bad, but I don't want to have a trial with former Nazis as witnesses he will accuse, because the people who know all about him *are* that. There is one in Germany who commanded a camp. He knows a lot about Wiesenthal, but he keeps silent because he also knows what Wiesenthal will use against him if he comes to court.'

In an interview in *profil* later that year, Kreisky re-affirmed his accusations and Wiesenthal took him to court once again. The case was still pending in the fall of 1988, when Kreisky pleaded that he couldn't come to court in Vienna because he was promoting the second volume of his memoirs at the Frankfurt Book Fair. As it turned out, Wiesenthal was presenting the second volume of *his* memoirs in Frankfurt, too.

'Look,' Wiesenthal protested, 'I also was in Frankfurt, but I could be in Vienna, too, for the trial.' But the case was postponed until January 1989. 'What happened next?' Wiesenthal reported rhetorically. 'He was twice, without apology, not coming to the trial. The judge spoke to the lawyers and said if Kreisky does not appear, he will give to me the verdict. So then his lawyer is bringing certification from his doctor that he is sick and cannot come from Mallorca. But two days later he is in Vienna presenting his book. When he does come to court, the judge suggests maybe he should apologize to me and get it over with. And what does he tell the judge? "Shortly before my death, I will apologize for this."

'The man hates me, but I am not a hater,' insisted Simon, two years Kreisky's senior, but in much better health. 'Still, for this apology, I will wait around.' He was still waiting when Bruno Kreisky died of heart failure in Vienna on 29 July 1990, at the age of seventy-nine.

– 34 –

Waldheim the conscience

Throughout the 1970s and most of the 1980s, Simon Wiesenthal wrestled with Jewish self-hate in the person of Bruno Kreisky, his most formidable and dangerous postwar enemy. In the second half of the eighties and well into the nineties, having outlasted Kreisky, his most formidable challenge was Jewish overkill. It took the form of the American Jewish Congress in New York and the Simon Wiesenthal Centre for Holocaust Studies in Los Angeles. And it took the face of Kurt Waldheim, about whom Wiesenthal personally made a principled stand which cost him Stateside lecture bookings, a rift with his own Wiesenthal Centre, and maybe even the Nobel Peace Prize. But, thanks to adept manoeuvring on his part as he turned eighty, he won respect, and even reverence, from his fellow Austrians.

As a diplomat and politician for most of his life, and as Secretary General of the United Nations for a decade, Kurt Waldheim was all things to all people. After all the twists and turns that took him in 1986 to both the Presidency of Austria and the summit of opprobrium, there are, according to Simon Wiesenthal, two things Waldheim never was: a Nazi or a war criminal.

'I must be the conscience of the world,' Kurt Waldheim proclaimed shortly after he was elected head of the UN in late 1971. *Conscience* was, in retrospect, an appropriate choice of word by Waldheim. At its old French and Latin literal roots, the word means 'with knowing'. In Waldheim's native German, however, the word *Mitwisser* (literally, 'with-knower') means 'accessory'.

His entry in the 1972 edition of *Who's Who in Austria* had at least one major omission:

Waldheim, Kurt, b. 21 December 1918, St Andrä-Wördern, Austria; s. of Walter W., civil servant, and Josefine W. n. Petrasch; m. 1944 Elisabeth Ritschel; **Educ.:** High Sch., Graduation from Consular Academy 1939; doctor of laws 1944; **Career:** entered Foreign service 1945; 1948–51 First Secretary Austrian Embassy Paris; 1951–55 Chief of Personnel Department, Foreign Ministry; 1955–56 Permanent Observer to the United Nations; 1956–58 Envoy in Canada; 1958–60 Ambassador to Canada; 1960–62 Head of Political Division West, Foreign ministry; 1962–64 Head of Political Section, Foreign Office; June 1964–January 1968 Ambassador to the United Nations; 1968–70 Federal Minister of Foreign Affairs; 1970–71 Ambassador to the United Nations; 1971– Secretary General of the United Nations.

This impressive record was followed by sixteen lines of awards. There was no mention of military service in World War II. I had heard that Waldheim had served in the German Army, but was not a Nazi. Since a friend of mine in New York had written that 'it's bizarre to listen to the UN these days and hear it presided over by a man who speaks English with the same accent as Paul Henreid', I made a note to fill in the wartime gap when I interviewed Waldheim in the summer of 1972 at his country home on the Attersee, a mountain lake in the Salzkammergut region of Austria.

Not that the omission was alarming. *Who's Who in Austria* had also neglected to mention Waldheim's 1971 campaign for the Presidency of Austria as candidate of the People's Party (so the post-war Blacks call themselves) against the beloved Socialist incumbent, Franz Jonas. Although I had just arrived in Austria, one could sense that Waldheim was destined to lose. 'He's a good man – too good to be President of Austria', I kept hearing, sometimes followed by 'He's too stiff' or 'He spends too much time outside of Austria.' When Waldheim did lose, the only surprise was that the margin was close, with Waldheim winning 47.2 per cent of the vote.

Losing that election was one of the best things that ever happened to Waldheim, for it made him available that autumn when the UN chose a successor to U Thant, who was bowing out of the $62,500-a-year post with a bleeding ulcer. As a compromise candidate whose most publicized qualification was his inoffensiveness to the five permanent members of the Security Council – Britain, France, the US, the Soviet Union, and newly arrived Red China –

Waldheim was expected to be as passive as his Buddhist predecessor. But nobody who knew him expected him to tiptoe in U Thant's footsteps.

To *Newsweek* cartoonist Ranan Lurie, Waldheim admitted at a sitting: 'Yes, I know I am colourless. But I must emphasize: I am not passive. If people were to look into my private life and my background, they would find out that I *have* to be active . . . However, I know from experience that you cannot force issues. I must be careful – but please let us not interpret caution as cowardice.' While questioning him, Lurie noted: 'He takes time to think out his reply. He is a sincere and open man; he does not try to evade questions.'

In Austria in 1986, as the Presidential election neared, two jokes surfaced in the anti-Waldheim campaign: a definition of 'Waldheimer's Disease: you grow so senile you forget you were a Nazi' and 'the man is so thick-skinned that he doesn't need a backbone to stand erect.' Neither was accurate, but it took four decades to fill in the gaps in Waldheim's biography – and autobiographies.

For Kurt Waldheim, the war really began where he often implied it ended: in the 1941 campaign against Russia after Hitler betrayed Stalin and the 'non-aggression' pact their two dictatorships had signed in August 1939, just days before they had invaded, divided, and gobbled up Poland. At 3 a.m. on 22 June 1941, Lieutenant Waldheim and his cavalry unit and their horses plunged into the River Bug – which had served as the dividing line between the German and Soviet zones of occupied Poland – and made their way across the water into the city of Brest-Litovsk. After four days of 'sanitizing' the Byelorussian city by wiping out snipers in its streets, sharpshooters in its citadel, and a Red Army squadron holed up in its railway station's cellar, Waldheim's mounted reconnaissance unit AA45 moved eastward.

By October, when the first snows fell and AA45 had been depleted by many casualties, Waldheim had received two medals and was put in charge of his division's First Mounted Squadron: 244 horses and 242 soldiers. In November, the temperature fell below zero – and stayed there. As Napoleon found out in 1812 and Hitler was about to learn, the Russian winter works to no invader's advantage.

At the beginning of December, when his division reached the area south-west of Orel, it was surrounded by the Red Army.

On Wednesday, 10 December 1941 – three days after the Japanese attack on Pearl Harbor and a day before Germany and Italy would declare war on the United States – a Russian grenade exploded near Waldheim and a splinter of it wounded him in the right leg. He was evacuated by sled, with an orderly trying to wash his wound in the snow and urging him to move his leg, despite the pain, to avoid losing it to frostbite. It was eight days before he and ninety other casualties reached a field hospital after German troops had punched a hole in the Russian encirclement. By then, the wound was infected. Though semi-conscious, Waldheim woke up when the first doctor to examine him said: 'I think I'm going to have to amputate the leg. If only I had real wool to wrap it in, then the surgeon might be able to save it.'

'I have real wool,' said Waldheim, reaching into his knapsack and producing a cherished scarf which a Dutch classmate at the Consular Academy, Susanne Kempers, had once improvised for him.

When he was anaesthetized for surgery, there was still some question whether he would come out of it with both legs. But he awoke to the lilting accent of a Viennese surgeon saying: 'My boy, one more day and your leg would have been gone.'

The Russians were advancing on the field hospital when Lieutenant Waldheim, successfully operated on, was to be evacuated on the last hospital train out. In a 1988 interview with me, he recalled his departure vividly: 'I was lying on the ground on straw, but just when the medical orderlies came to pick me up and carry me to the train, the doctor said: "Look, the man behind you has lost his leg. Your wound is not so bad. Would you agree to our taking him instead of you?" The man was shouting with heavy pain, so I couldn't say no. Then I lay back and waited to be captured. But, hours later, at four o'clock in the morning, suddenly somebody came in and said: "There's another train. It's not a hospital train, but a cattle train and we'll try getting the wounded people out on it if that's all right with you."' Relieved to travel westward cattle-class rather than eastward as a POW of the Russians, Waldheim was 'lifted on to a stretcher and so I was also rescued, but I couldn't know that beforehand. So you see, this was something that impressed me, shocked me, and concerned me directly: would I survive or not? And this I can remember as fresh as if it happened yesterday.'

This crucial episode does not appear in any of his memoirs. In 1985's *In the Eye of the Storm*, Waldheim wrote:

> I was evacuated home, but it took several months in a sanatorium in the mountains before my leg started to heal properly. I walked with a bad limp, and, to my undisguised relief, was discharged from further service at the front. I made a formal request to be permitted to resume my law studies . . . and, rather to my surprise, this was granted. I still had my pay as lieutenant and this helped to see me through.

And, in an earlier book, *The Challenge of Peace* (1977):

> The knowledge that I was serving in the German army was hard to bear. Deliverance from my bitter situation came when our unit moved into active combat on the Eastern front in 1941. I was wounded in the leg and medically discharged.

'It was impossible to leave Austria,' Kurt Waldheim wrote disarmingly and deceptively in *In the Eye of the Storm*:

> The borders had been closed and were heavily patrolled. Even ordinary movements were restricted and the authorities dealt arbitrarily with anyone who did not conform to the regulations. This complicated my studies for a doctorate in law because the university library had been dispersed as a result of the bombing raids and the books and documents I needed had been hidden in obscure and often widely scattered places. I had to dig out the information for my dissertation . . . in bits and pieces. The physical assembly of the source material proved more exhausting than the research and the writing; I finally obtained my degree in 1944.

In response to a 1980 inquiry by Representative Stephen J. Solarz, a Democratic Congressman from New York, Waldheim replied blithely: 'I myself was wounded on the eastern front and, being incapacitated for further service at the front, resumed my law studies at Vienna University, where I graduated in 1944.'

What Waldheim failed to mention both times (and on numerous other occasions) was that, between the beginning of 1942 and 14 April 1944, the date he received his Doctor of Laws degree, he spent no more than eight of those twenty-seven and a half months as a student. Where was he and what was he doing during the rest of that time?

In mid-March 1942, Lieutenant Waldheim completed his convalescence and returned to active duty – in Yugoslavia, which had been overrun eleven months earlier by Germany and three neighbours aligned with the Axis* through choice or necessity: Italy, Hungary, and Bulgaria. Classified as unfit for combat but qualified for staff duty, Lieutenant Waldheim was dispatched to the south central Yugoslavian town of Pljevlja, where his new unit, the Bader Combat Group, was working with the Italian Army's rugged alpine division, the Pusteria Mountain Infantry, to wipe out guerrilla resistance and its civilian support in the Dubrovnik-Sarajevo area. Since Italian was the strongest of Waldheim's three foreign languages (French and English were the others), he was put to work as an interpreter, with no command authority, in a radio truck manned by a Signal Corps team of technicians. Of his two months there, he contends: 'I committed no crime in the whole time. I sat there and the German command gave orders to the Italian units and the Italians gave messages back, so they needed someone to translate . . .'

Named after Paul Bader, the commanding general of German forces in Croatia, the Bader Combat Group was notorious for its harsh treatment of civilians as well as partisans. It had the authority to destroy villages and deport whole communities to concentration camps when sabotage occurred, or to take all males hostage and execute up to 'one hundred Serbs for each German killed, fifty Serbs for one German wounded.' Always, 'the most terrifying means of punishment' were the official guideline. A Bader Group quartermaster's report dated 20 May 1942 shows that, under German supervision, the Italian Pusteria Division turned 488 Yugoslav civilians over to the SS in Sarajevo for deportation to Norway as slave labour.

There is no evidence, however, that Lieutenant Waldheim and his communications team were ever present at deportations or

*Axis: a term stemming from the expression 'Rome-Berlin axis', referring to a 1936 accord between Hitler and Mussolini; later applied to the military alliance of Germany, Italy, and Japan with the on-and-off adherence of Hungary, Romania, Bulgaria, and the puppet states of Slovakia and Croatia.

'pacification operations'. In fact, what little is known portrays a relatively peaceful and sometimes conversationally daring twenty-three-year-old making the best of a faintly threatening assignment in the hinterlands. From Italian witnesses, we learn that he was well liked in Pljevjla, particularly by one of the daughters of the Rabrenovic family, in whose home he was billeted; from Yugoslav witnesses, that he was generous in sharing chocolates with the natives; and, from various eye-witnesses, that he was seen playing cards and chatting by candlelight with General Giovanni Esposito, chief of the Pusteria Division, over tea in a local pastry shop. Most remarkably, in a 1987 military history of Italy's campaigns in the area between 1941 and 1943, Giacomo Scoti writes:

> Many of our officers who belonged to the Pusteria Alpine Division remember Lt Kurt Waldheim with fondness due to his astonishing anti-Nazi position. Capt. Giuseppe Trabattoni, [now a] notary in Milan, recalls that the statements and attitudes of the young German liaison officer created a certain embarrassment and much concern among his interlocutors who were not used to discussing politics in public. Kurt Waldheim was also liked by our Alpinists for his cordial and informal behaviour, as is reported in the diary of Corporal Pompeo De Poli from Belluno.

De Poli's diary tells how Waldheim's mobile unit pulled into an Italian base at Cajnice for a couple of days. As soon as the team of four Germans disembarked, Lieutenant Waldheim was invited to the officers' mess, but insisted on eating with his men in the canteen: an example from which, De Poli hints, his superiors could have benefited. Be that as it may, hob-nobbing with his higher-ups and translating and transmitting radio traffic, Lieutenant Waldheim could scarcely have been unaware, as he steadfastly maintains, of what the Bader Combat Group and Pusteria Infantry Division were doing to civilians in Yugoslavia.

This was confirmed in 1988 by Zola Genazzini, an Italian former lieutenant in the division's Alpine Artillery, who remembers Waldheim in Pljevlja not only as 'the first German officer I ever saw', but also as a friend who, soon after joining the Italians, asked him at an Easter banquet whether it was true that some of the other guests had been killing civilians. In particular, Waldheim asked Genazzini whether a Major Ricci had killed captured, disarmed partisans in cold blood after a battle. When the answer was yes, Waldheim remarked that this meant General Esposito 'had not taken the necessary disciplinary provisions, measures, against these officers.' According to Genazzini, Waldheim added that he would talk to General Esposito about it.

Like so much about the recent Kurt Waldheim, this episode is a double-edged sword: used in his favour, it shows conscience, revulsion, and a desire to impose the traditional rules of war upon an immoral framework. Used against him, it indicates knowledge and awareness. In this case, the positive side of the sword so outshone the negative that I was surprised in 1989 – when I brought ex-Lieutenant Genazzini's recollection before President Waldheim for the first time he'd ever heard it – that he could not recollect Genazzini or their talk about the specific killings or, for that matter, an Easter dinner, though the name of Major Ricci struck a vague responsive chord.

'Frankly,' Waldheim told me, 'the Italian officers remember me much better than I remember them, but that's because there were so many of them and I was the only German officer there. A German colonel was supposed to be sent there as the liaison officer, but he took sick and never showed up, so although I was sent there just as an interpreter, to the Italians I was their liaison with the Germans. I wouldn't refute Genazzini's observations because the reactions sound like mine, but I wouldn't be saying the truth if I told you I remembered such a conversation.'

'Did you ever have that conversation with General Esposito?' I asked Waldheim.

'I had several conversations with General Esposito,' he replied. 'He was always very friendly to me and I always tried my best to see that there weren't any sort of retaliatory actions.' But Waldheim did not recall ever discussing Major Ricci's doings with the General and agreed with me that any lieutenant surely would remember dressing down a general for not maintaining military discipline if he had ever done so.

On the other hand, Yugoslav journalist Bozidar Dikic – to whom Waldheim in 1986 first acknowledged his 1942 presence in Pljevlja – points out that Waldheim worked inside the Pusteria Division's compound where scores of Yugoslav civilians were being held as hostages against partisan attacks. At the beginning of 1942, the Italian governor of Montenegro, General Alessandro Pircio Biroli, had decreed that, for every Italian soldier killed or wounded, fifty Yugoslavs would die. The Bader Combat Group was pressing its Italian allies to join an offensive against the partisans of communist leader Josip Broz, who had just assumed the *nom de guerre* of *Tito*, to the north and east. 'To cover up their reluctance to do battle,' says Dikic, 'the Pusteria Division carried out a bloodbath. On 4 May 1941, they shot thirty-two hostages.' Waldheim was seen by hostages from their prison windows, according to Dikic, who interviewed survivors of the Pljevlja arrests, two of whom told him that, while in custody, they saw Waldheim. 'He knew precisely about arrested civilians in the Italian prisons in Pljevlja,' Dikic insists, 'and of mass shootings of hostages.'

In mid-May 1942, its mission successfully completed, the Bader Group was dissolved. At the end of the month, Waldheim was transferred to the Command Staff of the West Bosnian Combat Group stationed in the spa of Banja Luka, some 140 miles north-west of Pljevlja. Again the mission was to liquidate partisan resistance and its civilian support – this time in the Kozara mountain range, where Tito was gathering strength.

Waldheim's new outfit was part of the German Army's 714th Infantry Regiment under the command of General Friedrich Stahl, who celebrated both his fifty-third birthday and the imminent launching of 'Operation Kozara' with a banquet in Banja Luka on Sunday, 14 June 1942. Among the ninety invitees who were serenaded with Handel's 'Water Music', the guest list showed twenty-five German officers, of whom the lowest ranked was Lt Kurt Waldheim. He was remembered by the evening's master of ceremonies, First Lt Heye Deepen, as 'shy about his slightly halting gait', but 'an upstanding young officer of uncommon politeness with Austrian charm, yet very reserved.' Also present was a Croatian minister named Oskar Turina, who was in charge of 'refugees' for the Ustashi, a fascist-inspired separatist and terrorist organization that had become the Nazi puppet government of an Independent State of Croatia in 1941. In Ustashi terms, Turina's 'refugee' work meant 'deportation' duty: euphemism within euphemism.

What was 'Operation Kozara'? A joint German-Croat sweep and purge in the summer of 1942, the entire action later came to be known as the Kozara Massacres. While thousands of partisan fighters were slaughtered in combat during late June and the first half of July, at least as many unarmed civilians were shot in 'reprisal' executions. Then, after the fighting died out on 18 July, the 'mop-up', which lasted through August, proved even more deadly. According to Mlado Stanic, a partisan commander, 'the Ustashi and the Germans destroyed everything they found that lived: chickens, cats, dogs, children, women, old folk – everyone! Anyone who somehow survived the first purge was swept away in the next wave.'

Some 68,000 people – *mostly women and children* – were deported to concentration camps set up by the Ustashi Minister of Interior, Andrija Artukovic (extradited from California, with some help from Simon and the Wiesenthal Centre, forty years after the war). Arriving prisoners were burned alive in the ovens of a converted brickyard at Jasenovac and, when that didn't alleviate overcrowding, Artukovic's ministry gave orders to poison the food of infants.

More than half the deportees never reached the makeshift Croatian concentration camps, but perished of starvation, exhaustion, and brutality during the long marches to their doom. All this was done with German approval. Captured German documents in the US National Archives in Washington praise the 'final liquidation' of 'sub-humans', carried out 'with neither pity nor mercy' because 'harshness alone can give peace to the country and only a cold heart can command what needs to be commanded in order to make this fertile godly garden of Bosnia bloom again for everybody.' Half a century later, the same language would be used by Serbs to justify genocide in Bosnia in the name of 'ethnic cleansing'.

Where was Waldheim while all this was happening with no little help from his Combat Group? For forty-four years, he never mentioned his presence in the area at all in public. Then, cornered by the press early in March 1986, he first said he'd played a minor role and knew of no war crimes or atrocities ascribed to his units. 'All I did was interpret between Italian and German commanders,' he told Reuters and the Columbia Broadcasting System (CBS).

Almost three weeks later, when his signature was found on documents mentioning casualties in the West Bosnian Division's 'mopping-up' activity (in all of Operation Kozara, only thirty-five Germans were killed and eighty-five wounded), he explained that it was routine for a staff officer to 'report on events . . . That was a perfectly normal activity and has nothing to do with atrocities or criminal acts. That was a completely correct and respectable activity . . . I was thoroughly aware of the hardness of the fighting, but . . . I never saw a partisan and never came into physical contact' with one.

Still sticking to his role as strictly an interpreter, Waldheim took to Austrian television to deny rumours that he'd been an intelligence officer interrogating prisoners and asked guilefully: 'I don't know a word of Serbo-Croatian, so with what language could I have interrogated Serbo-Croatian partisans? I was an interpreter of Italian and I don't believe there were any Italian prisoners and even fewer Germans, so the whole thing is completely far-fetched.' Nevertheless, he had listed Serbo-Croat among his language skills when applying to the Austrian Foreign Ministry after the war.

In Banja Luka, Waldheim says he served as 'a junior supply officer on temporary assignment' to the West Bosnian Combat Group. This was borne out by Ernst Wiesinger, a retired West German federal civil servant who testified in 1986 that, as an enlisted man in 1942, he had been a supply clerk for the West Bosnian Combat Group with an office in a government building next door to the Croatian State Bank in Banja Luka. In the adjoining room sat the quartermaster, a captain named Hermann Plume from the German Army Reserves, and his aide, Lieutenant Kurt Waldheim. Located in Cottbus, then in East Germany, in early 1988, the ninety-one-year-old ex-Captain Plume confirmed that Waldheim remained in Banja Luka the whole time he was stationed there.

On Wednesday, 22 July 1942 Lieutenant Kurt Waldheim was one of three members of the West Bosnian Combat Group to receive the Ustashi regime's Silver Medal of the Order of the Crown of King Zwonimir of Croatia with an oak leaf symbolizing 'courageous conduct in combat'. That the other two recipients were the paymaster and the assistant medical officer would tend to support Waldheim's claim, in May 1986, that King Zwonimir medals had been 'handed out like chocolates' to many general staff officers; so would his award's number, 916, showing how many such bonbons had already been bestowed in the medal's six months of existence. Unfortunately for his credibility, a month earlier our chocolate soldier had been saying: 'I do not remember anybody ever giving me such a medal, ever having it in my hands, and certainly never wearing it.'

Waldheim has protested: 'They cover me with garbage and then complain I stink.' In February 1988, the German weekly *Der Spiegel* printed a 'hitherto unknown' photograph taken a few days after the presentation of King Zwonimir medals. It showed a congratulatory visit by the Ustashi dictator of Croatia, Ante Pavelic, to General Stahl's headquarters in Banja Luka, with 'Lieutenant Waldheim' standing between Pavelic and Stahl the way an interpreter would. President Waldheim, however, said the man in the middle was some other officer, for he wasn't there.

That week in Banja Luka, on 27 and 28 July 1942, there was a violent round-up of some 300 local Jews, who were chased through the streets and hauled from their houses by the Ustashi. Waldheim says he knew none of this in his neighbourhood of Banja Luka, despite its being a compact community of fewer than 40,000 inhabitants. On Friday, 31 July, all the Jews of Banja Luka were deported by truck to the Jasenovac concentration camp, where to be Jewish meant instant extermination. Waldheim remembers where he was on that date: on his way to Kostajnica, a town some fifty miles away, for an inspection trip.

On 14 August, Lieutenant Waldheim was sent on a similar mission to another of his unit's outposts, in Novska. This was his last special assignment with the West Bosnian Combat Group, which was dissolved at the end of August, its grim mission accomplished.

'Look, I have the big disadvantage,' Kurt Waldheim conceded not long ago to his son, Gerhard, 'that nobody wants to put himself in my position. I was eight places in one year doing temporary work I don't care about, so if I don't remember where I was at a specific time, it's because nothing interesting happened, good or bad, and I couldn't have cared less.' Turning to me in our late 1988 interview, President Waldheim said: 'The one great problem I had to face is: if I ask you what you did half a century ago on a certain day and I ask you, "Where have you been on the twenty-fifth of July 1942?" you would have to think and probably wouldn't remember. And I didn't remember either . . . Sometimes, only by going through the files to answer some accusations could I find out on paper where I was, but I couldn't remember whether I ever really was in that village. And sometimes even today I don't know whether I was ever there. Imagine all the many villages in Yugoslavia if you go from Greece up to the Austrian border; how could I remember all these? If I was asked about the destruction of a village, then certainly I wasn't there.'

During the five months of 1942 that Lieutenant Waldheim spent in Yugoslavia on temporary duty with the Bader and West Bosnian Combat Groups, he was permanently assigned to the headquarters staff of the 12th German Army – based in Belgrade when he reported to it in March, but based in Arsakli in north-eastern Greece by the time he rejoined it in late September. His first stay in Arsakli was brief, but pleasant. On a high hill above Salonika (Thessaloniki) and overlooking an inlet of the Aegean Sea, Arsakli was a garden suburb cooled by a mountain breeze unknown to the Macedonian city below, where a German flier had recently measured the airport concrete runway's temperature at 75° Centigrade (167° Fahrenheit).

On 13 November 1942, Waldheim was granted a four-month 'study leave' to complete his work toward his law degree. He left for Austria six days later, reaching home just in time to enrol in a semi-unofficial seminar given by his favourite professor, Dr Alfred Verdross-Drossberg, at the University of Vienna. Banished from the Consular Academy after the Anschluss but narrowly retained on the University faculty, Verdross was permitted by the Nazi authorities to teach Public International Law; forbidden to give his popular course in Philosophy of Law, he gave it as a private tutorial to a handful of students who could be trusted. Among them in the winter semester of 1942–3 were Norbert Bischoff, later Austria's first postwar ambassador to Moscow; Franz König, later cardinal and Archbishop of Vienna, and Kurt Waldheim, who was promoted to First Lieutenant in the German Army while studying with the Austro-fascist, but often anti-Nazi, Professor Verdross.

Toward Christmas of 1942, the Kurt Waldheim who would write so eloquently in 1985 of how impossible it was to leave Austria during the war journeyed to occupied Holland to visit his Consular Academy classmate, Susanne Kempers. He wore civilian clothes: 'a fabulously elegant suit', she remembers, adding that it was tailor-made in Paris when he'd been stationed in France in 1940. While clothes alone did not make the man much different to her, she noted that her '*petit-bourgeois* provincial' admirer had become 'very much a cosmopolitan man of the world' since she'd seen him last. Though he thanked her for knitting the scarf that had saved his leg from amputation, his limp and his eyes told her more than he said to her in words about what he'd experienced in the interim. By bike and on foot, Susanne showed Kurt the devastation wrought by the

Germans in Amsterdam. And she told him about deportations of Jews, which had just begun.

'It's so terrible, so terrible,' he kept repeating. The next morning, at breakfast, he told her and her mother: 'If only this war will be over and I survive it, I'll devote the rest of my life to working for peace.' To this day, Susanne Kempers Lederer is convinced her old friend kept his promise.

Back in Vienna early in 1943, Waldheim asked Professor Verdross to assign him a topic for a dissertation that would fulfil the final requirement for his Doctor of Laws degree. Verdross introduced him to the writings of a nineteenth-century Prussian political theorist, Konstantin Frantz (1817–91).

In his two memoirs – *The Challenge of Peace* (1977) and *In the Eye of the Storm* (1985) – Kurt Waldheim *did* mention that he wrote his dissertation 'on the federalist principles of Konstantin Frantz'. In April 1986, during Waldheim's presidential campaign, the Wiesenthal Centre in Los Angeles announced that it had unearthed Waldheim's ninety-four-page dissertation in the Austrian National Library archives and proclaimed it to be an 'endorsement' of Nazi ideology.

While Waldheim's dissertation was neither delivered nor accepted until 1944, most of it was written in early 1943 during his 'study leave' from the Balkan front. This was also the time when Lieutenant Kurt Waldheim fell in love with a fellow law student, Elisabeth Charlotte Valerie Ritschel. Tall and pretty and pert with her tresses still in pigtails at twenty-one, she was sometimes called 'Liselotte' or 'Lilo', later 'Cissy'. Waldheim writes in his memoirs: 'Her family had been career officers in the Austro-Hungarian Empire and her father had been seriously wounded during the First World War. When his regiment was finally disbanded, he had become a modestly successful businessman.' And, Waldheim neglects to add, a member of the illegal Nazi Party in 1934.

After the Anschluss in 1938, Wilhelm Ritschel became the Nazi chief of the firm he worked for and not only took his family out of the Catholic Church, but enrolled his daughter Elisabeth, sixteen, in the League of German Maidens, the female Hitler Youth. Two years later, on 20 October 1940, Elisabeth Ritschel, having turned eighteen, applied to the Nazi Party, which granted her membership number 9027854 on 1 January 1941. The Waldheims (through their lawyer, Dr Theo Petter) claim that after she and Kurt announced their engagement later in 1943, she returned to the Church and left the Nazi Party under her fiancé's influence, but there is no record of her withdrawal.

While Lieutenant Waldheim was away from Arsakli on his highly rewarding study leave, his permanent unit, the 12th German Army, had been absorbed into Army Group E, commanded by General Alexander Löhr, an Austrian who was executed as a war criminal in Yugoslavia in 1947 for his role in the bombing of Belgrade six years earlier. On 15 January 1943, Adolf Eichmann had come to Salonika to assemble a team. Alois Brunner, his deputy in Greece; Dieter Wisliceny, his newly named representative in Salonika; Max Merten, a special envoy from Berlin, and General Löhr were chosen to implement 'the Final Solution' in Salonika. Order MV 1237, signed by Merten, required all Jews over the age of five to wear yellow stars and live in designated ghettoes. And Holocaust historian Gerald Reitlinger, author of *The Final Solution*, said in 1986 that General Löhr was 'perhaps more implicated in Jewish deportations than any other German Army commander.'

The deportation of the Jews of Salonika began in the middle of March 1943: the month Waldheim's leave ended. From mid-March to mid-May, German Army personnel commanded by General Löhr worked alongside the SS in shipping some 40,000 Greek Jews – one-fifth of the city's population – to the gas chambers of Poland. Nearly every day, some 2000 Jewish men, women, and children were crammed into German Army freight trains and hauled off to their doom. It was in Salonika that Eichmann added a lurid, but lucrative, feature to 'the Final Solution': each deportee had to pay his or her own way to the death camps; half-fare for children under ten; those under four rode free, and there were substantial reductions for the return tickets that everybody sought and nobody used. Eichmann had made elaborate arrangements with the German Ministry of Transport for the Gestapo to be billed by an official agency called the Middle European Travel Bureau, which also packaged Aryan holidays in the Greek islands and other resorts in the widening spectrum of the Third Reich at half-fare group tariffs. The 'resettlement' rate the Gestapo paid was four pfennigs per kilometre of railroad track per adult. The deportation of the Jews of Salonika cost almost two million marks, which the victims paid – first with their property and then with their lives.

In March 1986, when Waldheim first acknowledged his years of military service in the Balkans, he claimed that he had returned to duty on 31 March 1943, by flying to Salonika. But he insisted that a *New York Times* reporter who interviewed him forty-three years later was the first to tell him of the mass deportation of the Jews of Salonika, even though the assembly point for transports was directly across from the main railway station. 'I was situated up in the mountains in Arsakli,' he told the Viennese weekly *profil*. 'I swear to you that I didn't have the least thing to do with the deportation of Jews. I swear to you that I have just found out about it from the press.' Asked by the German weekly *Der Spiegel* whether he hadn't at least seen people wearing yellow stars, Waldheim replied: 'Not a one of them.'

When Colonel Roman Loos, the former chief of the German Secret Field Police in the Salonika area, heard this in 1986, he exclaimed incredulously, 'What?! He didn't know about that?! It was known to everybody!' Said Abraham Foxman of the Anti-Defamation League of B'nai B'rith: 'If he did not know what was going on . . . he was probably the world's most incompetent bureaucrat. If he knew, he is a liar.'

'Yes, he lies,' Simon Wiesenthal agreed, 'when he says he never knew about the deportation of the Jews of Salonika when he was there part of the time. How can one-fifth of a city's people disappear without someone noticing? To everything people say about him, he answers automatically "No", so sometimes he has to correct his statements. Through these lies, he loses all credibility. But that doesn't make him a war criminal, for a war criminal is a murderer too.'

In April 1986, his memory refreshed by controversy, Waldheim changed his personal military chronology to read 'returned via Tirana in early July 1943.' He now maintained that he was sent directly to the capital of Albania, which was under Italian occupation, as an interpreter. Subsequently, he produced a letter from his commander there and an affidavit from a fellow interpreter certifying Waldheim's presence in Tirana around the time he said he was there.

Waldheim's paybook also showed that, on 2 April 1943, he was in Belgrade, where he collected 1275 Yugoslavian diners in pay and expenses from Field Office 187 for Staff in Transit. One could quibble, as his critics do, that this still left him time to spend a day or more in Salonika. But a glance at a map shows it to be quite logical that Lieutenant Waldheim, while still in the Vienna area, could have been ordered to travel overland to Tirana via Belgrade, while the route from Salonika to Tirana would not have taken him anywhere near Belgrade. Besides, how much harm could he have done or seen in a few hours in Salonika? It is easy enough to believe that he didn't encounter a deportation – particularly if he wasn't there at all then. What is harder to believe is that he at first 'remembered' flying from that momentous home leave to somewhere he later said he wasn't.

– 35 –

The man who wasn't there

A photo from his forgotten-and-then-remembered 1943 Albanian assignment has done Kurt Waldheim more calculable harm than the thousands of words that have been written about his wartime work. On Saturday, 22 May of that year, Lieutenant Waldheim travelled from Tirana to Podgorica (later Titograd in Yugoslavia), a distance of less than a hundred miles, with his chief, Colonel Joachim Macholz, to co-ordinate a meeting between an Italian general and a couple of German generals. The famous picture shows four officers standing beside the wing of a plane (sometimes the wing is cropped out) after bidding farewell to one of the German generals, Rudolf Lüters, who had replaced Bader as German commander in Croatia and was about to fly off to his headquarters in Zagreb. Of the four on the ground, one is the Italian general, Ercole Roncaglia, and facing him is a *Waffen SS* General, Artur Phleps, holding an attaché case. Between them stand Colonel Macholz and Lieutenant Waldheim. The tallest, most central, and seemingly most commanding figure in the picture is the low man on the totem pole, Lieutenant Waldheim.

Waldheim's official defence, 'The White Book',* flies into a frenzy of righteous indignation reflecting the damage done by that one picture, which was unearthed by an amateur photographer in Innsbruck in 1985:

**Kurt Waldheim's Wartime Years: A Documentation* (1987), a 299-page book compiled by his son Gerhard, former Austrian Foreign Minister Karl Gruber (who hired Kurt Waldheim after the war), and two Foreign Ministry officials working for the President, Drs Ralph Scheide and Ferdinand Trauttmansdorff.

> At first, Dr Waldheim's critics attempted to present this photograph as evidence of a joint military mission shared by him and an SS general. These critics went so far as to describe the boots he wore as being part of an SS uniform. This absurd conjecture ignored the fact that most German officers wore high-top boots. In addition, Dr Waldheim was commissioned as a cavalry officer and high-top riding boots have traditionally been a standard item of a cavalry officer's uniform.

'The White Book' cites Macholz's testimony that Waldheim was there strictly as an interpreter and adds that 'in attributing to him the role of a principal because of his prominence in the photograph, his critics once again ignore the obvious: interpreters invariably appear in photographs with the principals they are serving, usually standing between them.'

To make matters worse, confronted by a *New York Times* correspondent when the celebrated photo first surfaced at the beginning of March 1986, Waldheim's initial response was: 'This is just part of a deliberate hate campaign.' Later, he would remember only that when, in translating, he softened some of Phleps' hard language exhorting the Italians to commit more manpower and energy to the war effort, the SS general – a German of Transylvanian origin – turned to him and murmured: 'You don't realize that I know Italian. Would you please translate what I say?'

Like many interpreters who serve as conduits of fast-moving conversation, Waldheim has no recollection of what he translated that day – and the same might have been true if he'd tried to recall it that very night. But there is no question that a topic of discussion at Podgorica on 22 May 1943 was Operation Black (*Unternehmen Schwarz*), which had been launched a week earlier to wipe out partisan resistance in the Yugoslav lands of Montenegro and Croatia. The 6 May operating order from the German command in Croatia had specified that 'troops must move against the hostile populace without consideration and with brutal severity.' On 23 May, the day after Waldheim was photographed with him, General Phleps, as commander of the *Waffen SS* Prinz Eugen Division, launched a clean-up of the Podgorica area. In 1986, the World Jewish Congress implied that Waldheim's chief, Colonel Macholz, stayed on to co-ordinate Italian participation in Operation Black. So where was Waldheim? His response: 'I don't remember anything.'

When Operation Black ended that June, more than 16,000 'enemies' of Germany were dead, of whom 12,000 were listed only as 'communists'. Just 1500 'enemies' were held as prisoners.

How did Kurt Waldheim evolve from a discreetly outspoken critic of the Nazi tyranny he served grudgingly as a self-described 'low-level desk lieutenant' into a passive accessory who saw no evil, heard no evil, and, if he spoke any evil, shrouded it in the kind of euphemisms ('special treatment', 'mopping-up' and 'cleansing operations', etc.) that were the coded language of the Third Reich? Robert Herzstein – a University of South Carolina historian who, working for the World Jewish Congress for ten days in March 1986, found no fewer than nineteen intelligence reports signed by Waldheim himself in the US National Archives in Washington – insists that, by the end of 1942, 'Waldheim was a highly competent, upwardly mobile, politically reliable, high level German intelligence officer.' But Markus Hartner, a non-commissioned officer who was cartographer for Army Group E in Waldheim's section, told Yugoslavian war-crimes investigators in early 1948 that, throughout the time he knew him, Waldheim 'rejected National Socialism [Nazism], not so much for social or scientific reasons, but much more for reasons of faith and conservatism.' Waldheim himself has boasted how Austrian soldiers who opposed the Anschluss greeted each other with a more Catholic '*Grüss Gott*!' instead of the official '*Heil Hitler*!' And his predecessor in the intelligence job at Arsakli, Dr Werner Schollen, a retired notary and lawyer more than four decades later, said that Waldheim used to speak openly in the officers' mess, where 'he certainly didn't have a reputation that he supported the Nazis. He was very critical about them.'

Hartner, who worked with Waldheim until 1945 and was captured at the end of the war, said that, when the new officer first arrived in Arsakli in mid-1942, 'he was not very popular owing to his volatile, unrestrained, and somewhat haughty nature', but 'later on, he became more considerate and friendly. As to myself, he treated me in a very accommodating manner since I was able to put calls through to his wife.' If this implies opportunism, it is not as devastating as former Israeli Foreign Minister Abba Eban's opinion of Waldheim's secret of subsequent success: 'Of my meetings with him, I have retained the impression that this man is living proof of the untruth of the dictum that nature abhors a vacuum. He is vacuum itself. Neuter and neutral. The opposite of an exceptional human being. He was ideal for the job of UN Secretary General, where no intellectual initiative is required.'

It is safe to say that, returning to the Balkans with his doctoral dissertation nearly completed and the girl that he'd marry constantly in mind, the young Lieutenant Waldheim had every incentive to stay alive and toe the line. Commuting between courtship in Vienna and combat zones on the fluctuating Balkan front, he had only to do 'nothing but my duty as a soldier' to stay out of trouble in wartime. For this, no unexceptional human being can be faulted. The questions that remain are not just *What were Waldheim's duties?* and *What were their consequences?*, but also the familiar American question asked of presidents from Nixon to Bush, from Watergate to Enron: *How much did he know and when did he know it?*

After reporting back to his base in Arsakli at the beginning of July 1943, First Lieutenant Waldheim was dispatched to Athens as one of three officers on the German general staff working with the 11th Italian Army in the Greek capital. From 19 July to 21 August, one of his duties was to write the staff's war diary. On 8 August, using his unit's approved terminology of referring to partisans as *bandits*, Waldheim noted:

> Appropriate instructions are being sent to the 1st Mountain Division concerning treatment of bandits. According to a new order from the *Führer*, bandits captured in battle are to be shot. Others suspected of banditry, etc., are to be taken prisoner and sent to Germany for use in labour details.

Slave labour was needed to fuel Germany's faltering war machine. Two days later, in Arsakli, General Löhr issued an order extending the net beyond the pool of suspected partisans:

> It may also be necessary to seize the entire male population – insofar as it does not have to be shot or hanged on account of participation in or support of the bandits, and insofar as it is incapable of work – and bring it to the prisoner collecting points for further transport into the Reich.

For weeks, the German Army's 1st Mountain Division – operating in the Pindus range of north-western Greece – had been seeking authorization to deport the entire male civilian populations of areas in which it was conducting sweeps against partisans. Hitler's order and Löhr's expansion of it (both of which were introduced at the postwar Nuremberg trials as evidence of wartime atrocities) hinted that the time might be at hand. On 15 August 1943, the Mountain Division radioed this message to Athens:

> From reports and Italian information, reinforced impression of heavy bandit concentrations in the area south-east of Arta. Bridgehead formations by groups seem particularly promising, for which reason scheduled clean-up operations in this area are deemed necessary. Hope of success only if all male civilians are seized and deported. . .
>
> Civilians continue to maintain waiting attitude. No doubt concerning total enemy engagement. Ioannina and Jewish Committee operating there must be regarded as centre of preparations for a resistance movement. . .

The transmission was received and certified 'correct' by Lieutenant Waldheim, who then forwarded it to the chief of the German general staff in Athens, General Heinz von Gyldenfeldt. In his reply, Gyldenfeldt told the 1st Mountain Division: 'Concerning the rounding up of the male civilian population, clarity should have been created by the recent order' of General Löhr. In other words: Go *ahead and do it, but don't blame me.*

Waldheim's 'White Book' argues with some merit and considerable acerbity that:

> . . . Dr Waldheim's critics contend that these entries make him liable for the actions of the troops operating pursuant to that order.
>
> The fact is that these entries do not indicate the initiation or implementation of any order or action, but merely show the recording by the German liaison staff of orders issued to a German unit by a higher command. Because Dr Waldheim had no role in the formulation, drafting, or issuance of these orders, he was in no position to modify their directives or to prevent their implementation.

Or, as Simon Wiesenthal put it: 'The war wouldn't have stopped if

Waldheim had protested. His chair might be empty for ten minutes, but then somebody else would be sitting in it.'

The German Army in Greece rode close herd on their balky Italian partners that summer as the Allies invaded Sicily on 10 July 1943. Mussolini was ousted and imprisoned two weeks later. His successor, Marshal Pietro Badoglio, dissolved the Fascist Party and, on 3 September in Algiers, signed an armistice with the Allies. Five days later, it was revealed that Italy had surrendered unconditionally. Freed by the Germans, Mussolini set up a fascist puppet government in northern Italy. Meanwhile, Badoglio's Italy – joining the Allies as a 'co-belligerent' – declared war on Germany.

Overnight, unreliable partners became prisoners of war in Greece – and Waldheim, with his command of the Italian language, was a go-between when his immediate superior, Lt-Col. Bruno Willers, met with his Italian counterpart to negotiate the surrender of the 11th Italian Army. After laying down their arms peaceably, the Italian troops waited, rather naïvely, for the Germans to ship them home – 'by way of Germany', they were told. There, however, tens of thousands of Italian officers and enlisted men were interned in forced labour camps.

From July in Arsakli, when his liaison team was briefed by Löhr and Gyldenfeldt on what to do if Italy suddenly left the Axis, to the end of September, when the last of the 11th Army was shipped north from Greece, Lieutenant Waldheim knew the score better than almost anybody else. Dr Hagen Fleischer, a history professor at the University of Crete who began investigating Waldheim's past the day he was named United Nations Secretary General in 1971, says he has ascertained that, after participating in the 11th Army's surrender negotiations, Waldheim 'personally interrogated Italian prisoners when the Germans, fearing the Italians would desert to . . . the underground resistance movement, embarked upon punitive operations.' Colonel Willers, however, insists to this day that Waldheim not only 'wouldn't have hurt a fly', but didn't have the authority to.

Upon his return to headquarters in Arsakli, above the city of Salonika, Waldheim became the third-ranking intelligence officer on General Löhr's staff. This, said a US Justice Department analysis in 1986, 'was no mean feat for a young lieutenant.' In a job that, at Army Group level, was held by captains or majors or even lieutenant-colonels more often than by a reserve lieutenant, Waldheim had two other first lieutenants working under him.

Waldheim's chief from late 1943 until the end of the war was another achiever: a thirty-year-old Silesian-born lieutenant-colonel named Herbert Warnstorff, who was twenty years younger than his deputy, Major Wilhelm Hammer, a Prussian reserve officer and spa director who walked with a cane thanks to a World War I wound.

Colonel Warnstorff, a successful textile manufacturer after the war, surfaced in 1986 to support Waldheim's claims that his lieutenant was a mere desk officer during their military months together. Most of the time, said Warnstorff, he let Waldheim give the daily intelligence briefing to General Löhr, who seemed more comfortable with his fellow Austrian than with Waldheim's Prussian and Silesian superiors. It soon was clear to everybody present that the tall lieutenant was the General's pet. Briefed by Warnstorff or Hammer, Löhr's first question would be, 'Where's Waldheim?' Reminded that Waldheim had gone back to Austria in late 1943 for a five-week Christmas-and-study leave, Löhr remarked with fond admiration: 'That's right. He's always studying.'

Waldheim was, indeed, revising his dissertation as well as plighting his troth to Liselotte Ritschel in Vienna. Despite political differences, the clerical-fascist family Waldheim and the Nazi family Ritschel warmed to each other and it was agreed that, if the war didn't interfere, Kurt and Cissy would marry sometime in mid-1944. Immediately after 1943's Christmas dinner at the Waldheims in Baden, the fiancé returned to active duty in Arsakli.

There, in addition to briefing General Löhr and important visitors, his duties were to gather and summarize information on enemy movements. In this job, Waldheim was, in the words of the University of Crete's Professor Fleischer (whose field of history is the German occupation of Greece), 'one of the best informed men in the German forces' with knowledge of 'virtually all aspects of the occupation of the Balkans', though Fleischer himself is guilty of scholarly over-reach when he adds that 'it is even probable that he personally attended executions in Yugoslavia.' With his access to wider information, Waldheim was also one of the first in a position to perceive that the war was lost.

University of South Carolina history professor (and World Jewish Congress researcher) Herzstein concurs that, by the end of 1943,

Waldheim 'had become a major intelligence figure in an Army Group of 300,000 men.' Dr Herzstein went on to say: 'In seventeen years of research in German bureaucratic records of that era, I have rarely come across so much responsibility in the hands of so junior an officer.' In early 1944, Lieutenant Waldheim won yet another medal: the German War Merit Cross, Second Class, with Swords, 'awarded for especially meritorious service in the zone of enemy action or for exceptional services in furthering the war effort.'

An Army Group E duty roster dated 1 December 1943 lists First Lieutenant Waldheim's other responsibilities:

> Signing the morning and evening daily intelligence reports to certify their correctness – and sometimes drafting them, too – based on information he received from the field and from his assistants . . .
>
> Personnel matters – including assessing the 'political reliability' of officers and enlisted men.
>
> Prisoner interrogation.

And 'special missions' – a catch-all euphemism which, in the Third Reich, could cover an unimaginable multitude of sins.

Waldheim denies that he ever interrogated a prisoner – insisting that, if anybody were to do such work, it would have been the job of Major Hammer, who was the counter-intelligence officer. One of his assistants, as well as ex-Colonel Warnstorff, support his claim.

It should be said here that neither this book nor any of the many books about the Waldheim affair have come up with more than circumstantial evidence against Waldheim. Nor is it likely that any future investigation will unearth a 'smoking gun' of the make so aptly described by Michael Graff – general secretary of the Austrian People's Party, whose presidential candidate Waldheim was in 1971 and 1986 – when he asserted in late 1987: 'So long as it's not proved he strangled six Jews with his own hands, no problem.' Graff had to resign for what Simon Wiesenthal protested as 'an insult to the worth of every Jew', but his cynical perception of what Waldheim's friends feared and foes hoped to find was deadly accurate.

The closest anyone has come to Graff's prescription for hard evidence against his hero was when, in 1986, a survivor of the 1944 deportations of the 2000 Jews of the north-western Greek city of Ioannina swore he had seen his brother beaten on 24 March by a

German officer he now identified as Kurt Waldheim; three other Ioannina deportees then came forth to testify that Lieutenant Waldheim had beaten them with a baton the next day in Larissa, where they were transferred from trucks to a train bound for Auschwitz. But Waldheim's military records show that, on 23 February 1944, due to thyroid trouble that had been diagnosed in January, he was granted a medical leave to go back to Austria. On 1 March, he entered the Military Treatment Centre in the mountain spa of Semmering, fifty miles from his family's home in Baden-bei-Wien, and was not released until 29 March.

While in Semmering, Waldheim put the finishing touches on his doctoral dissertation, which his fiancée – visiting him whenever she could free herself from her law classes in Vienna, sixty-five miles away – typed on a portable typewriter in a room at the nearby Hotel Panhans. Waldheim submitted his ninety-four-page thesis on Konstantin Frantz during his medical leave and, almost immediately, received a telegram from his professor: 'DISSERTATION ACCEPTED. CONGRATULATIONS. VERDROSS'. It led to another extension of Waldheim's leave – this time to receive his Doctor of Laws degree on Friday, 14 April 1944, at the University of Vienna, where his signature shows he accepted it personally. On the same day, his fiancée rejoined the Catholic Church. Two days later, Dr Kurt Waldheim returned to Arsakli.

His subsequent activities bear scrutiny, for the most formidable accusations lodged against him charge him with 'murder' and 'putting hostages to death' between April 1944 and May 1945. Astonishingly, these charges were contained in United Nations War Crimes Commission file number 79/724, a seven-page document which lay buried in the archives of UN headquarters in New York from 1948 to 1986, including the decade when Waldheim was at the helm of the world organization.

On 21 April 1944, right after Waldheim rejoined the intelligence command at Arsakli, Major Hammer issued a message estimating the number of Jews and foreigners on the Greek island of Corfu and ordering the Corps Group Ioannina to register them. On 28 April, the intelligence section of the Corps Group sent a letter to the intelligence command in Arsakli asking that the Nazi SD (Security Service) and Gestapo 'bring about implementation measures . . . for the purpose of settlement of the Jewish question' by 'evacuating' some 2000 Jews living on Corfu. On 12 May, General Löhr agreed to 'furnish transportation for an accelerated evacuation of the Jews.' On 17 June, the SS reported that 1795 Jews on Corfu had been 'seized and transported from the island' to Auschwitz, where most of them died.

Both April communications are reprinted in full in 'The White Book' (though not translated from German in its English version) and cited as clarification that, at Arsakli, deportations were dealt with exclusively by Major Hammer, the *counter*-intelligence officer, and not by Waldheim as a *military* intelligence officer.

Back on 7 April 1944, while Waldheim was still in Austria on his extended medical leave, a British 'Special Boat Squadron' of seven commandos and three Greek partisans – who had set out in a fishing boat flying a Turkish flag to raid the German-held Aegean islands of Khalki and Alimnia – were captured in a gun battle with a German patrol boat. They and their vessel were taken to the Greek island of Rhodes. The fishing boat's high-powered radio was a prize catch for German intelligence, which was able to monitor British marine and naval communications in the Aegean and eastern Mediterranean areas for several days before the British realized it was in enemy hands. The prisoners were sent on to Salonika for a fortnight of questioning – but not by Waldheim.

The interrogators sent what they had learned up the hill to Arsakli, where their report arrived on 24 April and was acknowledged with Waldheim's initial on the 'received' stamp. This is as far as Waldheim's involvement can be documented. Two days later, the intelligence section in Arsakli cabled the Commander-in-Chief South East in Belgrade that further interrogations would be 'fruitless' and to 'request decision whether prisoners now to be delivered to the SD', which meant torture, execution, or both. Six of the commandos were executed that spring. The only survivor of their ill-fated mission was the captain of the raiding party, who had been sent directly from Rhodes to a POW camp in Germany well before the death decrees were passed from Belgrade via Arsakli.

Late at night on 1 July, another British commando raid – this one on the island of Calino – met with similar results. The Germans took three prisoners: two wounded Britons and an American medic. The two Englishmen were flown to Athens, where one of them, a

Private Fishwick, died in hospital. The other, a sergeant named John Dryden, disappeared after being 'handed over to the SD in compliance with the Führer Order' of 18 October 1942 that captured Allied commandos were not to be allowed to surrender, but must be 'eliminated to the last man' – either right away or after interrogation. This post-mortem on John Dryden, dated 18 July 1944, bears Waldheim's initial.

The third captive – James Doughty, twenty-six, of Ipswich, Massachusetts, serving with the Royal Medical Corps – was taken to Salonika and interrogated, but was not turned over to the SD. Respecting his status as an unarmed non-combatant, the Germans shipped him to a POW camp in Germany. Doughty lived to contradict Waldheim in 1986, when the Austrian presidential candidate contended that 'there were no POW or partisan interrogations carried out at the Army Group command in Arsakli.' For Arsakli was precisely where Doughty was interrogated in July 1944, his lawyer told the World Jewish Congress almost forty-two years later. And the intelligence unit's monthly activity report for July 1944 – initialled by Waldheim – lists among its achievements 'interrogation of prisoners of the Anglo-American mission in Greece.'

This boast, like the various other initiallings, in no way implies involvement by Waldheim. Two British investigations of these and other commando cases have upheld him. In 1986, the Foreign Secretary declared that there was no 'evidence of any criminal activity on the part of Lieutenant Waldheim in relation to those men' and, three years later, the Ministry of Defence affirmed that 'the then Lieutenant Waldheim was a mere junior staff officer. There is no evidence . . . of any causative, overt act or omission from which his guilt of a war crime may be inferred.'

British and American captives were, however, few and far between. The daily briefings of General Löhr or a deputy were more immediate concerns of Lieutenant Waldheim's. German military documents which the World Jewish Congress found slumbering in the US National Archives in Washington show that Lieutenant Waldheim briefed Löhr's second-in-command, General Erich Schmidt-Richberg, on 'the situation in the Mediterranean, Italy, and the Balkans' on 20 May 1944, at a meeting that also discussed 'effective' use of hostages on a train in the Peloponnesus, mainland Greece's southern peninsula, 'to ensure the security of rail transport.' To discourage the Greek resistance from firing upon or sabotaging trains under German control, the Germans would round up Greek civilians and pack them into large cages that were attached to the fronts of trains. This exposed them to any gunfire, bombings, or derailments by their own partisans.

On 25 May 1944, Waldheim wrote a memorandum that was unearthed in 1987 in a Munich archive by Professor Herzstein (this time, not working for the World Jewish Congress, but for his own 1988 book, *Waldheim: the Missing Years*). It criticized indiscriminate killings in no uncertain terms:

> The reprisal measures imposed in response to acts of sabotage and ambush have, despite their severity, failed to achieve any noteworthy success, since our own measures have been only transitory, so that the punished communities or territories soon have to be abandoned once more to the bands. On the contrary, exaggerated reprisal measures undertaken without a more precise examination of the objective situation have only caused embitterment and have been useful to the bands.

Though his stated objections were pragmatic rather than moral, this protest does Waldheim credit. But it also shows that the young lieutenant was indeed aware of what was going on. Historian Herzstein says that, in examining thousands of documents of the German forces in Greece, 'I have seen few stronger protests of this kind, and then only from the pens of far more powerful men.'

On 13 June 1944, Waldheim briefed General Schmidt-Richberg on 'the situation in the West, Italy, the Mediterranean, and the Balkans' at a meeting that also discussed civilian slave labour.

On 9 August 1944, Waldheim briefed General Schmidt-Richberg on 'the far west, Italy, France, and the situation in the Balkans.' There was also a discussion of the daily success of 'Operation Viper', a series of ruthless 'cleansing operations' in which whole villages were wiped out to intimidate resistance; some researchers suspect that 'Viper' was also a round-up of the last remaining Jews in southern Greece. The next day, General Löhr issued an order that partisan activity 'must be retaliated in every case with shooting or hanging of hostages, destruction of the surrounding localities, etc.'

On the following day, Friday, 11 August, Lieutenant Waldheim's evening intelligence report noted, 'In Athens: several communists shot during raids', and identified an area south of the port of Herakleion on the island of Crete as a centre of 'bandit activity', meaning partisan operations. Two days later, German forces launched a 'cleansing' operation south-west of Herakleion and reported (to the intelligence command in Arsakli) that they had 'destroyed two bandit villages' and 'shot to death twenty hostages.'

It could be said (and has been said) that Waldheim's intelligence function was to point a finger and other hands would pull the trigger. Three years later, his 11 August 1944 evening intelligence report would be read in open court by US prosecutors in Nuremberg as evidence in the war crimes trial of General Wilhelm List, the Belgrade-based commander-in-chief of the German Army in the Balkans, and eleven other German officers charged with mass murder of hostages and 'reprisal' destruction of hundreds of towns and villages during Operation Viper. List received a life sentence,* but little or no attention was paid to the signature on just one of many incriminating documents; Kurt Waldheim, in 1947, mattered to barely a handful of people, all in Austria.

Those people – most of all, his fiancée – were waiting eagerly for his return from Greece on 15 August 1944, on 'compassionate leave' to wed. On Saturday the 19th, between Allied bombardments, Kurt Waldheim and Elisabeth Ritschel were married by Father Georg Plank beneath the green copper dome of Vienna's baroque Karlskirche. When they set out for their honeymoon in the pilgrimage shrine and mountain resort of Mariazell, some ninety miles from Vienna, their train had hardly cleared the city when air-raid sirens sounded. 'All the passengers were hustled off and we spent our wedding night in the crowded basement of the local railway station, listening to the bombs falling overhead,' Waldheim writes in his memoirs, without hinting he was still a soldier then.

By late summer of 1944, the Axis had lost the war, but millions of lives were yet to be lost before certainty would become reality. With external enemies massing on the rim of the Third Reich's Balkan boundaries, and internal enemies gathering strength, Hitler ordered General Löhr on 1 September to evacuate the Balkan Peninsula in order to mass German defences around Hungary,

*Pardoned and released in 1953, List died in Garmisch in 1971.

Austria, Czechoslovakia, and northern Italy as buffers against invasion from south or east.

In the first week of September, a cable from Arsakli aborted the Waldheims' honeymoon in Mariazell. Lieutenant Waldheim was summoned back to duty for Army Group E's gradual withdrawal from Greece into Yugoslavia. While ending more than a fortnight ahead of schedule, all was not lost on this honeymoon that had begun with a bombardment and ended with a retreat. The bride returned to Vienna pregnant.

'From Sept. 6 [1944] until the end of the year (after then, there are no documents) we find, almost without interruption, Waldheim's signature or the initial W on the intelligence reports of Army Group E,' writes Hanspeter Born, foreign editor of the Zurich weekly *Die Weltwoche*, in his 1987 study, *Certified Correct: Kurt Waldheim*. But it was not until 12 October, the day before Löhr and his staff transferred their headquarters from Arsakli to Kosovska Mitrovica in southern Yugoslavia, that Lieutenant Waldheim was implicated in events that led both the postwar United Nations War Crimes Commission and the Yugoslav State Commission on War Crimes to accuse him of murder.

On Thursday, 12 October 1944, the lead item in Lieutenant Waldheim's morning and evening intelligence reports noted a build-up of partisan activity along the thirty-five-mile stretch of winding road between the Yugoslavian towns of Stip and Kocani on the main route of Army Group E's imminent withdrawal through Macedonia to its new base. The next day, Waldheim and Colonel Warnstorff flew to Kosovska Mitrovica in General Löhr's plane. On Saturday, 14 October, late in the afternoon, most of Army Group E commenced the 200-mile road journey through a ghostly, ghastly moon landscape where corpses of partisans had been strung up as a warning message on every second telegraph pole. But no difficulties were encountered between Stip and Kocani.

The 1947 conclusion of the Yugoslav State Commission on War Crimes that 'Kurt Waldheim, Austrian, lieutenant, military intelligence office, was a war criminal' is based on how the perils to Germans on the Stip-Kocani stretch were eradicated in response to the warnings in Waldheim's reports. For, on Group E's moving day, 14 October, German troops set fire to three villages – Krupiste, Gorni Balvan, and Dolnyi Balvan – between Stip and Kocani and executed 114 of their inhabitants.

A hundred miles up the road, Lieutenant Kurt Waldheim – who had flown over the three villages the day before when they were still living, breathing places – had already resumed what his 'White Book' calls 'factual reporting of enemy military activity' which 'served as a basis for the orientation of the high command, but not for tactical field decisions by local commanders.' In 1986, Waldheim contended that the massacres hadn't taken place until 20 October, putting an additional six days between cause and effect. When corrected hours later, he had an alibi anyway: 'At the date of these atrocities, I was not in the area.' Nobody had said he was.

More damning than any of his defences was his own report on 'enemy losses' for the month of October 1944. Found by the World Jewish Congress (WJC) in the National Archives in Washington in 1986, Waldheim's calculation was 739 'bandits' killed and ninety-four taken prisoner. According to the WJC, 'the tell-tale data in Waldheim's report is his accompanying notation that these 833 purported resistance fighters had among them only sixty-three weapons (thirteen machine-guns, forty-nine rifles, and a submachine-gun). Thus, it would appear that many, if not most, of those killed were unarmed civilians' – presumably including the 114 people murdered in the 14 October reprisals in Krupiste, Gorni Balvan, and Dolnyi Balvan.

In 1947, Yugoslavia brought to trial the commander of the 14 October 1944 killing operation between Stip and Kocani: Captain Karl-Heinz Egberts-Hilker from Reconnaissance Battalion 22 of the German Army's 22nd Infantry Division. The WJC contended that Egberts-Hilker, who was hanged in Belgrade in 1948 for arson and murder, testified that Waldheim was responsible for the reprisal murders of which Egberts-Hilker was accused, and that the order for the operation had come from Waldheim.

The President of Austria's apologists scoffed at the notion that a low-level lieutenant had such authority and pointed out that in his statement of defence Egberts-Hilker told his Yugoslav judges: 'I have acknowledged this action from the first day of my interrogation. I have emphasized that I accept the entire responsibility, and that none of my subordinates and soldiers bear any guilt. Nor have I ever tried to shift the blame to my own superiors or use the earlier mentioned "general order" as an excuse.' In this case, the defendant was referring to a Hitler order that, when German Army units were attacked by partisans, all villages from which the partisans originated should be burned and all male inhabitants between sixteen and sixty killed.

'I was amazed,' Kurt Waldheim told me in 1989, 'when I saw in that war-crime file that I was made responsible for Stip-Kocani. First of all, I couldn't remember where it was and what it was. But I had to look deeply into the matter and my son Gerhard helped me very nicely to find out that this captain who was executed was a very honest man who took all responsibility himself. Before he died, he wrote a very moving letter to his mother that I have read. It is true that he destroyed these villages – but without any knowledge on my part or anybody else's. Anyway, there were several levels of command between him and headquarters of Army Group E. He said in his defence that his unit was attacked continuously from those villages. He had the order to protect a bridge so that the German Army could use it. And since he was continuously attacked by partisans from those villages, he then gave the order to destroy them in line with the general orders he had from Hitler. He said in his defence that he did not purposely kill women and children, but he had no choice. He made it crystal clear that he had no specific order to do this, but felt he had to on the basis of the general order. But, because I mentioned these incidents does not make me responsible for them. The language that crossed my desk did not refer to human tragedy, but to "counter-actions" and "self-defence". If I had seen any of this, I might have been shocked to death, but the way it was expressed, it mentioned "losses", not women and children.'

Clearly, Waldheim could identify more with his hanged fellow officer than with the eighty-two-year-old peasant from Krupiste who told *Newsweek* in 1986 how he survived the 1944 massacre only because two dead bodies fell on top of him. 'For me,' said Risto Ognjanov, 'October fourteenth is my second birthday. It was the beginning of my second life.'

The 'White Book' introduces a 1986 statement from the colonel who was the 22nd Infantry Division's operations officer in 1944. He insists that Egberts-Hilker was out of contact with division headquarters in mid-October 1944 and 'was forced to act independently. He had not – and could not have – received an order for the reprisal action during this withdrawal, neither from the division nor from the corps or even the highest commanding authority in the whole region, Army Group E.' The colonel concludes that 'participation of Army Group E, especially of a then-young orderly officer with the rank of first lieutenant like Dr Kurt Waldheim – and thus the inference of a responsibility (on Dr Waldheim's part) for the measures set off by Captain Egberts-Hilker – is impossible.'

Most tellingly of all, the 'White Book' points out that the Yugoslav war crimes file produced by the WJC contains '*no such statement made by Captain Egberts-Hilker*' implicating Waldheim in the atrocities and that *'Dr Waldheim's name is not mentioned at all in that testimony or, for that matter, in Captain Egberts-Hilker's defence and appeal statements prior to his being executed for that very incident.'* It would indeed appear that the WJC jumped to a conclusion that the defendant must have testified against Waldheim inasmuch as two key witnesses did so at the trial:

• Major Klaus Mellinghoff, General Löhr's aide-de-camp, who listed Lieutenant Waldheim as part of the chain of command conveying Hitler's 'wish for ruthless retaliation measures against the civilian population . . . down to the troops themselves.'

• Sergeant-Major Johann Mayer, who joined Army Group E headquarters in Arsakli as a personnel clerk in April 1944: 'Lieutenant Waldheim's job was to propose to his superior, Lieutenant-Colonel Warnstorff, all actions of *Ic* (Intelligence) and to prepare all the written reports for that purpose. These reports dealt with the question of hostages, retaliation measures, and behaviour with regard to war prisoners and the civilian population.' Shortly before the German withdrawal from Greece into Yugoslavia, 'a general order was issued according to which all retaliation measures, hostage questions, etc., should no longer depend upon decisions of field commanders and other troop commanders, but on Army Group E, that is, on its *Ic* (Intelligence) staff.'

Mayer's version of his unit's chain of command was that 'proposals would be worked out by Lieutenant Waldheim and submitted to his superior, Lieutenant-Colonel Warnstorff. If the latter agreed, he forwarded them for approval to the Chief of the General Staff, General [Schmidt-]Richberg, on whose decision the validation of such orders depended. In trivial cases, when no matter of principle was involved, Lieutenant-Colonel Warnstorff himself could make the decision.'

Army Group E was based in Stari Trg, near Mitrovica, for barely a month. Pristina, the principal city of Kosovo, the Yugoslav region bordering Albania, was fifteen miles to the south. In 1988, the chief archivist of Kosovo said he had seen evidence that Kurt Waldheim was present at the execution of 104 Albanian partisans in Pristina in the autumn of 1944. He said he had seen documents about 'the massacre of 104 Albanian patriots' while visiting a Tirana archive on a 1978 trip to Albania. The insular Albanian regime did not respond to requests for confirmation.

On 15 November 1944, Army Group E withdrew another 200 miles northwest through the mountains to Sarajevo, the Bosnian capital. 'On one occasion in Sarajevo,' personnel clerk Johann Mayer testified, 'certain civilians were killed . . . in November/December 1944.' The case involved some German Army deserters who had formed an anti-fascist underground organization with some Yugoslavs. According to Mayer, '*orders for shooting them were issued by Section* Ic, *based on information from the Gestapo . . . This order was issued by the Chief of the General Staff and the Commander of the Army Group.*'

The 'White Book' points out that, when Yugoslavia submitted its case against Waldheim to the UN War Crimes Commission at the end of 1947 – by which time ex-Lieutenant Waldheim was a rising star in the Austrian Foreign Ministry – the very same testimony by Mayer was altered to read: '*They were executed according to the order given by Waldheim in retaliation for desertion from the German Army of some other persons. . .*' This later usage, however, is favoured by the WJC and other Waldheim critics.

In 1986, Kurt Waldheim's initial response to evocation of ghosts from the past (Captain Egberts-Hilker and Sergeant-Major Mayer were both dead and Major Mellinghoff has never been traced) was to clone the hanged war criminal into two different officers he never knew: an 'Eckbert-Hilcer [whom] not a single member of the surviving officers and staff of Arsakli can remember', and a 'Captain Egberts' who 'seems to have given orders for the event [the 14 October 1944 massacres between Stip and Kocani], was convicted to death, and executed in Belgrade in 1948.' Of Mellinghoff, Waldheim spoke to me (in 1989) in the present tense: 'I can't remember him and I don't know why he is so mad at me.' As for Mayer, Waldheim had 'never heard of' him in 1986. Later, acknowledging that Mayer had indeed worked at Army headquarters,

Waldheim branded the deceased a 'liar' who was just 'trying to save his skin' after being captured by Yugoslav partisans at the end of the war. Somewhat more elegantly, the 'White Book' introduced an affidavit from Mayer's Viennese widow, Rosa, who swore that, from his release from Yugoslavian custody in duly 1948 to his death in 1972, 'my husband never told me anything about First Lieutenant Waldheim and his relationship to him during the war.'

Nonetheless, the accusations were so damaging in 1986 that Gerhard Waldheim phoned Simon Wiesenthal to implore him: 'Please, can you help my father?'

'No,' said Wiesenthal, 'your father can help himself. He should call Yugoslavia – or get on the first plane to Belgrade and go there himself and say, "Look, you have these documents and you say you have more. But I feel innocent, so please open up the whole file and release everything you have about me."'

According to Wiesenthal, Gerhard said: 'My father is too proud to ask this.'

Wiesenthal did a slow burn into the telephone: 'Too proud? Too proud! People are calling him "war criminal" and "murderer", but he is too proud to ask for the truth?'

– 36 –

The denazification of Lieutenant Waldheim

'Shortly before the end of the war, I was stationed in the Trieste area,' Kurt Waldheim wrote *in the 1985 German version* of his memoir, *In the Eye of the Storm*, but *not in the 1986 English version*. 'When the German troops in Italy surrendered, I made every effort to avoid capture and reach home.'

Preceded by 'At the end of my study leave and after my leg had healed, I was recalled to military service', this paragraph gives short shrift to Lieutenant Waldheim's 1942–5 military career in the Balkans. His wartime years rate even shorter shrift in the English version, in which those three sentences were deleted for what his 'White Book' defence claims at great length were space reasons.

As partisans and Allies narrowed the German hold on Yugoslavia, General Löhr's Army Group E withdrew from Sarajevo to Nova Gradiska in February 1945 and to Zagreb a month later. There, Lieutenant Waldheim was granted leave in late March and early April to move his pregnant wife from bombarded Vienna to relative safety in the mountains of Styria. In those days of difficulty, deprivation, and destruction as the war drew to an end, the Waldheims reached the village of Ramsau by train, thumb, and foot. Soon after rejoining his unit in Zagreb and receiving his second War Merit Cross – this one First Class, with Swords – the expectant father was reassigned to an infantry division near Trieste.

The direct route from Zagreb to Trieste was already in partisan hands, so Lieutenant Waldheim detoured north into Austria by way of Klagenfurt, but still was unable to make his way south through Italy to Trieste because the German lines were cut off. Returning to Klagenfurt around 1 May 1945, when the German Army capitulated in Italy, he reported himself 'unable to reach assigned unit' and, in the absence of further instructions, made his way back to Ramsau two days after his first child, Liselotte, was delivered by a mountain midwife and three days after what he calls – *in his memoir's English version, but not in its German version* – 'Austria's liberation by the Allied forces.'

With the immediate proclamation of Austria's revived existence, the Allies ordered all German military personnel to be formally discharged by occupation authorities. On 18 May 1945, Lieutenant Waldheim joined other soldiers in the nearby town of Schladming, where they were taken into custody and trucked across the German border to an American detention camp in Bad Tölz, Bavaria. With no SS tattoo and a non-combatant's (since 1941) military history as what he called 'just a sort of clerk', Waldheim was released by the Americans in June and returned to his wife and infant daughter.

The new father found the timing of Liselotte's arrival prophetic: 'The parallel with my own birth was poignant, coming on the heels of a terrible war. I prayed that out of this long agony and immediate desolation the world might fashion an abiding peace so that Liselotte and children everywhere might never again suffer such adversity.'

After a summer living off the land in Styria and on a farm in Upper Austria, the three Waldheims made their way back to Vienna in September and moved in with his parents in suburban Baden-bei-Wien. 'The pleasures of reunion,' says Waldheim, 'were dimmed by the conditions that awaited us. My parents' house had been bombed and the windows in the part we were due to occupy had all been blown out. We blocked them up as best we could, but we all nearly froze to death that winter. Fuel was hard to come by and material for repairs non-existent, but the biggest problem was finding enough to eat. The only way we survived was to walk far into the countryside and go from farm to farm asking for any surplus they might have for sale.'

A little later, Cissy Waldheim learned that the brand-new United Nations Organization had a Children's Fund. She sought out its representative in Vienna, where starving citizens were even eating the animals in the royal zoo at Schönbrunn Palace and the nearby Lainzer Tiergarten nature preserve. From UNO, as the UN was called then (and still is in Austria), the Waldheims obtained powdered milk and baby food for Liselotte, who, when she grew up, went to work for the UN in Geneva, not because she was her father's daughter, but because she owed her life to UNICEF.

Spruced up in his best knickerbockers, his hair combed straight back, and armed with three glowing letters of recommendation from staunch anti-Nazi politicians (two Blacks and one Red) in his old home town of Tulln and a résumé that made only passing mention of military service in the 'south-east', Kurt Waldheim appeared at the Austrian Foreign Ministry in Vienna's Ballhausplatz early in the morning of Monday, 8 October 1945 – having risen well before dawn to walk seven miles from Baden to Mödling, on the outskirts of the capital, and ride a rickety tram for more than an hour into the heart of the city.

Rebuilding Austria's dismantled diplomatic corps had been entrusted by the Allies to two dynamic young resistance heroes: Karl J. Gruber, a thirty-six-year-old Tyrolean conservative, and, as his deputy, Fritz Molden, a twenty-one-year-old liberal from Vienna who would later enjoy a boom-and-bust career as a publisher of German-language bestsellers. Gruber and Molden had met in Innsbruck during the last days of the war in the struggle to save the city from destruction by the retreating Germans.

Molden was in his office when the tall young applicant with the game leg poked his head in and asked where the Personnel Office was. They chatted briefly before Waldheim headed down the hall. Having been one of the first twelve postwar candidates to sit for the stiff competitive examination of the newly reconstituted Austrian Foreign Service – and one of only four to pass – Waldheim already owned a certain star status when he walked in. Molden looked on approvingly, for Waldheim's degrees in law and diplomacy, his foreign languages (English, French, Italian, and, he acknowledged, a smattering of Serbo-Croatian), and the deferential manner in which he clothed his ambition all marked him as a man to watch.

Thus, it came as no surprise to Molden when, a few hours later, Gruber informed him that he was considering Waldheim to be his personal diplomatic secretary. Molden agreed with Gruber that Waldheim's credentials were impressive, even though both resistance fighters recognized him as, in Molden's words, 'a man who is not a hero, not the type of guy who goes into the underground.' Gruber asked Molden to investigate Waldheim's past, for he was determined to have no Nazis, communists, or other security risks in any sensitive position in the Ministry.

Molden checked out Waldheim with the Minister of Interior, an old Socialist named Oskar Helmer, as well as with the American CIC and OSS, and came back with not just a clean bill of health, but statements from Nazi files in Lower Austria about the young man's negative attitude toward Hitlerism. 'Both CIC and OSS,' Molden recalls, 'said "Go ahead. As far as we know, this man was never a Nazi."'

On the personnel form that Waldheim submitted on 3 November 1945, he answered the section on military service by filling in the blanks for *duration* with '15 Aug. 1939 to 9 May 1945' . . . *campaigns*: 'France, Russia, Balkans' . . . and *injuries*: 'large splinter in right lower leg'. Six boxes later, when asked about *membership in military clubs, alliances, associations of the Nazi Party (SS, SA, etc.),* he noted 'NS [National Socialist] Riding Corps'. This was a reference to an equestrian society organized by students at the Consular Academy in November 1938, when Waldheim was finishing up his studies there. Though they rode out of a public riding school on the Rasumofskygasse in Vienna, the riding club, like all student equestrian groups, was absorbed into the Nazi SA brownshirted storm troops sometime in 1939, but Waldheim insists he was no longer there and never wore an SA uniform. While this led to a 1985 quip by Socialist Chancellor Fred Sinowatz, Bruno Kreisky's successor, that Waldheim 'wasn't a member of the SA; only his horse was', so pervasive was the Nazi absorption of existing Austrian organizations that, forty years earlier, Waldheim's rare acknowledgement was either overlooked or dismissed.

Kurt Waldheim was given a three-month probationary appointment as Provisional Attaché in the Chancellor's Office's Department of Foreign Affairs effective 1 December 1945. With his wife and daughter, he moved in with Cissy's parents in bombed-out Vienna until they could find a flat of their own.

The denazification of Kurt Waldheim was a perfunctory affair throughout. Having been linked – however tenuously and largely by absorption – to the Nazi Student Union as well as the SA Cavalry Corps, he became Denazification Case SK235 in an administrative inquiry that the Allies had required to purge all former Nazis from the new Austrian administrative machinery.

Complete with character references from anti-Nazis and his negative 1940 Nazi evaluation plus a two-page personal statement in which he stressed the 'sportslike' character of his SA Cavalry Corps connection, the application Kurt Waldheim submitted on 25 January 1946 also contained one clear-cut mis-statement:

> Finally, I would like to state that the grant from the Austrian Chamber of Industry and Commerce to attend the Consular Academy which I had received prior to March 1938 was cancelled as a result of my invariably pro-Austrian attitude and the dismissal of my father* which had resulted from the National Socialist seizure of power.

In reality, the 200-schilling grant was one of four held up after the Anschluss for review of the nominees' Aryan and Nazi credentials. Two of them were replaced by Nazi activists, but the other two, Kurt Waldheim and Hans Schernhorst, were sustained. Waldheim received his grant two months after the Anschluss.

Early in 1946, the Austrian government's Ministerial Committee for Denazification was given three months (later extended to 30 June) to investigate the wartime pasts of 13,000 federal employees ranging from janitors to Cabinet ministers. By 29 June, when the committee had resolved not quite half its caseload and had not yet taken up SK235, the Foreign Ministry took matters into its own hands. It simply retrieved Waldheim's dossier and appointed him to the Austrian Foreign Service as a career diplomat, retroactive to 1 June. In November 1946, he was formally notified that he was neither subject to any penalties arising from former Nazi affiliations nor required to register with the government as a former Nazi.

To Simon Wiesenthal, who opposes the concepts of collective guilt *and* collective innocence, the perfunctory denazification of postwar Austria 'was almost a case of collective amnesia.' In this regard, if in no other, Kurt Waldheim was a particularly ordinary Austrian. He began practising the art of forgetting as early as mid-1946, when Gruber was preparing to represent Austria at a crucial January 1947 meeting in London of the Deputy Foreign Ministers of the Big Four powers occupying his country. High on the agenda were Yugoslavia's claims to parts of southern Carinthia

*Kurt Waldheim's father, Walter, was arrested briefly by the Nazis in 1938 and forced to resign his post as a District Inspector of Schools because of his pro-Dollfuss, Austrofascist views.

which Tito's partisan army had 'liberated' bloodily in the last days of the war in Europe, only to be chased away when British troops arrived. As he and Gruber cast about for experts to serve in the delegation, Waldheim, though eager to see England for the first time, never mentioned his own wartime experience in Yugoslavia.

Waldheim went anyway – newly promoted to the rank of Legation Secretary, which qualified him for future assignment to an Austrian embassy abroad. As the delegates convened in London, the Austrians were greeted with a well-orchestrated Yugoslavian propaganda campaign against them. Waldheim's military superior, General Löhr, was put on trial in Belgrade for atrocities committed by Army Group E. Reminding the Four Powers that Löhr was an Austrian, the Yugoslavs in London accused Austria of having fought on Hitler's side and having forcibly 'Germanized' thousands of Slovenes living in Austria's southernmost province, Carinthia. Not only did Tito's team attack Austria for protecting war criminals and rehabilitating Nazis, but, on 30 January, they denounced a star member of Gruber's delegation – Hans Piesch, the Socialist governor of Carinthia – as a Nazi collaborator and demanded his expulsion from the conference.

Having cleared and worked with him, the British and the Americans angrily defended Piesch, but the Russians insisted upon a full investigation in Austria. To make matters worse, British investigators soon learned that Piesch had indeed worked for the Nazis as an official of Heinrich Himmler's Office for Race and Settlement. Piesch was forced to resign his governorship.

Bogged down in Balkan crossfire, the deputies' conference dissolved in late February with no decision reached. The next round would be the Big Four Foreign Ministers' meeting in Moscow at the end of March. In the meantime, Yugoslavia convicted and executed General Löhr as a war criminal, but, still respecting his military status, honoured his request to be shot instead of hanged.

In Moscow in 1947, the chief of Tito's delegation, Edvard Kardelj, renewed the attack on Austria by claiming that more than eighty of Hitler's generals had been Austrians and the execution of General Löhr should be just the beginning of compliance with 1943's Moscow Declaration. Austria was also a refuge for Ustashi and other Yugoslavian Nazis, said Kardelj, who declared that 'Austria should deliver all war criminals and traitors to the nation that was the victim of their crimes or treason.' The conference ended on 24 April 1947, with no decision on the territorial question that was really at issue.

In the summer of 1947, the Yugoslav Interior Ministry in Belgrade, studying the personnel rosters of General Löhr's Army Group E, recognized that the Lieutenant Kurt Waldheim on Löhr's intelligence staff was the same tall, quiet young man now sitting at Austrian Foreign Minister Gruber's side whenever he fought off Yugoslavia's territorial claims in London and Moscow. Around the same time, Captain Egberts-Hilker was hanged in Belgrade for the 1944 massacres of 114 villagers in the German response to Lieutenant Waldheim's intelligence reports of partisan activity on the road between Stip and Kocani. And the Yugoslavs discovered that sitting in their Kalvarija-Zemun POW camp was former Army Group E personnel clerk Johann Mayer, who already had the status of an informer. To further ingratiate himself with his captors and hasten his return to Vienna, Mayer stood ready to accuse Lieutenant Waldheim of everything from ordering murders to being a pre-1938 illegal Nazi.

Seeing that they were having no luck prying Ustashi fugitives loose from Austria, the Yugoslavs decided to take their case against Waldheim to the United Nations War Crimes Commission (UNWCC) in London. But UNWCC was one of the first casualties of the Cold War: because the US and the Soviet Union were unwilling to share intelligence with each other and reluctant to entrust information to a neutral body that might share it, the Commission was due to die on 31 March 1948. It would not consider any cases submitted after 31 December 1947. With this deadline in mind, on 12 December, the Yugoslav Interior Ministry prodded the Foreign Ministry 'to make a decision on Gruber's assistant, Lieutenant Waldheim, on the basis of which he could be registered by the United Nations War Crimes Commission' and 'bear in mind that the deadline for such registration will expire at the end of this year.'

Around that time, Anton Kolendic, deputy director of the Yugoslav military delegation in Vienna, received a secret list from Belgrade of thirty 'war criminals' living in Austria. Kolendic was surprised to see the name of Kurt Waldheim, with whom he had frequent contact, fourth on the list, heavily underlined, but was unable to contribute more to the investigation than the fact that Waldheim had never even mentioned to him that he'd served in Yugoslavia during the war.

'I looked carefully through his file because it was unusually detailed,' Kolendic recalled in 1986 to Dusko Doder of the *Washington Post*. 'We'd had such lists and files coming all the time, but, in the vast majority of cases, documentation was short and weak. We'd never had such a well-documented file before. At least, I don't remember seeing one.'

As instructed by Belgrade, Kolendic passed the secret list on to his Soviet counterpart, a Colonel Gonda. So it is certain that Russia knew at least a fragment of the truth Kurt Waldheim was concealing, which made him blackmailable by Soviet intelligence. And Kolendic, at least, is 'absolutely sure' the Russians approached Waldheim. 'When you are in the intelligence business,' he told Doder, 'you have a way of knowing such things. I dealt with Gonda regularly and we became quite friendly.'

'No such attempt perceivable to Dr Waldheim was made,' presidential spokesman Gerold Christian tried to assure Doder in late 1986. 'Dr Waldheim was never approached by any country in a manner implied by your question.' Groping for confirmation, Doder could only quote an unnamed 'former intelligence operative who held the rank of colonel in the Yugoslav secret police at the time' and said that, in early 1948, the Russians told Colonel Boro Leontic, a Yugoslav intelligence liaison man, that 'Waldheim was recruited and the Yugoslavs should stop their interference.' Colonel Leontic could not be located thirty-eight years later.

On 18 December 1947, the Yugoslav State Commission for the Determination of Crimes Committed by the Occupying Forces and their Collaborators indicted Kurt Waldheim for 'murders and slaughters, executions of hostages, [and] wanton destruction and arson', holding him responsible for 'preparing, issuing, and acting upon criminal orders while his group operated in Yugoslavia.' The seven-page indictment concluded that:

> Lieutenant [Kurt] Waldheim is a war criminal responsible for the war crimes described and assessed above.
>
> Placing this war criminal under arrest is obligatory under the terms of Article 4 Paragraph V of the Yugoslav law on criminal activities against the people and the State, and his surrender to the Yugoslav authorities for trial is obligatory under the terms of the Moscow Declaration of 30 October 1943.

Eight days later, the chairman of the commission informed the Yugoslav Foreign Ministry that it had declared Waldheim, 'at this time on the staff of the Austrian Minister Dr Gruber', a war criminal and asked it to lodge the indictment with UNWCC in London 'emphasizing the special importance we attach to this registration.'

Despite their demand for Waldheim's extradition, this was not the Yugoslavs' real aim. They wanted to plant a time-bomb they could explode at the next Big Four ministers' conference to embarrass Gruber the way they had with their accusations against Governor Piesch of Carinthia. With this in mind, their goal was to persuade UNWCC to put Waldheim on its 'A' list of alleged war criminals for whom there was good reason to assume that, if tried, they would be convicted.

While the Yugoslav delegation to UNWCC was translating the indictment against Waldheim into English for a hearing in February, the same UNWCC committee that would rule on Waldheim denied a Yugoslav request to put a former German Army intelligence officer, a Lieutenant Hanzer, on the 'A' list because just the job was not proof of a war crime in the absence of actual participation. Recognizing that this ruling would weaken their case against Waldheim, the Yugoslavs altered Johann Mayer's testimony that some German Army deserters were executed on orders from Army Group E's intelligence section (with the concurrence of the chief of staff, General Schmidt-Richberg, and General Löhr himself) to *'They were executed according to the order given by Waldheim.'* Similarly, testimony by Löhr's aide-de-camp, Major Mellinghoff, that reprisals against civilians were taken 'on the basis of the highest orders. *This is also valid for the sphere of activity of Section* Ic' (the intelligence section in which Waldheim worked) was altered to 'by the German general staff and high-ranking German officers. *The same line of action was taken by the accused'* (= Waldheim).

At that time, the people bent on incriminating Waldheim at all costs of truth had no notion that he had been at Kozara and close to the powers behind still other atrocities. Says historian Herzstein succinctly, if pejoratively: 'They framed the right guy.'

At its final session on 26 February 1948, attended by British and American representatives, Committee I of UNWCC placed Kurt Waldheim on its seventy-ninth 'A' list of wanted war-crimes suspects:

one of 37,000 names on what would be a total of eighty lists. Despite their keen interest in Waldheim, the Yugoslavs presented his file with eleven other cases and didn't hint that they knew where this fugitive from their justice was living and working. Another seventy-two Czech, Dutch, and Greek cases were submitted at the same session, so it is unlikely that the Waldheim dossier received more than a minute or two's cursory attention. A month later, just before going out of business, the full United Nations War Crimes Commission approved the committee's last lists.

In April, the Central Registry of War Criminals and Security Suspects (CROWCASS) of the Allied Control Council in Berlin, which assisted in the apprehension of war criminals, received the UNWCC lists from London and routinely added Waldheim's name to its index of 69,000 wanted war criminals, suspects, and witnesses. Though the Yugoslavs rejoiced because, back in May 1945, the Allies had decreed automatic extradition for anyone whose name appeared on the CROWCASS list, they made no effort to tell the hunters of war criminals where Waldheim could be found. Their time-bomb was still ticking . . .

But it was not destined to detonate at the Big Four ministers' conferences of 1949 – or for another thirty-eight years. Dislike between Stalin and Tito had widened into a breach that led Stalin to expel Yugoslavia's communist party from the Cominform* in June and impose an economic blockade by the communist world. This, in turn, left Yugoslavia with four opponents in the Big Four and a need to woo its Western neighbours, including occupied Austria, for closer economic ties. Such nasty issues as territory and war criminals were dropped from the table and, in fact, Yugoslavia informed Austria that all her POWs would be repatriated by the end of the year. Among them was the Yugoslavs' key living witness against Waldheim, Johann Mayer, released on 22 July 1948.

There was a more immediate reason, however, why Yugoslavia didn't explode its Waldheim bombshell at the ministerial meetings. Once again, with the luck and agility that lifted him to higher plateaus

**Cominform*: Communist Information Bureau, an international organization founded by Stalin in 1946 for the exchange of data among communist parties. It was dissolved in 1956 by Nikita Khrushchev as a gesture of reconciliation with Tito.

whenever the ground beneath him started to crumble, Waldheim was The Man Who Wasn't There. For, on 14 January 1948, Gruber had granted his request to be reassigned as First Secretary of the Austrian Legation in Paris, where Gerhard Waldheim was born three months later.

'Dr Herzstein tried very hard in his book to say that I was transferred from Vienna to Paris because the Austrian government was afraid the Yugoslavs would ask for my extradition,' President Kurt Waldheim told me ruefully in 1989. 'I tried to convince him that this was not so, because Dr Gruber didn't know what was happening with my file or even that there was one – and neither did I. Besides, if they had really wanted to extradite me to Yugoslavia, it would have been easier to get me from Paris than from Vienna.'

After three happy years in Paris, Waldheim was recalled to Vienna to head the Foreign Ministry's personnel department. His new job gave him access to and control over every employee's records, including his own.

Though bureaucrats throughout history have used that power to settle scores and blackmail rivals or superiors, Waldheim might have had other aims. 'It was around this time,' writes Herzstein, 'that a vague grey mist began to descend over Kurt Waldheim's past – when the crucial years between 1941 and 1945 seemed to go missing. Among other things, it became apparent in the early 1950s that Waldheim's doctoral dissertation on Konstantin Frantz had disappeared from the library of the University of Vienna . . . The disappearance of Waldheim's dissertation was consistent with a pattern of omission that was coming to characterize Waldheim's way of dealing with his war years. Waldheim rarely, if ever, actually lied about what he had done during the war; he simply neglected to mention the awkward parts.' By 1952, his official biography contained not a word about his ever having been in the military.

In the autumn of 1955 – thanks to negotiations led by Bruno Kreisky as Secretary of State, which, in Austria, means the chief civil servant in the Foreign Ministry – the Four-Power postwar occupation ended and the newly independent nation of Austria was admitted to the United Nations. Leading its first three-man delegation into the General Assembly Hall was thirty-six-year-old Kurt Waldheim.

Early in 1968, Austria's ambassador to the United Nations was presiding over a luncheon meeting of the UN Committee on the Peaceful Uses of Outer Space at his residence on Manhattan's East Side when he was summoned to the library to take a transatlantic phone call from his Chancellor, Josef Klaus. As he left the room, Kurt Waldheim heard the American delegate remark: 'Either he is going to be dismissed or be appointed Foreign Minister.'

After a brief discussion with his wife, Cissy, Waldheim accepted the job, 'convinced that I had now reached the peak of my career' at the age of forty-nine.

In his two years as Foreign Minister, Waldheim strengthened neighbourly relations with Yugoslavia by cultivating a personal friendship with Marshal Tito, who invited him often to his island residence of Brioni and presented him with the Order of the Grand Cross of the Yugoslav Flag. As biographer Herzstein points out: 'Waldheim had now been decorated by the Fascist Pavelic and the Communist Tito; he was indeed a flexible man.'

There had been much wrangling about whether Tito knew that he was negotiating with, entertaining, decorating, and, later, supporting for UN Secretary General a man wanted for murder in Yugoslavia – and, if so, why he went on with it. In the mid-1960s, Tito's government had purchased many reels of captured German military documents from the US National Archives and, in 1967, had updated its Waldheim file from them.

Tito's son, Misha Broz, is sure his father knew about his new friend's past, but considered Waldheim's wartime actions inconsequential. Tito's long-time chief of staff, Mirko Milutinovic, confirmed that 'I knew Waldheim had been compromised', but added that 'Tito did not regard Waldheim as a war criminal.' Other experts – aware of Tito's remoteness, communism's bureaucracies, and Yugoslavia's decentralization of paperwork – find it plausible that the Waldheim dossier could have eluded the dictator's notice. Still others suspect that, after the 1968 Warsaw Pact invasion of Czechoslovakia, Tito gave his highest priority to building up relations with Austria as a bulwark against another blitzkrieg.

At the beginning of the 1970s, the tallest man in Austria was neither Chancellor Klaus nor his six-foot-three Foreign Minister Waldheim, but five-foot-eight Bruno Kreisky, who had been out of office almost four years. The Austrian public had grown to like and respect him when he was playing key roles in coalition governments and negotiating the occupying armies (particularly the Red Army) out of Austria in 1955. Now, in opposition, they had come to trust and miss him. No People's Party politician, larger or smaller, measured up to Kreisky's stature.

In the national election of 1970, when Kreisky was elected Chancellor, there was no place for Kurt Waldheim in a Socialist Cabinet. But Waldheim was offered his UN position back. No sooner did he return to work in New York, however, than he took a leave of absence and went back to Austria when the People's Party asked him to run for President in 1971 against the ailing, but ever-popular, seventy-one-year-old Socialist incumbent, Franz Jonas. Waldheim's posters then, as in 1986, proclaimed him as 'THE MAN THE WORLD TRUSTS'. But, with Austrian socialism swept forward by Kreisky's new broom, Waldheim was foredoomed to defeat. Still, his 47.2 per cent slice of the vote surpassed even his own expectations and he returned to New York with more prestige than before: a familiar silhouette now in strong contention for UN Secretary General should U Thant not seek a third term at the end of 1971.

'The trouble with the Waldheims is that they are too good to be true,' *Time* correspondent Traudl Lessing would write from Vienna a few months later, when U Thant's health ruled out the Burmese's re-election. 'Waldheim's election committee during the presidential campaign put out the most insipid stories about the candidate's shaking of rough workers' hands to make the polished Dr Waldheim come to life. There are no anecdotes, there are no dark spots. From 1939 to 1945, Dr Waldheim "never took part in active politics." As a Foreign Minister in a People's Party government and as People's Party candidate for President, he never joined the party, but remained aloof and independent. Truly, he is the man who is always there, ready to serve, willing to negotiate, but never ready to rush into battle.' Not for another fifteen years would Waldheim recast himself as The Man Who Was Never There.

It was Bruno Kreisky who put forth Kurt Waldheim for Secretary General and activated his Socialist and Third World contacts to push his candidacy. For Kreisky recognized that, as a pair of French biographers of Waldheim put it, 'the man would be useful to him. He [Kreisky] was sufficiently familiar with the world to know that a diplomat of Waldheim's type, with neither the personality nor the ability to make his personal mark, can sometimes prove to be more useful than a Metternich, especially when one is representing a small country of negligible importance on the world scene.'

The invasion of neighbouring Czechoslovakia had alarmed Kreisky to such an extent that he hoped having an Austrian at the head of the UN might give the Russians second thoughts about violating Austrian sovereignty. As it turned out, Waldheim would go this one or two better by making Vienna the world's third official UN city (after New York and Geneva) in 1979 and, with Kreisky's co-operation, planting a huge new concave orange-striped eyesore of an edifice complex for UN agencies on the shore of the Danube: enough to make even the Red Army of the Brezhnev era think thrice before swooping.

The UN Secretary General is appointed by the General Assembly upon the recommendation of the Security Council, where each of the Big Five – Britain, China, France, Russia, and the US – has veto power. The Soviets supported Gunnar Jarring of Sweden, a former ambassador to Moscow, but others ruled him out early because two of the first three Secretary Generals had been Scandinavians (Trygve Lie of Norway and Dag Hammarskjöld of Sweden). China wanted another Oriental to succeed U Thant. The Americans supported Max Jakobson of Finland: a Socialist activist, journalist, and pro-Israel Jew who faced a sure Soviet veto. 'Our Arab friends in the General Assembly,' said a Soviet delegate, 'would never vote for a Jew.'

Only France favoured Waldheim from the outset – because he spoke French. But he quickly became almost everybody's second choice. Waldheim invited the Soviet delegate, Jacob Malik, to lunch and found him talking 'in rather friendly terms about my candidacy, although he would not commit himself. A few days later, I received a clue to the Soviet attitude when he invited me back to lunch.' George Bush, then the US ambassador to the UN, termed Waldheim 'ideally equipped' for the job, which Bush's deputy, Seymour Maxwell Finger, elaborated to mean that 'no one saw him as a man of principle. We believed him to be an opportunist, but in the 1970s we wanted a Secretary General who would be malleable.' In Peking, Kreisky's ambassador, Hans Thalberg, without ever mentioning Waldheim by name, lobbied in a low key with Chou En-lai for China to abstain rather than veto.

After the second ballot, only Jakobson and Waldheim were left in contention, but the Russians vetoed Jakobson and then China changed its mind about Waldheim. On Tuesday, 21 December 1971 – Waldheim's fifty-third birthday – the Security Council recommended that he be elected Secretary General. Oddly, of all the Western nations, only Britain abstained. The next day, the General Assembly ratified the choice.

'An odourless, colourless diplomat was required, and the criteria for the choice were specific,' a high UN official told Waldheim biographers Luc Rosenzweig and Bernard Cohen. But, on the day Waldheim was elected, one young Israeli television journalist, Haim Yavin, smelled a rat when a member of the Austrian delegation whispered to him that Waldheim had a Nazi past. Having just been granted a five-minute interview, Yavin asked Waldheim point-blank: 'Did you have any links with the Nazi Party? Were you a Party member?'

Waldheim gave a big smile and shook his head, saying: 'No links of any kind. On the contrary, my family had many problems during the Nazi period. My father was a teacher and a resolute anti-Nazi – as we all were: my brother and sister as well. My father was fired from his teaching post and thrown in jail. So you can be certain that there was no reason to cherish even the slightest friendly sentiment toward the Nazis. On the contrary, we suffered under their domination.'

'When did you hear about the Holocaust and what had been done to the Jews?' Yavin asked Waldheim.

'Well, I had Jewish friends when I was in high school. Some of them live in New York and have been in touch with me. I was deeply moved when I heard about that sort of thing and couldn't believe it. But there was not much we could do.' Yes, he had served as a German officer on the Russian front, but, after being wounded in 1941, 'the good Lord helped me and I was sent back home to resume my studies.' He concluded by reminding Yavin that nobody lifted a finger when Austria was occupied by the Nazis in 1938: 'The people who criticize us today ought to remember the call for help to Austria at the time of the Anschluss.'

When his interview was aired in Israel that night, Yavin 'felt as though the sky had fallen in on me and that I had done something terrible. The broadcasting authorities and the newspapers were furious with me for having dared to put such unpleasant questions to such a friendly man.' Recalling the episode in 1986, Yavin, by then Director of Israeli Television, said the Foreign Ministry feared that such aggressive questioning might jeopardize Austria's processing of Soviet Jews emigrating through Vienna, even though the Chancellor of Austria in 1971 was Jewish.

One of George Bush's successors at the UN, Daniel Patrick Moynihan, told Bush he would have much preferred Max Jakobson: 'Our candidate was a Socialist Jew, but instead we installed a German infantry officer.' Moynihan spoke hyperbole, for Waldheim never amounted to more in the war than a cavalry officer turned desk jockey. But, for the next decade, that low-level German lieutenant would be sitting on top of the world.

– 37 –

The man at the top

As Secretary General of the United Nations, Kurt Waldheim quickly came face to face-with the 'Jewish Problem' he had sidestepped in Salonika and Austria, Russia and the Balkans. A bland speech in Montreal early in his tenure was interrupted and enlivened by a young man who stood up and read a petition asking what the UN was doing on behalf of the emigration of Soviet Jews. The Secretary General simply stood still and silent until detectives came and dragged the man from the hall, still demanding an answer. Waldheim's reply came only after his heckler was gone. 'So you see,' he told his audience primly, 'my job is not as easy as it seems.' Then he resumed reading his set speech.

A different kind of distancing took place in September 1973, when Waldheim paid an official visit to Israel and was taken, as all visitors are, to place a wreath on the Yad Vashem memorial to Jewish victims of the Holocaust. While Yad Vashem is not a place of worship, male visitors are expected to cover their heads, just as in a synagogue, when they enter the 'Tent of Remembrance', where an eternal flame burns in semi-darkness. Twice offered *yarmulkahs* (skull-caps), Waldheim declined the first and stuck the second into his pocket. According to his escort, Eichmann prosecutor Gideon Hausner, 'Waldheim was the first visitor to Yad Vashem ever to have refused to cover his head during this ceremony.'

To Jewish eyes and ears around the world, Kurt Waldheim's two terms at the helm of the United Nations coincided with the ascendancy of the Third World and an anti-Israel bias; the image of Palestine Liberation Organization leader Yasser Arafat addressing the General Assembly in 1974 while wearing a revolver holster and bullets; and, above all, the 1975 resolution equating Zionism with racism. Even though Waldheim openly opposed that resolution as doing 'serious damage to the image of the United Nations', fought to put terrorism on the General Assembly agenda after the massacre of Israeli athletes at the 1972 Summer Olympic Games, and resisted numerous Third World initiatives, he was perceived and judged by what often transpired despite him in his era. 'The Secretary General of the United Nations is faced with one simple truth,' Waldheim said. 'He has no executive power . . . All I have is moral power. I have nothing behind me. I can write letters to people, I can speak personally to governments, but I have not got the power to force anyone to do anything.' Too often, however, the messenger was equated with the message.

The Third World, in fact, had turned on Waldheim with a vengeance and, through its one superpower, China, was able to veto any possibility of a third term as his mandate ran out in 1981. Long before then, however, hints about his past began to surface in print. As early as 25 August 1973, in the *New York Times Book Review*, Shirley Hazzard mentioned Waldheim's having been 'an officer in Hitler's army on the Russian front' and was chastized by a UN spokesman for having made 'a very injurious accusation', however true. One of Waldheim's first and most persistent critics, Hazzard, an Australian-born novelist, elaborated upon Waldheim's past in the 19 January 1980 issue of the Washington magazine *The New Republic*, by alleging that Waldheim had 'taken part in the Nazi youth movement and served in Hitler's army in various campaigns including the Eastern front.' *The New Republic's* editor, Martin Peretz, repeated the accusation in his 27 September issue.

Then, on 9 October 1980, Dr Hillel Seidman, a right-wing Zionist author and activist in his eighties who had survived the Nazi camps, went to a Waldheim press conference at the UN and asked him specifically whether he had been a member of the Nazi Student Union and the SA: precisely the first charges that would surface on the front pages five and a half years later. The Secretary General replied bluntly: 'That's nonsense!' – and, when Seidman went on to allege in addition that, while serving on the Russian front, Lieutenant Waldheim had played a role in the extermination of Eastern Jews, the other journalists present dismissed him as a crank.

Back in 1980, Congressman Stephen Solarz of New York had read enough to write to the Secretary General on 26 November asking about Shirley Hazzard's accusations. That was when Waldheim replied:

> It would be odd, to say the least, if the government of the United States and all the member governments voted twice to elect me as Secretary General of the United Nations if they had been in doubt as to my character and background

and, after assuring Solarz that these 'slanderous' rumours were a 'McCarthyesque lie', added that his omission of his 1942–5 military service in the Balkans was not meant to mislead: 'All I said was that after my wound I was no longer fit for service at the front. I meant to say that I could not be sent back to the Russian front.'

Retiring with honour from the UN in early 1982 on a pension of $83,000 a year (tax free), he taught a term as Distinguished Guest Professor at Georgetown University in Washington, where he also dictated his memoirs to two research assistants working with 200 boxes of files he took with him. Then he returned to Austria, where, outside the Hotel Imperial, he was promptly knocked down by a streetcar. Waldheim was treated for shock and bruises in a hospital. And a quip around town was: 'That's what happens when you live in limousines. You no longer know how to cross the street.'

Repeatedly nominated for a Nobel Peace Prize for his efforts at the UN, Waldheim gave lectures in Europe and America and talked of visiting the four countries to which his career hadn't taken him: 'Bolivia, Swaziland, Western New Guinea, and Botswana.' But when he started addressing colleagues and former subordinates in the familiar '*Du*' form instead of the formal '*Sie*', it soon became clear he had a nearer destination in mind: the Presidential Chancellery at the Ballhausplatz end of the Hofburg, the Winter Palace of the Habsburgs.

President Kirchschläger's second term would be expiring in 1986 and he wasn't permitted to try for a third. In the spring of 1985, the opposition People's Party asked Waldheim to be its presidential candidate again, as he had been in 1971. Waldheim said he would think it over.

Kurt Waldheim announced his candidacy in September 1985. From Lake Neusiedl on the Iron Curtain with Hungary to Lake Constance on the Swiss and German borders 500 miles to the west, Austria was blanketed with posters showing Waldheim at the UN or meeting with world leaders, or else Kurt and Cissy wearing their loden against a mountain backdrop – and the recurrent slogan: 'VOTE FOR A MAN THE WORLD TRUSTS'.

Unable to coax the ageing, ailing ex-Chancellor Bruno Kreisky out of retirement to die in office ('I want to save the country the cost of a State funeral,' he declared in declining), the Socialists put forth as their presidential candidate Dr Kurt Steyrer, a decent dermatologist who had been Minister of Health and Environment since 1981 under Kreisky and his successor, Fred Sinowatz. As Steyrer spoke of lowering unemployment, increasing pensions, and improving health care, one could feel and see the crowds wilting from disenchantment with fifteen years of socialism, which, entrenched in power, was reeling from scandals involving doctored wine, high-level insurance and tax frauds, and the hypocrisy of governing in coalition with the far-right Freedom Party of ex-SS man Friedrich Peter since 1983. This had brought into Sinowatz's cabinet a boyish Defence Minister with the Wagnerian name of Friedhelm Frischenschlager, who, in early 1985, embarrassed Austria by flying to Graz to give a red-carpet welcome (and Austrian citizenship back) to SS Major Walter Reder when Italy released its last war criminal from life imprisonment for massacring the villages of Marzabotto (1830 dead) and Lunigiana (1200 dead) in 1944.

It was Frischenschlager, too, who gave the Socialists the opening they thought would torpedo Waldheim's candidacy in a matter of days. Early in 1985, the daughter of executed General Löhr persuaded Frischenschlager to honour her father with a commemorative plaque on the house where he'd lived in Vienna. In making her case, she pointed out that, after all, Kurt Waldheim had been his adjutant. Frischenschlager was impressed; like many Austrians of all party affiliations, he took this as exoneration of Löhr, not implication of Waldheim.

Honouring Löhr infuriated a Viennese historian named Georg Tidl, who went to see Michael Graff, general secretary of the People's Party, in April 1985 to tell him that their potential candidate was linked to a war criminal. Graff brushed off Tidl with disbelief and the nonchalance of a politician who would eventually find 'no problem' with Waldheim 'so long as it's not proved he strangled six Jews with his own hands.'

Tidl did some more homework and, early in 1986, dug up parts of Lieutenant Waldheim's military career file. When he phoned Wiesenthal, Simon says Tidl asked for help in proving that the German Army division with which Waldheim was wounded in Russia in 1941 had been incorporated into an SS division in 1945, which Tidl insisted (according to Wiesenthal) would make Waldheim an SS man. Wondering at this logic, Wiesenthal nonetheless checked his files and found no record of such a merger.

When Frischenschlager allowed some Air Force officers to hang another plaque honouring General Löhr on a wall of the National Defence Academy in Vienna, Tidl took his research to the Socialist Party. Sensing that their candidate, Steyrer, was slipping behind Waldheim, the Socialists listened and, apparently, bought Tidl's story. Rather than attack Waldheim frontally with it and risk losing the votes of the 'formers' (as ex-Nazis are still called in Austria), they leaked it to the World Jewish Congress in New York.

Word of Tidl's work focused the attention of Hubertus Czernin, a *profil* magazine reporter, on the gaps in Waldheim's public war record. Czernin called the candidate and asked for his permission to look up his military files in the State Archives in the interest of dispelling all the gossip that was going around. Waldheim obliged graciously, says Czernin, and dispatched his secretary to assist the journalist with the necessary clearances and clarifications.

In the archives, Czernin found not just Waldheim's complete military career record, but details of his affiliations with the SA riding club and Nazi student union. When he went to see Waldheim about them, however, the candidate simply smiled and shook his head, saying, 'No, not me, not true.' Unable to elicit any more concrete answers at that evening meeting, Czernin went out to a café with two Waldheim aides – press secretary Gerold Christian and chief of staff Peter Marboe. They sat until one in the morning. Recalling that night, Czernin told Jane Kramer of the *New Yorker* how he exclaimed to Christian and Marboe: 'Wow! Waldheim must have had terrific contacts to be able to stay in Vienna and study law for two whole years in the middle of a world war.'

Marboe and Christian were so alarmed by Czernin's intimations that he says 'they went back to Waldheim, and then Waldheim said, "Well, maybe I was only sick for two months, and maybe then I went to the Balkans." But the thing is, he would never tell the whole story and this was very annoying, because it turned out that he was one of the best-informed officers in the Balkans. He knew everything.'

Czernin published his first exposé of Waldheim in *profil* on 3 March 1986. The next day, the *New York Times* carried a front-page story by John Tagliabue of its Bonn bureau. Datelined Vienna, it appeared under the headline: 'FILES SHOW KURT WALDHEIM SERVED UNDER WAR CRIMINAL'. Tagliabue wrote that his details came not just from *profil*, but from the World Jewish Congress, 'and were corroborated independently by *The Times*.' His story continued on to most of an inside page, which also contained the famous photo of Lieutenant Waldheim standing between Italian General Roncaglia and German SS General Phleps.

Tagliabue wrote that Waldheim, 'visibly shaken', told him: 'I regret these things most deeply, but I have to repeat that it is really the first time that I hear that such things happened. I never heard or learned anything of this while I was there. I hear for the first time that there were deportations from there.'

Though this disclaimer, oft repeated, would do more to destroy Waldheim's credibility than any other single episode in the daily flood of revelations soon to follow, Tagliabue had the perception to suggest early 'that the most serious accusation against him may ultimately turn out to be that he was not forthcoming about his past.' Or, as Tidl put it: 'The only thing behind the entire story is that Waldheim never volunteered any of this.'

Asked why he left his Balkan experience out of his 1985 autobiography, *In the Eye of the Storm: A Memoir,* Waldheim cited the opening words of his preface:

> This is not a book of memoirs in the ordinary sense, nor is it a comprehensive account of events during my term of office as Secretary General of the United Nations. . .
>
> Instead I have attempted to offer some insight into my background, actions, and aspirations. Without dwelling upon the routine and frustrations that are also the hallmarks of any arduous career, I have described those events and episodes which I feel bear some significance for the course of history.

Clearly, he did not yet consider his military career one of those. 'I never said that my book made any claim to completeness,' he told

Tagliabue. 'Otherwise it would have been so boring that no one would have read it.'

Simon Wiesenthal entered the Waldheim picture on 5 March 1986, with a statement that 'I consider it highly unlikely that he was ever a member of a Nazi organization.' As usual, Wiesenthal was not talking off the top of his head, for Tidl's call had not been Simon's first inquiry into Waldheim. Back in 1978, during the Secretary General's second term in office, Israeli intelligence had asked Wiesenthal whether Waldheim had a 'brown past'. Simon had said he had nothing on him in his files, but would check elsewhere. He called Berlin and asked his old friend and admirer, Axel Springer, the media mogul, to check out Waldheim with the two prime sources there: the American-controlled Berlin Documentation Centre (BDC), repository for SS files, and the French-controlled *Wehrmacht Archive* (WASt), a depository for all German Army records. The BDC's standard report form is a checklist of sixteen Nazi organizations, starting with the SS and Nazi Party; Waldheim had belonged to none of the sixteen. A day later, WASt issued a seemingly clean bill of health, too – or, at least, a report that dwelled more on Waldheim's ill health than on his active service:

> 1939: Taken into German Army and seconded to 45th Reconnaissance Section, cavalry squadron.
>
> 1941: Served with 1st Company of Reconnaissance Section 45; wounded in right knee; hospitalized at Reserve Field Hospital in Minsk.
>
> 1942: Transferred to Reserve Hospital XIII in Vienna. Left hospital, returned to service with cavalry section. Transferred to General Staff of Army Group E.
>
> 1944: Transferred due to illness of thyroid; hospitalized at Army Rest (Spa) Hospital at Semmering. Left hospital, conditionally fit for field service and returned to unit.

Though 'General Staff of Army Group E' should have spelled Löhr to Wiesenthal, he presumed that Waldheim had been a rather sickly low-level desk officer between hospitalizations and he was not enough of a Waldheim buff to recognize that his service in the Balkans varied from his official biographies. He told the Israelis there was no evidence against Waldheim.

Now, eight years later, Wiesenthal studied *profil* and the *New York Times,* but failed to find incriminating evidence against Waldheim. 'Deportations from Greece were organized by the SS under Alois Brunner – unfortunately also an Austrian,' he pointed out. While yet another Austrian, General Löhr, might have been a party to them, Wiesenthal saw no way Waldheim could have had any personal involvement. 'Still,' he added, 'it is hard to imagine that, in his position, Waldheim knew nothing at all.' And Simon challenged Waldheim's assertion that he had no knowledge of the deportation of Jews from Greece.

The next day, Wiesenthal went to Germany to open a Holocaust exhibit in Cologne. There, Waldheim reached him by phone to thank him for his support. 'But,' says Wiesenthal, 'he was very bitter and disappointed with me that I don't believe him when he says he didn't know about the deportations from Saloniki.

'So I say to him: "All the time I have known you, I take you to be an intelligent man. This does not speak for your intelligence that 70,000 people can disappear before your eyes – there were transports of 2000 people every couple of days for weeks and months – and you know nothing." So he says he was not in Saloniki most of the time and, when he was, he was five miles away. But I say to him: "How is it possible that you as an intelligence officer were unaware of these daily events when it is a known fact that the SS regularly transmitted reports on the deportations through the office of your superiors and when it is equally a known fact that these matters were regularly discussed among all officers? The transportation officers, the food officers, they all talked about it in the officers' casino, but where were you?"'

The Simon Wiesenthal Centre in Los Angeles made public Wiesenthal's 'rebuff' of Waldheim and added ominously that it was 'currently reviewing archival material dealing with German atrocities in Yugoslavia and Greece during World War II.' But the anti-Waldheim initiative had already been seized on the East Coast – by the World Jewish Congress in New York, where executive director Elan Steinberg issued a steady barrage of press releases 'exposing' Waldheim:

'WJC RELEASES DOCUMENTATION ON WALDHEIM'S NAZI PAST'

(5 March 1986)

'UN UNDER WALDHEIM TURNED DOWN U.S. REQUEST FOR NAZI ARCHIVES' (6 March)

'COVER-UP CITED IN WALDHEIM CAMPAIGN LITERATURE' (10 March)

'WALDHEIM BOOK GIVES FALSE ACCOUNT OF WARTIME RECORD' (17 March)

In the middle of March, the World Jewish Congress hired historian Herzstein to examine files on microfilm in the Captured German Records section of the Modern Military Branch of the National Archives in Washington with regard to Waldheim. Herzstein told Eli Rosenbaum, general counsel of the WJC, that he could give the project ten days, but no more. A forty-four-year-old New York native with an Oriental-looking moustache and beard, Herzstein had been sceptical about Waldheim ever since his university gave the Secretary General an honorary degree in 1979. Reading over the guest of honour's official biography, Herzstein had wondered: 'Who gets a law degree in Germany in 1944?' But his 1986 mission, he told me, 'was the same work I've been doing since 1969' while producing such books as *The Nazis; The War that Hitler Won,* and *Adolf Hitler and the German Trauma*. 'Researching Waldheim involved the same methodology, discipline, documents, and diplomacy' in prompting archivists to suggest sources and answer questions one hadn't thought to ask.

Toward the end of Herzstein's first week in Washington, on Friday, 21 March 1986, senior archivist John Mendelsohn beckoned him over to a Recordak microfilm-reader and pointed to a blurry document on the screen. 'Your friend,' he said quietly, 'was a war criminal.'

Startled, Herzstein blinked and asked: 'What were the charges? And who made them?'

'Murder,' Mendelsohn told him tersely. 'The Yugoslavs.'

They had discovered the 1947 *Odluka* (indictment) against Waldheim.

The next day in New York, the World Jewish Congress issued an announcement headed: 'US ARMY AND UNITED NATIONS LISTED KURT WALDHEIM AS SUSPECTED NAZI WAR CRIMINAL WANTED FOR "MURDER"' in time to make the Sunday papers. Then, on Tuesday, at a crowded press conference in WJC headquarters at 1 Park Avenue in New York, Herzstein gave his findings and analyses of Waldheim's links to the Kozara battle and massacre, 'Operation Black' and other anti-partisan actions, and prisoner interrogations. At the press conference, WJC Secretary General Israel Singer proclaimed, 'Our first accusation is that Kurt Waldheim was a Nazi. We should rest our case and say that he was unfit to serve as Secretary General of the United Nations. We have proven that point beyond a shadow of a doubt.' And then, as one Secretary General denouncing another, Singer went on to say: 'We have proven as well that Kurt Waldheim is a liar. We have proven that beyond the shadow of a doubt, and he himself has contradicted himself as each new information about his past came to light in the last few weeks.'

Thus began a campaign of invective in which, to the Austrian public and much of the world, Israel Singer would come to personify the abrasive Jew bent on vengeance. In the coming months, Singer would call Kurt Waldheim 'a sleazebag' on national television and, in an interview suggesting he was blackmailable by Tito, compare him to a two-bit whore who takes a quarter here, a quarter there, and builds a clientele with two-bit favours that add up to a lot of time in bed. He gave an interview to *profil* in which he told Austrians that if they elected Waldheim as their President, every bearer of an Austrian passport would face remorseless scrutiny, contempt, and mistrust abroad. When the President of Vienna's Jewish community pleaded with Singer to moderate his language before he made a bad situation worse for Austria's Jews, Singer asked him: 'How many Jews are living in Austria?'

'Seven thousand.'

'Then just let them emigrate,' Singer replied.

A New York lawyer and one-time college professor of Viennese descent, Israel Singer had ample reason to resent and perhaps even hate Austria. When Hitler annexed Austria in 1938, even before the German troops arrived in the capital, hordes of Nazified Viennese burst into Jewish homes and shops, looting and smashing, and made the most dignified of men – among them, rabbis – drop to their hands and knees and, sometimes with mere toothbrushes, scrub pro-Schuschnigg slogans from the pavements. In a famous photo, Israel Singer's father, president of Vienna's religious Zionist community, was one of those humiliated Jewish men.

Israel Singer was born in New York City three or four years after his father fled Austria, but that photo has haunted his career. 'And he has lived to avenge that moment,' his proud mentor, Rabbi Arthur Hertzberg, told me in a Viennese wine tavern in mid-1987. Hertzberg, professor of religion at Dartmouth and vice-president of the WJC, called Singer 'an acorn I planted that grew to be an oak.'

To Simon Wiesenthal, Singer was no oak, but a thorn in the healing process. 'I'll tell you who is reviving anti-Semitism in Austria!' Wiesenthal exclaimed to journalists during the 1986 presidential campaign. 'It is not the revelations about Waldheim's past. It is an interview with Israel Singer of the World Jewish Congress, telling Austrians that Bitburg* was one bitter day for President Reagan and that if Austrians elect Waldheim, the population of Austria is going to get six years of Bitburg. They have lit a fire. You cannot make a collective threat against an entire country and then pretend you can enforce it.'

In another conversation, Simon said he was appalled when 'a young man called me to ask, "Did the Jews before 1938 act like Singer and his friends?"' And he added that Singer reminded him 'a little of Rabbi [Meir] Kahane', the Jewish Defence League militant who – on the podium of Israel's parliament, the Knesset – would rip up a red-white-red Austrian flag and declare: 'May the name of the cursed Nazi Waldheim be wiped off the face of the earth.'†

On billboards across Austria, 'THE MAN THE WORLD TRUSTS' had been joined by 'WE AUSTRIANS WILL VOTE FOR WHOMEVER WE WANT!' and a more ominous 'JETZT ERST RECHT!' (best translated as 'NOW MORE THAN EVER'), a slogan Hitler had used on *his* posters, too. To make the threat clearer, the new posters used yellow – the colour of Hitler's anti-Semitic proclamations and of the Star of David he made the Jews wear.

The entire Waldheim campaign was a glitzy Alpine exercise in American-style politicking. The Waldheim motorcade of at least five cars and twenty jump-suited young people would sweep into a town or city, set up rostrum and microphones, and distribute felt

*The German town with an SS cemetery to which the President of the United States was tricked by his German hosts into visiting in 1985.

†Kahane was shot to death by an Egyptian-American in New York City on 5 November 1990.

pens, bumper stickers, and photos of their candidate. An entertainer warmed up the waiting crowd with song and dance and topical one-liners. The local brass band played rousing oompah-oompah marches.

Enter the Waldheims on foot: she in dirndl, he in loden suit. They worked the crowd easily, shaking hands, embracing old acquaintances, cuddling babies, and handing out autographed photos of the candidate. Making their way to the flag-draped platform, they nodded and waved to a cheering public. Waldheim usually left it to the local mayor or the town's most prominent People's Party politician to proclaim that 'we will not let foreigners dictate our politics' and call for 'an end to that slandering mafia in New York.' Then Waldheim would open his arms wide in a big, empty embrace of welcome and, when the crowd quieted, call for 'a return to Christian values, diligence, decency, and love of fatherland' with brief references to 'unjust attacks' for 'having only done my duty' as a soldier. Only occasionally did he grow so specific as to say that 'it is not these gentlemen from New York – Singer, Steinberg, and Rosenbaum – who will tell the Austrian people how to vote', but whenever he harped on the Semitic sound of those three WJC officials' names, the Waldheim Sonata played better than ever.

To tumultuous applause and resounding hymn-like music, the Waldheims would recede into a Mercedes waiting beside the platform while their mop-up team supervised clean-up and payments. The advance team was already on its way to the next speaking-stop. But Waldheim's long day would not end with the last rally at 10 p.m., for that was when he would take to the transatlantic telephone for long discussions with his son Gerhard, who was doing damage-control duty in the US: debating Rabbi Hier on TV and the Op Ed pages; visiting Washington to plead his father's case with Congressmen and the State and Justice Departments, and calling in old contacts, favours, and friendships from UN days to rally support.

Sometimes there were pickets carrying signs saying 'WALDHEIM WAR CRIMINAL' and 'MEMORY GAP FOR PRESIDENT!' Beate Klarsfeld came from Paris to try to disrupt Waldheim speeches in Linz and Vienna. Capitalizing on Chancellor Sinowatz's quip that 'Waldheim wasn't a Nazi; only his horse was', hecklers hoisted a four-foot-high papier mâché horse's head with the motto: 'A HORSE THE WORLD CAN TRUST'. When the Waldheim camp came up with a new slogan,

'SLANDER MUST NOT PAY!', demonstrators showed up carrying such placards, but with the first word crossed out and replaced by either 'CRIME . . .' or 'ANTI-SEMITISM. . .' At a rally in Vienna, hoodlums in loden and lederhosen beat up the protesters while the police looked on.

The national chairman of the People's Party, Alois Mock accused the World Jewish Congress of 'despicable infamy' and 'improper intervention in Austrian affairs'. When leaflets headed 'AUSCHWITZ, TREBLINKA, MAJDANEK – NOW IT'S THE TURN OF VIENNA' arrived in the mailboxes of prominent Jews, Mock denounced the hate-sheets as forgeries. The question, 'forgeries of what?' went unanswered. A Jewish art shop shut its door and adorned it with a sign, 'CLOSED DUE TO THREATS'. Simon Wiesenthal said, 'I know of several cases of taxi-drivers refusing to take Jewish passengers', and *Der Spiegel* reported:

> Not only are insults daily occurrences, but brutal attacks are increasing. Jews have been thrown out of cabs by cab drivers and spat upon in streets.

When three drunken youths tried to beat up Rabbi Jacob Biederman, he managed to flee, but shrugged off the attack as 'nothing special'.

Armed with overkill, People's Party general secretary Graff consistently took the low road and not only criticized Austria's Jewish community for not distancing itself from the 'dishonorable fellows' of the WJC, but warned against 'provoking feelings we all don't want to have.' When journalists asked Graff whether he wasn't provoking the very emotions he professed to deplore, he snapped back: 'You're only putting us down because we have the courage to stand up to a few Jews!'

From Mallorca, Bruno Kreisky talked on the telephone to *Time's* Vienna correspondent, Traudl Lessing, and, though no admirer of Waldheim, spoke up for him against the WJC. 'An extraordinary infamy!' the seventy-five-year-old Jewish ex-Chancellor growled. But he warned Mrs Lessing not to blame Jewish circles only. 'The Americans in general have an old score to settle with Waldheim. They never accepted the fact that he had to do the bidding of the majority at the UN.' Israel, Kreisky added, had always distrusted Waldheim because of the UN's Middle East policy. As for the reaction in Austria, Kreisky predicted: 'People will simply say, "we won't allow the Jews abroad to order us about and tell us who should be our President."' Though the latest polls showed Waldheim forging steadily ahead of Steyrer, Kreisky added a compassionate afterthought for his former Foreign Ministry colleague: 'I don't quite understand why Waldheim had to get himself into this mess.'

For once, Simon Wiesenthal and Bruno Kreisky were in agreement – about the 4 May 1986 Austrian election. 'Waldheim will win with the help of the World Jewish Congress,' Simon told me when we met on 9 April 1986, at the Hotel Doral Park Avenue in New York for breakfast. 'I know how people feel. I am an Austrian, too. Foreigners don't have the right to decide who will be our President.'

Simon told me that, after Herzstein had unearthed the Yugoslav *Odluka* accusing Lieutenant Waldheim of murder, candidate Waldheim had phoned again and they had talked more than thirty minutes: 'He wanted to say he didn't know what had happened to those three villages in Yugoslavia in 1944 until the documents were released in 1986. I said I would wait for more documents. And he asked me again to please believe him that he hadn't known about the deportations from Saloniki. How could he not have known?' But Wiesenthal told Waldheim: 'When this is only a matter of whether I believe you or not, then is this an Austrian affair between you as a candidate and me as a voter. But, if it is a matter of war crimes, then it is everybody's affair – the Yugoslavs', the Americans', the world's – because people from other countries were the victims.'

Now Wiesenthal told me at his breakfast table: 'In the moment I saw that there are accusations about Yugoslavs, I immediately become engaged. The same day, I drafted a two-hundred-word telegram to the Prime Minister of Yugoslavia [then Milka Planinc]. She happened to be in Vienna at the time. And I ask her to say why they have done nothing when there are such terrible accusations. What I say in the cable is that what I am doing is not for and not against Waldheim. As a citizen of Austria, I wish to know the truth. But the next day after she gets my cable, she is saying Yugoslavia is not mixing in Austrian elections. So I tell Waldheim: "You have to tell the Yugoslavs to let the world see everything. It's in your best interest."' Wiesenthal's guess was: 'If the Yugoslavs dropped the case, the only conclusion is that they had nothing.' He had no use for the possibility of blackmail: 'If they are using him for blackmail, then his dossier would never remain in the archive so a journalist in Yugoslavia could come and look at it.'

With a sigh, Simon said he wasn't looking forward to contending with the present state of 'Waldheim hysteria' in the US: 'That a man with my reputation has not the possibility to talk with people in a logical way about Waldheim says more about the hysteria than about Waldheim. Immediately, they say: "Ah, you protect Waldheim!" And I say: I wish to know the truth. Do what you wish, I will not change my attitude since forty years. I never accuse somebody without evidence and I never play the prosecutor and the judge for the same person. My line was always: the documents must be hard, but my language moderate – because, when both are hard, my judges will think, "This is a hater." And you know that I am not.'

There was a quaver in his voice and, to dispel emotion, he glanced at his breakfast-table *New York Times* and said a little more calmly:

'Look, for me, before I was ever coming to this country, was American press and American media the eminence of fairness. But I don't see this fairness now! There are big headlines, but in the article is not the contents that makes the headline true.'

He blamed the hysteria on World Jewish Congress demagoguery and said: 'If I had worked the way they do, I would be finished two years after I start. So this press conference will not be easy. I do not look forward.'

Later, at Simon's forty-minute meeting with Javier Perez de Cuellar, Waldheim's successor at the UN – for which Rabbi Hier of the Wiesenthal Centre* had flown in from Los Angeles – Perez de Cuellar began by expressing his personal admiration for Simon's forty years' work on behalf of justice.

'First we were talking about the troubles of Kurt Waldheim,' Simon reported, 'and the Secretary General told me that they were releasing to Israel and Austria – and now the United States has

*An institution founded in Los Angeles in 1977 by Rabbi Marvin Hier (pronounced *Hire*) for Holocaust education and remembrance as well as to 'honour a person who not only did something about our subject, but dedicated his whole life since Nineteen Forty-Five to it.' The Wiesenthal Centre also serves as tangible confirmation of Simon's immortality: the work he began will go on in his name long after his lifetime.

asked and will get it, too – the documents in possession of the United Nations that date from end of 1947 to beginning of 1948. I told the Secretary General that this was only a part of the file on Kurt Waldheim and the most important files are still in Belgrade.'

Perez de Cuellar agreed to intervene in the matter – to begin with, by calling the Yugoslav ambassador. (He did, but Yugoslavia's ruling Presidium declined 'to interfere in the internal affairs of our neighbours.') 'I told Perez de Cuellar that this has not only to do with Austria and Yugoslavia,' Simon informed me later, '"You must do something for the United Nations. Was a criminal for ten years the head of the UN?"'

Then Wiesenthal and Hier raised the other issue – which Simon introduced by telling Perez de Cuellar: 'It looks to me like in a thriller: 40,000 dead bodies in a cellar. These are the documents that were started collected in 1943 in London – first through the governments-in-exile of the occupied countries of Europe and then from the Jewish Agency, which took the testimony of people who escaped from those countries; and also from the French resistance, Dutch resistance, and other resistances; from Sweden, Hungary: documents, names, and descriptions of crimes. In 1948, the United Nations War Crimes Commission was closed and the papers were put away, even though they had a big historic value. Now, almost forty years later, they cannot remain in an archive in a cellar.'*

Perez de Cuellar asked Wiesenthal to draw up a memo outlining how and to whom, other than governments, the UNWCC files might be made available. The very next day, at Perez de Cuellar's request, the Waldheim files were opened to the US, Austrian, and Israeli governments; Israel was also granted access to the files of Alois Brunner, the Austrian SS aide to Eichmann who was still living in Syria, and Hermann Klenner, an East German diplomat and former Nazi Party member who was serving as vice president of the United Nations Human Rights Commission in Geneva. Months later, the archive was opened to scholars, historians, and researchers.

*Actually, the UN archive of 40,000 sealed files on war criminals, suspects, and witnesses was on the eleventh and twelfth floors of an office building on Park Avenue South.

At his press conference, however, Wiesenthal found the New York journalists much less interested in hearing about Perez de Cuellar than about his predecessor. 'Have you come to any conclusions about Waldheim?' Simon was asked.

'How could I?' he replied. 'Look, when I receive a dossier, I don't read it like a crime novel. I look at the first and last page to see the accusation and the conclusion – and then I go back to the beginning and read it all the way through, trying to see if one leads logically to the other . . . From this [UNWCC] document here, without the full Yugoslav documentation, what we have is an accusation from 1948 and nothing more.'

'As an Austrian citizen, how do you view the latest rise in Waldheim's popularity?'

Wiesenthal paused for a moment and then replied: 'You know, sixty-five per cent of the Austrian population are born after the war or were small children. And they feel very uncomfort[able] when are coming voices from abroad that give them advices whom they should elect. They feel adult enough to choose. . .'

Asked if the World Jewish Congress was premature, Wiesenthal said yes in the light of evidence thus far. Was there evidence? 'I don't know.' Then he pointed out: 'By 1948, the Yugoslavs knew he was already a small secretary in the Austrian Foreign Ministry. And they were going after everybody they could. In 1949, the Yugoslavs claimed for a number of people in Germany and Austria and other places and they started looking for Artukovic, who has just been extradited from California. But why did they not claim for Waldheim? The answer to this can only be given in Yugoslavia.'

After more than an hour of fielding rapid-fire questions in English, Wiesenthal was tiring and the queries were repeating themselves. When the press conference was over, I congratulated Simon and said goodbye. 'They weren't as hostile as I expected,' he remarked. 'Nobody even accused me of coming to protect him.'

But the next day's *New York Daily News* headline was: 'NAZI HUNTER SAYS: "HANDS OFF KURT!"'

– 38 –

The prisoner of the Hofburg

At Simon Wiesenthal's request, the respected, sometimes revered, incumbent President of Austria, Rudolf Kirchschläger – who could truly call himself 'the man Austria trusts' – had agreed to review all the evidence for and against Waldheim and to issue some sort of preliminary evaluation before the election. On 22 April 1986, with the voting for his successor a dozen days away, Kirchschläger went on national television to deliver his conclusions after closeting himself for ten days with three sets of papers: the UN War Crimes Commission files on Kurt Waldheim; a five-hundred-page 'preliminary set' of 'war documents transmitted to me by the World Jewish Congress, mainly from US war archives', and a defence prepared by Waldheim's son Gerhard.

As a former judge, Kirchschläger told his people: 'Do not expect from me any verdict. I have no right to pronounce a guilty verdict or an acquittal. Both would contradict the constitutional principle of the rule of law.' Furthermore, he had not conducted a hearing with witnesses. Nevertheless, he declared, 'if I were placed in the position of State Prosecutor, I would not dare . . . to level charges in an ordinary court on the basis of the pieces of evidence submitted to me.'

Kirchschläger gave six principal reasons why he wouldn't go into court: the order for ruthless reprisals ('expiation measures') bore a different departmental reference number from Waldheim's branch . . . Lieutenant Waldheim was never a counter-intelligence officer, as claimed in the charges; nor was he ever deputy head of Section *Ic*, but just an aide . . . 'As an aide, he had no power vested in him to order retaliatory measures' . . . 'All this must have been known to the key witness [the late Sergeant Johann] Mayer, owing to his assignment as personnel clerk' . . . Given his circumstances as a German captive under suspicion, Mayer might well have given false testimony to improve his own situation . . . and 'finally – and this seems to be decisive for me – the Socialist Federal Republic of Yugoslavia, which was the prosecutor then, obviously has not undertaken any steps towards actual prosecution.'

Saying he had taken on the assignment 'to inject some calm into the very vehement international reporting by the mass media, which has gripped the entire Western world and, to a certain extent, the Third World as well', Kirchschläger acknowledged only partial success. 'The wave of information has acquired a life of its own, which can be contained only with great difficulty. However, the press conferences of the World Jewish Congress, which were held daily or at two-day intervals in New York, have come to an end.' Also abating, he added, were the tensions provoked by 'mass solidarity towards an action that was interpreted as external interference in the presidential election campaign', which 'inevitably also had an impact on our Jewish fellow citizens.' Here, the tall, austere outgoing President sounded a stern warning in his most teary quaver:

'Today I again beseech all fellow citizens, and primarily those who bear political responsibility, to promote with all their strength this process of bringing internal calm. Throughout our history, anti-Jewish sentiments have never brought us any benefits or blessings. In addition, they are most deeply inhumane.'

Whether one's choice was Kurt Waldheim or Kurt Steyrer – or one of the two fringe candidates: 'Greens' nominee Frieda Meissner-Blau, a fifty-seven-year-old self-styled 'child of the '68 Revolution, though I could be their mother', and 'Germanic' nominee Otto Scrinzi, sixty-eight, a psychiatrist and former SA officer favouring restoration of the death penalty and opposing all things Jewish – one couldn't help wishing that Kirchschläger, whose own 'fulfilment of duty' at the end of the war cost some 1200 Austrian teenagers their lives, could stay on for a third term.

Simon Wiesenthal had no fault to find with Kirchschläger's analysis, 'except if he thinks the World Jewish Congress has quieted down, he will surely find out other.'

Sure enough, the WJC had been quick to rejoin that 'Dr Kirchschläger's conclusion was that he could neither convict nor acquit Waldheim.' Meanwhile, in an open letter to US Secretary of State George P. Shultz and Attorney General Edwin Meese III, the WJC's president, Seagram liquor heir Edgar M. Bronfman, denounced Waldheim as 'a man who is a proven liar . . . who participated in the most cruel behaviour of the National Socialists, and who is not only unrepentant of his past activities, but still has the nerve to stand before the world as one who simply obeyed orders and runs for the Presidency of Austria.' Waldheim said he would sue.

'Waldheim's deceit knows no bounds,' said the World Jewish Congress in late April. The WJC was seeking to have Waldheim placed on the US Immigration and Naturalization Service's 'Watch List'; based on a 1978 federal statute known as the 'Holtzman Amendment', it bars entry of aliens who 'ordered, incited, assisted, or otherwise participated in the persecution of any person because of race, religion, national origin, or political opinion.' By the end of April 1986, Neal Sher, who had succeeded Allan Ryan as director of the Justice Department's Office of Special Investigations, was reported to have said that if someone less prominent than Waldheim had been involved, 'a determination of excludability would be clearly and routinely made' on the basis of evidence already at hand. The OSI recommended to Attorney General Meese that Waldheim be barred from entering the country. Meese put it under consideration – which took a year.

Of the whole commotion in the States, Wiesenthal said with a sigh: 'This is so typically American. A great big cloud rises, but nothing comes of it. These World Jewish Congress people are young fellows who have never learned to read German military documents. A lot of people who read German don't know how to read a German military document. I myself needed a few years to become acquainted with the language: to know that when somebody signed a report on the left side, it was only for the accuracy. In all the [Waldheim] documents I have seen so far, they are signed by him on the left side. There are no conclusions by him what should be done.

'These boys from the WJC, they do not differentiate between an intelligence officer and a reconnaissance man. And it's nonsense to believe that the Yugoslavs by now don't know everything that happened in the Balkans. They've utilized or archived or published the war diaries of every German unit that was ever there.'

After what Rabbi Abraham Cooper called a 'bum rap in the *Daily News* headline, which registered on lots of American Jews who don't even read the *News*, but saw it on the stands', the associate dean of the Simon Wiesenthal Centre began to argue with Simon Wiesenthal about 'how his statements were being posited in the US and Canada. So we're *shreyen* [Yiddish for *screaming*] from the Pacific Coast all the way across America, all the way across the Atlantic Ocean, and halfway across Europe to try to tell him the harm he's doing himself over here and how frustrating this was to us.'

At the other end of the satellite connection, Simon simply explained the overheated political climate in Austria and the hyperbole heard there.

'Quite frankly, Simon, our main concern is that Gerhard Waldheim is over here and he and his father's Austro-American supporters are trying to cash in on your back,' Cooper told him – and he stopped Simon in his tracks when he told him Neal Sher of the OSI had called Waldheim 'legally excludable' from the US. After Cooper had explained this part of the Holtzman Amendment to Simon, he says Simon told him: 'Look, I have full confidence in Neal Sher, so if you are telling me that under US law an alien has no rights and is guilty until proven innocent, then you do whatever you want to do in America. I am not going to address the American issue. I am just going to say what I have to say here in Austria.'

Rabbis Cooper and Hier took this as a cue to launch a postcard campaign similar to a successful one they had used in 1979 to stave off expiration of the German statute of limitations on war crimes. On the front of the 1986 model, all in black and white: the newly unearthed and already world-famous photo of Lieutenant Waldheim standing between two generals at Podgorica in 1943; a portrait of Secretary General Waldheim at his UN desk, and the headline 'AMERICA SAYS NO TO WALDHEIM!' On the back: a pre-printed message – pre-addressed to Ronald Reagan in the White House with four lines at the bottom for the sender's full name and address. The text:

> Dear Mr President:
>
> In 1947 Kurt Waldheim was charged with 'murder and slaughter' by Yugoslavia. Those charges were accepted by the UN Crimes Commission, of which the United States was a member.

> As an 'alien' Mr Waldheim does not have the right to be allowed entry into the US unless he can exonerate himself of the war crimes charges.
>
> Because of the uniqueness and magnitude of Nazi crimes, we urge your administration to enforce the letter of the law and bar Mr Waldheim from our shores.

'We gave out a million postcards,' Rabbi Hier told me that summer, 'and the White House admits to receiving 100,000, which they say is an astronomical sum on any given issue.

Simon had said nothing to me about the postcard campaign, but had made an 'I-don't-want-to-hear-about-it' grimace when I'd mentioned it, so I asked Rabbi Hier whether he'd cleared it with him first.

'No,' he replied, 'but we told him what we were doing and that this was our point of view on the matter. It's great that we can sometimes disagree on issues. I don't consider Simon a defender of Waldheim. I think he is being more cautious than we are on the Waldheim case. He's operating like a jury and we're working like a grand jury. Our obligation is just to gather the information and present it to the authorities with a recommendation. At this point in time, I think there's no reason to give Waldheim the benefit of the doubt. I refuse to do so.'

'So you're saying that the Wiesenthal Centre is independent even of Wiesenthal?'

'Yes, we are independent. We're an American organization: totally American. You know, Mr Wiesenthal is not the head of the Simon Wiesenthal Centre – and, in this case, it's very clear and it's a good thing.'

Rabbi Hier even professed admiration for the World Jewish Congress: 'They had no other option. People called them to Vienna and said, "Here are documents." If the WJC had sat on those documents and done nothing about it, the people who gave it to them would have leaked it anyway and they would have said, "Look at these guys! We've given them decent documents and they don't even want to make it public." So I don't think any Jewish organization in the world, given those documents, would have behaved differently. They'd have made them public.'

'What if they'd given them to Simon Wiesenthal?' I asked. 'Wasn't he the logical place to bring them?'

'Well, maybe as Socialists, they felt he was too close to Waldheim's party and also anti-Kreisky,' Hier answered. 'I don't know.'

Rabbi Cooper added that the feud between Wiesenthal and the WJC had 'nothing to do with fund-raising, but with all the years Nahum Goldmann and the WJC shut the door in his face and made it easier for former Nazis to be accepted. Then they shafted him on Kreisky and left him standing all alone. No wonder it's a reflex that he bristles at the mention of the World Jewish Congress. So now, where there's no smoking gun, why should he go out and raise hell for a guy like Israel Singer? – who, by the way, doesn't come across as a normal human being to Simon. He just says "this guy is a frustrated *yeshiva bucher*" – a Yiddish term for an inexperienced, unrealistic Talmudic student. To me later that year, Wiesenthal would call Singer a 'young boy building his career on this case. I just had a talk with him in New York. He tried to tell me what is a Nazi. I say to Singer: "When I am meeting my first Nazi, you are not born yet."'

As the 4 May election neared, the campaign momentum was moving in Waldheim's direction. So intense was the anti-WJC backlash ('*The Jews didn't ask us if we objected to them making Begin their Prime Minister!*') that Socialist candidate Steyrer started pleading for the past to be forgotten as he plodded through 1200 election rallies and spoke to half a million voters in the hope that if no candidate won at least fifty per cent of the ballots cast on 4 May, there would have to be a run-off election in June between the top two vote-getters. But the front runner's newest poster offered to spare the public as well as himself that further ordeal: 'WALDHEIM ON MAY 4 WILL SAVE YOU A SECOND ROUND!'

Austrian elections are held on Sundays, with voting compulsory in some provinces. When the results were tallied that night, Kurt Waldheim had 2,343,227 votes – an impressive figure in a land of seven and a half million people (many of them minors ineligible to vote), but, at 49.6 per cent, 16,000 votes short of a majority. Steyrer had 43.7 per cent. Frau Meissner-Blau polled a surprisingly strong 5.5 per cent, and Dr Scrinzi a hard-core 1.2 per cent. A run-off election between the two Kurts – Steyrer and Waldheim – was set for 8 June 1986.

'True, I have only an outside chance,' Steyrer admitted, 'but if those who didn't vote on 4 May and those who voted for the

Environmentalist candidate come into my camp, I have a good chance of winning.'

Taking no chances, a weary Waldheim resumed his barn-storming, trying to touch all the bases he'd missed in his first 1986 campaign. But it all seemed grubbier as a re-run. By now, Waldheim had a sore throat and his Paul Henreid matinee-idol voice was a chronic croak as he said over and over: 'I have always been a practising Catholic and I can tell you my religion has helped me a lot. Our generation has suffered so much [but] I shall be able to stand anything that comes now: all the defamation and the rest.'

As one correspondent noted:

> Villagers approved. They will elect the Christian candidate against the attacks of a foreign world they neither know nor care about.

Though the Israeli government had remained remarkably cool toward the Waldheim controversy, it suddenly came to a boil when Yitzhak Shamir, then the Foreign Minister, urged Austrians not to vote for Waldheim: 'The election of such a man to such a position would be a tragedy.' Once again, Waldheim was being 'victimized' by outside interference in Austrian politics and he exploited this fully. At no meeting, no press conference, no TV interview did he fail to mention the WJC or Shamir and his terrorist past.* 'The media and the World Jewish Congress can go on hunting me, but I'll go right on saying that I had no knowledge,' Waldheim insisted from the outset, often referring to his nemesis as 'that private institution, the World Jewish Congress.' He told French journalist Claire Tréan in *Le Monde*: 'But the international press is dominated by the World Jewish Congress. It's well known!'

Throughout this reprise of the first campaign, Simon Wiesenthal, too, continued to vent his ire on the World Jewish Congress for 'demonizing' Waldheim. He told interviewers: 'I don't support him. I don't believe him. I have told that to him directly, and I will not defend him. But I can't kill a reputation of forty years over an outburst of hysteria in America. I find that to accuse someone of being a war criminal, a murderer, without evidence is not in accordance with

*As a leader of the extremist Stern Gang in 1948, Shamir was accused of complicity in the assassination of the UN's Swedish mediator in Palestine, Count Folke Bernadotte.

Jewish ethics.' And he pointed out that the World Jewish Congress 'has made people believe that Waldheim was one of the biggest war criminals', while to Wiesenthal 'Waldheim is a false symbol of the Nazis. He is a liar and an opportunist, but he never was a member of the Nazi Party. And there is no evidence that he was an assassin or a leader of the deportation of Jews.' Simon also blamed the WJC for suggesting that Waldheim was responsible for 'Austrian and UN policies hostile to Israel and the Jews.' Most of all, however, he blamed the WJC for making 'collective threats against all of Austria – and that, too, is not in accord with Jewish ethics.'

The backlash over Wiesenthal's attacks on the World Jewish Congress was being felt in the United States, where WJC President Bronfman merely professed puzzlement, but Vice-President Kalman Sultanik proclaimed that spring: 'Waldheim, who sent Jews to the gas chambers, is being backed and defended by that prominent Jew, Simon Wiesenthal.' And Barnett Zumoff, president of the Workmen's Circle organization, said at its national convention in Swan Lake, New York: 'Wiesenthal's actions represent a worst example of the type of internecine warfare within the Jewish community that seriously endangers that community and diverts our energies from dealing with the real problems that threaten all Jews.'

Answering attacks like Zumoff's and Sultanik's, the Simon Wiesenthal Centre was kept busy issuing statements clarifying Simon's position to a distracted, information-battered public. To seize the initiative, Rabbi Hier fanned the flames two days before the election with a press-released 'Reaction to the Projected Victory of Presidential Candidate Kurt Waldheim in Austria's June 8 Election' which began: 'Kurt Waldheim, a deliberate liar, was accused of "murder and slaughter" by the government of Yugoslavia. He has never disproved these charges; nor has his behaviour reflected that of an innocent man.' When Waldheim was elected President of Austria with a 53.9 per cent majority that Sunday night, Rabbi Hier was on NBC's Monday morning news telling the people of Austria that they had been given two chances to reject Waldheim and 'now we will keep your President busy cutting ribbons for the next six years.'

It was an easy threat to keep, for the Presidency of Austria can be, to a large extent, a ceremonial post – and ribbon-cutting is precisely what it's about (unless there is a parliamentary or cabinet emergency, in which case the President could dissolve a government, reject a cabinet, or call elections). Alone in his cluttered office in Vienna, Simon Wiesenthal went on speaking out not *for* Waldheim, but for fair play for Waldheim while others made demagogic pronouncements in Simon's *name*.

A poll taken in Vienna in mid-1986 showed that 'forty-three per cent of a representative sample said Jews were not Austrians – and a staggering seventy-nine per cent thought the Jews had at least been partly responsible for their own fate.'

Inaugurated on 8 July, President Kurt Waldheim was already known as 'The Prisoner of the Hofburg' (the winter palace of the Habsburgs in which the Presidential Chancellery lies) when I returned to Vienna from the US that August.

From the moment he was elected, the distancing had begun. The Socialist Chancellor, Fred Sinowatz, had resigned right away rather than pay ceremonial homage to Waldheim as head of state. He was followed by his Foreign Minister, Leopold Gratz, Kreisky's hatchet-man in the 1970 counter-attack on Wiesenthal for uncovering Nazis and an SS and SA man in the cabinet. Gratz could not bring himself to 'direct the Austrian Foreign Service in the defence of President Waldheim.' A forty-eight-year-old Viennese banker, Franz Vranitzky, who had been Sinowatz's finance minister, succeeded him as Chancellor. Yugoslavia, Albania, Greece, and the Netherlands withheld congratulations. Israel recalled its ambassador for consultations and sent a replacement of ambassadorial rank, but without the title of ambassador. The new US envoy, Ronald Lauder, a Jew who put a mezuzah* on his palatial residence's door, pleaded a prior commitment and didn't attend the inauguration. To retaliate, a number of prominent Austrians, including the editor of *Die Presse*, boycotted Ambassador Lauder's Fourth of July reception.

At the inauguration in Parliament, many Socialist MPs wore black ties in protest and, in the park between Parliament and the Presidential Chancellery, a dozen protesters, led by an American rabbi and a Roman Catholic nun, picketed in the striped uniforms of concentration camp inmates. State visitors bypassed Vienna for fear of being photographed shaking Waldheim's hand and, for similar

*An oblong container mounted to consecrate a Jewish home.

reasons, high foreign officials met their Austrian counterparts in border cities like Salzburg and Bregenz. American Jewish tourists cancelled their Austrian travel plans en masse.

The Waldheims had wanted to relax after the tiring election campaigns with a visit to Ireland, but Dublin gave them a polite 'no thank you'. When former Finnish President Urho Kekkonen died, a ceremonial visit to the funeral by the President of Austria was almost obligatory, but no invitation was forthcoming and Helsinki let it be known that rioting against Waldheim might mar the solemnity of the occasion. Then the Netherlands weighed in with word that an invitation, which had been extended to President Kirchschläger for the opening of a new dam, was not transferable. But the crowning insult came from the King of Belgium, Baudoin, whose father, Leopold III, had abdicated after the war in the wake of accusations that he had fascist sympathies and had collaborated with his German captors. King Baudoin let it be known that he wouldn't sponsor Belgium's 1987 Europalia festival honouring Austria if Waldheim was on its organizing committee. The Austrian Foreign Ministry had to pretend that the President would be too busy to participate or attend, even though Waldheim had already sounded out Belgian contacts about cutting the ribbon at the Europalia opening.

Not until March 1987 would Waldheim receive an acceptable invitation for a State visit – from King Hussein of Jordan, a nation still officially at war with neighbouring Israel. But even Hussein, who takes his winter ski vacations in Austria and owns a mansion on the edge of the Vienna Woods, later quailed at sharing the Presidential loge at the Opera Ball.

In the wine gardens of Vienna in 1986, the sounds of a summer night invariably reverberated with discussions of Waldheim, Wiesenthal, 'the Jews', 'the American Jews', and 'the Jews from New York'. At that autumn's Freedom Party Congress in Innsbruck, Norbert Steger, the moderate leader serving as Vice Chancellor in the post-Kreisky coalition that had governed Austria since 1983 was overthrown by Jörg Haider, a dashing, pipe-smoking thirty-six-year-old extreme rightist who was hailed as 'Hitler's adopted son' by fans who spoke of him fondly by the diminutive 'Jörgl'. His wealth came from inherited property (worth nine to twelve million dollars) in Carinthia that had been expropriated from a Jewish family.

Rather than rule in partnership with Haider, new chancellor Vranitzky dissolved the Red-Blue coalition. After President Waldheim called new elections, Haider made such a strong showing that the Socialists and the People's Party returned to their postwar Red-Black 'Grand Coalition', with Vranitzky at the helm this time, to keep Haider out of power. In 1989, however, after a strong second-place showing in provincial elections, Haider formed a regional Black and Blue coalition with the third-place People's Party to oust the Socialists in Carinthia and become Governor of the province. In 1990, after a Freedom Party candidate for mayor of a Carinthian village proclaimed that 'I told Simon Wiesenthal we're building ovens again, but not for you, Mr Wiesenthal; for you there's room in Jörgl's pipe', Wiesenthal, who had never met the man, sued him under an Austrian law prohibiting acts that spread or glorify Nazism, but Haider, puffing serenely above it all, chose to 'not even ignore' Simon's 'artificial agitation'.

Exacerbated by Attorney General Meese's decision in April 1987 to place Waldheim on the 'Watch List' of undesirable aliens excluded from the US and by Pope John Paul II's sudden invitation to Waldheim to visit the Vatican in mid-1987 as a devout Catholic man of peace (an opportunity Waldheim grasped so fast that it preceded his visit to Jordan), the hatred heated up that summer, when a group of orthodox Jews were cursed at, spat upon, and given the stiff-armed 'Heil Hitler!' salute in the streets of Vienna and some Jewish children were beaten up by Gentile children. The official Jewish community – representing less than one Austrian in a thousand – reported receiving an average of ten poison-pen letters per day. And Carl Hödl, the People's Party Deputy Mayor of Hitler's home city of Linz, wrote his hate-mail directly to WJC President Bronfman, comparing the attacks on Waldheim to

> those of your fellow believers, who two thousand years ago had Jesus Christ convicted in a show trial because he did not accommodate the lords of Jerusalem . . . It remained for you, and those like you, to bring such a Talmudic concept into the world.

Disowned by his party bosses amidst clamour for his removal, Hödl took early retirement at the age of sixty-three.

– 39 –

Wiesenthal vs Waldheim

'BACK TO THE FUTURE' proclaimed posters that had sprouted across Austria within hours of Kurt Waldheim's election victory in June 1986. Everybody in Austria agreed that the country had to resume its forward march from Western Europe's poorest land in 1970 to one of its most affluent in the eighties – a transition that coincided with the Kreisky era. But, by the time Waldheim was inaugurated a month later, everybody knew that even without the World Jewish Congress, the world's conscience would not let Austria and its President bury their past just yet.

For once, Waldheim had recognized this and, at his first presidential press conference two days after taking office, he had endorsed Simon Wiesenthal's proposal of an international commission of military historians to examine all relevant documents and evaluate the allegations against him. Speaking in bureaucratese, Waldheim told the press: 'I have no objection to such an idea because I am sure it would clarify, finally, my statement in this regard. But the technical aspects would have to be clarified before one would take a final position on such matters.'

'If Waldheim had his way,' one of the foreign correspondents present remarked, 'he'd kill this story through boredom.'

Pleased that his historical commission was moving from idea toward reality, Simon Wiesenthal said he didn't expect it to come up with a 'smoking gun'; in fact, he was quite sure there wasn't one. And he resumed speaking out on other aspects of the case. 'Waldheim should have sued a long time ago,' he told a couple of journalists. 'The media in the US are powerful, but the courts took care that the trees which make newsprint don't go all the way up into the sky.'

Expressing disappointment in Rabbi Hier's continued pronouncements (e.g., *'That such a man can still be elected President of Austria is an indictment of the Austrian people's unwillingness to squarely face up to the past . . . The Austrian people wanted Waldheim; they can have him!'*), Simon revealed to me that he had flirted with severing his ties to the Wiesenthal Centre and had even asked Hier to change its name.

'I have so many troubles with our Centre in connection with Waldheim,' he said with a sigh. 'Not with any other problems; just this. They are part of the hysteria, day and night. We have 320,000 members and I am getting letters from Jewish judges of the Supreme Courts of the States of New York and Connecticut and from other people of justice – not men off the street! – who could not understand my problem and so they resign their membership in the Centre. To each of these few people I send a letter telling them I will never change the style of my work; I will never accuse people without evidence. A judge should respect that. Later, they apologize and send letters to the Centre wanting to be reinstated as members. For a while, I was so unhappy with the situation that I revoked my name from the Centre. But, on the other hand, Waldheim is temporary and all the other work of the Centre is so important that, like those Supreme Court judges, I give my name back.'

Toward the end of October 1986, a Catholic university students' association took a stab at reconciliation with 'A Jewish Week' of readings, concerts, and lectures. On Thursday, Simon Wiesenthal shared the podium on anti-Semitism with Dr Erika Weinzierl, a non-Jewish historian who was Austria's leading analyst of the workings of bigotry. Wiesenthal went first. As his speech began, the organizers took a call from the President's office. Would there be three seats available in the audience if President Waldheim came right over? The organizers said yes and gave up their front-row seats. At a pause for questions, they announced that President Waldheim himself was on his way over. The capacity audience gasped. Wiesenthal gulped. Then he stood up and said: 'You will understand why I have to excuse myself.'

Not everybody did, but I could understand how, particularly with a couple of photographers present, Wiesenthal – his Stateside standing and lecture bookings at stake – could not afford to be seen in a situation involving hobnobbing with the controversial President. As Simon collected his coat in the vestibule, Waldheim and an aide and a bodyguard appeared. Waldheim gave Wiesenthal a warm 'Good evening, Mr Engineer!' Wiesenthal gave Waldheim a frostier 'Good evening, Mr President.' Glancing around to see that the photographers were still in the auditorium, Simon shook Waldheim's hand and left. Later, he would say: 'You cannot bring the President of the country in through the back door.'

The President of Austria took his front-row seat and listened attentively to Dr Weinzierl, but did not ask any questions. The audience behaved politely.

When the leaders of Democrats Abroad convened in Vienna in late 1986 to lay plans for the US presidential election two years later, I helped arrange a private briefing by Simon Wiesenthal over cocktails on a Saturday night at a home within walking distance of his – and he let me tape the conversation. Simon blamed the whole Waldheim affair, including his election, on middle level 'members of the Socialist Party in Vienna and the World Jewish Congress.' He did not condemn Waldheim for his memberships in the Nazi student union and SA riding club. 'Believe me,' said Simon, 'eighty per cent of students in those times had to be members of such organizations; they had no choice. And, if Waldheim had been a wise man, he could have said so and, by giving the right answer, win immediately. But his tactic was always evasion and no truth – and then the truth, when it was too late.'

He condemned Singer and Steinberg of the World Jewish Congress, but acknowledged the effect of their tactics: 'These two young boys: they knew the psychology of American Jews better than I do. In their subconscious, American Jews feel guilty. They haven't done enough against the Nazis in the war to help their fellow Jews in Europe. Now they have the golden chance to do all against Waldheim – verbally! On my lecture tours, they ask me: "What is the difference between Eichmann and Waldheim?" "Why is Waldheim not arrested?" "Why don't they hang him?" And when I say, "First give me evidence and then let us see", they say, "Why you protect him?" Nobody wish to know the truth!

'I have always had letters to the editor against me. Usually, they come from neo-Nazis. But now, to see them signed by Jews in Jewish newspapers: this is something new to me.'

Wiesenthal told the amateur politicians – American Democrats living in a dozen European countries and Israel – what he'd told

Singer and Steinberg when they visited him on his most recent lecture tour of the States. According to Wiesenthal, the 'two young boys' said to him: 'We cannot finish the matter of Waldheim without your moral support. We need your moral position in the world.' And Simon had replied:

'Well, let me tell you how to get it. You bring your evidence to me *before* you hold a press conference. And if your documents show me that the man was involved in war crimes, then I as an Austrian citizen will ask him to resign. People will believe me. But when you will come out and ask him to resign, it will be the same as it was in the presidential election. Out of the two and a half million votes he got, a few hundred thousand people voted for Waldheim who never would have voted for him without this interference from abroad. They say to me, "Do the Americans think we are a banana republic? that we cannot alone decide whom to elect?" And these quarter of a million people weren't voting for Waldheim so much as they were voting against the World Jewish Congress.'

Now Simon told the wide-eyed Democrats: 'To understand the Austrian position, I say: look, you had a problem with a president, Nixon. What would it have been like if the accusations against him had come not from the States, but only from abroad? Nixon would never have had to resign. So why should Singer and Steinberg imagine Waldheim should resign because they attacked him from abroad?'

Simon suggested that he, as an Austrian citizen, might call for Waldheim's resignation if the commission of military historians condemned him: 'They will read all the documents and they will make a conclusion. This is so easy when military historians talk; whether they are American or German or Greek, in half an hour, they have a common language of how these documents must be read. This commission must be created not for or against Waldheim, but only for the truth.'

Though Wiesenthal had high hopes for the historians' commission, others, including me, felt that any group empanelled by the Austrian government would have a built-in predisposition toward whitewash. This impression was heightened in 1987 when a part-time researcher at Wiesenthal's Jewish Documentation Centre, Silvana Konieczny-Origlia, copied a personal letter from one of the commission members, Gerald Fleming of Great Britain, to Wiesenthal enclosing evidence she said incriminated Waldheim. After she published letter and documents in the Italian magazine *Epoca*, it turned out that the documents – found by Fleming in Washington's National Archives and suggesting a link between Waldheim's intelligence unit and the killing of British prisoners of war in 1944 – had been analysed earlier, not only in Germany's *Der Spiegel*, but by the British Foreign Office, which found no evidence of 'any criminal activity' by Lieutenant Waldheim against British prisoners. Certifying the veracity of the documents, Wiesenthal pointed out that they contained only information that was already known. He added that Mrs Konieczny-Origlia 'disappeared about five days before and we have not heard from her since. I was very surprised to hear about this report.' She was no longer in his employ. Later, he would remark that this showed 'how the Waldheim case could induce a seemingly sensible, seemingly decent person to commit an incomprehensible action . . . believing that she could thereby prove Waldheim to be a war criminal who was being protected by me.'

Potentially more harmful to the historical commission was Fleming's covering letter, in which he wrote in German:

> Please destroy this letter. The documents are for your *private* files. They come from Washington. What I am telling you is absolutely confidential and must remain so.

Even though the letter was written before Fleming's appointment to the commission, some damage was done. An Italian journalist wrote that Simon had concealed the papers to help Waldheim. A week later, *Epoca* published an attack on Simon by the WJC's Elan Steinberg. And Serge Klarsfeld went on French TV to denounce Simon's role as a passive recipient of vital data.

The next attack on Simon Wiesenthal came from a more familiar direction. On the morning of 6 January 1988 – the Austrian holiday of Epiphany – Austrian Television transmitted nationwide a two-hour interview with Wiesenthal live from the stage of the Theater in der Josefstadt. A few minutes into the telecast, when Simon was explaining that he saw himself more as a 'researcher' than a 'Nazi-hunter', a voice from the third balcony shouted 'Murderer!' and another called out 'You are a liar!' as a shower of neo-Nazi hate-leaflets fluttered down upon the rococo auditorium. After a brief scuffle, three rightist hoodlums were apprehended by the police, but much more heartening was the immediate response when the interviewer, Franz Ferdinand Wolf, exhorted the capacity audience: '*This* is Austria 1988. I believe *that* was "The Other Austria". Shall we show it with applause?' – and all 850 Austrians on hand rose as one to give Wiesenthal a prolonged standing ovation.

Later, Simon told me: 'Letters to the editor in America are saying I am senile, but what I lose in America, I win in Austria.' He meant respect and respectability as he went from a non-person or worse in Kreisky's Austria to recognition as a symbol of justice and integrity in the Waldheim era. Indeed, nothing did Wiesenthal's heart more good than hearing a Socialist chancellor, Vranitzky, praise him publicly as 'Austria's incorruptible conscience, too long ignored or unacknowledged in our country.'

1988 was predestined to be a traumatic year for Austria with the fiftieth anniversary of the Anschluss in March preceded by delivery of the historians' commission report in February. As rumours flew that the panel would not be as kind to Waldheim as anticipated, pressure for his resignation mounted to a new frenzy. Though the *Jerusalem Post* claimed that People's Party leader Alois Mock had written to British Prime Minister Margaret Thatcher that President Waldheim would soon resign pleading ill health, the President himself, at the outset of his seventieth year, looked fitter than ever and seemed to thrive on controversy.

While the historians' 202-page report said that 'the question of Waldheim's guilty conduct in the war is not finally answered', it also concluded that 'he repeatedly assisted in connection with illegal actions and thereby facilitated their execution. He tried to let his military past slip into oblivion and, as soon as that was no longer possible, to portray it as harmless.' Though Waldheim termed the failure to attach 'personal guilt' to him a vindication, the Israeli member of the commission, Jehuda Wallach, said that not only had Waldheim twisted the panel's words, but that he believed there was enough evidence to prosecute the President of Austria.

At this point, Simon Wiesenthal beat the retreat that had begun when he'd left the Catholic students' seminar in haste upon hearing that Waldheim was coming. With his lecture bookings and his standing with world Jewry eroding from the principled position he had taken for two years, he now leaped to loftier moral ground by calling for Waldheim's resignation because a president must be an ethical role-model for a society. In various interviews, Wiesenthal said he hoped the President would take advantage of the report's ambiguity 'to make the decision to go without losing face, but in Austria's interest.' Terming the current situation a 'catastrophe', he said 'the way out lies with the President. Austria cannot live alone in the world. Sooner or later, the people will hold Dr Waldheim responsible for their isolation . . . The President must symbolize truth and not come in conflict with it.'

The Waldheim affair made Simon Wiesenthal and Bruno Kreisky into strange bedfellows. Kreisky, too, now called for the President to resign. Kreisky's initial defence of his former colleague against WJC 'infamy' and American 'score-settling' had turned to disenchantment with 'a candidate who will create a divided nation . . . It is not good for Austria to have a liar at the top of the State. It is not good for a people to have a President who is on the Watch List.'

The most startling response to the historians' report came from Karl Gruber, the Tyrolean resistance hero who, as Austrian Foreign Minister, gave Waldheim his first diplomatic job. Nearing eighty, Gruber gave an interview to Italian television and his words were re-broadcast on Austrian radio: 'The commission, they were not his friends. They were practically all his enemies. The German is a Socialist. The others are of Jewish descent.'

Gruber was promptly repudiated by everybody from Waldheim to Wiesenthal, from Chancellor Vranitzky to Gruber's own People's Party – and by the truth. The German panellist, Manfred Messerschmidt of the Research Institute for Military History in Freiburg, said he had never joined any political party and considered himself a liberal, not a socialist. Two commission members – Israel's Wallach and Britain's Fleming – were indeed Jewish, but the other three (including US Brigadier-General James Lawton Collins Jnr) were not. Gruber's words proved only one truth: the vocabulary of anti-Semitism was so pervasive in Austria that even a confirmed anti-fascist fighter spoke its language.

It was almost anticlimactic when Kurt Waldheim went on Austrian television to tell the nation (and the world) that he had ruled out resigning: 'It is a fundamental principle of our democracy that an election result cannot be subsequently corrected. A head of state must not retreat in the face of slanders, hateful demonstrations, and wholesale condemnations.'

As if to prove Waldheim's point, President Bronfman of the World Jewish Congress surfaced in the next day's *New York Times* with this condemnation:

> Mr Waldheim is clearly amoral. He is a man without conscience. He is a liar and an unrepentant man who was part and parcel of the Nazi killing machine.

On another occasion, Bronfman called upon the world to oppose Austria's application to enter the European Union: collective punishment for one man's unproven guilt.

Simon Wiesenthal took another tack. 'When the historians said Waldheim can't be tried,' he told me, 'I had hoped he would take this as a way to leave with dignity. When he didn't, I asked him to resign. But I spoke only as a citizen of Austria.'

While Waldheim's on-going sauna of cold snubs and hot exposures only seemed to invigorate him, he also appeared to have learned a certain humility that was almost becoming. In his TV response to the historians, he had acknowledged it was a mistake to say two years earlier that he was only doing his duty as a German soldier and now he paid his respects to 'the heroes and martyrs of that time'. He was not one of them, he admitted: 'We others in my generation were submerged in the machinery of war, in fear and the effort to survive.' But, he added, he had a 'clear conscience'.

'Maybe so,' Simon Wiesenthal remarked. 'The man was neither a Nazi nor a war criminal, a hero or a victim. He was an opportunist like ninety-nine per cent of the others. But should such an average person be president of a country?'

The fiftieth anniversary of the Anschluss fell on the same days of the week in 1988 that they did in 1938. On Friday, 11 March, the day Schuschnigg gave up, there would be a ceremony in the Hofburg, but enough Socialist and Green Members of Parliament threatened to boycott the event or walk out if the President spoke that he agreed to attend as a silent spectator. He was, however, given the opportunity to speak on national television the night before, and there he said that although Austria was the first victim of Hitler, some Austrians were guilty of committing Nazi crimes. 'Of course, there is no such thing as collective guilt,' he declared. 'Nevertheless, I should like to apologize as head of state.'

In 1988, Kurt Waldheim conjured up a ghost from Simon Wiesenthal's past: Eichmann-hunter Tuviah Friedman made a much-publicized return to Vienna from Haifa – at the invitation and expense of the offices of the President of Austria, the Austrian Foreign Ministry, and the Austrian Federal Press Service – as the self-proclaimed 'Conscience of Israel' come to Austria to pronounce President Kurt Waldheim 'innocent as a baby'. Friedman made no effort to contact Wiesenthal while being wined and dined by the Waldheims at the presidential villa in the garden district of Hohe Warte and by the Federal Press Service at the Noah's Ark Kosher Restaurant on the Judengasse in the old ghetto, where a press dinner for nine – Friedman, four officials shepherding him, and four journalists – cost the taxpayers some 400 dollars.

The last word on this whole fiasco, however, belonged to Simon Wiesenthal, who told the press that Friedman had snubbed him as a rival. 'We've been out of touch for more than thirty years,' Simon said. 'After Eichmann was captured, Friedman was once quoted as complaining: "They always talk about Wiesenthal, never about me." I feel sorry for Tuviah Friedman. He was recruited for something of which he wasn't intellectually capable . . . [But] nationally and internationally, Waldheim is in a situation where the only person who can help him is himself.'

The embarrassing resuscitation of Tuviah Friedman was part of a media offensive launched from the Hofburg in 1988. A spate of interviews with Waldheim began to appear in the world's English-language media. He told James M. Markham of the *New York Times* that he was slightly reluctant to make any gesture of reconciliation toward Austrian Jews: 'I have to be a little careful. I want to be sure I will be well received. There will always be people who will say, "Well, why is he coming?"' Then he launched into what Markham called 'a paean to the Jewish contribution to Austrian civilization' and recalled Jewish friendships in New York: 'I attended Jewish weddings. My family doctor in New York was a Jew.' He vowed to use his 'whole moral authority to fight anti-Semitism, which is a scourge of humanity. I shall do that out of deep conviction.'

Receiving Steve Lipman of *Jewish Week* at the Attersee, he rattled off his Jewish connections – the New York physician; a Jewish friend in the US who sends letters of 'moral support'; an English teacher from his early school years – and told Lipman how he attends Jewish weddings and funerals in Vienna wearing a conspicuous skull-cap. (Lipman did not mention the *yarmulkah* flap at Yad Vashem.)

He even granted a polite, if tense, interview to his nemesis, Professor Herzstein, the military historian who had 'unmasked' his 'hidden past' for the World Jewish Congress. Herzstein said that 'much of the information he offered was new and highly useful' to his book *Waldheim: the Missing Years*.

Just to analyse Herzstein's book and another (*Waldheim*, by French journalists Luc Rosenzweig and Bernard Cohen) for the *London Review of Books*, Gitta Sereny, the biographer of Franz Stangl, flew to Vienna for an interview with Waldheim. 'Why do they go on about me? Do you understand the reasons?' he asked Sereny in the Anschluss anniversary month of March 1988. When she observed that the historians' commission seemed to think he should have been a hero, he voiced his disappointment: 'I thought that the commission, who after all I asked for, would understand. Would I really have asked for such learned men to investigate my past if I had done something wrong? Those who think me bad, do they also think me mad? But it is true, of course. I could have resisted, deserted, and I didn't.'

From the moment in 1986 when the first 'revelations' about him began making daily headlines and Kurt Waldheim started to squirm like a schoolboy caught 'cheating', the 'character issue' was invoked on the world stage with the Final Solution as backdrop. And, on this canvas in an epic morality play which traumatized the Austria he symbolized for so many years and still symbolizes, President Kurt Waldheim – neither Nazi nor war criminal, but once the servant of both – has become as much a landmark of Holocaust remembrance as Simon Wiesenthal and Elie Wiesel, Adolf Eichmann and Anne Frank, and the bronze statue of a Jew scrubbing the pavement a few blocks from his Chancellery. Somewhere in time's no man's land between moral obtuseness and passive complicity, 'The Prisoner of the Hofburg' became today's 'Man in the Glass Booth' – with every day of his 2192-day presidency a Day of Judgement by the world.

– 40 –

A letter from Waldheim to Wiesenthal

The 1988 report of the historians' commission, proposed by Wiesenthal and activated by Waldheim, had given Simon a good opportunity to dismount the high horse of principle that had already cost him lecture bookings and rapport with the Simon Wiesenthal Centre, but it was too late for the Nobel Peace Prize which eluded him after his near-miss in 1983.

When, after two years of talk of Simon's sharing the honour with Elie Wiesel, the 1986 prize went to Wiesel alone, the timing was obvious. Simon's severest postwar test of character – the politically unfashionable stance of fair play he took early in the Waldheim affair and maintained for two turbulent years – had clearly taken its toll.

Simon saw something more sinister. In 1989, he complained to me that Israel Singer and the World Jewish Congress had torpedoed his last chance at the Nobel Peace Prize three years earlier in the heat of the Waldheim controversy: 'A member of the Nobel committee told me that they got "a letter from world Jewry" protesting any plan to give me the prize or have me share it with Wiesel. He wouldn't tell me any more than that, but I could guess where it was from. The World Jewish Congress is not world Jewry, but its name sounds like it.'

Singer denies that the WJC sent any such letter and says why he thinks the Nobel went to Wiesel alone: 'Hunters don't win peace prizes.'

As an Austrian citizen, Simon had every right to request the President's resignation, but no real reason to expect it. Still, he continued to call for it, even while acknowledging that Austrian interest in his work and his subject were never higher than when Kurt Waldheim ran for President.

Within President Waldheim, once he was installed in the Hofburg, some of the arrogance of office had given way to humility in power. Reviewing my tape of our 10 May 1989 interview with the president, I picked up on a reference he had made to a 'very clear letter' to Wiesenthal – and, the next day, back in the Hofburg once more, I was allowed to see a copy, but not to quote it. Dated 2 February 1989, on Dr Kurt Waldheim's personal (not his presidential) letterhead, it was two pages and nine paragraphs long.

Waldheim's letter began by acknowledging that he'd looked at Wiesenthal's new 1988 memoir with great interest, particularly because of the chapter about him. Then he thanked Simon for taking such a clear position against any and all allegations of wrong-doing by Lieutenant Waldheim and praised Wiesenthal's devotion to justice and his high moral standard – which was precisely why Waldheim was disturbed by Wiesenthal's doubts about his credibility, particularly concerning his purported knowledge of the deportation of the Jews of Salonika.

The tragedy was now forty-five years old, Waldheim went on, and allegations that he knew about it were based on assumptions, not proof. The same was true of the report of the historians, who operated on hypotheses, not facts.

The President acknowledged that once the historians' report and Wiesenthal's book had been issued, he could hardly hope for a change in position. Therefore, although it was too late to influence Simon's public judgement, he wanted to repeat once again – with the complete conviction of his conscience – that he knew nothing of the deportations.

Recalling a 1986 conversation with Wiesenthal that is cited in the memoir, Waldheim said Simon had suggested he would be more credible if he admitted knowing of the deportations. He had replied then and reiterated now that he had known nothing then and could not knowingly speak untruth.

Waldheim then reaffirmed that he was absent from Arsakli during the time of deportations and that the framework of his military activities precluded any involvement in the terrible events that took place.

Although Simon had jumped to political conclusions (that Waldheim should resign) from his doubts about the President's credibility, Waldheim insisted that, knowing the real truth, he could not accept Wiesenthal's statements in this regard.

Finally, Waldheim said that if a personal meeting would clarify matters, he stood ready to get together with Wiesenthal.

It was a remarkable letter for any president to send to a constituent.

Even more remarkably, three months after the letter from his President was sent to him, Wiesenthal had not answered it.

'Why should I answer him?' Simon asked me when I called him about it next morning. 'He is right that I will never change my position. This is what I believe. Him I can't believe.'

'But the President of your country writes to you!' I remonstrated, at least as shocked as I was years ago when Simon suggested Hitler caught syphilis from a Jewish prostitute.

'Yes, and already he is showing the letter to you!'

'Not him; one of his aides,' I argued. 'They're miffed that you didn't answer.'

'Look, if I write him a letter, immediately it will be in the press – but with two or three words missing.'

I asked him if he had ever suggested to Waldheim that he should say he knew about the deportations.

'Sure,' he said, 'because nobody can believe other. Listen, I am not going to answer his letter, but the last time I talked to him on the phone, I said to him: "I know during the war you could do nothing . . . After the war, however, you who have seen so much and known so much could have told us so much. But you say nothing."'

On 17 October 1989, Simon Wiesenthal had the last word on both Kurt Waldheim and the World Jewish Congress.

The previous afternoon, I'd attended a kosher banquet hosted by Mayor Helmut Zilk in Vienna's Rathaus (City Hall) for Arthur Hertzberg, a jovial, roly-poly New Jersey rabbi and professor (of religion at Dartmouth and history at Columbia) who happens to be vice president of the World Jewish Congress. After the feast, in his formal remarks, Hertzberg said:

'The Waldheim affair is dead, but could possibly be revived if he runs for President again. The less said about it the better – at least for a couple of years.'

Waldheim's term would expire in 1992. Remembering how Rabbi Hertzberg two years earlier had praised WJC secretary general Israel Singer to me as 'an acorn I planted that grew to be an oak', I asked him: 'Can we take your current concept as indicative of the thinking within the executive ranks of the World Jewish Congress?'

'I am vice president of the World Jewish Congress,' Hertzberg replied succinctly.

'Would Mr Singer and the others . . . ?' I persisted.

He cut me off by repeating, 'I am vice president of the World Jewish Congress' and adding, 'I don't speak lightly, OK?'

'OK,' I agreed as Hertzberg went on: 'But this is on the presumption that the problem is ending, not beginning again . . . I'm not entirely persuaded that the affair as a whole was brilliantly managed, not at all. It is, however, over – in the sense that it is very clear that the world will be better served if Mr Waldheim's term in office, when he ceases to be the Prisoner of the Hofburg, ends after one term, that's all.'

'Are you sounding this as a warning?' I asked.

'I'm not saying it as a warning or anything of the sort. I'm saying facts. I would imagine that if Mr Waldheim announced he were running for President again, inevitably the whole thing will revive. The World Jewish Congress would have to revive it, appropriately.'

After formal thanks by Karl Vak, chief of Vienna's Central Savings Bank, Hertzberg said: 'May I have one more word, Dr Vak? . . . I am going to speak officially. This is not a personal statement. I am talking with the full concurrence of my colleagues in the World Jewish Congress . . . We've said everything we're going to say in the matter of Waldheim. His future is a matter for the Austrian people to decide. We of the World Jewish Congress trust the good sense of the Austrian people. Or, to put it another way, Waldheim will neither live politically or cease to live politically from campaigning against the World Jewish Congress. That is over. Can I make myself clearer than that? The problem of Waldheim is the problem of Austria. It is no longer the problem of the World Jewish Congress. We have spoken our last word on the subject.'

Chatting with Hertzberg afterwards, I reminded him how he'd hailed Israel Singer as a sprout he'd nurtured. 'Yes,' the rabbi responded, 'but you know "The Sorcerer's Apprentice"* – and [it applies to] Elan Steinberg more than him.'

Of Waldheim, Hertzberg remarked: 'This man who didn't tell the truth about his past has been making some noises about running again . . . We are not going to provide him a target. He's not going to run against the World Jewish Congress. He's not going to run against *Weltjudentum* [world Jewry], thus allowing all the latent xenophobic feelings in this country to well up around supporting him. That game is not going to be played again. We are leaving him to the embarrassment – or to the support – of the Austrians. So he's not going to have such an easy time of it. The Austrians are embarrassed, but I hear he's living in a world of unreality. He thinks he's going to run.'

Later, I called the Austrian President's office, where his aide, Dr Scheide sounded pleased by the WJC's provisional withdrawal from the Austrian battlefield but said Waldheim had not yet decided whether to run for re-election and would make no comment on Hertzberg's words.

The next morning, I rang up Simon Wiesenthal, who remarked that he was 'glad to hear that a man of Rabbi Hertzberg's stature shares my opinion of Singer and Steinberg and says that the whole matter was badly run. I myself have suffered from this, so I am happy if it's over.'

When I asked Simon whether a Waldheim candidacy in 1992 might re-ignite the flames of controversy, he replied:

'He cannot run alone. No party will nominate him now. For him it is possible only to run around the table.'

In 1991, President Waldheim announced that he would not run for a second term in 1992 at the age of seventy-three.

* In a second-century Roman dialogue appropriated by Goethe and Walt Disney, the apprentice, in his master's absence, tries one of his spells and can't countermand it.

Part VII
Episodes and Epilogues

All too often in this part of the world, fear of one lie gives birth to another lie, in the foolish hope that by protecting ourselves from the first lie we will be protected from lies in general. But a lie can never protect us from a lie. Those who falsify history do not protect the freedom of a nation but rather constitute a threat to it.

The idea that a person can rewrite his autobiography is one of the traditional self-deceptions of Central Europe. Trying to do that means hurting oneself and one's fellow countrymen. When a truth is not given complete freedom, freedom is not complete.

– Czech (then Czechoslovak) President Václav Havel at the opening of the Salzburg Festival in Austria after he was introduced by President Kurt Waldheim on 26 July 1990 (translated from the Czech by Káča Poláčková-Henley).

– 41 –

Wiesenthal vs Wiesel

No Nobel for Simon Wiesenthal makes him no less noble. Rabbi Hier of the Wiesenthal Centre puts it most eloquently:

'Simon, to his credit, doesn't have to apologize to anyone for what he's done with his life. Without Simon Wiesenthal, the subject of the Holocaust would not really receive serious attention anywhere in the world. Let's also state for the record that, although the popular writers on the Holocaust began writing in the sixties – that's when Elie Wiesel first started getting published, too – there was still a big period of time between 1945 and the early sixties: a crucial period when there was the greatest pressure to forget. But if there was one person who kept it alive, that was Simon Wiesenthal. So this is all to his credit that nobody can take away from him. Without him, all this that we're talking about in America, the mere fact that there would be in Washington a President's Council, a Commission on the Holocaust headed by Elie Wiesel, would have been an impossibility, because the subject would have been forgotten. Simon was a stubborn man who kept it alive through the worst of times.'

When Elie Wiesel won the Nobel Peace Prize in 1986, Simon Wiesenthal did not rejoice at this recognition of Holocaust remembrance, for no love has been lost between these two titans of survivorship. Though Wiesel once came to Wiesenthal's rescue as a fund-raiser when his Viennese bank collapsed in 1974, Simon says that Wiesel later opposed his poaching on his turf when the Simon Wiesenthal Centre for Holocaust Studies was built in Los Angeles three years later. One bone of contention was Simon's insistence that the Wiesenthal Centre, despite being a division of Yeshiva University, should take a non-sectarian approach to the Holocaust:

'I was for over four years in different camps with people from fifteen nations: Jews, Gentiles, gypsies, communists. Through this experience, my view on the Holocaust and the whole problem of Nazism is a lot different from Elie Wiesel, who was *only* six months in camps and only with Jews. For me was the Holocaust not only a Jewish tragedy, but also a human tragedy. After the war, when I saw that the Jews were talking only about the tragedy of six million Jews, I sent letters to Jewish organizations asking them to talk also about the millions of others who were persecuted with us together – many of them only because they helped Jews. This made me unpopular with Jewish organizations – and, when the Wiesenthal Centre happened, I became a danger to them. Elie Wiesel wrote that what I was doing was "a diminution" of the tragedy. But he and they are the diminishers, for it is they who reduced the whole tragedy to a problem between Nazis and Jews instead of a crime against humanity.

'I know I am not only the bad conscience of the Nazis. I am also the bad conscience of the Jews. Because what I have taken up as my duty was *everybody's* duty.'

Relations between Wiesenthal and Wiesel soured not from their rivalry so much as from their disagreement over recognizing the role of gypsies as victims of Nazi genocide. 'Half a million gypsies are not the same to the world as six million Jews,' Simon acknowledges, 'even though the proportion is at least the same. But gypsies weren't well-organized people; they moved from place to place and many were illiterate. Besides, there was no Gypsy Documentation Centre – so nobody much cared about them until 1954.'

That was when Wiesenthal, on a research visit to Prague, stumbled on to some 1939 papers left by the Gestapo in the Moravian city of Ostrava. Piecing them together over the years like a jigsaw puzzle, Wiesenthal had established the chain of command in the extermination of the gypsies: with Adolf Eichmann at the top and a Captain Walter Braune, who has never been found, directly in charge of gypsy deportations to Poland which began in the fall of 1939. After more than a decade, Simon presented his findings to the Central Prosecutor's Office in Ludwigsburg, Germany. Later, he learned that other documents pertaining to the classification of gypsies under the Nuremberg laws of racial purity were in an archive at the

University of Tübingen under the care of Professor Sophie Erhard, the same 'race hygienist' who had drawn some of them up in 1942. A telegram from Wiesenthal to the German Minister of Justice was all it took to have the records transferred to the Federal Archives in Koblenz.

When four hard-working gypsy families in Darmstadt returned from a three-week vacation to find that their home – where they had lived for four years – had been torn down on the assumption they wouldn't be coming back, and besides, the authorities claimed, their living conditions posed a health menace, the Central Council of German Gypsies protested to the Mayor of Darmstadt that this was a 'continuation' of Nazi persecution. The mayor sued the gypsies for slander – and Simon Wiesenthal went to court in Frankfurt to testify 'on behalf of my fellow sub-humans' that this was indeed the 'same genocide, just new pogroms; the tragedy of the gypsies in Germany is by no means over.' The mayor's law suit was dismissed, but, says Simon, 'the gypsies got no restitution. The City can get away with murder.'

In 1979, a US Holocaust Memorial Council was founded to perpetuate awareness of history's greatest tragedy. Simon Wiesenthal, as an interested observer, was appalled to find that 'in addition to Jewish representatives, there are Poles, Russians, Ukrainians, and others who have seats and voices on the fifty-five-person council – but not the gypsies.' Hoping to win the gypsies a seat, Wiesenthal wrote a letter of polite protest to the council's chairman, 'my "friend" Wiesel'.

Many months later, Simon received a reply from a secretary stating that the selection of council members was in President Ronald Reagan's hands. On Wiesenthal's advice, gypsy leaders sent pleas to the White House, but their mail was forwarded to Elie Wiesel, who, says Simon, showed no sympathy.

Simon then wrote to Wiesel suggesting that one of the thirty-odd Jewish council members should vacate his seat and give it to a gypsy. Simon received no reply, but when he published his appeal in his 1985 annual report, he pricked enough Jewish consciences that Wiesel had to react to the criticism. The council held what Wiesenthal calls 'a kind of memorial hour' for the gypsies in September 1986, but Simon says that 'not until Elie Wiesel gave up the chairmanship a few months later were we able to get a gypsy on the council.' In 1987, Professor Ian F. Hancock, President of the World Romany Congress, was named to a vacant seat.

Simon's crusade for the gypsies posed a dilemma for him which he relates quite candidly in his 1988 memoir: when Wiesel won the 1986 Nobel Peace Prize, gypsy organizations wanted to go to Oslo to stage a demonstration against him. Wiesenthal pleaded with Roman Rose, president of the Central Council of German Gypsies, to call it off because, as a rival who had been considered for the prize, Wiesenthal would have been accused of inciting the protest to spite Wiesel. Out of long friendship and respect for his loyalty, the gypsies acceded.

In 1985, a happenstance of history had the World Jewish Congress holding its annual meeting in the convention centre of Vienna's Hofburg (at the other end of which palace President Waldheim would take up office a year later) at the very time when Austrian Minister of Defence Friedhelm Frischenschlager was extending a handshake of welcome to returning war criminal Walter Reder, the massacrist of Marzabotto. While the Congress wrestled with whether to pull out of Vienna and controversy swirled through the Hofburg with Chancellor Sinowatz trying to placate WJC President Bronfman, I saw Wiesenthal and Wiesel stalk a stately minuet of snubbing each other around the gefilte fish at a kosher buffet in the grand ballroom. It was not an appetizing spectacle.

No love has been lost between Wiesenthal and Wiesel since then. As late as 1989, Simon would tell me bitterly about Wiesel: 'That man, how he hates me!' For the only time I can remember, Simon failed to add his usual disclaimer: 'But I am not a hater.'

– 42 –

A hero at nightfall

One night a week for eight weeks at a time, I used to teach a four-hour journalism class in English at the Vienna campus of Webster University of St Louis. For 'Feature Writing' one Wednesday in 1983, the first half was devoted to 'The Difficult Interview' and the second half to 'The Celebrity Interview'. As it turned out, in the second half, from 8 to 10 p.m., we got both.

My celebrity was Simon Wiesenthal, then nearing his seventy-fifth birthday. Not all of my class of sixteen – Americans, Canadians, Nigerians, Arabs, a Venezuelan official of the Organization of Petroleum Exporting Countries (OPEC), a German count, and a Greek co-ed – had known that he was still alive, but everyone knew who he was. 'The man who caught Eichmann,' several of them said, even before starting their research. 'The man who won the Oscar playing Laurence Olivier,' said one of my lesser lights, who never did do her homework.

Arriving during the half-time break, Simon suffered smilingly through my brief introduction before giving the usual twenty-minute talk he makes for groups that know him mostly from the movies. He began in fluent and rhythmic, if accented, English by denying he was either a Jewish James Bond or Don Quixote: 'I am neither of them and I am nothing in between. I am only a survivor who was four and a half years in several concentration camps and lost, except for my wife, my whole family. My original profession was architect, at which I worked twelve years – two of them in the Soviet Union. I built many houses. I saw those houses destroyed during the war. After I was liberated in Mauthausen, as a living skeleton, the people who liberated me interrogated me and they offered to build me back up and then send me back home. My "home" used to be Lvov, then in Poland, now in the Soviet Union. But I said to them "Thank you, but no, thank you. Poland is for me a cemetery."'

Instead, he went on, 'I built the Jewish Documentation Centre in Linz without money, without any detective background, and without any official auspices because I felt we had – we have! – the right of the victim.'

The more he talked, the more he told the story of his life, the less he sounded like a creation of Cervantes or Ian Fleming, but rather an Old Testament prophet walking today's troubled earth. Wiesenthal told our class:

'We live in a modern world. We know there is pollution. The air is bad, the water is bad, the skies are dirty. But there is another sort of pollution that people ignore. In many countries, people are living between murderers – and that is the biggest pollution of all, believe me. Half the people in the world – most of the people in this room! – were born after the war and you have not the personal experience; you have only second-hand information. When you hear about millions, you cannot identify with millions.'

Here he told the story of Eichmann saying in Budapest in 1944 that a hundred dead people is a catastrophe, a million a statistic. Wiesenthal went on to say: 'He was absolutely right. Today you hear on the radio that there was a bus accident in which thirteen people died and this is a catastrophe. Then you read in the newspaper that in the Sahel region of Africa 25,000 people die of hunger and this is too bad, but you don't feel anything.'

When Wiesenthal had finished, there was a fervent round of applause, and then I threw the floor open to questions. The German count – working in Vienna as a bartender and taking courses to better himself – had read up on Simon's memoirs and addressed him by title: 'Diploma-Engineer Wiesenthal, I understand you twice attempted suicide in the concentration camps. Do you still have mental scars from your experience or has time healed the wounds?'

'This is not an easy question,' Simon began, and, after telling how he cut his wrists and overdosed on saccharine, he confronted the query's moral and psychological dimensions:

'People ask how someone could live with such bad luck. The first two years after the war, I could not sleep because all my thoughts were with people I'd lost. How could I go back to building houses when, without justice, people cannot build homes or families? First we had to rebuild justice – and I was naïve enough to think that it would take only a few hours. And now, if you ask me what I have made of those thirty-eight years, I must tell you that, at most, I have built only a warning – a warning for the criminals of tomorrow who are born today.'

He told how he could have had Franz Stangl killed for 500 dollars without risking all the perils of extradition, but had refused the offer: 'For me, the trial is a historical lecture with the help of the criminal – even when there is an acquittal because it happened too long ago and far away. For you, who were born after the war, the trial is more important than the sentence. Information is the best defence for future generations from the murderers of tomorrow. If you know from history the danger, then part of the danger is over because it may not take you by surprise as it did your ancestors.'

In the cases of Eichmann and Stangl, he said, 'no punishment could have been equated with the enormity of their crimes. The important thing is that guilt was established and justice done before the eyes of the world with Eichmann in that glass box.' But, asked whether it would have been better to let Eichmann live the rest of his life in prison as a warning to the murderers of tomorrow, Wiesenthal replied: 'Maybe. But the Israelis were the judges. It was their affair.'

It was when the subject shifted to 'Israeli affairs' a little later in the evening that the session turned contentious. We arrived there innocently enough by way of Geneva, where Wiesenthal once addressed the inhabitants of an Arab student residence: 'I get on very well with Arab young people. I told them that only through talking can people find a solution. Only the Syrians refused to talk to me. We had Lebanese, Jordanians, a couple of Arabs from Israel, a dozen Egyptians; and later an Iraqi joined us. I told him that "585 years before Christ, the Jews were going to Babylon and settling in your country, where they lived for more than two and a half thousand years. It was only after the creation of Israel that they had trouble."' Then, turning to my class, Wiesenthal asked rhetorically: 'Do you know that the number of Jews expelled from Arab countries is higher than the number of Palestinian refugees?'

In 1979, toward the end of Kurt Waldheim's tenure as United Nations Secretary General, his home city of Vienna had been designated as the third official UN city (after New York and Geneva).

A skyscraper complex was built on the Danube to house the headquarters of several UN organizations, including the International Atomic Energy Organization, the Industrial Development Agency (UNIDO), and the Relief and Works Agency (UNRWA) for Palestinian refugees. A number of my students either worked at the UN or had parents who did. The next question came from a Syrian girl who had no qualms about speaking to Simon. Rime (pronounced 'ream') Allaf was a leggy and very Westernized 'diplomatic brat' who grew up in Geneva and New York and whose father, UN Assistant Secretary General Mowaffak Allaf, happened to be the head of the whole UN operation in Vienna. Rime began:

'You've spoken to us tonight about enemies of our freedom, generations of victims, and the defence of future generations. And you've said that your conscience forces you to bring the guilty ones to trial. Now I'd like to ask you why you've never thought about living in Israel and whether you think the State of Israel is based upon the principles you subscribe to.'

'Look,' Wiesenthal replied patiently, 'if I did my work from Israel, immediately people would dismiss it as Israeli propaganda. My kind of work can only be done independently in such a way that people can't say that it's in my country's interest to accuse someone. This way, my contacts with Israel are that the Israeli police look for witnesses in Israel to the cases I am working on. Besides, I am an Austrian citizen. My daughter and grandchildren, they live in Israel. I knew [Prime Minister Menachem] Begin only fifty-two years. I don't agree with everything that's going on in Israel. . .'

'Do you agree with anything?' Rime interrupted.

'No, I agree with some and disagree with others. But the right to criticize openly belongs only to the people who live there because they pay the bills. My daughter and son-in-law, they have the right to open their mouths and say what is good and bad. It's very easy to sit in a safe country and give advice to people who are living in danger. After the affair in Lebanon last year, I spoke to a group of Italian leftist Jews and when they said what Israel was doing wrong, I told them to go to Israel and make it better. Every Jew can go to Israel.'

That 'affair in Lebanon last year' was the Israeli invasion of 1982, and now Wiesenthal was tiptoeing, all too willingly, into hot water: 'I could take an evening to tell you about the whole big manipulation of news that happened there.'

'From which side?' Rime asked softly.

Simon rose to the bait. 'You know,' he began, almost paternally, 'Beirut is like Vienna in one respect. Vienna is a hole in the Iron Curtain. When journalists are trying to find out what is going on in Prague, Budapest, or Belgrade, they don't go there. They come here to find out what is happening there! Beirut is the same for the Near East. Anything you want to know about Libya, Saudi Arabia, or Abu Dhabi, you can find out better in Beirut.

'That's why all the important media have offices there: *New York Times*, CBS, ABC, that's where they send their correspondents. The correspondents come and go, but who runs the offices for them? Palestinians! So when war breaks out, the correspondents are immediately on the leash of their offices. And I advise you to study the long list of journalists who were killed in Beirut since 1972. I cannot say that all the people running the offices of the media were members of the PLO [Palestinian Liberation Organization]. Maybe yes, maybe no. But they followed their directions.

'Through this, in the first days [of the 1982 affair in Lebanon], you were hearing about 600,000 homeless people. But the Israelis were only on the coastal side, where, in the whole territory, there were only 400,000 people, so how can there be 600,000 homeless?'

Simon's eyes rolled with amusement and there were a few knowing chuckles from the class, but I didn't find it funny. Sitting in the back row was my Palestinian pupil, Shawkat Hasan. A fortyish film-maker working for UNRWA, he had not seen his home since he was nine. And I had only to look at Shawkat to know that each life made homeless is a tragedy, while the difference between 400,000 and 600,000 is a statistic.

Shawkat sat silent as Simon rambled on. In July 1982, a month after the invasion, Wiesenthal had been in Israel and, in the lobby of a Hilton hotel, met a man from one of the big American TV networks who had just come from Beirut. Simon asked him: 'Did you buy a souvenir for your wife?'

'How did you know?!' the newsman exclaimed. 'I bought her a bracelet.'

'And how much did you pay for it?'

'Oh, 500 Lebanese pounds.'

'How much did they ask for?'

'Well, they asked 1200.'

'Are you sure you made a good buy?'

The newsman shrugged, saying: 'Maybe I could have bargained them down to 450.'

Simon said to him: 'You see, with the bracelet for your wife, you made deductions. When they said it was worth 1200, you felt this was not true. But every day you are buying information without making deductions. You supply your millions of audience with statistics that aren't true. Why don't you go on the air and apologize, saying: "Excuse me, I was a victim of false information. It was not 600,000 made homeless at the beginning; it was 150,000"?'

Red-faced and still quivering with righteous re-enacted rage at the TV newsman, Simon interrupted Philip Eguaseki from Nigeria when he challenged his assertion that all Beirut bureaus and correspondents were run by Palestinians: 'Look, you always saw on TV the firing Israeli tank. You saw the target: a house. But I have talked to the crews and now you can go to Beirut and you will hear – not just from Jews, but from other people – how the PLO put all their war machinery – whole installations! – in the houses.'

Philip persisted: 'Don't you believe that massacres took place in the refugee camps?' He was referring to the killings of more than 300 Palestinian men, women, and children in the camps of Sabra and Chatila on the southern edge of West Beirut on 17 September 1982. Although no Israeli troops were directly involved in the killings, they had sealed off the area and permitted Lebanese Christian militiamen to enter the camps and kill Arabs.

Simon said softly: 'Look, I was one of the first to ask for an inquiry committee into what has happened in Sabra and Chatila. On the other side, when you look at the whole history of the civil war from 1975, you see that massacres are the political language there. Look, according to newspapers, a few days ago, the Druze [Moslems] massacred a village of Christians. Maybe it's true, maybe it's not true, I don't know. But, in all of the criticism against the Israelis, people forget one small thing – that the Christian Phalangists, not the Israelis, killed those people!'

'In Sabra and Chatila?' Rime Allaf asked. 'But, two nights before then, the Israeli Army had encircled them and. . .'

'One moment! One moment!' Simon interjected. 'I will give you a counter question. I don't wish to give you a direct question about Syria. . .'

'Please do!' Rime interrupted.

'Because I could ask you what happened in Hama,' Simon went on, and when Rime said all right, he asked rhetorically: 'What happened in Hama? Almost 20,000 people were killed.' (In late 1982, the Syrian Army and ruling Ba'ath Party, using artillery and tanks, had repressed a rebellion in the clandestine Moslem Brotherhood's citadel of Hama in northern Syria.)

'Fine!' said Rime. 'But we are talking about military dictatorship. In Hama, what happened is that the Syrian government massacred its own people. In Lebanon, we are talking about an invading army coming into another country. It had control of the whole area. OK, you can say the Phalangists did it, you can say they killed. . .'

Now Wiesenthal interrupted her with a hypothetical question about innocent bystanders caught in a shoot-out between cops and the robbers they're chasing: 'Who is responsible? The police or the killers?'

'If there is an invading army in another country . . .' Rime reiterated, but then she shifted gear. 'OK, let's forget about Lebanon. Let's go back to 1948 in Deir Yassin. That was a massacre, wasn't it?'

'Yes,' Wiesenthal conceded. In April 1948, two Jewish terrorist organizations – Irgun Zvai Leumi (National Military Organization) and the Stern Gang, to which Menachem Begin and his successor, Yitzhak Shamir, once belonged – combined operations to storm the Palestinian village of Deir Yassin and killed some 250 inhabitants.

'Then what do you say about it?' Rime asked. 'I understand totally why you are looking for justice. You have every right to do this. But we must also look at other things. You say we should never be as good at killing as the Nazis . . .'

'You know,' said Wiesenthal, 'I have heard about Deir Yassin and I had talks, not only with Begin, but with other people. They say they had warned the people before and asked them to leave before someone would be shot. And these people, they say, ignored the warning.'

'Would you leave,' Rime wanted to know, 'if somebody comes around and says "if you don't go out by tomorrow, we're going to shoot you"? We're talking about a whole town, a little city of 250 people. And I'm talking about principles. I'm not accusing anybody. Everything you've said is great. But where are the principles when you look at the other side?'

'What you forget,' Wiesenthal said, 'is that, a few days before, a convoy of Jewish doctors and nurses was massacred on their way to the Jewish hospital in Jerusalem. Fifty-eight people were massacred, unarmed people, without any warning like in Deir Yassin. This was a time of war.'

I could hardly believe my ears. Here were two people I like and admire, both defending death and destruction. Rime, the diplomat's daughter par excellence, seemed to be saying that Syria has a right to destroy its own people, so long as they're Syrians! And Simon – that survivor of the camps, chronicler of genocide, conscience of the world, and symbol of justice – sought to justify the unjustifiable by applying collective guilt, if not selective genocide.

I decided that, as with most political arguments, the more we heard, the less we would want to hear. Besides, as journalists, my students had enough material without letting the war between Simon and Rime deteriorate into bickering, so I intervened as gently as I could, saying: 'I would like, when we can, to move the discussion back to Europe.'

William Rush, every inch the image of the all-American boy, had his hand up, so I asked: 'Is your question about Europe, Bill?'

'Yes,' he said, 'I have two.'

His first was a long hypothetical question, which – and that was the journalism lesson of the day! – is exactly what you don't ask a seventy-four-year-old man one hour and forty minutes into a two-hour interview late in the evening. To summate Rush's first question: *Suppose I'm the son of a Nazi officer and you awaken public attention to Nazi crimes and I go to my father and ask what this is about and he gives me an answer glamourizing what the Nazis did, isn't the effect of your work the opposite of what you set out to do?*

Wiesenthal bristled and, because I could see that not everyone understood that the question was hypothetical, I interjected that 'it's a little like what some of your Jewish enemies say about your "raking up the past."' Rush started to ask his second question, but Simon said: 'Let me answer your first question first.'

Almost compassionately, Wiesenthal might have been trying to 'justify' Rush's hypothetical father to him with his reply. If so, there was no need, for Rush's own father was an American soldier who, it turned out, had married an Austrian. Wiesenthal's answer was:

'The Nazi Party had ten and a half million members. Only one and a half per cent was involved in crimes. Among the membership was a large number of people who joined the party just to save their existence. It is the same as people in the Soviet Union who join the Communist Party because they have no other choice. So I am making differences among people who were Nazi Party members. Also, some of the people involved in crimes were not party members, but took advantage of the opportunities to kill, to rape people and property, in such times. With slaves, you can do anything.

'Austria had about 700,000 party members. My office is concerned mainly with two or three thousand of them. The rest are for me without any value. I recognize that Austria was a victim of Nazi expansion. As an Austrian citizen, however, I feel that a former Nazi Party member should not be a minister of the government. We should remember that Austria had over 100,000 victims of Nazism, not all of them Jews. This is only, you might say, a matter of hygiene . . . I should also tell you that very often to my office come people who were party members and I talk with them about it.'

Adding that whatever his callers told him was between him and them, and implying that the ones who would come to him have little or nothing to hide, but are people of conscience, Wiesenthal added: 'I have a dossier of letters from young people whose parents were in jail or even executed. They ask me to tell them if, in my opinion, their parents were guilty. I would say that I have a good name with such people if they ask me such a question.

'And now,' he said to Rush, 'to your second question.'

This one was more succinct: 'You've said you can't live in Israel and that Poland is for you a cemetery. But I'm wondering why you took refuge here in Austria, where eighty per cent of the SS men and a lot of the Nazi hierarchy came from and many of the concentration camps were. Why not somewhere with a better record, like Switzerland? Why Austria?'

Phrased in various ways, it is a legitimate question I'd heard Simon asked often, and I'd heard him answer it many times, with retorts ranging from 'I'm an Austrian citizen and I was born in the Austrian Empire! Why should I live somewhere else?' to 'The best way to keep an eye on the murderers of yesterday and tomorrow is to try to live among them.' I had never heard him take umbrage at it before. This time, however, his reaction was explosive:

'You know, I wish not to blame you, but I have talks with neo-Nazis and they are using your terminology absolutely – absolutely the same argument. And do you know what is my answer? So long as the criminals are free, the war has not ended for me. This is why I am in Austria. I work here. I have the right to be here. I was born in Austria. My father fought as an Austrian soldier. Why do you send me to Switzerland? Why don't you send me to other countries? Why don't you stop people on the street and say "Why do you live here? Why don't you go to Sweden?" Why are you doing this to me? Why are you inviting me to go to other countries?'

If Simon stopped there, it might have been a legitimate overreaction. One might have excused the personal outburst and the interrogator's finger pointing relentlessly at poor Rush. One could have chalked it up to a misunderstanding brought on by the unfocused first question, fatigue, and, above all, the Middle Eastern debate with Rime. But overreaction turned to overkill when Simon went on:

'Don't you see that this is an infection that we hoped was over? Before the Nazis started, there were here also a number of anti-Semites who said the Jews should go out.'

At this point, Rush put an apologetic word in edgewise, 'I didn't mean to ask you to make a choice', and I tried to change the subject diplomatically: 'We have time for two more questions.'

'No,' said Simon, standing up from his seat beside me at the head of the class. 'No more questions. This last question was enough.'

'I don't think it was meant the way you're taking it,' I started to say to Simon, but Webster University's European director, Dr Robert D. Brooks, who had been sitting in on this 'distinguished guest lecture', intervened, saying: 'I don't mean to be speaking for the student who asked it, but if I had asked it myself, I really would have meant whether you couldn't operate more effectively in one of these other countries. I think that is the connotation with which it was asked.'

Simon's response was: 'Look, I am tired. Thank you.' And he headed for the door.

Rime Allaf was the first to collect herself. With the instinct of a born hostess, even when it wasn't her party, she said 'Thank you very much', and the class gave Wiesenthal a spontaneous burst of applause as he stormed out of the door.

When I phoned Simon the next morning, he said both of Rush's questions were 'a provocation' and Rush was, after all, 'the son of a Nazi officer; he said so himself.' When I told him Rush's real, rather than hypothetical, background, Simon said nothing.

The following Wednesday, Rime Allaf turned in a paper entitled 'Justice, Wiesenthal Style'. Even in the heat of an argument in which she, too, had not distinguished herself morally, she had picked up the vibration that bothered me:

> . . . During the first few days of the war, continued Wiesenthal, it was said that 600,000 people were made homeless. According to Wiesenthal, however, this was impossible. He said that only 400,000 people had been living in the area! To my dismay, Wiesenthal was speaking the way Eichmann had spoken years ago.

She seized on another quote from Wiesenthal: 'My office is not working only against criminals that killed Jews. I am not making any difference as to who were the victims. As long as the criminals are free, the war is not over for me . . . My conscience forces me to bring the guilty ones to trial.' And she asked: 'Then why hasn't his conscience forced him to bring to trial criminals like Begin?'

After chronicling Wiesenthal's six prerequisites for genocide – hatred, dictatorship, bureaucracy, technology, time, and a minority as victim – Rime concluded:

> They applied when the Jews were massacred. They still prevail when the Palestinians are being massacred. Yet Wiesenthal hardly seems motivated to hunt for the latters' killers!
>
> Having looked forward to this meeting, all in all I was not disappointed; Simon Wiesenthal's words are not words one forgets. In him, my classmates and I saw the bitterness that is left over from so much suffering. We respected his work, understanding his need for 'justice', as he put it. I would have only wished that, as he spoke about the Arabs, he didn't sound like a Nazi speaking about the Jews. Is it justice or just revenge you're looking for, Mr Wiesenthal?

More than five years later, when I ran into Rime Allaf in Vienna – where her family had settled after her father retired from his $107,000-a-year UN post in 1987 – she took a certain perverse pride in having 'inspired' the title of Wiesenthal's latest autobiography: *Justice, Not Vengeance*. And the last time I talked to Rime – in late 1992, by which time she had married Juan Canizares, a Spanish classical and flamenco guitarist – she took particular pride that her father had come out of retirement to head the Syrian delegation to the first postwar peace talks with Israel.

To this day, Simon still inquires after the doings of 'your Syrian girl. I enjoyed arguing with her. She was good!' But he insists she had nothing to do with his book's title: 'My whole life did.'

Around the time I bumped into Rime, I picked up a curious echo of her reaction to Wiesenthal from – of all people! – Israel Singer of the World Jewish Congress: 'Wiesenthal makes it sound like 1100 or 1200 war criminals – all the ones he says he's caught plus a few others he's still looking into – killed six million Jews, so why should *we* be looking for more, particularly in *his* back yard? Look, I had a glorified view of him for many years and now that I've met him – well, I try to keep the view of him I already had no matter what he says about me. And you have to give him credit that, over so many years, sometimes all by himself, he kept the issue of Nazi criminals alive when the whole world, even the Jews, wanted to forget. But I'll tell you a couple of things I've learned about Wiesenthal since 1986: he may be a Galician by birth just as I'm one by ancestry, but he's lived in Austria long enough to be as litigious as any of the natives – and they're a litigious people. And the other thing about Wiesenthal is this: he only listens when *he's* talking.'

Asher Ben Nathan sat in the lobby of a shiny new motel in a workers' district of his native Vienna in 1987 spicing his breakfast with a fuming cigar. Having given a lecture on 'Israel Yesterday and Today: from the Viewpoint of an Ex-Austrian' at a Socialist Party institute the night before, the former Arthur Pier was free to reminisce about his postwar days in Austria forty years earlier. Head of the Jewish underground smuggling Displaced Persons into Palestine and founder of the first Documentation Centre in Vienna, the jaunty 'Arthur' had worked with Wiesenthal, Tuviah Friedman, and 'Manos' Diamant, among others, and remembered them well.

Reassigned back to Palestine in 1947, Asher Ben Nathan had entered the Foreign Service of the newborn nation of Israel in 1948 and risen through the ranks to become, in 1969, Israel's first ambassador to West Germany. After four and a half years in Bonn, he was named ambassador to Paris and subsequently served as adviser to Shimon Peres, later Prime Minister. A brief flirtation with Labour Party politics, in which he ran for mayor of Tel Aviv and lost, had done little to subdue the sixty-six-year-old 'Arthur', who reappeared as a visitor to Vienna in early 1987 wearing an undiplomatic plaid jacket over more traditional grey flannel slacks.

Recalling the Wiesenthal of the late 1940s, Asher Ben Nathan said 'our relationship was quite good for a while', but acknowledged a coolness, if not a rift, which developed between the two Nazi-hunters even before he returned to Palestine. Mostly, he says, Wiesenthal made a career of Nazi-hunting 'while I was concerned with refugees and Palestine and Israel in this hectic period, so I had no time for the politics and idiosyncrasies of the people with whom I worked – and, later, I went on to other tasks of my own. For me, it was a temporary mission; for him, it was his whole life.'

Still, there was more to it than that. 'Whenever we meet, Wiesenthal and I,' he volunteered, 'we meet by chance and then he will embrace me, but we keep our distance. He never attempts to contact me because he knows that I know things about him that other people don't know about. That's all, so let's leave it at that. I don't want to say more.'

Asked if their estrangement had anything to do with Bruno Kreisky's accusations that Simon collaborated in one way or another with the Gestapo, Asher Ben Nathan was quick to disclaim them: 'All these accusations have been looked into in Israel. We concluded that the man was no hero and no saint, but there's no proof of him being anything worse.' And, pressed for more, he concluded: 'Well, I've admired the way the man has grown into an elder statesman, an international personality. He's much more sure of himself than the chap I met who was still living in a camp when we got to know each other. All the time his reputation was growing, he never tried to contact me. He did what he did, but I have my own ideas and he knows what I think. When we do meet, he never tries to get close and I certainly have no reason to.'

In his 1960 autobiography, Tuviah Friedman sketches the self-styled 'desperado' Wiesenthal who 'had a dispute with "Arthur" and preferred to work on his own.' Wiesenthal had little use for the

Four Power politics among Austria's military occupation governments and their relations with Pier's ambitious fifth column of Jewish agents. 'Listen, Tadek,' Simon told Friedman. 'Maybe your "Arthur" cares *who* finds Eichmann, but I don't. I just want him found.' In Friedman's version of history (which both Simon and Asher Ben Nathan consider unreliable), Simon comes across as an any-means-to-an-end person and 'Arthur' doesn't.

If there has been a recurrent motif in Simon's later years, it has been his use of '*I am not a hater*' almost to the extent of cliché. Whether applied to Ukrainians, Kreisky, or the World Jewish congress (or anybody except, perhaps, Elie Wiesel), it has informed his life through the slings and arrows of the Waldheim affair and beyond. It made him, in his eighties, a more mature person than the man who stormed out of Webster University when nearing seventy-five – and this is not always the direction in which the elderly age. I caught a glimpse of this dimension (and of how grandly Simon was ageing) in late 1988, a few weeks before his eightieth birthday, when I confronted him with Asher Ben Nathan's 1987 quotes about him.

Simon reacted positively at first, as though congratulated: 'He is absolutely right that I was growing. Also he is right when he says I am no hero, no saint; I am just an ordinary man.' Then, after a brief pause to allow his listener to dispute this, Simon went on: 'This man was a hero of mine. In those times, we looked upon those people who were coming from Palestine to us as supermen. Later, we found out they were human beings just like us.

'My difficulties with him were never *about* him because he did very good work in Austria and later in Germany and France. They were about the people who worked for him. We disagreed over his friends. Some of his friends were not my friends. So there were little jealousies on their part, which must have hurt his opinion of me, but, more than that, some of the Jews he used had held functions under the Nazis. And, even when they had functioned honourably, it was my policy – *Lex Wiesenthal* – never to employ people who were compromised. OK, "Arthur" thought otherwise – and I should make it clear that he used them only for the benefit of his job, not for personal benefit.

'I still like the man very much. When his son died in the Yom Kippur War I went to him and his wife in Paris to tell them how sorry I felt that such a thing had happened to their son and to them and that such things still happen to people just because they are Jews. And, if we haven't spent much time together lately, it's because I think of him as too important and busy a man for me to waste his time. Like I said, he was a hero of mine.'

Was he still?

'Look,' said Simon, 'the next time he and I meet, I won't say anything to him about what he said to you, but I'll know to spend more time with him. So thank you. I would hate for either of us to go to the grave feeling coolness about the other.'

– 43 –

'I wish not to provoke the Lord'

In 1999, soon after turning ninety, Simon Wiesenthal gave up driving. He also stopped celebrating birthdays in Israel with his daughter, grandchildren and great-grandson. 'Instead, they come to me all year round. [Daughter] Pavlina is arriving with her husband next week. When they are here, this is for me vacation,' he told me in his own eloquent English when I visited him in Vienna early in 2002, three weeks after his ninety-third birthday on New Year's Eve. 'So I stay here all the time. I wish not to provoke the Lord.'

Life goes on for the venerable Nazi-hunter – and that in itself is his ultimate victory over the dwindling ranks of World War II criminals who survive uncaught: to outlive them.

'It's my situation,' he says philosophically, 'but I'm not responsible for it.'

Would he like to outlive Alois Brunner, the master genocidist? Four years Wiesenthal's junior, the Austrian-born Brunner was Eichmann's enforcer in Vienna and Prague in 1938–9 and later in Bratislava, Paris and Greece. Still in Syria after half a century, Brunner has been silent since the death of his protector, President Hafez al-Assad, in 2000. Wiesenthal's information is that 'Brunner is probably alive and somewhere in Syria, but is no more in the capital, Damascus. Still, he is safe in Syria because there to kill Jews is not a crime . . . But I don't think about outliving him and maybe he doesn't think about me. When I came out of the war alive in 1945, that was victory for me.'

His three secretaries take turns chauffeuring him to and from his Jewish Documentation Center in downtown Vienna. On doctor's orders, Wiesenthal spends only five mornings a week in the office, but one of the secretaries told me he takes his work home with him every noon.

'I am ninety-three years old and I am every day in the office. Why?' he said more rhetorically than boastfully. 'Because this is my life. After fifty-six years, you cannot overnight change and say "OK, I sit home." If I sit home, I am waiting for the death. Here, I still get many letters and I answer them. But some of the letters I am sorry I didn't get thirty years before.'

'Are there no more Nazis left to catch?' I asked him.

'No European Nazis more. Old Nazis, no,' he replied. 'If they are from my generation, they live now overseas – in South America. And their children and grandchildren are not more Nazis. They are hoping for a better life. But there are other young people, the new Nazis, who wish to carry on in the old way. They worry me.'

Across the border in the Czech Republic, where I live, that means skinheads, who bully and even murder Roma (Gypsies). But Wiesenthal was more general: 'There are people in Western Europe who cannot forgive that for more than fifty years we have had no war. So they make war.'

As a champion of Roma, who endure discrimination – by bourgeois Czechs and the school system – that can be as painful as a beating by skinheads, Wiesenthal had a simple solution to the country's 'Romany problem': 'Let the Roma live. Make them more intelligent. Give them an education and, after a time, the only question will be: "What are Roma?" Nobody will even know any more that this intelligent man or that one is Romany.'

Our conversation about the seamy side of Bohemian life only served to make a mellow Wiesenthal wax nostalgic for his student years in Prague (1928–32):

'Those four years were the best time of my young life. I came from Poland after being 'liberated' too many times by Cossacks and Ukrainians, Russians, Poles and Austrians – all at odds with each other, but all anti-Semites. The Czechs, on the other hand, were always fair to Jews; the Slovaks weren't. Only in Prague was I ever forgetting I was a Jew.'

Once, though, a Czech classmate from the provinces invited him home for a weekend. Wiesenthal remembers hearing his friend shout into the crank-up phone in the dormitory corridor: 'Mom, I'm bringing Wiesenthal with me. He's a Jew, but you'll like him.'

The old man recalls the episode fondly. If he has any regrets, it is that his self-curtailed travel schedule means he won't provoke the Lord by seeing Prague again. Even when US President Bill Clinton presented him with America's highest civilian honour, the Presidential Medal of Freedom, at the White House on 9 August 2000, Wiesenthal didn't make the trip, but gave a resounding acceptance speech via a special radio hookup:

'I am many times honoured, but that honour I particularly liked.'

Any regrets about the Nobel Peace Prize?

A sigh. *'Ach!* I got the Erasmus Prize – the Dutch Nobel Prize – in 1992. And I am a *Doctor honoris causa* nineteen times over.'

As I left, I heard him reciting by rote the universities that had granted him honorary doctorates – from Washington and Webster universities of St. Louis to Ohio Wesleyan to the University of Natal in South Africa. The man may have mellowed, but the mind is as agile as ever. Alois Brunner had better watch his step.

Vienna–Prague, April 2002

Index

Photo opposite: Simon Wiesenthal, © Heather A. Faulkner/*The Prague Post*